8/95

Historical Figures
in Fiction

Donald K. Hartman and Gregg Sapp

Oryx Press

1994

The rare Arabian Oryx is believed to have inspired the myth of the unicorn. This desert
antelope became virtually extinct in the early 1960s. At that time several groups of
international conservationists arranged to have 9 animals sent to the Phoenix Zoo
to be the nucleus of a captive breeding herd. Today the Oryx population
is nearly 800 and over 400 have been returned to reserves
in the Middle East.

Copyright © 1994 by The Oryx Press
4041 North Central at Indian School Road
Phoenix, Arizona 85012-3397

Published simultaneously in Canada
Printed and Bound in the United States of America

∞ The paper used in this publication meets the minimum requirements of American
National Standard for Information Science—Permanence of Paper for Printed Library
Materials, ANSI Z39.48, 1984.

Library of Congress Cataloging-in-Publication Data

Hartman, Donald K.
   Historical figures in fiction / by Donald Hartman and Gregg Sapp.
      p.   cm.
   Includes bibliographical references and index.
   ISBN 0-89774-718-6
   1. Historical fiction—History and criticism—Bibliography. 2. Young adult fiction—His-
tory and criticism—Bibliography. 3. History in literature—Bibliography. 4. Characters and
characteristics in literature—Bibliography. I. Sapp, Gregg. II. Title.
Z5917.H6H37   1994
[PN3441]
016.823'081089283—dc20   94-15105
                                                                              CIP

Contents

Preface

Biographical fiction is a diverse and extremely popular body of literature. Clearly, part of its enormous appeal is that it transports readers to another time and place, where they can experience famous events and gain insights into the lives and thoughts of people who have shaped history. In this way, biographical fiction stimulates both the imagination and the intellect. It can be read for pleasure as well as for edification.

Further, biographical fiction is versatile. It is a genre that subsumes all other literary categories—for example, a biographical novel can be written as a mystery, a Western, a romance, or even *belles lettres*. It can be written for juvenile, young adult, or adult readers. Finally, while a well-crafted biographical novel must be rooted in fact, the genre permits a fair degree of literary license, which allows the skillful author to exercise creative freedom and to employ certain literary techniques that are inappropriate in "straight" biography.[1] Irving Stone, one of the most prolific and widely read writers of fictional biographies, wrote in 1957:

> The biographical novel is based not merely on fact, but on feeling, the legitimate emotion arising from indigenous drama. Facts can get lost with almost too great a facility, but an emotional experience, once lived, can never be forgotten. . . . While a biography can be written purely out of a life's worthiness, with details of important names, places, and dates, the biographical must emerge naturally and organically from the conflicts of man against himself, man against man, or man against fate. . . . In a biographical novel therefore, the reading and the doing, through identification, become synonymous; the reader can live a thousand different lives during a relatively brief span of years.[2]

Because they represent such a vibrant and expansive genre, fictional biographies of one type or another might be found in almost any kind of library. In school libraries, these materials have been particularly recommended for uses in reading and writing programs.[3] Public librarians are well familiar with the popularity of fictional biographies, which can be measured in terms of circulations. In academic environments, fictional biographies can be read and studied by scholars interested in popular culture and certain fields of literary criticism.[4]

SCOPE

The problem for librarians and library patrons is that subject access to this literature—and, indeed, to any form of fiction—is difficult and sometimes nonexistent.[5] It is the purpose of this bibliography to help librarians identify and make effective use of this literature.

The book cites 4,200 novels in which almost 1,500 historical figures appear as significant characters. The historical figures were selected on the basis of their contribution to their respective art or profession, as well as for the fame and/or notoriety they have achieved in world history. We have included individuals of both popular and scholarly interest, living and deceased, from all fields of human endeavor. The books included are English-language juvenile, young adult, and adult books published since 1940. Some pre-1940 titles are listed if they have been reissued after that date. Translations were also included if they were listed in any of our sources, all of which appear following "References" at the end of this preface. *Roman à clef* were not included. Certainly, no work of this type can be truly comprehensive, but we have tried to identify and use the most significant sources providing subject access to fiction; thus, we hope that this book includes not only the most important fictional biographies, but also those most likely to be found in libraries.

Our intent is that only books in which the historical figures appear as major characters be included. Of course, the decision as to whether a character is major or minor within a novel can sometimes be subjective. In making that determination, we have generally relied upon the implicit judgment of our sources—for example, if one of our sources gives a name subject heading to a particular character, we assume that that person must play a fairly major role in the novel.

ARRANGEMENT

The main section of the book is arranged alphabetically by the names of the historical figures. Included under each entry are the person's birth and death dates (where applicable) and a brief note indicating profession and/or major fields of activity. Names were verified in the *Almanac of Famous People* (Gale 1989), and, as a general rule, only historical figures listed in that source are included in this book.

FORMAT OF ENTRIES

Beneath each main entry, citations are listed and give author, title, publisher, date, notes (such as indications of reading level for juvenile and young adult fiction, names of awards or honors won, titles of relevant secondary sources, information on reprints, etc.). Also listed are up to six citations to reviews of the book, wherever these could be found. (Abbreviations for review sources are found on page x.) Where more than six reviews were available, we have preferred to list book review sources that librarians would consider authoritative and that would also be likely to be found in libraries. See the sample entry shown below.

CONTENTS

No more than 100 novels are listed for any person. For any figure who appears in more than 100 novels, a sampling of titles published over the last five decades have been cited, although exceptions are made for pre-1940 "classic" novels or works by "major" writers. In making that determination, we relied upon various indexes, bibliographies, and reference resources, listed following under "Sources," as well as upon our own judgment.

In addition to the main section, there is an Occupation Index that provides access to the people listed in this book by their professions and/or fields of activity; multiple listings are given

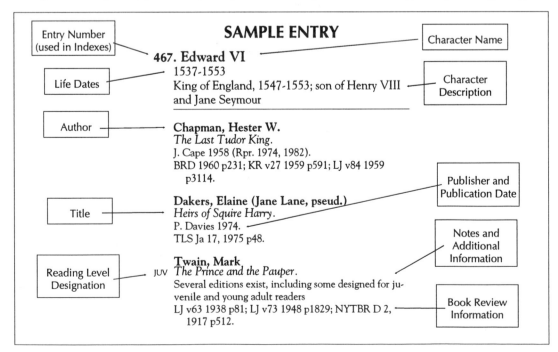

SAMPLE ENTRY

Entry Number (used in Indexes)

Character Name

467. Edward VI
1537-1553
King of England, 1547-1553; son of Henry VIII and Jane Seymour

Life Dates

Character Description

Author

Chapman, Hester W.
The Last Tudor King.
J. Cape 1958 (Rpr. 1974, 1982).
BRD 1960 p231; KR v27 1959 p591; LJ v84 1959 p3114.

Publisher and Publication Date

Dakers, Elaine (Jane Lane, pseud.)
Heirs of Squire Harry.
P. Davies 1974.
TLS Ja 17, 1975 p48.

Title

Notes and Additional Information

Reading Level Designation

Twain, Mark
JUV *The Prince and the Pauper.*
Several editions exist, including some designed for juvenile and young adult readers
LJ v63 1938 p81; LJ v73 1948 p1829; NYTBR D 2, 1917 p512.

Book Review Information

for figures who were prominent in more than one field. Some occupation terms are modified from the *Almanac of Famous People*. An Author Index and a Title Index are also included.

We invite librarians to examine this book and to provide us with their thoughts as to how it might be used and improved. If you are aware of any sources that we did not consult, or if you have any suggestions at all regarding this book, please feel free to contact us in care of The Oryx Press, 4041 N. Central Ave., Phoenix, AZ 85012-3397.

Donald Hartman
Gregg Sapp

REFERENCES

1. Ina Schabert, "Fictional Biography, Factual Biography, and their Contaminations," *Biography* 5 (winter 1982): 1-16.

2. Irving Stone, "The Biographical Novel," in *Literary Lectures Presented at the Library of Congress* (Washington, DC: GPO, 1973, 185-201.

3. Myra Zarnowski, "Learning about Fictionalized Biographies: A Reading and Writing Approach," *The Reading Teacher* 42 (November 1988): 136-142. See also chapter 5, "Fictionalized Versions," in Zarnowski's *Learning About Biographies* (National Council of Teachers of English, 1990).

4. See Naomi Jacobs, "The Character of Truth: Historical Figures in Contemporary Fiction" (Southern Illinois University Press, 1990) for one example of a recent scholarly study of the portrayals of notable historical figures in fiction.

5. Gregg Sapp, "The Levels of Access: Subject Approaches to Fiction," *RQ* 25 (summer 1986): 488-497; Shiela Inter, "The Fiction of Access to Fiction," *Technicalities* 7 (July 1987): 277-278.

SOURCES

Aaron Burr and the American Literary Imagination/ Charles F. Nolan—Westport, CT: Greenwood Press, 1980.

American History in Juvenile Books/ Seymour Metzner—NY: H.W. Wilson Company, 1966.

America in Fiction: An Annotated List of Novels That Interpret Aspects of Life in the United States, Canada, and Mexico/ Otis W. Coan and Richard G. Lillard—Palo Alto, CA: Pacific Books, 1967.

The American Historical Novel/ Ernest E. Leisy—Norman, OK: University of Oklahoma Press, 1950.

An Annotated Bibliography of California Fiction, 1664-1970/ Newton D. Baird and Robert Greenwood—Georgetown, CA: Talisman Literary Research, 1971.

An Annotated Bibliography of Florida Fiction, 1801-1980/ Janette C. Gardner—St. Petersburg, FL: Little Bayou Press, 1983.

The Assassination of John F. Kennedy: A Comprehensive Historical and Legal Bibliography, 1963-1979/ Westport, CT: Greenwood Press, 1980.

Benedict Arnold: The Traitor as Hero in American Literature/ David R. Johnson — Ph.D. dissertation, Pennsylvania State University, 1975.

The Biblical Novel: A Checklist with an Introductory Essay/ Arnold D. Ehlert—Anaheim, CA: BCH Publications, 1960.

Bibliography of California Fiction, Poetry, Drama in Three Volumes/ Edgar J. Hinkel—Oakland, CA: Alameda County Library, 1938.

A Bibliography of Novels Related to the American Frontier and Colonial History/ Jack Van Derhoof—Troy, NY: Whitston Publishing, 1971.

Billy the Kid: The Bibliography of a Legend/ J.C. Dykes—Albuquerque, NM: University of New Mexico Press, 1952.

Book Review Digest—NY: H.W. Wilson Company (1906-1992).

A Catalogue of Crime/ Jacques Barzun—NY: Harper & Row, 1971.

California in Fiction/ Alice K. Melcon—Berkeley, CA: California Library Association, 1961.

Characters from Young Adult Literature/ Mary Ellen Snodgrass — Englewood, CO: Libraries Unlimited, 1991.

Children's Catalog—NY: H.W. Wilson Company, 6th edition (1941) to 14th edition (1992).

Civil War Novels: An Annotated Bibliography/ Albert J. Menendez—NY: Garland Publishing, 1986.

A Classified Shakespeare Bibliography, 1936-1958/ University Park, PA: Pennsylvania State University Press, 1963.

Classified Washington Bibliography Compiled by a Special Committee of the American Library Association/ Washington, DC: U.S. George Washington Bicentennial Commission, 1931.

Crime Fiction, 1749-1980: A Comprehensive Bibliography/ Allen J. Hubin—NY: Garland Publishing, 1984.

Cumulated Fiction Index (1945-1984).

Dickinson's American Historical Fiction/ Metuchen, NJ: Scarecrow Press, 1986 (5th edition).

Fiction Catalog—NY: H.W. Wilson Company, 7th edition (1960) through 1991 supplement.

Florida in Fiction: A Bibliography/ Mary O. McRory—Tallahassee, FL: Florida State Library, 1958.

A Guide to Jewish Themes in American Fiction, 1940-1980/ Murray Blackman—Metuchen, NJ: Scarecrow Press, 1981.

A Guide to the Best Fiction, English and American, Including Translations from Foreign Languages/ Ernest A. Baker and James Packman—NY: Barnes & Noble, 1967.

The Guide to Supernatural Fiction/ Everett F. Bleiler—Kent, OH: Kent State University Press, 1983.

The Hollywood Novel and Other Novels about Film, 1912-1982: An Annotated Bibliography/ Nancy Brooker-Bowers—NY: Garland Publishing, 1985.

India in English Fiction, 1800-1970: An Annotated Bibliography/ Brijen K. Gupta—Metuchen, NJ: Scarecrow Press, 1973.

Jack the Ripper: A Bibliography and Review of the Literature/ Alexander Kelly—London: Association of Assistant Librarians, 1984.

John Brown: The Literary Image/ Leslie A. Wardenaar—Ph.D. dissertation, University of California at Los Angeles, 1974.

Junior High School Library Catalog—NY: H.W. Wilson Company, 1st edition (1965) to 1993 supplement.

Kentucky in Fiction: An Annotated Bibliography, 1951 to 1980/ Mary D. Foley—Lexington, KY: University of Kentucky Libraries, 1981.

*The Kentucky Novel/*Lawrence S. Thompson—Lexington, KY: University of Kentucky Press, 1958.

LC MARC—Dialog computer search of the database.

List of Novels and Short Stories about Workers/ Eleanor C. Anderson—NY: Woman's Press, 1938.

Literary Image of Daniel Boone: A Changing Heroic Ideal in Nineteenth and Twentieth Century Popular Literature/ Carolyn Smith—Ph.D. dissertation, University of Utah, 1974.

Literature by and about the American Indian: An Annotated Bibliography/ Urbana, IL: National Council of Teachers of English, 1979.

Literature of the American Southwest: A Selective Bibliography/ Kenneth Kurtz—Los Angeles: Occidental College, 1956.

Michigan Novels: An Annotated Bibliography/ Albert G. Black — Ann Arbor, MI: Michigan Council of Teachers of English, 1963.

A Mirror for the Nation: An Annotated Bibliography of American Social Fiction, 1901-1950/ Archibald Hanna—NY: Garland Publishing, 1985.

The Modern Presidency in American Fiction/ Louise D. Morrison — Ph.D. dissertation, Case Western Reserve University, 1972.

Mystery Index: Subjects, Settings, and Sleuths of 10,000 Titles/ Steven Olderr—Chicago: American Library Association, 1987.

New Jersey in the American Revolution: A Bibliography of Historical Fiction, from 1784/ Oral S. Coad—New Brunswick, NJ: New Brunswick Historical Club, 1980.

North Carolina Fiction, 1734-1957: An Annotated Bibliography/ Chapel Hill, NC: University of North Carolina Library, 1958.

The Novels of World War I: An Annotated Bibliography/ Philip E. Hager and Desmond Taylor—NY: Garland Publishing, 1981.

OCLC Online Union Catalog/ Database searched through OCLC's Epic Service.

Olderr's Fiction Index/ Chicago: St. James Press (1987-1990).

Olderr's Young Adult Fiction Index/ Chicago: St. James Press (1988-1990).

The Pioneer in the American Novel, 1900-1950/ Norman, OK: University of Oklahoma Press, 1967.

Poe in Imaginative Literature: A Study of American Drama, Fiction, and Poetry Devoted to Edgar Allen Poe or His Works/ John E. Reilly—Ph.D. dissertation, University of Virginia, 1965.

Reader's Guide to Prose Fiction/ Elbert Lenrow—NY: D. Appleton-Century Co., 1940.

The Russian Theme in English Literature from the Sixteenth Century to 1980: An Introductory Survey and Bibliography/ Anthony G. Cross—Oxford, England: Willen A. Meeuws, 1985.

Samuel Johnson: A Survey and Bibliography of Critical Studies/ James L. Clifford and Donald J. Greene—Minneapolis, MN: University of Minnesota Press, 1970.

Sea Fiction Guide/ Myron J. Smith—Metuchen, NJ: Scarecrow Press, 1976.

The Self-Made Image of Napoleon: A Challenge to Fiction/ Shoshana M. Knapp—Ph.D. dissertation, Stanford University, 1978.

Sixty Years of the Bible in Fiction: An Annotated Bibliography and Analysis of Fiction Based on the Bible, 1899-1959/ Helen E. Gilbert—Master's thesis, Atlanta University, 1960.

Sports Fiction for Adults: An Annotated Bibliography of Novels, Plays, Short Stories, and Poetry with Sporting Settings/ Suzanne Wise—NY: Garland Publishing, 1986.

Sports Pages: A Critical Bibliography of 20th Century American Novels and Stories Featuring Baseball, Basketball, and other Athletic Pursuits/ Grant Burns—Metuchen, NJ: Scarecrow Press, 1987.

Standard Catalog for High School Libraries—NY: H.W. Wilson Company, 6th edition (1952) to 1993 supplement. Note: Title is *Senior High School Library Catalog* after 1967.

Subject Index to High School Fiction/ Jeanne S. Van Nostrand — Chicago: American Library Association, 1938.

Themes and Settings in Fiction: A Bibliography of Bibliographies/ Donald K. Hartman and Jerome Drost—NY: Greenwood Press, 1988.

Thomas Jefferson: A Comprehensive, Annotated Bibliography of Writing about Him, 1826-1980/ Frank Shuffelton—NY: Garland Publishing, 1983.

War of 1812: An Annotated Bibliography/ Dwight L. Smith—NY: Garland Publishing, 1985.

War Story Guide: An Annotated Bibliography of Military Fiction/ Myron J. Smith—Metuchen, NJ: Scarecrow Press, 1980.

World Historical Fiction Guide/ Daniel D. McGarry and Sarah Harriman White—Metuchen, NJ: Scarecrow Press, 1973.

Book Review Source Abbreviations

Ja	= January	Jl	= July
F	= February	Ag	= August
Mr	= March	S	= September
Ap	= April	O	= October
My	= May	N	= November
Je	= June	D	= December

AB:	AB Bookman's Weekly	Books:	Books
ABR:	American Book Review	Boston R:	Boston Review
AH:	American Heritage	BRD:	Book Review Digest
AL:	American Literature	B Rpt:	Book Report
A Lib:	American Libraries	BritBkN:	British Book News
Am:	America	BS:	BestSellers
Am Q:	American Quarterly	Bus W:	Business Week
Amer R:	Americas Review	BW:	Book World
Am Spect:	American Spectator	BWatch:	Book Watch
Analog:	Analog Science Fiction/ Science Fact	BW(WP):	Book World (Washington Post)
Ant R:	Antioch Review	Callaloo:	Callaloo
Apo:	Apollo	Can Child Lit:	Canadian Children's Literature
Armchair Det:	Armchair Detective	Can Lit:	Canadian Literature
ASBYP:	Appraisal: Science Books for Young People	Can Mat:	CM: A Reviewing Journal of Canadian Materials for Young People
Atl:	Atlantic		
Aust Bk R:	Australian Book Review	CathW:	Catholic World
AW:	American West	CAY:	Come All Ye
		CBRS:	Children's Book Review Service
B&B:	Books and Bookmen	CC:	Children's Catalog
BALF:	Black American Literature Forum	Ch C:	Christian Century
Barron's:	Barron's	CCB-B:	Center for Children's Books. Bulletin
Belles Let:	Belles Lettres		
BFYC:	Books for Young Children	CE:	Childhood Education
BIC:	Books in Canada	CF:	Canadian Forum
BL:	Booklist	Ch Bk News:	Children's Book News
Bloom Rev:	Bloomsbury Review	Ch BWatch:	Children's Bookwatch
BM:	Burlington Magazine	CHE:	Chronicle of Higher Education

Child Lit: *Children's Literature*
ChLAQ: *Children's Literature Association. Quarterly*
Choice: *Choice*
ChSTrib: *Chicago Sunday Tribune*
Ch Today: *Christianity Today*
Clio: *Clio: A Journal of Literature, History and the Philosophy of History*
Comt: *Commentary*
Comw: *Commonweal*
Conn: *Connoisseur*
CQ: *Carolina Quarterly*
Cur R: *Curriculum Review*
CR: *Contemporary Review*
Cres: *Cresset*
Critiq: *Critique*
Critm: *Criticism*
CSM: *Christian Science Monitor*
CT: *Children Today*

Daedalus: *Daedalus*
Dal R: *Dalhousie Review*

EJ: *English Journal*
Esq: *Esquire*
Essence: *Essence*
FC: *Fiction Catalog*
Fic Int: *Fiction International*
Five Owls: *Five Owls*
Fortune: *Fortune*
Ga R: *Georgia Review*
GW: *Guardian Weekly*
GP: *Growing Point*

HB: *Horn Book Magazine*
HB Guide: *Horn Book Guide*
Hisp: *Hispania*
HM: *Harper's Magazine*
HMR: *Hungry Mind Magazine*
HR: *Hudson Review*
HT: *History Today*
Hum: *Humanist*
ILN: *Illustrated London News*
Inst: *Instructor*
Inter BC: *Interracial Books for Children Bulletin*

In Rev: *In Review*
JB: *Junior Bookshelf*
JHSLC: *Junior High School Library Catalog*
JPC: *Journal of Popular Culture*
JRead: *Junior Reader*
Ken R: *Kenyon Review*
KR: *Kirkus Reviews*
Kliatt: *Kliatt Young Adult Paperback Guide*

LA: *Language Arts*
LATBR: *Los Angeles Times Book Review*
Learning: *Learning*
Lis: *Listener*
LJ: *Library Journal*
Locus: *Locus*
Lon R Bks: *London Review of Books*

Mac: *Maclean's*
Meanjin: *Meanjin*
MFS: *Modern Fiction Studies*
MFSF: *Magazine of Fantasy and Science Fiction*
Moth Jones: *Mother Jones*
MQR: *Michigan Quarterly Review*
MR: *Minnesota Review*
Ms: *Ms.*

NAR: *North American Review*
Nat: *Nation*
NatR: *National Review*
Nature: *Nature*
NEQ: *New England Quarterly*
New Age: *New Age Journal*
New ER: *New England Review*
NewR: *New Republic*
New York: *New York Magazine*
NS: *New Statesman & Society*
NW: *Newsweek*
NY: *New Yorker*
NYHTBR: *New York Herald Tribune Book Review*
NYRB: *New York Review of Books*
NYT: *New York Times* (daily)
NYTBR: *New York Times Book Review*
NYTLa: *New York Times* (late edition)

Obs:	Observer		SLMQ:	School Library Media Quarterly
Outl:	Outlook		Sm Pr:	Small Press
			Sm Pr R:	Small Press Review
Par:	Parents Magazine		SN:	Saturday Night
Parabola:	Parabola		Soc:	Society
Phylon:	Phylon		South Car R:	South Carolina Review
PR:	Partisan Review		South Hum R:	Southern Humanities Review
Prog:	Progressive		South R:	Southern Review
PS:	Prairie Schooner		SPBR:	Small Press Book Review
Punch:	Punch		Spec:	Spectator
PW:	Publishers Weekly		Specu:	Speculum
			SSF:	Studies in Short Fiction
Queen's Q:	Queen's Quarterly		SWR:	Southwest Review
Quill & Q:	Quill & Quire			
			TCR:	Teachers College Record
R Contem Fic:	Review of Contemporary Fiction		TES:	Times Educational Supplement
Ref Bk R:	Reference Book Review		Time:	Time
Refl:	Reflections		TLS:	Times Literary Supplement
RMR:	Rocky Mountain Review of Language and Literature		TPR:	Threepenny Review
Roundup:	Roundup		Trib Bks:	Tribune Books
RQ:	RQ		TriQ:	TriQuarterly
R&RBk N:	Reference and Research Book News		USA T:	USA Today
RT:	Reading Teacher		Utne R:	Utne Reader
SatR:	Saturday Review		VLS:	Village Voice Literary Supplement
SB:	Science Books & Films		VOYA:	Voice of Youth Advocates
Sch Arts:	School Arts		VQR:	Virginia Quarterly Review
Sch Lib:	School Librarian		VV:	Village Voice
Science:	Science			
SCHSL:	Standard Catalog for High School Libraries		WAL:	Western American Literature
SE:	Social Education		WCRB:	West Coast Review of Books
SEP:	Saturday Evening Post		WER:	Whole Earth Review
Sew R:	Sewanee Review		WHR:	Western Humanities Review
SFCh:	San Francisco Chronicle		WJR:	Washington Journalism Review
SFChr:	Science Fiction Chronicle		Wil Q:	Wilson Quarterly
SFRB:	San Francisco Review of Books		WLB:	Wilson Library Bulletin
SFS:	Science-Fiction Studies		WLT:	World Literature Today
SHSLC:	Senior High School Library Catalog		W&M Q:	William & Mary Quarterly
SLJ:	School Library Journal		Wom R Bks:	Women's Review of Books
			WSJ:	Wall Street Journal
			Zygon:	Zygon

Historical Figures
in Fiction

Historical Figures in Fiction

1. Aaron, Hank (Henry Louis)
1934-
American baseball player

Rubin, Jeff; Rael, Rick
JUV *Baseball Brothers.*
Lothrop, Lee & Shepard 1976.
BL v73 1976 p328; KR v44 1976 p684; SLJ v23 D
1976 p70.

2. Abelard, Pierre
1079-1142
French theologian & philosopher

Finkelstein, Elizabeth
*Sinner Turned Saint: A Novel Based on the Life
and Times of Peter Abelard.*
Comet Press Books 1959.

Ince, Richard B.
Abelard of Paris.
Chancery Books 1969.

Meade, Marion
*Stealing Heaven: The Love Story of Heloise and
Abelard.*
Morrow 1979 (Rpr. 1989).
KR v47 1979 p536; LJ v104 1979 p1720; PW v217
My 23, 1980 p75.

Trouncer, Margaret
The Passion of Peter Abelard.
Heinemann 1965.

Waddell, Helen
Peter Abelard, a Novel.
Holt 1933 (Heavily reprinted).
BRD 1933 p973; NYTBR O 1, 1933 p7; SatR S 30,
1933 p145.

3. Abraham
Hebrew patriarch; commanded to sacrifice son
Isaac as test of faith

Bauer, Florence A.
Abram, Son of Terah.
Bobbs-Merrill 1948.
BRD 1948 p50; NYTBR Ap 18, 1948 p16.

Bendiner, Burton
Tell the Stars.
P. Davies 1970.

Chidsey, Alan
Abraham, Father of Nations.
Pageant Press 1956.

Gates, Susa Young
The Prince of Ur.
Bookcraft Co. 1945.

Hesky, Olga
Number the Dust.
Constable 1963.

Kellner, Esther
The Promise.
Westminster Press 1956.
BRD 1956 p506; LJ v81 1956 p828.

Kossak-Szczucka, Zofia
*The Covenant: A Novel of the Life of Abraham the
Prophet.*
Roy Publishers 1951.
BL v47 1951 p401; BRD 1951 p491; KR v19 1951
p308; NYTBR Jl 8, 1951 p10.

Penfield, Wilder
No Other Gods.
Little, Brown 1954.
BRD 1954 p699; LJ v79 1954 p383; NYTBR Mr 21,
1954 p25.

Rees, Jean A.
Road to Sodom: A Novel.
Random House 1961.

Rice, John R.
*Seeking a City: A Novel Based on the Biblical Story
of Abraham.*
W.B. Eerdmans 1957.

Simonhoff, Harry
And Abram Journeyed.
T. Yoseloff 1967.

Todres, Max
Man in the Ancient World.
Meador Publishing 1948.

4. Accoramboni, Vittoria
1557-1585
Italian noblewoman noted for her beauty &
tragic life

Merle, Robert
Vittoria.

Harcourt Brace Jovanovich 1990.
BL v86 1990 p1527; KR v58 1990 p299.

5. Adam
The first man; story told in Genesis, first book of the Bible

Bolt, David
Adam.
John Day Co. 1961.
BL v57 1961 p544; BRD 1961 p140; KR v29 1961 p176; LJ v86 1961 p1475.

Butcher, H. Maxwell
I, Adam.
Horizon House Publishers 1982.

Cannon, Ralph S.
Adam, Where Art Thou.
Carlton Press 1988.

Erskine, John
Adam and Eve; though He Knew Better.
Bobbs-Merrill 1927 (Rpr. 1963).
BRD 1927 p237; NYTBR N 20, 1927 p2; SatR D 3, 1927 p371.

6. Adams, Abigail Smith
1744-1818
Wife of John Adams & mother of John Quincy Adams

Morgan, Helen L.
YA *Liberty Maid: The Story of Abigail Adams.*
Westminster Press 1950.
BL v46 1950 p292; BRD 1950 p654; KR v18 1950 p66; LJ v75 1950 p883; NYTBR My 21, 1950 p18.

Stone, Irving
Those Who Love.
Doubleday 1965.
FC 11th p588; LJ v90 1965 p4113; NYTBR N 7, 1965 p56; Time v86 N 20, 1965 p48.

Wagoner, Jean Brown
JUV *Abigail Adams: Girl of Colonial Days.*
Bobbs-Merrill 1949 (Rpr. 1962, 1992).
LJ v75 1950 p328.

7. Adams, Henry Brooks
1838-1918
American historian

Conroy, Sarah Booth
Refinements of Love: A Novel About Clover and Henry Adams.
Pantheon 1993.
KR v60 1992 p1392; LJ v118 Ja 1993 p163.

8. Adams, John
1735-1826
Second US President

Stone, Irving
Those Who Love.
Doubleday 1965.
FC 11th p588; LJ v90 1965 p4113; NYTBR N 7, 1965 p56; Time v86 N 20, 1965 p48.

Wyckoff, Nicholas
The Braintree Mission: A Fictional Narrative of London and Boston, 1770-1771.
Macmillan 1957.
BRD 1957 p1015; FC 9th p569; KR v25 1957 p155; LJ v82 1957 p1069; NYTBR Ap 21, 1957 p6.

9. Adams, John Quincy
1767-1848
Sixth US President; catalyst behind Monroe Doctrine

Weil, Ann
JUV *John Quincy Adams, Boy Patriot.*
Bobbs-Merrill 1945 (Rpr. 1963).
BRD 1946 p868; KR v13 1945 p298; LJ v70 1945 p1093.

10. Adams, Samuel
1722-1803
American Revolutionary leader; force behind Boston Tea Party

Webb, Robert N.
JUV *We Were There at the Boston Tea Party.*
Grosset & Dunlap 1956.
BRD 1956 p974; KR v24 1956 p45; LJ v81 1956 p1045; NYTBR Mr 18, 1956 p40.

Wibberley, Leonard
YA *John Treegate's Musket.*
Ariel Books 1959.
BL v56 1959 p192; BRD 1960 p1432; KR v27 1959 p495; LJ v84 1959.

11. Adams, William
1564-1620
First Englishman to visit Japan

Blaker, Richard
The Needle-Watcher.
Heinemann 1932 (Rpr. 1973).
BRD 1932 p92; NYTBR O 9, 1932 p20; SatR S 24, 1932 p124.

Clavell, James
Shogun: A Novel of Japan.
Atheneum 1975.
BL v72 1975 p24; BRD 1975 p237; KR v43 1975 p474; LJ v100 1975 p1344; NYTBR Je 22, 1975 p5.

Lund, Robert
Daishi-san: A Novel.
John Day Co. 1961.
BL v57 1961 p606; BRD 1961 p883; KR v29 1961 p77; LJ v86 1961 p1478; NYTBR Ap 2, 1961 p16.

Nicole, Christopher
Lord of the Golden Fan.
Cassell 1973.
B&B v18 Jl 1973 p135; CR v223 O 1973 p217; PW
v207 Mr 3, 1975 p73.

12. Addams, Jane (Laura Jane)
1860-1935
American social reformer & pacifist

Hoobler, Thomas; Hoobler, Dorothy
JUV *The Summer of Dreams: The Story of a World's
Fair Girl.*
Silver Burdett Press 1993.

Jakes, John
Homeland.
Doubleday 1993.

Mark, Grace
The Dream Seekers.
Morrow 1992.

Wagoner, Jean Brown
JUV *Jane Addams, Little Lame Girl.*
Bobbs-Merrill 1944 (Rpr. 1962).
BRD 1944 p776; KR v12 1944 p373.

13. Aesop
Greek fabulist; hundreds of animal fables attributed to him

Wintle, Alfred D.
Aesop.
V. Gollancz 1943.

14. Agassiz, Louis (Jean Louis Radolphe)
1807-1873
Swiss-born American naturalist

MacKaye, David Loring
YA *Pat's New Worlds.*
Longmans, Green 1954.
BRD 1954 p574; KR v22 1954 p441; LJ v79 1954
p2501; SHSLC 7th p408.

McMahon, Thomas
McKay's Bees.
Harper & Row 1979.
BRD 1979 p816; KR v47 1979 p656; LJ v104 1979
p1590; NYTBR Ag 19, 1979 p12.

15. Aguinaldo, Emilio
1869-1964
Philippine revolutionary leader

Barnes, Tellfair B.
The Bamboo Caper.
T.B. Barnes 1990.

16. Ahab
d. 853 BC
King of Israel from about 876 to 853 BC; married Jezebel

Wilson, Dorothy Clarke
Jezebel.
McGraw-Hill 1955.
BRD 1956 p1009; KR v23 1955 p771; LJ v80 1955
p2616; NYTBR D 4, 1955 p57.

17. Akbar
1542-1605
Mogul emperor

Bothwell, Jean
YA *The Promise of the Rose.*
Harcourt, Brace & Co. 1958.
BRD 1959 p124; LJ v84 1959 p255; NYTBR F 22,
1959 p30.

Bothwell, Jean
YA *Ride, Zarina, Ride.*
Harcourt, Brace & World 1966.
KR v34 1966 p989; LJ v91 1966 p5243.

Myers, L. H.
The Near and the Far.
J. Cape 1929 (Rpr. 1943, 1956).
Also reprinted in the author's *The Root and the Flower.*
BRD 1930 p759; NYTBR F 16, 1930 p25.

Ponder, S. E. G.
*A Rose of Hindustan: A Romance of the Time of
Akbar, the Moghul Emperor.*
S. Paul 1946.

Sweet, Robert Burdette
Akbar the Great.
Heinemann Asia 1979.

18. Akhenaton
1372-1354 BC
King of Egypt

Caldecott, Moyra
The Son of the Sun.
Allison & Busby 1986.
LJ v111 D 1986 p133; PW v230 O 17, 1986 p59.

Drury, Allen
A God against the Gods.
Doubleday 1976.
BL v72 1976 p1451; LJ v101 1976 p1554; PW v209
My 17, 1976 p46.

Drury, Allen
Return to Thebes.
Doubleday 1977.
Sequel to *A God Against the Gods.*
BL v73 1977 p792; BRD 1977 p357; KR v45 1977
p111; LJ v102 1977 p512; NYTBR Mr 20, 1977 p29.

Greenhough, Terry
Friend of Pharaoh.
New English Library 1975.

Hawkes, Jacquetta
King of the Two Lands: The Pharaoh Akhenaten.
Random House 1966.
BRD 1967 p579; KR v34 1966 p856; LJ v91 1966
p4696; NYTBR Ja 22, 1967 p40.

Patterson, Emma L.
YA   *Sun Queen: A Novel about Nefertiti.*
D. McKay 1967.
BL v64 1968 p933; KR v35 1967 p1323; LJ v93 1968
p309.

Stacton, David
On a Balcony.
Faber & Faber 1958.
BRD 1960 p1267; SatR S 26, 1959 p20.

19. Albert, Prince
1819-1861
Consort of Queen Victoria of England

Anthony, Evelyn
Victoria and Albert: A Novel.
Crowell 1958.
BL v54 1958 p503; BRD 1958 p1012; FC 10th p17;
KR v26 1958 p90; NYTBR Mr 30, 1958 p35.

Benedictus, David
Who Killed the Prince Consort?.
Macmillan 1982.
Spec v249 N 6, 1982 p29.

Hibbert, Eleanor (Jean Plaidy, pseud.)
The Queen's Husband.
Hale 1973 (Rpr. 1978, 1982).
BL v74 1978 p1674; KR v46 1978 p131; LJ v103 1978
p899.

Long, Freda M.
For the Love of Albert.
Hale 1977.

McDonald, Eva
Queen Victoria's Prince.
Hale 1978.

Tyler-Whittle, Michael S.
Albert's Victoria.
St. Martin's Press 1972.
Sequel to *Young Victoria.*
BL v69 1973 p472; KR v40 1972 p883; LJ v97 1972
p2650.

Wilkins, Vaughan
Consort for Victoria.
Doubleday 1959.
BL v55 1959 p228; BRD 1959 p1062; KR v26 1958
p885; LJ v84 1959 p536.

20. Alcibiades
450?-404? BC
Athenian politician & general

Green, Peter
Achilles His Armour.
Doubleday 1967.
BS v27 O1, 1967; KR v35 Jl 15, 1967 p827; LJ v92
1967 p2811.

Levy, Gertrude R.
The Violet Crown: An Athenian Autobiography.
Faber & Faber 1954.

Marlowe, Stephen
The Shining.
Trident Press 1963.
LJ v88 1963 p3102; NYTBR S 8, 1963 p43.

Plowman, Stephanie
YA   *The Road to Sardis.*
Houghton Mifflin 1965.
BRD 1966 p961; LJ v91 1966 p2712; NYTBR My 8,
1966 p30.

Poole, Lynn
The Magnificent Traitor.
Dodd, Mead 1968.
BL v64 1968 p1023; KR v35 1967 p938; LJ v92 1967
p2811.

Stewart, Desmond
*The Memoirs of Alcibiades, Recently Discovered in
Thrace and for the First Time Put into English.*
Euphorion Books 1952.

Sutcliff, Rosemary
The Flowers of Adonis.
Coward-McCann 1970.
BL v66 1970 p884; BRD 1970 p1361; FC 9th p497;
KR v37 1969 p1287; LJ v95 1970 p84; NYTBR F
15, 1970 p45.

21. Alcott, Louisa May
1832-1888
American author

Brown, Pamela Beatrice
JUV *Louisa.*
Crowell 1955.
BRD 1957 p125.

Fisher, Aileen
YA   *We Alcotts: The Story of Louisa M. Alcott's Fam-
ily as Seen through the Eyes of "Marmee,"
Mother of Little Women.*
Atheneum 1968.
BRD 1968 p429; LJ v93 1968 p4731.

22. Alden, John
1599-1687
Pilgrim colonist; founded Duxbury, Massachusetts

Burt, Olive Woolley
JUV *John Alden, Young Puritan.*
Bobbs-Merrill 1964.

Friskey, Margaret
JUV *John Alden and the Pilgrim Cow.*
Childrens Press 1972.
LJ v98 1973 p1386.

Gaggin, Eva
YA *Down Ryton Water.*
Viking 1941.
BL v38 1941 p83; BRD 1941 p329; LJ v66 1941 p886;
NYTBR Ja 18,.

Gebler, Ernest
*The Plymouth Adventure: A Chronicle Novel of
the Voyage of the Mayflower.*
Doubleday 1950.
BRD 1950 p349; NYTBR Ap 30, 1950 p32; SatR Ap
29, 1950 p13.

Webb, Robert N.
JUV *We Were There with the Mayflower Pilgrims.*
Grosset & Dunlap 1956.

23. Alexander I
1777-1825
Czar of Russia, 1801-1825; grandson of Catherine the Great

Almedingen, Martha Edith
YA *The Retreat from Moscow.*
F. Warne 1968.
BRD 1969 p23; LJ v94 1969 p1788; NYTBR N 3,
1968 p32.

Anthony, Evelyn
Far Flies the Eagle.
Crowell 1955.
BL v51 1955 p468; BRD 1955 p862; KR v23 1955
p335; LJ v80 1955 p1381; NYTBR Jl 17, 1955 p18.

**Blech, William James (William J. Blake,
pseud.)**
The Angel: A Novel Based on the Life of Alexander I of Russia.
Doubleday 1950.
BRD 1950 p86; KR v18 1950 p264; LJ v75 1950 p862;
NYTBR Je 18, 1950 p22.

Dziewanowski, M. K.
Alexander I: Russia's Mysterious Tsar.
Hippocrene Books 1990.
BL v87 1990 p501.

Harrod-Eagles, Cynthia
YA *Anna: The Kirov Saga.*
St. Martin's 1991.
BL v88 1991 p120; KR v59 1991 p954; LJ v116 S 15,
1991 p110.

Leskov, N. S.
JUV *The Steel Flea.*
Harper & Brothers 1943 (Rpr. 1964).
BL v40 1944 p167; BRD 1943 p486; LJ v69 1944 p73;
NYTBR F 13, 1944 p14.

Sava, George
The Emperor Story: A Historical Romance.
Faber & Faber 1959.

Waldeck, R. G.
Lustre in the Sky.
Doubleday 1946.
BRD 1946 p329; KR v14 1946 p110; NYTBR Ap 28,
1946 p18; SatR Je 1, 1946 p8.

24. Alexander II
1818-1881
Czar of Russia, 1855-1881; son of Nicholas I

Phillips, Michael; Pella, Judith
The Crown and the Crucible.
Bethany House 1991.
Ch Today v35 N 25, 1991 p38.

25. Alexander the Great
356-323 BC
Macedonian king & conqueror of Greece,
Egypt, & Persia

Andrews, Mary Evans
YA *Hostage to Alexander.*
D. McKay 1961.
BRD 1962 p33; LJ v86 1961 p3072.

De Camp, Lyon Sprague
An Elephant for Aristotle.
Doubleday 1958.
BL v54 1958 p475; BRD 1958 p286; KR v26 1958
p93; LJ v83 1958 p1550; NYTBR Ap 6, 1958 p22.

Druon, Maurice
Alexander, the God.
Scribner 1960.
BL v58 1961 p191; BRD 1962 p323; LJ v86 1961
p4206; NYTBR D 10, 1961 p48.

Eiker, Karl V.
Star of Macedon.
Putnam 1957.
BRD 1957 p283; KR v25 1957 p228; LJ v82 1957
p1239; NYTBR My 19, 1957 p32.

Gerson, Noel Bertram
The Golden Lyre.
Doubleday 1963.

Kazantzakis, Nikos
YA *Alexander the Great.*
Ohio University Press 1982.
BS v42 Jl 1982 p130; LJ v106 1981 p2407.

Lamb, Harold
*Alexander of Macedon: The Journey to World's
End.*
Doubleday 1946.
BL v42 1946 p327; BRD 1946 p467; KR v14 1946
p117; NYTBR My 19, 1946 p6.

Marshall, Edison
The Conqueror.
Doubleday 1962.

Menen, Aubrey
A Conspiracy of Women.
Random House 1965.
BL v62 1965 p354; BRD 1965 p864; KR v33 1965
p943; LJ v90 1965 p5418; NYTBR N 14, 1965 p4.

Moray, Helga
Roxana and Alexander.
Hale 1971.

Payne, Pierre
Alexander the God.
A.A. Wyn 1954.
BRD 1954 p697; KR v22 1954 p644; NYTBR N 7,
1954 p48.

Renault, Mary
Fire from Heaven.
Pantheon 1969.
BL v66 1970 p543; BRD 1970 p1174; KR v37 1969
p1086; LJ v94 1969 p4541; NYTBR Je 7, 1970 p2.

Renault, Mary
Funeral Games.
Pantheon 1981.
BL v78 1981 p73; BRD 1982 p1116; KR v49 1981
p1251; LJ v106 1981 p2154; NYTBR Ja 17, 1982
p7.

Renault, Mary
The Persian Boy.
Pantheon 1972.
BRD 1973 p1081; KR v40 1972 p1115; LJ v98 1973
p2206; NYTBR Ja 7, 1973 p34.

Skipper, Mervyn
JUV *The Fooling of King Alexander.*
Atheneum 1967.
BL v64 1968 p595; BRD 1967 p1217; KR v35 1967
p1201; LJ v92 1967 p4606; NYTBR N 5, 1967 p71.

Wassermann, Jakob
Alexander in Babylon.
Ziff-Davis 1949.
BRD 1949 p959; LJ v74 1949 p496; NYTBR Mr 27,
1949 p31.

26. Alexander VI, Pope
1431-1503
Pope, 1492-1503; father of Cesare & Lucrezia
Borgia

Davis, Genevieve
A Passion in the Blood.
Simon & Schuster 1977.
KR v45 1977 p110; LJ v102 1977 p946; PW v211 My
23, 1977 p243.

Haasse, Hella S.
The Scarlet City: A Novel of 16th-Century Italy.
Academy Chicago Publishers 1990.

BL v87 1990 p140; KR v58 1990 p1026; LJ v115 Ag
1990 p141; NYTBR Je 16, 1991 p16.

Sava, George
Those Borgias.
Faber & Faber 1940.

27. Alexandra Feodorovna
1872-1918
Married Nicholas II, last Czar of Russia; slain
with family by Bolsheviks

Bloom, Ursula (Lozania Prole, pseud.)
The Last Tsarina.
Hale 1970.

Bownen, True
And the Stars Shall Fall.
Wyn 1951.
BRD 1951 p105; KR v19 1951 p190; NYTBR Jl 29,
1951 p11; SatR Je 2, 1951 p32.

Lambton, Antony
Elizabeth and Alexandra.
Dutton 1986.
BRD 1987 p1063; KR v54 1986 p237; LJ v111 Ap 15,
1986 p95; NYTBR My 18, 1986 p34.

28. Alfieri, Vittorio
1749-1803
Italian poet & dramatist

Rees, Joan
The Queen of Hearts.
Hale 1974.
TLS Ja 17, 1975 p48.

Wilkins, William V.
Crown without Sceptre.
Macmillan 1952.
BL v48 1952 p281; BRD 1952 p954; KR v20 1952
p163; NYTBR My 11, 1952 p20.

29. Alfred the Great
849-899
West Saxon king, 871-899

Berry, Erick
YA *The King's Jewel.*
Viking 1957.
BRD 1957 p80; KR v25 1957 p443; KR v82 1957
p2657; NYTBR D 29, 1957 p16.

Bonallack, Basil
The Flame in the Dark.
St. Martin's 1976.
KR v44 1976 p649; LJ v101 1976 p2084.

Duggan, Alfred Leo
The Right Line of Cerdic.
Pantheon 1961.
Also published as *King of Athelney.*
BL v58 1962 p369; BRD 1962 p327; LJ v87 1962
p853; NYTBR D 10, 1961 p49.

Farnol, Jeffery
The King Liveth.
Doubleday, Doran 1944.
BRD 1944 p231; KR v12 1944 p103.

Hodges, Cyril W.
YA   *The Marsh King.*
Coward-McCann 1967.
BRD 1967 p613; KR v35 1967 p349; LJ v92 1967
p2029; NYTBR My 7, 1967 p14.

Hodges, Cyril W.
JUV   *The Namesake.*
Coward-McCann 1964.
BRD 1964 p565; LJ v89 1964 p2229; NYTBR Ja 24,
1965 p26.

Ketchum, Philip
YA   *The Great Axe Bretwalda.*
Little, Brown 1955.
BL v52 1955 p39; BRD 1955 p494; KR v23 1955
p421; LJ v80 1955 p2391; NYTBR N 13, 1955 p24.

Leighton, Margaret
JUV   *Journey for a Princess.*
Ariel Books 1960.
BRD 1961 p822; LJ v85 1960 p4226; NYTBR Ag 21,
1960 p28; SatR D 17, 1960 p35.

Leighton, Margaret
JUV   *Voyage to Coromandel.*
Ariel Books 1965.
BRD 1965 p754; LJ v90 1965 p974; NYTBR My 2,
1965 p26.

Trease, Geoffrey
YA   *Escape to King Alfred.*
Vanguard Press 1958.
Also published as *Mist Over Athelney.*
BL v55 1959 p402; BRD 1959 p992; LJ v84 1959
p652; NYTBR F 15, 1959 p40.

Williams, Patry
Alfred the King.
Faber & Faber 1951.

Wolf, Joan
The Edge of Light.
NAL Books 1990.
BL v86 1990 p2974; KR v58 1990 p834; LJ v115 Je
15, 1990 p138.

30. Allen, Ethan
1738-1789
American Revolutionary soldier; organized
Green Mountain Boys

Alderman, Clifford L.
The Arch of Stars.
Appleton-Century-Crofts 1950.
BRD 1950 p10; KR v18 1950 p283; LJ v75 1950
p1044; NYTBR Je 25, 1950 p25.

Allen, Merritt P.
YA   *The Green Cockade.*
Longmans, Green 1942.

BL v39 1942 p123; BRD 1942 p14; LJ v67 1942
p1069; NYTBR O 18, 1942 p9.

Mason, F. van Wyck
Guns for Rebellion.
Doubleday 1977.
KR v45 1977 p743; LJ v102 1977 p2082.

Meigs, Cornelia
The Covered Bridge.
Macmillan 1936 (Rpr. 1964).
BL v33 1936 p127; BRD 1936 p668; LJ v62 1937
p303; NYTBR Ja 24, 1937 p9.

Peck, Robert Newton
YA   *Hang for Treason.*
Doubleday 1976.
BRD 1976 p931; KR v44 1976 p78; LJ v101 1976
p1050; NYTBR Ap 4, 1976 p32; SLJ v22 Mr 1976
p117.

Thompson, Daniel P.
The Green Mountain Boys.
M.M. Caldwell 1839 (Heavily reprinted).

Van de Water, Frederic F.
Catch a Falling Star.
Duell, Sloan and Pearce 1949.
BL v45 F 15, 1949 p210; BRD 1949 p936; FC 11th
p415; LJ v74 1949 p60; NYTBR Ja 30, 1949 p21.

Van de Water, Frederic F.
Rebel's Progress.
Skeffington & Son 1952.

Van de Water, Frederic F.
YA   *Reluctant Rebel.*
Duell, Sloan & Pearce 1948.
BL v44 1948 p314; BRD 1948 p863; FC 7th p359; KR
v16 1948 p30; LJ v73 1948 p474; NYTBR Ap 4,
1948 p5.

Webb, Robert N.
JUV   *We Were There with Ethan Ellen and the Green
Mountain Boys.*
Grosset & Dunlap 1956.
LJ v82 1957 p587.

31. Allen, Steve
1921-
Entertainer know for ad-libbed witticisms; early
host of *I've Got a Secret, Tonight Show*

Allen, Steve
Murder on the Glitter Box.
Kensington Publishing 1989.
BL v85 1989 p1849.

Allen, Steve
The Talk Show Murders.
Delacorte 1982.
BL v78 1981 p138; KR v49 1981 p1428; LJ v106 1981
p2334; NYTBR Ap 4, 1982 p29.

32. Allende, Salvador (Gossens)
1908-1973
Chilean president, 1970-1973; died in coup

Alegria, Fernando
Allende.
Stanford University Press 1993.
LJ v118 My 1993 p218.

Lindberg, Sue
Chicho: The Rise and Fall of Salvador Allende.
Lindberg Publishing 1982.

33. Allston, Washington
1779-1843
American painter & poet

Boelt, Martha
JUV *Boy Painter from Brookgreen: An Historical Novel
for Children.*
Copple House Books 1982.

34. Alston, Theodosia Burr
1783-1813
Daughter of Aaron Burr

Graff, Polly
YA *Theodosia, Daughter of Aaron Burr.*
Farrar & Rinehart 1941.

Harris, Cyril
Street of Knives.
Little, Brown 1950.
BL v47 1950 p75; BRD 1950 p407; KR v18 1950
p315; LJ v75 1950 p1291; NYTBR Ag 13, 1950 p22.

Seton, Anya
My Theodosia.
Houghton Mifflin 1941.
BRD 1941 p806; FC 7th p311; LJ v66 1941 p220;
NYTBR Mr 16, 1941 p7.

35. Altgeld, John Peter
1847-1902
Governor of Illinois, 1892-1896

Fast, Howard
The American: A Middle Western Legend.
Duell, Sloan & Pearce 1946.
BL v42 1946 p365; BRD 1946 p259; FC 7th p127; KR
v14 1946 p107; LJ v71 1946 p978; NYTBR Jl 21,
1946 p4.

36. Alva, Duke of
see Alvarez de Toledo, Fernando

37. Alvarado, Pedro de
1486-1541
Spanish adventurer; helped conquer Mexico &
Central America for Spain

Duncombe, Frances Riker
YA *The Quetzal Feather.*
Lothrop, Lee & Shepard 1967.
KR v35 1967 p1054; LJ v92 1967 p4258.

McAndrews, Anita
Conquistador's Lady.
Fithian Press 1990.

38. Alvarez de Toledo, Fernando
1507-1582
Spanish general

Stevenson, John P.
The Captain General.
Doubleday 1956.
BL v53 1956 p95; BRD 1956 p894; KR v24 1956
p452; SatR S 22, 1956 p29.

39. Ambrose, Saint
340-397
Bishop of Milan; most valuable legacy to the
church is his hymns

Raynolds, Robert
The Sinner of Saint Ambrose.
Bobbs-Merrill 1952.
BL v49 1952 p14; BRD 1952 p740; NYTBR Ag 10,
1952 p4; SatR Ag 9, 1952 p16.

40. Amenhotep IV
see Akhenaton

41. Amin, Idi
1925-
Ugandan dictator, 1971-1980

Ghanty, Yacoob H.
The Return of Big Dada.
Y. Ghanty 1981.

Watkins, Leslie
The Killing of Idi Amin.
Everest 1976.
Kliatt v11 Fall 1977 p9; LJ v102 1977 p1306; PW
v211 Ap 18, 1977 p60.

Westlake, Donald E.
YA *Kahawa.*
Viking 1982.
BL v78 1981 p522; KR v50 1982 p96; LJ v107 1982
p476; SLJ v28 Ag 1982 p132.

42. Amos
Eighth-century-BC Hebrew prophet

Davis, Eldon
The Man from Tekoa.
Gai-Garet Design & Publication 1990.

Wilson, Dorothy Clarke
The Herdsman.
Westminster Press 1946.

BL v43 1946 p118; BRD 1946 p897; KR v14 1946 p528; LJ v71 1946 p1465; NYTBR N 10, 1946 p9.

43. Amundsen, Roald Engelbregt
1872-1928
Norwegian polar explorer

Holt, Kare
The Race: A Novel of Polar Exploration.
Delacorte 1976.
Translation of *Kapplopet.*
BRD 1977 p625; KR v44 1976 p808; LJ v101 1976 p2086; NYTBR O 31, 1976 p42.

44. Andersen, Hans Christian
1805-1875
Danish author

Hubbard, Margaret A.
Flight of the Swan.
Bruce Publishing Co. 1946.
BL v43 1947 p191; BRD 1947 p439; LJ v72 1947 p87; NYTBR D 22, 1947 p11.

45. Andrassy, Julius, Count
1823-1890
Hungarian politician

Abrahams, William
Imperial Waltz.
Dial 1954.
BL v50 1954 p400; BRD 1954 p3; NYTBR Je 6, 1954 p24.

46. Andre, John
1750-1780
English soldier; hanged as Revolutionary spy

Bailey, Anthony
Major Andre.
Farrar, Straus, Giroux 1987.
BL v83 1987 p1649; KR v55 1987 p656; LJ v112 Je 15, 1987 p82; NYTBR Jl 5, 1987 p10.

D'Oyley, Elizabeth
Why, Soldiers, Why?.
M. Joseph 1957.

Groh, Lynn
YA *The Culper Spy Ring.*
Westminster Press 1969.
BRD 1970 p573; KR v37 1969 p941; LJ v94 1969 p4612.

Lancaster, Bruce
The Secret Road.
Little, Brown 1952.
BL v48 1952 p360; BRD 1952 p531; KR v20 1952 p287; LJ v77 1952 p1012; NYTBR Je 15, 1952 p5.

Longstreet, Stephen
Eagles Where I Walk.

Doubleday 1961.
LJ v86 1961 p3481.

Pleasants, Henry
Mars' Butterfly.
Christopher Publishing House 1941.
BRD 1942 p607.

47. Andree, Salomon August
1854-1897
Swedish explorer; first to explore Arctic in air by balloon

Sundman, Per Olof
The Flight of the Eagle.
Pantheon 1970.
BL v66 1970 p1382; BRD 1970 p1359; FC 9th p497; KR v38 1970 p203; LJ v95 1970 p2182; NYTBR My 31, 1970 p16.

48. Andropov, Yuri
1914-1984
Soviet politician

Gowing, Nik
The Wire: A Novel.
St. Martin's 1988.
KR v56 1988 p1694; NYTBR Mr 26, 1989 p16.

Salisbury, Harrison E.
The Gates of Hell.
Random House 1975.
KR v43 1975 p938; LJ v100 1975 p1846.

49. Andros, Edmund, Sir
1637-1714
English colonial administrator

Breslin, Howard
The Silver Oar.
Crowell 1954.
BL v51 1954 p83; BRD 1954 p110; KR v22 1954 p454; NYTBR N 14, 1954 p34.

50. Anne
1665-1714
Queen of Great Britain & Ireland, 1702-1714

Ansle, Dorothy P. (Hebe Elsna, pseud.)
The Elusive Crown.
Collins 1973 (Rpr. 1981).

Auchincloss, Louis
Exit Lady Masham.
Houghton Mifflin 1983.
FC 11th p28; KR v51 1983 p892; LJ v108 1983 p1806; PW v224 Ag 26, 1983 p369.

Bloom, Ursula (Lozania Prole, pseud.)
Marlborough's Unfair Lady.
Hale 1965 (Rpr. 1984).

Dakers, Elaine (Jane Lane, pseud.)
The Crown for a Lie.
F. Muller 1962.

Hibbert, Eleanor (Jean Plaidy, pseud.)
The Haunted Sisters.
Hale 1966 (Rpr. 1977).
BL v74 1978 p996; KR v45 1977 p1160.

Hibbert, Eleanor (Jean Plaidy, pseud.)
The Queen's Favourites.
Hale 1966 (Rpr. 1978).
KR v46 1978 p569; KR v46 1978 p644.

Kenyon, Frank Wilson
The Glory and the Dream.
Dodd, Mead 1963.

51. Anne of Cleves
1515-1557
Fourth wife of Henry VIII

Barnes, Margaret Campbell
My Lady of Cleves.
Macrae Smith Co. 1946.
BRD 1946 p41; FC 10th p34; KR v14 Ja 1946 p5;
    NYTBR Mr 10, 1946 p8: WLB v42 Ap 1946 p59.

Hamilton, Julia
Anne of Cleves.
Sphere 1972.
BS v32 Jl 1, 1972 p179.

Street, M. K.
The Flanders Mare.
Hale 1970.

52. Anson, George
1697-1762
English naval officer; circumnavigated globe,
1740-1744

Mason, F. van Wyck
Manila Galleon.
Little, Brown 1961.
BRD 1961 p945; FC 9th p349; KR v28 1960 p1042; LJ
    v86 1961 p114; NYTBR F 26, 1961 p46.

O'Brian, Patrick
YA *The Golden Ocean.*
John Day Co. 1956.
LJ v82 1957 p2199.

Styles, Showell
JUV *Centurion Comes Home.*
Faber & Faber 1980.
TLS D 26, 1980 p1458.

53. Anthony of Padua, Saint
1195-1231
Biblical scholar; patron saint of lost articles

Beahn, John E.
A Rich Young Man: Saint Anthony of Padua.
Bruce Pub. Co. 1953.

54. Anthony, Susan B.
1820-1906
American reformer

Jacobs, William J.
JUV *Mother, Aunt Susan and Me: The First Fight for
    Women's Rights.*
Coward, McCann & Geoghegan 1979.
BL v76 1979 p120; CBRS v8 1979 p9; KR v47 1979
    p1070.

Malm, Dorothea
The Woman Question.
Appleton-Century-Crofts 1957.
BL v55 1958 p23; BRD 1958 p712; KR v26 1958 p92;
    LJ v83 1958 p2079.

Monsell, Helen Albee
JUV *Susan Anthony, Girl Who Dared.*
Bobbs-Merrill 1960.

55. Antony, Marc
83?-30 BC
Roman politician & soldier; committed suicide
with Cleopatra

Butts, Mary
Scenes from the Life of Cleopatra.
Heinemann 1935 (Rpr. 1974).

Duggan, Alfred Leo
Three's Company.
Coward-McCann 1958.
BRD 1958 p316; FC 8th p128; KR v26 1958 p423; LJ
    v83 1958 p2840; TLS Ap 11, 1958 p193.

Gerson, Noel Bertram
That Egyptian Woman.
Doubleday 1956.
BRD 1956 p355; KR v24 1956 p487; NYTBR D 16,
    1956 p19; SatR Ag 25, 1956 p16.

56. Anza, Juan Bautista de
1735-1788
Explorer & Spanish colonial official; founded
San Francisco

Gray, Genevieve
JUV *How Far, Felipe?.*
Harper & Row 1978.
KR v46 1978 p242; NYTBR Ap 30, 1978 p38; SLJ
    v24 My 1978 p80.

Lauritzen, Jonreed
The Cross and the Sword.
Doubleday 1965.
BL v61 1965 p1055; FC 8th p251; KR v33 1965 p398;
    LJ v90 1965 p2583.

Summers, Richard A.
YA *Cavalcade to California.*
Oxford University Press 1941.
BRD 1941 p875; LJ v66 1941 p310; NYTBR Je 1,
1941 p9.

Wells, Evelyn
A City for St. Francis.
Doubleday 1967.
KR v35 1967 p580; LJ v92 1967 p2608.

57. Apollinaire, Guillaume
1880-1918
French poet, author, & critic

Frutkin, Mark
Atmospheres Apollinaire.
Porcupine's Quill 1988 (Rpr. 1990).
CanLit Autumn 1990 p139.

58. Appleseed, Johnny
1774-1847
American pioneer; according to legend he
planted & tended a trail of apple-seedling or-
chards over vast areas of the US

Atkinson, Eleanor
JUV *Johnny Appleseed: The Romance of the Sower.*
Harper & Brothers 1915 (Rpr. 1943, 1965).
BRD 1915 p15; FC 7th p22; NYTBR Ap 18, 1915
p143.

Douglas, Emily
JUV *Appleseed Farm.*
Abingdon Farm 1948.
BL v44 1948 p253, BRD 1948 p225; CC 1951 p183;
HB v24 My 1948 p193; KR v16 1948 p85; LJ v73
1948 p484.

Fast, Howard
YA *The Tall Hunter.*
Harper & Row 1942.
BRD 1942 p244; LJ v67 1942 p891; NYTBR Ja 24,
1943 p11.

Hunt, Irene
JUV *Trail of Apple Blossoms.*
Follett 1968.
BL v64 1968 p1186; LJ v93 1968 p2113; NYTBR Ap
14, 1968 p20; PW.

McMeekin, Isabel McLennan
JUV *Journey Cake.*
Messner 1942.
BRD 1942 p502; LJ v67 1942 p1069; NYTBR N 15,
1942 p32; SatR N 14, 1942 p27.

Nissenson, Hugh
The Tree of Life.
Harper & Row 1985.
BL v82 1985 p192; LATBR N 3, 1985 p14; NYTBR
O 27, 1985 p14; PW v228 Ag 16, 1985 p63; Time
v126 O 21, 1985 p87.

59. Aquinas, Thomas, Saint
1225-1274
Italian theologian & philosopher

Carroll, Malachy G.
Time Cannot Dim.
H. Regnery Co. 1955.
BL v52 1956 p251.

De Wohl, Louis
The Quiet Light.
Lippincott 1950.
BL v47 1950 p12; BRD 1950 p248; FC 7th p106; LJ
v75 1950 p1290; NYTBR S 3, 1950 p11.

60. Arbuckle, "Fatty" (Roscoe Conkling)
1887-1933
Involved in famous Hollywood manslaughter
scandal, 1921

Rogers, Garet
Scandal in Eden.
Dial 1963.
LJ v88 1963 p3103; NYTBR Jl 28, 1963 p22.

61. Archimedes
287?-212 BC
Greek mathematician

Lexau, Joan M.
JUV *Archimedes Takes a Bath.*
Crowell 1969.
CC 13th p543; KR v37 1969 p445; LJ v94 1969
p2104; SatR Je 28, 1969 p39.

62. Aristotle
384-322 BC
Greek philosopher

De Camp, Lyon Sprague
An Elephant for Aristotle.
Doubleday 1958.
BL v54 1958 p475; BRD 1958 p286; KR v26 1958
p93; LJ v83 1958 p1550; NYTBR Ap 6, 1958 p22.

Doody, Margaret
YA *Aristotle Detective.*
Harper & Row 1978.
KR v47 1979 p1456; TLS N 10, 1978 p1303.

Heller, Joseph
Picture This.
Putnam 1988.
BL v84 1988 p1754; BRD 1989 p726; KR v56 1988
p923; LJ v113 S 1, 1988 p182; NYTBR S 11, 1988
p9.

63. Arkwright, Richard, Sir
1732-1792
English inventor & manufacturer

Arkwright, Margaret
Cotton Arkwright, Master Spinner: A Novel Based on the Life of Sir Richard Arkwright.
D.J. Morton Publishers 1971.

64. Arnaz, Desi
1917-1986
Rumba bandleader; formed Desilu Productions with wife, Lucille Ball

Hijuelos, Oscar
The Mambo Kings Play Songs of Love.
Farrar, Straus, Giroux 1989.
BL v85 1989 p1943; BRD 1990 p817; KR v57 1989 p860; NYTBR Ag 27, 1989 p1.

65. Arnold, Benedict
1741-1801
American Revolutionary general & traitor

Bailey, Anthony
Major Andre.
Farrar, Straus, Giroux 1987.
BL v83 1987 p1649; KR v55 1987 p656; LJ v112 Je 15, 1987 p82; NYTBR Jl 5, 1987 p10.

Betz, Eva K.
JUV *Victory Drums.*
St. Anthony Guild Press 1955.

Callahan, North
Peggy.
Cornwall Books 1983.
LATBR Jl 15, 1984 p6.

Gerson, Noel Bertram
The Twisted Saber: A Biographical Novel of Benedict Arnold.
Dodd, Mead 1963.

Gessner, Robert
Treason.
Scribner 1944.
BRD 1944 p278; KR v12 1944 p106.

Lancaster, Bruce
The Secret Road.
Little, Brown 1952.
BL v48 1952 p360; BRD 1952 p531; KR v20 1952 p287; LJ v77 1952 p1012; NYTBR Je 15, 1952 p5.

Longstreet, Stephen
Eagles Where I Walk.
Doubleday 1961.
LJ v86 1961 p3481.

Mason, F. van Wyck
Guns for Rebellion.
Doubleday 1977.
KR v45 1977 p743; LJ v102 1977 p2082.

Nolan, Jeannette C.
YA *Treason at the Point.*
Messner 1944.

BL v41 1944 p80; BRD 1944 p560; KR v12 1944 p405; LJ v69 1944 p940.

Partington, Norman
The Sunshine Patriot: A Novel of Benedict Arnold.
St. Martin's 1975.
KR v43 1975 p582; LJ v100 1975 p1347; NYTBR D 28, 1975 p20; PW v207 Je 2, 1975 p46.

Peck, Robert Newton
YA *Fawn: A Novel.*
Little, Brown 1975.
BL v71 1975 p745; BRD 1975 p980; KR v42 1974 p1271; LJ v100 1975 p603; NYTBR F 2, 1975 p12; SLJ v21 My 1975 p66.

Pleasants, Henry
Mars' Butterfly.
Christopher Publishing House 1941.
BRD 1942 p607.

Roberts, Kenneth L.
Arundel: A Chronicle of the Province of Maine and of the Secret Expedition Led by Benedict Arnold against Quebec.
Doubleday, Doran 1930 (Rpr. 1933, 1938, 1945, 1947).
BL v26 Ap 30, 1930 p282; BRD 1930 p888; NYTBR Ja 12, 1930 p8; SHSLC 10th p526.

Roberts, Kenneth L.
Rabble in Arms: A Chronicle of Arundel and the Burgoyne Invasion.
Doubleday, Doran 1933 (Heavily reprinted).
Sequel to *Arundel.*
BL v30 1934 p150; BRD 1933 p797; NYTBR N 19, 1933 p8; SatR N 18, 1933 p269.

Spicer, Bart
Brother to the Enemy.
Dodd, Mead & Co. 1958.
BL v55 F 1, 1959 p288; BRD 1959 p933; FC 9th p480; NYTBR N 23, 1958 p50.

Taylor, David
Storm the Last Rampart.
Lippincott 1960.
BL v56 1960 p511; BRD 1960 p1320; KR v27 1959 p932; LJ v85 1960 p146; NYTBR My 29, 1960 p19.

Wolf, William J.
Benedict Arnold: A Novel.
Paideia Publishers 1990.
BL v87 1990 p258.

66. Arnold, Matthew
1822-1888
English poet & critic

MacDonald, Isobel
The Buried Self: A Background to the Poems of Matthew Arnold.
P. Davies 1949 (Rpr. 1969).

67. Artaud, Antonin
1896-1948
French actor & director; closely identified with "Theater of Cruelty"

Goldstein, Lisa
The Dream Years.
Bantam 1985.
BL v81 1985 p1637; KR v53 1985 p678; LJ v110 Ag 1985 p120; NYTBR O 20, 1985 p20; PW v227 Jl 15, 1985 p58.

68. Arthur, Chester Alan
1829-1886
21st US President

Fabian, Josephine C.
The Jackson's Hole Story: An Historical Novel Set in the Grand Teton Mountains of Wyoming.
Desert Book Co. 1963 (Rpr. 1972).

Wiegand, William
The Chester A. Arthur Conspiracy.
Dial 1983.
BL v79 1983 p1390; KR v51 1983 p682; LJ v108 1983 p1385; PW v224 Jl 1983 p56.

69. Arthur, King
Legendary king of the Britons

Barthelme, Donald
The King.
Harper & Row 1990.
BRD 1991 p123; LJ v115 Ap 1, 1990 p134; NYTBR My 27, 1990 p8.

Berger, Thomas
Arthur Rex: A Legendary Novel.
Delacorte 1978.
BRD 1979 p102; KR v46 1978 p701; LJ v103 1978 p2260; NYTBR N 12, 1978 p49.

Borowsky, Marvin
The Queen's Knight.
Random House 1955.
BL v51 1955 p366; BRD 1955 p95; KR v23 1955 p99; LJ v80 1955 p790; NYTBR Ap 10, 1955 p19.

Bowers, Gwendolyn
JUV *Brother to Galahad.*
H.Z. Walck 1963.
BRD 1963 p116; LJ v88 1963 p4078.

Bradley, Marion Zimmer
The Mists of Avalon.
Knopf 1982.
BL v79 1982 p409; KR v50 1982 p1200; LJ v107 1982 p2351; PW v222 N 12, 1982 p58.

Bulla, Clyde Robert
JUV *The Sword in the Tree.*
Crowell 1956.
BRD 1956 p138; CC 1961 p290; KR v24 1956 p1; LJ v81 1956 p764; NYTBR Ap 8, 1956 p38.

Canning, Victor
The Crimson Chalice.
Morrow 1978.
Originally published in three volumes under titles: *The Crimson Chalice*, *The Circle of the Gods*, and *The Immortal Wound.*
BL 74 1978 p1717; KR v46 1978 p649; LJ v103 1978 p1529.

Chant, Joy
The High Kings.
Bantam 1983.
LJ v108 1983 p2164; PW v224 S 2, 1983 p67.

Curry, Jane Louise
JUV *The Sleepers.*
Harcourt, Brace & World 1968.
BL v65 1968 p61; KR v36 1968 p459.

David, Peter
YA *Knight Life.*
Ace Fantasy Books 1987.
PW v231 Mr 13, 1987 p80; VOYA v10 O 1987 p176.

Ditmas, Edith
JUV *Gareth of Orkney.*
Faber & Faber 1956.

Finkel, George
YA *Watch Fires to the North.*
Viking 1967.
Also published as *Twilight Province.*
BRD 1968 p424; LJ v93 1968 p2546; NYTBR Ap 14, 1968 p20.

Gloag, John
Artorius Rex.
St. Martin's 1977.
KR v45 1977 p741; LJ v102 1977 p2081.

Godwin, Parke
Firelord.
Doubleday 1980.
KR v48 1980 p1101; LJ v105 1980 p2106.

Hadfield, Alice M.
JUV *King Arthur and the Round Table.*
Dutton 1958.

Housman, Clemence
The Life of Sir Aglovale de Galis.
Methuen 1905 (Rpr. 1954).

Jewett, Eleanore Myers
YA *The Hidden Treasure of Glaston.*
Viking 1946.
BL v43 1946 p38; BRD 1946 p423; KR v14 1946 p424; LJ v71 1946 p1336; NYTBR O 20, 1946 p30.

Jones, Courtway
In the Shadow of the Oak King.
Pocket Books 1991.
BWatch v12 O 1991 p3; Locus v27 S 1991 p60; SLJ v38 Ap 1992 p163.

Jones, Mary J.
Avalon.

Naiad Press 1991.
Locus v27 D 1991 p33.

Kennealy, Patricia
The Hawk's Gray Feather.
ROC 1990.
LJ v115 Mr 15, 1990 p116; PW v237 Mr 16, 1990 p64.

Malory, Thomas Sir
Le Morte d'Arthur.
Several editions exist; on which most other King Arthur stories are based.

Marshall, Edison
The Pagan King.
Doubleday 1959.
BL v56 1959 p28; BRD 1959 p678; KR v27 1959 p328; NYTBR Jl 19, 1959 p23.

Masefield, John
Badon Parchments.
Heinemann 1947.

Nathan, Robert
The Fair.
Knopf 1964.
BRD 1964 p866; LJ v89 1964 p1624; NYTBR Ap 12, 1964 p36.

Norton, Andre
JUV *Steel Magic.*
World Pub. Co. 1965.
CC 12th p438.

O'Meara, Walter
The Duke of War.
Harcourt, Brace & World 1966.
BL v62 1966 p434; KR v33 1965 p1204; LJ v91 1966 p716; NYTBR F 6, 1966 p40.

Powys, John Cowper
Porius, a Romance of the Dark Ages.
Macdonald 1952.
BRD 1952 p724; LJ v77 1952 p591; NYTBR Ap 27, 1952 p5.

Pyle, Howard
JUV *The Story of King Arthur and His Knights.*
Scribner 1903 (Heavily reprinted).

Pyle, Howard
JUV *The Story of the Grail and the Passing of Arthur.*
Scribner 1910 (Heavily reprinted).
NYTBR O 22, 1910 p589.

Roberts, Dorothy James
Kinsmen of the Grail.
Little, Brown 1963.
BRD 1963 p852; FC 9th p428; LJ v88 1963 p2538; SatR Ag 31, 1963 p26.

Roberts, Dorothy James
Launcelot, My Brother.
Appleton-Century-Crofts 1954.
BL v51 1954 p85; BRD 1954 p748; FC 9th p429; KR v22 1954 p458; NYTBR S 26, 1954 p5.

Robinson, Mabel L.
JUV *King Arthur and His Knights.*
Random House 1953.
BRD 1953 p797; LJ v78 1953 p1858; NYTBR N 15, 1953 p20.

Service, Pamela F.
YA *Tomorrow's Magic.*
Atheneum 1987.
BL v84 1987 p400; BRD 1988 p1562; PW v232 S 25, 1987 p111; SLJ v34 S 1987 p198.

Sterne, Emma Gelders
JUV *King Arthur and the Knights of the Round Table.*
Golden Press 1962.

Stewart, Mary
The Crystal Cave.
Morrow 1970.
BL v67 1970 p287; FC 9th p489; LJ v95 1970 p2830; NYTBR Ag 9, 1970 p33; PW v197 My 4, 1970 p59.

Stewart, Mary
The Hollow Hills.
Morrow 1973.
Sequel to *The Crystal Cave;* sequel *The Last Enchantment.*
BRD 1973 p1250; FC 9th p489; LJ v98 1973 p1845; NYTBR Jl 29, 1973 p13.

Stone, Eugenia
YA *Squire for King Arthur.*
Follett 1955.
CC 1956 p313.

Sutcliff, Rosemary
YA *The Road to Camlann.*
Dutton 1982.
BL v79 1983 p727; BRD 1983 p1398; SLJ v29 Ja 1983 p88.

Sutcliff, Rosemary
YA *Sword at Sunset.*
Coward-McCann 1963 (Rpr. 1987).
BRD 1963 p976; LJ v88 1963 p2786; NYTBR My 26, 1963 p26; SatR Ag 31, 1963 p26.

Treece, Henry
The Great Captains.
Random House 1956.
BL v52 1956 p363; BRD 1956 p934; FC 7th p351; KR v24 1956 p20; LJ v81 1956 p444; NYTBR Mr 18, 1956 p4.

Turton, Godfrey E.
The Emperor Arthur.
Doubleday 1967.
BL v64 1968 p770; KR v35 1967 p991; NYTBR N 12, 1967 p68.

White, T. H.
YA *The Book of Merlyn: The Unpublished Conclusion to The Once and Future King.*
University of Texas Press 1977.
BRD 1978 p1393; KR v45 1977 p750; LJ v102 1977 p1784; NYTBR Ag 28, 1977 p31; SLJ v24 Mr 1978 p142.

White, T. H.
YA *The Once and Future King.*
Putnam 1958.
Contains: *The Candle in the Wind, The Sword in the Stone, The Witch in the Wood,* and *The Ill-Made Knight.*
BRD 1958 p1111; KR v26 1958 p429; LJ v83 1958 p2184; NYTBR Ag 24, 1958 p4.

Wolf, Joan
The Road to Avalon.
New American Library 1988.
PW v235 Je 23, 1989 p56.

Woolley, Persia
Child of the Northern Spring.
Pocket Books 1988.

Woolley, Persia
YA *Queen of the Summer Stars.*
Poseidon Press 1990.
BL v86 1990 p1667; KR v58 1990 p533; LJ v115 Je 1, 1990 p186; SLJ v36 S 1990 p268.

Yolen, Jane
JUV *The Dragon's Boy.*
Harper & Row 1990.
BL v87 1990 p165; CC 16th p576; SLJ v36 O 1990 p122.

70. Ashley, William Henry
1778-1838
American fur trader & politician

Seifert, Shirley
Three Lives of Elizabeth.
Lippincott 1952.
BL v48 1952 p322; KR v20 1952 p166; NYTBR My 18, 1952 p23.

71. Asoka the Great
300-232 BC
Buddhist king of Magadha, 273-232 BC

Davar, Ashok
JUV *The Wheel of King Asoka.*
Follett 1977.
SLJ v24 Ja 1978 p77.

72. Astor, John Jacob
1763-1848
American fur trader & capitalist

Anderson, Dorothy S.
JUV *John Jacob Astor, Young Trader.*
Bobbs-Merrill 1961.

Derleth, August W.
Bright Journey.
Scribner 1940.
BL v37 1940 p154; BRD 1940 p242; NYTBR O 27, 1940 p7; SatR O 26, 1940 p20.

Jennings, John E.
River to the West: A Novel of the Astor Adventure.
Doubleday 1948.
BL v45 1948 p88; BRD 1948 p424; FC 8th p228; KR v16 1948 p488; LJ v73 1948 p1384; NYTBR N 7, 1948 p33.

Sperry, Armstrong
No Brighter Glory.
Macmillan 1942.
BRD 1942 p725; LJ v67 1942 p795; NYTBR S 13, 1942 p7.

73. Astor, Nancy Witcher Langhorne
1879-1964
American-born British politician

Marlowe, Derek
Nancy Astor, the Lady from Virginia.
Dell 1982.
Punch v282 Mr 10, 1982 p405.

74. Ataturk, Kemal
1880-1938
Turkish soldier & political leader

Bridge, Ann
The Dark Moment.
Macmillan 1952.
BRD 1952 p106; FC 9th p64; KR v19 1951 p639; LJ v76 1951 p1332; LJ v77 1952 p50; NYTBR Ja 6, 1952 p4.

Gavin, Catherine Irvine
The House of War.
Morrow 1970.
KR v38 1970 p820; LJ v95 1970 p3650; PW v198 Jl 27, 1970 p67.

75. Attila
406-453
King of the Huns

Costain, Thomas B.
YA *The Darkness and the Dawn.*
Doubleday 1959 (Rpr. 1974).
BL v56 1959 p117; BRD 1959 p244; FC 11th p133; LJ v85 1960 p361; NYTBR O 11, 1959 p6; SHSLC 10th p489.

De Wohl, Louis
Throne of the World.
Lippincott 1949.
Also published as *Attila.*
BRD 1949 p236; LJ v74 1949 p1556; NYTBR F 20, 1949 p22; SatR Mr 19, 1949 p26.

Fuller, Roger
Sign of the Pagan.
Dial 1954.
BRD 1955 p325; LJ v79 1954 p1824; NYTBR Ja 9, 1955 p23.

Gardonyi, Geza
Slave of the Huns.
Dent 1969.

Holland, Cecelia
The Death of Attila.
Knopf 1973.
BRD 1974 p566; LJ v97 1972 p3728; LJ v98 1973
p2015.

Johnstone, Paul
JUV *Escape from Attila.*
Criterion Books 1969.

Schreiber, Harvey K.
The Eagle and the Sword.
Popular Library 1979.
BL v75 1979 p856.

Simon, Edith
The Twelve Pictures: A Novel.
Putnam 1955.
KR v23 1955 p224; LJ v80 1955 p878; NYTBR My
22, 1955 p4; Time v65 Je 6, 1955 p118.

Tapsell, R. F.
The Year of the Horsetails.
Hutchinson 1967.
BRD 1967 p1287; LJ v92 1967 p2821; NYTBR S 24,
1967 p46.

76. Auden, W. H. (Wystan Hugh)
1907-1973
English-born American poet & author

Cross, Amanda
Poetic Justice.
Knopf 1970.
BRD 1970 p318; FC 10th p120; LJ v95 1970 p1394;
NYTBR Je 21, 1970 p18.

77. Audubon, John James
1785-1851
American ornithologist & artist

Brenner, Barbara
JUV *On the Frontier with Mr. Audubon.*
Coward McCann 1977.
BL v73 1977 p1086; CC 16th p453; KR v45 1977 p45;
PW v211 Ja 10, 1977 p62; SLJ v23 Ap 1977 p62.

Kennedy, Lucy
Mr. Audubon's Lucy.
Crown 1957.
BRD 1957 p489; FC 8th p238; LJ v82 1957 p751;
NYTBR My 12, 1957 p30.

Sanders, Scott R.
Wonders Hidden: Audubon's Early Years.
Capra Press 1984.
A "back-to-back" book bound with Ursula LeGuin's
The Visionary.
KR v52 1984 p643; LJ v109 1984 p1686; PW v226 Ag
17, 1984 p58.

Simon, Charlie M.
JUV *Joe Mason, Apprentice to Audubon.*
E.P. Dutton & Co. 1946.
BRD 1946 p754; LJ v71 1946 p1055; NYTBR Ag 25,
1946 p21.

78. Augustine, Saint
354-430
Philosopher; regarded as founder of Christian
theology

Coray, Henry W.
*Son of Tears: A Novel on the Life of Saint
    Augustine.*
Putnam 1957.
BRD 1957 p202; KR v25 1957 p501; LJ v82 1957
p2036; NYTBR S 22, 1957 p41.

De Wohl, Louis
The Restless Flame.
Gollancz 1952.
BRD 1952 p250; FC 7th p106; KR v19 1951 p408;
NYTBR Ja 6, 1952 p23; SatR Ja 26, 1952 p32.

Warner, Rex
The Converts: A Historical Novel.
Little, Brown 1967.
BL v64 1967 p239; BRD 1967 p1366; KR v35 1967
p446; LJ v92 1967 p2435; NYTBR Jl 30, 1967 p26.

79. Augustus
63 BC-AD 14
Roman emperor

Dored, Elisabeth
I Loved Tiberius.
Pantheon Books 1963.
LJ v88 1963 p574.
63 BC-14 AD

Duggan, Alfred Leo
Three's Company.
Coward-McCann 1958.
BRD 1958 p316; FC 8th p128; KR v26 1958 p423; LJ
v83 1958 p2840; TLS Ap 11, 1958 p193.

Graves, Robert
*I, Claudius: From the Autobiography of Tiberius
    Claudius, Born B.C. 10, Murdered and Deified
    A.D. 54.*
Modern Library 1934 (Heavily reprinted).

Massie, Allan
*Let the Emperor Speak: A Novel of Caesar Augus-
    tus.*
Doubleday 1987.
KR v55 1987 p1020; LJ v112 S 15, 1987 p95; PW
v232 Jl 24, 1987 p172.

Williams, John E.
Augustus.
Viking 1972.
BRD 1973 p1400; KR v40 1972 p975; LJ v97 1972
p2756; NYTBR Ap 8, 1973 p30.

80. Austen, Jane
1775-1817
English author

Ashton, Helen
Parson Austen's Daughter.
Dodd, Mead 1949.
BL v45 Jl 15, 1949 p382; BRD 1949 p26; LJ v74 1949
p1023; NYTBR S 11, 1949 p9.

Gould, Jean
YA *Jane.*
Houghton Mifflin 1947.
BRD 1947 p356; KR v15 1947 p192; LJ v72 1947
p895; NYTBR Je 22, 1947 p27.

Wilson, Barbara Ker
*Antipodes Jane: A Novel of Jane Austin in Austra-
lia.*
Viking 1985.
KR v53 1985 p350; NYTBR Jl 21, 1985 p12; PW
v227 Ap 5, 1985 p65.

81. Austin, Stephen Fuller
1793-1836
American colonizer & political leader

Krey, Laura Smith
On the Long Tide.
Houghton Mifflin 1940.
BRD 1940 p524; LJ v65 1940 p874; NYTBR N 10,
1940 p7.

82. Avicenna
980-1037
Arab physician & philosopher

Gordon, Noah
The Physician.
Simon & Schuster 1986.
KR v54 1986 p957; LJ v111 S 1, 1986 p214; NYTBR
Ag 17, 1986 p22; PW v230 Jl 4, 1986 p55.

83. Ba'al Shem Tov, Israel
1700-1760
Jewish religious leader

Singer, Isaac Bashevis
Reaches of Heaven: A Story of the Baal Shem Tov.
Landmark Press 1980.
BL v77 1980 p560; NY v56 N 10, 1980 p221.

Snitzer, Jacob Lazarus
*The Story the Baal Shem: Life, Love and Teachings
of the Founder of Chassidism and Jewish Mysti-
cism.*
Pardes Publishing House 1946.

84. Babbage, Charles
1792-1871
English mathematician & inventor

Slobodien, Ira
Doing Our Babbage.
ILEX Press 1992.

85. Babington, Anthony
1561-1586
English conspirator; planned to murder Elizabeth & install Mary Queen of Scots on throne

Pelham, Randolph
Tudor Traitor.
Hale 1971.

Uttley, Alison
YA *A Traveler in Time.*
Viking 1964.
BRD 1965 p1278; HB v40 1964 p612; LJ v89 1964
p4653; SHSLC 2nd p363.

86. Bach, Johann Sebastian
1685-1750
German composer

Meynell, Esther
The Little Chronicle of Magdalena Bach.
Schirmer 1934 (Rpr. 1949).

Ruber, Johannes
Bach and the Heavenly Choir.
World Pub. Co. 1956.

87. Bacon, Nathaniel
1647-1676
English-born colonist; led Bacon's Rebellion,
1676

Flannagan, Roy
*The Forest Cavalier: A Romance of America's
First Frontier and of Bacon's Rebellion.*
Bobbs-Merrill 1952.
BRD 1952 p309; NYTBR Ap 13, 1952 p17; SatR Je 7,
1952 p52.

Spector, Robert M.
The Greatest Rebel.
H.Z. Walck 1969.
KR v37 1969 p515; LJ v94 1969 p3869.

88. Bacon, Roger
1214-1294
English scientist & philosopher

Blish, James
Doctor Mirabilis.
Faber & Faber 1964 (Rpr. 1971, 1982).
BL v67 1971 p929; KR v39 1971 p128; LJ v96 1971
p2100.

Powys, John Cowper
The Brazen Head.
Macdonald 1956 (Rpr. 1969, 1978).

89. Bagration, Peter Ivanovich
1765-1812
Russian general who led campaigns against Napoleon

Golubov, Sergei
No Easy Victories: A Novel of General Bagration and the Campaign of 1812.
Hutchinson 1945.
Also published as *Bragration: The Honour and Glory.*

90. Baha'u'llah
1817-1892
Persian founder of Baha'i faith

Hatcher, John
Ali's Dream: The Story of Baha'u'llah.
G. Ronald 1980.

91. Bainbridge, William
1774-1833
American naval officer

Vail, Philip
The Sea Panther: A Novel about the Commander of the U.S.S. Constitution.
Dodd, Mead 1962.
LJ v87 1962 p2922.

92. Baker, Hobey (Hobart Amery Hare)
1892-1918
American hockey player

Goodman, Mark
Hurrah for the Next Man Who Dies.
Atheneum 1985.
BL v81 1985 p927; BRD 1985 p617; KR v53 1985 p9; LJ v110 Mr 1, 1985 p102; NYTBR My 19, 1985 p22.

93. Baker, Josephine
1906-1975
American-born French singer & entertainer

Schroeder, Alan
JUV *Ragtime Tumpie.*
Joy Street Books 1989.
BL v86 1989 p356; BRD 1990 p1629; KR v57 1989 p1409; NYTBR F 25, 1990 p33.

94. Balboa, Vasco Nunez de
1475-1517
Spanish explorer

Garrison, Omar V.
Balboa: Conquistador.
Lyle Stuart 1971.
Also published as *Conquistador.*
KR v39 1971 p962; LJ v96 1971 p2790.

95. Ball, Lucille
1911-1989
American comedienne & actress

Hijuelos, Oscar
The Mambo Kings Play Songs of Love.
Farrar, Straus, Giroux 1989.
BL v85 1989 p1943; BRD 1990 p817; KR v57 1989 p860; NYTBR Ag 27, 1989 p1.

96. Balzac, Honore de
1799-1850
French author

Gorham, Charles
Wine of Life: A Novel about Balzac.
Dial Press 1958.
BL v54 1958 p476; BRD 1958 p447; NYTBR Mr 9, 1958 p4.

97. Bankhead, Tallulah
1903-1968
American actress

Baxt, George
The Tallulah Bankhead Murder Case.
St. Martin's 1987.
BL v84 1987 p540; KR v55 1987 p1540; NYTBR F 12, 1989 p32; Time v131 F 1, 1988 p66.

98. Bar Kokhba, Simon
d.135
Led Jewish revolt against Roman domination, 131-135

Finch, Merton
Simon Bar Cochba: Rebellion in Judea.
Dobson 1969.

Gilner, Elias
Prince of Israel.
Exposition Press 1952.

Meisels, Andrew
Son of a Star.
Putnam 1969.
BL v66 1969 p107; KR v37 1969 p470.

Narell, Irena
JUV *Joshua, Fighter for Bar Kochba.*
Akiba Press 1978.

Opatoshu, Joseph
The Last Revolt: The Story of Rabbi Akiba.
Jewish Publication Society of America 1952.
NYTBR S 7, 1952 p29.

Segal, Brenda Lesley
If I Forget Thee.
St. Martin's 1983.
BL v79 1983 p1263; KR v51 1983 p599; LJ v108 1983 p1276.

Whiteman, Amram
JUV *Bar Kochba.*
Bloch Pub. Co. 1985.

99. Barabbas
Condemned thief who whose release was demanded instead of that of Jesus

Bekessy, Emery
Barabbas: A Novel of the Time of Jesus.
Prentice-Hall 1946.
BL v43 1947 p132; BRD 1946 p51; FC 10th p42; KR v14 1946 p436; LJ v71 1946 p1542; NYTBR N 24, 1946 p26.

Bloom, Ursula (Lozania Prole, pseud.)
Now Barabbas Was a Robber: The Story of the Man Who Lived That Christ Might Die.
Severn House 1977.
Originally published under the author's pseud., Deborah Mann.

Brooker, Bertram
The Robber: A Tale of the Time of the Herods.
Duell, Sloan & Pearce 1949.
BRD 1949 p107; SatR Jl 16, 1949 p18.

Corelli, Marie
Barabbas: A Dream of the World's Tragedy.
Methuen 1893 (Heavily reprinted).

Hancock, Edith
Glory of the Morn: A Story of Barabbas.
Bruce Humphries 1952.

Jones, Bob
Wine of Morning: A Novel of the First Century.
Van Kampen Press 1951.

Knab, Otto J. (Otto Michael, pseud.)
The Hour of Barabbas.
Sheed & Ward 1943.

Lagerkvist, Par
Barabbas.
Random House 1951 (Heavily reprinted).
BRD 1951 p496; BRD 1952 p528; FC 11th p355; KR v19 1951 p409; NYTBR O 7, 1951 p4; Time v58 D 3, 1951 p110.

100. Barents, Willem
1550-1597
Dutch arctic explorer

Schmeltzer, Kurt
YA *The Long Arctic Night.*
Franklin Watts 1952.
BL v49 1952 p52; BRD 1952 p789; KR v20 1952 p508; LJ v77 1952 p1524; NYTBR S 7, 1952 p31.

101. Barnum, P. T. (Phineas Taylor)
1810-1891
American showman

Stevenson, Augusta
JUV *P. T. Barnum, Circus Boy.*
Bobbs-Merrill 1964.

Thorp, Roderick
Jenny and Barnum: A Novel of Love.
Doubleday 1981.
KR v49 1981 p834; LJ v106 1981 p1755; PW v220 Jl 17, 1981 p80.

Trell, Max
The Small Gods & Mr. Barnum.
McCall Pub. Co. 1971.
BL v68 1971 p132; KR v39 1971 p574; LJ v96 1971 p2673.

102. Barry, John
1745-1803
American naval commander

Hinternhoff, John F.
JUV *Barry's Boys.*
Holt 1952.
LJ v77 1952 p2014.

103. Barth, Heinrich
1821-1865
German explorer

Seufert, Karl
YA *Caravan in Peril.*
Pantheon 1963.
LJ v88 1963 p2154.

104. Bartholdi, Auguste (Frederic Auguste)
1834-1904
French sculptor; designed Statue of Liberty

Eger, Jeffrey
JUV *The Statue in the Harbor: A Story of Two Apprentices.*
Silver Burdett 1986.
SLJ v32 My 1986 p90.

Fox, Mary Virginia
JUV *Apprentice to Liberty.*
Abingdon Press 1960.
BRD 1961 p451; KR v28 1960 p407; LJ v85 1960 p3215.

105. Bartholomew, Saint
One of the 12 apostles

Sutphen, William Gilbert van Tassel
I, Nathanael, Knew Jesus.
F.H. Revell 1941.
BRD 1942 p752.

106. Barton, Clara Harlowe

1821-1912
American nurse & founder of the American
Red Cross

Stevenson, Augusta
JUV *Clara Barton, Girl Nurse.*
Bobbs-Merrill 1946 (Rpr. 1962, 1986).
LJ v71 1946 p1718.

107. Bartram, John

1699-1777
American botanist

Stover, Herbert E.
Song of the Susquehanna.
Dodd, Mead 1949.
BL v45 1949 p338; BRD 1949 p885; NYTBR My 15,
1949 p21; SatR Je 4, 1949 p2.

108. Bass, Sam

1851-1878
American desperado

Rister, Claude (Buck Billings, pseud.)
The Owlhoot Trail.
Gateway Books 1942.

Woolley, Bryan
Sam Bass: A Novel.
Corona Pub. Co. 1983.
KR v51 1983 p790; LJ v108 1983 p1722.

109. Bates, Katharine Lee

1859-1929
American educator & poet

Myers, Elisabeth P.
JUV *Katharine Lee Bates, Girl Poet.*
Bobbs-Merrill 1961.

110. Bathsheba

Second wife of King David & mother of Solomon

Cassill, R. V.
After Goliath.
Ticknor & Fields 1985.
BL v81 1985 p756; KR v53 1985 p96; LJ v110 Mr 15,
1985 p70; NYTBR Je 16, 1985 p27.

Dorr, Roberta Kells
Bathsheba: The Love Story That Changed History.
Chosen Books 1980.

Ibu-Sahav, Ari
David and Bathsheba.
Crown 1951.
BRD 1952 p466; KR v19 1951 p621; LJ v76 1951
p1804; NYTBR N 25, 1951 p58.

Lindgren, Torgny
Bathsheba.

Harper & Row 1989.
KR v57 1989 p323; LJ v114 My 15, 1989 p90.

Shamir, Moshe
David's Stranger.
Abelard-Schuman 1965.
BRD 1966 p1094; KR v33 1965 p70; LJ v90 1965
p2901.

111. Batu Khan

d. 1255
Mongolian military leader; grandson of Genghis
Khan

Yan, V.
Batu-Khan: A Tale of the 13th Century.
Hutchinson International Authors 1945 (Rpr. 1977).

112. Baudelaire, Charles Pierre

1821-1867
French poet & critic

Perowne, Barry
A Singular Conspiracy.
Bobbs-Merrill 1974.
KR v42 1974 p266; LJ v99 1974 p776; NYTBR My
19, 1974 p41; PW v205 Ap 15, 1974 p47.

Wagner, Geoffrey
*The Wings of Madness: A Novel of Charles Baude-
laire.*
Borgo Press 1978 (Rpr. 1990).
BL v75 1978 p671.

White, Charles W. (Max White, pseud.)
*The Midnight Gardener, a Novel About Baude-
laire.*
Harper 1948.
BL v45 1948 p52; BRD 1948 p912; KR v16 1948
p288; LJ v73 1948 p1092; NYTBR S 12, 1948 p22.

113. Baxter, Richard

1615-1691
Nonconformist Puritan preacher

Derham, Arthur Morgan
No Darker Rooms.
Moody Press 1951.

114. Bean, Roy

1825-1903
American frontiersman

Garwood, W. R.; Breihan, Carl W.
West Wandering Wind.
Doubleday 1986.

McMurtry, Larry
Streets of Laredo.
Simon & Schuster 1993.

115. Beard, Dan (Daniel Carter)

1850-1941
American author, illustrator, & founder of the
American Boy Scouts

Mason, Miriam E.
JUV *Dan Beard, Boy Scout.*
Bobbs-Merrill 1953.
LJ v78 1953 p1244.

116. Beaumarchais, Pierre Augustin Caron de

1732-1799
French author

Feuchtwanger, Lion
Proud Destiny.
Viking 1947.
BRD 1947 p299; LJ v72 1947 p1193; NYTBR S 14,
1947 p3; SatR S 13, 1947 p9.

117. Beaumont, Francis

1584-1616
English dramatist

Bryher, Winifred
The Player's Boy.
Pantheon 1953.
BRD 1953 p128; LJ v78 1953 p1849; NYTBR My 17,
1953 p4.

118. Beaumont, William

1785-1853
American surgeon

Fox, Genevieve May
YA *Army Surgeon.*
Little, Brown 1944.
BL v40 1944 p288; BRD 1944 p256; LJ v69 1944
p356; NYTBR Mr 12, 1944 p6.

Myer, Alma M.
The Golden Page: A Biographical Novel.
Exposition Press 1977.

119. Beauregard, Pierre Gustav Toutant de

1818-1893
American Confederate general

Keyes, Frances Parkinson
Madame Castel's Lodger.
Farrar, Straus 1962.
FC 8th p240; NYTBR D 16, 1962 p24.

120. Becket, Thomas, Saint

1118-1170
Archbishop of Canterbury, 1162-1170; Roman
Catholic martyr

Bennetts, Pamela
The Angevin King.
Hale 1972.

Butler, Margaret
The Lion of Christ.
Coward, McCann & Geoghegan 1977.
Also published as *This Turbulent Priest.*
KR v45 1977 p299; LJ v102 1977 p1302.

Butler, Margaret
The Lion of Justice.
Coward, McCann & Geoghegan 1975.
BL v71 1975 p544; KR v42 1974 p1266; LJ v100 1975
p310; PW v207 Ja 6, 1975 p51.

Duggan, Alfred Leo
My Life for My Sheep.
Coward-McCann 1955.
Also published as *God and My Right.*
BRD 1955 p257; FC 8th p128; KR v23 1955 p573; LJ
v80 1955 p1828; NYTBR O 2, 1955 p5; Time v66
O 10, 1953 p131.

Follett, Ken
Pillars of the Earth.
Morrow 1989.
BL v86 Ja 15, 1990 p983; LJ v114 Jl 1989 p108;
NYTBR S 10, 1989 p41; PW v237 Je 22, 1990 p52.

Hainsworth, Annette
The Jewelled Crown.
Hale 1981.

Hibbert, Eleanor (Jean Plaidy, pseud.)
The Plantagenet Prelude.
Hale 1976 (Rpr. 1980).
BL v76 1980 p1411; KR v48 1980 p241; LJ v105 1980
p1103.

Meyer, Conrad F.
*The Saint: A Fictional Biography of Thomas
Becket.*
Brown University Press 1977.
PW v212 O 17, 1977 p72.

Mydans, Shelley
*Thomas: A Novel of the Life, Passions and Mir-
acles of Becket.*
Doubleday 1965.
BW Ag 22, 1965 p12; FC 11th p448; LJ v90 1965
p3073; NYTBR S 12, 1965 p4.

York, Robert
The Swords of December.
Scribner 1978.
KR v47 1979 p222; LJ v104 1979 p1359; PW v215 F
19, 1978 p103.

121. Beckford, William

1759-1844
English author

Menen, Aubrey
Fonthill.
Putnam 1974.

BL v71 1974 p138; KR v42 1974 p760; LJ v99 1974 p1985.

122. Becknell, William
1796-1865
American frontier explorer; established trading route known as Santa Fe Trail

Adams, Samuel Hopkins
YA *The Santa Fe Trail.*
Random House 1951.
BL v48 1951 p148; BRD 1951 p4; KR v19 1951 p439; LJ v77 1952 p65; NYTBR N 11, 1951 p36.

123. Beckwourth, James Pierson
1798-1867
American frontiersman

Brackett, Leigh
Follow the Free Wind.
Doubleday 1963.

Hotchkiss, Bill
Ammahabas: A Novel.
Norton 1983.
Sequel to *The Medicine Calf.*
KR v51 1983 p327; LJ v108 1983 p920; PW v223 Mr 25, 1983 p45.

Hotchkiss, Bill
YA *The Medicine Calf.*
Norton 1981.
KR v48 1980 p1479; KR v49 1981 p14; LJ v106 1981 p74; SLJ v28 Ja 1982 p30.

124. Beecher, Henry Ward
1813-1887
American clergyman, editor & abolitionist

McCall, Dan
Beecher: A Novel.
Dutton 1979.
BL v76 1979 p432; KR v47 1979 p880; LJ v104 1979 p1720; NYTBR Ja 20, 1980 p15; PW v216 Ag 6, 1979 p86.

125. Beethoven, Ludwig van
1770-1827
German composer

Brenner, Jacques
Nephew to the Emperor: A Novel Based on the Life of Beethoven.
World Pub. Co. 1959.
BL v56 1959 p153; BRD 1959 p136; KR v27 1959 p412; LJ v84 1959 p2518; NYTBR Ag 2, 1959 p4.

Chotzinoff, Samuel
Eroica: A Novel Based on the Life of Ludwig van Beethoven.
Simon & Schuster 1930 (Rpr. 1975).

BL v26 1930 p356; BRD 1930 p196; NYTBR Ap 13, 1930 p9; SatR Ap 5, 1930 p891.

Goss, Madeleine
YA *Beethoven: Master Musician.*
Doubleday, Doran 1931 (Rpr. 1946, 1961, 1966).
BRD 1931 p421; BRD 1947 p354; KR v14 1946 p391; LJ v57 1932 p580; NYTBR Ag 2, 1931 p12.

Malzberg, Barry
Chorale.
Doubleday 1978.
BL v75 1978 p459; KR v46 1978 p779; LJ v103 1978 p1770; PW v214 Jl 17, 1978 p166.

McHugh, Elisabeth
JUV *Beethoven's Cat.*
Atheneum 1988.
BL v84 1988 p1265; KR v56 1986 p541; NYTBR S 4, 1988 p26; PW v233 Ap 8, 1988 p95; SLJ v34 Ap 1988 p103.

Meynell, Esther
Grave Fairytale: A Romantic Novel.
Chapman & Hall 1931 (Rpr. 1950).
BRD 1932 p655; SatR F 13, 1932 p527.

Pidoll, Carl von
Eroica: A Novel about Beethoven.
Vanguard Press 1957.
BRD 1957 p728.

126. Behn, Aphra
1640-1689
First English woman to support herself by writing

Hahn, Emily
Purple Passage: A Novel about a Lady Both Famous and Fantastic.
Doubleday 1950.
Also published as *Aphra Behn.*
BRD 1950 p392; KR v18 1950 p365; LJ v75 1950 p1291; NYTBR S 10, 1950 p29.

127. Beiderbecke, Bix (Leon Bismark)
1903-1931
American jazz musician

Baker, Dorothy
Young Man with a Horn.
Houghton Mifflin 1938 (Rpr. 1953, 1957, 1961).
BRD 1938 p46; SatR Je 4, 1938 p12.

128. Belisarius
505-565
Byzantine military leader

Dixon, Pierson
The Glittering Horn: Secret Memoirs of the Court of Justinian.
J. Cape 1958.

Finkel, George
YA *Watch Fires to the North.*

Viking 1967.
Also published as *Twilight Province*.
BRD 1968 p424; LJ v93 1968 p2546; NYTBR Ap 14, 1968 p20.

Graves, Robert
Count Belisarius.
Random House 1938 (Rpr. 1970, 1982).
BL v35 1938 p133; BRD 1938 p385; NYTBR N 20, 1938 p6; NYTBR Ap 30, 1939 p8.

Masefield, John
Conquer: A Tale of the Nika Rebellion in Byzantium.
Macmillan 1941.
BL v38 1941 p113; BRD 1941 p606; NYTBR N 9, 1941 p7; SatR N 1, 1941 p8.

O'Connor, Richard
The Vandal.
Doubleday 1960.
BL v56 1960 p417; KR v27 1959 p817; LJ v85 1960 p678; NYTBR Ja 10, 1960 p34.

129. Bell, Alexander Graham
1847-1922
Invented telephone, 1876

McMahon, Thomas A.
Loving Little Egypt.
Viking 1987.
BW v17 F 22, 1987 p9; KR v54 1986 p1751; LJ v112 F 1, 1987 p93; NYTBR F 8, 1987 p16; PW v230 D 12, 1986 p42.

Widdemer, Mabel
JUV *Aleck Bell, Ingenious Boy*.
Bobbs-Merrill 1947 (Rpr. 1962).
BRD 1948 p920; LJ v72 1947 p1279.

130. Bell, Gertrude Margaret
1868-1926
English archaelogist

Cowlin, Dorothy
A Woman in the Desert: The Story of Gertrude Bell.
Muller 1967.
TLS My 25, 1967 p464.

131. Benedict, Saint
480-547
Italian founder of Benedictine monasticism

De Wohl, Louis
Citadel of God: A Novel of Saint Benedict.
Lippincott 1959.
BRD 1960 p352; KR v27 1959 p615; LJ v84 1959 p3585; NYTBR D 13, 1959 p27.

132. Benjamin, Judah Philip
1811-1884
American Confederate poltician

Abrahams, Robert D.
YA *Mr. Benjamin's Sword*.
Jewish Publication Society of America 1948.
BRD 1948 p2; LJ v73 1948 p1099; NYTBR Jl 25, 1948 p17.

Appel, Allan
Judah.
Leisure Books 1976.

Carr, John D.
Papa L'a-bas.
Harper & Row 1968.
BRD 1969 p219; LJ v93 1968 p4168; NYTBR N 10, 1968 p65.

Delmar, Vina
Beloved.
Harcourt, Brace 1956.
BL v52 1956 p339; BRD 1956 p250; FC 7th p104; NYTBR Mr 25, 1956 p4.

133. Benson, Arthur Christopher
1862-1925
English author

Aiken, Joan
The Haunting of Lamb House.
J. Cape 1991 (Rpr. 1993).
CR v259 Ag 1991 p111; TLS Ap 12, 1991 p19.

134. Beria, Lavrenti Pavlovich
1899-1953
Head of Soviet Intelligence, 1934-1953

Buckley, William F.
High Jinx.
Doubleday 1986.
BL v82 1986 p834; KR v54 1986 p69; LJ v111 Mr 15, 1986 p77; NYTBR Ap 6, 1986 p15; PW v229 Ja 31, 1986 p365.

Williams, Alan
The Beria Papers.
Simon & Schuster 1973.
BL v70 1974 p474; BRD 1974 p1310; KR v41 1973 p911; LJ v98 1973 p3285; NYTBR O 28, 1973 p49; PW v204 Ag 27, 1973 p437.

135. Bering, Vitus Jonassen
1680-1741
Danish navigator & explorer

Granberg, Wilbur J.
YA *Voyage into Darkness: To Alaska with Bering*.
Dutton 1960.
BRD 1961 p530; KR v28 1960 p239; LJ v85 1960 p2487; NYTBR Ag 28, 1960 p24.

136. Berkowitz, David
1953-
American murderer; better known as "Son of Sam"

Breslin, Jimmy
.44.
Viking 1978.
BL v74 1978 p1663; KR v46 1978 p447; LJ v103 1978
    p1288; NYTBR Jl 2, 1978 p6.

137. Berlioz, Louis Hector
1803-1869
French composer

Kenyon, Frank Wilson
Passionate Rebel: The Story of Hector Berlioz.
Dodd, Mead 1972.
BS v32 Ag 15, 1972 p232; PW v201 F 14, 1972 p66;
    TLS Ap 28, 1972 p501.

138. Bernadette of Lourdes
1844-1879
French peasant girl whose visions of the Virgin
Mary led to the establishment of the shrine at
Lourdes, France

Peters, Maureen
The Crystal and the Cloud.
Hale 1977.

Trouncer, Margaret
*A Grain of Wheat: The Story of Saint Bernadette
    of Lourdes, 1844-1879.*
Hutchinson 1958 (Rpr. 1976).

Werfel, Franz
The Song of Bernadette.
Viking 1942.
BL v38 1942 p347; BRD 1942 p818; LJ v67 1942
    p414; NYTBR My 10, 1942 p3.

139. Bernhardt, Sarah
1844-1923
French actress

Arnold, Alan
The Incredible Sarah: A Novel.
New American Library 1976.
Based on the screenplay by Ruth Wolff.

Gross, Joel
Sarah.
Morrow 1987.
KR v55 1987 p878; PW v231 Je 26, 1987 p59.

Lothar, Minda
Rage of Joy: The Divine Sarah Bernhardt.
Frewin 1968.

Sagan, Francoise
Dear Sarah Bernhardt.
Seaver Books 1988.
KR v56 1988 p815; LJ v113 Ag 1988 p176; PW v233
    My 27, 1988 p47.

140. Bethune, Norman
1890-1939
Canadian surgeon

Chou, Erh-fu
Doctor Norman Bethune.
Foreign Language Press 1982.

141. Bierce, Ambrose Gwinett
1842-1914
American author

Fuentes, Carlos
The Old Gringo.
Farrar, Straus, Giroux 1985.
BL v82 1985 p374; BRD 1986 p566; KR v53 1985
    p964; LJ v110 N 1, 1985 p109; NYTBR Ag 24,
    1986 p28; PW v230 Ag 15, 1986 p79.

Jakes, John
California Gold: A Novel.
Random House 1989.
BL v85 1989 p1922; NYTBR O 8, 1989 p24.

Lynch, Daniel
Yellow: A Novel.
Walker 1992.
KR v60 1992 p1276; LJ v117 N 15, 1992 p102.

142. Billington, John
d. 1630
One of pilgrims who arrived on the Mayflower;
first murderer in US

Coatsworth, Elizabeth
JUV *First Adventure.*
Macmillan 1950.
BL v47 1950 p140; BRD 1950 p185; KR v18 1950
    p463; LJ v75 1950 p157.

Webb, Robert N.
JUV *We Were There with the Mayflower Pilgrims.*
Grosset & Dunlap 1956.

143. Billy the Kid
1859-1881
American outlaw

Bean, Amelia
Time for Outrage.
Doubleday 1967.
BL v64 1968 p824; KR v35 1967 p982; LJ v92 1967
    p3657; PW v192 Ag 14, 1967 p47.

Burnett, W. R.
Mi Amigo: A Novel of the Southwest.
Knopf 1959 (Rpr. 1963).
BL v56 1959 p30; BRD 1959 p159; LJ v84 1959
    p2079; NYTBR Ag 2, 1959 p20; SatR Jl 25, 1959
    p23.

Corle, Edwin
Billy the Kid.

Duell, Sloan & Pearce 1953.
BRD 1953 p209; KR v21 1953 p311; LJ v78 1953
    p1148; NYTBR Ag 9, 1953 p12.

Everitt, David
The Story of Pat Garrett and Billy the Kid.
Knightsbridge Pub. Co. 1990.
BWatch v11 N 1990 p10.

Grey, Zane
Nevada: A Romance of the West.
Harper & Brothers 1928 (Heavily reprinted).
BRD 1928 p326; NYTBR Ap 15, 1928 p14.

Hough, Emerson
Heart's Desire: The Story of a Contented Town,
    Certain Peculiar Citizens and Two Fortunate
    Lovers.
Macmillan 1905 (Rpr. 1914, 1981).

McMurtry, Larry
Anything for Billy.
Simon & Schuster 1988.
BL v85 1988 p4; BRD 1989 p1111; KR v56 1988
    p1088; LJ v113 O 15, 1988 p104; NYTBR O 16,
    1988 p3.

Momaday, N. Scot
The Ancient Child: A Novel.
Doubleday 1989.
BL v86 S 1, 1989 p3; LJ v114 Ag 1989 p165.

Neider, Charles
The Authentic Death of Hendry Jones.
Harper 1956.
BL v53 1956 p72; BRD 1956 p680; KR v24 1956
    p371; NYTBR Ag 26, 1956 p26.

Nye, Nelson C.
Pistols for Hire.
Macmillan 1941 (Rpr. 1969).
Also published as *A Bullet for Billy the Kid.*
BRD 1941 p675; NYTBR N 9, 1941 p40.

Ondaatje, Michael
The Collected Works of Billy the Kid.
Penguin 1984.
NYTBR Mr 3, 1985 p34.

Whitlow, Duane
Lincoln County Diary.
Sunstone Press 1991.

144. Bingham, Hiram
1875-1956
American explorer; discovered ruins of last Inca
capital, Machu Picchu, Peru, 1911

Wilson, Carter
Treasures on Earth.
Knopf 1981.
BL v77 1981 p1435; KR v49 1981 p835; LJ v106 1981
    p2051; PW v220 Jl 10, 1981 p83.

145. Bismark, Otto Edward Leopold von
1815-1898
German political leader; first chancellor of German Empire

Fraser, George MacDonald
Royal Flash.
Knopf 1970.
FC 11th p215; LJ v95 1970 p2715; NYTBR O 18,
    1970 p4; Time v96 O 5, 1970 p92.

146. Black Hawk
1767-1838
Sauk Indian chief

Beckhard, Arthur J.
Black Hawk.
Messner 1957.
LJ v82 1957 p2663; LJ v83 1958 p235.

Cleven, Cathrine Seward
JUV *Black Hawk, Young Sauk Warrior.*
Bobbs-Merrill 1966.

Fuller, Iola
The Shining Trail.
Duell, Sloan & Pearce 1943.
BL v39 1943 p463; BRD 1943 p288; FC 9th p188; LJ
    v68 1943 p476; NYTBR Je 20, 1943 p4.

Laird, Charlton G.
Thunder on the River.
Little, Brown 1949.
KR v16 1948 p604; LJ v73 1948 p1743; NYTBR F 6,
    1949 p25.

Le Sueur, Meridel
JUV *Sparrow Hawk.*
Knopf 1950 (Rpr. 1987).
BL v47 1950 p121; BRD 1950 p553; KR v18 1950
    p387; LJ v75 1950 p1674; NYTBR N 12, 1950 p30.

147. Blackbeard
1680-1718
English pirate

Cochran, Hamilton
Rogue's Holiday: A Novel.
Bobbs-Merril 1947.
BL v43 1947 p272; BRD 1947 p172; KR v15 1947
    p76; NYTBR Ap 20, 1947 p14.

Hoffman, Margaret
Brethren of the Black Flag.
Coastal Plains 1982.

Johnson, Charles
JUV *Pieces of Eight.*
Discovery Press 1988.
BL v85 1989 p1300; PW v234 D 23, 1988 p82.

Powers, Tim
On Stranger Tides.
Ace Books 1987.
BL v84 1988 p752; KR v55 1987 p1279.

Tracy, Don
Carolina Corsair.
Dial 1955.
BRD 1955 p912; NYTBR Je 12, 1955 p14.

Wechter, Nell Wise
JUV *Teach's Light.*
J.F. Blair 1974.
SLJ v21 Ja 1975 p58.

Wirt, Mildred A.
Pirate Brig.
Scribner 1950.
NYTBR Jl 16, 1950 p16.

148. Blackwell, Antoinette Louisa Brown
1825-1921
American social reformer; first woman ordained minister in US, 1853

Kerr, Laura
Lady in the Pulpit.
Woman's Press 1951.
BRD 1951 p476.

149. Blackwell, Elizabeth
1821-1910
English-born American physician; first woman to receive MD in modern times, 1849

Henry, Joanne Landers
JUV *Elizabeth Blackwell, Girl Doctor.*
Bobbs-Merrill 1961.

150. Blake, William
1757-1827
English mystic, poet, & artist

Carter, Peter
JUV *The Gates of Paradise.*
Oxford University Press 1974.
GP v13 Mr 1975 p2574; JB v39 Ap 1975 p115; TLS Ap 4, 1975 p369.

151. Blanchard, Francois
1753-1809
Credited with first balloon crossing of English Channel

Whitney, Janet
Judith.
Morrow 1943.
BRD 1943 p865; NYTBR N 28, 1943 p46.

152. Blavatsky, Helena Petrovna
1831-1891
Russian-born theosophist

Hanson, Virginia
Masters and Men: The Human Story in the Mahatma Letters.
Theosophical Pub. House 1980.

153. Blessington, Marguerite Power, Countess
1789-1849
Renowned beauty; headed intellectual circle; wrote memoir of Byron

Leslie, Doris
Notorious Lady: The Life and Times of the Countess of Blessington.
Heinemann 1976.

154. Bligh, William, Captain
1754-1817
English naval officer

Bennett, Jack
YA *The Lieutenant: An Epic Tale of Courage and Endurance on the High Seas.*
Angus & Robertson 1977.
GP v16 Ap 1978 p3302; JB v42 Ag 1978 p197; TES Mr 17, 1978 p26.

Dark, Eleanor
Storm of Time.
Collins 1948 (Rpr. 1950, 1956, 1991).
BL v46 1950 p189; BRD 1950 p225; KR v18 1950 p38; NYTBR F 5, 1950 p30.

Maxwell, John
H.M.S. Bounty.
Cape 1977.
GP v16 O 1977 p3194; Obs O 30, 1977 p29.

McGinnis, Paul
Lost Eden.
McBride 1947.
BRD 1947 p584; LJ v72 1947 p639.

Miller, Stanley
Mr. Christian: The Journal of Fletcher Christian, Former Lieutenant of His Majesty's Armed Vessel "Bounty".
Macmillan 1973.
KR v41 1973 p832; LJ v98 1973 p3021; PW v204 Ag 13, 1973 p48.

Nicholson, Joyce
Man against Mutiny: The Story of Vice-Admiral Bligh.
Lutterworth 1961.

Nordhoff, Charles
Botany Bay.
Little, Brown 1941.
BRD 1941 p672; LJ v66 1941 p950; NYTBR N 9, 1941 p4; SatR N 15, 1941 p10.

Nordhoff, Charles
*The Bounty Trilogy: Comprising the Three Vol-
    umes, "Mutiny on the Bounty," "Men Against
    the Sea," and "Pitcairn's Island".*
Little, Brown 1936 (Heavily reprinted).
BRD 1937 p741; NYTBR D 6, 1936 p46.

Rienits, Rex
Stormy Petrel.
F. Muller 1963.

Vaughan, Crawford
The Last of Captain Bligh.
Staples Press 1950.

Wilson, Erle
Adams of the Bounty.
Angus & Robertson 1958.
BL v55 1959 p570; BRD 1959 p1072; KR v27 1959
    p186; LJ v84 1959 p2082; NYTBR My 3, 1959 p28.

155. Blixen, Karen Christentze
1885-1962
Danish author

Collin, Hedvig
JUV *Wind Island.*
Viking 1945.
BL v42 1946 p169; BRD 1945 p144; KR v13 1945
    p337; NYTBR N 11, 1945 p18.

156. Blood, Thomas
1618-1680
Irish adventurer

Quigley, Aileen
Bloodstone.
Hale 1972.

Robbins, Alan
On the Trail of Blood: A Participatory Mystery.
Holt 1988.
KR v56 1988 p166.

157. Boadicea
d. 62
Queen of ancient Britain

Allen, Kenneth S.
*Crimson Harvest: The Story of the Bloodiest Massa-
    cre Britain Has Ever Known.*
Hale 1966.
TLS Jl 28, 1966 p656.

Gedge, Pauline
The Eagle and the Raven.
Dial 1978.
KR v46 1978 p892.

King, Betty
Boadicea.
Hale 1975.

McDonald, Eva
Roman Conqueror.
Hale 1975.

Seton, Anya
The Mistletoe and the Sword.
Doubleday 1955 (Rpr. 1975).
BRD 1955 p817; LJ v80 1955 p1514; NYTBR Je 26,
    1955 p20.

Sinclair, James
Warrior Queen.
St. Martin's 1978.
BS v38 O 1978 p208; KR v46 1978 p331; LJ v103
    1978 p1085; PW v213 Mr 20, 1978 p56.

Stevens, Robert T. (R. T. Staples, pseud.)
Warrior Queen.
Toco Publications 1966 (Rpr. 1977).

Sutcliff, Rosemary
YA *Song for a Dark Queen.*
Pelham 1978.
BL v75 1979 p1214; BRD 1979 p1248; KR v47 1979
    p458; SLJ v25 Ap 1979 p72.

Treece, Henry
YA *The Queen's Brooch.*
Putnam 1967.
BL v64 1968 p936; BRD 1967 p1319; KR v35 1967
    p818; LJ v92 1967 p3206; NYTBR O 8, 1967 p40.

Treece, Henry
Red Queen, White Queen.
Random House 1958.
BL v55 1958 p128; BRD 1958 p1059; FC 9th p512;
    KR v26 1958 p527; NYTBR S 28, 1958 p44.

Wiat, Philippa
The Golden Chariot.
Hale 1979.

158. Bogart, Humphrey
1899-1957
American actor

Bergman, Andrew
Hollywood and LeVine.
Holt, Rinehart & Winston 1975 (Rpr. 1983).
BRD 1976 p104; LJ v100 1975 p1158; NYTBR S 7,
    1975 p39.

159. Bolden, "Buddy" (Charles)
1868-1931
Cornettist who is credited with originating jazz

Ondaatje, Michael
Coming through Slaughter.
Norton 1976 (Rpr. 1984).
BL v73 1977 p1146; BRD 1977 p1006; KR v45 1977
    p182; LJ v102 1977 p835; NYTBR Ap 24, 1977
    p14.

160. Boleyn, Anne
1507-1536
Second wife of Henry VIII

Ainsworth, William Harrison
Windsor Castle: An Historical Romance.
Henry Colburn 1843 (Heavily reprinted).

Albery, Peter
The Uncommon Marriage.
Elek Books 1960.

Anthony, Evelyn
Anne Boleyn.
Crowell 1957 (Rpr. 1986, 1991).
BL v53 1957 p528; BRD 1957 p877; FC 11th p19; KR
  v25 1957 p158; LJ v82 1957 p1064; NYTBR Ap
  28, 1957 p43.

Barnes, Margaret Campbell
Brief Gaudy Hour: A Novel of Anne Boleyn.
Macrae Smith 1949.
BRD 1949 p42; FC 11th p41; KR v17 1949 p371; LJ
  v74 1949 p1320; NYTBR O 2, 1949 p42.

Dakers, Elaine (Jane Lane, pseud.)
Sow the Tempest.
F. Muller 1960.

Fenton, Edward
Anne of the Thousand Days: A Novel.
New American Library 1970.

Hardwick, Mollie
Blood Royal: A Novel.
St. Martin's 1989.
BL v85 1989 p1248; KR v57 1989 p74; PW v235 Ja
  27, 1989 p452.

Heys, Margaret
The May Queen.
Hale 1967 (Rpr. 1972).
Also published as *Anne Boleyn.*
BS v32 Jl 1, 1972 p179.

Hibbert, Eleanor (Jean Plaidy, pseud.)
Murder Most Royal.
Hale 1949 (Rpr. 1972).

Lofts, Norah
*The Concubine: A Novel Based upon the Life of
  Anne Boleyn, Henry VIII's Second Wife.*
Doubleday 1963.
BRD 1963 p628; LJ v88 1963 p2726; NYTBR S 1,
  1963 p14.

Moody, Laurence
The Dark-Eyed Client.
Hale 1974.

Peters, Maureen
The Rose of Hever.
Hale 1969 (Rpr. 1976).

Wiat, Philippa
Sound Now the Passing-Bell.
Hale 1977.

York, Robert
*My Lord the Fox: The Secret Documents of An-
  thony Woodcott Concerning Queen Elizabeth I
  and Anne Boleyn.*
Vanguard 1986.
BL v82 1986 p1437; PW v229 My 16, 1986 p69.

161. Bolivar, Simon
1783-1830
Venezuelan soldier & South American liberator

Aguilera Malta, Demetrio
Manuela, La Caballeresa Del Sol, a Novel.
Southern Illinois University Press 1967.
Translation of *La Caballeresa Del Sol.*
LJ v92 1967 p2810.

Allis, Marguerite
*The Splendor Stays: An Historic Novel Based on
  the Lives of the Seven Hart Sisters of Saybrook,
  Connecticut.*
Putnam 1942.
BL v39 1942 p138; BRD 1942 p15; NYTBR N 8, 1942
  p12; SatR N 21,.

Garcia Marquez, Gabriel
The General in His Labyrinth.
Knopf 1990.
Translation of *El General en su Laberinto.*
BL v86 1990 p2041; BRD 1990 p638; KR v58 1990
  p951; NYTBR S 16, 1990 p1; PW v237 Jl 6, 1990
  p58.

Nelson, Cholmondeley
YA   *With Bolivar over the Andes.*
Reilly & Lee 1963.

162. Bonaparte, Elizabeth Patterson
1785-1879
Married to Napoleon's youngest brother, Jerome

Kane, Harnett T.
*The Amazing Mrs. Bonaparte: A Novel Based on
  the Life of Betsy Patterson.*
Doubleday 1963.
FC 9th p285; LJ v88 Ap 15, 1963 p1686.

163. Bonaparte, Jerome
1784-1860
Youngest brother of Napoleon; king of West-
phalia, 1807-1813

Kane, Harnett T.
*The Amazing Mrs. Bonaparte: A Novel Based on
  the Life of Betsy Patterson.*
Doubleday 1963.
FC 9th p285; LJ v88 Ap 15, 1963 p1686.

164. Bonaparte, Maria Letizia
1750-1836
Mother of Napoleon I

Coryn, Marjorie
Good-bye, My Son.
Appleton-Century 1943.
BL v39 1943 p293; BRD 1943 p178; LJ v68 1943
  p128; NYTBR F 21, 1943 p20.

Eaton, Evelyn
In What Torn Ship.
Harper & Brothers 1944.
BRD 1944 p217; KR v12 1944 p179; LJ v69 1944
  p502; NYTBR Jl 9, 1944 p12.

165. Bonhoeffer, Dietrich

1906-1945
Member of anti-Nazi resistance movement;
killed by Gestapo in concentration camp

Glazener, Mary
*The Cup of Wrath: The Story of Dietrich Bonhoef-
  fer's Resistance to Hitler.*
F.C. Beil 1991.

166. Bonneville, Benjamin Louie Eulalie de

1796-1878
French-born American soldier & explorer

Allen, Merritt P.
YA *Spirit of the Eagle.*
D. McKay 1947.
BRD 1947 p13; HB v23 S 1947 p363; KR v15 1947
  p310; NYTBR Ag 24,.

Giles, Janice H.
The Great Adventure.
Houghton Mifflin 1966.
BL v63 1967 p717; FC 9th p200; KR v34 1966 p709.

Gulick, Bill
The Land Beyond.
Houghton Mifflin 1958.
LJ v83 1958 p2629; NYTBR Mr 9, 1958 p32.

Miller, Helen Markley
JUV *Benjamin Bonneville, Soldier-Explorer, 1796-
  1878.*
Messner 1957.

Staffelbach, Elmer H.
Towards Oregon.
Macrae-Smith 1946.

167. Bonney, William H.

see Billy the Kid

168. Bonny, Anne

1700-1720?
Pirate; with a series of husbands operated in vi-
cinity of the West Indies

Gartner, Chloe
Anne Bonny.
Morrow 1977.

KR v45 1977 p637; LJ v102 1977 p1524; PW v211 Je
  20, 1977 p65.

Jekel, Pamela
*Sea Star: The Private Life of Anne Bonny, Pirate
  Queen.*
Harmony Books 1983.
BL v79 1983 p697; KR v51 1983 p137; PW v223 F 11,
  1983 p64.

Osborne, Anne
Wind from the Main.
Ballantine 1974.

York, Alison
The Fire and the Rope.
W.H. Allen 1979.
WCRB v5 Jl 1979 p19.

169. Boone, Daniel

1734-1820
Legendary American frontiersman

Bakeless, John E.
YA *Fighting Frontiersman: The Life of Daniel Boone.*
Morrow 1948.
BL v45 1948 p36; BRD 1948 p33; KR v16 1948 p338;
  LJ v73 1948 p1675; NYTBR N 14, 1948 p58.

Barrett, Neal
Daniel Boone, Westward Trail.
Miles Standish Press 1982.

Chambers, Catherine E.
JUV *Daniel Boone and the Wilderness Road.*
Troll Associates 1984.
SLJ v31 F 1985 p72.

Churchill, Winston
The Crossing.
Macmillan 1904 (Heavily reprinted).
FC 10th p99; NYTBR My 28, 1904 p354; NYTBR Je
  18, 1904 p405.

Eckert, Allan W.
The Court-Martial of Daniel Boone.
Little, Brown 1973.
BL v70 1974 p516; KR v41 1973 p904; LJ v98 1973
  p2879; NYTBR Ap 7, 1974 p32; PW v204 Ag 20,
  1973 p85.

Giles, Janice H.
The Kentuckians.
Houghton Mifflin 1953 (Rpr. 1980, 1987).
BRD 1953 p362; NYTBR Jl 26, 1953 p4.

Gordon, Caroline
Green Centuries.
Scribner 1941 (Rpr. 1971).
BL v38 1941 p113; BRD 1941 p357; NYTBR N 2,
  1941 p4.

Key, Alexander
JUV *With Daniel Boone on the Caroliny Trail.*
John C. Winston 1941.
BRD 1941 p501; LJ v66 1941 p143.

Mason, Miriam E.

JUV *Becky and Her Brave Cat, Bluegrass.*
Macmillan 1960.
BRD 1961 p944; KR v28 1960 p559; LJ v85 1960
p3224; NYTBR Ja 29, 1961 p38.

Meadowcroft, Enid La Monte

JUV *Holding the Fort with Daniel Boone.*
Crowell 1958.
Continues *On Indian Trails with Daniel Boone.*
BRD 1958 p739; LJ v83 1958 p967; NYTBR Ap 27,
1958 p36.

Meadowcroft, Enid La Monte

JUV *On Indian Trails with Daniel Boone.*
Crowell 1947.
BL v43 1947 p349; BRD 1947 p622; LJ v72 1947
p962; NYTBR Jl 27, 1947 p20.

Roberts, Elizabeth Madox
The Great Meadow.
Viking 1930 (Rpr. 1980).
BL v26 1930 p314; BRD 1930 p886; NYTBR Mr 2,
1930 p1; SatR Mr 15, 1930 p821.

Seifert, Shirley

YA *Never No More.*
Lippincott 1964.
LJ v89 1964 p4663.

Skinner, Constance L.
Becky Landers: Frontier Warrior.
Macmillan 1926 (Rpr. 1963).
BRD 1926 p646; SatR D 4, 1926 p403.

Steele, William O.

JUV *Daniel Boone's Echo.*
Harcourt, Brace 1957.
BL v54 1957 p146; BRD 1957 p873; HB v33 D 1957
p490; KR v25 1957 p771; LJ v82 1957 p2976;
NYTBR Ja 26, 1958 p30.

Steele, William O.

JUV *The Story of Daniel Boone.*
Grosset & Dunlap 1953.
BRD 1954 p838; KR v21 1953 p487; LJ v78 1953
p2228; NYTBR N 15, 1953 p30.

Stevenson, Augusta

JUV *Daniel Boone, Boy Hunter.*
Bobbs-Merrill 1943.
BRD 1943 p774; LJ v68 1943 p963.

Sutton, Margaret

YA *Jemima, Daughter of Daniel Boone.*
Scribner 1942.
BRD 1942 p752; HB v18 S 1942 p342; LJ v67 1942
p895; NYTBR Ag 30, 1942 p9.

Wheelwright, Jere H.

YA *Kentucky Stand.*
Scribner 1951.
BRD 1951 p939; LJ v76 1951 p719; NYTBR F 25,
1951 p20.

White, Stewart E.
The Long Rifle.
Doubleday 1932 (Heavily reprinted).

BRD 1932 p1011; FC 9th p553; NYTBR Mr 13, 1932
p5.

170. Boone, Rebecca B.
1739-1813
Wife of Daniel Boone

Seifert, Shirley

YA *Never No More.*
Lippincott 1964.
LJ v89 1964 p4663.

171. Booth, Catherine Mumford
1829-1890
Played leading role in founding & developing
the Salvation Army

Jackson, Dave; Jackson, Neta

YA *Kidnapped by River Rats.*
Bethany House Publishers 1991.

Ludwig, Charles
Mother of an Army.
Bethany House Publishers 1987.

172. Booth, John Wilkes
1838-1865
Assassin of Abraham Lincoln

Adicks, Richard
A Court for Owls.
Pineapple Press 1989.
BL v85 1989 p1778; KR v57 1989 p640; LJ v114 Jl
1989 p105.

Jordan, Jan
*Dim the Flaring Lamps: A Novel of the Life of John
Wilkes Booth.*
Prentice-Hall 1972.
BS v31 Mr 1, 1972 p528; KR v39 1971 p1275; LJ v96
1971 p4107.

Kennelly, Ardyth
The Spur.
Messner 1951.
BL v47 1951 p266; BRD 1951 p473; KR v19 1951
p78; LJ v76 1951 p514; NYTBR Ap 15, 1951 p17.

King, Benjamin
A Bullet for Lincoln: A Novel.
Pelican 1993.

Metcalf, Paul C.
Both.
Jargon Society 1982.
LJ v108 1983 p2300.

O'Toole, G. J. A.
*The Cosgrove Report: Being the Private Inquiry of
a Pinkerton Detective into the Death of President
Lincoln. . . .*
Rawson, Wade 1979.
BL v76 1980 p700; KR v47 1979 p1159; LJ v104 1979
p2484; PW v216 O 1, 1979 p75.

Russell, Pamela Redford
The Woman Who Loved John Wilkes Booth.
Putnam 1978.
KR v46 1978 p330; LJ v103 1978 p1199; PW v213 Ap 10, 1978 p66.

Stacton, David
The Judges of the Secret Court.
Pantheon 1961.
BRD 1962 p1140; LJ v86 1961 p2821; NYTBR Ag 13, 1961 p22.

Steward, Barbara; Steward, Dwight
The Lincoln Diddle.
Morrow 1979.
KR v47 1979 p825; LJ v104 1979 p1591; PW v215 Je 18, 1979 p80.

Wiegand, William
The Chester A. Arthur Conspiracy.
Dial 1983.
BL v79 1983 p1390; KR v51 1983 p682; LJ v108 1983 p1385; PW v224 Jl 1983 p56.

173. Booth, William
1829-1912
Founder of the Salvation Army

Jackson, Dave; Jackson, Neta
YA *Kidnapped by River Rats.*
Bethany House Publishers 1991.

La Bern, Arthur
Hallelujah!.
W.H. Allen 1973.
B&B v18 Jl 1973 p134.

174. Borden, Lizzie Andrew
1860-1927
Arrested for killing father, stepmother; acquitted

Engstrom, Elizabeth
Lizzie Borden.
Tor Books 1991.
KR v58 1990 p1479; LJ v115 D 1990 p160; PW v237 D 7, 1990 p70.

Hunter, Evan
Lizzie: A Novel.
Arbor House 1984.
BL v80 1984 p905; KR v52 1984 p268; LJ v109 1984 p1252; NYTBR Je 17, 1984 p20; PW v225 Mr 23, 1984 p65.

Satterthwait, Walter
Miss Lizzie.
St. Martin's 1989.
BL v86 1989 p40; KR v57 1989 p883; NYTBR O 15, 1989 p50.

175. Borghese, Maria Paolina
1780-1825
Sister of Napoleon I

Maass, Edgar
Imperial Venus: A Novel of Napoleon's Favorite Sister.
Bobbs-Merrill 1946.
BL v42 1946 p317; BRD 1946 p517; KR v14 1946 p180; NYTBR My 5, 1946 p10.

176. Borgia, Cesare
1475-1507
Italian diplomat & military leader; said to be prototype for Machiavelli's *The Prince*

Balchin, Nigel
The Borgia Testament.
Houghton Mifflin 1949.
BRD 1949 p36; FC 7th p26; KR v17 1949 p280; LJ v74 1949 p376; NYTBR Ag 7, 1949 p3.

Bennetts, Pamela
The Borgia Prince.
Hale 1968 (Rpr. 1975).
LJ v100 1975 p1650.

Davis, Genevieve
A Passion in the Blood.
Simon & Schuster 1977.
KR v45 1977 p110; LJ v102 1977 p946; PW v211 My 23, 1977 p243.

Haasse, Hella S.
The Scarlet City: A Novel of 16th-Century Italy.
Academy Chicago Publishers 1990.
BL v87 1990 p140; KR v58 1990 p1026; LJ v115 Ag 1990 p141; NYTBR Je 16, 1991 p16.

Holland, Cecelia
City of God: A Novel of the Borgias.
Knopf 1979.
KR v46 1978 p1375; LJ v104 1979 p648; PW v215 Ja 8, 1979 p69; Time v113 Ap 9, 1979 p83.

Lanzol, Cesare
The Serpent of Venice.
Roy 1970.

Maugham, W. Somerset
Then and Now: A Novel.
Heinemann 1946 (Rpr. 1956, 1967, 1977).
Also published as *Fools and Their Folly.*
BL v42 1946 p329; BRD 1946 p557; KR v14 1946 p129; NYTBR My 26, 1946 p4.

Sabatini, Rafael
Love at Arms.
Pan Books 1964.

Samuel, Maurice
Web of Lucifer: A Novel of the Borgia Fury.
Knopf 1947.
BL v42 1947 p242; BRD 1947 p784; FC 7th p301; LJ v72 1947 p320; NYTBR F 23, 1947 p5.

Sava, George
Those Borgias.
Faber & Faber 1940.

Shellabarger, Samuel
Prince of Foxes.
Little, Brown 1947.
BRD 1947 p813; FC 11th p550; KR v15 My 15, 1947
p259; LJ v72 1947 p1034; NYTBR Jl 13, 1947 p1.

177. Borgia, Lucrezia
1480-1519
Italian patron of learning & the arts; daughter of
Pope Alexander VI

Briggs, Jean
The Flame of the Borgias.
Harper & Row 1975.
KR v43 1975 p80; LJ v100 1975 p601; PW v207 Ja 27,
1975 p277.

Davis, Genevieve
A Passion in the Blood.
Simon & Schuster 1977.
KR v45 1977 p110; LJ v102 1977 p946; PW v211 My
23, 1977 p243.

Haasse, Hella S.
The Scarlet City: A Novel of 16th-Century Italy.
Academy Chicago Publishers 1990.
BL v87 1990 p140; KR v58 1990 p1026; LJ v115 Ag
1990 p141; NYTBR Je 16, 1991 p16.

Hibbert, Eleanor (Jean Plaidy, pseud.)
Light on Lucrezia.
Hale 1958 (Rpr. 1976).
Kliatt v11 Fall 1977 p8.

Hibbert, Eleanor (Jean Plaidy, pseud.)
Madonna of the Seven Hills.
Hale 1958 (Rpr. 1974).
LJ v99 1974 p3147.

Kenyon, Frank Wilson
The Naked Sword: The Story of Lucrezia Borgia.
Dodd, Mead 1968.
BS v28 O 15, 1968 p288; PW v194 S 16, 1968 p70.

Sava, George
Those Borgias.
Faber & Faber 1940.

Seymour, Miranda
Daughter of Shadows.
Coward, McCann & Geoghegan 1977.
PW v212 O 10, 1977 p59.

178. Bormann, Martin Ludwig
1900-1945
German Nazi politician

Egleton, Clive
The Bormann Brief.
Coward, McCann & Geoghegan 1974.
FC 9th p158; KR v41 1974 p1281; LJ v99 1974 p385;
PW v204 N 26, 1973 p28.

Forbes, Colin
The Leader and the Damned.

Collins 1983.
BL v81 1984 p190; KR v52 1984 p766.

Higgins, Jack
Thunder Point.
Putnam 1993.

Patterson, Harry
The Valhalla Exchange.
Stein & Day 1976.
BL v73 1977 p1558; KR v44 1976 p 1279; NYTBR Mr
20, 1977 p27; PW v210 D 27, 1976 p56.

Sherrett, J. A.
Operation Rat: A Novel.
Exposition Press 1973.

179. Boswell, James
1740-1795
Scottish biographer; wrote *Life of Johnson*, 1791

De La Torre, Lillian
The Return of Dr. Sam. Johnson, Detector.
International Polygonics 1985.
BL v82 1986 p732; PW v228 N 1, 1985 p63.

Moses, Joseph
JUV *The Great Rain Robbery.*
Houghton Mifflin 1975.
KR v43 1975 p455; NYTBR Ap 6, 1975 p12; SLJ v21
My 1975 p70.

Muir, Marie
Dear Mrs. Boswell.
St. Martin's 1953.
BRD 1953 p675; KR v21 1953 p141; LJ v78 1953
p1935.

180. Bothwell, James Hepburn, Earl of
1536-1578
Scottish nobleman & third husband of Mary
Queen of Scots

Balin, Beverly
King in Hell.
Coward-McCann 1971.
KR v38 1970 p1261; LJ v96 1971 p654.

Irwin, Margaret
The Gay Galliard: The Love Story of Mary,
Queen of Scots.
Harcourt, Brace 1942.
BL v38 1942 p251; BRD 1942 p391; FC 8th p222; LJ
v66 1942 p131; NYTBR F 15, 1942 p4.

181. Boudicca
see Boadicea

182. Boulanger, Georges Ernest Jean Marie
1837-1891
French military & political leader

Gorman, Herbert
Brave General.

Farrar 1942.
BL v38 1942 p234; BRD 1942 p302; NYTBR F 8,
  1942 p4; SatR F 7, 1942 p6.

183. Bouquet, Henry
1719-1765
Fought in French and Indian Wars, defeating Indians in Pontiac's Rebellion, 1763

Richter, Conrad
The Light in the Forest.
Knopf 1953 (Rpr. 1966, 1989).
BL v49 1953 p213; BRD 1953 p787; KR v21 1953
  p231; LJ v78 1953 p917; NYTBR My 17, 1953 p5.

184. Bowditch, Nathaniel
1773-1838
American mathematician & astronomer

Latham, Jean Lee
YA *Carry On, Mr. Bowditch.*
Houghton Mifflin 1955 (Rpr. 1983).
BRD 1955 p529; HB v31 S 15, 1955 p368; LJ v80
  1955 p2646; NYTBR Ja 29, 1956 p30.

185. Bowie, James
1796-1836
American-born Mexican colonist; died at the Alamo

Barrett, Monte
Tempered Blade.
Bobbs-Merrill 1946.
BRD 1946 p42; KR v14 1946 p24; NYTBR My 12,
  1946 p16; SatR Ap 20, 1946 p18.

Wellman, Paul I.
The Iron Mistress.
Doubleday 1951.
BRD 1951 p933; FC 8th p430; KR v19 1951 p278; LJ
  v76 1951 p1028; NYTBR Jl 29, 1951 p4.

186. Bowles, William Augustus
1763-1802
American adventurer; became director general of Creek Nation

Millard, Joseph
YA *The Incredible William Bowles.*
Chilton Books 1966.
LJ v91 1966 p1720.

187. Boycott, Charles Cunningham
1832-1897
Land agent ostracized for collecting excessive rents; the word "boycott" named after him

Rooney, Philip
Captain Boycott, a Romantic Novel.
Appleton-Century 1946 (Rpr. 1966).

BRD 1946 p698; KR v14 1946 p260; LJ v71 1946
  p1127; NYTBR S 8, 1946 p4.

188. Boyd, Belle
1843-1900
American Confederate spy

Kane, Harnett T.
*The Smiling Rebel: A Novel Based on the Life of
  Belle Boyd.*
Doubleday 1955.
BL v52 1955 p147; BRD 1955 p479; FC 9th p286; KR
  v23 1955 p609; LJ v80 1955 p2237; NYTBR O 23,
  1955 p39.

Kendricks, James
*She Wouldn't Surrender: The Wild Days and
  Nights of Belle Boyd, the Notorious Confederate
  Spy.*
Monarch Books 1960.

Nolan, Jeannette C.
YA *Belle Boyd, Secret Agent.*
Messner 1967.
KR v35 1967 p821; LJ v92 1967 p4263.

189. Braddock, Edward
1695-1755
English military leader

Frey, Ruby Frazier
Red Morning.
Putnam 1946.
BL v43 1946 p16; BRD 1946 p292; KR v14 1946
  p278; LJ v71 1946 p978; NYTBR Jl 28, 1946 p14.

Jennings, John E.
Gentleman Ranker.
Reynal & Hitchcock 1942.
BL v39 1942 p48; BRD 1942 p401; LJ v67 1942 p682;
  NYTBR Ag 30, 1942 p6.

190. Bradford, William
1590-1657
One of the Pilgrims who arrived on the Mayflower; governor of Plymouth Colony

Gebler, Ernest
*The Plymouth Adventure: A Chronicle Novel of
  the Voyage of the Mayflower.*
Doubleday 1950.
BRD 1950 p349; NYTBR Ap 30, 1950 p32; SatR Ap
  29, 1950 p13.

Gerson, Noel Bertram
The Land Is Bright.
Doubleday 1961.
FC 9th p198; LJ v86 1961 p3973.

Meigs, Cornelia
Rain on the Roof.
Macmillan 1925 (Rpr. 1950).
BRD 1925 p469; SatR N 28, 1925 p351.

Smith, Bradford
JUV *William Bradford, Pilgrim Boy.*
Bobbs-Merrill 1953 (Rpr. 1963).
LJ v78 1953 p930.

Webb, Robert N.
JUV *We Were There with the Mayflower Pilgrims.*
Grosset & Dunlap 1956.

191. Brady, Mathew B.
1823-1896
American photographer; photographed all aspects of the Civil War

Rogers, Frances
YA *Mr. Brady's Camera Boy.*
Lippincott 1951.
BRD 1951 p753; LJ v76 1951 p1717; NYTBR S 16, 1951 p28.

192. Brahms, Johannes
1833-1897
German composer

Deucher, Sybil
JUV *The Young Brahms.*
Dutton 1949.
BRD 1949 p233; LJ v74 1949 p1464.

Goss, Madeleine; Schauffler, Robert Haven
YA *Brahms the Master.*
Holt 1943.
BRD 1943 p317; NYTBR Mr 5, 1944 p6; SatR Ja 22, 1944 p36.

193. Brancusi, Constantin
1876-1957
Romanian-born sculptor

Neagoe, Peter
The Saint of Montparnasse: A Novel Based on the Life of Constantin Brancusi.
Chilton Books 1965.
KR v33 1965 p194; LJ v90 1965 p1746.

194. Brannan, Samuel
1819-1889
American pioneer & publisher; published San Francisco's first newspaper, the *California Star*, 1847

Bailey, Paul
The Gay Saint.
Murray & Gee 1944.
NYTBR F 27, 1944 p19.

Scott, Reva
Samuel Brannan and the Golden Fleece.
Macmillan 1944.
BL v40 1944 p390; BRD 1944 p670; KR v12 1944 p56; LJ v69 1944 p354; NYTBR Jl 9, 1944 p21.

195. Brant, Joseph
1742-1807
American Indian leader; loyal to British during Revolutionary War

Alderman, Clifford L.
JUV *Joseph Brant, Chief of the Six Nations.*
Messner 1958.
BRD 1959 p9; LJ v84 1959 p646; NYTBR Ja 18, 1959 p28.

Brick, John
Eagle of Niagara: The Story of David Harper and His Indian Captivity.
Doubleday 1955.
BL v51 1955 p346; BRD 1955 p111; KR v22 1954 p776; LJ v80 1955 p1008; NYTBR F 13, 1955 p28.

Brick, John
YA *The Raid.*
Duell, Sloan & Pearce 1960.
YA version of novel published in 1951 under the same title.
BL v47 1951 p310; BRD 1951 p113; FC 7th p51; KR v10 1951 p74; LJ v85 1960 p3229; NYTBR Ap 1, 1951 p29.

Chalmers, Harvey
West to the Setting Sun.
Macmillan 1943 (Rpr. 1965).
BRD 1944 p129.

Hine, Al
Brother Owl.
Doubleday 1980.
KR v48 1980 p928; LJ v105 1980 p1751; PW v218 Jl 18, 1980 p45.

Thomas, Howard
JUV *Joseph Brant.*
Prospect Books 1973 (Rpr. 1984).

196. Braun, Eva
1912-1945
German mistress of Adolf Hitler

Bloom, Ursula (Lozania Prole, pseud.)
Hitler's Eva.
Hutchinson 1954 (Rpr. 1976).

Dobbs, Michael
Last Man to Die.
HarperCollins 1992.

Melchior, Ib
Eva: A Novel.
Dodd, Mead 1984.
BL v80 1984 p1226; KR v52 1984 p317; LJ v109 1984 p916; PW v225 Mr 23, 1984 p65.

197. Brendan of Clonfert, Saint
484-577
Irish saint; founded the monastery of Clonfert

Buechner, Frederick
Brendan.
Atheneum 1987.
BL v83 1987 p1407; KR v55 1987 p489; LJ v112 Je 1,
    1987 p127; NYTBR Ag 9, 1987 p15.

Eberhart, Dikkon
YA *Paradise: A Novel.*
Stemmer House Publishers 1983.
KR v51 1983 p537; LJ v108 1983 p1277; SLJ v30 Ja
    1984 p91.

Fritz, Jean
JUV *Brendan the Navigator: A History Mystery about
    the Discovery of America.*
Coward, McCann & Geoghegan 1979.
BRD 1979 p441; NYTBR Ap 29, 1979 p30; SLJ v25
    My 1979 p61.

198. Brent, Margaret
1600-1671
English-born colonist & feminist

Grant, Dorothy
Margaret Brent, Adventurer.
Longmans, Green 1944.
BRD 1944 p294; KR v12 1944 p371; NYTBR O 22,
    1944 p27.

199. Breton, Andre
1896-1966
French poet, author, & critic

Collette, Jean Yves
The Death of Andre Breton.
Guernica Press 1984.

Goldstein, Lisa
The Dream Years.
Bantam 1985.
BL v81 1985 p1637; KR v53 1985 p678; LJ v110 Ag
    1985 p120; NYTBR O 20, 1985 p20; PW v227 Jl
    15, 1985 p58.

200. Brian Boru
926-1014
Irish king, 1002-1014

Brady, Charles A.
YA *Sword of Clontarf.*
Doubleday 1960.
HB v36 Je 1960 p220; KR v28 1960 p9; LJ v85 1960
    p1704.

Holland, Cecelia
The Kings in Winter.
Atheneum 1968.
BL v64 1968 p1219; BRD 1968 p623; FC 11th p300;
    KR v35 1967 p1384; LJ v92 1967 p4523; NYTBR
    Ja 28, 1968 p36.

Moeller, E. H.
Brian Boru.
Foster & Stewart 1944.

201. Bridger, James
1804-1881
American frontiersman & fur trader

Allen, Merritt P.
YA *Western Star: A Story of Jim Bridger.*
D. McKay 1941.
BL v38 O 1, 1941 p37; BRD 1941 p14; LJ v66 1941
    p735; SHSLC 8th p382.

Anderson, Anita M.
YA *Fur Trappers of the Old West.*
Harper & Row 1961.

Fleischman, Sid
JUV *Jim Bridger's Alarm Clock and Other Tall Tales.*
Dutton 1978.
BL v75 1979 p808; KR v47 1979 p124; SLJ v25 Ap
    1979 p55.

Hollmann, Clide
JUV *Jim Bridger, King of Scouts.*
Vantage Press 1953.

Kherdian, David
YA *Bridger: The Story of a Mountain Man.*
Greenwillow Books 1987.
BL v83 1987 p1127; BRD 1987 p1008; KR v55 1987
    p227; SLJ v33 Ap 1987 p111.

Parker, Laura
Jim Bridger, Mountain Man.
Miles Standish Press 1981.

Tousey, Sanford
JUV *Jim Bridger, American Frontiersman.*
A. Whitman 1952.
BRD 1952 p888; LJ v77 1952 p731; NYTBR Jl 13,
    1952 p18.

Winders, Gertrude
JUV *Jim Bridger, Mountain Boy.*
Bobbs-Merrill 1955.

202. Bronte, Anne
1820-1849
English author

Reid Banks, Lynne
Dark Quartet: The Story of the Brontes.
Delacorte 1977.
BL v73 1977 p1134; FC 10th p33; KR v44 1976
    p1284; LJ v102 1977 p830; SHSLC 12th p538.

White, Hilda
*Wild Decembers: A Biographical Portrait of the
    Brontes.*
Dutton 1957.
BRD 1957 p978.

203. Bronte, Charlotte
1816-1855
English author; wrote *Jane Eyre*

Cornish, Dorothy Helen
These Were the Brontes.
Macmillan 1940.
BRD 1940 p200; NYTBR Ja 28, 1940 p6; SatR F 17,
   1940 p12.

Dunlop, Agnes M. (Elizabeth Kyle, pseud.)
YA *Girl with a Pen: Charlotte Bronte.*
Holt, Rinehart & Winston 1964.
BRD 1964 p687; LJ v89 1964 p2230; NYTBR My 10,
   1964 p10; SatR My 16, 1964 p91.

Haire-Sargeant, Lin
*H: The Story of Heathcliff's Journey Back to Wuth-
   ering Heights.*
Pocket Books 1992.
BL v88 1992 p1994; LJ v117 Je 1, 1992 p176.

Reid Banks, Lynne
Dark Quartet: The Story of the Brontes.
Delacorte 1977.
BL v73 1977 p1134; FC 10th p33; KR v44 1976
   p1284; LJ v102 1977 p830; SHSLC 12th p538.

Reid Banks, Lynne
*Path to the Silent Country: Charlotte Bronte's
   Years of Fame.*
Delacorte 1977.
Sequel to *Dark Quartet.*
BL v74 1978 p1232; KR v46 1978 p142; LJ v103 1978
   p872; SLJ v25 1978 p168.

White, Hilda
*Wild Decembers: A Biographical Portrait of the
   Brontes.*
Dutton 1957.
BRD 1957 p978.

204. Bronte, Emily Jane
1818-1848
English author; wrote *Wuthering Heights*

Cornish, Dorothy Helen
These Were the Brontes.
Macmillan 1940.
BRD 1940 p200; NYTBR Ja 28, 1940 p6; SatR F 17,
   1940 p12.

Gater, Dilys
Emily.
Hale 1980.

Reid Banks, Lynne
Dark Quartet: The Story of the Brontes.
Delacorte 1977.
BL v73 1977 p1134; FC 10th p33; KR v44 1976
   p1284; LJ v102 1977 p830; SHSLC 12th p538.

White, Hilda
*Wild Decembers: A Biographical Portrait of the
   Brontes.*
Dutton 1957.
BRD 1957 p978.

205. Bronte, Patrick Branwell
1817-1848
English poet; brother of the Bronte sisters

Reid Banks, Lynne
Dark Quartet: The Story of the Brontes.
Delacorte 1977.
BL v73 1977 p1134; FC 10th p33; KR v44 1976
   p1284; LJ v102 1977 p830; SHSLC 12th p538.

Swindells, Robert E.
YA *Follow a Shadow.*
Holiday House 1990.
BL v87 1990 p819; SLJ V36 O 1990 p145.

White, Hilda
*Wild Decembers: A Biographical Portrait of the
   Brontes.*
Dutton 1957.
BRD 1957 p978.

206. Brown, John
1800-1859
American abolitionist; led raid at Harper's
Ferry, VA, 1859; executed

Ehrlich, Leonard
God's Angry Man.
Simon & Schuster 1932 (Rpr. 1941, 1954).
BRD 1932 p292; FC 10th p160.

Myers, Robert J.
The Slave of Frankenstein.
Lippincott 1976.
BL v72 1976 p1243; KR v44 1976 p216.

Nelson, Truman
The Surveyor.
Doubleday 1960.
BRD 1960 p989; KR v28 1960 p110; LJ v85 1960
   p1143; NYTBR Ap 17, 1960 p24.

Saddler, Harry D.
John Brown: The Magnificent Failure.
Dorrance 1951.

Stern, Philip Van Doren
The Drums of Morning.
Doubleday, Doran 1942.
BL v39 1942 p12; BRD 1942 p737; LJ v67 1942 p630;
   NYTBR Ag 9, 1942 p6.

Williams, Ben Ames
House Divided.
Houghton Mifflin 1947.
KR v15 1947 p368; LJ v72 1947 p1110; NYTBR S 7,
   1947 p3.

207. Browning, Elizabeth Barrett
1806-1861
English poet

Forster, Margaret
Lady's Maid.
Doubleday 1991.

BL v87 1991 p1177; BRD 1991 p621; KR v58 1990 p1694; LJ v116 Ja 1991 p150; NYTBR Mr 17, 1991 p14.

Iremonger, Lucille
How Do I Love Thee.
Morrow 1976.
BS v36 Jl 1976 p116; KR v44 1976 p214; LJ v101 1976 p1225; PW v209 Mr 1, 1976 p86.

McDonald, Eva
Dearest Ba.
Hale 1976.

Waite, Helen E.
How Do I Love Thee?: The Story of Elizabeth Barrett Browning.
Macrae Smith 1953.
BL v50 O 15, 1953 p84; HB v29 D 1953 p467; KR v21 1953 p394; LJ v78 1953 p1862; NYTBR N 15, 1953 p18.

Woolf, Virginia
Flush.
Harcourt, Brace 1933 (Heavily reprinted).
BRD 1933 p1041; NYTBR O 8, 1933 p2; SatR O 7, 1933 p159.

208. Browning, Robert
1812-1889
English poet; married Elizabeth Barrett, 1846

Forster, Margaret
Lady's Maid.
Doubleday 1991.
BL v87 1991 p1177; BRD 1991 p621; KR v58 1990 p1694; LJ v116 Ja 1991 p150; NYTBR Mr 17, 1991 p14.

Iremonger, Lucille
How Do I Love Thee.
Morrow 1976.
BS v36 Jl 1976 p116; KR v44 1976 p214; LJ v101 1976 p1225; PW v209 Mr 1, 1976 p86.

McDonald, Eva
Dearest Ba.
Hale 1976.

Urquhart, Jane
The Whirlpool: A Novel.
McClelland & Stewart 1986 (Rpr. 1990).
BRD 1988 p1767.

Woolf, Virginia
Flush.
Harcourt, Brace 1933 (Heavily reprinted).
BRD 1933 p1041; NYTBR O 8, 1933 p2; SatR O 7, 1933 p159.

209. Bruce, Lenny
1925-1966
American comedian

Kohler-Smith, Valerie
Lenny.
Grove Press 1974.
Based on the motion picture written by Julian Barry.

210. Bruckner, Anton
1824-1896
Austrian composer

Weiser, Theresa
Music for God.
Philosophical Library 1951.
BRD 1951 p930.

211. Bruegel, Pieter
1525-1569
Flemish painter

Hofmann, Gert
The Parable of the Blind.
Fromm International 1989.
Translation of *Der Blindensturz.*
BRD 1987 p858; LJ v111 F 15, 1986 p194; NYTBR Ja 26, 1986 p27.

Rocquet, Claude Henri
Bruegel; or, The Workshop of Dreams.
University of Chicago Press 1991.
BRD 1992 p1702; NYTBR Mr 29, 1992 p19; TLS D 13, 1991 p21.

212. Brunel, Isambard Kingdom
1806-1859
Constructed London's Thames Tunnel, 1825-1843

Buck, Alan
The Little Giant: A Life of I. K. Brunel.
David & Charles 1986.

213. Brunelleschi, Filippo
1377-1446
Italian architect

Manetti, Antonio
The Fat Woodworker.
Italica Press 1991.

214. Bruno, Giordano
1548-1600
Italian philosopher

Scott, Chris
Antichthon.
Quadrant 1982.
Also published as *The Heretic.*

215. Buchanan, James
1791-1868
15th US President

Gordon, Leo V.
Powderkeg.
Presido Press 1991.
KR v59 1991 p1109; LJ v116 O 15, 1991 p120; PW v238 S 27, 1991 p43.

Updike, John
Memories of the Ford Administration.
Knopf 1992.
Atl v271 Ja 1993 p125; LJ v117 O 1, 1992 p121; NYTBR N 1, 1992 p11.

216. Buck, Pearl S.
1892-1973
American author; won Pulitzer, 1932, Nobel Prize, 1938

Westervelt, Virginia
Pearl Buck, a Biographical Novel.
Elsevier/Nelson Books 1979.
LJ v104 1979 p1163.

217. Buddha
563-483 BC
Indian philosopher & founder of Buddhism

Barrett, William E.
Lady of the Lotus.
Doubleday 1975.
FC 11th p42; KR v43 1975 p192; LJ v100 1975 p781; PW v207 F 24, 1975 p109.

Hesse, Hermann
Siddhartha.
New Directions 1951.
Orginally published in 1923; this is the first English edition.
BRD 1952 p427; FC 9th p248; KR v19 1951 p594; NYTBR D 2, 1951 p52; SatR D 22, 1951 p34.

Landaw, Jonathan
JUV *The Story of Buddha.*
Hemkunt Press 1978.

Payne, Pierre
The Yellow Robe, a Novel of the Life of Buddha.
Dodd, Mead 1948.
BRD 1948 p651; LJ v73 1948 p198.

Payne, Robert
The Lord Comes: A Novel of the Life of Buddha.
Heinemann 1948.

Raina, Vimala
Ambapali.
Asia Pub. House 1962.
LJ v88 1963 p2028.

Siributr, M. R. Saisingh
JUV *The Golden Stag.*
Duang Kamol Pub. Co. 1978.

Wiloch, Thomas
Tales of Lord Shantih.
Unicorn Press 1989.

218. Buffalo Bill
see Cody, "Buffalo Bill" (William Frederick)

219. Buford, John
1826-1863
American Civil War general, Army of Potomac

Shaara, Michael
The Killer Angels.
McKay 1974.
Won 1975 Pulitzer prize.
BRD 1974 p1098; KR v42 1974 p702; LJ v99 1974 p2091; NYTBR O 20, 1974 p38.

220. Bunyan, John
1628-1688
English preacher & author; wrote *Pilgrim's Progress*

Barr, Gladys Hutchison
The Pilgrim Prince.
Holt, Rinehart & Winston 1963.
LJ v89 1964 p280.

Leeson, Muriel
JUV *The Bedford Adventure.*
Herald Press 1987.
SLJ v34 Mr 1988 p197.

221. Burgess, Guy Francis de Moncy
1911-1963
Member of British Foreign Office trio that passed classified data to Soviets in the 1950s

Garland, Rodney
The Troubled Midnight.
Coward McCann 1955.
KR v23 1955 p185; LJ v80 1955 p878; NYTBR My 8, 1955 p14.

Harling, Robert
The Enormous Shadow.
Harper 1955.
BRD 1956 p410; KR v24 1956 p602; NYTBR N 25, 1956 p67; SatR D 15, 1956 p40.

Llewellyn, Richard
Mr. Hamish Gleave.
Doubleday 1956.
BRD 1956 p577; LJ v81 1956 p442; NYTBR F 5, 1956 p23; SatR F 11, 1956 p43.

Pape, Richard
Arm Me Audacity.
A. Wingate 1955.

222. Burghley, William Cecil, Baron
1520-1598
English courtier and politician; Queen Elizabeth I's most trusted minister

Anthony, Evelyn
All the Queen's Men.

Crowell 1960.
BL v56 1960 p683; FC 11th p19; KR v28 1960 p250;
LJ v85 1960 p1616; TLS Je 3, 1960 p358.

223. Burgoyne, John
1722-1792
English general & playwright

Lancaster, Bruce
Guns of Burgoyne.
Frederick A. Stokes 1939 (Rpr. 1975).
BL v35 1939 p270; BRD 1939 p564; NYTBR Mr 26,
1939 p6.

Styles, Showell
Gentleman Johnny.
Macmillan 1962.
NYTBR Ap 21, 1963 p47.

224. Burkc, Martha Jane Cannary
see Calamity Jane

225. Burke, William
1792-1829
Irish murderer; with William Hare, killed 15
people

Byrd, Elizabeth
Rest without Peace.
Macmillan 1974.
B&B v19 Ap 1974 p91; GW v110 F 16, 1974 p25;
Obs F 3, 1974 p31; Spec v232 F 9, 1974 p171.

Goodwin, Inge
Bury Me in Lead.
A. Wingate 1952.

Thomas, Dylan
The Doctor and the Devils.
Dent 1953 (Heavily reprinted).
BL v50 1953 p116; BRD 1953 p932; LJ v78 1953
p2214; NYTBR D 6, 1953 p38.

226. Burney, Fanny (Frances)
1752-1840
English author

Stewart, Anna Bird
JUV *Young Miss Burney.*
Lippincott 1947.
BRD 1947 p862; LJ v72 1947 p1444; LJ v73 1948 p50.

227. Burns, Robert
1759-1796
Scottish poet

Barke, James
The Crest of the Broken Wave.
Macmillan 1953.
BL v49 1953 p349; BRD 1953 p37; KR v21 1953
p448; LJ v78 1953 p1529; NYTBR D 20, 1953 p15.

Barke, James
The Song in the Green Thorn Tree.
Collins 1947.
BL v44 1948 p352; BRD 1948 p42; FC 7th p28; KR
v16 1948 p152; NYTBR Jl 4, 1948 p5.

Barke, James
The Well of the Silent Harp.
Macmillan 1954.
BL v50 1954 p442; BRD 1954 p43; NYTBR S 5, 1954
p6.

Barke, James
The Wind That Shakes the Barley.
Macmillan 1947.
BRD 1947 p44; FC 7th p28; LJ v72 My 1, 1947 p732.

Barke, James
The Wonder of All the Gay World.
Collins 1949.
BRD 1950 p51; LJ v75 1950 p1180; NYTBR Jl 16,
1950 p18.

Bush-Brown, Louise
*Ploughman Poet: A Novel Based upon the Life of
Robert Burns.*
Dorrance 1972.

228. Burr, Aaron
1756-1836
US Vice President (1801-1805), soldier, & adventurer; killed Alexander Hamilton in a duel

Allis, Marguerite
To Keep Us Free.
Putnam 1953.
BL v49 1953 p204; BRD 1953 p9; CSM Mr 12, 1953
p11; NY v28 F 7, 1953 p103; SatR F 7, 1953 p21.

Bartlett, Jean Anne
Angelica.
Popular Library 1977.
PW v211 Ja 24, 1977 p331.

Graff, Polly
YA *Theodosia, Daughter of Aaron Burr.*
Farrar & Rinehart 1941.

Harris, Cyril
Street of Knives.
Little, Brown 1950.
BL v47 1950 p75; BRD 1950 p407; KR v18 1950
p315; LJ v75 1950 p1291; NYTBR Ag 13, 1950 p22.

Holland, Rupert S.
YA *Secret of Blennerhassett.*
Farrar & Rinehart 1941.
BRD 1941 p438; LJ v66 1941 p269.

Kurland, Michael
The Whenabouts of Burr.
Daw Books 1975.
PW v207 Je 2, 1975 p56.

Seton, Anya
My Theodosia.

Houghton Mifflin 1941.
BRD 1941 p806; FC 7th p311; LJ v66 1941 p220;
  NYTBR Mr 16, 1941 p7.

Stanley, Edward
The Rock Cried Out.
Duell, Sloan & Pearce 1949.
BRD 1949 p868; KR v17 1949 p238; LJ v74 1949
  p892; NYTBR Jl 3, 1949 p13.

Vidal, Gore
Burr: A Novel.
Random House 1973 (Rpr. 1982).
BRD 1973 p1338; BRD 1974 p1254; FC 11th p633;
  KR v41 1973 p988; LJ v98 1973 p3284; NYTBR D
  2, 1973 p76; Time v102 N 5, 1973 p109.

229. Burton, Richard Francis, Sir
1821-1890
English explorer & Orientalist; discovered Lake
Tanganyika, 1858; noted for 16 volume translation of *Arabian Nights*

Farmer, Philip Jose
To Your Scattered Bodies Go.
Putnam 1971.
KR v38 1970 p1267; LJ v96 1971 p1389; PW v198 N
  16, 1970 p71.

Harrison, William
Burton and Speke.
St. Martin's 1982.
BL v79 1982 p92; KR v50 1982 p951; LJ v107 1982
  p1895; PW v222 Ag 13, 1982 p67.

Rayner, William
The Trail to Bear Paw Mountain.
Collins 1974.
Obs Ap 21, 1974 p37.

230. Bush, George Herbert Walker
1924-
41st US President; Vice President under Ronald
Reagan

Fisher, David E.
Hostage One.
Random House 1989.
BL v85 1989 p1612; KR v57 1989 p715; NYTBR S
  17, 1989 p30; PW v235 My 19, 1989 p66.

Searls, Hank
Kataki: A Novel.
McGraw-Hill 1987.
BL v84 1987 p112; KR v55 1987 p1028.

231. Butler, Benjamin Franklin
1818-1893
American politician & military leader

Bromfield, Louis
Wild Is the River.
Harper & Brothers 1941.
BRD 1941 p112; LJ v66 1941 p949.

Roberts, W. Adolphe
*Brave Mardi Gras: A New Orleans Novel of the
  '60s.*
Bobbs-Merrill 1946.
BL v42 1946 p266; BRD 1946 p691; KR v14 1946 p3;
  NYTBR Mr 10, 1946 p8.

232. Butler, Samuel
1835-1902
English author; wrote novel *Way of All Flesh*

Hopkins, Kenneth
*Samuel Butler and Miss E. M. A. Savage: Further
  Correspondence.*
Warren House Press 1976.

233. Byrd, Richard, Admiral
1888-1957
American naval officer & polar explorer

Strong, Charles S.
JUV *We Were There with Byrd at the South Pole.*
Grosset & Dunlap 1956.
BRD 1956 p904; LJ v81 1956 p1049; NYTBR Mr 18,
  1956 p40.

234. Byron, George Gordon Noel Byron, Baron
1788-1824
English poet

Aldanov, Mark
For Thee the Best.
Scribner 1945.
BL v42 1945 p110; BRD 1945 p403; KR v13 1945
  p378; NYTBR N 4, 1945 p1.

Box, Sydney
The Bad Lord Byron.
Convoy Publications 1949.

Combuchen, Sigrid
Byron: A Novel.
Heinemann 1991.
NYTBR Ja 24, 1993 p19.

Dessau, Joanna
Lord of the Ladies.
Hale 1981 (Rpr. 1983).
TLS Ja 8, 1982 p35.

Edwards, Anne
Haunted Summer.
Coward, McCann & Geoghegan 1972.
KR v40 1972 p1043; LJ v97 1972 p3727; LJ v98 1973
  p273; PW v202 S 18, 1972 p72.

Gray, Austin K.
Teresa; or, Her Demon Lover.
Scribner 1945.
BRD 1945 p282; KR v13 1945 p448; NYTBR N 4,
  1945 p1.

Iremonger, Lucille
My Sister, My Love.
Morrow 1981.
KR v48 1980 p1479; LJ v105 1980 p2588.

Kenyon, Frank Wilson
The Absorbing Fire.
Dodd, Mead 1966.
B&B v11 Ap 1966 p35; BS v26 N 15, 1966 p310; LJ
v91 1966 p6000.

Marlowe, Derek
A Single Summer with Lord B..
Viking 1970.
Also published as *A Single Summer With L. B..*
BRD 1970 p933; KR v37 1969 p1030; LJ v95 1970
p1048; NYTBR F 15, 1970 p47.

McDonald, Eva
Lord Byron's First Love.
Hale 1968 (Rpr. 1973).

Nicole, Christopher
The Secret Memoirs of Lord Byron.
Lippincott 1978.
BL v75 1978 p664; KR v46 1978 p1087; LJ v104 1979
p421; PW v214 O 2, 1978 p128.

Nye, Robert
The Memoirs of Lord Bryon.
Hamish Hamilton 1989.
GW v141 O 1, 1989 p28; Obs S 17, 1989 p47.

Prantera, Amanda
*Conversations with Lord Byron on Perversion, 163
Years after His Lordship's Death.*
Atheneum 1987.
KR v55 1987 p1026; LJ v112 Ag 1987 p144; PW v232
S 11, 1987 p80.

Prokosch, Frederic
The Missolonghi Manuscript.
Farrar, Straus & Giroux 1968 (Rpr. 1984).
BRD 1968 p1089; BS v27 Ja 15, 1968 p403; Choice
v5 O 1968 p958; LJ v92 D 1, 1967 p4525; SatR Ja
13, 1968 p82; Time v91 F 9, 1968 p95.

Seymour, Miranda
Count Manfred.
Coward, McCann & Geoghegan 1977.
KR v44 1976 p1186.

West, Paul
Lord Byron's Doctor.
Doubleday 1989.
BL v86 1989 p147; BRD 1991 p1968; KR v57 1989
p1034; LJ v114 S 1, 1989 p298; NYTBR F 3, 1991
p32; PW v236 Jl 21, 1989 p50.

235. Cabeza de Vaca, Alvar Nunez
1490-1557
Spanish explorer

Baker, Betty
JUV *Walk the World's Rim.*
Harper & Row 1965.

BRD 1965 p61; CC 11th p323; LJ v90 1965 p1546;
NYTBR Jl 11, 1965 p34.

Cheavens, Sam Frank
*Child of the Sun: A Historical Novel Based on the
Journey of Cabeza de Vaca across North Amer-
ica.*
Sun Publishing Co. 1986.

Hall, Oakley
The Children of the Sun.
Atheneum 1983.
KR v51 1983 p474; LJ v108 1983 p1156; NYTBR O
23, 1983 p24.

Mirsky, Jeannette
YA *The Gentle Conquistadors.*
Pantheon 1969.
KR v37 1969 p566; LJ v94 1969 p3222.

Panger, Daniel
Black Ulysses.
Viking 1978 (Rpr. 1982).
BL v79 1982 p298; LJ v107 1982 p2110.

Slaughter, Frank G.
YA *Apalachee Gold: The Fabulous Adventures of Ca-
beza de Vaca.*
Doubleday 1954.
BL v51 1955 p285; BRD 1955 p836; KR v22 1954
p408; LJ v79 1954 p2502; NYTBR F 13, 1955 p28.

Wojciechowska, Maia
JUV *Odyssey of Courage: The Story of Alvan Nunez
Cabeza de Vaca.*
Atheneum 1965.
BRD 1965 p1366; LJ v90 1965 p2040.

236. Cabot, John
1450-1498
Italian-born explorer

Hill, Kay
YA *And Tomorrow the Stars: The Story of John
Cabot.*
Dodd, Mead 1968.
KR v36 1968 p701; LJ v94 1969 p884; NYTBR D 22,
1968 p12.

237. Cabot, Sebastian
1476-1557
Italian-born explorer & cartographer; son of
John Cabot

Smith, A. C. H.
Sebastian the Navigator.
Weidenfeld & Nicolson 1985.

238. Cabrillo, Juan Rodriguez
1520-1543
Portuguese explorer

Lovelace, Maud
JUV *What Cabrillo Found: The Story of Juan Rodriguez Cabrillo*.
Crowell 1958.
BRD 1959 p639; KR v26 1958 p712; LJ v84 1959 p252.

Merrell, Elizabeth
YA *Tenoch*.
T. Nelson 1954.
BL v51 1954 p180; BRD 1954 p613; KR v22 1954 p443; NYTBR O 10, 1954 p38.

239. Caesar, Gaius Julius
see Julius Caesar

240. Cagliostro, Alessandro, Conte di
1743-1795
Italian adventurer & magician

Dumas, Alexandre
Memoirs of a Physician.
T.B. Peterson 1850 (Heavily reprinted).
Translation of *Memoires d'un Medecin*.

Dumas, Alexandre
The Queen's Necklace.
G. Routledge & Sons 1880 (Heavily reprinted).
Translation of *Le Collier de la Reine*.
FC 11th p172.

Susac, Andrew
God's Fool: A Biographical Novel of Cagliostro.
Doubleday 1972.
KR v40 1972 p867; LJ v98 1973 p1016.

241. Calamity Jane
1852-1903
American frontier heroine

Berger, Thomas
Little Big Man.
Dial 1964 (Heavily reprinted).
BRD 1964 p97; LJ v89 1964 p4560; NYTBR O 11, 1964 p42; SatR O 3, 1964 p38.

McMurtry, Larry
Buffalo Girls: A Novel.
Simon & Schuster 1990.
BL v87 1990 p5; BRD 1991 p1266; KR v58 1990 p1033; LJ v115 O 1, 1990 p118; NYTBR O 7, 1990 p3; Time v136 O 29, 1990 p103.

242. Caligula
12-41
Roman emperor, 37-41

Burroughs, Edgar Rice
I Am a Barbarian.
E.R. Burroughs, Inc. 1967.
LJ v93 1968 p1018.

Douglas, Lloyd C.
The Robe.
Houghton Mifflin 1942.
BL v39 1942 p71; BRD 1942 p217; FC 11th p166; NYTBR O 25, 1942 p7; SatR O 31, 1942 p16.

Slaughter, Frank G.
The Sins of Herod: A Novel of Rome and the Early Church.
Doubleday 1968.
KR v36 1968 p483; LJ v93 1968 p1920.

243. Calvin, John
1509-1564
French-born Swiss Protestant theologian; established Calvinism

Barr, Gladys Hutchison
The Master of Geneva: A Novel Based on the Life of John Calvin.
Holt, Rinehart & Winston 1961.
LJ v86 1961 p3490; LJ v87 1962 p1334; NYTBR N 19, 1061 p61.

Norton-Taylor, Duncan
God's Man: A Novel on the Life of John Calvin.
Baker Book House 1979.
BRD 1981 p1060; LJ v107 1980 p744; Time v115 Ap 7, 1980 p85.

244. Campanella, Tommaso
1568-1639
Italian philosopher, poet, & author

Cyrano de Bergerac, Savinien
Other Worlds; the Comical History of the States and Empires of the Moon and the Sun.
Oxford University Press 1965.
Translation of *Histoire Comique*.
Choice v3 1966 p656.

245. Capone, Al (Alphonse)
1899-1947
American gangster; dominated Chicago's crime scene in the 1920s; implicated in St. Valentine's Day massacre, 1929

Adamic, Louis
Grandsons: A Story of American Lives.
Harper 1935 (Rpr. 1990).
BL v31 1935 p299; BRD 1935 p2; NYTBR Mr 24, 1935 p5.

Albert, Marvin
The Untouchables: A Novel.
Ivy Books 1987.
Based on a screenplay written by David Mamet.

Burnett, William Riley
Little Caesar.
Dial 1929 (Heavily reprinted).
BL v26 1929 p32; BRD 1929 p139; NYTBR Je 2, 1929 p8; SatR Je 15, 1929 p1110.

Roeburt, John
Al Capone: A Novel.
Pyramid Books 1959.

246. Caravaggio, Michelangelo da
1573-1610
Italian painter

Calitri, Charles J.
The Goliath Head: A Novel about Caravaggio.
Crown 1972.
KR v40 1972 p493; LJ v97 1972 p2429; PW v201 Ap
   24, 1972 p41.

Murray, Linda
The Dark Fire: A Novel.
Morrow 1977.
BL v74 1977 p463; KR v45 1977 p595; LJ v102 1977
   p1679.

Payne, Robert
Caravaggio: A Novel.
Little, Brown 1968.
BL v65 1968 p152; KR v36 1968 p422; LJ v93 1968
   p2692.

247. Carlos
1947-
Venezuelan-born terrorist

Phillips, David Atlee
The Carlos Contract: A Novel of International Terrorism.
Macmillan 1978.
KR v46 1978 p1088.

248. Carlota
1840-1927
Belgian-born empress of Mexico as wife of Archduke Maximilian of Austria

Barnes, Nancy
YA *Carlota, American Empress.*
Messner 1943.
BL v40 1943 p150; BRD 1943 p43; NYTBR Ja 30,
   1944 p6; SatR N 13, 1943 p46.

Bourne, Peter
Flames of Empire.
Putnam 1949.
BRD 1949 p466; KR v17 1949 p438; LJ v74 1949
   p1461; NYTBR S 25, 1949 p30.

Gavin, Catherine Irvine
The Cactus and the Crown.
Doubleday 1962.
BL v58 1962 p477; BRD 1962 p441; FC 11th p231;
   KR v29 1961 p1094; LJ v87 1962 p2038; NYTBR F
   11, 1962 p34.

Gorman, Herbert
The Breast of the Dove.
Rinehart 1950.

BRD 1950 p368; KR v18 1950 p75; LJ v75 1950 p560;
   NYTBR Ap 16, 1950 p43.

Meadows, Rose
Imperial Pawn.
Hurst & Blackett 1972.

249. Carnegie, Andrew
1835-1919
American industrialist & philanthropist

Kaup, Elizabeth
Not for the Meek.
Macmillan 1941.
BRD 1941 p491; LJ v66 1941 p80; NYTBR F 2, 1941
   p7; SatR Mr 8, 1941 p10.

250. Carr, Emily
1871-1945
Canadian painter & author

Gaitskell, Susan
JUV *Emily.*
Three Tree Press 1986.

Leger, Diane
JUV *The Attic of All Sorts.*
Orca Book Publishers 1991.
BIC v20 O 1991 p52; Can Mat v19 S 1991 p230.

251. Carroll, Anna Ella
1815-1893
American political pamphleteer & author

Noble, Hollister
*Woman with a Sword: The Biographical Novel of
   Anna Ella Carroll of Maryland.*
Doubleday 1948.
BRD 1948 p624; FC 9th p381; KR v16 1958 p240; LJ
   v73 1948 p1027.

252. Carroll, Lewis, pseud.
1832-1898
English mathematician & author; wrote *Alice's
Adventures in Wonderland* and *Through the Looking Glass*

Slavitt, David R.
Alice at 80: A Novel.
Doubleday 1984.
BL v1984 p1600; KR v52 1984 p501; LJ v109 1984
   p1349; NYTBR Ag 19, 1984 p12.

Thomas, Donald S.
Mad Hatter Summer.
Viking 1983.
Also published as *Belladonna: A Lewis Carroll Nightmare.*
BL v80 1983 p470; KR v51 1983 p974; NYTBR Ja 1,
   1984 p24; PW v224 O 14, 1983 p44.

253. Carson, "Kit" (Christopher)
1809-1868
American frontiersman & Indian agent

Allen, Merritt P.
YA *The Silver Wolf.*
Longmans, Green 1951.
BL v47 1951 p260; BRD 1951 p12; KR v18 1950
    p693; LJ v76 1951 p606; NYTBR Jl 29, 1951 p12.

Bell, Margaret E.
JUV *Kit Carson, Mountain Man.*
Morrow 1952.
BL v49 1952 p18; BRD 1952 p61; KR v20 1952 p339;
    LJ v77 1952 p1520; NYTBR N 16, 1952 p32.

Collier, Edmund
YA *The Story of Kit Carson.*
Grosset & Dunlap 1953.
LJ v78 1953 p2107; NYTBR N 15, 1953 p20.

Fergusson, Harvey
Wolf Song.
Knopf 1927 (Rpr. 1936, 1978).
BRD 1927 p248.

Gentry, Claude
Kit Carson.
Magnolia Publishers 1956.

Holland, Cecelia
The Bear Flag.
Houghton Mifflin 1990.
BL v86 1990 p1957; BRD 1991 p877; KR v58 1990
    p521; LJ v115 Je 15, 1990 p134.

McCall, Edith S.
YA *Message from the Mountains.*
Walker 1985.
BRD 1986 p1061; SLJ v32 N 1985 p99.

O'Dell, Scott
Hill of the Hawk.
Bobbs-Merrill 1947.
BL v44 1947 p69; BRD 1947 p684; LJ v72 1947
    p1194; NYTBR O 5, 1947 p22.

Stevenson, Augusta
JUV *Kit Carson, Boy Trapper.*
Bobbs-Merrill 1945 (Rpr. 1962).
BRD 1945 p678; LJ v70 1945 p980.

Tousey, Sanford
JUV *Kit Carson, American Scout.*
A. Whitman 1949.
BRD 1949 p921; KR v17 1949 p509; LJ v74 1949
    p1681.

254. Carter, Howard
1874-1939
English Egyptologist; discovered tomb of Tutankhamun, 1922

Holland, Cecelia
Valley of the Kings: A Novel of Tutankhamun.

V. Gollancz 1978.
Obs Je 18, 1978 p28; TLS Ag 4, 1978 p897.

255. Carter, Jimmy (James Earl, Jr.)
1924-
39th US President

Cockburn, Alexander; Ridgeway, James
Smoke: Another Jimmy Carter Adventure.
Times Books 1978.
BL v75 1979 p794; KR v46 1978 p1081; LJ v103 1978
    p2535; PW v214 S 25, 1978 p127.

256. Carter, Mrs. Leslie
1862-1937
American actress

Young, Agnes
Blaze of Glory.
Random House 1950.
BRD 1950 p1004; KR v18 1950 p437; LJ v75 1950
    p1507; NYTBR O 22, 1950 p35.

257. Cartier, Jacques
1491-1557
French explorer; discovered St. Lawrence River

Oswald, Gwendoline C.
JUV *A Young Explorer from Brittany: A Boy's Visit to
    "New France".*
Initiative Pub. House 1978.
Can Child Lit #27 1982 p190.

Syme, Ronald
JUV *Cartier, Finder of the St. Lawrence.*
Morrow 1958.
BL v54 1958 p398; BRD 1958 p1031; KR v25 1957
    p842; LJ v83 1958 p653.

258. Caruso, Enrico
1873-1921
Italian operatic singer

Paul, Barbara
A Cadenza for Caruso.
St. Martin's 1984.
BL v80 1984 p1380; KR v52 1984 p430; NY v60 S 3,
    1984 p98; PW v225 My 11, 1984 p262.

Paul, Barbara
A Chorus of Detectives.
St. Martin's 1987.
BL v83 1987 p1493; KR v55 1987 p894; NYTBR N 8,
    1987 p62.

Paul, Barbara
Prima Donna at Large.
St. Martin's 1985.
BL v82 1985 p31; KR v53 1985 p756; LJ v110 S 1,
    1985 p215; NYTBR O 13, 1985 p29; PW v227 Jl 5,
    1985 p58.

Thiess, Frank
Neapolitan Legend.
Heinemann 1949.

259. Carver, George Washington
1864-1943
American educator & scientist; discovered industrial uses for peanut, sweet potato, soybean

Means, Florence
JUV *Great Day in the Morning.*
Houghton Mifflin 1946.
BL v43 1946 p57; BRD 1946 p563; KR v14 1946
p426; LJ v71 1946 p1720; NYTBR N 10, 1946 p50.

Stevenson, Augusta
JUV *George Carver, Boy Scientist.*
Bobbs-Merrill 1944 (Rpr. 1959).
BL v41 1944 p95; BRD 1944 p719; KR v12 1944 p401.

260. Cary, Alice
1820-1871
American poet

Long, Laura
YA *Singing Sisters.*
Longmans, Green 1941.
BL v38 1941 p37; BRD 1941 p559; LJ v66 1941 p737;
NYTBR Mr 1, 1942 p10.

261. Cary, Phoebe
1824-1871
American poet; sister of Alice Cary

Long, Laura
YA *Singing Sisters.*
Longmans, Green 1941.
BL v38 1941 p37; BRD 1941 p559; LJ v66 1941 p737;
NYTBR Mr 1, 1942 p10.

262. Casanova (de Seingalt), Giovanni Giacomo
1725-1798
Venetian adventurer & author

Aldington, Richard
The Romance of Casanova.
Duell, Sloan & Pearce 1946.
BRD 1946 p10; KR v14 1946 p182; NYTBR Jl 7, 1946
p5; SatR Je 15, 1946 p16.

Erskine, John
Casanova's Women, Eleven Moments of a Year.
Frederick A. Stokes 1941.
BRD 1941 p280; NYTBR Mr 9, 1941 p7; SatR Ag 2,
1941 p16.

Mankowitz, Wolf
A Night with Casanova.
Sinclair-Stevenson 1991.
TLS Ag 16, 1991 p23; Spec v267 N 30, 1991 p38.

Marshall, Rosamond
Rogue Cavalier.
Doubleday 1955.
NYTBR Je 19, 1955 p16.

Schnitzler, Arthur
Casanova's Homecoming.
Thomas Seltzer 1922 (Rpr. 1930, 1948, 1971).

263. Cassatt, Mary Stevenson
1844-1926
American impressionist painter; noted for paintings of mother and child

King, Joan
Impressionist: A Novel of Mary Cassatt.
Beaufort 1983.
BL v79 1983 p1014; KR v51 1983 p201; LJ v108 1983
p517; PW v223 Mr 4, 1983 p87.

264. Cassidy, Butch
1867-1912?
American outlaw

Cooke, John Byrne
South of the Border.
Bantam 1989.
BL v85 1989 p1248; KR v57 1989 p4; LJ v114 F 15,
1989 p175; NYTBR My 7, 1989 p24; PW v235 Ja
6, 1989 p92.

Garwood, W. R.
Catch Kid Curry.
Bath Street Press 1982.

Halladay, Wilford M.
Long Shadows.
Cedar Fork 1991.

Henry, Will
Alias Butch Cassidy.
Random House 1968.
FC 10th p253; KR v35 1967 p1394; LJ v93 1968
p1020.

Kennelly, Ardyth
Good Morning, Young Lady.
Houghton Mifflin 1953.
BL v49 1953 p322; BRD 1953 p504; FC 7th p206; KR
v21 1953 p125; LJ v78 1953 p54; NYTBR Ap 19,
1953 p4.

265. Castro (Ruz), Fidel
1926-
Cuban revolutionary leader; president of Cuba
1959-

Alexander, Karl
Papa and Fidel.
T. Doherty Associates 1989.
KR v57 F 1, 1989 p136; LATBR My 7, 1989 p4; LJ
v114 Ap 1, 1989 p109; PW v235 F 1, 1989 p55.

Armstrong, Campbell
Mambo.
Harper & Row 1990.
BL v86 1990 p1609; KR v58 1990 p198; PW v237 Mr 2, 1990 p73.

Krich, John
A Totally Free Man: An Unauthorized Autobiography of Fidel Castro.
Creative Arts 1981 (Rpr. 1988).
KR v49 1981 p1308; LJ v106 1981 p2332; NYTBR S 26, 1982 p39.

Mailer, Norman
Harlot's Ghost.
Random House 1991.
BL v88 1991 p5; BRD 1991 p1197; KR v59 1991 p960; LJ v116 S 1, 1991 p231; NYTBR S 29, 1991 p1.

Miller, Warren
Flush Times.
Little, Brown 1962.
BRD 1963 p708; LJ v87 1962 p3689; NYTBR S 30, 1962 p43; SatR N 10, 1962 p49.

266. Cather, Willa Sibert
1873-1947
American novelist; won Pulitzer for novel *One of Ours*

Franchere, Ruth
YA *Willa.*
Crowell 1958.
BL v55 1958 p52; BRD 1958 p391; KR v26 1958 p611; LJ v83 1958 p3007; NYTBR O 12, 1958 p29.

267. Catherine de Medici
1519-1589
Wife of Henry II; daughter of Lorenzo de Medici

Grey, Shirley
The Crescent Moon: A Romance Set in the Time of Diane de Poitiers.
Milton House Books 1973.
B&B v19 N 1973 p132.

Hibbert, Eleanor (Jean Plaidy, pseud.)
Madame Serpent.
Appleton-Century-Crofts 1951 (Rpr. 1957, 1975).
BL v47 1951 p230; BRD 1951 p401; KR v19 1951 p7; NYTBR Mr 11, 1951 p22.

Hibbert, Eleanor (Jean Plaidy, pseud.)
Queen Jezebel.
Hale 1953.
BL v50 1953 p34; BRD 1953 p427; KR v21 1953 p446; NYTBR S 13, 1953 p32.

Pelham, Randolph
The Medici Murderess.
Hale 1972.

Ross Williamson, Hugh
The Florentine Woman.

Joseph 1970 (Rpr. 1973).
BL v69 1973 p973; LJ v98 1973 p3652; Obs Ja 10, 1971 p28.

Ross Williamson, Hugh
Paris Is Worth a Mass.
St. Martin's 1973.
BL v70 1973 p369; LJ v98 1973 p3652.

268. Catherine II
see Catherine the Great

269. Catherine of Aragon
1485-1536
Queen of England; first wife of Henry VIII

Bloom, Ursula (Lozania Prole, pseud.)
Henry's Golden Queen.
Hale 1964 (Rpr. 1985).

Hibbert, Eleanor (Jean Plaidy, pseud.)
Katharine of Aragon.
Hale 1968.

Hibbert, Eleanor (Jean Plaidy, pseud.)
Katharine, the Virgin Widow.
Hale 1961.

Hibbert, Eleanor (Jean Plaidy, pseud.)
The Shadow of the Pomegranate.
Hale 1962.

Lofts, Norah
The King's Pleasure.
Doubleday 1969.
BL v66 1969 p495; FC 9th p323; KR v37 1969 p694; LJ v94 1969 p2641.

Macleod, Alison
The Hireling.
Houghton Mifflin 1968.
Also published as *The Trusted Servant.*
BRD 1969 p844; FC 9th p337; LJ v93 1968 p4167; NYTBR S 22, 1968 p37.

Street, M. K.
The Princess from Spain.
Hale 1974.

270. Catherine of Siena
1347-1380
Italian religious leader; influenced Pope Gregory XI to return papacy to Rome from Avignon, 1376

De Wohl, Louis
Lay Siege to Heaven.
Lippincott 1961.
BL v57 1961 p292; BRD 1961 p345; FC 9th p133; KR v28 1960 p932; NYTBR Ja 8, 1961 p49.

Unruh, Fritz von
The Saint: A Novel.
Random House 1950.

BRD 1950 p921; KR v18 1950 p398; LJ v75 1950
p1409; NYTBR D 10, 1950 p25.

271. Catherine of Valois
1401-1437
Wife of Henry V of England; lived in obsurity after death of Henry V, due to unpopular remar-
riage to poor commoner

Davies, Iris
Tudor Tapestry.
Hale 1974.

Hibbert, Eleanor (Jean Plaidy, pseud.)
Epitaph for Three Women.
Putnam 1983.
BL v79 1983 p1328.

Hibbert, Eleanor (Jean Plaidy, pseud.)
The Queen's Secret.
Putnam 1990.
CSM v82 Ap 26, 1990 p14.

Jarman, Rosemary Hawley
Crown in Candlelight.
Popular Library 1978.
FC 11th p325; KR v46 1978 p125; LJ v103 1978 p775.

Lewis, Hilda
Wife to Henry V.
Jarrolds 1954.
BL v53 1957 p404; BRD 1957 p550; KR v25 1957
p91; LJ v82 1957 p1365; NYTBR Mr 3, 1957 p34.

Long, Freda M.
The Bartered Queens.
Hale 1971.

Ridge, Antonia
The Royal Pawn.
Appleton-Century 1963.
Also published as *The Thirteenth Child.*
LJ v88 1963 p4100; LJ v88 1963 p4397.

Sisson, Rosemary Anne
The Queen and the Welshman.
W.H. Allen 1979 (Rpr. 1987).

272. Catherine the Great
1729-1796
Empress of Russia, 1762-1796

Almedingen, Martha Edith
YA *Anna.*
Farrar, Straus & Giroux 1972.
BL v68 1972 p818; BRD 1972 p25; KR v40 1972 p72;
LJ v97 1972 p1611.

Anthony, Evelyn
Rebel Princess.
Crowell 1953.
Also published as *Imperial Highness.*
BL v50 1953 p80; BRD 1953 p893; KR v21 1953
p404; LJ v78 1953 p1424; NYTBR O 25, 1953 p40.

Anthony, Evelyn
Royal Intrigue.
Crowell 1954.
Also published as *Curse Not the King.*
BL v51 1954 p16; BRD 1954 p841; KR v22 1954
p366; LJ v79 1954 p1399.

Carnegie, Sacha
Kasia and the Empress.
Dodd, Mead 1973.
Also published as *The Banners of Power.*
B&B v18 Ja 1973 p120.

Kay, Mara
JUV *In Place of Katia.*
Scribner 1963.
LJ v88 1963 p1766.

Lehr, Helene
*Star of the North: A Novel Based on the Life of
Catherine the Great.*
St. Martin's 1990.
KR v58 1990 p297.

273. Catherwood, Frederick
1799-1854
Made archaeological recordings of antiquities of
Arabia, Nile Valley, Palestine, & the Mayan cities of Central America

Highwater, Jamake
*Journey to the Sky: A Novel about the True Adven-
tures of Two Men in Search of the Lost Mayan
Kingdom.*
Crowell 1978.
KR v46 1978 p963; PW v214 S 25, 1978 p127.

274. Catlin, George
1796-1872
American painter & author

Olsen, Theodore V.
Mission to the West.
Doubleday 1973 (Rpr. 1987).

275. Catullus, Gaius Valerius
84-54 BC
Roman poet

Dayton, Eldorous L.
Chantefable.
Gardnor House 1982.

De Maria, Robert
Clodia.
St. Martin's 1965.
KR v33 1965 p124; LJ v90 1965 p1346.

Dixon, Pierson
Farewell, Catullus.
House & Maxwell 1953.
BRD 1960 p360; LJ v85 1960 p1472; NYTBR Mr 20,
1960 p38; SatR Ap 9, 1960 p30.

Hardy, W. G.
The City of Libertines.
Appleton-Century-Crofts 1957.
BRD 1957 p396; KR v25 1957 p700; LJ v82 1957
　p3109; NYTBR D 8, 1957 p41.

Jaro, Benita Kane
The Key.
Dodd, Mead 1988.
KR v56 1988 p645; NYTBR S 4, 1988 p21.

Wilder, Thorton
The Ides of March.
Harper 1948.
BRD 1948 p922; FC 11th p663; KR v15 1947 p675; LJ
　v73 1948 p338; NYTBR F 22, 1948 p1; Time v51 F
　23, 1948 p102.

276. Cavendish, Thomas
1555-1592
English navigator

Westcott, Jan
Captain for Elizabeth.
Crown 1948.
BL v45 1948 p121; BRD 1948 p909; NYTBR O 24,
　1948 p36.

277. Caxton, William
1422-1491
First English printer

Grohskopf, Bernice
YA　*Blood & Roses.*
Atheneum 1979.
BS v39 S 1979 p229; CBRS v7 Ag 1979 p137; KR
　v47 1979 p331; PW v215 F 5, 1979 p95; SLJ v25
　Mr 1979 p148.

Harnett, Cynthia
YA　*Caxton's Challenge.*
World 1960.
Also published as *The Load of Unicorn* and *The Cargo
of the Madalena.*
BL v57 1960 p100; BRD 1961 p591; KR v28 1960
　p631; LJ v85 1960 p3230; NYTBR N 13, 1960 p24.

278. Cecil, William
see Burghley, William Cecil, Baron

279. Celine, Louis-Ferdinand
1894-1961
French author

Clark, Tom
The Exile of Celine.
Random House 1986.
KR v54 1986 p1740; LJ v112 F 15, 1987 p160;
　NYTBR F 8, 1987 p28.

280. Cellini, Benvenuto
1500-1571
Italian goldsmith & designer of intricate metal-
work

Spinatelli, Carl J.
The Florentine.
Prentice-Hall 1953.
BL v50 1953 p15; BRD 1953 p885; KR v21 1953
　p233; LJ v78 1953 p917; NYTBR Je 21, 1953 p4.

281. Cenci, Beatrice
1577-1599
Italian noblewoman; hanged for patricide

Kircher, Susanne
A Roman Scandal: The Story of Beatrice Cenci.
Mason/Charter 1976.
KR v44 1976 p919; LJ v101 1976 p2394; PW v210 Ag
　16, 1976 p119.

Lindsay, Philip
The Fall of the Axe.
Hutchinson 1940.

Prokosch, Frederic
A Tale for Midnight.
Little, Brown 1955.
BL v52 S 1, 1955 p15; BRD 1955 p739; KR v23 1955
　p310; LJ v80 1955 p1494; NYTBR Jl 31, 1955 p5.

282. Cermak, Anton Joseph
1873-1933
Mayor of Chicago, 1931-1933

Collins, Max Allan
True Detective.
St. Martin's 1983.
BL v80 1984 p716; KR v51 1983 p1172; LJ v109 1984
　p113; NYTBR F 5, 1984 p18; PW v224 N 18, 1983
　p61.

283. Cervantes (Saavedra), Miguel de
1547-1616
Spanish poet, novelist, & dramatist; wrote *Don
Quixote*

Chapman, Robin
The Duchess's Diary.
Faber & Faber 1985.
KR v53 1985 p6; NYTBR Mr 17, 1985 p23.

Gidley, Charles
Armada.
Viking 1988.
BL v84 1988 p749; KR v55 1987 p1640; LJ v113 Ja
　1988 p98.

Newcomb, Covelle
YA　*Vagabond in Velvet: The Story of Miguel de Cer-
vantes.*
Longmans, Green 1942.
BRD 1942 p564; LJ v67 1942 p798.

284. Cezanne, Paul
1839-1906
French painter

McLeave, Hugh
A Man and His Mountain: The Life of Paul Cezanne.
Macmillan 1977.
BRD 1978 p848; LJ v103 1978 p88.

285. Chaka
1773-1828
African leader; founded Zulu Empire

Bond, Geoffrey
Chaka the Terrible.
Arco Publications 1961.

Hall, Lynn Bedford
JUV *Shaka, Warrior King of the Zulu.*
Struik 1987.

Langa, James
Shaka.
Longman 1982.

McMenemy, Nickie
Assegai.
Saturday Review Press 1973.
KR v41 1973 p656; LJ v98 1973 p2146; LJ v98 1973 p3165; PW v203 Je 18, 1973 p66.

Mofolo, Thomas
Chaka the Zulu.
Oxford University Press 1949 (Rpr. 1965, 1977).

Roberts, Esther
The Black Spear.
W. Earl 1950.

Schoeman, P. J.
Phampatha, the Beloved of King Shaka.
Timmins 1983.

Scholefield, Alan
Great Elephant.
Morrow 1967.
KR v35 1967 p1340; LJ v92 1967 p4526; NYTBR Ja 7, 1968 p39.

Seed, Jenny
JUV *The Voice of the Great Elephant.*
Hamilton 1968 (Rpr. 1986).
KR v37 1969 p1259; LJ v95 1970 p2536.

286. Champlain, Samuel de
1567-1635
French explorer & founder of Quebec

Kent, Louise Andrews
JUV *He Went with Champlain.*
Houghton Mifflin 1959.
BRD 1960 p735; LJ v84 1959 p2226; NYTBR Ag 30, 1959 p28; SHSLC 8th p424.

Leitch, Adelaide
JUV *The Great Canoe.*
St. Martin's 1963.

Tharp, Louise Hall
YA *Champlain, North-West Voyager.*
G.G. Harrap 1946.
BL v41 1944 p128; BRD 1944 p744; KR v12 1944 p375; LJ v69 1944 p1052; NYTBR N 12, 1944 p7.

287. Chandler, Raymond Thornton
1888-1959
American author; created the private detective Philip Marlowe

Conteris, Hiber
Ten Percent of Life.
Simon & Schuster 1987.
KR v55 1987 p1479.

Larsen, Gaylord
A Paramount Kill.
Dutton 1988.
BL v84 1988 p972; KR v55 1987 p1701.

288. Chanel, "Coco" (Gabrielle)
1882-1971
French fashion designer; created Chanel No. 5 perfume

Soliman, Patricia B.
Coco, the Novel.
Putnam 1990.
KR v58 1990 p757.

289. Chaplin, Charlie
1889-1977
Movie actor & director; considered greatest comic actor of silent movies

Coover, Robert
Charlie in the House of Rue.
Penmaen Press 1980.
BL v76 1980 p1182; LJ v104 1979 p2663.

290. Chapman, John
see Appleseed, Johnny

291. Chares
b. 320 BC
Greek sculptor; carved Colossus of Rhodes

De Camp, Lyon Sprague
The Bronze God of Rhodes.
Doubleday 1960 (Rpr. 1983).
BL v56 1960 p510; BRD 1960 p336; KR v27 1959 p846; LJ v85 1960 p777; NYTBR F 7, 1960 p34.

292. Charlemagne
742-814
King of the Franks & Roman emperor

Andrews, Frank E.
YA *For Charlemagne!*.
Harper 1949.
BL v46 1949 p144; BRD 1949 p19; KR v17 1949
p511; LJ v74 1949.

Boyce, Burke
JUV *The Emperor's Arrow*.
Lippincott 1967.
KR v35 1967 p412; LJ v92 1967 p2448.

Lebrun, Francoise
JUV *The Days of Charlemagne*.
Silver Burdett 1985.

Manson, Christopher
JUV *Here Begins the Tale of the Marvellous Blue
Mouse*.
Holt 1992.
BL v88 1992 p2018; SLJ v38 Ag 1992 p144.

Serraillier, Ian
JUV *The Ivory Horn: Retold from the Song of Roland*.
Oxford University Press 1960.

Willard, Barbara
Son of Charlemagne.
Doubleday 1959.

293. Charles I
1600-1649
King of England, Ireland, 1625-1649

Anthony, Evelyn
Charles the King.
Doubleday 1961.
LJ v86 S 1, 1961 p2813.

Barnes, Margaret Campbell
Mary of Carisbrooke.
Macrae Smith 1955.
BL v52 1956 p209; BRD 1956 p49; FC 9th p32; KR
v23 1955 p816; LJ v80 1955 p2771.

Beardsworth, Millicent M.
King's Contest.
Hale 1975.

Beardsworth, Millicent M.
King's Victory.
Hale 1978.

Bibby, Violet
Many Waters Cannot Quench Love.
Morrow 1974.
NS v88 N 8, 1974 p666; TLS S 20, 1974 p1012.

Bridge, S. R.
For Love or the King.
Hale 1979.

Dakers, Elaine (Jane Lane, pseud.)
The Severed Crown.
P. Davies 1972.
BL v70 1973 p151; KR v41 1973 p619; LJ v98 1973
p2334; PW v203 Je 11, 1973 p147.

Dakers, Elaine (Jane Lane, pseud.)
The Young and Lonely King.
Muller 1969.

Evans, Jean
The Phoenix Rising.
St. Martin's 1976.
KR v44 1976 p1316; LJ v102 1977 p630.

Fitz, Virginia White
Sweete Jane: Mistress of a Martyr King.
Carlgate Press 1988.

Helwig, David
The King's Evil.
Oberon Press 1981 (Rpr. 1984).
BRD 1982 p593; KR v52 1984 p157; LJ v109 1984
p733; NYTBR Jl 8,.

Hibbert, Eleanor (Jean Plaidy, pseud.)
YA *Myself, My Enemy*.
Hale 1983.
LJ v108 1983 p2263; NYTBR Ja 15, 1984 p18.

Long, Freda M.
The People's Martyr.
Hale 1969.

294. Charles II
1630-1685
King of England, Ireland, 1660-1685

Ansle, Dorothy P. (Hebe Elsna, pseud.)
The King's Bastard.
Collins 1971 (Rpr. 1982).

Arthur, Frank
*The Abandoned Woman: The Story of Lucy Wal-
ter*.
Heinemann 1964.

Barnes, Margaret Campbell
With All My Heart.
Macrae Smith 1951.
BRD 1951 p50; FC 7th p30; KR v19 1951 p327; LJ
v76 1951 p1219.

Barnes, Margaret Campbell; Elsna, Hebe
Lady on the Coin.
Macrae Smith 1963.
LJ v89 1964 p966.

Bell, Josephine
In the King's Absence.
Bles 1973.
B&B v18 Jl 1973 p136.

Binner, Ina
The Royal Blackbird.
Hale 1978.

Bloom, Ursula (Lozania Prole, pseud.)
Pretty, Witty Nell.
Hale 1952 (Rpr. 1972).

Dakers, Elaine (Jane Lane, pseud.)
Prelude to Kingship.
Rich & Cowan 1936 (Rpr. 1969).

Denis, Charlotte
King's Bastard.
Wingate 1977.

Denis, Charlotte
King's Wench.
Pocket Books 1976 (Rpr. 1987).

Dryden, Kathryn
Prisoner at Large.
Hale 1971.

Evans, Jean
The King's Own.
Hale 1977.

Fletcher, Inglis C.
Bennett's Welcome.
Bobbs-Merrill 1950 (Rpr. 1978).
BRD 1950 p313; NYTBR O 29, 1950 p30; SatR D 2, 1950 p67.

Gluyas, Constance
The King's Brat.
Prentice-Hall 1972.
KR v40 1972 p875; LJ v97 1972 p3181.

Goudge, Elizabeth
The Child from the Sea.
Coward-McCann 1970.
FC 9th p211; KR v38 1970 p620; LJ v95 1970 p3650; PW v198 Jl 6, 1970 p55.

Heyer, Georgette
The Great Roxhythe.
Small, Maynard 1923 (Rpr. 1977, 1983).
BRD 1923 p238; NYTBR Je 24, 1923 p17.

Heyer, Georgette
Royal Escape.
Heinemann 1938 (Rpr. 1939, 1961, 1967).
BL v35 1939 p230; BRD 1939 p455; NYTBR F 5, 1939 p7; SatR F 4, 1939 p7.

Hibbert, Eleanor (Jean Plaidy, pseud.)
A Health unto His Majesty.
Hale 1956 (Rpr. 1972).

Hibbert, Eleanor (Jean Plaidy, pseud.)
Here Lies Our Sovereign Lord.
Putnam 1973.
BL v69 1973 p1008; KR v41 1973 p475.

Hibbert, Eleanor (Jean Plaidy, pseud.)
The Wandering Prince.
Putnam 1971.
BL v68 1972 p380; KR v39 1971 p1141; LJ v97 1972 p1626.

Leslie, Doris
The Sceptre and the Rose.
Heinemann 1967.
PW v202 D 18, 1972 p41.

Lewis, Hilda
Catherine.
Putnam 1966.
Also published as *Wife to Charles II.*
B&B v11 N 1965 p38; Obs O 31, 1965 p27.

Macleod, Alison
The Portingale.
Hodder & Stoughton 1976.
TLS Mr 19, 1976 p310.

Neill, Robert
Traitor's Moon.
Doubleday 1952.
BL v49 1952 p90; KR v20 1952 p516; NYTBR O 5, 1952 p36.

Oliver, Marina
Masquerade for the King.
Hale 1978.

Quigley, Aileen
King's Pawn.
Hale 1971.

Strong, Bethany
First Love.
Parable Press 1976.

Tremain, Rose
Restoration: A Novel of Seventeenth Century England.
Viking 1990.
KR v58 1990 p79; LJ v115 F 1, 1990 p109; NYTBR Ap 15, 1990 p7; PW v237 F 2, 1990 p75.

Winsor, Kathleen
Forever Amber.
Macmillan 1944.
BRD 1944 p821; KR v12 1944 p346; LJ v69 1944 p884; NYTBR O 15, 1944 p7.

295. Charles V
1500-1558
Emperor of Germany & king of Spain

Zara, Louis
Against This Rock.
Creative Age Press 1943.
BL v40 1943 p115; BRD 1943 p900; LJ v68 1943 p669; NYTBR O 3, 1943 p6.

296. Charles XII
1682-1718
King of Sweden, 1697-1718

Heidenstam, Verner von
The Charles Men.
American-Scandinavian Foundation 1920 (Rpr. 1933, 1961, 1970).

297. Charles Edward, Prince
see Stuart, Charles Edward Louis Philip

298. Charles Martel
689-741
Ruler of the Frankish empire

Gladd, Arthur A.
YA *The Saracen Steed.*
Dodd, Mead 1960.
BRD 1961 p506; KR v28 1960 p94; LJ v85 1960 p2048; NYTBR My 8, 1960 p6.

299. Charles, Prince of Wales
1948-
Son of Queen Elizabeth, heir apparent to the British throne

Heald, Tim
Caroline R..
Arbor House 1980.
PW v218 O 31, 1980 p77.

King, Norman
The Prince and the Princess: The Love Story.
Simon & Schuster 1983.

Krin, Sylvie
Heir of Sorrows.
Private Eyes 1988.
Punch v295 D 9, 1988 p66.

Ross, Caroline
Miss Nobody.
Congdon & Lattes 1981.
KR v49 1981 p382; LJ v106 1981 p905; PW v219 Ap 3, 1981 p68.

300. Chateaubriand, Francois Rene de
1768-1848
French author

Brady, Charles A.
Crown of Grass.
Doubleday 1964.

301. Chatterton, Thomas
1752-1770
English poet

Ackroyd, Peter
Chatterton.
Grove Press 1988.
NYTBR Ja 17, 1988 p1; PW v232 N 13, 1987 p60; Time v131 Ja 18, 1988 p65.

Bell, Neil
Cover His Face: A Novel of the Life and Times of Thomas Chatterton, the Marvellous Boy of Bristol.
Collins 1943.

Kruger, Rayne
Young Villain with Wings.
Longmans, Green 1953.

302. Chaucer, Geoffrey
1340-1400
English poet; wrote *The Canterbury Tales*

Chute, Marchette
YA *The Innocent Wayfaring.*
Dutton 1943.
BRD 1943 p151; LJ v68 1943 p672; NYTBR Ag 15, 1943 p7.

Crowley, Duane
Riddle Me a Murder.
Blue Boar Press 1986.
BL v83 1987 p1179; LJ v112 Mr 1, 1987 p95.

Darby, Catherine
The Love Knot.
Hale 1989 (Rpr. 1991).
BL v87 1991 p1177; KR v59 1991 p3; LJ v116 F 15, 1991 p220; PW v238 F 15, 1991 p73.

Faulkner, Nancy
YA *The Yellow Hat.*
Doubleday 1958.
BL v55 1958 p219; BRD 1959 p348; KR v26 1958 p505; LJ v84 1959 p256.

Philip, Lindsay
The Gentle Knight.
Chivers 1977.

303. Chekhov, Anton Pavlovich
1860-1904
Russian novelist, dramatist, & short story writer

Watson, Ian
Chekhov's Journey.
V. Gollancz 1983 (Rpr. 1989, 1991).
BL v86 1989 p430; KR v57 1989 p1369; PW v236 O 6, 1989 p84; Obs F 20, 1983 p33.

Wetherell, W. D.
Chekhov's Sister: A Novel.
Little, Brown 1990.
BRD 1991 p1970; KR v58 1990 p17; LJ v115 F 15, 1990 p214; NYTBR Mr 25, 1990 p12; PW v237 Ja 26, 1990 p402.

304. Chippendale, Thomas
1718-1779
English cabinetmaker

Laker, Rosalind
Gilded Splendour.
Doubleday 1982.
KR v50 1982 p362; LJ v107 1982 p1011; PW v221 Ap 9, 1982 p44.

305. Chopin, Frederic
1810-1849
Polish pianist & composer

Byrne, Marie
Softly, Softly.
Blond 1958.

Golden, Grace
JUV *Seven Dancing Dolls.*
Bobbs-Merrill 1961.
NYTBR D 24, 1961 p12.

Gronowicz, Antoni
YA *Chopin.*
T. Nelson & Sons 1943.
BL v40 1943 p82; BRD 1943 p330; LJ v68 1943 p895;
NYTBR N 14, 1943 p8.

Leslie, Doris
Polonaise.
Hutchinson 1944.

McDonald, Eva
November Nocturne.
Hale 1975.

Ruttkay, G.
JUV *Chopin, His Life Told in Anecdotal Form.*
Hyperion Press 1945.
BRD 1945 p614; KR v13 1945 p201; LJ v70 1945
p534; NYTBR Je 10, 1945 p18.

306. Chouteau, Rene Auguste
1749-1829
Frontiersman & public official;

Wooldridge, Rhoda
JUV *Chouteau and the Founding of Saint Louis.*
Independence Press 1975.

307. Christian, Fletcher
1764-1793
Ringleader in mutiny on the "Bounty"

Dark, Eleanor
Storm of Time.
Collins 1948 (Rpr. 1950, 1956, 1991).
BL v46 1950 p189; BRD 1950 p225; KR v18 1950
p38; NYTBR F 5, 1950 p30.

Maxwell, John
H.M.S. Bounty.
Cape 1977.
GP v16 O 1977 p3194; Obs O 30, 1977 p29.

Miller, Stanley
*Mr. Christian: The Journal of Fletcher Christian,
Former Lieutenant of His Majesty's Armed Ves-
sel "Bounty".*
Macmillan 1973.
KR v41 1973 p832; LJ v98 1973 p3021; PW v204 Ag
13, 1973 p48.

Nordhoff, Charles
Botany Bay.
Little, Brown 1941.
BRD 1941 p672; LJ v66 1941 p950; NYTBR N 9,
1941 p4; SatR N 15, 1941 p10.

Nordhoff, Charles
*The Bounty Trilogy: Comprising the Three Vol-
umes, "Mutiny on the Bounty," "Men Against
the Sea," and "Pitcairn's Island".*
Little, Brown 1936 (Heavily reprinted).
BRD 1937 p741; NYTBR D 6, 1936 p46.

308. Christie, Agatha Miller, Dame
1890-1976
English detective story writer

Larsen, Gaylord
Dorothy and Agatha.
Dutton 1990.
BL v87 1990 p804; KR v58 1990 p1571; SLJ v37 My
1991 p126.

Tynan, Kathleen
Agatha.
Ballantine 1978.
BL v75 1978 p159; BRD 1979 p1298; KR v46 1978
p613; LJ v103 1978 p1663; PW v215 F 5, 1979 p94.

309. Christie, John Reginald Halliday
1899-1953
English murderer

Bradley, Matthew
Lay Down Dead.
New International Library 1964.

310. Christina
1626-1689
Queen of Sweden, 1632-1654

Stephan, Ruth W.
The Flight.
Knopf 1956.
BL v53 1956 p149; BRD 1956 p890; FC 7th p329; KR
v24 1956 p490; LJ v81 1956 p1994; NYTBR O 21,
1956 p52.

Stephan, Ruth W.
My Crown, My Love.
Knopf 1960.
BRD 1960 p1355; LJ v85 1960 p3465; NYTBR N 6,
1960 p32.

311. Christophe, Henri
1767-1820
Ruler of Haiti, 1811-1820

Bourne, Peter
Drums of Destiny.
Putnam 1947.
Also published as *Black Saga.*
BL v44 1947 p32; BRD 1947 p464; FC 9th p57; KR
v15 1947 p369; LJ v72 1947 p1269.

Carpentier, Alejo
The Kingdom of This World.
Knopf 1957.

Atl v200 Ag 1957 p84; FC 11th p99; NYTBR My 19,
1957 p4.

Horner, Lance
The Black Sun.
Fawcett 1966.
B&B v14 Ag 1969 p43.

Levin, Benjamin
Black Triumvirate: A Novel of Haiti.
Citadel Press 1972.
KR v40 1972 p93; LJ v97 1972 p1826.

Newcomb, Covelle
YA *Black Fire: A Story of Henri Christophe.*
Longmans, Green 1940 (Rpr. 1947).
BRD 1940 p679; HB v16 S 1940 p349; LJ v65 1940
p662; SatR D 7, 1940 p38.

Strother, Elsie W.
Drums at Sunset.
National Writers Press 1990.

Taylor, Angeline
Black Jade.
R.M. McBride 1947.
BRD 1948 p828; LJ v72 1947 p1540.

Vandercook, John W.
*Black Majesty: The Life of Christophe, King of
Haiti.*
Harper & Brothers 1928 (Rpr. 1950).
BL v24 1928 p406; BRD 1928 p783; NYTBR Ap 1,
1928 p10.

312. Chrysler, Walter Percy
1875-1940
American auto manufacturer; founded Chrysler
Corp., 1925

Weddle, Ethel H.
JUV *Walter Chrysler, Boy Machinist.*
Bobbs-Merrill 1960.

313. Chrysostom, John, Saint
345-407
Religious leader; archbishop of Constantinople,
398-404

Groseclose, Elgin
Olympia: A Novel.
D.C. Cook Pub. Co. 1980.
LJ v105 1980 p2432.

314. Churchill, Winston Leonard Spencer, Sir
1874-1965
English political leader & author; prime minister during WW II

Chaput, W. J.
The Man on the Train.
St. Martin's 1986.
BL v83 1986 p474; KR v54 1986 p1532.

Garfield, Brian Wynne
The Paladin: A Novel Based on Fact.
Simon & Schuster 1980.
BL v76 1980 p815; KR v48 1980 p149; LJ v105 1980
p1001; NYTBR Mr 30, 1980 p6; PW v217 F 15,
1980 p103.

315. Cicero, Marcus Tullius
106-43 BC
Roman orator, political leader, & philosopher

Benton, Kenneth
Death on the Appian Way.
Chatto & Windus 1974.
Obs Je 16, 1974 p33; TLS My 17, 1974 p517.

Caldwell, Taylor
A Pillar of Iron.
Doubleday 1965.
BRD 1965 p189; FC 9th p90; NYTBR Je 27, 1965 p31.

Saylor, Steven
Roman Blood.
St. Martin's 1991.
BL v88 1991 p496; KR v59 1991 p1186; PW v238 O
4, 1991 p80.

Wagner, John; Wagner, Esther
The Gift of Rome.
Little, Brown 1961.
BL v57 1961 p547; BRD 1961 p1477; KR v29 1961
p29; LJ v86 1961 p596; NYTBR Mr 19, 1961 p30.

316. Cid, El
1040-1099
Spanish hero; celebrated in literature

Goldston, Robert C.
JUV *The Legend of the Cid.*
Bobbs-Merrill 1963.
BRD 1964 p474; LJ v88 1963 p4863; NYTBR N 10,
1963 p62.

Taylor, Georgia E.
The Infidel.
St. Martin's 1979.
KR v46 1978 p1383; LJ v104 1979 p421; PW v215 Ja
1, 1979 p47.

317. Cinque, Joseph
1811-1852
African slave who led mutiny aboard ship, 1839

Chase-Riboud, Barbara
Echo of Lions.
Morrow 1989.
BL v85 1989 p974; KR v56 1988 p1756; LJ v114 F 1,
1989 p81; NYTBR My 14, 1989 p22.

Historical Figures in Fiction

Claudius I / 55

318. Clairmont, Claire (Clara Mary Jane)
1798-1879
Stepdaughter of William Godwin; mother of
Lord Byron's daughter, Allegra; friend of Percy,
Mary Shelley

Chernaik, Judith
Love's Children: A Novel.
Knopf 1992.
Also published as *Mab's Daughters.*
KR v60 1992 p199.

319. Clark, George Rogers
1752-1818
American frontiersman & Revolutionary general

Churchill, Winston
The Crossing.
Macmillan 1904 (Heavily reprinted).
FC 10th p99; NYTBR My 28, 1904 p354; NYTBR Je
18, 1904 p405.

Havighurst, Walter
YA *Proud Prisoner.*
Holt, Rinehart & Winston 1964.
BRD 1965 p554; LJ v89 1964 p4648; NYTBR N 29,
1964 p34.

Lancaster, Bruce
YA *The Big Knives.*
Little, Brown 1964.
BRD 1964 p695; LJ v89 1964 p2884; LJ v89 1964
p3184; NYTBR Ag 16, 1964 p21.

Nolan, Jeannette C.
YA *The Victory Drum.*
Messner 1953.
LJ v78 1953 p742.

Schindall, Henry
Let the Spring Come.
Appleton-Century-Crofts 1953.
BRD 1953 p832; LJ v78 1953 p520; NYTBR My 31,
1953 p11.

Seifert, Shirley
Waters of the Wilderness.
J.B. Lippincott 1941.
BRD 1941 p805; LJ v66 1941 p669.

Sinclair, Harold
Westward the Tide.
Doubleday 1940.
BRD 1940 p843.

Skinner, Constance L.
Becky Landers: Frontier Warrior.
Macmillan 1926 (Rpr. 1963).
BRD 1926 p646; SatR D 4, 1926 p403.

Thom, James Alexander
From Sea to Shining Sea.
Ballantine 1984.
BL v80 1984 p1524; KR v52 1984 p502; NYTBR O 7,
1984 p22.

Thompson, Maurice
Alice of Old Vincennes.
Bowen-Merrill 1900 (Rpr. 1908, 1970, 1985).
NYTBR O 6, 1900 p670; NYTBR D 8, 1900 p864.

Van Every, Dale
Bridal Journey.
Messner 1950.
BRD 1950 p928; KR v18 1950 p35; LJ v75 1950 p398;
NYTBR Mr 26, 1950 p35.

Van Every, Dale
The Captive Witch.
Messner 1951.
BRD 1951 p907; KR v19 1951 p406; NYTBR N 4,
1951 p37.

Van Every, Dale
Westward the River.
Putnam 1945.
BRD 1945 p728.

Zara, Louis
This Land Is Ours.
Houghton Mifflin 1940.
BL v36 1940 p346; BRD 1940 p1024; NYTBR Ap 21,
1940 p2; SatR Ap 27, 1940 p7.

320. Clark, William
1770-1838
American explorer; co-leader in the Lewis and
Clark expedition

Charbonneau, Louis
Trail: The Story of the Lewis and Clark Expedition.
Doubleday 1989.
BL v86 1989 p426; KR v57 1989 p1347; LJ v114 O
15, 1989 p101; PW v236 S 8, 1989 p54.

Fisher, Vardis
Tale of Valor: A Novel of the Louis and Clark Expedition.
Doubleday 1958.
BRD 1958 p374; KR v26 1958 p322; LJ v83 1958
p2179; NYTBR Je 29, 1958 p20.

Munves, James
JUV *We Were There with Lewis and Clark.*
Grosset & Dunlap 1959.

Thom, James Alexander
From Sea to Shining Sea.
Ballantine 1984.
BL v80 1984 p1524; KR v52 1984 p502; NYTBR O 7,
1984 p22.

Wilkie, Katharine
JUV *Will Clark, Boy in Buckskins.*
Bobbs-Merrill 1953 (Rpr. 1963).
LJ v78 1953 p2106.

321. Claudius I
10 BC-AD 54
Emperor of Rome, AD 41-54

Dored, Elisabeth
I Loved Tiberius.
Pantheon Books 1963.
LJ v88 1963 p574.
10 BC-54 AD

Graves, Robert
Claudius the God and His Wife Messalina.
Arthur Barker 1934 (Heavily reprinted).
BL v31 1935 p266; BRD 1935 p399; NYTBR Ap 14,
    1935 p1; SatR Ap 6, 1935 p601.

Graves, Robert
*I, Claudius: From the Autobiography of Tiberius
    Claudius, Born B.C. 10, Murdered and Deified
    A.D. 54.*
Modern Library 1934 (Heavily reprinted).

322. Clay, Cassius Marcellus
1810-1903
American abolitionist & diplomat

Sherburne, James
Hacey Miller: A Novel.
Houghton Mifflin 1971.
BL v67 1971 p855; KR v39 1971 p24; LJ v96 1971
    p207.

323. Clay, Henry
1777-1852
American politician & orator

Cochran, Louis
The Fool of God.
Duell, Sloan & Pearce 1958.
BL v54 1958 p502; BRD 1958 p231; KR v26 1958
    p15; NYTBR Ag 3, 1958 p18.

Crabb, Alfred L.
Home to Kentucky.
Bobbs-Merrill 1953.
BL v50 1953 p12; BRD 1953 p216; FC 7th 93 p93;
    NYTBR Ag 16, 1953 p12.

Harper, Robert S.
The Road to Baltimore.
M.S. Mill 1942.
BRD 1942 p332; NYTBR Jl 26, 1942 p22.

324. Cleaveland, Moses
1754-1806
Founded Cleaveland, Ohio, 1796; spelling later
changed to Cleveland

Gaines, Edith
JUV *Free!.*
New Day Press 1972.

325. Clemens, Samuel Langhorne
see Twain, Mark, pseud.

326. Cleopatra
69-30 BC
Queen of Egypt; mistress of Julius Caesar &
Marc Antony

Balderston, John L.
A Goddess to a God.
Macmillan 1948.
BRD 1948 p37; KR v16 1948 p412; LJ v73 1948
    p1510; NYTBR N 14, 1948 p11.

Butts, Mary
Scenes from the Life of Cleopatra.
Heinemann 1935 (Rpr. 1974).

Cowlin, Dorothy
Cleopatra: Queen of Egypt: A Biographical Novel.
Wayland 1970.

Davis, William Stearns
*A Friend of Caesar: A Tale of the Fall of the Ro-
    man Republic.*
Macmillan 1900 (Rpr. 1919, 1928, 1968).
NYTBR Je 16, 1900 p386.

Gerson, Noel Bertram
That Egyptian Woman.
Doubleday 1956.
BRD 1956 p355; KR v24 1956 p487; NYTBR D 16,
    1956 p19; SatR Ag 25, 1956 p16.

Haggard, H. Rider
Cleopatra.
Longman's, Green 1889 (Heavily reprinted).

Lindsay, Kathleen
Enchantress of the Nile.
Hurst & Blackett 1965.

Mitchison, Naomi
Cleopatra's People.
Heinemann 1972.
GW v106 Je 24, 1972 p23; Lis v88 Jl 6, 1972 p22.

Rice, Anne
The Mummy; or, Ramses the Damned.
Ballantine 1989.
BL v85 1989 p1051; KR v57 1989 p328; NYTBR Je
    11, 1989 p9; PW v235 My 5, 1989 p70.

Rofheart, Martha
The Alexandrian: A Novel.
Crowell 1976.
BL v73 1976 p588; KR v44 1976 p858; LJ v101 1976
    p2195; PW v210 Jl 26, 1976 p70.

327. Cleveland, Grover (Stephen Grover)
1837-1908
22nd & 24th US President

Conroy, Sarah Booth
*Refinements of Love: A Novel About Clover and
    Henry Adams.*
Pantheon 1993.
KR v60 1992 p1392; LJ v118 Ja 1993 p163.

Fitch, James Monroe
The Ring Buster: A Story of the Erie Canal.
F. H. Revell 1940.

Glidden, Frederick (Luke Short, pseud.)
And the Wind Blows Free.
Macmillan 1945 (Rpr. 1955).
BL v42 1945 p38; BRD 1945 p266; KR v13 1945
    p116; NYTBR My 20, 1945 p17.

Statham, Frances P.
The Roswell Legacy.
Fawcett Columbine 1988.
PW v234 Ag 12, 1988 p452.

328. Clinton, Bill (William Jefferson)
1946-
42nd US President

Archer, Jeffrey
Honor among Thieves.
HarperCollins 1993.
KR v61 1993 p735.

329. Clinton, DeWitt
1769-1828
American politician; promoted the construction
of the Erie Canal

Casey, Jack
A Land beyond the River.
Bantam 1988.

330. Clinton, Henry, Sir
1738-1795
Commander of British troops in the American
Revolution

Bell, Kensil
Danger on the Jersey Shore.
Dodd, Mead 1959.
LJ v84 1959 p3933.

Davis, Burke
Yorktown.
Rinehart 1952.
BL v49 1952 p125; BRD 1952 p228; FC 7th p99; KR
    v20 1952 p520; LJ v77 1952 p1654; NYTBR N 2,
    1952 p22.

331. Clive, Robert
1725-1774
British general & colonist; founded Empire of
British India

Henty, G. A.
JUV *With Clive in India.*
Blackie 1884 (Heavily reprinted).

Leigh, Mary
The Company's Servant.
MacDonald 1947.

Partington, Norman
Master of Bengal: A Novel of Clive of India.
St. Martin's 1974.
KR v42 1974 p1220; LJ v100 1975 p502; NYTBR Ja
    19, 1975 p36; PW v206 N 18, 1974 p45.

332. Cochise
1815-1874
Apache Indian chief

Arnold, Elliott
Blood Brother.
Duell, Sloan & Pearce 1947 (Rpr. 1950, 1979).
BL v43 1947 p223; BRD 1947 p26; KR v14 1946
    p600; LJ v72 1947 p319; NYTBR Mr 2, 1947 p20.

Arnold, Elliott
YA *Broken Arrow.*
Duell, Sloan & Pearce 1954.
Containing much of the material and story of the
    author's *Blood Brother.*
LJ v80 1955 p492.

Johnson, Enid
YA *Cochise, Great Apache Chief.*
Messner 1953.
BRD 1953 p484; LJ v78 1953 p2110.

La Farge, Oliver
JUV *Cochise of Arizona: The Pipe of Peace Is Broken.*
Aladdin Books 1953.
BRD 1953 p533; KR v21 1953 p582; LJ v78 1953
    p2226; NYTBR N 15, 1953 p22.

Wyatt, Edgar
YA *Cochise, Apache Warrior and Statesman.*
Whittlesey House 1953.
BL v50 1953 p107; BRD 1953 p1032; KR v21 1953
    p336; LJ v78 1953 p1548.

333. Cody, "Buffalo Bill" (William Frederick)
1846-1917
American Indian fighter, army scout, & showman

Blackburn, Thomas Wakefield
A Good Day to Die.
D. McKay 1967.
BL v63 1967 p1032; BRD 1967 p132; KR v35 1967
    p17; LJ v92 1967 p1029; NYTBR Mr 19, 1967 p49.

Estleman, Loren D.
This Old Bill.
Doubleday 1990.
BL v80 1984 p1437.

Mark, Grace
The Dream Seekers.
Morrow 1992.

McMurtry, Larry
Buffalo Girls: A Novel.
Simon & Schuster 1990.

BL v87 1990 p5; BRD 1991 p1266; KR v58 1990 p1033; LJ v115 O 1, 1990 p118; NYTBR O 7, 1990 p3; Time v136 O 29, 1990 p103.

Moran, Mabel
YA *Red Eagle: Buffalo Bill's Adopted Son.*
Lippincott 1948.
BRD 1948 p597; LJ v73 1948 p1285.

Stevenson, Augusta
JUV *Buffalo Bill, Boy of the Plains.*
Bobbs-Merrill 1948.
BL v44 1948 p269; BRD 1948 p804; LJ v73 1948 p485.

334. Coeur, Jacques
1395-1456
Influential financial adviser to Charles VII

Costain, Thomas B.
The Moneyman.
Doubleday 1947.
Atl v180 S 1947 p122; BRD 1947 p195; FC 11th p133; LJ v72 1947 p1033; NYTBR Jl 13, 1947 p1; Time v50 Jl 21, 1947 p94.

Schoonover, Lawrence
The Burnished Blade.
Macmillan 1948.
BRD 1948 p746; KR v16 1948 p340; LJ v73 1948 p1091; NYTBR O 3, 1948 p26.

335. Coffin, Levi
1798-1877
American abolitionist

Ludwig, Charles
Levi Coffin and the Underground Railroad.
Herald Press 1975.

336. Coleridge, Samuel Taylor
1772-1834
English poet; wrote *The Rime of the Ancient Mariner* and *Kubla Khan*

Phillips, Jill M.
Walford's Oak.
Carol Pub. Group 1990.
BL v86 1990 p1880; KR v58 1990 p682.

337. Colgate, William
1783-1857
English-born American manufacturer; started company that later became Colgate-Palmolive

Carver, Saxon Rowe
YA *William Colgate: Yeoman of Kent.*
Broadman Press 1957.
LJ v83 1958 p236.

338. Collins, Michael
1890-1922
Irish politician & Sinn Fein leader

Fitz Gibbon, Constantine
High Heroic: A Novel.
Norton 1969.
BRD 1969 p434; LJ v95 1970 p82; NYTBR N 9, 1969 p68.

339. Collins, Wilkie (William)
1824-1889
English novelist

Carr, John D.
The Hungry Goblin: A Victorian Detective Novel.
Harper & Row 1972.
KR v40 1972 p430; LJ v97 1972 p2654; NYTBR Jl 16, 1972 p32.

Palmer, William
The Detective and Mr. Dickens: A Secret Victorian Journal Attributed to Wilkie Collins.
St. Martin's 1990.
BL v87 1990 p420; KR v58 1990 p1356; NYTBR D 16, 1990 p33.

340. Columba, Saint
521-597
Irish missionary

Desjarlais, John
The Throne of Tara.
Crossway Books 1990.
Locus v25 S 1990 p58; VOYA v13 D 1990 p279.

Macnicol, Eona K.
Colum of Derry.
Sheed & Ward 1954.

Oliver, Jane
Isle of Glory.
Collins 1947 (Rpr. 1964).
LJ v89 1964 p3338.

341. Columban, Saint
543-615
Irish religious figure

Polland, Madeleine A.
YA *Fingal's Quest.*
Doubleday 1961.
LJ v86 1961 p3076.

342. Columbus, Christopher
1451-1506
Italian navigator; traditional discoverer of America

Bailey, Bernadine
YA *Christopher Columbus: Sailor and Dreamer.*
Houghton Mifflin 1960.
LJ v85 1960 p2033.

Belfrage, Cedric
My Master, Columbus.
Doubleday 1961 (Rpr. 1992).

Bonde, Cecil von
Columbus Redivivus.
Timmins 1975.

Carpentier, Alejo
The Harp and the Shadow.
Mercury House 1990.
BL v86 1990 p1683; BRD 1991 p303; LJ v115 Ap 15,
1990 p121; NYTBR Je 3, 1990 p18; PW v237 My
4, 1990 p56.

Cooper, James Fenimore
Mercedes of Castile; or, The Voyage to Cathay.
Lea & Blanchard 1840 (Heavily reprinted).

Foreman, Michael
JUV *The Boy Who Sailed with Columbus.*
Arcade Publishing 1992.

Forester, C. S.
To the Indies.
Little, Brown 1940 (Rpr. 1951, 1963).
Also published as *The Earthly Paradise.*
BL v36 1940 p429; FC 11th p207; LJ v65 1940 p591;
Time v36 Jl 29, 1940 p60.

Frohlich, Newton
1492.
St. Martin's 1990.
BL v87 1990 p255; KR v58 1990 p1191; LJ v115 O 1,
1990 p115.

Ghisalberti, Mario
Christopher Columbus: A Romance.
Heinemann 1949.

Goll, Reinhold W.
JUV *Pedro Sails with Columbus.*
R.W. Goll 1981.

Harmon, Seth
YA *Sons of the Admiral: The Story of Diego and Fer-
nando Columbus.*
Junior Literary Guild 1940.
BRD 1940 p401; LJ v65 1940 p596; LJ v65 1940 p857.

Hays, Wilma Pitchford
JUV *Noko, Captive of Columbus.*
Coward-McCann 1967.
KR v35 1967 p1206; LJ v92 1967 p4251.

Hughes, Alice
JUV *Cajun Columbus.*
Pelican Pub. Co. 1975 (Rpr. 1991).

Huntford, Roland
Sea of Darkness.
Scribner 1975.
KR v43 1975 p866; LJ v100 1975 p1949; NYTBR N
16, 1975 p76.

Kent, Louise Andrews
JUV *He Went with Christopher Columbus.*
Houghton Mifflin 1940.
BL v37 1940 p158; BRD 1940 p504; LJ v65 1940
p926; NYTBR F 23, 1941 p10.

Lawson, Robert
JUV *I Discover Columbus.*
Little, Brown 1941.
BRD 1941 p534; LJ v66 1941 p908; NYTBR N 2,
1941 p7.

Litowinsky, Olga
JUV *The High Voyage: The Final Crossing of Christo-
pher Columbus.*
Delacorte Press 1991.
BL v88 1991 p376; KR v59 1991 p395; NYTBR N 10,
1991 p56.

Marlowe, Stephen
The Memoirs of Christopher Columbus.
Scribner 1987.
BL v83 1987 p1075; KR v55 1987 p329; LJ v112 My
1, 1987 p84; TLS Mr 6, 1987 p245.

Martin, Susan
JUV *I Sailed with Columbus: The Adventure of a Ship's
Boy.*
Overlook Press 1991.
BRD 1992 p1283; NYTBR N 10, 1991 p29; SLJ v37 S
1991 p281.

Meadowcroft, Enid La Monte
JUV *Ship Boy with Columbus.*
Crowell 1942.
BRD 1942 p525; HB v18 Jl 1942 p262; LJ v67 1942
p583.

O'Connor, Genevieve A.
JUV *The Admiral and the Deck Boy: One Boy's Journey
with Christopher Columbus.*
Shoe Tree Press 1991.
NYTBR N 10, 1991 p56; SLJ v38 Ja 1992 p137.

Parini, Jay
Bay of Arrows.
Holt 1992.
KR v60 1992 p744; LJ v117 Ag 1992 p151; NYTBR S
20, 1992 p14.

Posse, Abel
The Dogs of Paradise.
Atheneum 1989.
BRD 1991 p1498; KR v57 1989 p1557; LJ v115 Ja
1990 p150; NYTBR Mr 18, 1990 p22.

Powers, Alfred
JUV *Chains for Columbus.*
Westminster Press 1948.
BL v45 1949 p181; BRD 1949 p744; KR v16 1948
p444; LJ v74 1949 p316; NYTBR Je 26, 1949 p22.

Reit, Seymour
JUV *Voyage with Columbus.*
Bantam 1986.
SLJ v33 Ja 1987 p89.

Sabatini, Rafael
Columbus: A Romance.
Houghton Mifflin 1942.
BL v38 1942 p210; BRD 1942 p669; NYTBR Ja 25,
1942 p7.

Schllein, Miriam
JUV *I Sailed with Columbus.*
HarperCollins 1991.
BRD 1992 p1780; NYTBR N 10, 1991 p29; SLJ v37
    O 1, 1991 p128.

Sperry, Armstrong
YA *The Voyages of Christopher Columbus.*
Random House 1950.
BL v47 1950 p142; BRD 1950 p850; KR v18 1950
    p423; NYTBR N 12, 1950 p6.

Street, James
The Velvet Doublet.
Doubleday 1953.
BRD 1953 p907; FC 9th p494; KR v20 1952 p724; LJ
    v78 1953 p55.

Syme, Ronald
JUV *Columbus, Finder of the New World.*
Morrow 1952.
BL v49 1952 p53; BRD 1952 p866; KR v20 1952
    p408; SatR N 15, 1952 p72.

Wiggs, Susan
JUV *The Canary Who Sailed with Columbus.*
Panda Books 1989.
SLJ v36 Jl 1990 p65.

Wilhelm, Ida Mills
The Son of Dolores.
Field-Doubleday 1945.

Yolen, Jane
JUV *Encounter.*
Harcourt Brace Jovanovich 1992.
BL v88 1992 p1281; KR v60 1992 p402; SLJ v38 My
    1992 p117.

343. Confucius
551-479 BC
Chinese philosopher

Linklater, Eric
The Cornerstones: A Conversation in Elysium.
Macmillan 1942.
BRD 1942 p473.

344. Constantine I
280-337
Roman emperor, 306-337

De Wohl, Louis
The Living Wood.
Lippincott 1947.
BL v44 1947 p70; BRD 1947 p984; SatR O 4, 1947
    p18.

Slaughter, Frank G.
Constantine: The Miracle of the Flaming Cross.
Doubleday 1965.
BRD 1967 p1220; KR v33 1965 p645; LJ v90 1965
    p5116; NYTBR S 12, 1965 p47.

Thubron, Colin
Emperor: A Novel.
Heinemann 1978 (Rpr. 1991).
Lis v100 S 7, 1978 p318; Obs S 3, 1978 p26.

Upson, Frieda S.
Constantine, the Great.
Holy Cross Orthodox Press 1986.

345. Constantine the Great
see Constantine I

346. Constantine XI Palaeologus
1404-1453
Last Byzantine emperor

Bellairs, John
JUV *The Trolley to Yesterday.*
Dial 1989.
BL v85 1989 p1719; KR v57 1989 p686; PW v235 My
    12, 1989 p295.

Paton Walsh, Jill
YA *The Emperor's Winding Sheet.*
Farrar, Straus & Giroux 1974.
BL v70 1974 p1203; BRD 1974 p1269; KR v42 1974
    p490; LJ v99 1974 p1234.

347. Cook, James, Captain
1728-1779
English navigator & explorer

Blunden, Godfrey
Charco Harbour.
Vanguard Pres 1968.
BL v65 1969 p732; KR v36 1968 p836; LJ v93 1968
    p3797; NYTBR N 10, 1968 p5.

Borden, Charles A.
YA *He Sailed with Captain Cook.*
Crowell 1952 (Rpr. 1968).
BL v48 1952 p268; BRD 1952 p92; KR v20 1952 p73;
    LJ v77 1952 p365; NYTBR Ap 13, 1952 p22.

Bushnell, O. A.
*The Return of Lono: A Novel of Captain Cook's
    Last Voyage.*
Little, Brown 1956.
Also published as *Last Days of Captain Cook.*
BL v53 1956 p94; BRD 1956 p146; KR v24 1956
    p255; LJ v81 1956 p1620; NYTBR Je 17, 1956 p18.

Finkel, George
YA *James Cook, Royal Navy.*
Angus & Robertson 1970 (Rpr. 1987).
B&B v15 Ap 1970 p36.

Hooker, John
Captain James Cook.
Penguin Books 1987.
Based on the screenplay by Peter Yeldham.

Innes, Hammond
The Last Voyage: Captain Cook's Lost Diary.
Knopf 1979.

Atl v243 Ap 1979 p99; BRD 1979 p627; FC 11th
    p314; LJ v104 1979 p512; SatR Ap 28, 1979 p46.

Latham, Jean Lee
YA *Far Voyager: The Story of James Cook.*
Harper & Row 1970.
BRD 1970 p824; LJ v95 1970 p2541.

McGinnis, Paul
Lost Eden.
McBride 1947.
BRD 1947 p584; LJ v72 1947 p639.

Rodgers, Paul
To Kill a God.
Heinemann 1987.
ILN v275 Ap 1987 p68.

348. Coolidge, Calvin
1872-1933
30th US President

Webb, Kenneth
JUV *From Plymouth Notch to President: The Farm Boy-
hood of Calvin Coolidge.*
Countryman Press 1978.

349. Cooper, "Gary" (Frank James)
1901-1961
American actor; starred in *High Noon* and *Sergeant York*

Kaminsky, Stuart M.
High Midnight.
St. Martin's 1981.
KR v49 1981 p656; LJ v106 1981 p1246.

350. Cooper, James Fenimore
1789-1851
American novelist; wrote *The Last of the Mohi-
cans*

Proudfit, Isabel
James Fenimore Cooper.
Messner 1946.
BRD 1947 p729; KR v14 1946 p392; LJ v72 1947
    p229; SatR F 15, 1947 p46.

351. Cooper, Peter
1791-1883
American manufacturer, inventor, & philanthropist

Knight, Ruth Adams
YA *Certain Harvest: A Novel of the Time of Peter
Cooper.*
Doubleday 1960.
BRD 1960 p752; KR v27 1959 p817; LJ v85 1960
    p303; NYTBR Ja 10, 1960 p34.

352. Copernicus, Nicolaus
1473-1543
Polish astronomer

Banville, John
Doctor Copernicus: A Novel.
Norton 1976 (Rpr. 1984, 1987).
BL v73 1977 p1067; BRD 1977 p68; KR v44 1976
    p1313; LJ v102 1977 p511; PW v210 D 27, 1976
    p56.

Kelly, Eric P.
YA *From Star to Star: A Story of Krakow in 1493.*
Lippincott 1944.
BL v41 1944 p94; BRD 1944 p411; KR v12 1944
    p453; LJ v69 1944 p1006.

353. Copley, John Singleton
1738-1815
American portrait painter

Coatsworth, Elizabeth
JUV *Boston Bells.*
Macmillan 1952.
BL v49 1952 p144; BRD 1952 p187; LJ v77 1952
    p2012.

354. Corelli, Marie, pseud.
1855-1924
English novelist

Ansle, Dorothy P. (Hebe Elsna, pseud.)
The Lonely Dreamer.
Hale 1961 (Rpr. 1975).

355. Cornell, Katharine
1898-1974
American actress

Malvern, Gladys
YA *Curtain Going Up! The Story of Katharine Cor-
nell.*
Messner 1943.
BL v40 1943 p151; BRD 1943 p541; SatR N 13, 1943
    p46.

356. Cornwallis, Charles, Marquis
1738-1805
English military & political leader; surrendered
to George Washington at Yorktown

Davis, Burke
The Ragged One.
Rinehart 1951.
BL v47 1951 p301; BRD 1951 p222; KR v19 1951
    p138; NYTBR My 13, 1951 p18.

Davis, Burke
Yorktown.
Rinehart 1952.

BL v49 1952 p125; BRD 1952 p228; FC 7th p99; KR
v20 1952 p520; LJ v77 1952 p1654; NYTBR N 2,
1952 p22.

Graves, Robert
Proceed, Sergeant Lamb.
Random House 1941.
BRD 1941 p363; LJ v66 1941 p793; NYTBR O 19,
1941 p6.

McDonald, Eva
The Lady from Yorktown.
Ulverscroft 1972.

357. Coronado, Francisco Vasquez de
1510-1554
Spanish explorer

Baker, Betty
YA *A Stranger and Afraid.*
Macmillan 1972.
BL v69 1973 p491; KR v40 1972 p1034; LJ v98 1973
p640; NYTBR N 5, 1972 p14.

Campbell, Camilla
YA *Coronado and His Captains.*
Follett Pub. Co. 1958.
BL v55 1959 p243; BRD 1959 p170; LJ v83 1958
p3576.

Clendenin, Mary Joe
JUV *Gonzalo, Corondado's Shepherd Boy.*
Eakin Publications 1990.

Hersch, Virginia Davis
The Seven Cities of Gold.
Duell, Sloan & Pearce 1946.
BRD 1946 p376; KR v14 1946 p260; LJ v71 1946
p1050; NYTBR S 1, 1946 p5.

Price, G. G.
Coranado Comes.
Signal Publishing Co. 1940.

358. Cortez, Hernando
1485-1547
Spanish explorer & conquistador

Appel, Benjamin
JUV *We Were There with Cortes and Montezuma.*
Grosset & Dunlap 1959.

Baggett, Samuel G.
Gods on Horseback.
McBride 1952.
BL v49 1953 p223; BRD 1953 p29.

Baker, Betty
JUV *The Blood of the Brave.*
Harper & Row 1966.
BRD 1966 p53; LJ v91 1966 p3262.

Baron, Alexander
The Golden Princess.
Washburn 1954.

BL v51 1954 p161; BRD 1955 p44; KR v22 1954
p734; LJ v79 1954 p2319; NYTBR Ja 9, 1955 p22.

Berg, William A.
The White God of the Aztecs.
B. Humphries 1961.

Coleman, Eleanor S.
YA *The Cross and the Sword of Cortes.*
Simon & Schuster 1968.
JHSLC 2nd p327; KR v36 1968 p558; LJ v93 1968
p4412.

Hayton-Keeva, Sally
Unholy Sacrifice.
Sagn Books 1992.

Lobdell, Helen
YA *Golden Conquest.*
Houghton Mifflin 1953.
BL v50 1954 p190; BRD 1953 p577; KR v21 1953
p587; LJ v78 1953 p1860; NYTBR S 13, 1953 p30.

Mantel, S. G.
YA *The Youngest Conquistador.*
McKay 1963.
LJ v88 1963 p4865.

Marshall, Edison
Cortez and Marina.
Doubleday 1963.

Nevins, Albert J.
YA *The Young Conquistador.*
Dodd, Mead 1960.

Porter, Elizabeth
*Cortes the Conqueror, His Romance with Donna
Marina.*
Dorrance 1944.

Shedd, Margaret
Malinche and Cortes.
Doubleday 1971.
BL v67 1971 p896; KR v39 1971 p74; LJ v96 1971
p658; PW v199 Ja 11, 1971 p61.

Shellabarger, Samuel
Captain from Castile.
Little, Brown 1945.
BL v41 1945 p140; BRD 1945 p641; KR v12 1944
p485; LJ v69 1944 p1103; NYTBR Ja 7, 1945 p5.

Strousse, Flora
YA *The Friar and the Knight.*
P.J. Kenedy 1957.
NYTBR N 17, 1957 p24.

Syme, Ronald
JUV *Cortes of Mexico.*
Morrow 1951.
BRD 1951 p863; KR v19 1951 p353; LJ v76 1951
p1717; NYTBR Ja 13, 1952 p28.

359. Cotton, John
1584-1652
English-born American clergyman

Rushing, Jane Gilmore
Covenant of Grace.
Doubleday 1982.
BL v78 1982 p1301; KR v50 1982 p367; LJ v107 My
1, 1982 p906; PW v221 Mr 26, 1982 p66.

360. Coughlin, Father (Charles Edward)
1891-1979
American priest & political activist; famous for
his radio broadcasts

Angoff, Charles
Summer Storm.
T. Yoseloff 1963.
LJ v89 1964 p880; NYTBR D 15, 1963 p23; SatR Ja 4,
1964 p82.

Costello, Anthony
Jericho.
Bantam 1982.
KR v50 1982 p153; LJ v107 1982 p649.

361. Crabtree, Lotta
1847-1924
American actress; began career entertaining in
California mining camps

Place, Marian T. (Dale White, pseud.)
JUV *Lotta Crabtree, a Girl of the Goldrush.*
Bobbs-Merrill 1958 (Rpr. 1962).
LJ v84 1959 p248.

362. Crane, Stephen
1871-1900
American author; wrote *The Red Badge of Courage*

Zara, Louis
*Dark Rider: A Novel Based on the Life of Stephen
Crane.*
World Pub. Co. 1961.
BL v58 1961 p128; BRD 1962 p1337; KR v29 1961
p512; LJ v86 1961 p2823; NYTBR S 17, 1961 p42.

363. Cranmer, Thomas
1489-1556
English religious reformer; Archbishop of Canterbury

Malpass, Eric
Of Human Frailty.
Hale 1987.
BritBkN Jl 1987 p444.

Street, M. K.
YA *Henry's Archbishop.*
Hale 1968.

Turton, Godfrey E.
My Lord of Canterbury.
Doubleday 1967.

BL v63 1967 p767; BRD 1967 p1327; KR v34 1966
p1244; LJ v92 1967 p598; NYTBR Mr 5, 1967 p42;
PW v190 D 12, 1966 p49.

364. Crassus, Marcus Licinius Dives
115-53 BC
Roman military leader & politician

Ghnassia, Maurice
Arena: A Novel.
Viking 1969.
BL v66 1969 p438; KR v37 1969 p579; LJ v94 1969
p2807; PW v195 My 26, 1969 p49.

Saylor, Steven
Arms of Nemesis.
St. Martin's 1992.
BL v89 1992 p242; KR v60 1992 p1093; NYTBR O
18, 1992 p34.

365. Crazy Horse
1842-1877
American Indian chief

Henry, Will
No Survivors.
Random House 1950.
BRD 1950 p426; LJ v75 1950 p1660; NYTBR N 26,
1950 p36; SatR D 23, 1950 p35.

Meadowcroft, Enid La Monte
JUV *The Story of Crazy Horse.*
Grosset & Dunlap 1954.
BL v51 1955 p270; BRD 1955 p627; KR v22 1954
p727; LJ v80 1955 p491; NYTBR N 14, 1954 p28.

Sale, Richard
The White Buffalo.
Simon & Schuster 1975.
BL v72 1975 p30; KR v43 1975 p801; LJ v100 1975
p1846; PW v208 Jl 14, 1975 p58.

366. Crippen, Hawley Harvey
1862-1910
American-born English murderer

Bloom, Ursula (Lozania Prole, pseud.)
The Girl Who Loved Crippen.
Hutchinson 1957 (Rpr. 1981).

Gordon, Richard
The Private Life of Dr. Crippen.
Heinemann 1981.

Lewis, Hilda
The Case of the Little Doctor.
Random House 1949.
Also published as *Said Dr. Spendlove.*
BRD 1949 p554; KR v16 1948 p580; NYTBR Ja 16,
1949 p16; SatR Ja 22, 1949 p32.

Raymond, Ernest
We, the Accused.

Frederick A. Stokes Co. 1935 (Rpr. 1968, 1981).
BRD 1935 p827; SatR Ag 24, 1935 p6.

Williams, Emlyn
Dr. Crippen's Diary: An Invention.
Robson Books 1987.
KR v57 1989 p500.

367. Crittenden, John Jordan
1787-1863
American lawyer & politician

Seifert, Shirley
Three Lives of Elizabeth.
Lippincott 1952.
BL v48 1952 p322; KR v20 1952 p166; NYTBR My
18, 1952 p23.

368. Crockett, Davy (David)
1786-1836
American frontiersman; died at the Alamo

Brown, Dee
Wave High the Banner.
Macrae-Smith 1942.
BRD 1942 p95.

Coatsworth, Elizabeth
JUV *Old Whirlwind: A Story of Davy Crockett.*
Macmillan 1953 (Rpr. 1964).
BRD 1953 p192; LJ v78 1953 p1856; NYTBR O 11,
1953 p30.

Cohen, Caron Lee
JUV *Sally Ann Thunder Ann Whirlwind Crockett.*
Greenwillow Books 1985.
BL v81 1985 p1190; BRD 1987 p347; SLJ v32 S 1985
p114.

Davis, Hazel H.
JUV *Davy Crockett.*
Random House 1955.
BRD 1956 p243; KR v23 1955 p784; LJ v81 1956
p564.

Dewey, Ariane
JUV *The Narrow Escapes of Davy Crockett.*
Greenwillow Books 1990.
BL v86 1990 p1339; BRD 1990 p460; SLJ v36 My
1990 p83.

Foreman, L. L.
The Road to San Jacinto.
Dutton 1943.
BL v39 1943 p426; BRD 1943 p275; LJ v68 1943
p366; NYTBR Ap 11, 1943 p16.

Hazen, Barbara Shook
JUV *Davy Crockett, Indian Fighter.*
Pyramid Communications 1975.
SLJ v22 Mr 1976 p101.

Le Sueur, Meridel
*Chanticleer of Wilderness Road: A Story of Davy
Crockett.*

Knopf 1951 (Rpr. 1982, 1990).
BL v48 1952 p174; BRD 1951 p517; KR v19 1951
p531; LJ v76 1951 p2014; NYTBR F 17, 1952 p34.

Matthews, Billie L.; Hurlburt, Virginia E.
JUV *Davy's Dawg.*
Hendrick-Long 1989.

Meadowcroft, Enid La Monte
JUV *The Story of Davy Crockett.*
Grosset & Dunlap 1952.
LJ v77 1952 p1908.

Shapiro, Irwin
YA *Yankee Thunder: The Legendary Life of Davy
Crockett.*
Messner 1944.
BRD 1944 p679; HB v20 My 1944 p206; LJ v69 1944
p506; SatR Mr 11, 1944 p26.

Steele, William O.
JUV *Davy Crockett's Earthquake.*
Harcourt, Brace 1956.
BL v52 1956 p346; BRD 1956 p888; CC 10th p350;
KR v24 1956 p242; LJ v81 1956 p2045; NYTBR Jl
15, 1956 p20.

Street, James
Oh, Promised Land.
Dial Press 1940.
BRD 1940 p892; NYTBR Ap 28, 1940 p4.

Walt Disney Productions
JUV *Walt Disney's Davy Crockett and Mike Fink.*
Simon & Schuster 1955.

369. Cromwell, Oliver
1599-1658
English military & political leader; ruled England as Lord Protector, 1653-1658

Bell, Josephine
In the King's Absence.
Bles 1973.
B&B v18 Jl 1973 p136.

Linington, Elizabeth
The Kingbreaker.
Doubleday 1958.
BRD 1958 p675; KR v26 1958 p296.

Macken, Walter
Seek the Fair Land.
Macmillan 1959.
BL v56 1959 p28; BRD 1960 p865; KR v27 1959
p361; LJ v84 1959 p2213; NYTBR Ag 9, 1959 p22.

Sanders, John
Cromwell's Cavalier.
Hale 1968.

370. Crook, George
1829-1890
American general & Indian fighter

Burnett, William Riley
Adobe Walls: A Novel of the Last Apache Rising.
Knopf 1953.
BL v50 1953 p34; BRD 1953 p138; KR v21 1953
p314; LJ v78 1953 p1330; NYTBR Ag 16, 1953 p4.

371. Crosby, Fanny (Frances Jane)
1820-1915
American songwriter; wrote over 6,000 hymns

Barrett, Ethel
Fanny Crosby.
Regal Books 1984.

372. Crowley, Aleister (Edward Alexander)
1875-1947
Writer of occult lore, Black Magic rites

Collins, Randall
The Case of the Philosopher's Ring.
Crown 1978.
KR v46 1978 p1216.

373. Cuauhtemoc
1495-1525
Last Aztec ruler; hanged by Cortez

De Cesco, Federica
YA *The Prince of Mexico.*
John Day Co. 1970.
BS v30 Jl 1, 1970 p144; KR v38 1970 p558; LJ v95
1970 p4051.

374. Culpeper, Nicholas
1616-1654
English physician; believed astrology influenced
disease

Tyrell, Mabel L.
The Affairs of Nicholas Culpeper.
Macrae-Smith 1946.
BL v42 1946 p330; BRD 1946 p832; KR v14 1946
p79; NYTBR My 5, 1946 p14.

375. Cushing, William Barker
1842-1874
American Civil War naval hero

Shirreffs, Gordon D.
Roanoke Raiders.
Westminster Press 1959.
LJ v84 1959 p3642.

376. Custer, George Armstrong
1839-1876
American general; killed at the Battle of Little
Big Horn

Berger, Thomas
Little Big Man.
Dial 1964 (Heavily reprinted).
BRD 1964 p97; LJ v89 1964 p4560; NYTBR O 11,
1964 p42; SatR O 3, 1964 p38.

Birney, Hoffman
The Dice of God.
Holt 1956.
BL v52 1956 p362; BRD 1956 p84; KR v24 1956 p59;
NYTBR Mr 25, 1956 p32.

Chadwick, Joseph
YA *The Sioux Indian Wars.*
Monarch Books 1962.

Curry, Thomas A.
Riding for Custer.
Arcadia House 1947.

Downey, Fairfax
YA *The Seventh's Staghound.*
Dodd, Mead 1948.
BRD 1948 p226; LJ v73 1948 p1828; NYTBR N 14,
1948 p4; SatR N 13, 1948 p42.

Goble, Paul
JUV *Red Hawk's Account of Custer's Last Battle.*
Pantheon 1969 (Rpr. 1992).
BL v67 1970 p341; BRD 1971 p504; KR v38 1970
p879; LJ v95 1970 p4350; NYTBR N 8, 1970 p22.

Grey, Zane
The U.P. Trail: A Novel.
Harper & Brothes 1918 (Rpr. 1982).

Gruber, Frank
Bugles West.
Rinehart 1954 (Rpr. 1977).
NYTBR O 3, 1954 p20.

Haycox, Ernest
Bugles in the Afternoon.
Little, Brown & Co. 1944.
BL v40 Mr 15, 1944 p251; BRD 1944 p329; NYTBR F
13, 1944 p6.

Henry, Will
YA *Custer's Last Stand: The Story of the Battle of the
Little Big Horn.*
Chilton Books 1966.
BRD 1966 p539; KR v34 1966 p632; LJ v91 1966
p5760.

Henry, Will
No Survivors.
Random House 1950.
BRD 1950 p426; LJ v75 1950 p1660; NYTBR N 26,
1950 p36; SatR D 23, 1950 p35.

Henry, Will
Yellow Hair.
Ballantine 1953.
NYTBR N 15, 1953 p36.

Johnston, Terry
YA *Long Winter Gone.*

Bantam 1990.
Kliatt v25 S 1991 p10.

Johnston, Terry
YA *Seize the Sky.*
Bantam 1991.
Kliatt v25 S 1991 p10.

Johnston, Terry
YA *Whisper of the Wolf.*
Bantam 1991.
Roundup v4 Winter 1991 p48.

Jones, Douglas C.
The Court-Martial of George Armstrong Custer.
Scribner 1976.
BL v73 1976 p122; BRD 1977 p686; KR v44 1976
　　p855; LJ v102 1977 p127; NYTBR N 21, 1976 p20.

Kaufman, Fred S.
Custer Passed Our Way.
North Plains Press 1971.

Magorian, James
*The Great Injun Carnival: The Secret Diary of
　　General George Armstrong Custer.*
Black Oak Press 1982.
SFRB v7 S 1982 p27.

Mills, Charles K.
A Mighty Afternoon.
Doubleday 1980.
LJ v106 1981 p166.

Patten, Lewis B.
Cheyenne Captives.
Doubleday 1978.
BL v74 1978 p1539; FC 10th p410.

Patten, Lewis B.
Proudly They Die.
Doubleday 1964.

Patten, Lewis B.
The Red Sabbath.
Doubleday 1968.
BL v65 1968 p230.

Place, Marian T. (Dale White, pseud.)
JUV *The Boy Who Came Back.*
Criterion Books 1967.
KR v34 1966 p1139; LJ v92 1967 p1755.

Shiflet, Kenneth E.
The Convenient Coward.
Stackpole 1961.

Smith, Terry
*Reprieve from Little Big Horn: A Novel of General
　　Custer's Cavalry.*
Exposition Press 1957.

Stevenson, Augusta
JUV *George Custer, Boy of Action.*
Bobbs-Merrill 1963.

Ulyatt, Kenneth
YA *Custer's Gold: A Story of the American West at
　　the Time of the Battle of the Little Big Horn.*
Collins 1971.
TLS O 22, 1971 p1319.

377. Cutpurse, Moll
1589-1662
English female criminal; pickpocket & highway
robber; dressed as man

Galford, Ellen
Moll Cutpurse: Her True Story.
Firebrand Books 1985.
LJ v110 Jl 1985 p76.

378. Cyrus the Great
600-529 BC
Persian king & founder of Persian empire

Nagel, Sherman A.
Cyrus the Persian.
Wm. B. Eerdmans 1941.

Petty, Thurman C.
The Open Gates.
Pacific Press Pub. Association 1992.

379. D'Annunzio, Gabriele
1863-1938
Italian author & poet

Macbeth, George
The Lion of Pescara.
Cape 1984.

Shaine, L. C.
Tamara.
Ballantine 1989.

380. DaGama, Vasco
1460-1524
Portuguese explorer & navigator

Bailey, Ralph E.
Argosies of Empire.
Dutton 1947.
BL v44 1948 p174; BRD 1947 p37; KR v15 1947
　　p398; LJ v72 1947 p1693.

381. Dali, Salvador
1904-1989
Spanish artist; leader of Surrealist Movement

Kaminsky, Stuart M.
The Melting Clock.
Mysterious Press 1991.
NYTBR D 22, 1991 p21.

382. Dalton, Emmett
1871-1937
American outlaw

Hansen, Ron
Desperadoes: A Novel.
Knopf 1979 (Rpr. 1980, 1990).
BL v75 1979 p1517; BRD 1979 p532; KR v47 1979
p212; LJ v104 1979 p1077; NYTBR Je 3, 1979 p14.

383. Damien, Father
1840-1889
Catholic missionary; devoted life to leper colony in Hawaii

Bushnell, O. A.
Molokai.
World Pub. Co. 1963 (Rpr. 1975).
BRD 1963 p155; LJ v88 1963 p3224; NYTBR O 13,
1963 p46.

384. Dampier, William
1652-1715
English explorer & author

Andrews, Robert Hardy
Burning Gold.
Doubleday 1945.
BRD 1945 p635; KR v13 1945 p227; LJ v70 1945
p635; NYTBR Ag 19, 1945 p25.

Chester, Alan
Brother Captain.
P. Davies 1964.

Chester, Alan
The Cygnet Adventure.
Rigby 1984.

Rush, Philip
JUV *He Went with Dampier.*
Roy Publishers 1958.

385. Daniel
Hebrew prophet; escaped from lion's den

Petty, Thurman C.
The Open Gates.
Pacific Press Pub. Association 1992.

Wagoner, Jean Brown
JUV *The Captive Lad: A Story of Daniel, the Lion-Hearted.*
Bobbs-Merrill 1954.
BRD 1955 p940; LJ v80 1955 p492; NYTBR Ja 16,
1955 p28.

386. Dante Alighieri
1265-1321
Italian poet; wrote *The Divine Comedy*

Barbeau, Clayton
Dante & Gentucca: A Love Story.
Capra Press 1974.

Langley, Noel
The Inconstant Moon.
A. Barker 1949.

Schachner, Nathan
The Wanderer: A Novel of Dante and Beatrice.
Appleton-Century 1944.
BL v41 1944 p124; BRD 1944 p664; KR v12 1944
p381; LJ v69 1944 p883.

Tutaev, David
A Comedy but Not Divine: A Gothic Novel.
Macdonald 1971.
NS v82 O 8, 1971 p483.

387. Danton, Georges Jacques
1759-1794
French revolutionary leader; guillotined by
Robespierre

Mantel, Hilary
A Place of Greater Safety.
Atheneum 1993.
LJ v118 F 15, 1993 p193; NYTBR My 9, 1993 p21.

388. Dare, Virginia
b. 1587
First child of English parents born in America

Bothwell, Jean
YA *Lady of Roanoke.*
Holt, Rinehart & Winston 1965.
KR v33 1965 p252; NYTBR Je 13, 1965 p24.

Hooks, William H.
JUV *The Legend of the White Doe.*
Macmillan 1988.
BL v84 1988 p1432; KR v56 1988 p363; SLJ v34 Je
1988 p105.

Stevenson, Augusta
JUV *Virginia Dare, Mystery Girl.*
Bobbs-Merrill 1959.
LJ v83 1958 p1289.

389. Darius I
548-486 BC
King of Persia, 521-486 BC

Coolidge, Olivia E.
YA *Marathon Looks on the Sea.*
Houghton Mifflin 1967.
BL v64 1968 p773; JHSLC 2nd p327; KR v35 1967
p1216; LJ v93 1968 p302.

Tapsell, R. F.
Shadow of Wings.
Hutchinson 1972.

390. Darrow, Clarence Seward

1857-1938

American lawyer; defense attorney in the
Scopes "monkey" trial and the Leopold-Loeb
murder trial

Levin, Meyer
Compulsion.
Simon & Schuster 1956.
BL v53 1956 p199; BRD 1956 p562; FC 11th p372;
    KR v24 1956 p600; LJ v81 1956 p2324; NYTBR O
    28, 1956 p7.

Mark, Grace
The Dream Seekers.
Morrow 1992.

391. Darwin, Charles Robert

1809-1882

English naturalist; expounded theory of evolu-
tion through natural selection; wrote *Origin of
the Species*

Eisenberg, Philip
JUV *We Were There with Charles Darwin on H.M.S.
    Beagle.*
Grosset & Dunlap 1960.
LJ v85 1960 p2674.

Law, Felicia
JUV *Darwin and the Voyage of the Beagle: A Fictional
    Account of Charles Darwin's Work and Adven-
    tures during the Five-Year-Long Voyage.*
A. Deutsch 1985.
BL v81 1985 p1667; BRD 1986 p943; NYTBR Jl 14,
    1985 p36; SLJ v32 N 1985 p87.

Stone, Irving
*The Origin: A Biographical Novel of Charles Dar-
    win.*
Doubleday 1980.
BL v76 1980 p1465; BRD 1981 p1389; FC 11th p587;
    KR v48 1980 p737; LJ v105 1980 p1663; NYTBR S
    14, 1980 p12.

Subercaseaux, Benjamin
Jeremy Button.
Macmillan 1954.
BL v50 1954 p298; BRD 1954 p858; FC 7th p338; KR
    v22 1954 p41; LJ v79 1954 p552.

392. Davenant, William, Sir

1606-1668

English dramatist & poet

Ashton, Winifred (Clemence Dane, pseud.)
The Godson: A Fantasy.
Norton 1964.

393. Davenport, Thomas

1802-1851

American inventor; discovered principle of start-
ing, stopping electric current over wire

Meigs, Cornelia
YA *Call of the Mountain.*
Little, Brown 1940.
BL v37 1940 p140; BRD 1940 p631; LJ v65 1940
    p1045; NYTBR N 10, 1940 p10.

394. David, King of Israel

Second king of Israel & Judah

Cassill, R. V.
After Goliath.
Ticknor & Fields 1985.
BL v81 1985 p756; KR v53 1985 p96; LJ v110 Mr 15,
    1985 p70; NYTBR Je 16, 1985 p27.

Chinn, Laurene
The Unanointed.
Crown 1958.
BRD 1959 p203; FC 7th p77; KR v26 1958 p808; LJ
    v84 1959 p861; NYTBR Ap 12, 1959 p40.

Daugherty, Sonia
JUV *Wings of Glory.*
Oxford University Press 1940.
BRD 1940 p225; LJ v65 1940 p214.

Davey, Charles Foster
David.
Muhlenberg Press 1960.

Davis, Elmer H.
Giant Killer.
John Day Co. 1928 (Rpr. 1943).
BL v25 1928 p120; BRD 1928 p187; NYTBR O 14,
    1928 p6; SatR O 27, 1928 p293.

De Wohl, Louis
David of Jerusalem.
Lippincott 1963.

Grimes, Ruby Evans
*I Shall Dwell: The Youthful Years of David, King of
    Israel.*
Wm. B. Eerdmans 1947.

Hamilton, Wallace
David at Olivet.
St. Martin's 1979.
KR v46 1978 p1374; LJ v104 Je 1979 p1277.

Heller, Joseph
God Knows.
Knopf 1984.
BL v80 1984 p1570; KR v52 1984 p639; LJ v109 1984
    p1772; NYTBR S 23, 1984 p1; PW v226 Ag 3,
    1984 p52.

Heym, Stefan
The King David Report, a Novel.
Putnam 1973.

BL v70 1973 p320; BRD 1974 p546; KR v41 1973
    p829; LJ v98 1973 p3283.

Ibu-Sahav, Ari
David and Bathsheba.
Crown 1951.
BRD 1952 p466; KR v19 1951 p621; LJ v76 1951
    p1804; NYTBR N 25, 1951 p58.

Israel, Charles E.
Rizpah: A Novel.
Simon & Schuster 1961.
BL v57 1961 p635; BRD 1961 p687; KR v29 1961
    p32; LJ v86 1961 p1794; NYTBR Ap 2, 1961 p17.

Jacobson, Dan
The Rape of Tamar.
Macmillan 1970.
FC 9th p271; KR v38 1970 p655; LJ v95 1970 p2717;
    PW v197 Je 15, 1970 p59.

Jenkins, Gwyn
King David.
Doubleday 1961.
Also published as *The Son of Jesse.*
LJ v86 1961 p2963.

Jones, Juanita Nuttall
David, Warrior of God.
Association Press 1954.
BRD 1955 p474; KR v22 1954 p629; LJ v79 1954
    p2500; NYTBR Ja 16, 1955 p28.

King, Marian
JUV *Young King David.*
Lippincott 1948.
BRD 1948 p455; LJ v73 1948 p1198.

Lindgren, Torgny
Bathsheba.
Harper & Row 1989.
KR v57 1989 p323; LJ v114 My 15, 1989 p90.

Malvern, Gladys
YA *Saul's Daughter.*
Longmans, Green 1956.
BRD 1956 p608; KR v24 1956 p608; LJ v81 1956
    p301; NYTBR Ap 8, 1956 p38.

Martin, Malachi
King of Kings: A Novel.
Simon & Schuster 1980.
BL v77 1981 p1079; BRD 1981 p941; FC 11th p416;
    KR v49 1981 p32; LJ v106 1981 p472; NYTBR Ap
    5, 1981 p30.

Rodale, J. I.
The Stones of Jehoshaphat.
Rodale Books 1954.

Schmitt, Gladys
David, the King.
Dial Press 1946 (Rpr. 1973).
BL v42 1946 p227; BRD 1946 p723; FC 10th p463;
    KR v14 1946 p40; LJ v71 1946 p182; NYTBR F 24,
    1946 p5.

Shamir, Moshe
David's Stranger.
Abelard-Schuman 1965.
BRD 1966 p1094; KR v33 1965 p70; LJ v90 1965
    p2901.

Slaughter, Frank G.
David, Warrior and King: A Biblical Biography.
World Pub. Co. 1962.
BL v58 1962 p702; BRD 1962 p1115; KR v30 1962
    p73; LJ v87 1962 p1152.

Wagoner, Jean Brown
JUV *The Shepherd Lad: A Story of David of Bethlehem.*
Bobbs-Merrill 1953.
BRD 1953 p975; LJ v78 1953 p1942; NYTBR N 15,
    1953 p40.

Weil, Grete
The Bride Price.
Godine 1991.
LJ v117 Ap 1, 1992 p152; NYTBR My 10, 1992 p6.

395. Davis, Jefferson
1808-1889
President of Confederacy, 1861-1865

Kane, Harnett T.
*Bride of Fortune: A Novel Based on the Life of
    Mrs. Jefferson Davis.*
Doubleday 1948.
BRD 1948 p440; FC 9th p285; KR v16 1948 p410; LJ
    v73 1948 p1384; NYTBR O 10, 1948 p4.

Olsen, Theodore V.
*There Was a Season: A Biographical Novel of Jef-
    ferson Davis.*
Doubleday 1972.
BL v68 1972 p648; LJ v97 1972 p86.

Seifert, Shirley
The Proud Way.
Lippincott 1948.
BRD 1948 p755; NYTBR Je 20, 1948 p20.

Vaughan, Matthew
Major Stepton's War.
Doubleday 1978.
KR v46 1978 p572; LJ v103 1978 p1662.

396. Davis, Richard Harding
1864-1916
American journalist

Lynch, Daniel
Yellow: A Novel.
Walker 1992.
KR v60 1992 p1276; LJ v117 N 15, 1992 p102.

397. Davis, Sam
1844-1863
Confederate soldier

Rowell, Adelaide C.
On Jordan's Stormy Banks, a Novel of Sam Davis,
    the Confederate Scout.
Bobbs-Merrill 1948.
BRD 1948 p719; LJ v73 1948 p708; NYTBR My 23,
    1948 p34.

398. Deborah
Hebrew prophetess

Jenkins, Sara L.
JUV *Song of Deborah: A Novel.*
John Day Co. 1963.

Jones, Juanita Nuttall
Deborah: The Woman Who Saved Israel.
Association Press 1956.

Weinreb, Nathaniel Norsen
The Sorceress.
Doubleday 1954.
BL v51 1954 p134; BRD 1954 p935; FC 7th p372; KR
    v22 1954 p455; NYTBR Ja 2, 1955 p20.

399. Debs, Eugene Victor
1855-1926
American labor organizer & socialist leader

Mark, Grace
The Dream Seekers.
Morrow 1992.

Nissenson, Aaron
Song of Man: A Novel Based upon the Life of
    Eugene V. Debs.
Whittier Books 1964.
LJ v89 1964 p1985.

Stone, Irving
Adversary in the House.
Doubleday 1947.
BL v44 O 1, 1947 p51; BRD 1947 p866; FC 9th p491;
    LJ v72 1947 p1195; NYTBR S 28, 1947 p4; WLB
    v43 N 1947 p154.

400. Debussy, Claude
1862-1918
French composer

La Mure, Pierre
Clair de Lune: A Novel about Claude Debussy.
Random House 1962.
NYTBR N 4, 1962 p56.

401. Decatur, Stephen
1779-1820
American naval officer

Burland, Brian
Stephen Decatur, the Devil, and the Endymion.
Allen & Unwin 1975.
Obs N 23, 1975 p31; Spec v235 N 1, 1975 p572.

Hoyt, Edward Palmer
Against Cold Steel.
Pinnacle Books 1974.

Vinton, Iris
JUV *The Story of Stephen Decatur.*
Grosset & Dunlap 1954.
LJ v80 1955 p491.

Wilson, Hazel Hutchins
JUV *Tall Ships.*
Little, Brown 1958.
BL v54 1958 p451; BRD 1958 p1121; KR v26 1958
    p3; LJ v83 1958 p973.

402. Dee, John
1527-1608
English alchemist, mathematician & magician

Ackroyd, Peter
The House of Doctor Dee.
Hamilton 1993.

Jerrold, Ianthe
Love and the Dark Crystal.
Hale 1955.

Meyrink, Gustav
The Angel of the West Window.
Dedalus 1991.

Wrede, Patricia C.
Snow White and Rose Red.
T. Doherty Associates 1989.
BL v85 1989 p1511; BL v86 1990 p907; KR v57 1989
    p510.

403. Deere, John
1804-1886
American manufacturer & inventor

Bare, Margaret Ann
JUV *John Deere, Blacksmith Boy.*
Bobbs-Merrill 1964.

404. DeGaulle, Charles
1890-1970
French general & statesman

Fabre-Luce, Alfred
The Trial of Charles de Gaulle.
Praeger 1963.
Translation of *Haute Cour.*

Forsyth, Frederick
The Day of the Jackal.
Viking 1971.
Atl v228 S 1971 p114; FC 11th p208; LJ v96 1971
    p2669; NYTBR Ag 15, 1971 p3; Time v98 Ag 23,
    1971 p56.

Koch, Eric
The French Kiss: A Tongue-in-Cheek Political Fantasy.
McClelland & Stewart 1969.

Martin, Les
JUV *Prisoner of War.*
Random House 1993.

405. Delacroix, Eugene
1798-1863
French painter

Hersch, Virginia Davis
To Seize a Dream.
Crown 1948.
BL v45 1949 p159; BRD 1948 p377; KR v16 1948
　p453; NYTBR N 14, 1948 p10.

406. Demetrius I
337-283 BC
King of Macedonia, 294-285 BC

Duggan, Alfred Leo
Besieger of Cities.
Pantheon 1963.
BDR 1963 p285; LJ v88 1963 p3642; NYTBR S 22,
　1963 p40; SatR Ja 11, 1964 p62.

407. DeMille, Cecil B.
1881-1959
American movie director & producer

Myers, Hortense
JUV *Cecil B. DeMille, Young Dramatist.*
Bobbs-Merrill 1963.

408. Desmoulins, Camille
1760-1794
French revolutionary; guillotined by Robespierre

Mantel, Hilary
A Place of Greater Safety.
Atheneum 1993.
LJ v118 F 15, 1993 p193; NYTBR My 9, 1993 p21.

409. DeSoto, Hernando
1500-1542
Spanish explorer

Jennings, John E.
*The Golden Eagle: A Novel Based on the Fabulous
　Life and Times of the Great Conquistador Her-
　nando de Soto, 1500-1542.*
Putnam 1958.
BRD 1959 p532; KR v26 1958 p785; LJ v83 1958
　p3441.

Lytle, Andrew
At the Moon's Inn.
Bobbs-Merrill 1941 (Rpr. 1990).

BRD 1941 p571; NY N 22, 1941 p110; NYTBR N 23,
　1941 p7.

410. Dessalines, Jean Jacques
1758-1806
Haitian ruler, 1804-1806

Strother, Elsie W.
Drums at Sunset.
National Writers Press 1990.

411. Devereaux, Robert
1566-1601
English nobleman & favorite of Elizabeth I

Eckerson, Olive
My Lord Essex.
Holt 1955.
BL v51 Ap 15, 1955 p342; BRD 1955 p268; FC 7th
　p121; LJ v80 1955 p561; NYTBR Mr 27, 1955 p31.

Evans, Jean
Essex, Traitor Earl.
Hale 1976.

Garrett, George
Death of the Fox.
Doubleday 1971 (Rpr. 1991).
BL v68 1971 p182; BRD 1971 p477; FC 11th p229;
　KR v39 1971 p1036; LJ v96 1971 p2540; NYTBR S
　26, 1971 p52.

412. Dewey, George
1837-1917
American naval officer

Long, Laura
JUV *George Dewey, Vermont Boy.*
Bobbs-Merrill 1963.
BRD 1952 p567; LJ v77 1952 p909; NYTBR Jl 13,
　1952 p18.

413. Dewey, John
1859-1952
American philosopher & educator

Rosen, Norma
John and Anzia: An American Romance.
Dutton 1989.
BRD 1991 p1594; KR v57 1989 p1426; NYTBR Ja 28,
　1990 p23.

414. Diamond, "Legs" (Jack)
1896-1931
American gangster

Kennedy, William
Legs: A Novel.
Coward, McCann & Geoghegan 1975.
BL v71 1975 p893; BRD 1975 p686; KR v43 1975
　p195; LJ v100 1975 p878.

415. Diana, Princess of Wales

1961-

Married Prince Charles, 1981; known as "Princess Di"

Brown, Alan
Princess.
Firecrest 1990.
KR v58 1990 p202; LJ v115 Mr 1, 1990 p113.

Fenton, Julia
Black Tie Only.
Contemporary Books 1990.
BL v86 1990 p1607; KR v58 1990 p289; LJ v115 Ap 1, 1990 p136.

King, Norman
The Prince and the Princess: The Love Story.
Simon & Schuster 1983.

Krin, Sylvie
Heir of Sorrows.
Private Eyes 1988.
Punch v295 D 9, 1988 p66.

Lefcourt, Peter
Di and I.
Random House 1994.
NYTBR Je 15, 1994 p45.

416. Diane de Poitiers

1499-1566

Mistress of Henry II of France

Grey, Shirley
The Crescent Moon: A Romance Set in the Time of Diane de Poitiers.
Milton House Books 1973.
B&B v19 N 1973 p132.

417. Dickens, Charles

1812-1870

English author; wrote *Tale of Two Cities, Christmas Carol, Pickwick Papers*, as well as several other classic works

Ackroyd, Peter
English Music.
Hamish Hamilton 1992.
KR v60 1992 p1002; Obs v5 My 24, 1992 p60; PW v239 1992 p485; TLS v268 My 22, 1992 p29.

Ansle, Dorothy P. (Hebe Elsna, pseud.)
Consider These Women.
Hale 1954.

Bloom, Ursula (Lozania Prole, pseud.)
The Romance of Charles Dickens.
Hale 1960 (Rpr. 1983).

Busch, Frederick
The Mutual Friend.
Harper & Row 1978 (Rpr. 1983).

BL v74 1978 p1163; BRD 1978 p184; KR v46 1978 p57; LJ v103 1978 p1079; NYTBR Ap 9, 1978 p10.

Curry, Jane Louise
JUV *What the Dickens!.*
McElderry Books 1991.
BL v88 1991 p326; BRD 1992 p449; SLJ v37 S 1991 p250.

Dale, W. V. Y.
I Rest My Claims.
Staples Press 1948.

Hardwick, Michael
The Gaslight Boy.
Weidenfeld & Nicolson 1976.
Novel based on Yorkshire Television's series, Dickens of London.
Lis v96 D 9, 1976 p745.

Kyle, Elisabeth
YA *Great Ambitions: A Story of the Early Years of Charles Dickens.*
Holt, Rinehart & Winston 1968.
BL v64 1968 p928; BRD 1968 p763; KR v35 1967 p1480; NYTBR Je 23, 1968 p22.

Lincoln, Victoria
Charles: A Novel.
Little, Brown 1962.
BL v58 1962 p751; BRD 1962 p723; FC 9th p320; KR v30 1962 p531; LJ v87 1962 p1151; NYTBR Ag 26, 1962 p30.

Manley, Seon
JUV *A Present for Charles Dickens.*
Westminster Press 1983.
CBRS v12 Ja 1984 p53; PW v224 O 14, 1983 p54.

McHugh, Stuart
Knock on the Nursery Door: Tales of the Dickens Children.
Joseph 1972.
LJ v98 1973 p1844.

Palmer, William
The Detective and Mr. Dickens: A Secret Victorian Journal Attributed to Wilkie Collins.
St. Martin's 1990.
BL v87 1990 p420; KR v58 1990 p1356; NYTBR D 16, 1990 p33.

Palmer, William
The Highwayman and Mr. Dickens.
St. Martin's 1992.
KR v60 1992 p884; LJ v117 Ag 1992 p151; PW v239 Jl 20, 1992 p230.

Rowland, Peter
The Disappearance of Edwin Drood.
St. Martin's 1992.
BL v88 1992 p1092; KR v60 1992 p81; PW v239 Ja 20, 1992 p50.

Watts, Alan S.
The Confessions of Charles Dickens: A Very Factual Fiction.
Peter Lang 1991.

418. Dickinson, Emily Elizabeth
1830-1886
American poet

Bedard, Michael
JUV *Emily.*
Doubleday 1992.
HB v69 Ja 1993 p72; PW v239 N 16, 1992 p63; SLJ v38 N 1992 p88.

Benet, Laura
Come Slowly, Eden: A Novel about Emily Dickinson.
Dodd, Mead 1942.
BL v39 1942 p33; BRD 1942 p55; NYTBR S 20, 1942 p6; SatR O 10, 1942 p11.

Edwards, Anne
The Hesitant Heart.
Random House 1974.
BRD 1974 p327; LJ v99 1974 p3282; NYTBR Mr 31, 1974 p40; PW v204 D 31, 1973 p21.

Fisher, Aileen
YA *We Dickinsons: The Life of Emily Dickinson as Seen through the Eyes of Her Brother Austin.*
Atheneum 1965.
BRD 1965 p406; HB v41 D 1965 p642; LJ v90 1965 p3804; NYTBR Ja 16, 1966 p36.

Gould, Jean
YA *Miss Emily.*
Houghton Mifflin 1946.
BRD 1946 p327; KR v14 1946 p72; LJ v71 1946 p764; NYTBR Ap 28, 1946 p32.

Malzberg, Barry
The Remaking of Sigmund Freud.
Ballantine 1985.
LJ v110 Ag 1985 p121; NYTBR Ag 4, 1985 p20.

Vernon, John
Peter Doyle: A Novel.
Random House 1991.
BL v87 1991 p980; KR v59 1991 p212; LJ v116 Mr 15, 1991 p119; NYTBR Jl 14, 1991 p9.

419. Didrikson, Mildred "Babe"
see Zaharias, "Babe" Didrikson

420. Digby, Kenelm, Sir
1603-1665
English diplomat & author

Hill, Pamela
Digby.
Hale 1987.
BritBkN Ap 1987 p213.

421. Dillinger, John Herbert
1902-1934
American bank robber

Collins, Max Allan
True Crime.
St. Martin's 1984.
BL v81 1985 p619; KR v52 1984 p1120; NYTBR Mr 10, 1985 p24; PW v226 N 2, 1984 p68.

Kelly, Jack
Mad Dog.
Atheneum 1992.
BL v88 1992 p1010; KR v60 1992 p11; LJ v117 F 1, 1992 p126.

Patterson, Harry
Dillinger: A Novel.
Stein & Day 1983.
KR v51 1983 p80; LJ v108 1983 p602; PW v223 Ja 14, 1983 p69.

422. Dinesan, Isak
see Blixen, Karen Christentze

423. Dinwiddie, Robert
1693-1770
British colonial administrator; governor of Virginia, 1751-1758

Frey, Ruby Frazier
Red Morning.
Putnam 1946.
BL v43 1946 p16; BRD 1946 p292; KR v14 1946 p278; LJ v71 1946 p978; NYTBR Jl 28, 1946 p14.

424. Diocletian
245-313
Roman emperor, 284-305

Mary, Cornelius, Sister
JUV *Marc's Choice: A Story of the Time of Diocletian.*
Bruce Pub. Co. 1957.

Mora, Ferenc
The Gold Coffin.
Corvina Press 1964.

425. Diogenes
412-323 BC
Greek philosopher

Jicinski, Blanca
Diogenes: A Novel Based on an Apocryphal Biography of the Greek Philosopher.
William-Frederick Press 1964.

426. Disney, Walt
1901-1966
American cartoonist, showman, & film producer; created the animated figure Mickey Mouse

Apple, Max
The Propheteers: A Novel.
Harper & Row 1987.
BL v83 1986 p529; BRD 1987 p58; KR v54 1986
p1810; LJ v112 Ja 1987 p103; NYTBR Mr 15, 1987
p13; PW v230 D 26, 1986 p53.

Collins, David R.
JUV *Walt Disney's Surprise Christmas Present.*
Broadman Press 1971.
LJ v96 1971 p3487.

Powers, Richard
Prisoner's Dilemma.
Beachtree/Morrow 1989.

427. Disraeli, Benjamin
1804-1881
British prime minister, author, & diplomat

Bonnet, Theodore
The Mudlark.
Doubleday 1949 (Rpr. 1978).
BRD 1949 p87; FC 11th p64; LJ v74 1949 p1092;
NYTBR Ag 14, 1949 p5.

Buruma, Ian
Playing the Game.
Farrar, Straus & Giroux 1991.
BL v87 1991 p2090; KR v59 1991 p620; LJ v116 Jl
1991 p131; NYTBR Ag 4, 1991 p11.

Edelman, Maurice
Disraeli in Love.
Stein & Day 1972.
BL v68 1972 p972; BRD 1972 p365; KR v40 1972
p344; LJ v97 1972 p2430; NYTBR Jl 9, 1972 p28;
TLS Jl 7, 1972 p765.

Edelman, Maurice
Disraeli Rising.
Stein & Day 1975.
BL v71 1975 p1107; BRD 1975 p364; KR v43 1975
p135; LJ v100 Mr 15, 1975 p602.

Leslie, Doris
The Prime Minister's Wife.
Doubleday 1960.
Also published as *The Perfect Wife.*
BRD 1961 p827; FC 8th p256; LJ v85 1960 p4391;
NYTBR Ja 15, 1961 p35.

Macbeth, George
Dizzy's Woman.
Cape 1986.
B&B O 1986 p35; Obs Ag 31, 1986 p20; PW v230 N
14, 1986 p51; TLS O 31, 1986 p1225.

428. Dix, Dorothea Lynde
1802-1887
American reformer, educator, & humanitarian

Melin, Grace Hathaway
JUV *Dorothea Dix, Girl Reformer.*
Bobbs-Merrill 1963.

429. Dixon, Jeremiah
d. 1777
English-born surveyor; with Charles Mason de-
termined boundary between Maryland and
Pennsylvania, called Mason-Dixon Line

Lefever, Barbara S.
The Stargazers: Story of Mason and Dixon.
Printing Express 1986.

430. Dodge, Mary Elizabeth Mapes
1831-1905
American author; editor of children's magazine
St. Nicholas; wrote *Hans Brinker & the Silver
Skates*

Mason, Miriam E.
JUV *Mary Mapes Dodge, Jolly Girl.*
Bobbs-Merrill 1949.
BRD 1949 p614; LJ v74 1949 p666; NYTBR Jl 17,
1949 p22.

431. Dodgson, Charles Lutwidge
see Carroll, Lewis, pseud.

432. Donatello
1386-1466
Italian sculptor

Manetti, Antonio
The Fat Woodworker.
Italica Press 1991.

433. Donne, John
1573-1631
English poet

Sandys, Elseph
Catch a Falling Star.
Blond & Briggs 1978.

Vining, Elizabeth Gray
Take Heed of Loving Me.
Lippincott 1964.
BRD 1964 p1200; FC 11th p634; LJ v89 1964 p137;
NYTBR Ja 5, 1964 p22; TLS Ja 14, 1965 p21.

434. Donnelly, Ignatius
1831-1901
American politician, reformer, & author

Sullivan, Oscar M.
North Star Sage: The Story of Ignatius Donnelly.
Vantage Press 1953.

435. Dostoyevsky, Fyodor Mikhailovich
1821-1881
Russian author; wrote the novels *Crime and Pun-
ishment, The Idiot, & Brothers Karamazov*

Coulter, Stephen
The Devil Inside: A Novel of Dostoevsky's Life.
Doubleday 1960.
BRD 1961 p296; KR v28 1960 p771; LJ v85 1960
p3461; NYTBR N 27, 1960 p48.

436. Doubleday, Abner
1819-1893
American army officer & reputed inventor of
baseball

Dunham, Montrew
JUV *Abner Doubleday, Young Baseball Pioneer.*
Bobbs-Merrill 1965.

437. Douglas, Alfred Bruce, Lord
1870-1945
English poet noted for his intimate relationship
with Oscar Wilde

Reilly, Robert
The God of Mirrors.
Atlantic Monthly Press 1986.
KR v53 1985 p1354; LJ v111 F 1, 1986 p95; NYTBR
Mr 2, 1986 p17; PW v228 N 29, 1985 p38.

438. Douglas, Stephen Arnold
1813-1861
American politician; noted for his debates with
Abraham Lincoln

Neyhart, Louise A.
JUV *Henry's Lincoln.*
Holiday House 1945 (Rpr. 1958).
BRD 1945 p523; HB v21 Jl 1945 p274; KR v13 1945
p271; LJ v70 1945 p688; NYTBR Jl 29, 1945 p21.

Seifert, Shirley
The Senator's Lady.
Lippincott 1967.
BL v64 1967 p491; KR v35 1967 p620; LJ v92 1967
p2434; PW v191 My 15, 1967 p40.

439. Douglass, Frederick
1817-1895
American abolitionist, author, & journalist

Doherty, Ivy Duffy
JUV *Rainbows of Promise.*
Review & Herald Pub. Association 1983.

Fuller, Edmund
A Star Pointed North.
Harper 1946.
BL v43 1946 p102; BRD 1946 p295; KR v14 1946
p431; LJ v71 1946 p1464; NYTBR N 3, 1946 p7.

440. Dowland, John
1563-1626
English composer & lutenist

Pollock, John Hackett
The Lost Nightingale.
Carter 1951.

441. Doyle, Arthur Conan, Sir
1859-1930
English author; created the character Sherlock
Holmes

Frost, Mark
The List of 7.
Morrow 1993.
NYTBR O 17, 1993 p49.

Harper, Leslie Vernet
The Secret Conan-Doyle Correspondence.
Mascom Publishers 1986.

Marks, Peter
Skullduggery.
Carroll & Graf 1987.
BL v83 1987 p1718; KR v55 1987 p882; LJ v112 Jl
1987 p96; NYTBR Ag 23, 1987 p11.

Saffron, Robert
The Demon Device: A Novel.
Putnam 1979.
KR v47 1979 p35.

Trow, M. J.
The Supreme Adventure of Inspector Lestrade.
Stein & Day 1985.
Originally published as *The Adventures of Inspector Les-*
trade.
KR v53 1985 p759.

Walsh, Ray
The Mycroft Memoranda.
St. Martin's 1984.
CR v245 Jl 1984 p45; Punch v286 Mr 21, 1984 p22;
TLS Mr 16, 1984 p270.

442. Drake, Francis, Sir
1540-1596
English naval officer & explorer; first Englishman to circumnavigate the globe

Foltz, Mary Jane
Awani.
Morrow 1964.
LJ v89 1964 p3470.

Fredman, John
Does the Queen Still Live?.
W.H. Allen 1979.
B&B v25 D 1979 p18.

Heyer, Georgette
Beauvallet.
Longmans, Green 1930 (Rpr. 1952, 1968, 1969).
BL v27 1930 p28; BRD 1930 p488; NYTBR Je 8, 1930
p8; SatR Mr 8, 1930 p809.

Hurd, Edith Thacher
JUV *The Golden Hind.*

Crowell 1960.
BRD 1961 p673; KR v28 1960 p452; LJ v85 1960
p3863; SatR Ja 21, 1961 p75.

Kent, Louise Andrews
JUV *He Went with Drake.*
Houghton Mifflin 1961.
LJ v87 1962 p848; NYTBR D 10, 1961 p46.

Latham, Jean Lee
YA *Drake, the Man They Called a Pirate.*
Harper 1960.
BRD 1961 p808; KR v28 1960 p96; LJ v85 1960
p2040.

Leadabrand, Russ
JUV *The Secret of Drake's Bay.*
Ritchie Press 1969.
LJ v95 1970 p1945.

Martini, Steven Paul
The Simeon Chamber.
D.I. Fine 1988.
KR v56 1988 p1089.

Mason, F. van Wyck
Golden Admiral.
Doubleday 1953.
BL v49 1953 p238; BRD 1953 p626; KR v20 1952
p770; LJ v78 1953 p374; NYTBR Mr 1, 1953 p30.

Smith, Ralph (S. H. Paxton, pseud.)
YA *The Dragon in New Albion.*
Little, Brown 1953.
BRD 1953 p730; KR v21 1953 p336; LJ v78 1953
p1702; NYTBR Ag 16, 1953 p14.

Strang, Herbert
On the Spanish Main.
Bobbs-Merrill 1907 (Rpr. 1944).
Reprinted in 1944 under title: *With Drake on the Spanish Main.*

Wibberley, Leonard
YA *The King's Beard.*
Ariel Books 1952.
BL v48 1952 p304; BRD 1952 p951; KR v20 1952
p192; LJ v77 1952 p912; NYTBR My 4, 1952 p30.

Young, Delbert A.
JUV *The Ghost Ship.*
Clarke, Irwin 1972.

443. Dreiser, Theodore
1871-1945
American author & editor; wrote *Sister Carrie* &
An American Tragedy

Burke, J. F.
Noah.
Sherbourne Press 1968.
KR v36 1968 p200.

444. Dreyfus, Alfred
1859-1935
French army officer wrongly convicted of high
treason

France, Anatole
Penguin Island.
J. Lane 1909 (Heavily reprinted).
BRD 1910 p141; NYTBR Ag 21, 1938 p17; SatR D
31, 1938 p19.

Hardwick, Michael
Prisoner of the Devil.
Proteus 1979.
Obs Ag 5, 1979 p36; PW v218 Jl 11, 1980 p87; WLB
v55 Ja 1981 p375.

Proust, Marcel
Jean Santeuil.
Weidenfeld & Nicolson 1955.
BRD 1956 p755; LJ v81 1956 p726; NYTBR F 12,
1956 p1.

445. Du Barry, Marie Jeanne, Comtesse
1746-1793
Mistress of Louis XV; guillotined

Bloom, Ursula (Lozania Prole, pseud.)
The Enchanting Courtesan.
Hale 1955 (Rpr. 1975).

Dumas, Alexandre
Memoirs of a Physician.
T.B. Peterson 1850 (Heavily reprinted).
Translation of *Memoires d'un Medecin.*

Smythe, David Mynders
Golden Venus.
Doubleday 1960.
LJ v85 1960 p1475; NYTBR Ap 24, 1960 p50.

446. Du Guesclin, Bertrand
1320-1380
French military commander

Carr, Shirley Niles
The King's Constable.
Garrett & Massie 1951.

447. Dulles, Allen Welsh
1893-1969
American lawyer & diplomat; director of CIA,
1953-1961

Mailer, Norman
Harlot's Ghost.
Random House 1991.
BL v88 1991 p5; BRD 1991 p1197; KR v59 1991
p960; LJ v116 S 1, 1991 p231; NYTBR S 29, 1991
p1.

Wiseman, Thomas
The Day before Sunrise.

Holt 1976.
BL v72 1976 p1094; KR v44 1976 p384; Lis v95 My 6,
  1976 p578; PW v209 Mr 1, 1976 p85.

448. Dumas, Alexandre
1802-1870
French author, novelist, & playwright; wrote
The Three Musketeers & *The Count of Monte
Cristo*

Endore, Guy
King of Paris.
Simon & Schuster 1956.
BL v53 1956 p146; BRD 1956 p293; FC 11th p163;
  KR v24 1956 p363; LJ v81 1956 p1915.

449. Dumas, Alexandre (fils)
1824-1895
French author & dramatist; son of Alexandre
Dumas (1802-1870)

Endore, Guy
King of Paris.
Simon & Schuster 1956.
BL v53 1956 p146; BRD 1956 p293; FC 11th p163;
  KR v24 1956 p363; LJ v81 1956 p1915.

450. Dunbar, Paul Laurence
1872-1906
American author & poet

Gould, Jean
JUV *That Dunbar Boy.*
Dodd, Mead 1958.

451. Duncan, Isadora
1878-1927
American dancer

Stokes, Sewell
Recital in Paris: A Novel.
P. Davies 1954.

Weiss, David
*The Spirit and the Flesh: A Novel Inspired by the
  Life of Isadore Duncan.*
Doubleday 1959.
BRD 1960 p1414; KR v27 1959 p615; LJ v84 1959
  p3493; NYTBR N 15, 1959 p56.

452. Duplessis, Marie
1824-1847
French courtesan & model; well-known in Paris
in the 1840s

Winwar, Frances
The Last Love of Camille.
Harper 1954.
BL v50 1954 p269; BRD 1954 p965; KR v22 1954
  p71; NYTBR Ap 18, 1954 p20.

453. Durer, Albrecht
1471-1528
German painter & engraver

Fisher, Frances Hope
*Written in the Stars: A Novel about Albrecht
  Durer.*
Harper 1951.
BRD 1951 p291; KR v19 1951 p163; NYTBR Jl 1,
  1951 p15.

454. DuSable, Jean Baptiste
1750-1818
American pioneer; opened first trading post on
site of modern-day Chicago

Du Bois, Shirley Graham
YA *Jean Baptiste Pointe de Sable: Founder of Chicago.*
Messner 1953.
BRD 1953 p377; LJ v78 1953 p746; NYTBR Ag 2,
  1953 p14.

455. Duse, Eleanora
1859-1924
Italian actress

Stubbs, Jean
The Passing Star.
Macmillan 1970 (Rpr. 1985).
B&B v15 Je 1970 p39.

456. Dvorak, Anton
1841-1904
Czech composer

Purdy, Claire Lee
YA *Antonin Dvorak, Composer from Bohemia.*
Messner 1950.
BL v47 1951 p191; BRD 1951 p721; KR v18 1950
  p521; LJ v76 1951 p123.

Skvorecky, Josef
Dvorak in Love.
Knopf 1986.
Translation of *Scherzo Capriccioso*
BRD 1987 p1737; KR v54 1986 p1756; LJ v112 F 15,
  1987 p163; NYTBR F 22, 1987 p11; PW v230 D
  19, 1986 p46.

457. Earhart, Amelia
1898-1937
American aviator; first woman to fly solo across
Atlantic; disappeared in trans-Pacific flight

Tanous, Peter
The Earhart Mission.
Simon & Schuster 1978.
BL v75 1978 p528; KR v46 1978 p1214; PW v214 D
  4, 1978 p59.

Thayer, James Stewart
The Earhart Betrayal.

Putnam 1980.
KR v48 1980 p535; PW v217 Ap 18, 1980 p77; SLJ
  v27 S 1980 p93.

458. Early, Jubal Anderson
1816-1894
American Confederate general

Bellah, James Warner
The Valiant Virginians.
Ballantine 1953.

459. Earp, Wyatt
1848-1929
Deputy marshall in Dodge City, KS; survived famous gunfight at the OK Corral, 1881

Berger, Thomas
Little Big Man.
Dial 1964 (Heavily reprinted).
BRD 1964 p97; LJ v89 1964 p4560; NYTBR O 11,
  1964 p42; SatR O 3, 1964 p38.

Estleman, Loren D.
Bloody Season.
Bantam 1987.
BL v84 1987 p513; KR v55 1987 p1593; LJ v113 Ja
  1988 p98.

Everitt, David
Legends.
PaperJacks 1988.

Garfield, Brian
Sliphammer.
Dell 1970.

Henry, Will
Who Rides with Wyatt.
Random House 1955 (Rpr. 1989).
NYTBR Ap 3, 1955 p31.

Holbrook, Stewart
YA *Wyatt Earp, U.S. Marshall*.
Random House 1956.
BL v53 1956 p29; BRD 1956 p451; LJ v81 1956
  p2051; NYTBR N 25, 1956 p56.

Johnson, Enid
YA *Wyatt Earp: Gunfighting Marshall*.
J. Messner 1956.

Jones, Kathy
Wild Western Desire.
Kensington Pub. Corp. 1993.
BL v89 1993 p970.

Krepps, Robert W.
Hour of the Gun.
Fawcett 1967.

Swarthout, Glendon
The Old Colts.
Thorndike Press 1985.
BL v81 1985 p1297; KR v53 1985 p347; LJ v110 Je 1,
  1985 p146; PW v227 Mr 29, 1985 p65.

460. Eastman, George
1854-1932
American inventor & philanthropist; invented roll film & the Kodak camera

Clune, Henry W.
By His Own Hand.
Macmillan 1952.
BL v49 1952 p105; BRD 1952 p186; KR v20 1952
  p612; LJ v77 1952 p1896.

Henry, Joanne Landers
YA *George Eastman, Young Photographer*.
Bobbs-Merrill 1959.

461. Eddy, Mary Baker Morse
1821-1910
American religious leader; founder of Christian Science Religious Movement

Vidal, Gore
Live from Golgotha.
Random House 1992.
NYTBR O 4, 1992 p13; NW v120 Ag 31, 1992 p69;
  Time v140 S 28, 1992 p64.

462. Edison, Thomas Alva
1847-1931
American inventor; over 1,000 inventions including the phonograph and incandescent lamp

Dandola, John
West of Orange.
Tory Corner Editions 1990.

Davis, Christopher
A Peep into the 20th Century.
Harper & Row 1971 (Rpr. 1985).
BRD 1971 p318; KR v39 1971 p313; LJ v96 1971
  p3913; NYTBR My 30, 1971 p4.

Guthridge, Sue
JUV *Tom Edison, Boy Inventor*.
Bobbs-Merrill 1947 (Rpr. 1959, 1986).
Also published as *Thomas A. Edison, Young Inventor*.

McCreary, Lew
Mount's Mistake.
Atlantic Monthly Press 1987.
KR v55 1987 p1416; NYTBR D 27, 1987 p18.

McMahon, Thomas A.
Loving Little Egypt.
Viking 1987.
BW v17 F 22, 1987 p9; KR v54 1986 p1751; LJ v112 F
  1, 1987 p93; NYTBR F 8, 1987 p16; PW v230 D
  12, 1986 p42.

Meadowcroft, Enid La Monte
JUV *The Story of Thomas Alva Edison*.
Grosset & Dunlap 1952.

Serviss, Garrett Putnam
Edison's Conquest of Mars.

Carcosa House 1947.
Published serially in the *New York Evening Journal*,
1898.

Villiers de L'Isle-Adam, Comte de
Eve of the Future Eden.
Coronado Press 1981.
Translation of *L'Eve Future.*

Zagst, Michael
"M.H." Meets President Harding.
D.I. Fine 1987.
KR v55 1987 p258; LJ v112 Ap 15, 1987 p102; PW
v231 Mr 13, 1987 p71.

463. Edward I
1239-1307
King of England, 1272-1307

Bennetts, Pamela
A Dragon for Edward.
St. Martin's 1975.
KR v43 1975 p580; LJ v100 1975 p1344.

Doherty, P. C.
Angel of Death.
St. Martin's 1990.
KR v58 1990 p223; LJ v115 Ap 1, 1990 p140.

Doherty, P. C.
The Crown in Darkness.
St. Martin's 1988.
KR v56 1988 p574; PW v233 My 13, 1988 p267.

Doherty, P. C.
Satan in St. Mary's.
St. Martin's 1986.
KR v55 1987 p258; LJ v112 Ap 1, 1987 p166; PW
v231 F 20, 1987 p74.

Fairburn, Eleanor
*The Green Popinjays: A Novel Based on Historical
Fact.*
Ulverscroft 1962.

Haycraft, Molly
The King's Daughters.
Lippincott 1971.
BL v68 1971 p328; KR v39 1971 p764; LJ v96 1971
p2791.

Hibbert, Eleanor (Jean Plaidy, pseud.)
Edward Longshanks.
Hale 1979.
BL v78 1982 p942; HT v30 Ja 1980 p55.

McGraw, Barbara
Dona Eleanora and Lord Edward.
Scott, Foresman 1982.

Trease, Geoffrey
JUV *The Baron's Hostage.*
T. Nelson 1975.
BL v72 1975 p459; KR v43 1975 p667; LJ v78 1953
p1340; SLJ v22 S 1975 p127.

Trevaskis, Eve
The Lion of England.
Hale 1975 (Rpr. 1979).

464. Edward II
1284-1327
King of England, 1307-1327

Barnes, Margaret Campbell
Isabel the Fair.
Macrae Smith 1957.
BL v54 1957 p135; BRD 1957 p47; FC 11th p41.

Bennetts, Pamela
The She-Wolf.
Hale 1975.

Clarke, Brenda (Brenda Honeyman, pseud.)
The King's Minions.
Hale 1974.

Dakers, Elaine (Jane Lane, pseud.)
A Secret Chronicle.
P. Davies 1977.

Druon, Maurice
The She-Wolf of France.
Scribner 1960.
BRD 1961 p372; FC 10th p149; NYTBR Ja 15, 1961
p5; SatR Ja 14, 1961 p32.

Dymoke, Juliet
The Lion of Mortimer.
Ace Books 1979.

Evans, Jean
A Brittle Glory.
Hale 1977.

Graham, Alice Walworth
The Vows of the Peacock.
Doubleday 1955.
BL v51 1955 p367; BRD 1955 p947; KR v23 1955
p16; NYTBR My 22, 1955 p24.

Hibbert, Eleanor (Jean Plaidy, pseud.)
The Follies of the King.
Hale 1980 (Rpr. 1982).
BL v78 1982 p942; KR v50 1982 p92; PW v221 F 19,
1982 p59.

Lewis, Hilda
Harlot Queen.
D. McKay 1970.
KR v38 1970 p78; LJ v95 1970 p1503; LJ v95 1970
p3078.

Penford, John Colin
The Gascon.
Wild Rose Books 1984.

Trevaskis, Eve
The Lord of Misrule.
Hale 1972.

465. Edward III
1312-1377
King of England, 1327-1377

Bennetts, Pamela
The She-Wolf.
Hale 1975.

Clarke, Brenda (Brenda Honeyman, pseud.)
Edward, the Warrior.
Hale 1975.

Clarke, Brenda (Brenda Honeyman, pseud.)
The Golden Griffin.
Hale 1976.

De Angeli, Marguerite
JUV *The Door in the Wall.*
Doubleday 1949.
Won the 1950 Newbery award.
BL v46 1949 p85; BRD 1949 p224; KR v17 1949
   p552; LJ v75 1950 p50; NYTBR N 20, 1949 p58.

Doherty, P. C.
The Death of a King: A Medieval Mystery.
St. Martin's 1985.
KR v53 1985 p1204; PW v228 N 15, 1985 p48.

Druon, Maurice
The Lily and the Lion.
Scribner 1961.
Final volume of *The Accursed Kings* series.
BL v58 1962 p476; BRD 1962 p324; LJ v87 1962
   p1629; NYTBR F 18, 1962 p40.

Eaton, Evelyn
The King Is a Witch.
Cassell 1965 (Rpr. 1974).
AB v56 O 20, 1975 p1707; NatR v27 Ag 15, 1975
   p897.

Hibbert, Eleanor (Jean Plaidy, pseud.)
The Vow of the Heron.
Hale 1980.
Sequel to *Follies of the King.*
BL v78 1982 p1129; KR v50 1982 p513.

Kalechofsky, Roberta
*Bodmin, 1349: An Epic Novel of Christians and
   Jews in the Plague Years.*
Micah 1988.
PW v233 My 20, 1988 p86.

Powers, Anne
Ride with Danger.
Bobbs-Merrill 1958.
BRD 1958 p871; LJ v83 1958 p2076; NYTBR Je 8,
   1958 p44.

Trevaskis, Eve
King's Wake.
Hale 1977.

466. Edward IV
1442-1483
King of England, 1461-1470, 1471-1483

Andrew, Prudence
A Question of Choice.
Hutchinson 1962.
NYTBR D 9, 1962 p38.

Bennetts, Pamela
The Black Plantagenet.
Hale 1969 (Rpr. 1972).

Evans, Jean
The Divided Rose.
Hale 1972.

Hibbert, Eleanor (Jean Plaidy, pseud.)
The Goldsmith's Wife.
Appleton-Century-Crofts 1950 (Rpr. 1974).
BRD 1950 p431; KR v18 1950 p70; LJ v99 1974
   p1565; NYTBR Mr 12, 1950 p29.

Jarman, Rosemary Hawley
The King's Grey Mare.
Little, Brown 1973.
BRD 1974 p608; KR v41 1973 p576; LJ v98 1973
   p2333.

Watson, Julia
Son of York: A Novel of Edward IV.
Sphere Books 1973.

Westcott, Jan
The White Rose.
Putnam 1969.
Also published as *The Lion's Share.*
KR v37 1969 p533; LJ v94 1969 p3470.

467. Edward VI
1537-1553
King of England, 1547-1553; son of Henry VIII
and Jane Seymour

Chapman, Hester W.
The Last Tudor King.
J. Cape 1958 (Rpr. 1974, 1982).
BRD 1960 p231; KR v27 1959 p591; LJ v84 1959
   p3114.

Churchill, Rosemary
*Conflict for a Crown: The Story of King Edward
   VI's Reign.*
Hale 1977.

Dakers, Elaine (Jane Lane, pseud.)
Heirs of Squire Harry.
P. Davies 1974.
TLS Ja 17, 1975 p48.

Twain, Mark
JUV *The Prince and the Pauper.*
Several editions exist, including some designed for ju-
   venile and young adult readers.
LJ v63 1938 p81; LJ v73 1948 p1829; NYTBR D 2,
   1917 p512.

468. Edward VII

1841-1910
King of England, 1901-1910; son of Queen Victoria

Butler, David E.
Edward VII, Prince of Hearts.
Weidenfeld & Nicolson 1974.
Also published as *Edward the King.*
Obs Ap 13, 1975 p30.

Cartland, Barbara
The Race for Love.
Duron 1978.

Hall, Robert L.
The King Edward Plot.
McGraw-Hill 1980.
BRD 1981 p604; KR v47 1979 p1390; LJ v105 1980
p641; NYTBR Mr 23, 1980 p33.

Hardwick, Mollie
The Duchess of Duke Street.
Holt 1976.
First published in England in two volumes: book one,
This Way Up, and book two, *The Golden Years.*
FC 11th p270.

Tyler-Whittle, Michael S.
Bertie, Albert Edward, Prince of Wales.
St. Martin's 1974.
KR v42 1974 p1324; LJ v100 1975 p411.

Tyler-Whittle, Michael S.
Edward: Edward the Seventh King and Emperor.
St. Martin's Press 1975.
KR v43 1975 p940; PW v208 S 8, 1975 p52.

469. Edward VIII

1894-1972
King of England, 1936; abdicated throne to
marry American Wallis Simpson; thereafter
Duke of Windsor

Edwards, Anne
Wallis: The Novel.
Morrow 1991.
BL v87 1991 p1282; KR v59 1991 p345; NYTBR Je 9,
1991 p40.

Findley, Timothy
Famous Last Words.
Clarke, Irwin 1981.
BRD 1982 p421; KR v50 1982 p434; LJ v107 1982
p1010; NYTBR Ag 15, 1982 p10.

Fisher, Graham
The Plot to Kill Wallis Simpson.
St. Martin's 1989.
KR v57 N 1, 1989 p1549; PW v236 O 27, 1989 p55.

Kilian, Michael
Dance on a Sinking Ship.
St. Martin's 1988.

KR v55 1987 p1692; LJ v113 Mr 1, 1988 p77; PW
v232 Ja 8, 1988 p72.

Patterson, Harry
To Catch a King.
Stein & Day 1979.
KR v47 1979 p884; LJ v104 1979 p2239; NYTBR O
28, 1979 p49; WCRB v5 S 1979 p27.

Smith, A. C. H.
Edward and Mrs. Simpson.
Weidenfeld & Nicolson 1978.

470. Edward the Black Prince

1330-1376
Eldest son of Edward III; Prince of Wales

Bennetts, Pamela
Don Pedro's Captain.
St. Martin's 1978.
KR v46 1978 p447.

Doyle, Arthur Conan
The White Company.
Tauchnitz 1891 (Heavily reprinted).
FC 9th p145.

471. Edward the Confessor

1002-1066
King of England, 1042-1066

Anand, Valerie
Gildenford.
Scribner 1977.
KR v45 1977 p366; LJ v102 1977 p1403.

Anand, Valerie
The Norman Pretender.
Scribner 1979.
KR v47 1979 p1272; LJ v105 1980 p118; PW v216 D
10, 1979 p59.

Duggan, Alfred Leo
The Cunning of the Dove.
Pantheon 1960.
BL v56 1960 p568; BRD 1960 p385; KR v28 1960
p244; LJ v85 1960 p1935; NYTBR Ap 10, 1960 p4.

Oliver, Jane
JUV *Faraway Princess.*
St. Martin's 1962.
LJ v87 1962 p3204; NYTBR O 14, 1962 p34.

Rice, Sile
The Saxon Tapestry.
Arcade 1992.
BL v88 1991 p681; PW v238 N 1, 1991 p73.

472. Edwards, Jonathan

1703-1758
American theologian & philosopher; wrote *Freedom of the Will*

Coombe, Jack
Consider My Servant: A Novel Based upon the Life of Jonathan Edwards.
Exposition Press 1957.

473. Einstein, Albert
1879-1955
German-born American physicist; formulated theories of relativity; won Nobel Prize, 1921

Appel, Allen
Till the End of Time.
Doubleday 1990.
BL v87 1990 p24; KR v58 1990 p893; LJ v115 S 1, 1990 p253; PW v237 Je 29, 1990 p85.

Gitlin, Todd
The Murder of Albert Einstein.
Farrar Straus Giroux 1992.
KR v60 1992 p737; PW v239 Je 22, 1992 p44.

Kaminsky, Stuart M.
Smart Moves.
St. Martin's 1986.
BL v83 1987 p983; KR v55 1987 p177; PW v231 Ja 23, 1987 p64.

Lightman, Alan P.
Einstein's Dreams.
Pantheon 1993.
BL v89 1992 p580; KR v60 1992 p1276; NYTBR Ja 3, 1993 p10.

Sinclair, Upton
A World to Win.
Viking 1946.
BRD 1946 p756; LJ v71 1946 p759.

474. Eisenhower, Dwight David
1890-1969
American general & 34th US President

Beckhard, Arthur J.
YA *The Story of Dwight D. Eisenhower.*
Grosset & Dunlap 1956.
BRD 1957 p64; KR v24 1956 p755; LJ v82 1957 p224; NYTBR Ja 27, 1957 p30.

Phillippi, Wendell C.
Dear Ike.
Two-Star Press 1991.

Ridgway, James M.
Eisenhower and the Great Rebellion, 1861-1863.
Cannonade Press 1982.

Shavelson, Melville
Ike.
Warner Books 1989.
LJ v104 1979 p1162.

475. Eleanor of Aquitaine
1122-1204
Marriage to Louis VII of France annulled; married Henry II of England, 1154

Bourne, Peter
The Court of Love.
Hutchinson 1958 (Rpr. 1974).

Cooke, Carol Phillips
Through a Glass Darkly: The Story of Eleanor of Aquitaine.
M.H.I., Concord Printing Co. 1990.

Hibbert, Eleanor (Jean Plaidy, pseud.)
The Courts of Love.
Putnam 1988.
CSM v80 F 12, 1988 p20; KR v56 1988 p96; PW v233 Ja 22, 1988 p104.

Hibbert, Eleanor (Jean Plaidy, pseud.)
The Plantagenet Prelude.
Hale 1976 (Rpr. 1980).
BL v76 1980 p1411; KR v48 1980 p241; LJ v105 1980 p1103.

Hibbert, Eleanor (Jean Plaidy, pseud.)
The Revolt of the Eaglets.
Hale 1977 (Rpr. 1980).
BL v76 1980 p1658; KR v48 1980 p734.

Holland, Sheila
Eleanor of Aquitaine.
Hale 1978.

Hutchins, Linda
Mortal Love: A Novel of Eleanor of Aquitaine.
Doubleday 1980.
BS v40 Jl 1980 p158; KR v48 1980 p154; LJ v105 1980 p878; PW v217 F 1, 1980 p103.

Konigsburg, E. L.
JUV *A Proud Taste for Scarlet and Miniver.*
Atheneum 1973.
BL v70 1973 p287; BRD 1974 p672; KR v41 1973 p685; LJ v98 1973 p3147; NYTBR O 14, 1973 p8.

Lee, Rowena
The Diadems of a Duchess: A Reconstruction of the Life and Times of Eleanor of Aquitaine.
Hale 1972.

Lofts, Norah
Eleanor the Queen: The Story of the Most Famous Woman of the Middle Ages.
Doubleday 1955.
Also published as *Queen in Waiting.*
BL v52 1955 p16; BRD 1955 p568; KR v23 1955 p330; LJ v80 1955 p2650; NYTBR Jl 24, 1955 p18.

Mackin, Jeanne
The Queen's War: A Novel of Eleanor of Aquitaine.
St. Martin's 1991.
BL v87 1991 p1780; KR v59 1991 p202; LJ v116 Mr 15, 1991 p116.

Trouncer, Margaret
Eleanor: The Two Marriages of a Queen.
Heinemann 1967.
Punch v252 F 22, 1967 p282.

476. Elgar, Edward William
1857-1934
English composer & conductor

Alldritt, Keith
Elgar on the Journey to Hanley.
St. Martin's 1979.
BL v76 1979 p216; LJ v104 1979 p1481.

Hamilton-Paterson, James
Gerontius.
Macmillan 1989.
BL v87 1991 p1692; BRD 1991 p783; KR v59 1991
p129; LJ v116 Ap 1, 1991 p149; NYTBR Je 30,
1991 p22.

477. Elgin, Thomas Bruce
1766-1841
English diplomat & art connoiseur

Vrettos, Theodore
YA *Lord Elgin's Lady.*
Houghton Mifflin 1982.
BL v78 1982 p1425; BW v12 Je 6, 1982 p6; KR v50
1982 p371; LJ v107 1982 p906.

478. Elijah
Old Testament prophet

Bothwell, Jean
YA *Flame in the Sky: A Story of the Days of the
Prophet Elijah.*
Vanguard Press 1954.
BRD 1955 p97; KR v22 1954 p754; LJ v79 1954
p2499; NYTBR Ja 16, 1955 p28.

Paul, Louis
Dara the Cypriot.
Simon & Schuster 1959.
BL v55 1959 p417; BRD 1959 p784; KR v27 1959
p22; LJ v84 1959 p1153.

Zador, Henry B.
Hear the Word: A Novel about Elijah and Elisha.
McGraw-Hill 1962.

479. Eliot, George, pseud.
1819-1880
English novelist; wrote *The Mill on the Floss*

Glover, Halcott
Both Sides of the Blanket.
Constable 1945.

Glover, Halcott
Louise and Mr. Tudor.
Constable 1946.

White, Terence De Vere
Johnnie Cross: A Novel.
St. Martin's 1983.
BL v80 1984 p718; KR v51 1983 p1138; PW v224 O
21, 1983 p60.

480. Elizabeth I
1533-1603
Queen of England, 1558-1603; daughter of
Henry VIII & Anne Boleyn

Ansle, Dorothy P. (Hebe Elsna, pseud.)
Prelude for Two Queens.
Collins 1972.

Ansle, Dorothy P. (Hebe Elsna, pseud.)
The Queen's Ward.
Collins 1967 (Rpr. 1980).

Anthony, Evelyn
All the Queen's Men.
Crowell 1960.
BL v56 1960 p683; FC 11th p19; KR v28 1960 p250;
LJ v85 1960 p1616; TLS Je 3, 1960 p358.

Beatty, John; Beatty, Patricia
YA *Holdfast.*
Morrow 1972.
BL v69 1972 p200; KR v40 1972 p946; LJ v97 1972
p3810; PW v202 O 16, 1972 p50.

Bennetts, Pamela
Envoy from Elizabeth.
St. Martin's 1973.
KR v41 1973 p825; LJ v98 1973 p3281.

Bennetts, Pamela
My Dear Lover England.
St. Martin's 1975.
KR v43 Ja 15, 1975 p80; LJ v100 1975 p500.

Birkhead, Margaret
Trust and Treason.
St. Martin's 1991.
BL v87 1990 p801; KR v58 1990 p1473; LJ v115 D
1990 p157; PW v237 N 9, 1990 p45.

Bloom, Ursula (Lozania Prole, pseud.)
The Little Wig-Maker of Bread Street.
Hale 1959.

Bloom, Ursula (Lozania Prole, pseud.)
The Loves of a Virgin Princess.
Hale 1968 (Rpr. 1984).

Byrd, Elizabeth
Immortal Queen.
Ballantine 1956.
BRD 1956 p150; FC 8th p64; NYTBR S 9, 1956 p32.

Cartland, Barbara
Messenger of Love.
Hutchinson 1961.

Coates, Sheila
The Queen's Letter.
Hale 1973.

Davenat, Colette
Deborah.
Morrow 1973.
KR v41 1973 p472; LJ v98 1973 p2331.

Delves-Broughton, Josephine
The Heart of a Queen.
Whittlesey House 1950.
Also published as *Crown Imperial.*
BL v46 1950 p275; BRD 1950 p239; KR v18 1950
   p108; NYTBR Ap 9, 1950 p17.

Dessau, Joanna
Absolute Elizabeth.
St. Martin's 1979.
KR v47 1979 p77; LJ v104 1979 p647.

Dessau, Joanna
The Red-Haired Brat.
St. Martin's 1979.
KR v46 1978 p1263; LJ v104 1979 p127.

Eagar, Frances
JUV *Time Tangle.*
T. Nelson 1976.
GP v15 My 1976 p2880; KR v45 1977 p539; SLJ v24
   O 1977 p88.

Eckerson, Olive
My Lord Essex.
Holt 1955.
BL v51 Ap 15, 1955 p342; BRD 1955 p268; FC 7th
   p121; LJ v80 1955 p561; NYTBR Mr 27, 1955 p31.

Eldridge, Denise
JUV *The Queen's Choyce.*
Macmillan 1974.

Ellis, Amanda M.
Elizabeth, the Woman.
Dutton 1951.
BL v48 1951 p85; BRD 1951 p266; KR v19 1951
   p306; LJ v76 1951 p1220; NYTBR S 2, 1951 p10.

Evans, Jean
The Rose and Ragged Staff.
Hale 1974.

Finney, Patricia
The Firedrake's Eye.
St. Martin's 1992.
LJ v117 Je 1, 1992 p176; TLS Ja 24, 1992 p22.

Garrett, George
Death of the Fox.
Doubleday 1971 (Rpr. 1991).
BL v68 1971 p182; BRD 1971 p477; FC 11th p229;
   KR v39 1971 p1036; LJ v96 1971 p2540; NYTBR S
   26, 1971 p52.

Garrett, George
The Succession: A Novel of Elizabeth and James.
Doubleday 1983 (Rpr. 1991).
BL v80 1983 p313; BRD 1984 p557; KR v51 1983
   p1013; LJ v108 1983 p2100; NYTBR D 25, 1983 p6.

Hamilton, Julia
The Last of the Tudors.
Hale 1971.

Harnett, Cynthia
YA *Stars of Fortune.*
Methuen 1956 (Rpr. 1984, 1990).
BL v53 1957 p283; BRD 1957 p398; NYTBR F 17,
   1957 p30; SatR D 22, 1956 p38.

Harwood, Alice
So Merciful a Queen, So Cruel a Woman.
Bobbs-Merrill 1958.
BL v54 1958 p611; BRD 1958 p497; FC 9th p231.

Heaven, Constance
The Queen and the Gypsy.
Coward, McCann & Geoghegan 1977.
BL v73 1977 p1646; KR v44 1976 p1317; LJ v102
   1977 p512; SLJ v23 My 1977 p83.

Hibbert, Eleanor (Jean Plaidy, pseud.)
Gay Lord Robert.
Putnam 1971.
BL v68 1971 p36; KR v39 1971 p696; LJ v96 1971
   p3488.

Hibbert, Eleanor (Jean Plaidy, pseud.)
Queen of This Realm: The Story of Elizabeth I.
Hale 1984.

Irwin, Margaret
Elizabeth and the Prince of Spain.
Harcourt, Brace 1953.
BL v50 1953 p168; BRD 1953 p467; FC 10th p278;
   KR v21 1953 p552; LJ v78 1953 p1686; NYTBR N
   29, 1953 p46.

Irwin, Margaret
YA *Elizabeth: Captive Princess.*
Harcourt, Brace 1948.
Sequel to *Young Bess.*
BL v45 D 15, 1948 p137; BRD 1948 p413; LJ v73
   1948 p1665; NYTBR D 5, 1948 p47; SHSLC 10th
   p508.

Irwin, Margaret
Young Bess.
Harcourt, Brace & Co. 1945.
Part of a trilogy entitled *The Story of Elizabeth Tudor.*
BRD 1945 p353; LJ v70 1945 p219.

Kay, Susan
YA *Legacy.*
Crown 1986.
BL v82 1986 p834; Kliatt v21 S 1987 p16; KR v54
   1986 p234; LJ v111 Ap 1, 1986 p161; NYTBR My
   11, 1986 p24.

Kenyon, Frank Wilson
*Shadow in the Sun: A Novel about the Virgin
   Queen Elizabeth I.*
Crowell 1958.
BRD 1959 p559; KR v26 1958 p526; NYTBR O 26,
   1958 p54; SatR D 20, 1958 p25.

Letton, Jennette; Letton, Francis
The Robsart Affair.
Harper 1956 (Rpr. 1978).
BL v53 1957 p224; BRD 1956 p561; FC 7th p219; KR
 v24 1956 p560; NYTBR N 18, 1956 p60.

Letton, Jennette; Letton, Francis
The Young Elizabeth.
Harper & Brothers 1953.
BL v49 1953 p340; BRD 1953 p560; KR v21 1953
 p271; LJ v78 1953 p1164; NYTBR Je 7, 1953 p23.

Long, Freda M.
The Queen's Progress.
Hale 1971.

Malpass, Eric
A House of Women: A Novel.
St. Martin's 1975.
KR v43 1975 p936; PW v208 Ag 25, 1975 p284.

Melnikoff, Pamela
JUV *Plots and Players.*
Blackie 1988.
BRD 1989 p1125; NYTBR My 21, 1989 p34; SLJ v35
 Jl 1989 p83.

O'Neill, Joseph
Chosen by the Queen.
V. Gollancz 1947.

Osborne, Maggie
Chase the Heart.
Morrow 1987.
KR v54 1986 p1681; LJ v112 Ja 1987 p110; PW v230
 N 28, 1986 p66.

Peters, Maureen
The Peacock Queen.
Hale 1972.

Preston, Hugh
A Time to Lose.
St. Martin's 1977.

Roberts, Keith
Pavane.
Doubleday 1968.
KR v36 1968 p930; LJ v94 1969 p1347.

Robertson, R. Garcia
The Spiral Dance.
Morrow 1991.
KR v59 1991 p1050.

Ross Williamson, Hugh
The Sisters.
Joseph 1958.
Also published as *Conspirators and the Crown.*
BL v55 1959 p503; BRD 1959 p858; NYTBR Ap 19,
 1959 p6.

Schoonover, Lawrence
To Love a Queen.
Little, Brown 1973.
BL v69 1973 p791; KR v40 1972 p1444; LJ v98 1973
 p86.

Scott, Walter Sir
YA *Kenilworth.*
A. Constable 1821 (Heavily reprinted).
BRD 1905 p311; NYTBR D 5, 1908 p763.

Sheedy, Alexandra E.
YA *She Was Nice to Mice: The Other Side of Eliza-
 beth's I's Character Never before Revealed by
 Previous Historians.*
McGraw-Hill 1975.
KR v43 1975 p849; PW v208 Jl 28, 1975 p121; SLJ
 v22 O 1975 p108.

Stolz, Mary
JUV *Bartholomew Fair.*
Greenwillow 1990.
BL v86 1990 p2182; KR v58 1990 p1092.

Strode-Jackson, Myrtle
Tansy Taniard.
Scribner 1945.
Also published as *Queen and Tansy Taniard.*
BL v42 1945 p57; BRD 1945 p687; KR v13 1945
 p228; NYTBR S 23, 1945 p22.

Sutcliff, Rosemary
JUV *The Queen Elizabeth Story.*
Oxford University Press 1950.
BL v47 1950 p48; BRD 1950 p880; KR v18 1950
 p417; LJ v75 1950 p1515; NYTBR Ag 20, 1950 p16.

Thorpe, Helen
Elizabeth, Queen and Woman.
Roy Publishers 1972.
BL v68 1972 p588; KR v40 1972 p96.

Turner, Judy
Cousin to the Queen: The Story of Lettice Knollys
Constable 1972.

Westcott, Jan
The Tower and the Dream.
Putnam 1974.
BL v70 1974 p774; KR v41 1973 p1286; LJ v99 1974
 p154; PW v204 D 10, 1973 p30.

Wheelwright, Jere H.
The Strong Room.
Scribner 1948.
BL v44 1948 p217; BRD 1948 p910; KR v15 1947
 p659; LJ v73 1948 p198; NYTBR Mr 7, 1948 p26.

York, Robert
*My Lord the Fox: The Secret Documents of An-
 thony Woodcott Concerning Queen Elizabeth I
 and Anne Boleyn.*
Vanguard 1986.
BL v82 1986 p1437; PW v229 My 16, 1986 p69.

481. Elizabeth II
1926-
Queen of England; succeeded father George VI
to throne upon his death in 1952

Gallico, Paul
Coronation.

Doubleday 1962 (Rpr. 1981).
LJ v87 1962 p3066; NYTBR O 14, 1962 p42.

Mann, Paul
The Britannia Contract.
Carroll & Graf 1993.

Shute, Nevil
In the Wet.
Morrow 1953.
BL v49 1953 p285; BRD 1953 p700; FC 9th p459; KR
    v21 1953 p80; LJ v78 1953 p595; TLS My 15, 1953
    p313.

Van Greenaway, Peter
*The Man Who Held the Queen to Ransom and
    Sent Parliament Packing.*
Weidenfeld & Nicolson 1968.
BL v65 1969 p1166; KR v37 1969 p139; LJ v94 1969
    p1649; NYTBR Mr 30, 1969 p43.

482. Elizabeth of Hungary, Saint
1207-1231
Daughter of Andrew II of Hungary; canonized,
1235

Haughton, Rosemary
Elizabeth's Greeting.
Lippincott 1968.
BL v65 1969 p482; BRD 1969 p572; KR v36 1968
    p1072; LJ v94 1969 p566; NYTBR N 3, 1968 p52.

483. Elssler, Fanny
1810-1884
Austrian dancer

Grun, Bernard
Fanny Beloved.
W.H. Allen 1960.

484. Emmet, Robert
1778-1803
Irish patriot; led uprising in Dublin for independence, 1803; hanged

Brophy, John
Sarah: A Novel.
Collins 1948.

Browne, Gretta Curran
Tread Softly on My Dreams.
Headline 1990.

Maher, Nellie
Robert Emmet, His Two Loves.
Celsius Press 1975.

485. Erasmus, Desiderius
1469-1536
Dutch author, philosopher, & scholar

Trease, Geoffrey
YA *Shadow of the Hawk.*

Harcourt, Brace 1949.
BL v46 1949 p17; BRD 1949 p923; KR v17 1949
    p362; LJ v74 1949 p1209; NYTBR Ag 21, 1949 p26.

Vernon, Louise A.
JUV *The Man Who Laid the Egg.*
Herald Press 1977.
SLJ v24 Mr 1978 p134.

486. Ericson, Leif
b. 975
Norwegian explorer; discovered North American coast, circa 1000 AD

Benchley, Nathaniel
YA *Beyond the Mists.*
Harper & Row 1975.
BRD 1976 p97; BS v35 D 1975 p300; NYTBR F 8,
    1976 p14; SLJ v22 S 1975 p116.

Brady, Charles A.
This Land Fulfilled.
Dutton 1958.
BRD 1958 p133; KR v26 1958 p475; LJ v83 1958
    p2320; NYTBR D 14, 1958 p16.

Marshall, Edison
West with the Vikings.
Doubleday 1961.

487. Esau
Old Testament figure; son of Isaac who sold his
birthright to younger brother, Jacob

Cabries, Jean
Jacob.
Dutton 1958.
BL v55 1958 p97; BRD 1958 p177; KR v26 1958
    p477; LJ v83 1958 p3152; NYTBR S 14, 1958 p30.

Fineman, Irving
Jacob; an Autobiographical Novel.
Random House 1941.
BRD 1941 p297; NYTBR O 5, 1941 p6; SatR O 11,
    1941 p14.

488. Estevanico
1500-1540
Moroccan explorer; led Spanish expedition into
US Southwest, 1538

Mirsky, Jeannette
YA *The Gentle Conquistadors.*
Pantheon 1969.
KR v37 1969 p566; LJ v94 1969 p3222.

O'Dell, Scott
JUV *The King's Fifth.*
Houghton Mifflin 1966.
Won the 1967 Newbery award.
BRD 1966 p904; CC 16th p539; HB v42 D 1966 p721.

Panger, Daniel
Black Ulysses.

Viking 1978 (Rpr. 1982).
BL v79 1982 p298; LJ v107 1982 p2110.

Parish, Helen R.
JUV *Estebanico.*
Viking 1974.
BL v71 1974 p179; KR v42 1974 p1104.

489. Esther
Persian queen in the Old Testament who saved the Jews from massacre

Andrews, Gini
Esther: A Novel.
HarperCollins 1991.

Andrews, Gini
Esther: The Star and the Sceptre.
Zondervan 1980.

Cotton, Ella Earls
Queen of Persia: The Story of Esther Who Saved Her People.
Exposition Press 1960.

Frischauer, Paul
So Great a Queen: The Story of Esther, Queen of Persia.
Scribner 1950.
BRD 1950 p330; KR v18 1950 p432; LJ v75 1950 p1406; NYTBR Ja 7, 1951 p26.

Hutchinson, Polly A.
Oh, King, Live Forever.
Beta Books 1977.

Lofts, Norah
Esther.
Macmillan 1950.
BRD 1950 p571; FC 11th p378; KR v18 1950 p598; NY v26 O 7, 1950 p133.

Malvern, Gladys
YA *Behold Your Queen.*
Longmans 1951.
BRD 1951 p573; KR v19 1951 p351; LJ v76 1951 p1716; NYTBR N 11, 1951 p6.

Marshall, Effie Lawrence
Queen Esther.
Falmouth Pub. House 1950.

Weinreb, Nathaniel Norsen
Esther.
Doubleday 1955.
BL v52 1956 p191; BRD 1956 p976; LJ v81 1956 p1053.

490. Eugenie
1826-1920
Wife of Napoleon III and empress of France

Chapman, Hester W.
Eugenie: A Novel.
Little, Brown 1961.

BL v58 1961 p157; BRD 1962 p212; KR v29 1961 p474; LJ v86 1961 p2677.

Kenyon, Frank Wilson
That Spanish Woman.
Dodd, Mead 1962.
First published with the title *I, Eugenia.*
FC 9th p293.

Lowndes, Marie A.
She Dwelt with Beauty.
Macmillan 1949.

McGregor, Iona
Death Wore a Diadem.
St. Martin's 1989.
KR v57 1989 p1637.

Meadows, Rose
The Crinoline Empress.
Hale 1976.

491. Euripides
480-406 BC
Greek tragic dramatist

Plowman, Stephanie
YA *The Road to Sardis.*
Houghton Mifflin 1965.
BRD 1966 p961; LJ v91 1966 p2712; NYTBR My 8, 1966 p30.

492. Evans, Mary Ann
see Eliot, George, pseud.

493. Evans, Oliver
1755-1819
American inventor & steam-engine manufacturer

Teilhet, Darwin Le Ora
Trouble Is My Master.
Little, Brown 1942.
BL v38 1942 p369; BRD 1942 p764.

494. Eve
First woman, created from rib of first man, Adam

Bolt, David
Adam.
John Day Co. 1961.
BL v57 1961 p544; BRD 1961 p140; KR v29 1961 p176; LJ v86 1961 p1475.

Erskine, John
Adam and Eve; though He Knew Better.
Bobbs-Merrill 1927 (Rpr. 1963).
BRD 1927 p237; NYTBR N 20, 1927 p2; SatR D 3, 1927 p371.

495. Fairfax, Thomas
1612-1671
English Civil War military leader

Dymoke, Juliet
Born for Victory.
Jarrolds 1960 (Rpr. 1974).

Sutcliff, Rosemary
Rider on a White Horse.
Coward-McCann 1959.
BL v56 1959 p219; BRD 1960 p1306; FC 11th p59;
    KR v27 1959 p611; NYTBR O 18, 1959 p50.

496. Fargo, William George
1818-1881
American transportation pioneer; with Henry
Wells, started express service, Wells, Fargo &
Co.

Wilkie, Katharine
JUV *William Fargo, Young Mail Carrier.*
Bobbs-Merrill 1962.

497. Farinelli (Carlo Broschi)
1705-1782
Italian opera singer

Goldman, Lawrence
The Castrato: A Novel.
John Day Co. 1973.
KR v41 1973 p268; LJ v98 1973 p1308; PW v203 F
    26, 1973 p122.

498. Farouk I
1920-1965
Egyptian king, 1936-1952; abdicated

Slavitt, David R.
The Killing of the King.
Doubleday 1974.
BRD 1975 p1177; KR v42 1974 p652; LJ v99 1974
    p1987; NYTBR O 27, 1974 p50.

499. Farragut, David Glasgow
1801-1870
Civil War naval officer remembered for saying
"Damn the torpedoes, full speed ahead"

Gerson, Noel Bertram
Clear for Action!.
Doubleday 1970.
BL v67 1971 p728; KR v38 1970 p985; PW v198 Ag
    31, 1970 p278.

Latham, Jean Lee
YA *Anchors Aweigh.*
Harper & Row 1968.
KR v36 1968 p1119; LJ v93 1968 p4420; PW v194 O
    14, 1968 p65.

Long, Laura
JUV *David Farragut, Boy Midshipman.*
Bobbs-Merrill 1950.
BL v47 1950 p161; BRD 1951 p538; LJ v75 1950
    p1911.

Mudra, Marie
YA *David Farragut, Sea Fighter.*
Messner 1953.
BL v50 1954 p225; BRD 1954 p640; KR v21 1953
    p493; LJ v79 1954 p77.

Reyher, Ferdinand
JUV *David Farragut, Sailor.*
Lippincott 1953.
BRD 1954 p739; KR v21 1953 p632; LJ v79 1954 p77;
    SatR F 13, 1954 p53.

Street, James
By Valour and Arms.
Sun Dial Press 1944.
BRD 1944 p728; KR v12 1944 p304; LJ v69 1944
    p762; NYTBR S 24, 1944 p7.

500. Farrar, Geraldine
1882-1967
American opera singer

Paul, Barbara
A Chorus of Detectives.
St. Martin's 1987.
BL v83 1987 p1493; KR v55 1987 p894; NYTBR N 8,
    1987 p62.

Paul, Barbara
Prima Donna at Large.
St. Martin's 1985.
BL v82 1985 p31; KR v53 1985 p756; LJ v110 S 1,
    1985 p215; NYTBR O 13, 1985 p29; PW v227 Jl 5,
    1985 p58.

501. Faulkner, William
1897-1962
American author; wrote *The Sound and the Fury*;
won Nobel Prize, 1949, Pulitzer Prize, 1962

Kaminsky, Stuart M.
Never Cross a Vampire.
St. Martin's 1980.
BL v77 1980 p31; KR v48 1980 p1029; LJ v105 1980
    p1754; NYTBR D 7, 1980 p45.

502. Faust (Faustus)
1480?-1540?
German magician of the 1500s who actually ex-
isted, but concerning whom a great body of legend and myth grew up; archetype character used
in the writings of Goethe, Marlowe, and Mann

Nye, Robert
Faust.
Putnam 1981.
BL v77 My 1, 1981 p1187; KR v49 1981 p167; LJ
    v106 1981 p992; PW v219 Ja 23, 1981 p119.

Zelazny, Roger; Sheckley, Robert
If at Faust You Don't Succeed.
Bantam 1993.

503. Fawkes, Guy
1570-1606
English conspirator; executed

Kirby, Kate
Scapegoat for a Stuart.
St. Martin's 1976.
KR v45 1977 p115; LJ v102 1977 p948.

Ross Williamson, Hugh
JUV *Guy Fawkes.*
Collins 1964.
LJ v91 1966 p3550.

504. Fellini, Federico
1920-
Italian screenwriter & director

Fellini, Federico
Trip to Tulum.
Fleetway 1992.

505. Ferdinand V
1452-1516
Spanish ruler; best known for marrying Isabella
of Castile; financed the voyages of Columbus

Hibbert, Eleanor (Jean Plaidy, pseud.)
Isabella and Ferdinand.
Hale 1970.
Composed of three novels by the author originally
published under their respective titles: *Castile for Is-
abella, Spain for the Sovereigns, & Daughters of Spain.*

Kesten, Hermann
Ferdinand and Isabella.
A.A. Wyn 1946.
BRD 1946 p447; KR v14 1946 p399; LJ v71 1946
p1465; NYTBR N 24, 1946 p20.

Kidwell, Carl
Granada, Surrender!.
Viking 1968.
KR v36 1968 p115; LJ v94 1969 p886.

Schoonover, Lawrence
*The Queen's Cross: A Biographical Romance of
Queen Isabella of Spain.*
W. Sloane Associates 1955.
BL v52 1956 p190; BRD 1955 p807; KR v23 1955
p615; LJ v80 1955 p2163; NYTBR O 30, 1955 p38.

506. Fermi, Enrico
1901-1954
Italian-born American physicist; discovered ura-
nium fission; won Nobel Prize, 1938

Silman, Roberta
Beginning the World Again.
Viking 1990.
BL v87 1990 p258; KR v58 1990 p1038; LJ v115 O 1,
1990 p118; NYTBR N 4, 1990 p29.

507. Ferris, George Washington Gale
1859-1896
Invented Ferris Wheel for the World's Colum-
bian Exposition, 1893

Lawson, Robert
JUV *The Great Wheel.*
Viking 1957 (Rpr. 1993).
BL v54 1957 p113; BRD 1957 p534; KR v25 1957
p417; LJ v82 1957 p2658; NYTBR S 22, 1957 p36.

508. Field, Cyrus West
1819-1892
American merchant & financier

Latham, Jean Lee
YA *Young Man in a Hurry: The Story of Cyrus W.
Field.*
Harper 1958.
BL v55 1958 p80; BRD 1958 p643; KR v26 1958
p464; LJ v83 1958 p3307; NYTBR Ja 18, 1959 p28.

509. Field, Eugene
1850-1895
American journalist, author, & poet

Nolan, Jeannette C.
YA *The Gay Poet: The Story of Eugene Field.*
Messner 1940.
BL v37 1940 p123; BRD 1940 p683; LJ v65 1940
p856; NYTBR D 8, 1940 p10.

510. Fielding, Henry
1707-1754
English author; wrote *Tom Jones*

Bosse, Malcolm J.
The Vast Memory of Love.
Ticknor & Fields 1992.
KR v60 1992 p793; LJ v117 Ag 1992 p144; NYTBR S
6, 1992 p7; PW v239 Jl 6, 1992 p38.

511. Fink, Mike
1770?-1823
American frontiersman

Bennett, Emerson
Mike Fink: Legend of the Ohio.
Robinson & Jones 1848 (Rpr. 1970).

Bowman, James Cloyd
JUV *Mike Fink, Snapping Turtle of the O-hi-o-o, Snag
of the Massassip.*
Little, Brown 1957.
BL v53 1957 p365; BRD 1957 p106; KR v24 1956
p871; LJ v82 1957 p880.

Cohen, Caron Lee
JUV *Sally Ann Thunder Ann Whirlwind Crockett.*
Greenwillow Books 1985.
BL v81 1985 p1190; BRD 1987 p347; SLJ v32 S 1985
p114.

Walt Disney Productions
JUV *Walt Disney's Davy Crockett and Mike Fink.*
Simon & Schuster 1955.

512. Fisk, Jim (James)
1834-1872
American railroad financier & speculator

Porter, Donald
Jubilee Jim and the Wizard of Wall Street.
Dutton 1990.
BL v86 1990 p1071; KR v58 1990 p133; LJ v115 Ap
1, 1990 p138.

513. Fitch, John
1743-1798
American inventor & steamboat pioneer

Stevenson, Augusta
JUV *John Fitch: Steamboat Boy.*
Bobbs-Merrill 1966.

514. Fitzgerald, F. Scott
1896-1940
American author; wrote *This Side of Paradise* and
The Great Gatsy

Aldridge, James
One Last Glimpse.
Little, Brown 1977.
BL v73 My 1, 1977 p1325; ILN v265 My 1977 p83; LJ
v102 1977 p945; NYTBR Jl 10, 1977 p45.

Schulberg, Budd
The Disenchanted.
Random House 1950 (Rpr. 1952, 1987).
BL v47 1950 p116; BRD 1950 p803; KR v18 1950
p316; LJ v75 1950 p1181; NYTBR O 29, 1950 p1.

515. Fitzgerald, Zelda
1900-1948
American author; wife of F. Scott Fitzgerald

Zuckerman, George
The Last Flapper.
Little, Brown 1969.
BS v29 Je 1, 1969 p97; LJ v94 1969 p1525; NYTBR Je
22, 1969 p33; PW v195 Mr 17, 1969 p49.

516. Flaubert, Gustave
1821-1880
French novelist; wrote *Madame Bovary*

Barnes, Julian
Flaubert's Parrot.
J. Cape 1984.
KR v52 1984 p1152; LJ v110 Ap 1, 1985 p155;
NYTBR Mr 10, 1985 p7; NYTBR F 23, 1986 p38;
PW v226 D 21, 1984 p83.

517. Fleming, Ian
1908-1964
English author; created the James Bond adventure series

Kaminsky, Stuart M.
You Bet Your Life.
St. Martin's 1978.
KR v47 1979 p154; LJ v104 1979 p650; NYTBR Ap
22, 1979 p20.

518. Flinders, Matthew
1774-1814
English explorer; known for charting the coasts
of Australia & Tasmania

Hill, Ernestine
*My Love Must Wait; the Story of Matthew Flin-
ders.*
Angus & Robertson 1942.
BRD 1944 p349; NYTBR Ja 30, 1944 p7; SatR F 19,
1944 p20.

519. Flynn, Errol
1909-1959
American actor

Kaminsky, Stuart M.
Bullet for a Star.
St. Martin's 1977.
BL v74 1977 p356; KR v45 1977 p60; NYTBR Ag 21,
1977 p35; PW v211 Je 13, 1977 p100.

McDonald, Roger
Flynn: A Novelisation.
Penguin 1992.
Based on the screenplay by Frank Howson and Alister
Webb.

520. Ford, Gerald R.
1913-
38th US President; succeeded Richard Nixon after his resignation

Updike, John
Memories of the Ford Administration.
Knopf 1992.
Atl v271 Ja 1993 p125; LJ v117 O 1, 1992 p121;
NYTBR N 1, 1992 p11.

521. Ford, Henry
1863-1947
American automobile manufacturer

McMahon, Thomas A.
Loving Little Egypt.
Viking 1987.
BW v17 F 22, 1987 p9; KR v54 1986 p1751; LJ v112 F
1, 1987 p93; NYTBR F 8, 1987 p16; PW v230 D
12, 1986 p42.

Sinclair, Upton
The Flivver King: A Story of Ford-America.
United Automobile Workers of America 1937 (Rpr. 1984).
BRD 1937 p901; BRD 1938 p977; NYTBR My 22, 1938 p7; SatR N 13, 1937 p11.

522. Forrest, Nathan Bedford
1821-1877
American Confederate general; first head of original Klu Klux Klan

Crabb, Alfred L.
Home to Tennessee.
Bobbs-Merrill 1952.
BL v48 1952 p214; NYTBR Mr 2, 1952 p25; SatR F 16, 1952 p44.

Crabb, Alfred L.
Lodging at the Saint Cloud, a Tale of Occupied Nashville.
Bobbs-Merrill 1946.
BL v42 1946 p317; BRD 1946 p178; KR v14 1946 p49; NYTBR Ap 21, 1946 p26.

Crabb, Alfred L.
A Mockingbird Sang at Chickamauga.
Bobbs-Merrill 1949.
BRD 1949 p198; FC 7th p93; LJ v74 1949 p1201; NYTBR O 9, 1949 p34; SatR N 19, 1949 p44.

Legard, Garald
Leaps the Live Thunder.
Morrow 1955.
BRD 1955 p521; KR v23 1955 p223; LJ v80 1955 p1141; NYTBR My 29, 1955 p12.

Norton, Andre
YA *Ride Proud, Rebel!.*
World Pub. Co. 1961 (Rpr. 1981).
BL v57 1961 p609; BRD 1962 p885; KR v29 1961 p223; LJ v86 1961 p1996; NYTBR My 14, 1961 p6.

Parks, Aileen Wells
JUV *Bedford Forrest, Boy on Horseback.*
Bobbs-Merrill 1952 (Rpr. 1963).
BRD 1952 p694; LJ v77 1952 p730; NYTBR Jl 13, 1952 p18.

Yeager, Charles Gordon
Fightin' with Forrest.
Dixie Pub. Co. 1987.

523. Forten, James
1766-1842
American reformer & businessman; influential spokesman for the abolition movement

Johnston, Brenda
JUV *I Cannot Be a Traitor.*
New Day Press 1972.

524. Foster, Stephen Collins
1826-1864
American composer; wrote songs *My Old Kentucky Home,* & *Oh Susannah*

Douty, Esther Morris
JUV *The Story of Stephen Foster.*
Grosset & Dunlap 1954.
BRD 1955 p251; KR v22 1954 p727; LJ v80 1955 p494; NYTBR N 14, 1954 p2.

Higgins, Helen Boyd
JUV *Stephen Foster, Boy Minstrel.*
Bobbs-Merrill 1944 (Rpr. 1953).

Purdy, Claire Lee
YA *He Heard America Sing: The Story of Stephen Foster.*
Messner 1940.
BL v36 1940 p370; BRD 1940 p743; LJ v65 1940 p400; NYTBR Ap 14, 1940 p10.

525. Foster, William Zebulon
1881-1961
American labor leader & radical politician

Gibbons, Floyd Phillips
The Red Napoleon.
J. Cape & H. Smith 1929 (Rpr. 1976).
BRD 1929 p351; NYTBR Ag 25, 1929 p9; SatR O 12, 1929 p274.

526. Fouche, Joseph
1759-1820
French politician & revolutionary

Carr, John D.
Captain Cut-Throat.
Harper 1955 (Rpr. 1980, 1988).
BL v51 1955 p290; BRD 1955 p150; KR v23 1955 p96; NYTBR Ap 3, 1955 p28.

527. Fox, George
1624-1691
Religious leader; founded the Society of Friends or Quakers

Hartog, Jan de
Peaceable Kingdom: An American Saga.
Atheneum 1971.
BS v31 Mr 1, 1972 p526; BRD 1972 p568; FC 11th p275; LJ v97 F 1, 1972 p515; NYTBR Ja 16, 1972 p32.

Vernon, Louise A.
JUV *Key to the Prison.*
Herald Press 1968.

528. Fox, Margaret
1833-1893
American spiritualist medium

Walz, Jay
The Undiscovered Country.
Duell, Sloan & Pearce 1958.
BL v54 1958 p402; BRD 1958 p1093; KR v26 1958
p97; NYTBR My 11, 1958 p29.

529. Francesca da Rimini
d. 1285
Italian noblewoman; her story is woven into
Dante's *Inferno*

Fleetwood, Frances
*Concordia: The Story of Francesca da Rimini's
Daughter.*
St. Martin's 1973.
KR v41 1973 p206; LJ v98 1973 p1190; PW v203 Mr
5, 1973 p73.

530. Francis I
1494-1547
King of France, 1515-1547

Shellabarger, Samuel
The King's Cavalier.
Garden City Books 1950.
BRD 1950 p820; KR v17 1949 p608; NYTBR Ja 8,
1950 p5; SatR Ja 21, 1950 p17.

531. Francis of Assisi, Saint
1182-1226
Italian monk & founder of the Franciscan order

Borden, Lucille
Sing to the Sun.
Macmillan 1933 (Rpr. 1944).
BRD 1933 p98.

Bruckenberger, Raymond
*The Seven Miracles of Gubbio and the Eighth: A
Parable.*
McGraw 1948.
BL v45 1949 p158; BRD 1948 p111; FC 7th p55; KR
v16 1948 p535; NYTBR N 14, 1948 p24.

De Wohl, Louis
*The Joyful Beggar: A Novel of St. Francis of As-
sisi.*
Lippincott 1958.
FC 9th p133.

Jewett, Eleanore Myers
YA *Big John's Secret.*
Viking 1962.
LJ v88 1963 p872.

Kantor, MacKinlay
JUV *The Work of Saint Francis.*
World Pub. Co. 1958.
Also published as *Unseen Witness.*
BL v55 1958 p99; BRD 1959 p547; KR v26 1958
p527; LJ v83 1958 p3018; NYTBR D 7, 1958 p48.

Kazantzakis, Nikos
Saint Francis: A Novel.
Simon & Schuster 1962 (Rpr. 1966).
BL v58 1962 p750; BRD 1962 p637; FC 11th p338;
KR v30 1962 p298; LJ v87 1962 p1630; NYTBR Je
10, 1962 p7.

Kossak, Zofia
*Blessed Are the Meek: A Novel about St. Francis
of Assisi.*
Roy Publishers 1944.
BL v40 1944 p318; BRD 1944 p424; KR v12 1944
p46; LJ v69 1944 p262; NYTBR Mr 19, 1944 p1.

Lechner, Michael
My Beautiful White Roses.
Smoketree Press 1971.

Leclerc, Eloi
The Wisdom of the Poor One of Assisi.
Hope Pub. House 1992.

Milhous, Katherine
JUV *The First Christmas Crib.*
Scribner 1944.
BL v41 1944 p94; BRD 1944 p523; CC 7th p1015;
KR v12 1944 p431; LJ v69 1944 p940; NYTBR D
3, 1944 p26.

O'Dell, Scott
YA *The Road to Damietta.*
Houghton Mifflin 1985.
BRD 1986 p1205; SLJ v32 D 1985 p104.

Pauli, Hertha
JUV *Pietro and Brother Francis.*
Washburn 1971.
Am v125 D 4, 1971 p487.

Timmermans, Felix
Perfect Joy of St. Francis.
Farrar, Straus & Young 1952.
BRD 1952 p886; NYTBR Jl 13, 1952 p16; SatR Ag
23, 1952 p36.

White, Helen C.
Bird of Fire: A Tale of St. Francis of Assisi.
Macmillan 1958.
BRD 1958 p1109; FC 7th p378; KR v26 1958 p562; LJ
v83 1958 p2324; NYTBR S 28, 1958 p46.

Williamson, Glen
Repair My House.
Creation House 1973.

532. Francis Xavier, Saint
1506-1557

De Wohl, Louis
Set All Afire: A Novel about Saint Francis Xavier.
Lippincott 1953.
BL v50 1953 p167; BRD 1953 p256; FC 8th p115; KR
v21 1953 p675; NYTBR N 29, 1953 p47.

533. Francisco, Peter

1760-1831

American soldier who served in Continental army under Layfayette; many anedotes told about his physical strength

Shaffer, Janet
Peter Francisco, Virginia Giant.
Moore Pub. Co. 1976.

Wilson, Charles G.
YA *Sword of Francisco.*
Crowell 1956.
BRD 1957 p996; KR v24 1956 p573; LJ v82 1957 p884.

534. Franck, Cesar Auguste

1822-1890

French organist & composer

Harwood, Ronald
Cesar and Augusta.
Little, Brown 1978.
KR v48 1980 p308; LJ v105 1980 p1408; TLS My 5, 1978 p493.

535. Franco, Francisco

1892-1975

Spanish military dictator

Marlowe, Stephen
The Man with No Shadow.
Prentice-Hall 1974.
BS v34 Je 15, 1974 p145; KR v42 1974 p72; LJ v99 1974 p1848; NYTBR Je 30, 1974 p31.

536. Frankau, Gilbert

1884-1952

English novelist; wrote the novel *World without End*

Frankau, Gilbert
Gilbert Frankau's Self-Portrait: A Novel of His Own Life.
Dutton 1940.

537. Franklin, Benjamin

1706-1790

American political leader; author, scientist, & printer; helped draft Declaration of Independence, Constitution

Bourne, Miriam Anne
JUV *What Is Papa Up to Now?.*
Coward, McCann & Geoghegan 1977.
BL v73 1977 p1494; KR v45 1977 p424; SLJ v24 O 1977 p98.

Feuchtwanger, Lion
Proud Destiny.
Viking 1947.
BRD 1947 p299; LJ v72 1947 p1193; NYTBR S 14, 1947 p3; SatR S 13, 1947 p9.

Frey, Ruby Frazier
Red Morning.
Putnam 1946.
BL v43 1946 p16; BRD 1946 p292; KR v14 1946 p278; LJ v71 1946 p978; NYTBR Jl 28, 1946 p14.

Hall, Robert L.
YA *Benjamin Franklin and a Case of Christmas Murder.*
St. Martin's 1991.
BL v87 1991 p1009; KR v58 1990 p1570; PW v237 N 30, 1990 p61.

Hall, Robert L.
YA *Benjamin Franklin Takes the Case: The American Agent Investigates Murder in the Dark Byways of London.*
St. Martin's 1988.
BL v84 1988 p1479; KR v56 1988 p654; LJ v113 My 1, 1988 p94; PW v233 My 6, 1988 p96.

Hall, Robert L.
YA *Murder at Drury Lane.*
St. Martin's 1992.
BL v89 1992 p491; KR v60 1992 p1153.

Lancaster, Bruce
Blind Journey.
Little, Brown 1953.
BRD 1953 p537; KR v21 1953 p400; LJ v78 1953 p1425; NYTBR S 20, 1953 p5.

Lawson, Robert
JUV *Ben and Me: A New and Astonishing Life of Benjamin Franklin as Written by His Good Mouse Amos.*
Little, Brown 1939 (Rpr. 1950, 1973, 1983, 1988).
BRD 1939 p575; LJ v65 1940 p125; NYTBR D 10, 1939 p10; PW v233 Ap 29, 1988 p80; SHSLC 8th p428.

Lerangis, Peter
JUV *The Amazing Ben Franklin.*
Bantam 1987.
SLJ v34 O 1987 p41.

Mathieson, Theodore
The Devil and Ben Franklin.
Simon & Schuster 1961.
NYTBR My 21, 1961 p30; SatR Ag 5, 1961 p16.

Meadowcroft, Enid La Monte
JUV *The Story of Benjamin Franklin.*
Grosset & Dunlap 1952.
BRD 1953 p635; LJ v78 1953 p156.

Meigs, Cornelia
YA *Mounted Messenger.*
Macmillan 1943.
BRD 1943 p564; CC 7th p1015; HB v19 My 1943 p175; LJ v68 1943 p434.

Monjo, F. N.
JUV *Poor Richard in France.*

Holt, Rinehart & Winston 1973.
KR v41 1973 p1167; LJ v98 1973 p3690; LJ v98 1973
p3701; NYTBR N 4, 1973 p57.

Neilson, Winthrop
Edge of Greatness.
Putnam 1951.
BRD 1951 p651; NYTBR My 6, 1951 p17; SatR My
19, 1951 p30.

O'Toole, G. J. A.
YA *Poor Richard's Game.*
Delacorte 1982.
CSM v75 F 11, 1983 pB3; WCRB v8 S 1982 p25.

Tweedt, Craig L.
JUV *Zak and Ben.*
Modern Curriculum Press 1986.

Zochert, Donald
Murder in the Hellfire Club.
Holt, Rinehart & Winston 1978.
BL v75 1979 p797; KR v46 1978 p1330; LJ v104 1979
p132; PW v214 D 11, 1978 p58.

538. Franklin, John, Sir
1786-1847
English arctic explorer; died in search of North-
west Passage

Cato, Nancy
North-West by South.
Heinemann 1965.

Godfrey, Martyn
JUV *Mystery in the Frozen Lands.*
J. Lorimer 1988.
Can Mat v17 My 1989 p123; Can Child Lit #56 1989
p91; Mac v101.

Nadolny, Sten
The Discovery of Slowness.
Viking 1987.
Translation of *Die Entdeckung der Langsamkeit.*
BL v84 1987 p362; KR v55 1987 p1345; LJ v112 S 15,
1987 p96; NYTBR D 20, 1987 p15.

Tapley, Caroline
YA *John Come down the Backstay.*
Atheneum 1974.
BL v70 1974 p1156; KR v42 1974 p434; LJ v99 1974
p1232; NYTBR Jl 21, 1974 p8.

539. Franz Ferdinand
1863-1914
Archduke of Austria, whose assassination in
1914 led to outbreak of World War I

Powell, William
The First Casuality.
L. Stuart 1979.
KR v47 1979 p1023.

540. Franz Joseph I
1830-1916
Emperor of Austria, 1848-1916 & king of Hungary, 1867-1916

Janetschek, Ottokar
The Emperor Franz Joseph.
W. Laurie 1953.

541. Frazer, James George, Sir
1854-1941
Scottish anthropologist

Crowley, Aleister
Golden Twigs.
Teitan Press 1988.

542. Frederick II
1194-1250
German emperor; ruled Holy Roman Empire,
1212-1250

Berdach, Rachel
The Emperor, the Sages and Death.
T. Yoseloff 1962.
LJ v87 1962 p2911.

De Chair, Somerset
The Star of the Wind.
Constable 1974.
Obs Ag 25, 1974 p23.

De Wohl, Louis
*The Joyful Beggar: A Novel of St. Francis of As-
sisi.*
Lippincott 1958.
FC 9th p133.

De Wohl, Louis
The Quiet Light.
Lippincott 1950.
BL v47 1950 p12; BRD 1950 p248; FC 7th p106; LJ
v75 1950 p1290; NYTBR S 3, 1950 p11.

Holland, Cecelia
Antichrist: A Novel of Emperor Frederick II.
Atheneum 1970.
BRD 1970 p669; KR v37 1969 p1339; LJ v95 1970
p513; NYTBR F 22, 1970 p46.

Holland, Cecelia
JUV *The King's Road.*
Atheneum 1970.
BL v67 1971 p450; KR v38 1970 p1106; LJ v95 1970
p3627.

MacKaye, David Loring
JUV *The Silver Disk.*
Longmans, Green 1955.
BL v52 1955 p79; BRD 1955 p593; KR v23 1955
p601; LJ v80 1955 p2391; NYTBR O 16, 1955 p34.

543. Frederick Louis

1707-1751

Prince of Wales; son of George II & father of George III

Walthew, Kenneth
The Prince from Hanover.
Hale 1978.

Wilkins, Vaughan
Fanfare for a Witch.
J. Cape 1954.
BL v50 1954 p250; BRD 1954 p955; KR v22 1954
p135; LJ v79 1954 p552; NYTBR Ag 15, 1954 p18.

544. Frederick the Great

1712-1786

King of Prussia, 1740-1786; noted for social reforms

Frank, Bruno
The Days of the King.
Knopf 1928 (Rpr. 1935, 1942, 1970).
BL v24 1928 p322; BRD 1928 p270; NYTBR D 11,
1927 p7; SatR Ja 7, 1928 p502.

Sabatini, Rafael
The Birth of Mischief.
Houghton Mifflin 1945.
BRD 1945 p614; NYTBR Ag 5, 1945 p12.

545. Fremont, John Charles

1813-1890

American explorer & US presidential nominee,
1856

Hawthorne, Hildegarde
No Road Too Long.
Longmans, Green 1940.
BRD 1940 p411; LJ v65 1940 p91; LJ v65 1940 p455;
NYTBR Jl 7, 1940 p10.

Holland, Cecelia
The Bear Flag.
Houghton Mifflin 1990.
BL v86 1990 p1957; BRD 1991 p877; KR v58 1990
p521; LJ v115 Je 15, 1990 p134.

Nevin, David
Dream West.
Putnam 1983.
BL v80 1984 p649; KR v51 1983 p1177; LJ v108 1983
p2262; NYTBR Ja 29, 1984 p10; PW v224 N 25,
1983 p57.

Stone, Irving
Immortal Wife.
Doubleday, Doran 1944.
BRD 1944 p725; FC 9th p491; KR v12 1944 p356; LJ
v69 1944 p762; NYTBR O 1, 1944 p4.

546. French, Daniel Chester

1850-1931

American sculptor

Longstreth, Thomas Morris
YA *The Great Venture.*
Macmillan 1948.
BL v45 1949 p181; BRD 1948 p513; KR v16 1948
p442; LJ v73 1948 p1675.

547. Freud, Sigmund

1856-1939

Austrian psychiatrist & author; founder of psychoanalysis

Burgess, Anthony
The End of the World News.
McGraw-Hill 1983.
BL v79 1983 p641; BRD 1983 p217; FC 11th p87; KR
v51 1983 p14; LJ v108 1983 p411; NYTBR Mr 6,
1983 p3; Time v121 Mr 21, 1983.

Daniels, Kathleen
*Minna's Story: The Secret Love of Doctor Sigmund
Freud.*
Health Press 1990.

Doctorow, E. L.
Ragtime.
Random House 1975.
BL v72 1975 p24; BRD 1975 p338; BRD 1976 p313;
KR v43 1975 p529; LJ v100 1975 p1344; NYTBR Jl
6, 1975 p1.

Harrison, Carey
Freud: A Novel.
Weidenfeld & Nicolson 1984.
BritBkN My 1984 p302.

Hill, Carol DeChellis
Henry James' Midnight Song.
Poseidon Press 1993.
NYTBR S 5, 1993 p10.

Mackworth, Cecily
Lucy's Nose.
Carcanet 1992.
TLS Mr 6, 1992 p22.

Malzberg, Barry
The Remaking of Sigmund Freud.
Ballantine 1985.
LJ v110 Ag 1985 p121; NYTBR Ag 4, 1985 p20.

Meyer, Nicholas
The Seven-Per-Cent Solution.
Dutton 1974.
BL v71 1974 p23; BRD 1974 p827; BRD 1975 p867;
FC 11th p429; KR v42 1974 p650; LJ v99 1974
p2176; NYTBR S 29, 1974 p41.

Millar, Thomas P.
Who's Afraid of Sigmund Freud?.
Palmer Press 1985.
BIC v15 Ap 1986 p38.

Soothill, Rayner
My Friend Freud: An Intimate Memoir.
Angus & Robertson 1983.

Stone, Irving
The Passions of the Mind.
Doubleday 1971.
Atl v227 Ap 1971 p91; BRD 1971 p1313; FC 11th
    p587; LJ v96 Ap 1, 1971 p1292; NYTBR Mr 14,
    1971 p7; Time v97 Ap 5, 1971 p91.

Thomas, D. M.
The White Hotel.
Viking 1981.
BRD 1981 p1425; FC 11th p605; LJ v106 1981 p370;
    NYTBR Mr 15, 1981 p1.

Trachtenberg, Inge
An Arranged Marriage.
Norton 1975.
BL v71 1975 p991; KR v42 1974 p1323; LJ v100 1975
    p504; PW v207 Ja 6, 1975 p50.

548. Fritz, Jean Guttery
1915-
American author of children's books

Fritz, Jean
JUV *Homesick, My Own Story.*
Putnam 1982.
BL v79 1982 p42; BRD 1983 p536; KR v50 1982
    p1002; NYTBR N 14, 1982 p41; SLJ v29 S 1982
    p120.

549. Frontenac, Louis de Buade de
1620-1698
French colonial governor of Canada

Cather, Willa
Shadows on the Rock.
Knopf 1931 (Heavily reprinted).
BL v28 1931 p26; BRD 1931 p181; NYTBR Ag 2,
    1931 p1; SatR Ag 22, 1931 p67.

550. Frost, Robert Lee
1874-1963
American poet; won four Pulitzers

Reed, Meredith
JUV *Our Year began in April.*
Lee & Shepard 1963.
BRD 1964 p974; LJ v88 1963 p4867; NYTBR D 22,
    1963 p10.

551. Fulton, Robert
1765-1815
American engineer & inventor; first to develop
a practical, profitable steamboat

Henry, Marguerite
JUV *Robert Fulton, Boy Craftman.*
Bobbs-Merrill 1945.

BRD 1945 p320; KR v13 1945 p340; LJ v70 1945
    p1027.

Lane, Carl D.
The Fire Raft.
Little, Brown 1951.
BL v47 1951 p405; BRD 1951 p501; LJ v76 1951
    p1236; SCHSL 6th p1054.

Wilkins, William V.
Being Met Together.
Macmillan 1944.
BRD 1944 p813; KR v12 1944 p181; LJ v69 1944
    p651; NYTBR S 3, 1944 p5.

552. Funston, Frederick
1865-1917
American military leader

Barnes, Tellfair B.
The Bamboo Caper.
T.B. Barnes 1990.

553. Gage, Thomas
1721-1787
English army officer & colonial governor of Massachusetts

Barker, Shirley
The Last Gentleman.
Random House 1960.
BL v57 1960 p87; BRD 1960 p65; KR v28 1960 p336;
    LJ v85 1960 p2616.

Payne, Robert
Concord Bridge.
Bobbs-Merrill 1952.
BL v48 1952 p378; BRD 1952 p445; NYTBR Je 29,
    1952 p16; SatR Ag 23, 1952 p37.

554. Galen
129-199
Greek physician & author

Prantera, Amanda
The Side of the Moon.
Bloomsbury 1991.
Books v6 Jl 1992 p17; Lon R Bks v13 My 9, 1991 p23;
    TLS My 10, 1991 p18.

555. Galileo
1564-1642
Italian astronomer; constructed first astronomi-
cal telescope

Brighton, Catherine
JUV *Five Secrets in a Box.*
Dutton 1987.
BRD 1988 p206; PW v231 Jl 10, 1987 p67; SLJ v34 N
    1987 p87.

Rosen, Sidney
YA *Galileo and the Magic Numbers.*

Little, Brown 1958.
BL v54 1958 p421; BRD 1958 p910; KR v26 1958 p40; LJ v83 1958 p971; NYTBR S 14, 1958 p32.

556. Gama, Vasco da
see DaGama, Vasco

557. Gamaliel the Elder
d. 50
Palestinian religious leader & scholar

Heard, Gerald
The Gospel According to Gamaliel.
Harper 1945.
BRD 1945 p314; KR v13 1945 p508; NYTBR Ja 6, 1946 p7.

558. Gandhi, Indira
1917-1984
Prime minister of India, 1966-1977, 1978-1984

Rawla, N. D.
All the Prime Minister's Men.
Pankaj Books 1977.

559. Gandhi, Mahatma
1869-1948
Hindu nationalist leader; known for fasts & civil disobedience against British rule in India; assassinated

Jacob, Helen Pierce
JUV *A Garland for Gandhi.*
Parnassus Press 1968.
HB v45 F 1969 p47; LJ v94 1969 p2102.

Narayan, R. K.
Waiting for the Mahatma.
Michigan State University Press 1955 (Rpr. 1981).
BRD 1955 p666; LJ v80 1955 p2868; NYTBR D 25, 1955 p10.

Tharoor, Shashi
The Great Indian Novel.
Viking 1989.
BRD 1991 p1837; KR v59 1991 p76; LJ v116 Mr 1, 1991 p118; NYTBR Mr 24, 1991 p16.

Wolpert, Stanley A.
Nine Hours to Rama.
Random House 1962.
BRD 1962 p1319; LJ v87 1962 p1153; NYTBR Mr 18, 1962 p5; SatR My 26, 1962 p31.

560. Garcia Lorca, Federico
1899-1936
Spanish poet & dramatist

Thornton, Lawrence
Under the Gypsy Moon.
Doubleday 1990.
KR v58 1990 p1041; NYTBR O 14, 1990 p14.

561. Garfield, James Abram
1831-1881
20th US President; assassinated

Davis, Hazel H.
General Jim.
Bethany Press 1958.

562. Garibaldi, Giuseppe
1807-1882
Italian patriot & soldier

Baker, Nina
YA *Garibaldi.*
Vanguard Press 1944.
BL v41 1945 p141; BRD 1944 p34; KR v12 1944 p453; LJ v70 1945 p36; NYTBR N 12, 1944 p16.

Trease, Geoffrey
YA *Follow My Black Plume.*
Vanguard Press 1963.
BRD 1964 p1172; HB v39 Ag 1963 p392; LJ v88 1963 p3371.

Trease, Geoffrey
YA *A Thousand for Sicily.*
Vanguard Press 1964.
Sequel to *Follow My Black Plume.*
HB v42 Ag 1966 p440; LJ v91 1966 p3548.

563. Garland, Judy
1922-1969
American actress; played Dorothy in *The Wizard of Oz*; mother of Liza Minnelli

Kaminsky, Stuart M.
Murder on the Yellow Brick Road.
St. Martin's 1977.
KR v46 1978 p138; NYTBR Jl 1, 1979 p21.

Ryman, Geoff
Was: A Novel.
Knopf 1992.
BL v88 1992 p1663; KR v60 1992 p349; NYTBR Jl 5, 1992 p7.

564. Garrett, Patrick Floyd
1850-1908
American lawman; best known for killing Billy the Kid

Everitt, David
The Story of Pat Garrett and Billy the Kid.
Knightsbridge Pub. Co. 1990.
BWatch v11 N 1990 p10.

565. Garrick, David
1717-1779
English actor & dramatist

Stewart, Anna Bird
YA *Enter David Garrick.*

Lippincott 1951.
BL v48 1951 p87; BRD 1951 p844; KR v19 1951
p583; LJ v76 1951 p2017; NYTBR N 11, 1951 p16.

566. Garvey, Marcus
1887-1940
American Black leader; led Back to Africa
movement

Austin, Edmund O.
The Black Challenge.
Vantage Press 1958.

Childress, Alice
YA *A Short Walk.*
Coward, McCann & Geoghegan 1979.
BL v76 1979 p429; KR v47 1979 p1012; LJ v104 1979
p2234; NYTBR N 11, 1979 p14; PW v216 Ag 20,
1979 p76.

Williams, Gershom A.
*A Hero for Jamaica: A Novel of the Living Legend
of Marcus Garvey.*
Exposition Press 1973.

567. Gauguin, Paul (Eugene Henri Paul)
1848-1903
French postimpressionist painter

Gorham, Charles
*The Gold of Their Bodies: A Novel about
Gauguin.*
Dial Press 1955.
BL v51 1955 p367; BRD 1955 p358; LJ v80 1955
p452; NYTBR F 27, 1955 p31.

Lucas, Christopher
JUV *Tiki and the Dolphin: The Adventures of a Boy in
Tahiti.*
Vanguard 1974.
KR v42 1974 p634; PW v206 Jl 8, 1974 p75.

Maugham, W. Somerset
The Moon and Sixpence.
Heinemann 1919 (Heavily reprinted).
BRD 1919 p340; FC 10th p365; NYTBR Ag 3, 1919
p389; NYTBR Ja 30, 1955 p2.

568. Gehrig, Lou (Henry Louis)
1903-1941
American baseball player; died of disease now
commonly called Lou Gehrig's disease

Van Riper, Guernsey
JUV *Lou Gehrig, Boy of the Sand Lots.*
Bobbs-Merrill 1949 (Rpr. 1959, 1986).
BL v45 1949 p299; BRD 1949 p939; LJ v74 1949
p667; NYTBR Jl 17,.

569. Genghis Khan
1162-1227
Mongul conqueror

Alberts, Frances Jacobs
JUV *A Gift for Genghis Khan.*
Whittlesey House 1961.
LJ v86 1961 p2352.

Baumann, Hans
YA *Sons of the Steppe: The Story of How the Con-
queror Genghis Khan Was Overcome.*
H.Z. Walck 1957 (Rpr. 1961).
BL v54 1958 p449; BRD 1958 p73; KR v26 1958
p376; LJ v83 1958 p2074; NYTBR Mr 16, 1958 p42.

Caldwell, Taylor
*The Earth Is the Lord's: A Tale of the Rise of
Genghis Khan.*
Scribner 1941.
BL v37 1941 p270; BRD 1941 p138; LJ v65 1940
p808; NYTBR Ja 5, 1941 p6.

Clou, John
A Caravan to Camul.
Bobbs-Merrill 1954.
BL v50 1954 p419; BRD 1954 p182; NYTBR Jl 4,
1954 p10.

Dandrea, Don
YA *Orlok.*
Pineapple Press 1986.
KR v54 1986 p320; PW v229 Mr 21, 1986 p74.

David, Kurt
JUV *Black Wolf of the Steppes.*
Houghton Mifflin 1972.
BL v69 1973 p855; LJ v98 1973 p2008; TLS Ap 28,
1972 p85.

Lamb, Harold
The Sea of the Ravens.
D.M. Grant 1983.

Mather, Berkely
Genghis Khan.
Dell 1965.

Ritchie, Rita
YA *The Golden Hawks of Genghis Khan.*
Dutton 1958.
BL v55 1958 p137; BRD 1959 p842; KR v26 1958
p417; LJ v84 1959 p259; NYTBR Ja 25, 1959 p32.

Ritchie, Rita
YA *Secret beyond the Mountains.*
Dutton 1960.
BL v57 1960 p129; BRD 1961 p1193; LJ v85 1960
p3874.

Ritchie, Rita
YA *The Year of the Horse.*
Dutton 1957.
BRD 1957 p778; KR v25 1957 p642; LJ v82 1957
p2981.

Sargent, Pamela
Ruler of the Sky: The Saga of Genghis Khan.
Crown 1993.
BL v89 1992 p580; LJ v117 D 1992 p188.

Sproat, Robert
Chinese Whispers.
Faber 1988.
KR v56 1988 p568; NS v115 Mr 25, 1988 p26; TLS
    Mr 25, 1988 p337.

Yan, V.
Jenghiz-Khan: A Tale of 13th Century Asia.
Hyperion Press 1978.
Reprint of the 1945 ed. published by Hutchinson's In-
    ternational Authors.

570. Gentileschi, Artemisia
1597-1651
Italian artist

Banti, Anna
Artemisia.
University of Nebraska Press 1988.
BL v85 1988 p537; LJ v114 My 1, 1989 p76.

571. George I
1660-1727
King of Great Britain, 1714-1727

Lehr, Helene
Princess of Hanover: A Novel.
St. Martin's 1989.
KR v57 1989 p575.

572. George II
1683-1760
King of Great Britain, 1727-1760

Hibbert, Eleanor (Jean Plaidy, pseud.)
Caroline, the Queen.
Hale 1968 (Rpr. 1986).
KR v54 1986 p665.

Marshall, Edison
The Upstart.
Farrar & Rinehart 1945.
KR v13 1945 p20; NYTBR Ap 15, 1945 p10.

573. George III
1738-1820
King of Great Britain, 1760-1820

Ashton, Helen
Footman in Powder.
Dodd, Mead 1954.
BL v51 1954 p62; BRD 1954 p27; NYTBR O 3, 1954
    p29.

Gibbs, Mary Ann
Enchantment: A Pastoral.
P. Davies 1952 (Rpr. 1974).

Hibbert, Eleanor (Jean Plaidy, pseud.)
Perdita's Prince.
Hale 1969 (Rpr. 1987).
PW v232 S 18, 1987 p160.

Hibbert, Eleanor (Jean Plaidy, pseud.)
The Prince and the Quakeress.
Hale 1968 (Rpr. 1986).
BL v83 1986 p548.

Hibbert, Eleanor (Jean Plaidy, pseud.)
The Third George.
Hale 1969 (Rpr. 1974, 1987).
PW v231 My 29, 1987 p64.

Maughan, A. M.
The King's Malady.
Hodder & Stoughton.

Meadows, Rose
Pretty Maids All in a Row.
Hale 1976.

Monjo, F. N.
JUV *King George's Head Was Made of Lead.*
Coward, McCann & Geoghegan 1974.
KR v42 1974 p1156; NYTBR N 3, 1974 p26.

Walthew, Kenneth
A Queen for Royal George.
Hale 1977.

574. George IV
1762-1830
King of Great Britain, 1820-1830

Ashton, Helen
Footman in Powder.
Dodd, Mead 1954.
BL v51 1954 p62; BRD 1954 p27; NYTBR O 3, 1954
    p29.

Bloom, Ursula (Lozania Prole, pseud.)
The Lass a King Loved.
Hale 1975.

Bloom, Ursula (Lozania Prole, pseud.)
A Queen for the Regent.
Hale 1971 (Rpr. 1983).

Burke, J. F.
Prince Regent.
Fontana 1979.
Based on the BBC serial originated by Ian and Joan
    Curteis.

Condon, Richard
The Abandoned Woman.
Dial 1977.
BL v73 1977 p1326; BRD 1977 p259; LJ v102 1977
    p1206; NYTBR Je 5, 1977 p17; Time v109 My 30,
    1977 p73.

Hardwick, Michael
Regency Royal.
Coward, McCann & Geoghegan 1978.
KR v46 1978 p962; PW v214 S 18, 1978 p161.

Hibbert, Eleanor (Jean Plaidy, pseud.)
Indiscretions of the Queen.
Hale 1970 (Rpr. 1988).
Obs Ja 10, 1971 p28.

Hibbert, Eleanor (Jean Plaidy, pseud.)
Perdita's Prince.
Hale 1969 (Rpr. 1987).
PW v232 S 18, 1987 p160.

Hibbert, Eleanor (Jean Plaidy, pseud.)
Sweet Lass of Richmond Hill.
Hale 1970 (Rpr. 1988).

McDonald, Eva
The Gretna Wedding.
Hale 1967 (Rpr. 1988).

Meadows, Rose
To Be My Wedded Wife.
Pocket Books 1974.
PW v205 Mr 18, 1974 p55.

575. George V
1865-1936
King of Great Britain, 1910-1936

Clarke, Thomas Ernest Bennett
Murder at Buckingham Palace.
St. Martin's 1981.
KR v49 1981 p1549; LJ v107 1982 p275.

576. George, Saint
d. 303
Christian martyr; known for his legendary fight
with the dragon

Grahame, Kenneth
The Reluctant Dragon.
Holiday House 1938 (Heavily reprinted).

Hays, Edward
*St. George and the Dragon and the Quest for the
    Holy Grail.*
Forest of Peace Books 1986.

Rose, Elizabeth; Rose, Gerald
JUV *St. George and the Fiery Dragon.*
Norton 1964.

577. Gericault, Jean Louis Andre Theodore
1791-1824
French painter

Aragon, Louis
Holy Week.
Putnam 1961.
BL v58 1961 p156; BRD 1961 p39; KR v29 1961
    p640; LJ v86 1961 p2813; NYTBR S 24, 1961 p4.

578. Geronimo
1829-1909
Apache Indian leader

Bond, Geoffrey
Geronimo Rides Out.
Arco Publications 1962.

Burroughs, Edgar Rice
Apache Devil.
Grosset & Dunlap 1933 (Rpr. 1978).
BRD 1933 p143; NYTBR My 21, 1933 p19.

Carter, Forrest
Watch for Me on the Mountain.
Delacorte Press 1978.
BL v75 1978 p457; KR v46 1978 p762; LJ v103 1978
    p2260; NYTBR Mr 18, 1979 p12; PW v214 Jl 24,
    1978 p80.

Dugan, Bill
YA *Geronimo.*
Harper 1991.
Kliatt v26 Ap 1992 p6.

Ingram, Hunter
Fort Apache.
Ballantine 1975.

Shirreffs, Gordon D.
Son of the Thunder People.
Westminster Press 1957.
LJ v83 1958 p246.

579. Gibbon, Edward
1737-1794
English historian; wrote *The Decline and Fall of
the Roman Empire*

Brophy, Brigid
*The Adventures of God in His Search for the Black
    Girl.*
Macmillan 1973.
A novella in a collection of short stories.
BRD 1974 p150; Choice v11 O 1974 p1132; FC 9th
    p68; NYTBR Ag 25, 1974 p4; TLS N 23, 1973
    p1417.

580. Gibbons, Floyd Phillips
1887-1939
American journalist; war correspondent, covered WW I, Russian revolution, & Spanish civil
war

Gibbons, Floyd Phillips
The Red Napoleon.
J. Cape & H. Smith 1929 (Rpr. 1976).
BRD 1929 p351; NYTBR Ag 25, 1929 p9; SatR O 12,
    1929 p274.

581. Gibbons, Grinling
1648-1721
English sculptor & woodcarver

Clare, Austin
JUV *The Carved Cartoon: A Picture of the Past.*
Stacey 1972.
Reprint of 1873 edition.
TLS Je 15, 1973 p673.

582. Gilbert, William Schwenck, Sir

1836-1911
English light opera librettist; collaborated with
A. S. Sullivan

Power-Waters, Alma

YA *The Melody Maker.*
Dutton 1959.
BRD 1960 p1085; LJ v84 1959 p3939.

583. Gilmore, Gary Mark

1941-1977
American murderer; first person to be executed
by firing squad following reinstatement of death
penalty

Mailer, Norman

The Executioner's Song.
Little, Brown 1979.
BL v76 1979 p422; BRD 1979 p824; BRD 1980 p793;
    FC 11th p405; KR v47 1979 p1049; LJ v104 1979
    p2329; NYTBR O 7, 1979 p1.

584. Ginsberg, Allen

1926-
American poet; associated with the "Beat"
movement

Craddock, William J.

Be Not Content.
Doubleday 1970.
BL v66 1970 p1380; KR v38 1970 p75; LJ v95 1970
    p881; NYTBR Ap 26, 1970 p46.

585. Gioconda, Lisa Gherardini

b. 1479
Italian noblewoman; subject of Leonardo da
Vinci's famed portrait "Mona Lisa"

La Mure, Pierre

The Private Life of Mona Lisa.
Little, Brown 1976.
BL v73 1976 p235; BRD 1977 p763; KR v44 1976
    p753; LJ v101 1976 p1658.

Mayfield, Sara

Mona Lisa, the Woman in the Portrait.
Grosset & Dunlap 1974.
KR v42 1974 p618; LJ v99 1974 p2176.

586. Giraud, Henri Honore

1879-1949
French general

Frizell, Bernard

Timetable for the General.
Collins 1972.
B&B v18 O 1972 p75; Spec v229 Ag 26, 1972 p320.

587. Glendower, Owen

1359-1415
Welsh revolutionary; self-proclaimed prince of
Wales; figures prominently in Shakespeare's
Henry IV

Crawshay-Williams, Eliot

The Wolf from the West.
Long 1947.

Powys, John Cowper

Owen Glendower, an Historical Novel.
Simon & Schuster 1940 (Rpr. 1974, 1978).
BRD 1941 p725; NYTBR Ja 26, 1941 p7; SatR F 1,
    1941 p10.

Rofheart, Martha

Glendower Country.
Putnam 1973.
Also published as *Cry God for Glendower.*
BL v70 1973 p31; KR v41 1973 p476; LJ v98 1973
    p2148; LJ v98 1973 p3727.

Trease, Geoffrey

JUV *Bent Is the Bow.*
Nelson 1967.
LJ v92 1967 p2455.

588. Glover, John

1732-1797
American Revolutionary leader

Lancaster, Bruce

Trumpet to Arms.
Little, Brown 1944.
BRD 1944 p433; LJ v69 1944 p502.

589. Goddard, Robert Hutchings

1882-1945
American physicist; launched first liquid-fueled
rocket, 1926

Coombs, Charles I.

YA *Rocket Pioneer.*
Harper & Row 1965.
SB v1 Mr 1966 p237.

590. Godiva, Lady

Made legendary ride naked through Coventry to
win tax relief for townspeople

Faure, Raoul Cohen

Lady Godiva and Master Tom.
Harper 1948.
BRD 1948 p260; KR v15 1947 p629; LJ v73 1948 p39;
    NYTBR F 1, 1948 p12.

Mackail, Denis G.

Her Ladyship.
Hutchinson 1949.

591. Godwin, Edward William
1833-1886
English designer; best known as designer of wall-
paper, furniture, costumes, & theatrical scenery

Ansle, Dorothy P. (Hebe Elsna, pseud.)
The Sweet Lost Years.
Hale 1955 (Rpr. 1974).

592. Goering, Hermann Wilhelm
1893-1946
German Nazi leader; founder of Gestapo

Leffland, Ella
The Knight, Death, and the Devil.
Morrow 1990.
BL v86 1989 p705; BRD 1991 p1116; KR v57 1989
    p1701; LJ v115 F 1, 1990 p108; NYTBR F 11, 1990
    p8; PW v239 D 1, 1989 p48.

Willis, Ted
The Lions of Judah.
Macmillan 1979.
BL v76 1980 p1493; KR v48 1980 p322; LJ v105 1980
    p1191; NYTBR Ag 17, 1980 p19.

593. Goethe, Johann Wolfgang von
1749-1832
German poet, novelist, & dramatist; wrote *Faust*
and *The Sorrows of Werther*

Kundera, Milan
Immortality.
Grove Weidenfeld 1991.
BRD 1991 p1065; BL v87 1991 p1531; KR v59 1991
    p351; NYTBR My 5, 1991 p30.

Mann, Thomas
The Beloved Returns.
Knopf 1940 (Rpr. 1957, 1964, 1983).
Translation of *Lotte in Weimar.*
FC 11th p409; LJ v65 1940 p652.

Nichols, Wallace B.
Old Apollo.
N. Wolsey 1946.

594. Gogh, Vincent Willem van
1853-1890
Dutch painter

Marcogliese, Catherine
JUV *Emily's Portfolio.*
Studio 123 1991.

Poldermans, Joost
Vincent: A Novel Based on the Life of van Gogh.
Holt, Rinehart & Winston 1962.
BL v58 1962 p683; BRD 1962 p959; FC 9th p405; KR
    v30 1962 p251; LJ v87 1962 p1632.

Stone, Irving
Lust for Life: The Novel of Vincent van Gogh.

Longmans, Green 1934 (Heavily reprinted).
BL v31 1934 p91; BRD 1934 p902; NYTBR S 30,
    1934 p2; SatR S 29, 1934 p137.

595. Goldman, Emma
1869-1940
American anarchist

Burke, J. F.
Noah.
Sherbourne Press 1968.
KR v36 1968 p200.

Day, Douglas
The Prison Notebooks of Ricardo Flores Magon.
Harcourt Brace Javanovich 1991.
BL v88 1991 p676; KR v59 1991 p1106; LJ v116 O
    15, 1991 p119.

Doctorow, E. L.
Ragtime.
Random House 1975.
BL v72 1975 p24; BRD 1975 p338; BRD 1976 p313;
    KR v43 1975 p529; LJ v100 1975 p1344; NYTBR Jl
    6, 1975 p1.

Mannin, Ethel Edith
*Red Rose: A Novel Based on the Life of Emma
    Goldman.*
Jarrolds 1941.

Rose, Howard
The Pooles of Pismo Bay.
Raymond Saroff 1990.
LJ v115 Je 1, 1990 p184.

596. Goldwater, Barry Morris
1909-
American politician; defeated by Lyndon
Johnson in 1964 US presidential election

Buckley, William F.
Tucker's Last Stand.
Random House 1990.
BL v87 1990 p691; KR v58 1990 p1550; NYTBR F 17,
    1991 p15; PW v237 N 16, 1990 p44.

597. Gollancz, Victor, Sir
1893-1967
English publisher

Bingham, John
Murder Plan Six.
V. Gollancz 1958.
BRD 1959 p102; NYTBR F 15, 1959 p44.

598. Gompers, Samuel
1850-1924
American labor leader; president of AFL, 1886-
1924

Barber, Elsie Marion
Hunt for Heaven.

Macmillan 1950.
BRD 1950 p49; KR v18 1950 p316; LJ v75 1950
p1044; NYTBR Ag 6, 1950 p17.

Hughes, Rupert
The Giant Wakes: A Novel about Samuel Gompers.
Borden Pub. Co. 1950.
BRD 1950 p457; NYTBR Jl 23, 1950 p19; SatR S 9,
1950 p34.

599. Goodnight, Charles
1836-1929
American cattleman

McMurtry, Larry
Streets of Laredo.
Simon & Schuster 1993.

600. Gorbachev, Mikhail Sergeyevich
1931-
Russian political leader; initiated policy of glasnost in attempt to revive Soviet society

Flannery, Sean
Counterstrike.
Morrow 1990.
KR v58 1990 p1113; LJ v115 S 15, 1990 p98; PW
v237 Ag 24, 1990 p55.

Gaillard, Frye
The Secret Diary of Mikhail Gorbachev.
Imprimatur Books 1990.
LJ v115 N 1, 1990 p124.

Jones, Dennis
Concerto.
St. Martin's 1989.
KR v58 1990 p366; LJ v115 My 1, 1990 p112;
NYTBR Je 17, 1990 p19; PW v237 Ap 20, 1990
p57.

601. Gordon, Charles George
1833-1885
English soldier who fought in many parts of the
British Empire

Maugham, Robin
The Last Encounter.
McGraw-Hill 1973.
BRD 1974 p808; LJ v99 1974 p382; NYTBR O 21,
1973 p51.

602. Gorky, Maxim, pseud.
1868-1936
Russian novelist & dramatist; wrote *Lower
Depths*

Gouzenko, Igor
The Fall of a Titan.
Cassell 1954.

BL v50 1954 p450; BRD 1954 p368; FC 7th p158; KR
v22 1954 p343; LJ v79 1954 p1225; NYTBR Jl 18,
1954 p1.

603. Gottschalk, Louis Moreau
1829-1869
American musician & composer

Breslin, Howard
Concert Grand.
Dodd, Mead 1963.

604. Gould, Glenn Herbert
1932-1982
Canadian pianist & composer

Bernhard, Thomas
The Loser.
Knopf 1991.
BL v88 1991 p27; KR v59 1991 p803; LJ v116 Ag
1991 p140; NYTBR S 8, 1991 p15.

605. Gould, Jay (Jason)
1836-1892
American railroad financier & speculator

Porter, Donald
Jubilee Jim and the Wizard of Wall Street.
Dutton 1990.
BL v86 1990 p1071; KR v58 1990 p133; LJ v115 Ap
1, 1990 p138.

606. Goya y Lucientes, Francisco Jose de
1746-1828
Spanish painter

Braider, Donald
*Rage in Silence: A Novel Based on the Life of
Goya.*
Putnam 1969.
BL v66 1969 p30; FC 9th p61; KR v37 1969 p193; LJ
v94 1969 p1897; NYTBR Ap 13, 1969 p46.

Feuchtwanger, Lion
This Is the Hour.
Viking 1951.
BL v47 1951 p346; BRD 1951 p287; FC 7th p132; KR
v19 1951 p157; LJ v76 1951 p772; NYTBR My 20,
1951 p5.

Gerson, Noel Bertram
The Naked Maja.
McGraw-Hill 1959.

Larreta, Antonio
The Last Portrait of Duchess of Alba.
Adler & Adler 1988.
KR v56 1988 p563; LJ v113 My 15, 1988 p93;
NYTBR O 23, 1988 p38.

Marlowe, Stephen
*Colossus: A Novel about Goya and a World Gone
Mad.*

Macmillan 1972.
BL v69 1972 p329; LJ v97 1972 p2753; PW v202 Jl
31, 1972 p68.

Porter, Eric
*Saturn's Child: A Romantic Novel Based on the
Life of Francisco Goya y Lucientes, 1746-1828.*
Rockliff 1947.

Sandstrom, Flora
*The Dancing Giant: A Novel Based on the Life of
Goya.*
A. Barker 1948.

White, Charles W. (Max White, pseud.)
In the Blazing Light.
Duell, Sloan & Pearce 1946.
BRD 1946 p882; KR v13 1945 p548; NYTBR F 17,
1946 p14.

607. Grable, Betty
1916-1973
American actress; WW II pin-up girl

Appel, Allen
Till the End of Time.
Doubleday 1990.
BL v87 1990 p24; KR v58 1990 p893; LJ v115 S 1,
1990 p253; PW v237 Je 29, 1990 p85.

608. Graham, Billy (William Franklin)
1918-
American evangelist

Dennison, Dorothy
Physician, Heal Thyself: A Novel.
Paternoster Press 1954.

609. Grant, Ulysses S.
1822-1885
Commander-in-chief of the Union Army;
forced surrender of Robert E. Lee; 18th US President

Adams, Henry
Democracy: An American Novel.
Holt 1880 (Heavily reprinted).
NYTBR Ja 23, 1921 p8; NYTBR O 26, 1952 p3; SatR
O 25, 1952 p37.

Devon, Louis
Aide to Glory.
Crowell 1952.
BL v49 1952 p125; BRD 1952 p248; LJ v77 1952
p1758.

Jones, Ted
Grant's War: A Novel of the Civil War.
Presido Press 1992.
KR v60 1992 p206; LJ v117 Je 1, 1992 p176; PW v239
F 10, 1992 p71.

Kantor, MacKinlay
JUV *Lee and Grant at Appomattox.*

Random House 1950.
BL v47 1950 p142; BRD 1950 p494; KR v18 1950
p422; LJ v76 1951 p54; NYTBR N 12, 1950 p6.

Lampman, Evelyn
YA *The Runaway.*
Lippincott 1953.
BL v50 1954 p262; BRD 1954 p518; KR v21 1953
p432; LJ v79 1954 p72; NYTBR Ja 31, 1954 p22.

Miers, Earl Schenck
YA *The Guns of Vicksburg.*
Putnam 1957.
BL v54 1958 p421; BRD 1958 p751; LJ v83 1958
p970; SatR Mr 22, 1958 p53.

Miers, Earl Schenck
JUV *We Were There When Grant Met Lee at Appomat-
tox.*
Grosset & Dunlap 1960.

Monjo, F. N.
JUV *The Vicksburg Veteran.*
Simon & Schuster 1971.
BL v67 1971 p835; KR v39 1971 p174; LJ v96 1971
p2365; NYTBR Ap 25, 1971 p40.

Nolan, Jeannette C.
YA *The Story of Ulysses S. Grant.*
Grosset & Dunlap 1952.

Seifert, Shirley
Captain Grant: A Novel.
Lippincott 1946.
Also published as *Uncounted Years.*
BL v42 1946 p300; BRD 1946 p736; FC 7th p310; KR
v14 1946 p129; NYTBR Je 2, 1946 p16.

Stevenson, Augusta
JUV *U.S. Grant, Young Horseman.*
Bobbs-Merrill 1962.

Todd, Helen
A Man Named Grant.
Houghton Mifflin 1940.
BRD 1940 p919; LJ v65 1940 p591; SatR S 21, 1940
p6.

610. Grasse, Count Francois Joseph Paul de
1722-1788
French naval officer; aided Continental forces
in American Revolution

Haislip, Harvey
Sea Road to Yorktown.
Doubleday 1960.
LJ v85 1960 p3101; LJ v85 1960 p3814.

611. El Greco
1541-1614
Spanish painter

Andres, Stefan Paul
El Greco Paints the Grant Inquisitor.
Dimension Press 1989.

Braider, Donald
Color from a Light Within.
Putnam 1967.
Also published as *The Private Life of El Greco.*
BL v63 1967 p1032; KR v35 1967 p616; NYTBR N
    12, 1967 p66; PW v192 Ag 21, 1967 p71.

De Osa, Veronica
The Mystic Finger Symbol.
Hale 1956.

Trevino, Elizabeth Borton
*The Greek of Toledo: A Romantic Narrative about
    El Greco.*
Crowell 1959.
BL v56 1959 p242; BRD 1960 p130; LJ v84 1959
    p3154; NYTBR O 25, 1959 p66.

612. Greene, Nathanael
1742-1786
American Revolutionary general

Davis, Burke
The Ragged One.
Rinehart 1951.
BL v47 1951 p301; BRD 1951 p222; KR v19 1951
    p138; NYTBR My 13, 1951 p18.

Hopkins, Joseph G.
Retreat and Recall.
Scribner 1966.
BL v62 1966 p993; KR v34 1966 p266; LJ v91 1966
    p2087; NYTBR Jl 3, 1966 p20.

Seifert, Shirley
Let My Name Stand Fair.
Lippincott 1956.
BL v53 1956 p23; BRD 1956 p836; FC 7th p311; KR
    v24 1956 p322; SatR Jl 28, 1956 p29.

Wiener, Willard
Morning in America.
Farrar & Rinehart 1942.
BRD 1942 p832; LJ v67 1942 p952; NYTBR N 1,
    1942 p22.

613. Gregory the Great
540-604

Schmirger, Gertrud (Gerhart Ellert, pseud.)
Gregory the Great.
Harcourt, Brace & World 1963.
BRD 1964 p361; LJ v88 1963 p4663; NYTBR O 20,
    1963 p47.

614. Gregory the Great, Saint
540-604
Pope & canonized saint

Mann, Thomas
The Holy Sinner.
Knopf 1951.
Translation of *Der Erwahlte.*
BL v48 1951 p32; BRD 1951 p575; KR v19 1951
    p355; LJ v76 1951 p1221; NYTBR S 9, 1951 p1.

615. Grenville, Richard
1541-1591
British naval hero; led colonizing expedition to
Roanoke Island, NC, 1585

Du Maurier, Daphne
The King's General.
Doubleday 1946 (Heavily reprinted).
BL v42 1946 p165; BRD 1946 p232; FC 9th p150; KR
    v13 1945 p476; NYTBR Ja 6, 1946 p6.

Fletcher, Inglis C.
Roanoke Hundren: A Novel.
Bobbs-Merrill 1948 (Rpr. 1952, 1972).
BL v45 1948 p88; BRD 1948 p273; FC 9th p177; LJ
    v73 1948 p1384; NYTBR O 24, 1948 p35.

Fullerton, Alexander
The Thunder and the Flame.
Hodder & Stoughton 1964 (Rpr. 1978).

Landells, Richard
Grenville's Revenge.
Hale 1971.

616. Grey, Jane, Lady
1537-1554
Queen of England; ruled for nine days; executed

Ainsworth, William Harrison
The Tower of London.
Richard Bentley 1840 (Heavily reprinted).
FC 7th p12.

Barrow, Pamela
Traitor Queen.
Hale 1974.

Bloom, Ursula (Lozania Prole, pseud.)
My Love! My Little Queen!.
Hale 1961 (Rpr. 1985).

Bloom, Ursula (Lozania Prole, pseud.)
The Ten-Day Queen.
Hale 1972 (Rpr. 1983).

Bradford, Karleen
JUV *The Nine Days Queen.*
Scholastic-TAB Publications 1986.
Quill & Q v52 D 1986 p14.

Evans, Jean
Nine Days a Queen.
Hale 1970.
Also published as *Lady Jane Grey.*

Eyre, Katherine
YA *Another Spring: The Story of Lady Jane Grey.*

Oxford University Press 1949.
BRD 1949 p293; HB v25 N 1949 p537; LJ v75 1950
p112.

Harwood, Alice
The Lily and the Leopards.
Bobbs-Merrill 1949.
Also published as *She Had to Be Queen.*
BRD 1949 p400; FC 8th p193; LJ v74 1949 p1094;
NYTBR Ag 28, 1949 p26; SatR S 24, 1949 p18.

Kenyon, Frank Wilson
*Henry VIII's Secret Daughter: The Tragedy of
Lady Jane Grey.*
Hutchinson 1974.

Lindsay, Philip
There Is No Escape.
Hutchinson 1974.
Originally published in 1950.

Malvern, Gladys
YA *The World of Lady Jane Grey.*
Vanguard Press 1964.
LJ v89 1964 p4208.

May, Beatrice
Sister to Jane: The Story of Lady Katharine Grey.
Hale 1983 (Rpr. 1992).

Mullally, Margaret
*A Crown in Darkness: A Novel about Lady Jane
Grey.*
St. Martin's 1975.
KR v43 1975 p869; PW v208 S 15, 1975 p46.

Peters, Maureen
Jewel of the Greys.
Hale 1972.
B&B v18 Ja 1973 p120.

Smith, A. C. H.
YA *Lady Jane: A Novel.*
Holt, Rinehart & Winston 1985.
B Rpt v4 Mr 1986 p31; BritBkN Ap 1986 p202; Kliatt
v20 Spring 1986 p14.

Vance, Marguerite
YA *Lady Jane Grey, Reluctant Queen.*
Dutton 1952.
BL v49 1952 p114; BRD 1952 p904; KR v20 1952
p661; LJ v78 1953 p229; NYTBR N 16, 1952 p22.

617. Grieg, Edvard Hagerup
1843-1907
Norwegian composer

Purdy, Claire Lee
YA *Song of the North: The Story of Edvard Grieg.*
Messner 1941.
BL v37 1941 p516; BRD 1941 p732; LJ v66 1941
p466; NYTBR Je 22, 1941 p10.

618. Grimaldi, Joseph
1779-1837
English clown; popular attraction in Covent
Gardens, 1806-1823

Hardwick, Mollie
Lovers Meeting.
St. Martin's 1979.
BL v76 1979 p331; KR v47 1979 p875; LJ v104 1979
p1718.

619. Grimke, Angelina Emily
1805-1879
American abolitionist & author; sister of Sarah
Grimke

Bushkovitch, Mary
The Grimkes of Charleston.
Southern Historical Press 1992.

Stevenson, Janet
Sisters and Brothers.
Crown 1966.
LJ v91 1966 p1248.

620. Grimke, Sarah Moore
1792-1873
American abolitionist; with sister Angelina, lec-
tured for American Anti-Slavery Society &
rights of women

Bushkovitch, Mary
The Grimkes of Charleston.
Southern Historical Press 1992.

Stevenson, Janet
Sisters and Brothers.
Crown 1966.
LJ v91 1966 p1248.

621. Groves, Leslie Richard
1896-1970
Director of the Manhattan Project

Smith, Martin Cruz
Stallion Gate.
Random House 1986.
BL v82 1986 p1043; LJ v111 My 1, 1986 p132;
NYTBR My 4, 1986 p14; PW v229 Mr 14, 1986
p102.

622. Gruber, Franz Xaver
1787-1863
Austrian musician; wrote music for the Christ-
man song *Silent Night*

Wenning, Elizabeth
JUV *The Christmas Mouse.*
Holt 1959 (Rpr. 1983).
BRD 1960 p1420; KR v27 1959 p756; LJ v84 1959
p3627; NYTBR N 29, 1959 p68; SatR D 19, 1959
p43.

623. Guarnieri, Giuseppe Antonio
1863-1745
Italian violin maker; commonly known because
he signed his violins with I.H.S. after his name

Wibberley, Leonard
YA *Guarneri: Story of a Genius.*
Farrar, Straus & Giroux 1974.
BS v34 N 15, 1974 p379; HB v50 Ag 1974 p387; LJ
v99 1974 p2750.

624. Guevara, Che Ernesto
1928-1967
Argentine revolutionary; associated with Castro
in Cuban takeover

Buckley, William F.
See You Later Alligator.
Doubleday 1985.
BL v81 1985 p802; FC 11th p85; KR v53 1985 p4;
NYTBR Mr 3, 1985 p12; PW v227 Ja 18, 1985 p61.

Cantor, Jay
The Death of Che Guevara: A Novel.
Knopf 1983.
BL v80 1983 p134; BRD 1984 p241; KR v51 1983
p825; LJ v108 1983 p2099; NYTBR N 27, 1983 p3.

Reynolds, Steve; Carver, Gene
The Murder of Che Guevara.
Wild Goose Publishing 1983
BL v81 1984 p187.

625. Gustavus Adolphus
1594-1632
King of Sweden, 1611-1632

Henty, G. A.
JUV *The Lion of the North: A Tale of the Times of Gus-
tavus Adolphus and the Wars of Religion.*
Blackie 1885.

Ronalds, Mary Teresa
The Lion at Midnight.
Macdonald & Co. 1971.
Obs D 12, 1971 p27.

626. Gutenberg, Johannes
1400-1468
German printer; reputedly first printer in Europe
to use moveable type

Marcuse, Katherine
JUV *The Devil's Workshop.*
Abingdon 1979.
BL v75 1979 p1296; RT v33 D 1979 p360; SLJ v25
Ap 1979 p59.

Ritchie, Ward
*1440 John Gutenberg 1940: A Fanciful Story of
the 15th Century.*
Ward Ritchie Press 1940.

Vernon, Louise A.
JUV *Ink on His Fingers.*
Herald Press 1972.

627. Guthrie, Woody (Woodrow Wilson)
1912-1967
American folksinger & songwriter; wrote the
song *This Land is Your Land*

McAlpine, Gordon
Joy in Mudville.
Dutton 1989.
KR v57 1989 p152; LJ v114 Mr 1, 1989 p88.

628. Gwyn, Nell (Eleanor)
1650-1687
English actress; mistress of Charles II

Bloom, Ursula (Lozania Prole, pseud.)
The Orange Girl.
Hale 1972 (Rpr. 1985).

Bloom, Ursula (Lozania Prole, pseud.)
Pretty, Witty Nell.
Hale 1952 (Rpr. 1972).

Hibbert, Eleanor (Jean Plaidy, pseud.)
Here Lies Our Sovereign Lord.
Putnam 1973.
BL v69 1973 p1008; KR v41 1973 p475.

Kenyon, Frank Wilson
Mistress Nell.
Appleton-Century-Crofts 1961.
Also published as *Mrs. Nelly.*
LJ v86 1961 p2963; NYTBR O 8, 1961 p38

King, Betty
Nell Gwyn.
Hale 1979.

Leigh, Olivia
Nell: The Life of Nell Gwynn.
Hale 1960.

Sudworth, Gwynedd
Three Charles for Nell.
Hale 1979.

Sumner, Richard
Mistress of the Boards.
Random House 1976.
KR v44 1976 p995; LJ v101 1976 p2303.

Turner, Judy
The Merry Jade.
Hale 1978.

629. Hadrian
76-138
Roman emperor, 117-138

Gray, Charles Edward
Murder Defies the Roman Emperor.

B. Humphries 1957.
NYTBR Ap 27, 1958 p18.

Ish-Kishon, Sulamith
Drusilla: A Novel of the Emperor Hadrian.
Pantheon 1970.
HB v46 Ag 1970 p393; LJ v95 1970 p385.

Schmidt, Joel
Hadrian.
Gay Sunshine Press 1984.

Siegel, Benjamin
The Sword and the Promise.
Harcourt, Brace 1959.
BL v55 1959 p478; BRD 1959 p909; KR v27 1959
    p105; LJ v84 1959 p1628; NYTBR Mr 29, 1959 p31.

Trease, Geoffrey
YA *Message to Hadrian.*
Vanguard Press 1955.
BRD 1956 p933; LJ v81 1956 p1553; NYTBR Ag 12,
    1956 p24.

Yourcenar, Marguerite
Memoirs of Hadrian.
Farrar, Straus & Young 1954.
BL v51 1954 p176; BRD 1954 p982; FC 7th p392; KR
    v22 1954 p592; LJ v79 1954 p2100; NYTBR N 21,
    1954 p6.

630. Hale, Nathan
1755-1776
American Revolutionary patriot; hanged as spy
by the British

Brown, Marion Marsh
YA *Young Nathan.*
Westminster Press 1949.
BL v46 1949 p51; BRD 1949 p114; KR v17 1949
    p397; LJ v74 1949 p1550; NYTBR Ja 22, 1950 p18.

Decker, Malcolm
The Rebel and the Turncoat.
Whittlesey House 1949.
BL v45 1949 p297; BRD 1949 p225; KR v17 1949
    p62; LJ v74 1949 p828.

Mann, Martha
YA *Nathan Hale, Patriot.*
Dodd, Mead & Co. 1944.
BRD 1944 p500; LJ v69 1944 p1006; SatR F 10, 1945
    p25.

Monjo, F. N.
JUV *A Namesake for Nathan.*
Coward, McCann & Geoghegan 1977.
KR v45 1977 p856; NYTBR Ja 1, 1978 p20; SLJ v24
    N 1977 p60.

Stevenson, Augusta
JUV *Nathan Hale, Puritan Boy.*
Bobbs-Merrill 1959.
LJ v84 1959 p3932.

631. Hall, Charles Francis
1821-1871
American arctic explorer

Steelman, Robert J.
Call of the Arctic.
Coward-McCann 1960.
BL v57 1961 p547; BRD 1961 p1347; KR v28 1960
    p804; LJ v85 1960 p3651.

632. Hamilton, Sir William
1730-1803
English diplomat and archaeologist; husband of
Lady Emma Hamilton

Bloom, Ursula (Lozania Prole, pseud.)
The Magnificent Couresan.
McBride 1950.
Also published as *Our Dearest Emma.*
NYTBR Je 4, 1950 p27.

Dessau, Joanna
The Blacksmith's Daughter.
Hale 1983.

Field, Bradda
Bride of Glory.
Greystone Press 1942.
Also published as *Miledi.*
BL v38 1942 p275; BRD 1942 p254; LJ v67 1942
    p182; NYTBR Mr 1, 1942 p6.

Foxell, Nigel
Loving Emma.
Harvester Press 1986.
BritBKN D 1986 p710; Lon R Bks v9 Ja 8, 1987 p17;
    TLS D 5, 1986 p1380.

Frye, Pearl
The Sleeping Sword: A Biographical Novel.
Little, Brown 1952.
BRD 1952 p330; KR v20 1952 p304; LJ v77 1952
    p1304; NYTBR Jl 6, 1952 p11.

Graham, Molly
*Emma: The Lives and Loves of Emma, Lady Ham-
    ilton.*
Hale 1967.

Hodge, Jane
Shadow of a Lady.
Coward, McCann & Geoghegan 1973.
BL v70 1974 p516; FC 9th p253; KR v41 1973 p906;
    LJ v98 1973 p3392.

Kenyon, Frank Wilson
Emma.
Crowell 1955.
BL v51 1955 p316; BRD 1955 p492; FC 7th p207; KR
    v23 1955 p16; LJ v80 1955 p561; NYTBR Mr 13,
    1955 p24.

Schuyler, Vera
Beloved Upstart.
W.H. Allen 1974.

Sontag, Susan
The Volcano Lover: A Romance.
Farrar, Straus, Giroux 1992.
BL v88 1992 p1733; KR v60 1992 p635; LJ v117 Je
  15, 1992 p103; NYTBR Ag 9, 1992 p1; Time v140
  Ag 17, 1992 p66.

Stacton, David
Sir William: or, A Lesson in Love.
Putnam 9163.
BRD 1963 p958; LJ v88 1963 p4398; NYTBR O 20,
  1963 p46; SatR O 5, 1963 p41.

Styles, Showell
The Admiral's Fancy.
Faber & Faber 1958.
BL v55 1958 p157; BRD 1959 p957; KR v26 1958
  p672.

633. Hamilton, Alexander
1757-1804
American politician; first secretary of the treasury; died from wounds inflicted in duel with
Aaron Burr

Atherton, Gertrude Franklin
*The Conqueror: Being the True and Romantic
  Story of Alexander Hamilton.*
Macmillan 1902 (Heavily reprinted).
Most reprints carry the subtitle *A Dramatized Biography of Alexander Hamilton.*
FC 8th p20; NYTBR Ap 12, 1902 p244; NYTBR Ap
  19, 1902 p265; NYTBR Ag 6, 1911 p485.

Desmond, Alice Curtis
*Alexander Hamilton's Wife: A Romance of the
  Hudson.*
Dodd, Mead 1952.
BL v49 1952 p16; BRD 1952 p246; LJ v77 1952
  p1312; NYTBR N 16, 1952 p20.

Flood, Charles B.
Monmouth.
Houghton Mifflin 1961.
BRD 1962 p395; LJ v86 1961 p3300; NYTBR O 8,
  1961 p5; SatR N 4, 1961 p41.

Harte, Bret
*Thankful Blossom: A Romance of the Jerseys,
  1779.*
J.R. Osgood 1877 (Heavily reprinted).

Laing, Alexander K.
Jonathan Eagle.
Duell, Sloan & Pearce 1955.
BRD 1955 p521; LJ v80 1955 p1588; NYTBR Ag 21,
  1955 p4.

St. George, Judith
YA *Turncoat Winter, Rebel Spring.*
Chilton Book Co. 1970.
BL v30 Je 1, 1970 p106; LJ v95 1970 p3640.

Taylor, David
Mistress of the Forge.
Lippincott 1964.
FC 9th p501; LJ v89 1964 p1117; LJ v89 1964 p2246;
  NYTBR Ap 12, 1964 p37.

634. Hamilton, Emma
1761-1815
Wife of Sir William Hamilton; Mistress of Horatio Nelson

Bloom, Ursula (Lozania Prole, pseud.)
The Magnificent Courtesan.
McBride 1950.
Also published as *Our Dearest Emma.*
NYTBR Je 4, 1950 p27.

Dessau, Joanna
The Blacksmith's Daughter.
Hale 1983.

Field, Bradda
Bride of Glory.
Greystone Press 1942.
Also published as *Miledi.*
BL v38 1942 p275; BRD 1942 p254; LJ v67 1942
  p182; NYTBR Mr 1, 1942 p6.

Foxell, Nigel
Loving Emma.
Harvester Press 1986.
BritBKN D 1986 p710; Lon R Bks v9 Ja 8, 1987 p17;
  TLS D 5, 1986 p1380.

Frye, Pearl
The Sleeping Sword: A Biographical Novel.
Little, Brown 1952.
BRD 1952 p330; KR v20 1952 p304; LJ v77 1952
  p1304; NYTBR Jl 6, 1952 p11.

Graham, Molly
Emma: The Lives and Loves of Emma, Lady Hamilton.
Hale 1967.

Hodge, Jane
Shadow of a Lady.
Coward, McCann & Geoghegan 1973.
BL v70 1974 p516; FC 9th p253; KR v41 1973 p906;
  LJ v98 1973 p3392.

Kenyon, Frank Wilson
Emma.
Crowell 1955.
BL v51 1955 p316; BRD 1955 p492; FC 7th p207; KR
  v23 1955 p16; LJ v80 1955 p561; NYTBR Mr 13,
  1955 p24.

Schuyler, Vera
Beloved Upstart.
W.H. Allen 1974.

Sontag, Susan
The Volcano Lover: A Romance.
Farrar, Straus, Giroux 1992.
BL v88 1992 p1733; KR v60 1992 p635; LJ v117 Je
  15, 1992 p103; NYTBR Ag 9, 1992 p1; Time v140
  Ag 17, 1992 p66.

Stacton, David
Sir William: or, A Lesson in Love.
Putnam 1963.
BRD 1963 p958; LJ v88 1963 p4398; NYTBR O 20,
 1963 p46; SatR O 5, 1963 p41.

Styles, Showell
The Admiral's Fancy.
Faber & Faber 1958.
BL v55 1958 p157; BRD 1959 p957; KR v26 1958
 p672.

635. Hammett, (Samuel) Dashiell
1894-1961
American writer of detective fiction; wrote *The
Maltese Falcon*

Gores, Joseph N.
Hammett: A Novel.
Putnam 1975.
BL v72 1975 p283; BRD 1976 p455; KR v43 1975
 p796; LJ v100 1975 p1573; NYTBR N 9, 1975 p55;
 PW v208 Jl 21, 1975 p62.

636. Hampton, Wade
1818-1902
American Confederate general

Allen, Merritt P.
YA *Johnny Reb.*
D. McKay 1952.
BRD 1952 p13; JHSLC 3rd p379; KR v20 Ja 1, 1952
 p2; LJ v77 1952 p604; NYTBR Mr 9, 1952 p22.

McGiffin, Lee
YA *Rebel Rider.*
Dutton 1959.
BL v56 1959 p248; BRD 1960 p859; KR v27 1959
 p498; LJ v84 1959 p3640.

637. Hancock, John
1737-1793
American Revolution politician; first to sign
Declaration of Independence

Cleven, Cathrine Seward
JUV *John Hancock, New England Boy.*
Bobbs-Merrill 1963.

Gerson, Noel Bertram
*Yankee Doodle Dandy: A Biographical Novel of
 John Hancock.*
Doubleday 1965.
BL v62 1965 p195.

638. Handel, George Frederick
1685-1759
German-born English composer; *The Messiah* is
his best-known work

Wheeler, Opal
JUV *Handel at the Court of Kings.*

Dutton 1943.
BRD 1944 p803; LJ v69 1944 p74; SatR Ag 19, 1944
 p27.

639. Hanks, Nancy
1784-1818
Mother of Abraham Lincoln

Stevenson, Augusta
Nancy Hanks, Kentucky Girl.
Bobbs-Merrill 1954 (Rpr. 1962).

Wilson, Dorothy Clarke
Lincoln's Mothers.
Doubleday 1981.
BL v77 1981 p1014; LJ v106 1981 p371; PW v218 D
 26, 1980 p51.

640. Hannibal
247-183 BC
Carthaginian general; known for his tactical
genius, & for his crossing of the Alps with elephants

Baumann, Hans
YA *I Marched with Hannibal.*
H.Z. Walck 1962.
BL v58 1962 p480; BRD 1962 p74; HB v38 Ap 1962
 p178; KR v30 1962 p117; LJ v87 1962 p2030;
 NYTBR Mr 4, 1962 p34.

Bryher, Winifred
Gate to the Sea.
Pantheon 1958.
BL v55 1958 p97; BRD 1958 p161; LJ v83 1958
 p2763; NYTBR S 14, 1958 p5.

De Beer, Gavin
Alps and Elephants.
Dutton 1956.
BL v53 1956 p66; BRD 1956 p247; NYTBR S 16,
 1956 p26.

Dolan, Mary
YA *Hannibal of Carthage.*
Macmillan 1955.
Also published as *Hannibal: Scourge of Imperial Rome.*
BL v51 1955 p354; BRD 1955 p247; FC 8th p119; KR
 v23 1955 p220; LJ v80 1955 p1217: NYTBR Je 26,
 1955 p18.

Hirsh, Marilyn
JUV *Hannibal and His 37 Elephants.*
Holiday House 1977.
KR v45 1977 p1043; PW v212 Jl 18, 1977 p138; SLJ
 v24 N 1977 p48.

Houghton, Eric
JUV *The White Wall.*
McGraw-Hill 1961.
LJ v88 1963 p1362; SatR F 23, 1963 p46.

Kent, Louise Andrews
JUV *He Went with Hannibal.*

Houghton Mifflin 1964.
LJ v89 1964 p2878.

Lindsay, Jack
Hannibal Takes a Hand.
A. Dakers 1941.

Powers, Alfred
JUV *Hannibal's Elephants.*
Longmans, Green 1944.
BL v41 1944 p111; BRD 1944 p610; KR v12 1944
p374; LJ v69 1944 p1052; NYTBR D 17, 1944 p18.

Taleb, Mirza
Hannibal, Man of Destiny.
Branden Press 1974.

641. Harding, Warren G.
1865-1923
29th US President

Plunket, Robert
My Search for Warren Harding.
Knopf 1983 (Rpr. 1992).
KR v51 1983 p206; LJ v108 1983 p921.

Reed, Ishmael
Mumbo Jumbo.
Doubleday 1972 (Rpr. 1988).
BL v69 1972 p69; BRD 1972 p1073; KR v40 1972
p641; LJ v97 1972 p3182; NYTBR Ag 6, 1972 p1.

Zagst, Michael
"M.H." Meets President Harding.
D.I. Fine 1987.
KR v55 1987 p258; LJ v112 Ap 15, 1987 p102; PW
v231 Mr 13, 1987 p71.

642. Hare, William
1792-1870
Irish murderer; with partner William Burke,
committed a series of infamous murders; sold
bodies to supply dissection subjects to school of
anatomy

Byrd, Elizabeth
Rest without Peace.
Macmillan 1974.
B&B v19 Ap 1974 p91; GW v110 F 16, 1974 p25;
Obs F 3, 1974 p31; Spec v232 F 9, 1974 p171.

Goodwin, Inge
Bury Me in Lead.
A. Wingate 1952.

Thomas, Dylan
The Doctor and the Devils.
Dent 1953 (Heavily reprinted).
BL v50 1953 p116; BRD 1953 p932; LJ v78 1953
p2214; NYTBR D 6, 1953 p38.

643. Harold II
1022-1066
Last Saxon king of England

Anand, Valerie
The Norman Pretender.
Scribner 1979.
KR v47 1979 p1272; LJ v105 1980 p118; PW v216 D
10, 1979 p59.

Bulwer-Lytton, Edward
Harold, the Last of the Saxon Kings.
B. Tauchnitz 1848 (Heavily reprinted).

Clarke, Brenda (Brenda Honeyman, pseud.)
Harold of the English.
Hale 1979.

Lewis, Hilda
YA *Harold Was My King.*
D. McKay 1970.
BL v67 1971 p602; LJ v96 1971 p1528.

Llywelyn, Morgan
The Wind from Hastings.
Houghton Mifflin 1978.
KR v46 1978 p327; LJ v103 1978 p1196.

Muntz, Hope
The Golden Warrior: The Story of Harold and William.
Scribner 1949.
BL v45 1949 p225; BRD 1949 p665; FC 9th p372; KR
v16 1948 p581; LJ v74 1949 p312; NYTBR Mr 6,
1949 p26.

Oliver, Jane
JUV *Faraway Princess.*
St. Martin's 1962.
LJ v87 1962 p3204; NYTBR O 14, 1962 p34.

Treece, Henry
YA *Hounds of the King.*
Bodley Head 1955.

Viney, Jayne
The Last Saxon.
Hale 1976.

644. Harris, Joel Chandler
1848-1908
American journalist & author; created Uncle
Remus character

Harlow, Alvin Fay
YA *Joel Chandler Harris, Plantation Storyteller.*
Messner 1941.
BL v37 1941 p516; BRD 1941 p397; LJ v66 1941
p465; NYTBR S 7, 1941 p9.

Weddle, Ethel H.
JUV *Joel Chandler, Young Storyteller.*
Bobbs-Merrill 1964.

645. Harrison, William Henry
1773-1841
American general & ninth US President

Peckham, Howard
JUV *William Henry Harrison, Young Tippecanoe.*
Bobbs-Merrill 1951.
BRD 1951 p694; LJ v76 1951 p880; NYTBR My 20,
1951 p26.

646. Harvey, William
1578-1657
English physician; discoverer of the circulation
of blood

Hamburger, Jean
The Diary of William Harvey: The Imaginary Journal of the Physician Who Revolutionized Medicine.
Rutgers University Press 1992.
BL v89 1992 p238; KR v60 1992 p1009.

Weiss, David
Physician Extraordinary: A Novel of the Life and Times of William Harvey.
Delacorte 1975.
BL v72 1975 p116; KR v43 1975 p681; PW v207 Je
16, 1975 p74.

647. Hastings, Warren
1732-1818
English colonial administrator; first governor-general of India

Dereham, Francis
The Governor and the Lady.
Hale 1975.

Minney, R. J.
The Governor's Lady.
Jarrolds 1951.
Complete revision of the author's *Governor General.*

648. Hathaway, Anne
1557-1623
Wife of William Shakespeare

Nye, Robert
Mrs. Shakespeare: The Complete Works.
Sinclair-Stevenson 1993.
Obs Ja 24, 1993 p53; TLS Ja 29, 1993 p21.

649. Hatshepsut
d. 1481? BC
Egyptian queen

Carter, Dorothy Sharp
YA *His Majesty, Queen Hatshepsut.*
Lippincott 1987.
BRD 1988 p275; KR v55 1987 p1236; NYTBR D 20,
1987 p20; SLJ v34 O 1987 p137.

Gedge, Pauline
Child of the Morning.
Dial 1977.

BL v74 1977 p22; KR v45 1977 p444; LJ v102 1977
p1405.

Lumpkin, Beatrice
Senefer and Hatshepsut: A Novel of Egyptian Genius.
DuSable Museum Press 1983.

McGraw, Eloise J.
Pharaoh.
Coward-McCann 1958.
BRD 1958 p697; LJ v83 1958 p1551; NYTBR Jl 6,
1958 p12; SatR Je 7, 1958 p16.

Wadoud, Jain
Hatshepsut: Foremost of the Noble Ladies, King of Queens.
Horus Pub. Inc. 1987.

650. Hatton, Christopher, Sir
1540-1591
English courtier and politician; Lord chancellor,
1587; favorite of Elizabeth I

Howard, Liz
The Squire of Holdenby.
Hale 1986.

651. Hawthorne, Nathaniel
1804-1864
American author; wrote *The Scarlet Letter* and
The House of Seven Gables

Byron, May
A Day with Nathaniel Hawthorne.
Folcroft Library Editions 1978.
Reprint of the 1912 ed. published by Hodder &
Stoughton.

Plante, David
Slides: A Novel.
Gambit 1971.
BRD 1971 p1079; KR v39 1971 p654; LJ v96 1971
p2546; NYTBR Ag 22, 1971 p28.

Thorn, Michael
Pen Friends.
Macmillan 1988.

652. Haydn, Franz Joseph
1732-1809
Austrian composer

Ewen, David
YA *Haydn, a Good Life.*
Holt 1946.
BL v43 1946 p104; BRD 1947 p284; KR v14 1946
p225; LJ v71 1946 p1811.

653. Hayes, Roland
1887-1976
American tenor; sang arias & folk songs

Smith, Eunice Young
YA *A Trumpet Sounds: A Novel Based on the Life of Roland Hayes.*
Lawrence Hill 1985.
BS v45 Mr 1986 p445; VOYA Ag 1986 p151.

654. Hearn, Lafcadio
1850-1904
Author who introduced Japanese culture to the West through his writings

Rose, Dennis
Lafcadio: His Sun Was Dark.
Book Guild 1987.

Wedeck, Harry E.
Mortal Hunger; a Novel Based on the Life of Lafcadio Hearn.
Sheridan House 1947.
BRD 1947 p949; NYTBR S 14, 1947 p29; SatR Ag 23, 1947 p11.

655. Hearne, Samuel
1745-1792
English explorer

Lambert, Richard S.
North for Adventure.
McClelland & Stewart 1952.

656. Hearst, William Randolph
1863-1951
American journalist, publisher, & politician

Hall, Robert L.
Murder at San Simeon.
St. Martin's 1988.
BL v84 F 15, 1988 p972; KR v56 Ja 15, 1988 p89; PW 232 Ja 8, 1988 p73.

Jakes, John
California Gold: A Novel.
Random House 1989.
BL v85 1989 p1922; NYTBR O 8, 1989 p24.

Martini, Steven Paul
The Simeon Chamber.
D.I. Fine 1988.
KR v56 1988 p1089.

McMahon, Thomas A.
Loving Little Egypt.
Viking 1987.
BW v17 F 22, 1987 p9; KR v54 1986 p1751; LJ v112 F 1, 1987 p93; NYTBR F 8, 1987 p16; PW v230 D 12, 1986 p42.

657. Heck, Barbara Ruckle
1734-1804
Irish-born religious leader; helped established first Methodist chapel in America

Withrow, William H.
Barbara Heck: A Tale of Early Methodism.
Hunt & Eaton 1895 (Rpr. 1961).

658. Heine, Heinrich
1797-1856
German poet, author, & critic

Meynell, Esther
Grave Fairytale: A Romantic Novel.
Chapman & Hall 1931 (Rpr. 1950).
BRD 1932 p655; SatR F 13, 1932 p527.

659. Heisman, John William
1869-1936
Football coach; Heisman Trophy named for him

Wells, Lawrence
Let the Band Play Dixie.
Doubleday 1987.
KR v55 1987 p888; LJ v112 Ag 1987 p145.

660. Helen of Troy
Greek legendary figure

Erskine, John
The Private Life of Helen of Troy.
Bobbs-Merrill 1925 (Heavily reprinted).
BRD 1925 p209; FC 7th p125; NYTBR D 6, 1925 p2.

Hansen, Eva Hemmer
Scandal in Troy.
Random House 1956.
BL v53 1956 p71; BRD 1956 p406; NYTBR O 21, 1956 p54; SatR S 29, 1956 p26.

Hopkins, Kenneth
Helen of Troy.
Beverly Books 1956.

Jackson, Laura Riding
A Trojan Ending.
Random House 1937 (Rpr. 1984).
LATBR Je 30, 1985 p4.

Seymour, Miranda
The Goddess.
Coward, McCann & Geoghegan 1979.
KR v47 1979 p350.

661. Heliogabalus
204-222
Roman emperor

Duggan, Alfred Leo
Family Favorites.
Pantheon 1961.
BL v57 1961 p519; BRD 1961 p376; KR v28 1960 p937; LJ v86 1961.

662. Heloise
1101-1164
French religious figure; wife of Peter Abelard

Ince, Richard B.
Abelard of Paris.
Chancery Books 1969.

Meade, Marion
Stealing Heaven: The Love Story of Heloise and Abelard.
Morrow 1979 (Rpr. 1989).
KR v47 1979 p536; LJ v104 1979 p1720; PW v217 My 23, 1980 p75.

Trouncer, Margaret
The Passion of Peter Abelard.
Heinemann 1965.

Waddell, Helen
Peter Abelard, a Novel.
Holt 1933 (Heavily reprinted).
BRD 1933 p973; NYTBR O 1, 1933 p7; SatR S 30, 1933 p145.

663. Hemings, Sally
1773-1835
One of Thomas Jefferson's slaves; alleged to be his mistress

Chase-Riboud, Barbara
Sally Hemings: A Novel.
Viking 1979.
BRD 1979 p225; FC 11th p106; KR v47 1979 p539; LJ v104 1979 p1355; NYTBR O 28, 1979 p14.

Erickson, Steve
Arc D'X.
Poseidon Press 1993.
NYTBR My 2, 1993 p9.

Rinaldi, Ann
YA *Wolf by the Ears.*
Scholastic 1991.
BL v87 1991 p1125; BRD 1991 p1571; SLJ v37 Ap 1991 p142; VOYA v14 Je 1991 p101.

Woodson, Minnie Shumate
The Sable Curtain.
Stafford Lowery Press 1987.

664. Hemingway, Ernest Miller
1899-1961
American author & journalist; wrote *A Farewell to Arms* & *For Whom the Bell Tolls*; won Nobel Prize in 1954

Aldridge, James
One Last Glimpse.
Little, Brown 1977.
BL v73 My 1, 1977 p1325; ILN v265 My 1977 p83; LJ v102 1977 p945; NYTBR Jl 10, 1977 p45.

Alexander, Karl
Papa and Fidel.
T. Doherty Associates 1989.
KR v57 F 1, 1989 p136; LATBR My 7, 1989 p4; LJ v114 Ap 1, 1989 p109; PW v235 F 1, 1989 p55.

Donnell, David
The Blue Ontario Hemingway Boat Race.
Coach House Press 1985.
BIC v14 O 1985 p22.

Gilmore, Christopher Cook
Hemingway: A Novel.
St. Martin's 1988.

Haldeman, Joe
The Hemingway Hoax.
Morrow 1990.
BL v86 1990 p1784; KR v58 1990 p696; LJ v115 My 1, 1990 p112.

Henderson, William M.
I Killed Hemingway.
St. Martin's Press 1993.
KR v61 1993 p11; NYTBR My 9, 1993 p9; PW v240 Ja 25, 1993 p77.

Kaminsky, Stuart M.
High Midnight.
St. Martin's 1981.
KR v49 1981 p656; LJ v106 1981 p1246.

Murphy, Michael
Hemingsteen.
Autolycus Press 1978.
BL v74 1978 p1412.

Whelan, Gloria
YA *The Pathless Woods.*
Lippincott 1981.
KR v49 S 1, 1981 p1088; SLJ v27 Ap 1981 p144.

665. Henri, Robert
1865-1929
American artist

Sandoz, Mari
Son of the Gamblin' Man: The Youth of an Artist.
C.N. Potter 1960 (Rpr. 1976).
BL v56 1960 p434; BRD 1960 p1175; LJ v85 1960 p1144; NYTBR Jl 10, 1960 p26.

666. Henry I
1068-1135
King of England, 1100-1135

Dymoke, Juliet
Henry of the High Rock.
Dobson 1971.
TLS D 24, 1971 p1597.

Dymoke, Juliet
The Lion's Legacy.
Dobson 1974.

Hibbert, Eleanor (Jean Plaidy, pseud.)
The Lion of Justice.
Putnam 1979.

667. Henry II
1133-1189
King of England, 1154-1189

Andrew, Prudence
Ordeal by Silence: A Story of Medieval Times.
G.P. Putnam's Sons 1961.
BRD 1962 p33; LJ v86 1961 p2960; NYTBR O 29,
    1961 p44.

Barnes, Margaret Campbell
The Passionate Brood.
Macrae Smith 1945 (Rpr. 1972).
Also published as *Like Us They Live.*
BRD 1945 p37; FC 10th p34; KR v13 F 15, 1945 p72;
    WLB v40 O 1945 p101.

Bennetts, Pamela
The Angevin King.
Hale 1972.

Bourne, Peter
The Court of Love.
Hutchinson 1958 (Rpr. 1974).

Butler, Margaret
The Lion of Christ.
Coward, McCann & Geoghegan 1977.
KR v45 1977 p299; LJ v102 1977 p1302.

Butler, Margaret
The Lion of England.
Coward, McCann & Geoghegan 1973.
BL v70 1973 p273; KR v41 1973 p700; LJ v98 1973
    p3391; PW v204 Jl 9, 1973 p41.

Butler, Margaret
The Lion of Justice.
Coward, McCann & Geoghegan 1975.
BL v71 1975 p544; KR v42 1974 p1266; LJ v100 1975
    p310; PW v207 Ja 6, 1975 p51.

Duggan, Alfred Leo
My Life for My Sheep.
Coward-McCann 1955.
Also published as *God and My Right.*
BRD 1955 p257; FC 8th p128; KR v23 1955 p573; LJ
    v80 1955 p1828; NYTBR O 2, 1955 p5; Time v66
    O 10, 1953 p131.

Hibbert, Eleanor (Jean Plaidy, pseud.)
The Courts of Love.
Putnam 1988.
CSM v80 F 12, 1988 p20; KR v56 1988 p96; PW v233
    Ja 22, 1988 p104.

Hibbert, Eleanor (Jean Plaidy, pseud.)
The Plantagenet Prelude.
Hale 1976 (Rpr. 1980).
BL v76 1980 p1411; KR v48 1980 p241; LJ v105 1980
    p1103.

Hibbert, Eleanor (Jean Plaidy, pseud.)
The Revolt of the Eaglets.
Hale 1977 (Rpr. 1980).
BL v76 1980 p1658; KR v48 1980 p734.

Holland, Cecelia
The Earl.
Knopf 1971.
BS v31 N 1, 1971 p356; FC 11th p300; LJ v96 1971
    p2346.

Hutchins, Linda
Mortal Love: A Novel of Eleanor of Aquitaine.
Doubleday 1980.
BS v40 Jl 1980 p158; KR v48 1980 p154; LJ v105
    1980 p878; PW v217 F 1, 1980 p103.

Lofts, Norah
*Eleanor the Queen: The Story of the Most Famous
    Woman of the Middle Ages.*
Doubleday 1955.
Also published as *Queen in Waiting.*
BL v52 1955 p16; BRD 1955 p568; KR v23 1955
    p330; LJ v80 1955 p2650; NYTBR Jl 24, 1955 p18.

Mydans, Shelley
*Thomas: A Novel of the Life, Passions and Mir-
    acles of Becket.*
Doubleday 1965.
BW Ag 22, 1965 p12; FC 11th p448; LJ v90 1965
    p3073; NYTBR S 12, 1965 p4.

Trouncer, Margaret
Eleanor: The Two Marriages of a Queen.
Heinemann 1967.
Punch v252 F 22, 1967 p282.

York, Robert
The Swords of December.
Scribner 1978.
KR v47 1979 p222; LJ v104 1979 p1359; PW v215 F
    19, 1978 p103.

668. Henry III
1207-1272
King of England, 1216-1272

Bennetts, Pamela
The De Montfort Legacy.
St. Martin's 1973.
B&B v18 Jl 1973 p135; BL v70 1973 p207; KR v41
    1973 p265.

Graham, Alice Walworth
Shield of Honor.
Doubleday 1957.
BRD 1957 p958; FC 7th p158; KR v25 1957 p453; LJ
    v82 1957 p2038.

Pargeter, Edith (Ellis Peters, pseud.)
The Scarlet Seed.
Heinemann 1963 (Rpr. 1991).

Penman, Sharon Kay
YA *Falls the Shadow.*
Holt 1988.

BL v84 1988 p1202; KR v56 1988 p396; LJ v113 Jl
1988 p96; SLJ v35 S 1988 p211.

Trease, Geoffrey
JUV *The Baron's Hostage.*
T. Nelson 1975.
BL v72 1975 p459; KR v43 1975 p667; LJ v78 1953
p1340; SLJ v22 S 1975 p127.

669. Henry IV
1367-1413
King of England, 1399-1413

Heyer, Georgette
Simon the Coldheart.
Heinemann 1925 (Rpr. 1979, 1993).
KR v47 1979 p1157; LJ v104 1979 p2370.

Hibbert, Eleanor (Jean Plaidy, pseud.)
The Star of Lancaster.
Hale 1981.
BL v79 1982 p2; KR v50 1982 p1119; LJ v107 1982
p2004; PW v222 O 8, 1982 p55.

Pargeter, Edith (Ellis Peters, pseud.)
The Bloody Field.
Viking 1973.
BRD 1974 p931; KR v41 1973 p410; LJ v98 1973
p1601.

Pyle, Howard
YA *Men of Iron.*
Harper & Brothers 1891 (Heavily reprinted).

670. Henry V
1387-1422
King of England, 1413-1422

Bennetts, Pamela
Royal Sword at Agincourt.
St. Martin's 1971 (Rpr. 1977).
BL v68 1972 p846; KR v39 1971 p1139; LJ v97 1972
p1738.

Clarke, Brenda (Brenda Honeyman, pseud.)
Harry the King.
Hale 1971.

Doherty, P. C.
The Whyte Harte.
St. Martin's 1988.
BL v85 1988 p617; KR v56 1988 p1566; LJ v114 Ja
1989 p105; PW v234 O 28, 1988 p64.

Giardina, Denise
Good King Harry.
Harper & Row 1984.
BL v80 1984 p1293; KR v52 1984 p213; LJ v109 1984
p732; NYTBR Jl 29, 1984 p20.

Hibbert, Eleanor (Jean Plaidy, pseud.)
The Queen's Secret.
Putnam 1990.
CSM v82 Ap 26, 1990 p14.

Hibbert, Eleanor (Jean Plaidy, pseud.)
The Star of Lancaster.
Hale 1981.
BL v79 1982 p2; KR v50 1982 p1119; LJ v107 1982
p2004; PW v222 O 8, 1982 p55.

Jackson, Dorothy V. S.
Walk with Peril.
Putnam 1959.
BL v55 1959 p314; BRD 1959 p525; KR v26 1958
p855; LJ v84 1959 p209.

Jarman, Rosemary Hawley
Crown in Candlelight.
Popular Library 1978.
FC 11th p325; KR v46 1978 p125; LJ v103 1978 p775.

Lewis, Hilda
Wife to Henry V.
Jarrolds 1954.
BL v53 1957 p404; BRD 1957 p550; KR v25 1957
p91; LJ v82 1957 p1365; NYTBR Mr 3, 1957 p34.

Maughan, A. M.
Harry of Monmouth.
Sloane Associates 1956.
Atl v197 Ap 1956 p76; BRD 1956 p624; FC 11th
p421; LJ v81 1956 p1053; NYTBR Mr 18, 1956 p38.

Pargeter, Edith (Ellis Peters, pseud.)
The Bloody Field.
Viking 1973.
BRD 1974 p931; KR v41 1973 p410; LJ v98 1973
p1601.

Peters, Maureen
Seven for St. Crispin's Day.
Hale 1971.

Rofheart, Martha
Fortune Made His Sword.
Putnam 1972.
Also published as *Cry God for Harry.*
BL v68 1972 p702; BRD 1972 p1100; KR v39 1971
p1332; LJ v97 1972 p517; NYTBR F 27, 1972 p46.

671. Henry VI
1421-1471
King of England; ruled during the War of the
Roses

Hibbert, Eleanor (Jean Plaidy, pseud.)
The Queen's Secret.
Putnam 1990.
CSM v82 Ap 26, 1990 p14.

Hibbert, Eleanor (Jean Plaidy, pseud.)
Red Rose of Anjou.
Putnam 1983.

Lewis, Hilda
YA *Here Comes Harry.*
Criterion Books 1960.
BL v57 1960 p218; BRD 1961 p834; KR v28 1960
p760; LJ v85 1960 p3873; NYTBR O 9, 1960 p52.

Long, Freda M.
The Coveted Crown.
Hale 1966.

672. Henry VII
1457-1509
King of England, 1485-1509

Barnes, Margaret Campbell
The Tudor Rose.
Macrae Smith 1953.
BL v50 1953 p100; CSM S 24, 1953 p7; FC 11th p41;
    KR v21 1953 p495.

Clarke, Brenda (Brenda Honeyman, pseud.)
Richmond and Elizabeth.
Hale 1970.

Farrington, Robert
Tudor Agent.
St. Martin's 1974.
B&B v19 Jl 1974 p111; LJ v99 1974 p1847; Obs F 3,
    1974 p31.

Gellis, Roberta
The Dragon and the Rose.
Playboy Press 1977.
PW v210 D 6, 1976 p60.

Hibbert, Eleanor (Jean Plaidy, pseud.)
Uneasy Lies the Head.
Hale 1982 (Rpr. 1984).
KR v52 1984 p649; PW v226 Jl 27, 1984 p138.

Jarman, Rosemary Hawley
The King's Grey Mare.
Little, Brown 1973
BRD 1974 p608; KR v41 1973 p576; LJ v98 1973
    p2333.

Kilbourne, Janet
Wither One Rose.
Hale 1973.

Palmer, Marian
The Wrong Plantagenet.
Doubleday 1972.
BL v68 1972 p974; FC 9th p394; Obs D 17, 1972 p33;
    PW v201 Mr 15, 1972 p1020.

Stephens, Peter J.
YA *Battle for Destiny.*
Atheneum 1967.
BRD 1967 p1256; LJ v92 1967 p3206; NYTBR Jl 9,
    1967 p34.

Stubbs, Jean
An Unknown Welshman.
Stein & Day 1972.
B&B v17 Jl 1972 p63; BL v69 1972 p30; KR v40 1972
    p429; PW v201 Ap 17, 1972 p57.

Sudworth, Gwynedd
The King of Destiny.
Hale 1973.

673. Henry VIII
1491-1547
King of England, 1509-1547; most renowned of
English kings

Abbey, Anne M.
Kathryn, in the Court of Six Queens.
Bantam 1989.
PW v235 Ap 7, 1989 p131.

Ainsworth, William Harrison
Windsor Castle: An Historical Romance.
Henry Colburn 1843 (Heavily reprinted).

Albery, Peter
The Uncommon Marriage.
Elek Books 1960.

Ansle, Dorothy P. (Hebe Elsna, pseud.)
The Wise Virgin.
Collins 1967 (Rpr. 1982).

Anthony, Evelyn
Anne Boleyn.
Crowell 1957 (Rpr. 1986, 1991).
BL v53 1957 p528; BRD 1957 p877; FC 11th p19; KR
    v25 1957 p158; LJ v82 1957 p1064; NYTBR Ap
    28, 1957 p43.

Barnes, Margaret Campbell
Brief Gaudy Hour: A Novel of Anne Boleyn.
Macrae Smith 1949.
BRD 1949 p42; FC 11th p41; KR v17 1949 p371; LJ
    v74 1949 p1320; NYTBR O 2, 1949 p42.

Barnes, Margaret Campbell
King's Fool.
Macrae Smith 1959.
BL v56 1959 p241; BRD 1960 p66; FC 7th p29; KR
    v27 1959 p613; LJ v85 1960 p361.

Barnes, Margaret Campbell
My Lady of Cleves.
Macrae Smith Co. 1946.
BRD 1946 p41; FC 10th p34; KR v14 Ja 1946 p5;
    NYTBR Mr 10, 1946 p8; WLB v42 Ap 1946 p59.

Bloom, Ursula (Lozania Prole, pseud.)
Henry's Golden Queen.
Hale 1964 (Rpr. 1985).

Bloom, Ursula (Lozania Prole, pseud.)
Henry's Last Love.
Hale 1958 (Rpr. 1978).

Bloom, Ursula (Lozania Prole, pseud.)
The King's Wife.
Lythway Press 1973.
Originally published by Hutchinson, 1950.

Bloom, Ursula (Lozania Prole, pseud.)
The Last Love of a King.
Hale 1974 (Rpr. 1983).

Bloom, Ursula (Lozania Prole, pseud.)
Six Wives but One Love.
Hale 1972.

Brady, Charles A.
Stage of Fools.
Dutton 1953.
BL v49 1953 p213; BRD 1953 p102; FC 8th p51; KR
    v21 1953 p55; LJ v78 1953 p444; NYTBR Ap 5,
    1953 p19.

Buchan, John
The Blanket of the Dark.
Houghton Mifflin 1931 (Rpr. 1933, 1952, 1964).
BRD 1931 p142; NYTBR S 20, 1931 p22; SatR S 26,
    1931 p152.

Dakers, Elaine (Jane Lane, pseud.)
Sow the Tempest.
F. Muller 1960.

Fenton, Edward
Anne of the Thousand Days: A Novel.
New American Library 1970.

George, Margaret
The Autobiography of Henry VIII.
St. Martin's 1986.
BL v82 1986 p1562; KR v54 1986 p1045; LJ v111 S
    15, 1986 p99; NYTBR O 12, 1986 p28; PW v232
    Ag 7, 1987 p444.

Hardwick, Mollie
Blood Royal: A Novel.
St. Martin's 1989.
BL v85 1989 p1248; KR v57 1989 p74; PW v235 Ja
    27, 1989 p452.

Haycraft, Molly
The Reluctant Queen.
Lippincott 1962.
BL v59 1962 p30; BRD 1962 p526; FC 11th p279; KR
    v30 1962 p400; LJ v87 1962 p2156.

Hibbert, Eleanor (Jean Plaidy, pseud.)
Murder Most Royal.
Hale 1949 (Rpr. 1972).

Hibbert, Eleanor (Jean Plaidy, pseud.)
The Shadow of the Pomegranate.
Hale 1962.

Hibbert, Eleanor (Jean Plaidy, pseud.)
The Sixth Wife.
Ulverscroft 1953 (Rpr. 1969).

Leigh, Olivia
The Fifth Wife of Bluebeard.
Hale 1969.

Lewis, Hilda
I Am Mary Tudor.
McKay 1972.
BRD 1972 p788; Choice v9 S 1972 p815; FC 11th
    p373; LJ v97 1972 p1740.

Lindsay, Philip
The Heart of a King.
Howard Baker Ltd. 1968.

Lofts, Norah
*The Concubine: A Novel Based upon the Life of
    Anne Boleyn, Henry VIII's Second Wife*.
Doubleday 1963.
BRD 1963 p628; LJ v88 1963 p2726; NYTBR S 1,
    1963 p14.

Lofts, Norah
The King's Pleasure.
Doubleday 1969.
BL v66 1969 p495; FC 9th p323; KR v37 1969 p694;
    LJ v94 1969 p2641.

Luke, Mary M.
The Ivy Crown.
Doubleday 1984.
BL v80 1984 p944; KR v52 1984 p58; LJ v109 1984
    p509; PW v225 Ja 20, 1984 p76.

Macleod, Alison
The Heretic: A Novel.
Houghton Mifflin 1966.
BRD 1966 p767; FC 8th p272; LJ v91 1966 p2876;
    NYTBR Ap 10, 1966 p28.

Macleod, Alison
The Hireling.
Houghton Mifflin 1968.
Also published as *The Trusted Servant*.
BRD 1969 p844; FC 9th p337; LJ v93 1968 p4167;
    NYTBR S 22, 1968 p37.

Malvern, Gladys
YA *The Six Wives of Henry VIII*.
Vanguard Press 1972.
JHSLC 3rd p417.

Minard, Rosemary
JUV *Long Meg*.
Pantheon 1982.
BL v79 1983 p725; BRD 1983 p1010; NYTBR Ja 23,
    1983 p29; SLJ v29 F 1983 p80.

Peters, Maureen
Henry VIII and His Six Wives.
St. Martin's 1972.
BL v69 1972 p329; KR v40 1972 p1045; LJ v97 1972
    p2862.

Plunkett, Robert L.
A California Dreamer in King Henry's Court.
Silver Dawn Media 1989.
Locus v24 Mr 1990 p65; SFChr v12 N 1990 p40;
    WCRB v15 #3 1990 p54.

Stefik, Paul
My Will Be Done.
Dorrance Pub. Co. 1991.

Westcott, Jan
The Queen's Grace.
Crown 1959.
BL v56 1960 p328; BRD 1960 p1424; KR v27 1959
    p710.

674. Henry the Navigator

1394-1460

Portuguese prince; known for establishing a
school of navigation & dispatching voyagers on
expeditions around the coast of Africa

Baumann, Hans
YA *The Barque of the Brothers: A Tale of the Days of
     Henry the Navigator.*
    H.Z. Walck 1958.

Burt, Olive Woolley
JUV *I Challenge the Dark Sea.*
    J. Day 1962.
    LJ v87 1962 p2428.

Slaughter, Frank G.
*The Mapmaker: A Novel of the Days of Prince
     Henry, the Navigator.*
Doubleday 1957.
BRD 1957 p851; LJ v82 1957 p2544.

675. Henry, O., pseud.

1862-1910

American journalist & short story writer; wrote
the *Gift of the Magi*

Kramer, Dale
The Heart of O. Henry.
Rinehart 1954.
BL v51 1954 p107; BRD 1954 p505; KR v22 1954
     p559; LJ v79 1954 p1822; NYTBR O 24, 1954 p12.

676. Henry, Patrick

1736-1799

American orator & patriot

Barton, Thomas Frank
JUV *Patrick Henry, Boy Spokesman.*
    Bobbs-Merrill 1960.

Campion, Nardi Reeder
JUV *Patrick Henry, Firebrand of the Revolution.*
    Little, Brown 1961.

Erskine, John
*Give Me Liberty: The Story of an Innocent By-
     stander.*
Frederick A. Stokes 1940.
BL v37 1941 p175; BRD 1940 p286; NYTBR N 3,
     1940 p6.

Gerson, Noel Bertram
Give Me Liberty: A Novel of Patrick Henry.
Doubleday 1966.
FC 8th p168; LJ v91 1966 p2234.

677. Herbert, Alan Patrick, Sir

1890-1971

English humorist & political leader

Herbert, Alan Patrick
Made for Man.

Doubleday 1958.
BL v55 1958 p155; BRD 1958 p518; KR v26 1958
     p569; NYTBR O 12, 1958 p33.

678. Herbert, Victor

1859-1924

American conductor & composer

Purdy, Claire Lee
YA *Victor Herbert, American Music-Master.*
    Messner 1944.
    BL v41 1945 p198; BRD 1945 p575; LJ v70 1945 p165.

679. Hereward the Wake

Anglo-Saxon rebel; led rebellion against William the Conqueror

Anand, Valerie
The Disputed Crown.
Scribner 1982.
BL v79 1982 p188; KR v50 1982 p880; LJ v107 S 15,
     1982 p1767; PW v222 S 10, 1982 p65.

Bell, Anne
Wake the Brave.
Hale 1980.

Kingsley, Charles
Hereward the Wake.
Tauchnitz 1866 (Heavily reprinted).
FC 7th p209.

Lewis, Hilda
YA *Harold Was My King.*
    D. McKay 1970.
    BL v67 1971 p602; LJ v96 1971 p1528.

Rice, Sile
The Saxon Tapestry.
Arcade 1992.
BL v88 1991 p681; PW v238 N 1, 1991 p73.

Thorndike, Russell
The First Englishman.
Rich & Cowan 1949 (Rpr. 1971).

Treece, Henry
YA *Man with a Sword.*
    Bodley Head 1962 (Rpr. 1964, 1979).
    BS v24 N 15, 1964 p347; BRD 1965 p1260; LJ v89
         1964 p4652; NYTBR Ja 31, 1965 p26.

Weenolsen, Hebe
*The Last Englishman: The Story of Hereward the
     Wake.*
Doubleday 1951.
BL v48 1951 p58; BRD 1951 p929; KR v19 1951
     p493; LJ v77 1952 p366; NYTBR N 25, 1951 p59.

680. Herod Antipas

4 BC-AD 39

Ruler of Gailiee; son of Herod the Great; sent Jesus to Pontius Pilate

Bekessy, Emery
Barabbas: A Novel of the Time of Jesus.
Prentice-Hall 1946.
BL v43 1947 p132; BRD 1946 p51; FC 10th p42; KR
    v14 1946 p436; LJ v71 1946 p1542; NYTBR N 24,
    1946 p26.

681. Herod the Great
73-4 BC
Procurator of Judea who ordered the killing of
all males under the age of two for fear of losing
his throne to Jesus

Hunt, Leslie
At the Point of the Sword.
Vantage 1984.

Lagerkvist, Par
Herod and Mariamne.
Knopf 1968.
Also published as *Mariamne.*
Atl v222 N 1968 p144; BRD 1969 p742; FC 8th p247;
    KR v36 1968 p844; LJ v93 1968 p3799.

Nightingale, H. Ellsworth
Herod.
Vantage Press 1967.

Sullivan, Richard
The Three Kings.
Harcourt, Brace & Co. 1956.
LJ v81 1956 p2325; NYTBR D 16, 1956 p18.

682. Herrick, Robert
1591-1674
English poet & author

Macaulay, Rose
They Were Defeated.
Collins 1932 (Rpr. 1960, 1981).

683. Herzl, Theodor
1860-1904
Hungarian-born, Austrian-Jewish journalist &
writer; founder of Zionism

Baker, Nina
YA *Next Year in Jerusalem; the Story of Theodor
    Herzl.*
Harcourt, Brace 1950.
BRD 1950 p45; LJ v75 1950 p704; NYTBR F 26, 1950
    p24; SatR My 13, 1950 p42.

Kotker, Norman
Herzl, the King.
Scribner 1972.
BL v69 1972 p68; KR v40 1972 p640; LJ v97 1972
    p2645.

684. Hess, Rudolf
1894-1987
Nazi leader; sentenced to life imprisonment for
war crimes

Barwick, James
Shadow of the Wolf.
Coward, McCann & Geoghegan 1979.
BL v76 1979 p93; KR v47 1979 p464; LJ v104 1979
    p1481.

Carney, Daniel
The Square Circle.
Corgi 1982.

Eden, Matthew
Document of the Last Nazi.
H. Hamilton 1979.

Iles, Greg
Spandau Phoenix.
Dutton 1993.
BL v89 1993 p1569; KR v61 1993 p247.

Lear, Peter
The Secret of Spandau: A Novel.
Joseph 1986.
BritBkN Jl 1986 p390.

Tuccille, Jerome
*The Mission: A Novel about the Flight of Rudolf
    Hess.*
Fine 1991.
KR v58 1990 p1706.

685. Heydrich, Reinhard
1904-1942
Nazi terrorist & deputy-chief of the Gestapo;
known as "the hangman of Europe"

Barwick, James
The Hangman's Crusade.
Macmillan 1980.

686. Hickok, "Wild Bill" (James Butler)
1837-1876
American frontiersman; toured with Buffalo Bill
as legendary gunfighter

Berger, Thomas
Little Big Man.
Dial 1964 (Heavily reprinted).
BRD 1964 p97; LJ v89 1964 p4560; NYTBR O 11,
    1964 p42; SatR O 3, 1964 p38.

Charyn, Jerome
YA *Darlin' Bill: A Love Story of the Wild West.*
Arbor House 1980.
LJ v105 1980 p2343; NYTBR D 7, 1980 p11; SLJ v28
    Ja 1982 p29.

Dexter, Pete
Deadwood.
Random House 1986.

BL v82 1986 p834; BRD 1987 p459; KR v54 1986 p227; LJ v111 Ap 1, 1986 p160; NYTBR Ap 20, 1986 p9; PW v229 F 21, 1986 p155; Time v127 Je, 1986 p76.

Estleman, Loren D.
Aces & Eights.
Doubleday 1981.

Sale, Richard
The White Buffalo.
Simon & Schuster 1975.
BL v72 1975 p30; KR v43 1975 p801; LJ v100 1975 p1846; PW v208 Jl 14, 1975 p58.

Weidt, Maryann
JUV *Wild Bill Hickok.*
Lothrop, Lee & Shepard 1992.
BL v89 1993 p806; SLJ v38 D 1992 p93.

687. Hidalgo y Costilla, Miguel
1753-1811
Mexican revolutionary; led fight for Mexican independence from Spain

Gorman, Herbert
The Cry of Dolores.
Rinehart 1948.
BL v44 1948 p202; BRD 1948 p326; FC 7th p157; KR v15 1947 p653; LJ v73 1948 p39; NYTBR F 8, 1948 p5.

688. Hildegard of Bingen, Saint
1098-1179
German religious figure; noted for her prophecies

Lachman, Barbara
The Journal of Hildegard of Bingen, Advent 1151 - Epiphany 1153.
Bell Tower 1993.

689. Hill, James Jerome
1838-1916
American railroad magnate

Dempsey, Al
Path of the Sun.
TOR 1992.
KR v60 1992 p1392; LJ v117 1992 p185.

690. Hill, Joe, pseud.
1879-1915
American labor union leader

Stegner, Wallace Earle
The Preacher and the Slave.
Houghton Mifflin 1950 (Rpr. 1990).
Also published as *Joe Hill, a Biographical Novel.*
BRD 1950 p858; KR v18 1950 p361; LJ v75 1950 p1182; NYTBR S 10, 1950 p4.

691. Hillstrom, Joseph
see Hill, Joe, pseud.

692. Hippocrates
460-377 BC
Greek physician

Penfield, Wilder
The Torch.
Little, Brown 1960.
BL v57 1960 p241; BRD 1961 p1114; KR v28 1960 p640; LJ v85 1960 p3104.

693. Hitchcock, Alfred
1899-1980
English film director; movies include *North by Northwest*, *Rear Window*, & *Psycho*; won 1940 Oscar for *Rebecca*

Baxt, George
The Alfred Hitchcock Murder Case.
St. Martin's 1986.
BL v82 1986 p946; KR v54 1986 p252; LJ v111 Mr 1, 1986 p111; PW v229 Ja 31, 1986 p360.

694. Hitler, Adolf
1889-1945
German dictator & Nazi leader

Bainbridge, Beryl
Young Adolf.
Duckworth 1978.
BRD 1979 p62; LJ v104 1979 p972; NYTBR Mr 11, 1979 p15; TLS D 1, 1978 p1385.

Beymer, William G.
12:20 P.M.: A Novel.
Whittlesey House 1944.
BRD 1944 p64; KR v12 1944 p470; SRL N 25, 1944 p20.

Bloom, Ursula (Lozania Prole, pseud.)
Daughter of the Devil.
Hale 1963 (Rpr. 1974).

Bloom, Ursula (Lozania Prole, pseud.)
Hitler's Eva.
Hutchinson 1954 (Rpr. 1976).

Bonker, Frances
The Mad Dictator: A Novel of Adolph Hitler.
Chapman & Grimes 1950.

Born, Edith de
The House in Vienna.
Knopf 1960.
Sequel to *Felding Castle.*
BL v56 1960 p326; BRD 1960 p129; FC 7th p45; LJ v85 1960 p144.

Dobbs, Michael
Last Man to Die.
HarperCollins 1992.

Ebersohn, Wessel
Klara's Visitors.
Gollancz 1987.
Obs Ja 18, 1987 p23; TLS Ja 30, 1987 p108.

Erickson, Steve
Tours of the Black Clock.
Poseidon Press 1989.
VLS D 1989 p10; VV v35 Ap 3, 1990 p75.

Fadiman, Edwin
Who Will Watch the Watchers.
Little, Brown 1970.
KR v38 1970 p76; LJ v95 1970 p1390; NYTBR My
   10, 1970 p37.

Fitz Gibbon, Constantine
In the Bunker: A Novel.
Norton 1973.
BRD 1973 p394; LJ v98 1973 p2144; NYTBR Je 17,
   1973 p28.

Fleming, Peter
The Flying Visit.
Scribner 1940.
BL v37 1940 p90; BRD 1940 p312; NYTBR Ag 25,
   1940 p17.

Forbes, Colin
The Leader and the Damned.
Collins 1983.
BL v81 1984 p190; KR v52 1984 p766.

Forman, James
YA *The White Crow.*
Farrar, Straus & Giroux 1976.
KR v44 1976 p1268; SLJ v23 F 1977 p71.

Gronowicz, Antoni
Hitler's Wife.
Paramount Pub. Co. 1942.

Gurr, David
The Ring Master.
McClelland & Stewart 1987.
KR v55 1987 p1014; LJ v112 O 1, 1987 p108; NYTBR
   N 1, 1987 p24.

Harris, Robert
Fatherland.
Random House 1992.
NYTBR Je 27, 1992 p28.

Heywood, Joseph
The Berkut.
Random House 1987.
BL v83 1987 p1538; KR v55 1987 p1015; LATBR S
   6, 1987 p13; NY v63 S 28, 1987 p98; NYTBR N
   29, 1987 p20; PW v231 Jl 10, 1987 p57.

Hugo, Richard
The Hitler Diaries.
Macmillan 1982.
KR v50 1982 p1204; NYTBR My 22, 1983 p42; PW
   v222 N 12, 1982 p57; TLS Ag 6, 1982 p865.

Kirst, Hans H.
Soldiers' Revolt.

Harper & Row 1966.
BL v62 1966 p1078; BRD 1966 p653; KR v34 1966
   p448; LJ v91 1966 p4698; NYTBR Jl 17, 1966 p29;
   PW v189 My 2, 1966 p54.

Levine, Jacques
Hitler's Secret Diaries.
Aiglon Press 1988.
PW v234 Ag 5, 1988 p80.

Marlowe, Stephen
The Valkyrie Encounter.
Putnam 1978.
BL v74 1978 p1165; BS v38 Je 1978 p75; KR v45
   1977 p1134.

Melchior, Ib
Eva: A Novel.
Dodd, Mead 1984.
BL v80 1984 p1226; KR v52 1984 p317; LJ v109 1984
   p916; PW v225 Mr 23, 1984 p65.

Mullally, Frederic
Hitler Has Won.
Simon & Schuster 1975.
KR v43 1975 p732; LJ v100 1975 p1346; PW v208 Jl
   14, 1975 p59.

Nathanson, E. M.
Knight's Cross: A Novel.
Carol Pub. Group 1993.

Prior, Allan
Fuhrer.
Sinclair Stevenson 1991.

Puccetti, Roland
The Death of the Fuhrer.
St. Martin's 1972.
KR v41 1973 p143; LJ v98 1973 p2147; NYTBR Ap
   22, 1973 p24.

Radin, Max
The Day of Reckoning.
Knopf 1943.
BL v39 1943 p464; BRD 1943 p670; NYTBR Je 13,
   1943 p14; SatR Jl 3, 1943 p9.

Richard, Andre
Lisa: A Novel of the Postwar Life of Adolf Hitler.
Exposition Press 1956.

Spinrad, Norman
The Iron Dream.
Avon 1972 (Rpr. 1977).
Analog v103 Ja 1983 p159; BS v35 Ag 1975 p147; Kli-
   att v13 Spring 1979 p20.

Steiner, George
The Portage to San Cristobal of A.H..
Faber & Faber 1981.
BRD 1982 p1287; FC 11th p579; KR v50 1982 p300;
   LJ v107 1982 p906; NYTBR My 2, 1982 p13; SLJ
   v29 O 1982 p170.

Tute, Warren
Hitler: The Last Ten Days.
Fontana 1973.

Based on the original screenplay by Ennio de Concini, Maria Pia Fusco, and Wolfgang Reinhardt.

Van Rjndt, Phillipe
The Trial of Adolf Hitler.
Summit Books 1978.
BS v39 Ap 1979 p10; Kliatt v14 Spring 1980 p12; LJ v104 1979 p212; PW v214 O 16, 1978 p108.

Wallace, Irving
The Seventh Secret.
Dutton 1986.
LJ v111 Mr 15, 1986 p79; NYTBR Ja 12, 1986 p20; PW v230 S 26, 1986 p71.

Weiss, Ernst
The Eyewitness.
Houghton Mifflin 1977.
BL v73 1977 p1634; KR v45 1977 p598; LJ v102 1977 p1681; NYTBR N 13, 1977 p92; PW v211 My 23, 1977 p242.

West, Paul
The Very Rich Hours of Count von Stauffenberg.
Harper & Row 1980 (Rpr. 1989).
BL v76 1980 p1660; LJ v105 1980 p1664; NYTBR N 9, 1980 p14.

Young, Michael
The Trial of Adolf Hitler.
Dutton 1944.
BRD 1944 p837; LJ v69 1944 p204.

695. Hobson, Richmond Pearson
1870-1937
Confederate military leader; commander of the Merrimac

Donovan, Frank R.
The Unlucky Hero.
Duell, Sloan & Pearce 1963.
LJ v88 1963 p4483.

696. Hoffa, Jimmy (James Riddle)
1913-1975?
American labor union leader; President of Teamsters, 1957-1971

Hannibal, Edward
Blood Feud.
Ballantine 1979.
KR v47 1979 p281; LJ v104 1979 p751; NYTBR Je 10, 1979 p24.

697. Hoffmann, Ernst Theodor Amadeus
1776-1822
German author

Davies, Robertson
The Lyre of Orpheus.
Viking 1989.
BRD 1989 p374; LJ v114 Ja 1989 p100; NYTBR Ja 8, 1989 p7.

698. Hogarth, William
1697-1764
English painter & engraver

Ackroyd, Peter
English Music.
Hamish Hamilton 1992.
KR v60 1992 p1002; Obs v5 My 24, 1992 p60; PW v239 1992 p485; TLS v268 My 22, 1992 p29.

699. Holliday, "Doc" (John Henry)
1851-1887
American frontier gambler; friend of Wyatt Earp

Estleman, Loren D.
Bloody Season.
Bantam 1987.
BL v84 1987 p513; KR v55 1987 p1593; LJ v113 Ja 1988 p98.

Hamill, Pete
Doc.
Paperback Library 1971.

Hogan, Ray
Betrayal in Tombstone.
Popular Library 1975.

Kelland, Clarence B.
Tombstone.
Harper 1952.
KR v20 1952 p331; NYTBR Jl 27, 1952 p19.

Krepps, Robert W.
Hour of the Gun.
Fawcett 1967.

Lewis, Preston
The Lady and Doc Holliday.
Diamond Books 1989.
LJ v114 N 15, 1989 p106.

700. Holly, "Buddy" (Charles Hardin Holley)
1936-1959
American rock-and-roll singer

Denton, Bradley
Buddy Holly Is Alive and Well on Ganymede.
Morrow 1991.
BL v87 1991 p2098; KR v59 1991 p895.

701. Homer
Greek epic poet

Graves, Robert
Homer's Daughter.
Doubleday 1955 (Rpr. 1982).
BRD 1955 p365; FC 7th p160; KR v22 1954 p734; LJ v80 1955 p158; NYTBR F 27, 1955 p4.

702. Hood, John Bell
1831-1879
Confederate general

Crabb, Alfred L.
Home to Tennessee.
Bobbs-Merrill 1952.
BL v48 1952 p214; NYTBR Mr 2, 1952 p25; SatR F
16, 1952 p44.

Perenyi, Eleanor Spencer
The Bright Sword.
Rinehart 1955.
BL v51 1955 p343; FC 7th p274; KR v23 1955 p17; LJ
v80 1955 p801; NYTBR Mr 6, 1955 p27.

703. Hoover, Herbert
1874-1964
31st US President

Comfort, Mildred
JUV *Herbert Hoover, Boy Engineer.*
Bobbs-Merrill 1965.

704. Hoover, J. Edgar
1895-1972
Director of FBI, 1924-1972

Ludlum, Robert
The Chancellor Manuscript.
Dial 1977.
BS v37 Je 1977 p71; FC 11th p336; LJ v102 1977
p834; NYTBR My 27, 1977 p8.

Thomas, D. M.
Flying in to Love.
Scribner 1992.
BL v89 1992 p5; KR v60 1992 p946; NYTBR O 11,
1992 p13.

705. Horn, Tom
1860-1903
American murderer

Fenady, Andrew
YA *Claws of the Eagle.*
Walker 1984.
LATBR Ap 29, 1984 p12; SLJ v30 My 1984 p106.

Henry, Will
I, Tom Horn.
Lippincott 1975.

706. Hosea
Old Testament prophet

Lawrence, Deborah
Chase the Wind.
Nelson Publishers 1983.

Lehman, Yvonne
In Shady Groves.
Chosen Books 1983.

Mand, Evald
The Unfaithful.
Muhlenberg Press 1954.

Osgood, Phillips
*The Sinner Beloved: A Novel of the Life and Times
of Hosea the Prophet.*
American Press 1956.

Patai, Irene
The Valley of God.
Random House 1956.
KR v24 1956 p180; LJ v81 1956 p1189; NYTBR Ap
22, 1956 p31.

707. Houdini, Harry
1874-1926
American magician; famous for escape feats

Bethancourt, Ernesto
YA *The Tomorrow Connection.*
Holiday House 1984.
BL v81 1984 p517; BS v44 D 1984 p356; SLJ v31 D
1984 p88.

Doctorow, E. L.
Ragtime.
Random House 1975.
BL v72 1975 p24; BRD 1975 p338; BRD 1976 p313;
KR v43 1975 p529; LJ v100 1975 p1344; NYTBR Jl
6, 1975 p1.

Howard, Elizabeth
YA *Mystery of the Magician.*
Random House 1987.
SLJ v34 O 1987 p139.

Levy, Elizabeth
YA *Running Out of Magic with Houdini.*
Knopf 1981.
BL v78 1981 p390; SLJ v28 D 1981 p86.

Selznick, Brian
JUV *The Houdini Box.*
Knopf 1991.
Five Owls v6 N 1991 p39; NW v118 D 16, 1991 p72.

Stashower, Daniel
The Adventure of the Ectoplasmic Man.
Morrow 1985.
KR v53 1985 p20; Kliatt v20 Fall 1986 p28; LJ v110 F
15, 1985 p115; NYTBR Ap 28, 1985 p24.

708. Houston, Sam
1793-1863
American general & politician; first president of
the Republic of Texas

Crook, Elizabeth
The Raven's Bride.
Doubleday 1991.
BL v87 1991 p1177; KR v58 1990 p1625.

Gant, Matthew
The Raven and the Sword.

Coward-McCann 1960.
LJ v85 1960 p1935; NYTBR Je 5, 1960 p36.

Garner, Claud W.
YA *Sam Houston: Texas Giant.*
Naylor Co. 1969.
SWR v55 Winter 1970 pR6.

Gerson, Noel Bertram
Sam Houston: A Biographical Novel.
Doubleday 1968.
KR v36 1968 p712; LJ v93 1968 p3576.

Giles, Janice H.
Savanna.
Houghton Mifflin 1961.
BL v58 1961 p253; BRD 1962 p452; KR v29 1961
   p479; LJ v86 1961 p2816.

Latham, Jean Lee
YA *Retreat to Glory: The Story of Sam Houston.*
Harper & Row 1965.
BL v61 1965 p996; BRD 1965 p736; KR v33 1965
   p318; LJ v90 1965 p2407; NYTBR Je 13, 1965 p24.

Long, Jeff
*Empire of Bones: A Novel of Sam Houston and the
   Texas Revolution.*
Morrow 1993.
BL v89 1993 p1036; LJ v118 Mr 15, 1993 p107.

Michener, James A.
The Eagle and the Raven.
State House Press 1990.
BL v86 1990 p1932; KR v58 1990 p827; NYTBR S
   30, 1990 p28; PW v237 Jl 20, 1990 p49.

Owen, Dean
*The Sam Houston Story: A Swashbuckling Ac-
   count of the Man Whose Daring Exploits Altered
   the Course of Texan History.*
Monarch Books 1961.

Robson, Lucia St Clair
Walk in My Soul.
Ballantine 1985.
BL v81 1985 p1437; KR v53 1985 p391.

Stevenson, Augusta
JUV *Sam Houston, Boy Chieftain.*
Bobbs-Merrill 1944.
BRD 1944 p720; LJ v69 1944 p405.

Wellman, Paul I.
*Magnificent Destiny: A Novel about the Great Se-
   cret Adventure of Andrew Jackson and Sam
   Houston.*
Doubleday 1962.
BRD 1962 p477; FC 9th p542; KR v30 1962 p477; LJ
   v87 1962 p2779; NYTBR S 23, 1962 p45.

709. Howard, Catherine
1520-1542
Fifth wife of Henry VIII; beheaded

Bloom, Ursula (Lozania Prole, pseud.)
The Last Love of a King.
Hale 1974 (Rpr. 1983).

Evans, Jean
The Tudor Tragedy.
Hale 1972.

Ford, Ford Madox
The Fifth Queen Crowned.
E. Nash 1908 (Rpr. 1986).
Spec v256 My 3, 1986 p32.

Hammond, Jane
Shadow of the Headsman.
Hale 1975.

Hibbert, Eleanor (Jean Plaidy, pseud.)
Murder Most Royal.
Hale 1949 (Rpr. 1972).

Leigh, Olivia
The Fifth Wife of Bluebeard.
Hale 1969.

Mawson, Christian
Ramping Cat.
Cape 1941.
NYTBR O 12, 1941 p8.

Miall, Wendy
No Other Will But His.
Hale 1972.

Peters, Maureen
Katheryn, the Wanton Queen.
Hale 1967 (Rpr. 1973).

Smith, Jessica
Katharine Howard.
Sphere 1972.
Also published as *Henry Betrayed.*
BS v32 Jl 1, 1972 p179.

Wiat, Philippa
Maid of Gold.
Hale 1978.

710. Howard, Oliver Otis
1830 1909
Union Civil War general

Arnold, Elliott
Blood Brother.
Duell, Sloan & Pearce 1947 (Rpr. 1950, 1979).
BL v43 1947 p223; BRD 1947 p26; KR v14 1946
   p600; LJ v72 1947 p319; NYTBR Mr 2, 1947 p20.

711. Howe, Elias
1819-1867
American inventor of the sewing machine

Corcoran, Jean
JUV *Elias Howe, Inventive Boy.*
Bobbs-Merrill 1962.

712. Howe, Julia Ward

1819-1910

American poet & author; wrote poem *Battle Hymn of the Republic*

Hayes, Marjorie

YA *Green Peace.*

Lippincott 1945.

BL v42 1945 p96; BRD 1945 p312; CC 7th p1002; KR v13 1945 p317; LJ v71 1946 p59; NYTBR Ja 20, 1946 p22.

Jennings, John E.

Banners against the Wind.

Little, Brown 1954.

BL v51 1954 p41; BRD 1954 p470; FC 7th p199; KR v22 1954 p344; LJ v79 1954 p1953; NYTBR Ag 8, 1954 p14.

Wagoner, Jean Brown

JUV *Julia Ward Howe, Girl of Old New York.*

Bobbs-Merrill 1945.

BRD 1945 p738; KR v13 1945 p340; LJ v70 1945 p1028.

713. Howe, Samuel Gridley

1802-1876

American educator & philanthropist

Hayes, Marjorie

YA *Green Peace.*

Lippincott 1945.

BL v42 1945 p96; BRD 1945 p312; CC 7th p1002; KR v13 1945 p317; LJ v71 1946 p59; NYTBR Ja 20, 1946 p22.

Jennings, John E.

Banners against the Wind.

Little, Brown 1954.

BL v51 1954 p41; BRD 1954 p470; FC 7th p199; KR v22 1954 p344; LJ v79 1954 p1953; NYTBR Ag 8, 1954 p14.

714. Howe, William, Viscount

1729-1814

British commander and chief in the American Revolution

Flood, Charles B.

Monmouth.

Houghton Mifflin 1961.

BRD 1962 p395; LJ v86 1961 p3300; NYTBR O 8, 1961 p5; SatR N 4, 1961 p41.

Nutt, Frances T.

Three Fields to Cross.

Stephen-Paul 1947.

BL v44 1948 p203; BRD 1948 p628; NYTBR D 21, 1947 p12.

715. Hubble, Edwin Powell

1889-1953

American astronomer

Bezzi, Tom

Hubble Time.

Mercury House 1987.

BL v84 1987 p107; KR v55 1987 p1335; PW v232 S 18, 1987 p161.

716. Hudson, Henry

1575-1611

English navigator & explorer; Hudson River is named after him

Baker, Nina

YA *Henry Hudson.*

Knopf 1958.

BL v54 1958 p449; BRD 1958 p52; KR v25 1957 p904; LJ v83 1958 p1599; NYTBR Ap 20, 1958 p36.

Lambert, Richard S.

YA *Mutiny in the Bay: Henry Hudson's Last Voyage.*

St. Martin's 1963.

Scott, J. M.

YA *Hudson of Hudson's Bay.*

Methuen 1950 (Rpr. 1973).

BL v47 1951 p333; BRD 1951 p795; KR v19 1951 p65; LJ v76 1951 p607; NYTBR My 13, 1951 p26.

Syme, Ronald

JUV *Henry Hudson.*

Morrow 1955.

Also published as *Hudson of the Bay.*

BRD 1955 p883; KR v22 1954 p810; LJ v80 1955 p1515; NYTBR Jl 31, 1955 p16.

717. Hughes, Howard Robard

1905-1976

American capitalist, aviator, & movie producer

Kaminsky, Stuart M.

The Howard Hughes Affair.

St. Martin's 1979.

BL v76 1979 p332; BW v9 O 21, 1979 p6; KR v47 1979 p895; LJ v104 1979 p1723; NYTBR O 7, 1979 p35.

718. Hugo, Victor Marie

1802-1885

French dramatist & author; wrote *Les Miserables*

Crockett, Clarence V.

Three Loves Claim Victor Hugo.

Liveright Pub. Corp. 1964.

719. Hull, Isaac

1773-1843

American naval officer

Allis, Marguerite

The Splendor Stays: An Historic Novel Based on the Lives of the Seven Hart Sisters of Saybrook, Connecticut.

Putnam 1942.
BL v39 1942 p138; BRD 1942 p15; NYTBR N 8, 1942
p12; SatR N 21, 1942 p9.

Beebe, Ralph
Who Fought and Bled.
Coward-McCann 1941.
BRD 1941 p65.

720. Hunt, E. Howard
1918-
Consultant for Richard Nixon; jailed for involvement in Watergate scandal

Mailer, Norman
Harlot's Ghost.
Random House 1991.
BL v88 1991 p5; BRD 1991 p1197; KR v59 1991
p960; LJ v116 S 1, 1991 p231; NYTBR S 29, 1991
p1.

721. Hunter, John
1728-1793
Scottish physiologist & surgeon to George III

Rogers, Garet
Lancet: A Novel.
Putnam 1956.
BRD 1956 p792; KR v24 1956 p763; NYTBR D 9,
1956 p42; SatR N 17, 1956 p40.

722. Hunter, William
1718-1783
Scottish anatomist & obstetrician; brother of
John Hunter

Rogers, Garet
Lancet: A Novel.
Putnam 1956.
BRD 1956 p792; KR v24 1956 p763; NYTBR D 9,
1956 p42; SatR N 17, 1956 p40.

723. Hus, Jan
1369-1415
Bohemian religious reformer; burned at stake

Alcock, Deborah
A Torch to Bohemia.
Lutterworth Press 1940.

724. Hussein, Saddam
1935-
President of Iraq, 1979-

Archer, Jeffrey
Honor among Thieves.
HarperCollins 1993.
KR v61 1993 p735.

Hagberg, David
Desert Fire.
Tor 1993.

725. Huston, John
1906-1987
Actor & director; directed *The African Queen &
Prizzi's Honor*; won Oscar for *Treasure of the Sierra Madre*

Hamblett, Charles
The Crazy Kill: A Fantasy.
Sidgwick & Jackson 1956.

726. Hutchinson, Anne
1591-1643
American religious leader

Auchincloss, Louis
The Winthrop Covenant.
Houghton Mifflin 1976.
BRD 1976 p57; LJ v101 1976 p546; NYTBR Mr 28,
1976 p10.

Heidish, Marcy
Witnesses: A Novel.
Houghton Mifflin 1980.
BL v77 1980 p31; KR v48 1980 p666; LJ v105 1980
p1540; NYTBR S 14, 1980 p12; SLJ v27 N 1980
p92.

Rimmer, Robert
The Resurrection of Anne Hutchinson.
Prometheus 1987.

Rushing, Jane Gilmore
Covenant of Grace.
Doubleday 1982.
BL v78 1982 p1301; KR v50 1982 p367; LJ v107 My
1, 1982 p906; PW v221 Mr 26, 1982 p66.

727. Huxley, Aldous Leonard
1894-1963
English novelist & essayist; wrote *Brave New
World*

Kreeft, Peter
*Between Heaven and Hell: A Dialog Somewhere
beyond Death with John F. Kennedy, C. S. Lewis, and Aldous Huxley.*
InterVarsity Press 1982.

728. Hypatia
d. 415
Alexandrian philosopher & mathematician

Kingsley, Charles
Hypatia: or, New Foes with an Old Face.
Tauchnitz 1857 (Heavily reprinted).

729. Ignatius of Loyola, Saint
1491-1556
Spanish founder of the Jesuit order

De Wohl, Louis
The Golden Thread.

Lippincott 1952.
BRD 1952 p250; KR v20 1952 p630; NYTBR O 26, 1952 p30.

730. Ikhnaton, Pharaoh
see Akhenaton

731. Irving, Henry, Sir
1838-1905
English actor; known for Shakespearian roles

Johnson, Pamela Hansford
Catherine Carter: A Novel.
Macmillan 1952.
BL v48 1952 p369; BRD 1952 p484; KR v20 1952 p305; LJ v77 1952 p1814; NYTBR Jl 20, 1952 p4.

Malvern, Gladys
YA *Curtain's at Eight.*
Macrae Smith 1957.
BL v53 1957 p562; BRD 1957 p600; KR v25 1957 p183; LJ v82 1957 p2198.

732. Irving, Washington
1783-1859
American author; wrote *Rip Van Winkle* and *Legend of Sleepy Hollow*

Benet, Laura
Washington Irving, Explorer of American Legend.
Dodd, Mead & Co. 1944.
LJ v69 1944 p1051; SatR N 11, 1944 p46.

733. Isaac
Old Testament figure; son of Abraham and Sarah

Fineman, Irving
Jacob; an Autobiographical Novel.
Random House 1941.
BRD 1941 p297; NYTBR O 5, 1941 p6; SatR O 11, 1941 p14.

Stern, Chaim
Isaac: The Link in the Chain.
R. Speller 1977.
LJ v102 1977 p1045.

734. Isabella I
1451-1504
Queen of Castile; financed Columbus' voyage to America

Hibbert, Eleanor (Jean Plaidy, pseud.)
Isabella and Ferdinand.
Hale 1970.
Composed of three novels by the author originally published under their respective titles: *Castile for Isabella, Spain for the Sovereigns, & Daughters of Spain.*

Kesten, Hermann
Ferdinand and Isabella.

A.A. Wyn 1946.
BRD 1946 p447; KR v14 1946 p399; LJ v71 1946 p1465; NYTBR N 24, 1946 p20.

Kidwell, Carl
Granada, Surrender!.
Viking 1968.
KR v36 1968 p115; LJ v94 1969 p886.

Lofts, Norah
Crown of Aloes.
Doubleday 1974.
KR v41 1973 p1224; LJ v98 1973 p2464.

Schoonover, Lawrence
The Queen's Cross: A Biographical Romance of Queen Isabella of Spain.
W. Sloane Associates 1955.
BL v52 1956 p190; BRD 1955 p807; KR v23 1955 p615; LJ v80 1955 p2163; NYTBR O 30, 1955 p38.

735. Isaiah
Old Testament prophet

Asch, Sholem
The Prophet.
Putnam 1955.
BL v52 O 15, 1955 p65; BRD 1955 p25; FC 11th p24; LJ v80 1955 p2161; NYTBR N 6, 1955 p4.

Head, Constance
Isaiah: The Prophet Prince.
Living Books 1988.

736. Jack the Ripper
English murderer; killed five London women, 1888-1889; never apprehended

Alexander, David
Terror on Broadway.
Random House 1954.
BRD 1954 p8; KR v22 1954 p251; NYTBR Je 27, 1954 p15; SatR Jl 10, 1954 p31.

Alexander, Karl
Time after Time.
Delacorte 1979.
BS v39 My 1979 p43; KR v47 1979 p74; LJ v104 1979 p850; PW v215 Ja 29, 1979 p106.

Bailey, Hilary
The Cry from Street to Street.
Constable 1992.

Barry, John
The Michaelmas Girls.
A. Deutsch 1975.
TLS Jl 11, 1975 p784.

Bloch, Robert
Fear and Trembling.
Tor 1989.
BL v85 1989 p1431; WCRB v14(6) 1989 p26.

Bloch, Robert
The Night of the Ripper.

Doubleday 1984.
BL v81 1984 p189; KR v52 1984 p634; LJ v109 S 15, 1984 p1770; PW v226 Jl 27, 1984 p140.

Brown, Frederic
The Screaming Mimi.
Dutton 1949.
BRD 1949 p109; KR v17 1949 p564; NYTBR N 27, 1949 p45.

Clark, Mark
Ripper.
Byren House 1987.

Daniel, Mark
YA   *Jack the Ripper.*
New American Library 1988.
Kliatt v23 Ja 1989 p6.

Dibdin, Michael
The Last Sherlock Holmes Story.
Pantheon 1978.
BRD 1978 p330; KR v46 1978 p516.

Frost, Mark
The List of 7.
Morrow 1993.
NYTBR O 17, 1993 p49.

Gordon, Richard
Jack the Ripper.
Atheneum 1980.
BL v77 1980 p197; KR v48 1980 p926; LJ v105 1980 p1878; NYTBR S 28, 1980 p14; PW v218 Jl 25, 1980 p147.

Hanna, Edward B.
The Whitechapel Horrors.
Carroll & Graf 1992.
BL v89 1992 p239; KR v60 1992 p1020; NYTBR O 18, 1992 p34.

Queen, Ellery
A Study in Terror.
Lodestone Publishing 1966.
Also published as *Sherlock Holmes versus Jack the Ripper.*

Walsh, Ray
The Mycroft Memoranda.
St. Martin's 1984.
CR v245 Jl 1984 p45; Punch v286 Mr 21, 1984 p22; TLS Mr 16, 1984 p270.

West, Pamela
Yours Truly, Jack the Ripper.
St. Martin's 1987.
KR v55 1987 p1485; LJ v112 O 1, 1987 p111; PW v232 O 16, 1987 p73.

West, Paul
The Women of Whitechapel and Jack the Ripper.
Random House 1991.
BRD 1991 p1969; LJ v116 Mr 1, 1991 p118; NYTBR My 12, 1991 p11.

Wilson, Colin
Ritual in the Dark.

Houghton Mifflin 1960.
BRD 1960 p1445; KR v28 1960 p58; LJ v85 1960 p1619; NYTBR Mr 6, 1960 p4.

737. Jackson, "Stonewall" (Thomas Jonathan)
1824-1863
American Confederate general

Brown, Jack I.
The Shade of the Trees: A Narrative Based on the Life and Career of Lieutenant General Thomas "Stonewall" Jackson.
Todd & Honeywell 1988.

Grubb, Davis
A Dream of Kings.
Scribner 1955.
BL v52 1955 p125; BRD 1955 p375; KR v23 1955 p511; LJ v80 1955 p1914; NYTBR S 25, 1955 p4.

Herrin, Lamar
The Unwritten Chronicles of Robert E. Lee.
St. Martin's 1991.
Kliatt v25 S 1991 p10; KR v57 1989 p1270; LJ v114 O 1, 1989 p118; PW v236 S 22, 1989 p40; SLJ v36 D 1990 p27.

Hinkins, Virginia
JUV   *Stonewall's Courier: The Story of Charles Randolph and General Jackson.*
Whittlesey House 1959.
BRD 1959 p484; KR v27 1959 p180; LJ v84 1959 p1338; NYTBR Je 21, 1959 p22.

Kane, Harnett T.
The Gallant Mrs. Stonewall: A Novel Based on the Lives of General and Mrs. Stonewall Jackson.
Doubleday 1957.
BL v54 1957 p65; BRD 1957 p479; KR v25 1957 p600; LJ v82 1957 p2452; NYTBR N 3, 1957 p55.

Keneally, Thomas
Confederates.
Harper & Row 1979.
BL v77 1980 p198; BRD 1980 p652; KR v48 1980 p860; LJ v105 1980 p1752; NYTBR O 5, 1980 p3; SLJ v27 D 1980 p79.

King, Benjamin
YA   *A Bullet for Stonewall.*
Pelican 1990.
BL v86 1990 p1687; LJ v115 Je 1, 1990 p179.

Monsell, Helen Albee
JUV   *Tom Jackson, Young Stonewall.*
Bobbs-Merrill 1961.
Also published as *Young Stonewall, Tom Jackson.*

Slaughter, Frank G.
Stonewall Brigade.
Doubleday 1975 (Rpr. 1986).
BL v71 1975 p1163; KR v43 1975 p141; LJ v100 1975 p692.

738. Jackson, Andrew
1767-1845
American general & seventh US President;
nicknamed "Old Hickory"

Angell, Polly
YA *Andy Jackson: Long Journey to the White House.*
Aladdin Books 1956.
BRD 1956 p20; KR v24 1956 p404.

Crabb, Alfred L.
Home to Hermitage.
Bobbs-Merrill 1948.
BL v44 1948 p282; BRD 1948 p181; FC 7th p93; LJ
v73 1948 p395; NYTBR Ap 4, 1948 p21.

Davis, Louise Littleton
JUV *Snowball Fight in the White House.*
Westminster Press 1974.
LJ v99 1974 p2721.

Downes, Anne Miller
The Quality of Mercy.
Lippincott 1959.

Evernden, Margery
JUV *Lyncoya.*
H.Z. Walck 1973.
BL v70 1974 p655; KR v41 1973 p1369; LJ v99 1974
p571.

Gerson, Noel Bertram
Old Hickory.
Doubleday 1964.
FC 9th p198; LJ v89 1964 p1776; LJ v89 1964 p2243.

Kaufelt, David A.
American Tropic.
Poseidon Press 1986.
BL v83 1987 p751; KR v54 1986 p1605; LJ v112 F 1,
1987 p92; NYTBR F 1, 1987 p20.

Miller, Helen Topping
JUV *Her Christmas at the Hermitage: A Tale about Ra-
chel and Andrew Jackson.*
Longmans, Green 1955.
BL v52 1955 p167; BRD 1956 p644; KR v23 1955
p562; LJ v80 1955 p1819; NYTBR N 6, 1955 p50.

Nolan, Jeannette C.
YA *Andrew Jackson.*
Responsive Environments Corp. 1949.
BL v45 1949 p285; BRD 1949 p686; KR v17 1949
p113; LJ v74 1949 p739; NYTBR Jl 3, 1949 p10.

Nolan, Jeannette C.
YA *Patriot in the Saddle.*
Messner 1945.
BRD 1945 p529; HB v21 S 1945 p351; LJ v70 1945
p822; SatR F 10, 1945 p26.

Palmer, Bruce; Giles, John C.
Horseshoe Bend.
Simon & Schuster 1962.
BL v58 1962 p719; KR v30 1962 p31; LJ v87 1962
p1152; NYTBR My 20, 1962 p32.

Shepard, Odell
Holdfast Gaines.
Macmillan 1946.
BL v43 1946 p103; BRD 1946 p746; KR v14 1946
p428; LJ v71 1946 p1543; NYTBR N 24, 1946 p28.

Slate, Sam J.
As Long as the Rivers Run.
Doubleday 1972.
BL v69 1972 p329; KR v40 1972 p822; LJ v97 1972
p3616.

Steele, William O.
JUV *Andy Jackson's Water Well.*
Harcourt, Brace 1959.
BL v55 1959 p426; BRD 1959 p938; KR v27 1959
p224; LJ v84 1959 p1700; NYTBR My 10, 1959
p23.

Stevenson, Augusta
JUV *Andy Jackson: Boy Soldier.*
Bobbs-Merrill 1942 (Rpr. 1952, 1962).
BRD 1942 p739; LJ v67 1942 p847.

Stone, Irving
*The President's Lady: A Novel about Rachel and
Andrew Jackson.*
Doubleday 1951.
BL v48 O 15, 1951 p66; BRD 1951 p849; FC 11th
p588; LJ v76 1951 p1421; NYTBR S 30, 1951 p4;
Time v58 O 8, 1951 p122.

Street, James
Oh, Promised Land.
Dial Press 1940.
BRD 1940 p892; NYTBR Ap 28, 1940 p4.

Trumbo, Dalton
*The Remarkable Andrew, Being the Chronicle of a
Literal Man.*
Lippincott 1941.
BL v37 1941 p271; BRD 1941 p902; NYTBR F 2,
1941 p6; SatR F 15, 1941 p10.

Wellman, Paul I.
*Magnificent Destiny: A Novel about the Great Se-
cret Adventure of Andrew Jackson and Sam
Houston.*
Doubleday 1962.
BRD 1962 p477; FC 9th p542; KR v30 1962 p477; LJ
v87 1962 p2779; NYTBR S 23, 1962 p45.

Young, Stanley
YA *Young Hickory, a Story of the Frontier Boyhood
and Youth of Andrew Jackson.*
Farrar & Rinehart 1940.
BRD 1940 p1024; HB v17 Ja 1941 p59; LJ v65 1940
p855; NYTBR N 24, 1940 p10.

739. Jackson, Joe (Joseph Jefferson)
1888-1951
American baseball player; banned from game for
the part he played in the "Black Sox" scandal of
1919; nicknamed "Shoeless Joe"

Kinsella, W. P.
Shoeless Joe.
Houghton Mifflin 1982.
BL v78 1982 p941; BRD 1982 p732; KR v50 1982
 p159; LJ v107 1982 p745; NYTBR Jl 25, 1982 p10;
 SLJ v28 Ag 1982 p131.

740. Jackson, Rachel Donelson Robards
1767-1828
Wife of Andrew Jackson

Crabb, Alfred L.
Home to Hermitage.
Bobbs-Merrill 1948.
BL v44 1948 p282; BRD 1948 p181; FC 7th p93; LJ
 v73 1948 p395; NYTBR Ap 4, 1948 p21.

Gerson, Noel Bertram
Old Hickory.
Doubleday 1964.
FC 9th p198; LJ v89 1964 p1776; LJ v89 1964 p2243.

Govan, Christine
JUV *Rachel Jackson, Tennessee Girl.*
Bobbs-Merrill 1955.
LJ v80 1955 p1507.

Miller, Helen Topping
JUV *Her Christmas at the Hermitage: A Tale about Ra-
 chel and Andrew Jackson.*
Longmans, Green 1955.
BL v52 1955 p167; BRD 1956 p644; KR v23 1955
 p562; LJ v80 1955 p1819; NYTBR N 6, 1955 p50.

Stone, Irving
*The President's Lady: A Novel about Rachel and
 Andrew Jackson.*
Doubleday 1951.
BL v48 O 15, 1951 p66; BRD 1951 p849; FC 11th
 p588; LJ v76 1951 p1421; NYTBR S 30, 1951 p4;
 Time v58 O 8, 1951 p122.

Wellman, Paul I.
*Magnificent Destiny: A Novel about the Great Se-
 cret Adventure of Andrew Jackson and Sam
 Houston.*
Doubleday 1962.
BRD 1962 p477; FC 9th p542; KR v30 1962 p477; LJ
 v87 1962 p2779; NYTBR S 23, 1962 p45.

741. Jacob
Old Testament figure; son of Isaac

Buechner, Frederick
The Son of Laughter.
Harper 1993.

Cabries, Jean
Jacob.
Dutton 1958.
BL v55 1958 p97; BRD 1958 p177; KR v26 1958
 p477; LJ v83 1958 p3152; NYTBR S 14, 1958 p30.

Fineman, Irving
Jacob; an Autobiographical Novel.

Random House 1941.
BRD 1941 p297; NYTBR O 5, 1941 p6; SatR O 11,
 1941 p14.

Hoyer, Robert
Jabbok.
Muhlenberg Press 1958.

Mann, Thomas
Joseph and His Brothers.
Knopf 1948 (Heavily reprinted).
First published in English in four separate parts: *The
 Tales of Jacob, Young Joseph, Joseph in Egypt,* and
 Joseph the Provider..

Rees, Jean A.
Jacob Have I Loved.
Eerdmans 1963.
LJ v88 1963 p4238.

742. James (the Greater), Saint
Apostle of Jesus

Mosley, Jean Bell
The Crosses at Zarin.
Broadman Press 1967.
KR v35 1967 p664.

743. James I
1394-1437
King of Scotland, 1406-1437

Bridge, S. R.
Captive King.
Hale 1978.

Cummins, Mary
Heir to Balgennan.
Hale 1978.

Fremantle, Anne
James and Joan.
Holt 1948.
BRD 1948 p288; LJ v73 1948 p122; NYTBR F 29,
 1948 p5; SatR Mr 6, 1948 p28.

Oliver, Jane
Crown for a Prisoner.
Collins 1953.

Simpson, Evan John (Evan John, pseud.)
Crippled Splendour.
Dutton 1938 (Rpr. 1971).
BL v35 1938 p24; BRD 1938 p875; NYTBR S 11,
 1938 p2; SatR S 10, 1938 p7.

Tranter, Nigel G.
Lion Let Loose.
Hodder & Stoughton 1967.

744. James I
1566-1625
King of England, 1603-1625, & as James VI,
King of Scotland, 1567-1625; son of Mary
Queen of Scots

Beamish, Annie O'Meara
The Wayward Wench.
Hale 1963.

Bibby, Violet
Many Waters Cannot Quench Love.
Morrow 1974.
NS v88 N 8, 1974 p666; TLS S 20, 1974 p1012.

Binner, Ina
Monarch of Two Kingdoms.
Hale 1976.

Garrett, George
The Succession: A Novel of Elizabeth and James.
Doubleday 1983 (Rpr. 1991).
BL v80 1983 p313; BRD 1984 p557; KR v51 1983
    p1013; LJ v108 1983 p2100; NYTBR D 25, 1983 p6.

Hibbert, Eleanor (Jean Plaidy, pseud.)
The Murder in the Tower.
Hale 1964 (Rpr. 1974).
BL v71 1974 p238.

Lewis, Hilda
A Mortal Malice.
Hutchinson 1963 (Rpr. 1972).

Lewis, Hilda
Wife to Great Buckingham.
Jarrolds 1959.
BRD 1960 p816; KR v28 1960 p193; LJ v85 1960
    p1618.

Long, Freda M.
Royal Clown.
Hale 1973.
B&B v18 Ag 1973 p134.

Peters, Maureen
Bride for King James.
Hale 1968.

Stewart, Stanley
The King James Version: A Novel.
Random House 1977.
FC 10th p504; LJ v101 1976 p2598.

Tranter, Nigel G.
*The Courtesan: The Second of Three Novel about
    the Master of Gray.*
Coronet 1973.

Tranter, Nigel G.
Past Master.
Hodder & Stoughton 1965.

Tranter, Nigel G.
*The Wisest Fool: A Novel of James the Sixth and
    First.*
Hodder & Stoughton 1974.

745. James II
1633-1701
King of England, 1685-1688; & as James VII,
King of Scotland,

Clark, J. Kent
The King's Agent.
Scribner 1958.
BL v55 1959 p236; BRD 1959 p210; KR v26 1958
    p471; LJ v83 1958 p2320; NYTBR N 30, 1958 p68.

Dakers, Elaine (Jane Lane, pseud.)
The Phoenix and the Laurel.
Hale 1954 (Rpr. 1974).

Kersey, Clare
The Cinderella Duchess.
Hale 1971.

Neill, Robert
The Golden Days.
Hutchinson 1972.
BL v70 1973 p152; KR v41 1973 p340; LJ v98 1973
    p1309.

Ross Williamson, Hugh
James, by the Grace of God.
Joseph 1955.
BRD 1956 p799; SatR O 27, 1956 p26.

746. James IV
1473-1513
King of Scotland, 1488-1513

Hill, Pamela
The King's Vixen.
Putnam 1954.
Also published as *Flaming Janet: A Lady of Galloway.*
BRD 1954 p424; KR v22 1954 p77; SatR Jl 24, 1954
    p36.

Maclaren, Deanna
A Dagger in the Sleeve.
W.H. Allen 1979 (Rpr. 1986).

Oliver, Jane
Sunset at Noon.
Collins 1955 (Rpr. 1963).
LJ v88 1963 p2028.

Orr, Christine
Gentle Eagle, a Stewart Portrait.
International Pub. Co. 1947.

Steele, Hunter
*Chasing the Gilded Shadow: A Tale of the Time of
    James IV of Scotland.*
St. Martin's 1986.
BL v82 1986 p1059; BritBkN Jl 1986 p425; KR v54
    1986 p338; LJ v111 Mr 15, 1986 p79; NYTBR My
    25, 1986 p16; PW v229 My 28, 1986 p52.

Stewart, A. J.
*Falcon: The Autobiograhy of His Grace James the
    4, King of Scots.*
P. Davies 1970.
B&B v15 Je 1970 p39; LJ v96 1971 p1139; TLS Ag
    14, 1970 p894.

Tranter, Nigel G.
Chain of Destiny.
Hodder & Stroughton 1964 (Rpr. 1977, 1991).

Trotter, Sallie
Royal Paladin.
Serif Books 1950.

Westcott, Jan
The Hepburn.
Crown 1950.
BL v46 1950 p211; BRD 1950 p960; KR v18 1950 p109; NYTBR Ap 23, 1950 p31.

747. James V
1512-1542
King of Scotland, 1513-1542

Gal, Laszlo
JUV *The Goodman of Ballengiech.*
Methuen 1987.

Hill, Pamela
My Lady Glamis.
St. Martin's 1985.

Tranter, Nigel G.
James, by the Grace of God.
Beaufort Books 1985.
BritBkN Ja 1986 p48; LJ v111 Mr 1, 1986 p110; TLS My 9, 1986 p498.

Tranter, Nigel G.
The River Realm.
Beaufort Books 1984.
KR v53 1985 p158; LJ v110 Ap 1, 1985 p161; PW v227 Mr 1, 1985 p69; TLS My 17, 1985 p561.

748. James, Henry, Jr.
1843-1916
American novelist

Aiken, Joan
The Haunting of Lamb House.
J. Cape 1991 (Rpr. 1993).
CR v259 Ag 1991 p111; TLS Ap 12, 1991 p19.

Goldstein, Rebecca
The Dark Sister.
Viking 1991.
BL v87 1991 p1858; KR v59 1991 p553; LJ v116 Je 1, 1991 p191; NYTBR Ag 11, 1991 p29.

Hill, Carol DeChellis
Henry James' Midnight Song.
Poseidon Press 1993.
NYTBR S 5, 1993 p10.

749. James, Jesse Woodson
1847-1882
American outlaw; known for daring bank & train robberies

Hansen, Ron
The Assassination of Jesse James by the Coward, Robert Ford.
Knopf 1983.
BRD 1984 p660; KR v51 1983 p898; LJ v108 1983 p1720; NYTBR F 5, 1984 p18.

Henry, Will
Death of a Legend.
Random House 1954.

Ross, James R.
I, Jesse James.
Dragon Pub. Corp. 1988.
BWatch v10 Je 1989 p5.

Taylor, Robert
Loving Belle Starr.
Algonquin Books 1984.
KR v52 1984 p169; LATBR Jl 29, 1984 p8; LJ v109 1984 p997; PW v225 F 24, 1984 p125.

750. Jefferson, Martha
1772-1836
Eldest daughter of Thomas Jefferson

Bourne, Miriam Anne
JUV *Patsy Jefferson's Diary.*
Coward, McCann & Geoghegan 1976.
KR v44 1976 p467; SatR S 1976 p110.

751. Jefferson, Martha Wayles Skelton
1748-1782
Wife of Thomas Jefferson

Grimes, Roberta
My Thomas: A Novel of Martha Jefferson's Life.
Doubleday 1993.

752. Jefferson, Thomas
1743-1826
Third US President; wrote Declaration of Independence

Bourne, Miriam Anne
JUV *Patsy Jefferson's Diary.*
Coward, McCann & Geoghegan 1976.
KR v44 1976 p467; SatR S 1976 p110.

Byrd, Max
Jefferson: A Novel.
Bantam 1993.

Chase-Riboud, Barbara
Sally Hemings: A Novel.
Viking 1979.
BRD 1979 p225; FC 11th p106; KR v47 1979 p539; LJ v104 1979 p1355; NYTBR O 28, 1979 p14.

Cochran, Louis
The Fool of God.
Duell, Sloan & Pearce 1958.
BL v54 1958 p502; BRD 1958 p231; KR v26 1958 p15; NYTBR Ag 3, 1958 p18.

Delmar, Vina
A Time for Titans.
Harcourt Brace Jovanovich 1974.
FC 9th p130; KR v42 1974 p69; LJ v99 1974 p774;
    PW v205 Ja 21, 1975 p79.

Erickson, Steve
Arc D'X.
Poseidon Press 1993.
NYTBR My 2, 1993 p9.

Fox, Mary Virginia
JUV *Treasure of the Revolution.*
Abingdon Press 1961.

Gerson, Noel Bertram
The River Devils.
Doubleday 1968.
KR v36 1968 p529; LJ v93 1968 p2523.

Goodrum, Charles A.
The Best Cellar.
St. Martin's 1987.
KR v55 1987 p891; LJ v112 Jl 1987 p100.

Grimes, Roberta
My Thomas: A Novel of Martha Jefferson's Life.
Doubleday 1993.

Holland, Janice
JUV *They Built a City: The Story of Washington,*
    D.C..
Scribner 1953.
BRD 1953 p441; KR v21 1953 p70; LJ v78 1953 p454;
    NYTBR F 15, 1953 p26.

Miller, Helen Topping
JUV *Christmas at Monticello with Thomas Jefferson.*
Longmans, Green 1959.
LJ v84 1959 p2522.

Monjo, F. N.
JUV *Grand Papa and Ellen Aroon.*
Holt, Rinehart & Winston 1974.
KR v43 1975 p23.

Peden, William
Twilight at Monticello.
Houghton Mifflin 1973.
KR v41 1973 p340; LJ v98 1973 p1196; NYTBR Je 3,
    1973 p33; PW v203 Ap 9, 1973 p63.

Rinaldi, Ann
YA *Wolf by the Ears.*
Scholastic 1991.
BL v87 1991 p1125; BRD 1991 p1571; SLJ v37 Ap
    1991 p142; VOYA v14 Je 1991 p101.

753. Jenner, Edward
1749-1823
English physician; discovered vaccine used
against smallpox

Gibbs, Willa
The Dedicated: A Novel.
Morrow 1960.

Also published as *The Two Doctors.*
BL v56 1960 p444; BRD 1960 p521; FC 7th p149; KR
    v27 1959 p894; LJ v85 1960 p2054; NYTBR F 21,
    1960 p34.

754. Jeremiah
Old Testament prophet

Chinn, Laurene
Voice of the Lord: A Novel.
Crown 1961.
LJ v86 1961 p3971.

Millikin, Virginia Greene
YA *Jeremiah, Prophet of Disaster.*
Association Press 1954.
NYTBR Ap 4, 1954 p26.

Pitzer, Robert
Daughter of Jerusalem: A Biblical Novel of the
    Days of Jeremiah.
Liveright Pub. Corp. 1956.

Weinreb, Nathaniel Norsen
The Babylonians.
Doubleday 1953.
BL v50 1953 p15; BRD 1953 p991; FC 9th p542; KR
    v21 1953 p272; NYTBR Je 21, 1953 p14.

755. Jesus Christ
Christianity is based on his teachings

Absire, Alain
Lazarus.
Harcourt Brace Jovanovich 1988.
KR v56 1988 p68; LJ v113 Mr 15, 1988 p66.

Asch, Sholem
Mary.
Putnam 1949 (Rpr. 1985).
BRD 1949 p25; FC 11th p24; KR v17 1949 p436; LJ
    v74 1949 p1460; NYTBR O 9, 1949 p5.

Asch, Sholem
The Nazarene.
Putnam 1939 (Rpr. 1984).
BL v36 N 1, 1939 p88; BRD 1939 p32; FC 11th p24;
    LJ v65 1940 p587; NYTBR O 29, 1939 p3.

Bauer, Florence A.
Behold Your King.
Bobbs-Merrill 1945.
BL v42 1945 p18; BRD 1945 p40; KR v13 1945 p259;
    NYTBR S 30, 1945 p32.

Bauer, Ludwig
The Quest: The Story of the Shepherds of Bethle-
    hem.
Concordia Publishing House 1945.

Bell, Sallie Lee
Until the Day Break: A Novel of the Time of
    Christ.
Zondervan 1950.
BRD 1950 p65; LJ v75 1950 p104.

Bishop, James A.
The Day Christ Died.
Harper 1957.
BL v53 1957 p444; BRD 1957 p87; KR v25 1957
p198; LJ v82 1957 p1311; NYTBR My 19, 1957
p10.

Blythe, LeGette
Bold Galilean.
Grosset & Dunlap 1948.
BRD 1948 p81; KR v16 1948 p515; LJ v73 1948
p1192; NYTBR N 7, 1948 p30.

Brelich, Mario
The Work of Betrayal.
Marlboro Press 1988.
NYTBR Ag 27, 1989 p18.

Brod, Max
The Master.
Philosophical Library 1951.
BRD 1951 p116; KR v19 1951 p611; LJ v76 1951
p1332; NYTBR N 11, 1951 p5.

Brown, John P.
The Lost Years of Jesus.
Pageant Press 1954.

Bulgakov, Mikhail A.
The Master and Margarita.
Harper & Row 1967 (Heavily reprinted).
BRD 1967 p189; Choice v5 1968 p632; LJ v92 1967
p3657; NYTBR O 22, 1967 p1.

Burgess, Anthony
The Kingdom of the Wicked.
Arbor House 1985.
BL v81 1985 p1474; LJ v110 O 15, 1985 p100;
NYTBR S 22, 1985 p20; PW v228 Ag 30, 1985
p416; TLS My 31, 1985 p598.

Burgess, Anthony
Man of Nazareth.
McGraw-Hill 1979.
Atl v243 My 1979 p94; BRD 1979 p178; KR v47 1979
p206; LJ v104 1979 p972; NYTBR Ap 15, 1979 p1.

Caldwell, Taylor
I, Judas.
Atheneum 1977.
BL v73 1977 p1631; KR v45 1977 p678; PW v212 Jl
11, 1977 p74.

Callaghan, Mary Lloyd
The Cedar Block.
Judson Press 1949.

Ceder, Georgiana Dorcas
JUV *Ann of Bethany.*
Abingdon Cokesbury 1951.
BRD 1951 p159; CC 1951 p115; LJ v76 1951 p879;
WLB v47 1951 p191.

Crowell, Grace
JUV *The Little Serving Maid.*
Augsburg Pub. House 1953.

De Wohl, Louis
The Spear.
Lippincott 1955.
BL v51 1955 p366; BRD 1955 p238; KR v23 1955
p49; LJ v80 1955 p1014; NYTBR Mr 20, 1955 p24.

Douglas, Lloyd C.
The Robe.
Houghton Mifflin 1942.
BL v39 1942 p71; BRD 1942 p217; FC 11th p166;
NYTBR O 25, 1942 p7; SatR O 31, 1942 p16.

Fisher, Vardis
Jesus Came Again: A Parable.
A. Swallow 1956.

Fox, Paul H.
The Daughter of Jairus.
Little, Brown 1951.
BRD 1951 p306; KR v18 1950 p706; LJ v76 1951
p179; NYTBR F 11, 1951 p20.

Gibran, Kahlil
*Jesus the Son of Man, His Words and His Deeds as
Told and Recorded by Those Who Knew Him.*
Knopf 1928 (Heavily reprinted).
BRD 1928 p300; NYTBR D 23, 1928 p18.

Goldthorpe, John
The Same Scourge.
Putnam 1956.
BRD 1956 p369; KR v24 1956 p59; LJ v81 1956 p530;
NYTBR Jl 29, 1956 p18.

Graves, Robert
King Jesus.
Farrar, Straus & Cudahy 1946 (Heavily reprinted).
BRD 1946 p332; KR v14 1946 p548; LJ v71 1946
p1206; NYTBR S 29, 1946 p5.

Hamon, Marcel
Nightfall at Noon.
Ziff-Davis 1949.
BRD 1949 p388; LJ v74 1949 p1202; NYTBR S 11,
1949 p37.

Harington, Joy
Jesus of Nazareth.
Doubleday 1956.
BRD 1958 p489; LJ v82 1957 p2821.

Harrison, Marcus
The Memoirs of Jesus Christ.
Arlington Books 1975.
PW v211 Ja 3, 1977 p67.

Haughton, Rosemary
JUV *The Carpenter's Son.*
Macmillan 1967.
BRD 1967 p576; KR v35 1967 p7; LJ v92 1967 p1734;
NYTBR Ap 16, 1967 p22.

Holmes, Marjorie
The Messiah.
Harper & Row 1987.
Sequel to *Three from Galilee.*

BL v84 1987 p1; KR v55 1987 p1261; LJ v112 O 15,
1987 p94; PW v232 S 4, 1987 p53.

Holmes, Marjorie
Three from Galilee.
Harper & Row 1985.
BL v81 1985 p1596; KR v53 1985 p657; LJ v110 S 15,
1985 p93; PW v227 Je 28, 1985 p62.

Ingles, James W.
A Woman of Samaria.
Longmans, Green 1949.
BRD 1949 p452.

Joers, Lawrence E. C.
Thou Art Peter.
Vantage Press 1952.

Kagawa, Toyohiko
Behold the Man.
Harper & Brothers 1941.
BL v38 1941 p35; BRD 1941 p488; NYTBR Je 29,
1941 p7.

Kazantzakis, Nikos
The Greek Passion.
Simon & Schuster 1953.
BL v50 1954 p221; BRD 1954 p484; KR v21 1953
p715; LJ v78 1953 p2212; NYTBR Ja 10, 1954 p5.

Kazantzakis, Nikos
The Last Temptation of Christ.
Simon & Schuster 1960.
Atl v206 S 1960 p114; BRD 1960 p726; FC 11th
p338; KR v28 1960 p517; LJ v85 1960 p2957;
NYTBR Ag 7, 1960 p4.

Keepler, James H.
The Jordan Beachhead: A Novel of Biblical Times.
Exposition Press 1956.

Keyes, T.
The Second Coming.
W.H. Allen 1972.

Kinstler, Clysta
The Moon under Her Feet.
HarperCollins 1991.

Knab, Otto J. (Otto Michael, pseud.)
The Hour of Barabbas.
Sheed & Ward 1943.

Komroff, Manuel
His Great Journey.
Pyramid Books 1956.

Komroff, Manuel
In the Year of Our Lord.
Harper & Brothers 1942.
LJ v67 1942 p319; LJ v67 1942 p676; SatR Ap 11,
1942 p8.

Konstantinovic, Radomir
Exitus: A Novel.
Calder & Boyars 1965.

Kossoff, David
The Little Book of Sylvanus.
St. Martin's 1975.
FC 10th p311.

Langguth, A. J.
Jesus Christs.
Harper & Row 1968.
BRD 1968 p773; LJ v93 1968 p572; NYTBR Mr 10,
1968 p31.

Lapham, Arthur L.
Justus.
Concordia Pub. House 1973.
LJ v98 1973 p2463.

Leslie, Desmond
The Jesus File.
Sidgwick & Jackson 1975.
PW v207 Ja 20, 1975 p70.

Lillie, Amy Morris
JUV *Nathan, Boy of Capernaum.*
Dutton 1945.
BRD 1945 p431; HB v21 My 1945 p199; KR v13 1945
p134; LJ v70 1945 p355.

Lofts, Norah
YA *How Far to Bethlehem?.*
Doubleday 1965.
FC 9th p323; LJ v90 1965 p2871.

Lovelace, Delos Wheeler
YA *Journey to Bethlehem.*
Crowell 1953.
BL v50 1953 p90; BRD 1953 p581; KR v21 1953 p451.

Lowenstein, Hubertus
The Lance of Longinus.
Macmillan 1946.
BRD 1946 p503; KR v14 1946 p100; LJ v71 1946
p121; SatR F 23, 1946 p37.

MacGregor, Mary E. (Marian Keith, pseud.)
JUV *Boy of Nazareth.*
Abington-Cokesbury Press 1950.
BRD 1950 p594; KR v18 1950 p385; LJ v75 1950
p1307.

Malvern, Gladys
YA *Tamar.*
Longmans, Green 1952.
BL v49 1952 p36; BRD 1952 p597; KR v20 1952
p341; LJ v77 1952 p1523; NYTBR S 28, 1952 p36.

Mills, James R.
The Gospel According to Pontius Pilate.
San Francisco Club 1977.
KR v45 1977 p1038; PW v212 Ag 22, 1977 p61.

Monterosso, Carlo
The Salt of the Earth.
Faber & Faber 1967.
LJ v92 1967 p3660.

Moore, George
The Brook Kerith: A Syrian Story.
Macmillan 1916 (Heavily reprinted).

BRD 1916 p392; NYTBR Ag 27, 1916 p329; SatR S
2, 1916 p228.

Newcomb, Robert Thomas
Janissa.
Destiny Publishers 1943.
BRD 1943 p606.

Oursler, Fulton
The Greatest Story Ever Told: A Tale of the Greatest Life Ever Lived.
Doubleday 1949 (Heavily reprinted).
BL v45 1949 p210; BRD 1949 p707; KR v17 1949
p52; LJ v74 1949 p57; NYTBR F 6, 1949 p10.

Payne, Pierre
The Lord Jesus.
Abelard-Schuman 1964.
BRD 1965 p981; NYTBR N 15, 1964 p58; SatR O 3,
1964 p38.

Payne, Pierre
The Shepherd.
Horizon Press 1959.
BRD 1960 p1046; KR v27 1959 p667; NYTBR N 8,
1959 p60.

Perkins, Jacob R.
The Emperor's Physician.
Bobbs-Merrill 1944.
BL v40 1944 p390; BRD 1944 p593; KR v12 1944
p236; NYTBR Jl 16, 1944 p14.

Perri, Francesco
The Unknown Disciple.
Macmillan 1950.
BL v46 1950 p262; BRD 1950 p721; KR v18 1950 p73.

Ranger, Mary
JUV *Simon the Small: A Young Galilean Wonders Why
Peter Becomes a Fisher of Men.*
Concordia Pub. House 1977.

Rayner, William
The Last Days.
Morrow 1969.
BL v65 1969 p733; FC 8th p337; LJ v94 1969 p2251.

Robey, John B.
The Innovator.
Doubleday, Doran 1945.
BRD 1945 p600; KR v12 1944 p538; LJ v70 1945
p117; NYTBR F 11, 1945 p6.

Ronalds, Mary Teresa
The Eyewitness: The Testimony of John.
Abingdon Press 1967.
LJ v92 1967 p4264.

Slaughter, Carolyn
Magdalene: A Novel.
M. Evans 1979.
KR v47 1979 p219.

Slaughter, Frank G.
The Crown and the Cross: The Life of Christ.
World Pub. Co. 1959.

BRD 1959 p918; KR v27 1959 p64; LJ v84 1959
p1257; NYTBR Ap 5, 1959 p37.

Speare, Elizabeth George
YA *The Bronze Bow.*
Houghton Mifflin 1961 (Rpr. 1973).
Won the 1962 Newbery award.
BRD 1962 p1134; HB v37 O 1961 p432; KR v29 1961
p615; LJ v86 1961 p3077; NYTBR N 12, 1961 p20.

Storey, Anthony
The Saviour: A Novel.
Boyars 1978.
B&B v24 D 1978 p62; CR v234 Ja 1979 p48.

Sutphen, William Gilbert van Tassel
I, Nathanael, Knew Jesus.
F.H. Revell 1941.
BRD 1942 p752.

Thornton, Francis
*The Donkey Who Always Complained: A Parable
for Moderns.*
P.J. Kenedy 1956.

Tournier, Michel
The Four Wise Men.
Doubleday 1982.
KR v50 1982 p899; NYTBR O 24, 1982 p14; PW
v222 Ag 13, 1982 p66.

Vance, Marguerite
JUV *While Sheperds Watched.*
Dutton 1946.
CC 1951 p651.

Vidal, Gore
Live from Golgotha.
Random House. 1992.
NYTBR O 4, 1992 p13; NW v120 Ag 31, 1992 p69;
Time v140 S 28, 1992 p64.

Wallace, Irving
The Word.
Simon & Schuster 1972.
Atl v230 S 1972 p96; LJ v97 1972 p1035; NYTBR Mr
19, 1972 p39.

Wallace, Lew
Ben-Hur: A Tale of the Christ.
Harper & Brothers 1880 (Heavily reprinted).
NYTBR F 3, 1900 p78; NYTBR D 5, 1908 p748; LJ
v81 1956 p1053.

Waltari, Mika
The Secret of the Kingdom.
Putnam 1961.
BL v57 1960 p241; BRD 1961 p1486; KR v28 1960
p967; LJ v85 1960 p4489; NYTBR Ja 15, 1961 p5.

Wibberley, Leonard
The Centurion.
Morrow 1966.
BRD 1966 p1294; FC 9th p556; LJ v91 1966 p4704;
NYTBR O 30, 1966.

Wibberley, Leonard
The Testament of Theophilus: A Novel of Christ and Caesar.
Morrow 1973.
Also published as *Merchant of Rome.*
BL v69 1973 p973; NYTBR O 7, 1973 p34.

Wilson, Dorothy Clarke
The Gifts: A Story of the Boyhood of Jesus.
McGraw-Hill 1957.
BRD 1957 p998; KR v25 1957 p654; LJ v82 1957 p2544.

Wright, Herbert W.
Jesus' Kingdom of Love: The Unwritten Story of the Lost Kingdom of Agape.
Exposition Press 1957.

Yanikian, Gourgen
The Resurrected Christ: A Novel.
Exposition Press 1955.

Yerby, Frank
Judas, My Brother; the Story of the Thirteenth Disciple.
Dial Press 1968.
KR v36 1968 p1006.

Zehnpfennig, Gladys
Son of Nazareth.
T.S. Denison 1957.

Zeldis, Chayym
Golgotha.
Avon Books 1974.
LJ v99 1874 p1567.

756. Jezebel
Wife of King Ahab; name is used symbolically for a wicked woman

Hesky, Olga
The Painted Queen.
A. Blond 1961.
BRD 1962 p542; LJ v87 1962 p1629.

Paul, Louis
Dara the Cypriot.
Simon & Schuster 1959.
BL v55 1959 p417; BRD 1959 p784; KR v27 1959 p22; LJ v84 1959 p1153.

Slaughter, Frank G.
The Curse of Jezebel: A Novel of the Biblical Queen of Evil.
Doubleday 1961.
NYTBR N 5, 1961 p53.

Wilson, Dorothy Clarke
Jezebel.
McGraw-Hill 1955.
BRD 1956 p1009; KR v23 1955 p771; LJ v80 1955 p2616; NYTBR D 4, 1955 p57.

757. Joan of Arc, Saint
1412-1431
French heroine & saint; tried for heresy, burned at stake

Dana, Barbara
YA *Young Joan: A Novel.*
HarperCollins 1991.
BL v87 1991 p1794; BRD 1991 p432; SLJ v37 My 1991 p108; VOYA v14 Je 1991 p94.

Doherty, P. C.
Serpent amongst the Lilies.
Hale 1990.
KR v58 1990 p1131.

Fadiman, Edwin
The Voice and the Light.
Crown 1949.
BRD 1949 p284; KR v17 1949 p339; LJ v74 1949 p1093; NYTBR O 30, 1949 p51.

Goodwin, Marie D.
YA *Where the Towers Pierce the Sky.*
Four Winds Press 1989.
BL v86 1989 p742; BRD 1990 p692; SLJ v35 N 1989 p126.

Hibbert, Eleanor (Jean Plaidy, pseud.)
Epitaph for Three Women.
Putnam 1983.
BL v79 1983 p1328.

Keneally, Thomas
Blood Red, Sister Rose.
Viking 1974 (Rpr. 1984, 1991).
BL v71 1974 p321; KR v42 1974 p960; LJ v100 1975 p145; NYTBR F 9, 1975 p7.

Long, Freda M.
The Divine Fantasy.
Hale 1976.

Masefield, Judith
YA *Shepherdess of France: Remembrances of Jeanne d'Arc.*
Coward-McCann 1969.
BRD 1970 p942; KR v37 1969 p1127; LJ v95 1970 p1204; NYTBR Mr 29, 1970 p18.

Peters, Maureen
Joan of the Lilies.
Hale 1969 (Rpr. 1972).

Schoonover, Lawrence
The Burnished Blade.
Macmillan 1948.
BRD 1948 p746; KR v16 1948 p340; LJ v73 1948 p1091; NYTBR O 3, 1948 p26.

Stoker, M. Brooke
Virgin-at-Arms.
Hale 1978.

Tournier, Michel
Gilles & Jeanne.
Grove Weidenfeld 1990.

First published in 1987 by Methuen.
BL v86 1990 p1530; Choice v28 S 1990 p122.

Twain, Mark
Personal Recollections of Joan of Arc.
Harper & Brothers 1896 (Heavily reprinted).
FC 10th p533.

Wagenknecht, Edward (Julian Forrest, pseud.)
The Glory of the Lilies: A Novel about Joan of Arc.
Bles 1969.

758. Job
Old Testament figure

Shaw, Jean
Job's Wife: A Novel.
Wolgemuth & Hyatt 1990.

759. John of Gaunt
1340-1399
Duke of Lancaster; fourth son of Edward III

Clarke, Brenda (Brenda Honeyman, pseud.)
The Golden Griffin.
Hale 1976.

Crowley, Duane
Riddle Me a Murder.
Blue Boar Press 1986.
BL v83 1987 p1179; LJ v112 Mr 1, 1987 p95.

Hibbert, Eleanor (Jean Plaidy, pseud.)
Passage to Pontefract.
Hale 1981.
BL v79 1982 p2; KR v50 1982 p897; PW v222 O 8, 1982 p127.

Seton, Anya
Katherine.
Houghton Mifflin 1954.
BL v51 S 15, 1954 p42; BRD 1954 p797; FC 11th p545; LJ v80 1955 p499; NYTBR O 3, 1954 p28.

760. John of the Cross, Saint
1542-1591
Spanish religious figure & poet

Rohrbach, Peter T.
Bold Encounter: A Novel Based on the Life of St. John of the Cross.
Bruce Pub. Co. 1960.

761. John Paul II, Pope
1920-
First non-Italian Pope since Renaissance

Quinnell, A. J.
In the Name of the Father.
New American Library 1987.
BL v83 1987 p1627; KR v55 1987 p1106; NYTBR N 8, 1987 p62; PW v234 Ag 5, 1988 p83.

762. John the Baptist
New Testament figure; baptized Jesus in the river Jordan

Brown, Slater
YA *John the Baptist, Prophet of Christ.*
Association Press 1955.
LJ v80 1955 p1260; NYTBR Mr 27, 1955 p32.

Dieterle, William (William Sidney, pseud.)
The Good Tidings.
Farrar, Straus 1950.
BRD 1950 p249; KR v18 1950 p283; LJ v75 1950 p1045; NYTBR Je 18, 1950 p22.

763. John, King of England
1167-1216
Youngest son of Henry II; forced by English barons to sign Magna Carta

Bennetts, Pamela
The Barons of Runnymede.
St. Martin's 1974.
KR v42 1974 p260; LJ v99 1974 p1845; PW v205 Mr 18, 1974 p48.

Chidsey, Donald Barr
This Bright Sword.
Crown 1957.
BL v53 1957 p452; BRD 1957 p174; LJ v82 1957 p749.

Costain, Thomas B.
Below the Salt: A Novel.
Doubleday 1957.
BRD 1957 p204; FC 11th p132; KR v25 1957 p 493; LJ v82 1957 p1904; NYTBR S 22, 1957 p4.

Farely, Alison
King Wolf.
Hale 1974.

Farely, Alison
Kingdom under Tyranny.
Hale 1974.

Farely, Alison
Last Howl of the Wolf.
Hale 1975.

French, Allen
YA *The Lost Baron: A Story of England in the Year 1200.*
Houghton Mifflin 1940.
BL v36 1940 p385; BRD 1940 p326; LJ v65 1940 p502; NYTBR My 12, 1940 p10.

Gellis, Roberta
Masques of Gold.
Jove 1988.
PW v234 Ag 5, 1988 p79.

Goldman, James
Myself as Witness.
Random House 1979.

BL v76 1980 p756; BRD 1980 p466; FC 11th p243;
KR v47 1979 p1279; LJ v104 1979 p2664; NYTBR
F 10, 1980 p18.

Hibbert, Eleanor (Jean Plaidy, pseud.)
The Prince of Darkness.
Hale 1978 (Rpr. 1981).
BL v77 1981 p1141; KR v49 1981 p169; PW v219 F
13, 1981 p78.

Lindsay, Philip
The Devil and King John.
Hutchinson 1943 (Rpr. 1972).

Penman, Sharon Kay
YA *Here Be Dragons.*
Holt, Rinehart & Winston 1985.
BL v81 1985 p1418; KR v53 1985 p552; LJ v110 Jl
1985 p95; NYTBR S 1, 1985 p15; SLJ v32 S 1985
p155.

Shelby, Graham
The Wolf at the Door.
Collins 1975.
KR v43 1975 p627; LJ v100 1975 p1654.

764. Johnson, Andrew
1808-1875
17th US President

Crabb, Alfred L.
*Supper at the Maxwell House: A Novel of Recap-
tured Nashville.*
Bobbs-Merrill 1943.
BL v39 1943 p463; BRD 1943 p182; LJ v68 1943
p530; NYTBR Jl 11, 1943 p4.

Crane, William D.
YA *Andrew Johnson, Tailor from Tennessee.*
Dodd, Mead 1968.
BRD 1968 p288; KR v35 1967 p1479; LJ v93 1968
p879.

Gerson, Noel Bertram
The Yankee from Tennessee.
Doubleday 1960.

McSpaden, J. Walker
Storm Center: A Novel about Andy Johnson.
Dodd, Mead 1947.
BRD 1947 p595; NYTBR Mr 9, 1947 p32; SatR My 3,
1947 p11.

765. Johnson, James Weldon
1871-1938
American author; wrote *The Book of American
Negro Poetry* & *Negro Americans, What Now?*

Reed, Ishmael
Mumbo Jumbo.
Doubleday 1972 (Rpr. 1988).
BL v69 1972 p69; BRD 1972 p1073; KR v40 1972
p641; LJ v97 1972 p3182; NYTBR Ag 6, 1972 p1.

766. Johnson, Lyndon Baines
1908-1973
36th US President

Bernau, George
Promises to Keep.
Warner Books 1988.
BL v84 1988 p1865; KR v56 1988 p1170; LJ v113 O
15, 1988 p100.

Buckley, William F.
Tucker's Last Stand.
Random House 1990.
BL v87 1990 p691; KR v58 1990 p1550; NYTBR F 17,
1991 p15; PW v237 N 16, 1990 p44.

Montgomery, Vivian
JUV *Mr. Jellybean.*
Shoal Creek Publishers 1980.
SLJ v27 F 1981 p59.

Savitt, Sam
A Day at the LBJ Ranch.
Random House 1965.
LJ v90 1965 p2410.

Thomas, D. M.
Flying in to Love.
Scribner 1992.
BL v89 1992 p5; KR v60 1992 p946; NYTBR O 11,
1992 p13.

767. Johnson, Samuel
1709-1784
English lexicographer, critic, & author

Beatty, John; Beatty, Patricia
YA *At the Seven Stars.*
Macmillan 1963.
BRD 1963 p65; LJ v88 1963 p2558; NYTBR S 1, 1963
p12.

Carter, Winifred
Dr. Johnson's Dear Mistress.
Selwyn & Blount 1949.
BRD 1950 p152; LJ v75 1950 p1397; NYTBR Ja 21,
1951 p20; SatR N 18, 1950 p29.

De La Torre, Lillian
The Detections of Dr. Sam Johnson.
Doubleday 1960 (Rpr. 1984, 1989).
BRD 1961 p337; KR v28 1960 p830; NYTBR N 27,
1960 p42; SatR Ja 28, 1961 p31.

De La Torre, Lillian
*Dr. Sam: Johnson, Detector; Being a Light-Hearted
Collection of Recently Reveal'd Episodes in the
Career of the Great Lexicographer Narrated as
from the Pen of James Boswell.*
Knopf 1946 (Rpr. 1983).
BL v43 1946 p69; BRD 1946 p208; KR v14 1946
p353; NYTBR S 22, 1946 p6.

De La Torre, Lillian
The Return of Dr. Sam. Johnson, Detector.

International Polygonics 1985.
BL v82 1986 p732; PW v228 N 1, 1985 p63.

Huffman, Lambert
The Magnificent Delinquent: The Tragic but Tender Story of Samuel Johnson and His Wife, Tetty.
Creative Publishers 1979.

Moses, Joseph
JUV *The Great Rain Robbery.*
Houghton Mifflin 1975.
KR v43 1975 p455; NYTBR Ap 6, 1975 p12; SLJ v21 My 1975 p70.

Norman, Charles
Mr. Oddity, Samuel Johnson.
Bell Pub. Co. 1951.
BRD 1951 p661; NYTBR O 14, 1951 p42; SatR O 13, 1951 p38.

768. Johnson, William, Sir
1715-1774
British colonial government official in America

Tebbel, John W.
The Conqueror: A Novel.
Dutton 1951.
BRD 1951 p873; KR v19 1951 p32; LJ v76 1951 p514; NYTBR Ap 8, 1951 p22.

Widdemer, Margaret
Lady of the Mohawks.
Doubleday 1951.
BL v48 1951 p102; BRD 1951 p946; KR v19 1951 p539; NYTBR D 2, 1951 p52.

Widdemer, Margaret
Red Cloak Flying.
Doubleday 1950.
BL v46 1950 p233; BRD 1950 p971; KR v17 1949 p610; LJ v75 1950 p43; NYTBR Ja 8, 1950 p26.

769. Jones, John Paul
1747-1792
American naval officer

Churchill, Winston
Richard Carvel.
Macmillan 1899 (Heavily reprinted).
FC 10th p99; NYTBR Jl 1, 1899 p433; NYTBR Ap 14, 1900 p247.

Cooper, James Fenimore
The Pilot: A Tale of the Sea.
Charles Wiley 1823 (Heavily reprinted).
FC 11th p129.

Dodge, Constance
The Dark Stranger.
Penn Publishing 1940.
BL v36 1940 p429; BRD 1940 p251; NYTBR Je 16, 1940 p6; SatR Jl 20, 1940 p14.

Dumas, Alexandre
Paul Jones: A Nautical Romance.
F. Warne 1889.
Translation of *Le Capitaine Paul.*

Ellsberg, Edward
Captain Paul.
Dodd, Mead & Co. 1941.
BL v37 1941 p491; BRD 1941 p274; CSM Jl 5, 1941 p11; LJ v66 1941 p463; LJ v66 1941 p886; NYTBR Je 1, 1941 p6.

Ellsberg, Edward
YA *"I Have Just Begun to Fight!": The Story of John Paul Jones.*
Dodd, Mead 1942.
BL v38 1942 p344; BRD 1942 p234; LJ v67 1942 p368.

Frye, Pearl
Gallant Captain: A Biographical Novel Based on the Life of John Paul Jones.
Little, Brown 1955.
BL v52 1956 p189; BRD 1956 p340; KR v23 1955 p815; LJ v80 1955 p2601; NYTBR Ja 8, 1956 p26.

Haislip, Harvey
Sailor Named Jones.
Doubleday 1957.
BL v53 1957 p500; BRD 1957 p385; KR v25 1957 p156; LJ v82 1957 p1065; NYTBR Ap 28, 1957 p42.

Haugaard, Erik Christian
JUV *A Boy's Will.*
Houghton Mifflin 1983.
BRD 1984 p684; HB v59 D 1983 p708; PW v224 O 21, 1983 p67; SLJ v30 F 1984 p71.

Hungerford, Edward B.
JUV *Escape to Danger.*
Follett Pub. Co. 1949.
BL v46 1950 p161; BRD 1949 p444; KR v17 1949 p626; LJ v75 1950 p329.

Karig, Walter
Don't Tread on Me.
Rinehart 1954.
BL v50 1954 p369; BRD 1954 p483; FC 7th p204; KR v22 1954 p274; LJ v79 1954 p1225; NYTBR Je 27, 1954 p4.

Kent, Louise Andrews
JUV *He Went with John Paul Jones.*
Houghton Mifflin 1958.
BL v54 1958 p592; BRD 1958 p606; LJ v83 1958 p2509; NYTBR My 4, 1958 p32.

McNamara, Tom
Henry Lunt and the Ranger.
Nuventures 1991.

Melville, Herman
Israel Potter: His Fifty Years of Exile.
Putnam 1855 (Heavily reprinted).
Also published under the titles: *The Refugee* and *His Fifty Years of Exile.*

Ripley, Clements
Clear for Action: A Novel about John Paul Jones.
Appleton-Century 1940.
BL v37 1940 p91; BRD 1940 p769; NYTBR Ag 4, 1940 p7; SatR S 28, 1940 p20.

Royal, Lorene Thompson
The Ember's Glow: The Love-Life of John Paul Jones, Founder of the American Navy.
Story Book Press 1949.

Schoonover, Lawrence
The Revolutionary.
Little, Brown 1958.
BL v54 1958 p535; BRD 1958 p946; FC 9th p448; KR v26 1958 p94; LJ v83 1958 p1552.

Snow, Dorothea J.
JUV *John Paul Jones, Salt-Water Boy.*
Bobbs-Merrill 1950.
LJ v76 1951 p186.

Vinton, Iris
JUV *The Story of John Paul Jones.*
Grosset & Dunlap 1953.
BRD 1954 p913; KR v21 1953 p487; LJ v78 1953 p2228; NYTBR N 15, 1953 p30.

770. Jones, Mary Harris
1830-1930
American labor union leader; commonly referred to as "Mother Jones"

Houston, Robert
Bisbee '17: A Novel.
Pantheon 1979.
KR v47 1979 p213; LJ v104 1979 p1077; NYTBR Je 10, 1979 p24.

Rappaport, Doreen
JUV *Trouble at the Mines.*
Crowell 1987.
BL v83 1987 p1370; HB v63 Mr 1987 p212; KR v55 1987 p558; NYTBR My 17, 1987 p33; SLJ v33 Ap 1987 p102.

Settle, Mary Lee
The Scapegoat.
Random House 1980.
FC 11th p545; LJ v105 1980 p1881; NYTBR O 26, 1980 p1.

771. Joseph
Old Testament figure; son of Jacob; sold into slavery by his brothers

Cabries, Jean
Jacob.
Dutton 1958.
BL v55 1958 p97; BRD 1958 p177; KR v26 1958 p477; LJ v83 1958 p3152; NYTBR S 14, 1958 p30.

Cantrell, Grady
Joseph, Slave of Mystery.
Vulcan Books 1949.

Eberle, Gertrude
Charioteer: A Story of Old Egypt in the Days of Joseph.
Wm. B. Eerdmans 1946.
BRD 1946 p238; NYTBR O 27, 1946 p25.

Fineman, Irving
Jacob; an Autobiographical Novel.
Random House 1941.
BRD 1941 p297; NYTBR O 5, 1941 p6; SatR O 11, 1941 p14.

King, Marian
YA *Coat of Many Colors: The Story of Joseph.*
Lippincott 1950.
BRD 1950 p511; KR v18 1950 p472; LJ v75 1950 p1913; NYTBR Ja 21, 1951 p26.

Landorf, Joyce
Joseph: A Novel.
Revell 1980.
PW v217 My 16, 1980 p200.

Lau, Josephine
JUV *The Story of Joseph.*
Abingdon-Cokesbury Press 1950.
BRD 1950 p537; KR v18 1950 p98; LJ v75 1950 p640; NYTBR Mr 12, 1950 p22.

Mann, Thomas
Joseph and His Brothers.
Knopf 1948 (Heavily reprinted).
First published in English in four separate parts: *The Tales of Jacob, Young Joseph, Joseph in Egypt,* and *Joseph the Provider.*

Parker, Norton S.
Table in the Wilderness.
Ziff-Davis Publishing 1947.
BRD 1947 p696; NYTBR Ap 13, 1947 p20.

Phillips, Leroy
Joseph the Dreamer.
W.A. Wilde 1949.

Rees, Jean A.
Jacob Have I Loved.
Eerdmans 1963.
LJ v88 1963 p4238.

772. Joseph of Arimathea
New Testament figure; rich Israelite who went to Pilate and begged the body of Jesus, placing it in his own tomb

Brooker, Bertram
The Robber: A Tale of the Time of the Herods.
Duell, Sloan & Pearce 1949.
BRD 1949 p107; SatR Jl 16, 1949 p18.

Hughes, Thomas Rowland
The Story of Joseph of Arimathea.
G. Aberystwyth 1961.

Slaughter, Frank G.
The Thorn of Arimathea.

Doubleday 1959.
BRD 1959 p918; FC 9th p471; KR v26 1958 p855; LJ
v84 1959 p120.

Steedman, Marguerite
Refuge in Avalon.
Doubleday 1962.
BL v58 1962 p787; BRD 1962 p1146; KR v30 1962
p252; LJ v87 1962 p1810.

773. Joseph, Chief
1840-1904
Chief of Nez Perce Indians

Byrd, Sigman
The Valiant.
Jason Press 1955.
BRD 1955 p137; LJ v80 1955 p2169; NYTBR O 2,
1955 p29.

Cheshire, Gifford P.
Thunder on the Mountain.
Doubleday 1960.

Forman, James D.
JUV *People of the Dream.*
Farrar, Straus & Giroux 1972.
BL v68 1972 p997; KR v40 1972 p589; LJ v97 1972
p3813; NYTBR N 5, 1972 p14.

Fox, Norman A.
Rope the Wind.
Dodd, Mead 1958 (Rpr. 1992).
NYTBR Ja 11, 1959 p35.

Hanes, Frank Borden
The Fleet Rabble: A Novel of the Nez Perce War.
L.C. Page 1961 (Rpr. 1989).
BRD 1962 p510; KR v29 1961 p346; LJ v86 1961
p2491; NYTBR Ag 27, 1961 p28.

Henry, Will
From Where the Sun Now Stands.
Random House 1960 (Rpr. 1978).
NYTBR F 21, 1960 p35.

Hubler, Richard G.
The Earthmother Drinks Blood.
Creek House 1975.

Patton, Oliver B.
My Heart Turns Back.
Popular Library 1978.
LJ v103 1978 p1662.

Payne, Robert
The Chieftan: A Story of the Nez Perce People.
Prentice-Hall 1953.
BL v49 1953 p323; BRD 1953 p731; KR v21 1953
p229; LJ v78 1953 p994; NYTBR My 17, 1953 p26.

Perry, Frederick
Thunder on the Mountain.
Dorrance 1973.

Rush, William
Red Fox of the Kinapoo.

Longmans, Green 1950.
BRD 1949 p793; KR v17 1949 p302; LJ v74 1949
p1107; NYTBR Ag 21, 1949 p26.

774. Joseph, Saint
Husband of the Virgin Mary

Holmes, Marjorie
Two from Galilee: A Love Story.
Revell 1972.
BS v32 S 1, 1972 p247; KR v40 1972 p691; PW v201
Je 19, 1972 p58.

Lofts, Norah
YA *How Far to Bethlehem?.*
Doubleday 1965.
FC 9th p323; LJ v90 1965 p2871.

775. Josephine
1763-1814
Empress of France; first wife of Napoleon I

Chambers, Rosamund M.
Little Creole: A Story of Napoleon and Josephine.
Cassell 1952.

Coryn, Marjorie
Alone among Men.
Appleton-Century 1947.
BL v44 1947 p50; BRD 1947 p194; KR v15 1947
p402; LJ v72 1947 p1193; NYTBR D 28, 1947 p18.

Coryn, Marjorie
The Marriage of Josephine.
Appleton-Century 1945.
BRD 1945 p153; KR v13 1945 p380; LJ v70 1945
p1026.

Kenyon, Frank Wilson
*The Emperor's Lady: A Novel Based on the Life of
the Empress Josephine.*
Crowell 1953.
BRD 1953 p506; KR v21 1953 p198; NYTBR My 31,
1953 p11; SatR Je 13, 1953 p17.

Lancaster, Sheila
Mistress of Fortune.
Hodder & Stoughton 1982 (Rpr. 1984).

Lofts, Norah
*A Rose for Virtue: The Very Private Life of
Hortense, Stepdaughter of Napoleon I.*
Doubleday 1971.
BL v68 1971 p319; FC 11th p379; KR v39 1971 p829;
PW v200 Ag 9, 1971 p40.

Mackie, Philip
Napoleon and Love.
Quartet Books 1974.

Malvern, Gladys
YA *Stephanie.*
Macrae Smith 1956.
BL v52 1956 p391; BRD 1956 p608; KR v24 1956
p77; LJ v81 1956 p1553.

Schonthan, Gaby von
The Roses of Malmaison: The Turbulent Life of the
   Beautiful Josephine.
Meredith Press 1968.
LJ v93 1968 p1919.

Unwin, Monica
The Tragic Empress.
Hale 1970.
TLS Ag 21, 1970 p934.

Wheatley, Dennis
The Dark Secret of Josephine.
Edito-Service 1973.

776. Josephus, Flavius
37-101
Jewish historian; governor of Galilee; wrote *History of the Jewish War*

Feuchtwanger, Lion
Josephus.
Viking 1932 (Heavily reprinted).
BL v29 1932 p114; FC 11th p198; NYTBR O 16,
   1932 p6.

Finch, Matthew
A Fox Called Flavius.
Dobson 1974.

777. Joshua
Old Testament figure; led Israelites into Canaan

Gerson, Noel Bertram
The Hittite.
Doubleday 1961.

Noller, Ella M.
Ahira, Prince of Naphtali: The Story of the Journey
   into Canaan.
Wm. B. Eerdsmans 1947.

Slaughter, Frank G.
The Scarlet Cord: A Novel of the Woman of
   Jericho.
Doubleday 1956.
BL v52 1956 p276; BRD 1956 p862; KR v23 1955
   p868; NYTBR F 5, 1956 p4.

778. Joyce, James
1882-1941
Irish author & poet; wrote *Ulysses*

Cross, Amanda
The James Joyce Murder.
Macmillan 1967 (Rpr. 1982).
BRD 1967 p306; FC 9th p120; LJ v92 My 1, 1967
   p1856; SatR Ap 29, 1967 p36.

Gold, Alison L.
Clairvoyant: The Imagined Life of Lucia Joyce.
Hyperion 1992.
BW v22 Jl 19, 1992 p6; KR v60 1992 p415; NYTBR
   Ag 16, 1992 p18.

779. Joyce, William ("Lord Haw-Haw")
1906-1946
British traitor; made English language propaganda broadcasts for the Nazis; executed for treason

Raymond, Ernest
The Lord of Wensley.
Cassell 1956.

780. Juarez, Benito Pablo
1806-1872
President of Mexico, 1861-1863, 1867-1872

Baker, Nina
YA *Juarez, Hero of Mexico.*
Vanguard Press 1942.
BRD 1942 p36; LJ v67 1942 p896; NYTBR N 15,
   1942 p30.

781. Judas Iscariot
One of the 12 apostles of Christ; betrayed Jesus
for 30 pieces of silver

Asch, Sholem
The Nazarene.
Putnam 1939 (Rpr. 1984).
BL v36 N 1, 1939 p88; BRD 1939 p32; FC 11th p24;
   LJ v65 1940 p587; NYTBR O 29, 1939 p3.

Bloom, Ursula (Lozania Prole, pseud.)
Judas Iscariot—Traitor?.
Hale 1971 (Rpr. 1981).

Blythe, LeGette
A Tear for Judas.
Bobbs-Merrill 1951.
BRD 1951 p95; NYTBR Je 24, 1951 p17; SatR Je 2,
   1951 p30.

Brelich, Mario
The Work of Betrayal.
Marlboro Press 1988.
NYTBR Ag 27, 1989 p18.

Brooker, Bertram
The Robber: A Tale of the Time of the Herods.
Duell, Sloan & Pearce 1949.
BRD 1949 p107; SatR Jl 16, 1949 p18.

Caldwell, Taylor
I, Judas.
Atheneum 1977.
BL v73 1977 p1631; KR v45 1977 p678; PW v212 Jl
   11, 1977 p74.

Callahan, Morley
A Time for Judas.
St. Martin's 1984.
BL v80 1984 p1150; KR v52 1984 p262; LJ v109 1984
   p994; PW v225 Mr 30, 1984 p43.

Dillon, Philip R.
Judas of Kerioth: A Romance of Old Judea.
Exposition Press 1953.

Kazantzakis, Nikos
The Last Temptation of Christ.
Simon & Schuster 1960.
Atl v206 S 1960 p114; BRD 1960 p726; FC 11th
  p338; KR v28 1960 p517; LJ v85 1960 p2957;
  NYTBR Ag 7, 1960 p4.

Konstantinovic, Radomir
Exitus: A Novel.
Calder & Boyars 1965.

Nash, Richard N.
Behold the Man.
Doubleday 1986.
BL v83 1986 p324; KR v54 1986 p1239.

Nicole, Albert
Judas, the Betrayer.
Baker Book House 1957.

Panas, Henryk
The Gospel According to Judas.
Hutchinson 1977.

Peto, James
Iscariot.
Jarrolds 1962.

Rayner, William
The Knifeman.
Morrow 1969.
KR v37 1969 p407; PW v195 Ap 7, 1969 p54.

Sanders, Jack H.
Chains of Shadows: A Romance of Judas Iscariot.
F. H. Revell 1943.

Schnieder, Isador
The Judas Time.
Dial 1946.
BRD 1947 p795; LJ v72 1947 p464; SatR Ap 12, 1947
  p24.

Van Greenaway, Peter
The Judas Gospel.
Atheneum 1972.
BRD 1972 p1327; FC 9th p526; KR v40 1972 p752; LJ
  v97 1972 p3186; NYTBR S 17, 1972 p45.

Yanikian, Gourgen
The Triumph of Judas Iscariot.
Research Pub. Co. 1950.

782. Judith
Old Testament figure

Wilchek, Stella
Judith.
Harper & Row 1969.
BL v65 1969 p1261; FC 8th p440; KR v37 1969 p409;
  LJ v94 1969 p2252.

783. Julian (Flavius Claudius Julianus)
331-363
Emperor of Rome, 361-363

De Chair, Somerset
*Bring Back the Gods: The Epic Career of the Em-
  peror Julian, the Great.*
Harrap 1962.

De Wohl, Louis
Imperial Renegade.
Lippincott 1950.
BRD 1950 p248; LJ v75 1950 p43; NYTBR Ja 22,
  1950 p27; SatR Mr 4, 1950 p31.

Merezhkovsky, Dmitry
The Death of the Gods.
Putnam 1901 (Rpr. 1929, 1989).
Also published as *Julian the Apostate.*
NYTBR S 7, 1901 p622.

Vidal, Gore
Julian: A Novel.
Little, Brown 1964 (Rpr. 1977, 1981, 1984).
BRD 1964 p1199; FC 11th p633; LJ v89 1964 p1625;
  NYTBR My 31, 1964 p4; TLS N 12, 1964 p1013.

784. Julius Caesar
100-44 BC
Roman general & dictator

Anderson, Paul L.
Swords in the North.
Biblo & Tannen 1964.
First published in 1935 by Appleton.
SHSLC 9th p377.

Balderston, John L.
A Goddess to a God.
Macmillan 1948.
BRD 1948 p37; KR v16 1948 p412; LJ v73 1948
  p1510; NYTBR N 14, 1948 p11.

Brown, Esther Fisher
Gaul Is Divided.
William-Frederick Press 1952.

Butts, Mary
Scenes from the Life of Cleopatra.
Heinemann 1935 (Rpr. 1974).

Coolidge, Olivia E.
Caesar's Gallic War.
Houghton Mifflin 1961 (Rpr. 1991).
LJ v87 1962 p338; NYTBR N 12, 1961 p26.

Davis, William Stearns
*A Friend of Caesar: A Tale of the Fall of the Ro-
  man Republic.*
Macmillan 1900 (Rpr. 1919, 1928, 1968).
NYTBR Je 16, 1900 p386.

Duggan, Alfred Leo
Winter Quarters.
Coward-McCann 1956.
BRD 1956 p273; FC 7th p117; KR v24 1956 p590; LJ
  v81 1956 p1993; NYTBR S 23, 1956 p4.

Gerson, Noel Bertram
That Egyptian Woman.

Doubleday 1956.
BRD 1956 p355; KR v24 1956 p487; NYTBR D 16,
1956 p19; SatR Ag 25, 1956 p16.

Hardy, W. G.
The Bloodied Toga: A Novel of Julius Caesar.
Macmillan 1979.
BIC v9 Ap 1980 p16.

Hardy, W. G.
The Scarlet Mantle: A Novel of Julius Caesar.
Macmillan 1978 (Rpr. 1984).

Mabie, Mary L.
Prepare Them for Caesar.
Little, Brown 1949.
BRD 1949 p578; FC 7th p226; LJ v74 1949 p495;
NYTBR Jl 31, 1949 p14; SatR F 4, 1950 p21.

Taylor, Anna
The Gods Are Not Mocked.
Morrow 1968.
BRD 1969 p1291; LJ v94 1969 p216; NYTBR F 2,
1969 p38.

Warner, Rex
Imperial Caesar.
Little, Brown 1960.
Sequel to *The Young Caesar.*
BL v56 1960 p654; BRD 1961 p1493; KR v28 1960
p336; LJ v85 1960 p1826; NYTBR Je 12, 1960 p6.

Warner, Rex
The Young Caesar.
Little, Brown 1958.
BL v54 1958 p504; BRD 1958 p1095; FC 11th p34;
KR v26 1958 p45; LJ v83 1958 p766; NYTBR Mr
16, 1958 p5.

Webb, Robert N.
JUV *We Were There with Caesar's Legions.*
Grosset & Dunlap 1960.

Wilder, Thorton
The Ides of March.
Harper 1948.
BRD 1948 p922; FC 11th p663; KR v15 1947 p675; LJ
v73 1948 p338; NYTBR F 22, 1948 p1; Time v51 F
23, 1948 p102.

Winn, Derek
I Served Caesar.
Tom Stacey Ltd. 1972.
Lis v87 My 11, 1972 p628; Obs Ag 13, 1972 p27.

785. Jumel, Eliza
1769-1865
Social climber known for her marriages to
Aaron Burr & coffee planter Stephen Jumel

Beyea, Basil
The Golden Mistress.
Simon & Schuster 1975.
KR v43 1975 p473; LJ v100 1975 p877; PW v207 Ap
28, 1975 p40.

Beyea, Basil
*Notorious Eliza: A Novel about the Woman Who
Married Aaron Burr.*
Simon & Schuster 1978.
KR v46 1978 p604; LJ v103 1978 p1287; PW v213 Je
19, 1978 p92.

Brown, Raymond B.
Madam Jumel.
Magna Carta Press 1965.
AB v37 F 21, 1966 p762.

Falkner, Leonard
Painted Lady; Eliza Jumel, Her Life and Times.
Dutton 1962.
BRD 1962 p368; LJ v87 1962 p1452.

786. Jung, Carl Gustav
1875-1961
Swiss psychiatrist; wrote *Psychology of the Unconscious*

West, Morris L.
The World Is Made of Glass.
Morrow 1983.
BL v79 1983 p1167; KR v51 1983 p402; Time v122 Jl
25, 1983 p72.

787. Justinian I (Flavius Anicius Justinianus)
483-565
Byzantine emperor, 527-565

Bradshaw, Gillian
The Bearkeeper's Daughter.
Houghton Mifflin 1987.
BL v84 1987 p604; KR v55 1987 p1411; LJ v112 N
15, 1987 p89; PW v232 O 30, 1987 p51.

Dixon, Pierson
*The Glittering Horn: Secret Memoirs of the Court
of Justinian.*
J. Cape 1958.

Lamb, Harold
Theodora and the Emperor: The Drama of Justinian.
Doubleday 1952.
BRD 1952 p528; FC 8th p240; KR v20 1952 p312; LJ
v77 1952 p1188; NYTBR Ag 3, 1952 p7.

Masefield, John
Basilissa: A Tale of the Empress Theodora.
Macmillan 1940.
BL v37 1940 p36; BRD 1940 p614; LJ v65 1940 p709;
NYTBR S 22, 1940 p6.

Wellman, Paul I.
The Female: A Novel of Another Time.
Doubleday 1953.
BL v50 1953 p80; BRD 1953 p994; KR v21 1953
p546; NYTBR S 27, 1953 p35.

788. Kamehameha II
1797-1824
Hawaiian ruler, 1819-1824

Judd, Walter F.
Let Us Go: The Narrative of Kamehameha II, King of the Hawaiian Islands, 1819-1824.
Topgallant Pub. Co. 1976.

789. Kane, Elisha Kent
1820-1857
American arctic explorer & physician

Walz, Jay
The Undiscovered Country.
Duell, Sloan & Pearce 1958.
BL v54 1958 p402; BRD 1958 p1093; KR v26 1958 p97; NYTBR My 11, 1958 p29.

790. Kauffmann, Angelica
1741-1807
Swiss painter

Schreiner, Samuel A.
Angelica.
Arbor House 1978.
LJ v103 1978 p2262; PW v214 S 11, 1978 p77.

791. Kean, Edmund
1787-1833
English actor; best known for his Shakespearian roles

Berstl, Julius
Kean, the Imaginary Memoirs of an Actor.
Orion Press 1962.
First published in 1946 as *The Sun's Bright Child.*
BRD 1962 p99; LJ v87 1962 p1805; NYTBR Ap 15, 1962 p36.

792. Kearny, Stephen Watts
1794-1848
American general in the Mexican War

O'Dell, Scott
Hill of the Hawk.
Bobbs-Merrill 1947.
BL v44 1947 p69; BRD 1947 p684; LJ v72 1947 p1194; NYTBR O 5, 1947 p22.

793. Keaton, "Buster" (Joseph Francis)
1896-1966
American actor & comedian

Sill, Harold D.
YA *Keaton Comedies: A Toby Bradley Adventure.*
Addison-Wesley 1977.
SLJ v23 Ap 1977 p80.

794. Keats, John
1795-1821
English poet

Burgess, Anthony
Abba Abba.
Little, Brown 1977.
BL v75 My 15, 1979 p1419; BRD 1979 p177; NYTBR Ap 29, 1979 p14; TLS Je 3, 1977 p669.

Holdsworth, Jean
Our Brightest Brother: A Novel of the Life of John Keats.
Constable 1978.

Rees, Joan
Bright Star: The Story of John Keats and Fanny Brawne.
Harrap 1968.
B&B v14 O 1968 p53.

Roberts, Cecil
The Remarkable Young Man.
Macmillan 1954.
BL v51 1954 p42; BRD 1954 p747; KR v22 1954 p318; NYTBR Jl 25, 1954 p4.

795. Keller, Helen Adams
1880-1968
American blind & deaf author & lecturer

Brown, Marion Marsh
YA *The Silent Storm.*
Abingdon Press 1963.
BRD 1964 p161; LJ v88 1963 p3346; NYTBR Ja 26, 1964 p26.

Hickok, Lorena A.
YA *The Story of Helen Keller.*
Grosset & Dunlap 1958.
LJ v83 1958 p3572.

796. Kellogg, John Harvey
1852-1943
American physician; developed grain cereal flakes

Boyle, T. Coraghessan
Road to Wellville: A Novel.
Viking 1993.
NYTBR Ap 25, 1993 p1.

797. Kelly, Emmett
1898-1979
American clown; created character of "Weary Willie"

Kaminsky, Stuart M.
Catch a Falling Clown.
St. Martin's 1982.
BL v78 1982 p586; KR v49 1981 p1430; LJ v107 1982 p110.

798. Kelly, Michael
1762-1826
Irish opera singer

Jacob, Naomi Ellington
The Irish Boy: A Romantic Biography.
Hutchinson 1955.

799. Kelly, Ned (Edward)
1854-1880
Australian outlaw

Chandler, A. Bertram
Kelly Country.
Penquin 1983.

Drewe, Robert
Our Sunshine.
Picador Press 1991.
AustBkR D 1991 p15.

Lambert, Eric
Kelly.
F. Muller 1964.

Phillips, J. H.
The Trial of Ned Kelly.
Law Book Co. 1987.

800. Kemble, Fanny (Frances Anne)
1809-1893
English actress; noted for her Shakespearian
roles

Buckmaster, Henrietta
Fire in the Heart.
Harcourt, Brace 1948.
BL v45 1948 p88; BRD 1948 p375; FC 7th p58; KR
   v16 1948 p407; LJ v73 1948 p1272; NYTBR O 24,
   1948 p31.

801. Kennedy, Edward Moore
1932-
American politician; brother of John F. Kennedy; involved in Chappaquiddick incident

Reybold, Malcolm
*The Inspector's Opinion: The Chappaquiddick Inci-
dent.*
Saturday Review Press 1975.
BRD 1976 p1000; KR v43 1975 p1016; LJ v101 1976
   p548; NYTBR N 30, 1975 p8; PW v208 S 15, 1975
   p48.

802. Kennedy, John Fitzgerald
1917-1963
35th US President; assassinated

Appel, Allen
Till the End of Time.
Doubleday 1990.

BL v87 1990 p24; KR v58 1990 p893; LJ v115 S 1,
   1990 p253; PW v237 Je 29, 1990 p85.

Ballard, J. G.
The Atrocity Exhibition.
Cape 1970.
KR v38 1970 p529; LJ v95 1970 p2512.

Bealle, Morris Allison
*Guns of the Regressive Right: The Only Reconstruc-
tion of the Kennedy Assassination That Makes
Sense.*
Columbia Pub. Co. 1964.

Bernau, George
Promises to Keep.
Warner Books 1988.
BL v84 1988 p1865; KR v56 1988 p1170; LJ v113 O
   15, 1988 p100.

Bourjaily, Vance Nye
The Man Who Knew Kennedy.
Dial Press 1967.
BRD 1967 p152; KR v34 1966 p1191; LJ v91 1966
   p6108; NYTBR Ja 29, 1967 p4.

Buckley, William F.
Mongoose, R.I.P..
Random House 1987.
BL v84 1987 p657; KR v55 1987 p1635; LJ v113 F 1,
   1988 p75; NYTBR Ja 24, 1988 p11; PW v232 D 11,
   1987 p47.

Burke, Phyllis
Atomic Candy.
Atlantic Monthly Press 1989.
KR v57 1989 p228; LJ v114 Ap 1, 1989 p110; PW
   v235 F 24, 1989 p220.

DeLillo, Don
Libra.
Viking 1988.
BL v84 1988 p1625; KR v56 1988 p843; NYTBR Jl
   24, 1988 p1; Time v132 Ag 1, 1988 p65.

Freed, Donald
Executive Action: Assassination of a Head of State.
Dell 1973.
BS v33 S 1, 1973 p259; PW v203 Mr 26, 1973 p72.

Gerson, Jack
The Back of the Tiger: A Novel.
Beaufort Books 1984.
PW v227 My 3, 1985 p64.

Graves, Wallace
Trixie.
Knopf 1969.
BL v66 1970 p651; KR v37 1969 p882; LJ v94 1969
   p3083; NYTBR N 30, 1969 p65; PW v196 Ag 18,
   1969 p55.

Ions, Edmund S. (Edmund Aubrey, pseud.)
Sherlock Holmes in Dallas.
Dodd, Mead 1980.
Also published as *The Case of the Murdered President.*
KR v48 1980 p942; LJ v105 1980 p2103.

Korda, Michael
The Immortals: A Novel.
Poseidon Press 1992.
BL v88 1992 p1972; KR v60 1992 p870; LJ v117 Ag
   1992 p149; NYTBR S 13, 1992 p9.

Kreeft, Peter
*Between Heaven and Hell: A Dialog Somewhere
   beyond Death with John F. Kennedy, C. S. Lewis, and Aldous Huxley.*
InterVarsity Press 1982.

Mailer, Norman
Harlot's Ghost.
Random House 1991.
BL v88 1991 p5; BRD 1991 p1197; KR v59 1991
   p960; LJ v116 S 1, 1991 p231; NYTBR S 29, 1991
   p1.

Mayer, Robert
I, J.F.K..
Dutton 1989.
KR v57 1989 p653; LJ v114 Ap 15, 1989 p100; PW
   v235 My 12, 1989 p283.

McCarry, Charles
The Tears of Autumn.
Saturday Review Press 1975.
BL v71 1975 p669; FC 9th p329; KR v42 1974 p1225;
   LJ v100 1975 p67; NYTBR Mr 23, 1975 p35.

Morris, Wright
One Day.
Atheneum 1965 (Rpr. 1976).
BRD 1965 p905; LJ v90 1965 p1933; NYTBR Mr 7,
   1965 p4; SatR F 20, 1965 p23.

O'Donnell, Mary Paula King
You Can Hear the Echo.
Simon & Schuster 1966.
LJ v91 1966 p967.

Reginald, R.; Elliot, Jeffrey M.
If J.F.K. Had Lived: A Political Scenario.
Borgo Press 1982.
A revised edition of *The Attempted Assassination of
   John F. Kennedy.*

Shapiro, Stanley
A Time to Remember.
Random House 1986.
BL v82 1986 p1663; KR v54 1986 p1061; WCRB v12
   S 1986 p36.

Thomas, D. M.
Flying in to Love.
Scribner 1992.
BL v89 1992 p5; KR v60 1992 p946; NYTBR O 11,
   1992 p13.

Webb, Lucas
*The Attempted Assassination of John F. Kennedy:
   A Political Fantasy.*
Borgo Press 1976.

Woolley, Bryan
November 22.

Seaview Books 1981.
KR v49 1981 p655; LJ v106 1981 p1325; PW v219 Je
   12, 1981 p46.

803. Kennedy, John Patrick
1888-1969
American financier & diplomat; father of the
Kennedy family

Harris, Robert
Fatherland.
Random House 1992.
NYTBR Je 27, 1992 p28.

804. Kennedy, Robert Francis
1925-1968
US Attorney General, 1961-1964; brother of
John F. Kennedy; assassinated

Buckley, William F.
Tucker's Last Stand.
Random House 1990.
BL v87 1990 p691; KR v58 1990 p1550; NYTBR F 17,
   1991 p15; PW v237 N 16, 1990 p44.

Gordon, Robert Ellis
When Bobby Kennedy Was a Moving Man.
Black Heron Press 1993.
NYTBR N 28, 1993 p26.

Hannibal, Edward
Blood Feud.
Ballantine 1979.
KR v47 1979 p281; LJ v104 1979 p751; NYTBR Je 10,
   1979 p24.

Korda, Michael
The Immortals: A Novel.
Poseidon Press 1992.
BL v88 1992 p1972; KR v60 1992 p870; LJ v117 Ag
   1992 p149; NYTBR S 13, 1992 p9.

Lynn, Jack
The Factory.
Harper & Row 1982.
KR v51 1983 p331; PW v223 Mr 25, 1983 p47.

Rechy, John
Marilyn's Daughter.
Carroll & Graf 1988.
BL v84 1988 p1755; KR v56 1988 p852; NYTBR N 6,
   1988 p22.

805. Kepler, Johannes
1571-1630
German astronomer

Banville, John
Kepler: A Novel.
Secker & Warburg 1981 (Rpr. 1983).
BRD 1983 p83; FC 11th p39; KR v51 1983 p192; LJ
   v108 1983 p1153; NYTBR My 29, 1983 p10.

Saile, Olaf
Troubadour of the Stars: The Romantic Life of Johannes Kepler.
O. Piest 1940.
BRD 1940 p800.

Schuder, Rosemarie
Witch's Son.
Seven Seas Pub. 1965.

806. Key, Francis Scott
1779-1843
American lawyer; wrote *The Star-Spangled Banner*

Bakeless, Katherine
JUV *The Birth of a Nation's Song.*
F.A. Stokes 1942.
BRD 1942 p34; LJ v67 1942 p268.

Brown, Marion Marsh
YA *Broad Stripes and Bright Stars.*
Westminster Press 1955.
LJ v80 1955 p997.

Holland, Rupert S.
YA *Freedom's Flag: The Story of Francis Scott Key.*
Macrae-Smith 1943.
BRD 1943 p387; NYTBR Ag 8, 1943 p12.

Mandrell, Louise
JUV *Sunrise over the Harbor.*
Summit Group 1993.

Stevenson, Augusta
JUV *Francis Scott Key, Maryland Boy.*
Bobbs-Merrill 1960.

Swanson, Neil H.
YA *The Star-Spangled Banner: The Thrilling Story of a Boy Who Lived the Words of Our National Anthem.*
Winston 1958.
BL v54 1958 p593; BRD 1958 p1029; KR v26 1958 p286; LJ v83 1958 p2076.

807. Khrushchev, Nikita Sergeyevich
1894-1971
Premier of the U.S.S.R., 1958-1964

Beal, John Robinson
The Secret Speech: The Failure of Comrade Khrushchev's Leadership.
Duell, Sloan & Pearce 1961.
BRD 1961 p91; LJ v86 1961 p2119.

Burdick, Eugene; Wheeler, Harvey
Fail-Safe.
McGraw-Hill 1962.
Atl v210 D 1962 p166; BL v59 1962 p244; FC 11th p86; KR v30 1962 p776; LJ v87 1962 p3466.

Creighton, Christopher; Hynd, Noel
The Khrushchev Objective.
Doubleday 1987.

BL v83 1987 p8821; KR v54 1986 p1815; LJ v112 F 15, 1987 p160; PW v231 Ja 9, 1987 p79.

Krotkov, Yuri
The Nobel Prize.
Simon & Schuster 1980.
BRD 1980 p689; LJ v105 1980 p1187; NYTBR Jl 13, 1980 p1.

808. Kidd, William (Captain)
1645-1701
Scottish privateer & pirate

Chidsey, Donald Barr
The Legion of the Lost.
Crown 1967.
KR v35 1967 p362; LJ v92 1967 p1641.

Lawson, Robert
JUV *Captain Kidd's Cat.*
Little, Brown 1956 (Rpr. 1984).
BL v52 1956 p282; BRD 1956 p553; KR v24 1956 p3; LJ v81 1956 p767; NYTBR F 12, 1956 p30.

Raine, Norman Reilly
Captain Kidd.
World Publishing Co. 1945.
A novelization of the screen play by Norman Reilly Raine, from an original story by Robert N. Lee.

809. Kierkegaard, Soren Aabye
1813-1855
Danish philosopher & theologian; regarded as founder of existentialism

Anderson, Barbara
Kierkegaard: A Fiction.
Syracuse University Press 1974.
Choice v12 Ap 1975 p235.

810. King, Martin Luther, Jr.
1929-1968
American clergyman and leader in Civil Rights movement; won Nobel Prize, 1964; assassinated

Bailey, Anne
JUV *You Can Make a Difference: The Story of Martin Luther King, Jr..*
Bantam 1990.

Graves, Wallace
Trixie.
Knopf 1969.
BL v66 1970 p651; KR v37 1969 p882; LJ v94 1969 p3083; NYTBR N 30, 1969 p65; PW v196 Ag 18, 1969 p55.

Johnston, William
YA *King.*
St. Martin's 1978.
Based on a screenplay written by Abby Mann.
BS v38 Jl 1978 p104; LJ v103 1978 p994; SLJ v25 S 1978 p174.

Kilcommons, Denis
The Dark Apostle.
Magna Print Books 1987.
Punch v293 O 21, 1987 p59; Spec v260 F 27, 1988
p30.

Tate, Eleanora E.
JUV *Thank You, Dr. Martin Luther King.*
F. Watts 1990.
BL v86 1990 p1636; BRD 1990 p1803; KR v58 1990
p186; SLJ v36 Mr 1990 p220.

811. King, William Lyon Mackenzie

1874-1950
Canadian politician & prime minister

Robertson, Heather
Igor: A Novel of Intrigue.
J. Lorimer 1989.
BIC Ja 1990 p45; SN v105 Ja 1990 p44.

Robertson, Heather
Lily, a Rhapsody in Red.
J. Lorimer 1986.
BIC v15 O 1986 p21; Quill & Q v52 S 1986 p80.

812. Kipling, (Joseph) Rudyard

1865-1936
English novelist & poet; won Nobel Prize, 1907;
wrote *The Jungle Book*

Otto, Margaret Glover
JUV *Mr. Kipling's Elephant.*
Knopf 1961.
LJ v86 1961 p4040; NYTBR Ja 7, 1962 p32.

813. Kirov, Sergei Mironovich

1886-1934
Russian Communist leader; one of Stalin's chief
aides

Ulam, Adam
The Kirov Affair.
Harcourt Brace Jovanovich 1988.
BL v84 1988 p1575; BRD 1989 p1689; KR v56 1988
p323; LJ v113 Je 1, 1988 p144; NYTBR Je 12, 1988
p13.

014. Kleist, Heinrich von

1777-1811
German dramatist & poet; wrote *The Broken Jug*
and *Michael Kohlhaus*

Wolf, Christa
No Place on Earth.
Farrar, Straus & Giroux 1982.
KR v50 1982 p700; LJ v107 1982 p1678; NYTBR O
10, 1982 p11; PW v221 Je 25, 1982 p102.

815. Knox, Henry

1750-1806
American Revolutionary general; US Secretary
of War, 1785-1794

Downey, Fairfax
JUV *Guns for General Washington.*
T. Nelson 1961.
LJ v86 1961 p3678.

Peck, Robert Newton
The King's Iron.
Little, Brown 1977.
KR v45 1977 p952; LJ v102 1977 p2182.

Reit, Seymour
JUV *Guns for General Washington: A Story of the
American Revolution.*
Harcourt Brace Jovanovich 1990.
BL v87 1991 p921; BRD 1991 p1553; SLJ v37 Ja 1991
p96.

816. Knox, John

1505-1572
Scottish religious reformer

Nygaard, Norman E.
Tempest over Scotland: The Story of John Knox.
Zondervan 1960.

817. Kopechne, Mary Jo

1940-1969
Died in automobile accident involving Edward
Kennedy

Reybold, Malcolm
*The Inspector's Opinion: The Chappaquiddick Inci-
dent.*
Saturday Review Press 1975.
BRD 1976 p1000; KR v43 1975 p1016; LJ v101 1976
p548; NYTBR N 30, 1975 p8; PW v208 S 15, 1975
p48.

818. Kruger, Paul

1825-1904
President of Transvaal, 1883-1900

Cloete, Stuart
Rags of Glory.
Doubleday 1963.
BRD 1963 p203; LJ v88 1963 p2925; NYTBR Ag 25,
1963 p5; SatR Ag 24, 1963 p48.

Haggard, H. Rider
Jess: A Tale of the Transvaal.
Smith, Elder 1887 (Rpr. 1950).

Hope, Christopher
Kruger's Alp.
Heinemann 1984.
NS v108 S 28, 1984 p30; Obs S 23, 1984 p22; Spec
v253 O 6, 1984 p33; TLS S 28, 1984 p1085.

Sinclair, Kathleen H. (Brigid Knight, pseud.)
The Sun Climbs Slowly.
Cassell 1942.
Also published as *Westward the Sun.*
BL v38 1942 p330; BRD 1942 p708; LJ v67 1942
 p268; NYTBR Mr 29, 1942 p7.

Young, Francis Brett
The City of Gold.
Heinemann 1939 (Rpr. 1966, 1971).
BL v36 1939 p69; BRD 1939 p1076; NYTBR O 8,
 1939 p6; SatR O 14, 1939 p12.

819. Krutch, Joseph Wood
1893-1970
American critic

Green, Gerlad
An American Prophet.
Doubleday 1977.
FC 10th p222; LJ v102 1977 p833; NYTBR Ap 10,
 1977 p14.

820. Kublai Khan
1216-1294
Founder of the Mongol dynasty of China; grandson of Genghis Khan

Baumann, Hans
YA *Sons of the Steppe: The Story of How the Con-
 queror Genghis Khan Was Overcome.*
H.Z. Walck 1957 (Rpr. 1961).
BL v54 1958 p449; BRD 1958 p73; KR v26 1958
 p376; LJ v83 1958 p2074; NYTBR Mr 16, 1958 p42.

Calvino, Italo
Invisible Cities.
Harcourt Brace Jovanovich 1974.
BRD 1975 p198; Choice v12 Ap 1975 p227; FC 9th
 p82; LJ v99 1974 p2088; NYTBR N 17, 1974 p35.

Inoue, Yasushi
Wind and Waves: A Novel.
University of Hawaii Press 1989.
PW v234 D 23, 1988 p66; TLS Ap 28, 1989 p466;
 WLT v63 Summer 1989 p537.

Marshall, Edison
Caravan to Xanadu: A Novel of Marco Polo.
Farrar, Straus & Young 1953.
BRD 1953 p620; KR v21 1953 p155; LJ v78 1953
 p520; NYTBR Mr 29, 1953 p22.

Price, Olive M.
YA *The Valley of the Dragon: A Story of the Times of
 Kublai Khan.*
Bobbs-Merrill 1951.
BRD 1951 p716; LJ v76 1951 p714; NYTBR Jl 8, 1951
 p12.

Shea, Robert
Shike: Time of the Dragons.
Jove 1981.
PW v219 Ap 24, 1981 p73.

821. Kutuzov, Mikhail Ilarionovich
1745-1813
Russian military leader

Almedingen, Martha Edith
YA *The Retreat from Moscow.*
F. Warne 1968.
BRD 1969 p23; LJ v94 1969 p1788; NYTBR N 3,
 1968 p32.

822. L'Enfant, Pierre Charles
1754-1825
French architect & city planner; designed plan
for Washington, DC

Holland, Janice
JUV *They Built a City: The Story of Washington,
 D.C..*
Scribner 1953.
BRD 1953 p441; KR v21 1953 p70; LJ v78 1953 p454;
 NYTBR F 15, 1953 p26.

823. Laclos, (Pierre) Choderlos de
1741-1803
French novelist; wrote *Les Liaisons Dangereuses*

Mantel, Hilary
A Place of Greater Safety.
Atheneum 1993.
LJ v118 F 15, 1993 p193; NYTBR My 9, 1993 p21.

824. Lafarge, Marie
1816-1852
French murderer

Bowen, Marjorie
The Lady and the Arsenic.
Heinemann 1937 (Rpr. 1944).
BRD 1944 p467; KR v12 1944 p1; NYTBR F 20, 1944
 p5; SatR F 12, 1944 p30.

825. Lafayette, Marie Joseph Paul, Marquis
1757-1834
French political leader & American Revolutionary War hero

Foster, Martha S.
JUV *A Red Carpet for Lafayette.*
Bobbs-Merrill 1961.
LJ v86 1961 p2533; NYTBR N 5, 1961 p50.

Schoeler, William
That Man Lafayette: A Historical Novel.
Vantage Press 1957.

Wiener, Willard
Morning in America.
Farrar & Rinehart 1942.
BRD 1942 p832; LJ v67 1942 p952; NYTBR N 1,
 1942 p22.

Wilson, Hazel Hutchins
JUV *The Little Marquise: Madame Lafayette.*
Knopf 1957.
BL v54 1958 p288; BRD 1958 p1121; KR v25 1957
p532; LJ v83 1958 p246.

Wright, Constance
A Chance for Glory.
Holt 1957.
BL v53 1957 p380; BRD 1957 p1011; KR v25 1957
p14; NYTBR Mr 10, 1957 p7.

826. Laffite, Jean
1780-1825
French pirate who operated in the Gulf of Mexico; fought for the US in the War of 1812

Ingraham, J. H.
Lafitte, the Pirate of the Gulf.
Harper & Brothers 1836 (Heavily reprinted).

Kent, Madeleine
*The Corsair: A Biographical Novel of Jean Lafitte,
Hero of the Battle of New Orleans.*
Doubleday 1955.
BRD 1955 p491; KR v23 1955 p715; LJ v80 1955
p2612; NYTBR N 6, 1955 p51.

Shepard, Odell
Holdfast Gaines.
Macmillan 1946.
BL v43 1946 p103; BRD 1946 p746; KR v14 1946
p428; LJ v71 1946 p1543; NYTBR N 24, 1946 p28.

Sperry, Armstrong
YA *Black Falcon, a Story of Piracy and Old New Orleans.*
J.C. Winston 1949.
BRD 1949 p863; KR v17 1949 p513; LJ v74 1949
p1548; NYTBR D 4, 1949 p42.

Townsend, Tom
YA *Powderhorn Passage.*
Eakin Press 1988.
SLJ v35 N 1988 p133.

827. Laing, Alexander Gordon
1793-1826
Scottish explorer

Schlee, Ann
Laing.
Macmillan 1987.
GW v141 Jl 23, 1989 p28; Lis v118 D 31, 1987 p24;
NS v114 N 27, 1987 p32; TLS D 11, 1987 p1374.

828. Lamb, Caroline, Lady
1785-1828
English novelist; noted for her affair with Lord
Byron; wife of William Melbourne

Ansle, Dorothy P. (Hebe Elsna, pseud.)
The Love Match.
Lythway Press 1976.

Leslie, Doris
This for Caroline.
Heinemann 1964.

McDonald, Eva
Lord Byron's First Love.
Hale 1968 (Rpr. 1973).

829. Lamb, Charles
1775-1834
English author & essayist; wrote *Essays of Elia*;
brother of Mary Ann Lamb

Bell, Neil
So Perish the Roses.
Macmillan 1940.
BL v37 1940 p69; BRD 1940 p859; LJ v65 1940 p808;
NYTBR S 29, 1940 p6.

830. Lamb, Mary Ann
1764-1847
English poet & writer; sister of Charles Lamb

Bell, Neil
So Perish the Roses.
Macmillan 1940.
BL v37 1940 p69; BRD 1940 p859; LJ v65 1940 p808;
NYTBR S 29, 1940 p6.

831. Landru, Henri Desire
1869-1922
French murderer; executed

Masson, Rene
Landru.
Doubleday 1965.
Also published as *Number One.*
BL v62 1965 p140; BRD 1966 p800; LJ v90 1965
p3076; NYTBR Jl 4, 1965 p12.

Wiser, William
Disappearances.
Atheneum 1980 (Rpr. 1984, 1986, 1992).
BL v76 1980 p1261; KR v48 1980 p537; LJ v105 1980
p1329; NYTBR Ag 10, 1980 p14; PW v217 Ap 11,
1980 p74; WLB v55 O 1980 p148.

832. Lang, Fritz
1890-1976
Austrian-born film director

Rodman, Howard
Destiny Express: A Novel.
Atheneum 1990.
BRD 1991 p1584; KR v57 1989 p1629; LJ v114 D
1989 p175; NYTBR Mr 4, 1990 p13.

833. Langtry, Lillie
1853-1929
English actress; noted for her beauty

Butler, David
Lillie.
Warner 1979.

Sichel, Pierre
The Jersey Lily.
W.H. Allen 1958.
BRD 1959 p909; JL v84 1959 p776; NYTBR N 23,
    1958 p22.

834. Lansdale, Edward Geary
1908-1987
American military leader

Mailer, Norman
Harlot's Ghost.
Random House 1991.
BL v88 1991 p5; BRD 1991 p1197; KR v59 1991
    p960; LJ v116 S 1, 1991 p231; NYTBR S 29, 1991
    p1.

835. LaSalle, Robert Cavelier, Sieur de
1643-1687
French explorer

Allen, Merritt P.
YA *The Wilderness Way*.
Longmans, Green 1954.
BRD 1954 p12; KR v22 1954 p4; LJ v79 1954 p788;
    NYTBR Ap 18, 1954 p22.

Fuller, Iola
The Gilded Torch.
Putnam 1957.
BL v53 1957 p453; BRD 1957 p333; FC 7th p143; KR
    v25 1957 p156; LJ v82 1957 p1239; NYTBR Ap
    21, 1957 p18.

Tebbel, John W.
Touched with Fire.
Dutton 1952.
BL v49 1953 p156; KR v20 1952 p494; LJ v77 1952
    p1502; NYTBR N 23, 1952 p36.

Vernon, John
La Salle.
Viking 1986.
Kliatt v21 S 1987 p21.

836. Lassalle, Ferdinand
1825-1864
German socialist leader

Heym, Stefan
Uncertain Friend.
Cassell 1969.
NS v78 Jl 18, 1969 p88.

Meredith, George
*The Tragic Comedians: A Study in a Well-Known
    Story*.
Chapman & Hall 1880 (Heavily reprinted).

837. Laval, Pierre
1883-1945
French premier; leader of Vichy regime; executed for treason

Beeding, Francis
There Are Thirteen.
Harper & Brothers 1946.
BL v42 1946 p300; BRD 1946 p50; KR v14 1946 p8;
    SatR Mr 2, 1946 p40.

Strachey, John
The Frontiers.
Random House 1952.
BL v49 1952 p33; BRD 1952 p853; KR v20 1952
    p421; LJ v77 1952 p1402; NYTBR S 7, 1952 p28.

838. Lawrence, T. E. (Thomas Edward)
1888-1935
English author, archaeolologist, & adventurer

Aldridge, James
Heroes of the Empty View.
Knopf 1954.
BL v51 1954 p41; BRD 1954 p8; KR v22 1954 p344;
    LJ v79 1954 p1399; NYTBR Ag 8, 1954 p4.

Booth, Martin
Dreaming of Samarkand.
Morrow 1990.
KR v58 1990 p444; LJ v115 Ap 15, 1990 p121;
    NYTBR Jl 1, 1990 p14; PW v237 Mr 9, 1990 p52.

Eden, Matthew
The Murder of Lawrence of Arabia.
Crowell 1979.
BL v75 1979 p913; KR v47 1979 p77; LJ v104 1979
    p750; PW v215 F 5, 1979 p92.

Irving, Clive
Promise the Earth.
Harper & Row 1982.
BL v79 1982 p296; KR v50 1982 p890; LJ v107 1982
    p1769; NYTBR N 28, 1982 p12; Obs O 17, 1982
    p33.

Stine, Megan
The Mummy's Curse.
Random House 1992.

839. Lawrence, Thomas, Sir
1769-1830
English portrait painter

Durman, Hilda
Artist in Love.
Roy 1954 (Rpr. 1973, 1980, 1989).

840. Lazarus

New Testament figure; Jesus raised him from the dead

Absire, Alain
Lazarus.
Harcourt Brace Jovanovich 1988.
KR v56 1988 p68; LJ v113 Mr 15, 1988 p66.

Holton, Bill
The Lazarus Legacy: There Is Life after Death.
Alpha Pub. 1985.

McGerr, Patricia
Martha, Martha.
P.J. Kenedy 1960.
BRD 1960 p859; FC 7th p229; KR v28 1960 p271; LJ v85 1960 p781.

Preus, Johan
The Friend of the Prince.
Augsburg Pub. House 1948.

841. Leah

Old Testament figure; Jacob's first wife; sister of Rachel

Cabries, Jean
Jacob.
Dutton 1958.
BL v55 1958 p97; BRD 1958 p177; KR v26 1958 p477; LJ v83 1958 p3152; NYTBR S 14, 1958 p30.

842. Lecouvreur, Adrienne

1692-1730
French actress

Dunlap, Katharine
The Glory and the Dream.
Morrow 1951.
BL v47 1951 p329; BRD 1951 p253; KR v19 1951 p136; NYTBR My 13, 1951 p19.

Levy, Barbara
Adrienne.
Holt, Rinehart & Winston 1960.
BRD 1961 p831; KR v28 1960 p698; LJ v85 1960 p3675; NYTBR O 23, 1960 p52.

843. Lee, Charles

1731-1782
American Revolutionary general

Taylor, David
Farewell to Valley Forge.
Lippincott 1955.
BL v52 1955 p126; BRD 1955 p889; KR v23 1955 p559; LJ v80 1955 p2522; NYTBR N 27, 1955 p47.

Wiener, Willard
Morning in America.
Farrar & Rinehart 1942.
BRD 1942 p832; LJ v67 1942 p952; NYTBR N 1, 1942 p22.

844. Lee, Francis Lightfoot

1734-1797
American Revolutionary patriot; signed Declaration of Independence

Roberts, Carey
YA *Tidewater Dynasty: The Lees of Stratford Hall.*
Harcourt Brace Jovanovich 1981.
Kliatt v18 Winter 1984 p18; KR v49 1981 p456; LJ v106 1981 p1324; PW v219 Ap 17, 1981 p48.

845. Lee, Gypsy Rose

1914-1970
American burlesque queen

Lee, Gypsy Rose
The G-String Murders.
Simon 1941 (Rpr. 1984).
BRD 1941 p535; NYTBR O 12, 1941 p24.

Lee, Gypsy Rose
Mother Finds a Body.
Simon & Schuster 1942.
BRD 1942 p460; NYTBR O 25, 1942 p38; SatR O 24, 1942 p41.

846. Lee, Henry

1756-1818
Governor of Virginia; father of Robert E. Lee

Roberts, Carey
YA *Tidewater Dynasty: The Lees of Stratford Hall.*
Harcourt Brace Jovanovich 1981.
Kliatt v18 Winter 1984 p18; KR v49 1981 p456; LJ v106 1981 p1324; PW v219 Ap 17, 1981 p48.

Seifert, Shirley
Let My Name Stand Fair.
Lippincott 1956.
BL v53 1956 p23; BRD 1956 p836; FC 7th p311; KR v24 1956 p322; SatR Jl 28, 1956 p29.

Spicer, Bart
Brother to the Enemy.
Dodd, Mead & Co. 1958.
BL v55 F 1, 1959 p288; BRD 1959 p933; FC 9th p480; NYTBR N 23, 1958 p50.

847. Lee, Jason

1803-1845
American missionary; helped establish territorial government in Oregon

Brooks, Anne
The Singing Fiddles: A Story of the Jason Lee Mission in Early Oregon.
Arcadia House 1950.

848. Lee, Richard Henry

1732-1794
American Revolutionary poltician; a signer of the Declaration of Independence

Roberts, Carey
YA *Tidewater Dynasty: The Lees of Stratford Hall.*
Harcourt Brace Jovanovich 1981.
Kliatt v18 Winter 1984 p18; KR v49 1981 p456; LJ
    v106 1981 p1324; PW v219 Ap 17, 1981 p48.

849. Lee, Robert E.

1807-1870
Commander-in-chief of the Confederate Army
in the Civil War

Adams, Richard
Traveller.
Knopf 1988.
BL v84 1988 p1369; KR v56 1988 p470; LJ v113 Je
    15, 1988 p67; NYTBR Je 5, 1988 p13; PW v233 Ap
    22, 1988 p63.

Altsheler, Joseph A.
*The Shades of the Wilderness: A Story of Lee's
    Great Stand.*
Appleton 1916 (Rpr. 1944, 1987).
BL v12 1916 p486; BRD 1916 p10; NYTBR My 7,
    1916 p199.

Cannon, Ralph
Lee on the Levee.
Saravan House 1940.

Commager, Henry Steele
YA *America's Robert E. Lee.*
Houghton Mifflin 1951.
BL v48 1951 p51; BRD 1951 p188; KR v19 1951
    p531; LJ v76 1951 p1944; NYTBR S 9, 1951 p30.

Davis, Burke
To Appomattox: Nine April Days, 1865.
Rinehart 1959.
BL v55 1959 p473; KR v26 1958 p650; LJ v83 1958
    p2747.

Davis, Paxton
YA *Three Days.*
Atheneum 1980.
HB v56 Ap 1980 p182; NYTBR Ap 1980 p50; SLJ
    v27 S 1980 p82.

Downey, Fairfax
JUV *A Horse for General Lee.*
Scribner 1953.
KR v21 1953 p438; LJ v78 1953 p78; NYTBR Ag 23,
    1953 p20.

Eaton, Jeanette
JUV *Lee: The Gallant General.*
Morrow 1953.
BL v50 1953 p39; BRD 1953 p283; KR v21 1953
    p487; LJ v78 1953 p1940.

Harper, M. A.
For the Love of Robert E. Lee.
Soho Press 1992.

Hart, Scott
Eight April Days.
Coward-McCann 1949.

BL v46 1949 p4; BRD 1949 p398; LJ v74 1949 p1202;
    NYTBR O 9, 1949 p34.

Henty, G. A.
JUV *With Lee in Virginia: A Story of the American
    Civil War.*
Blackie 1889 (Heavily reprinted).

Herrin, Lamar
The Unwritten Chronicles of Robert E. Lee.
St. Martin's 1991.
Kliatt v25 S 1991 p10; KR v57 1989 p1270; LJ v114
    O 1, 1989 p118; PW v236 S 22, 1989 p40; SLJ v36
    D 1990 p27.

Johnson, Grace
A Hand Raised at Gettysburg.
Bruce 1955.

Kane, Harnett T.
*The Lady of Arlington: A Novel Based on the Life
    of Mrs. Robert E. Lee.*
Doubleday 1953.
BL v50 1953 p79; BRD 1953 p495; FC 11th p334; KR
    v21 1953 p497; NYTBR O 25, 1953 p40.

Kantor, MacKinlay
JUV *Lee and Grant at Appomattox.*
Random House 1950.
BL v47 1950 p142; BRD 1950 p494; KR v18 1950
    p422; LJ v76 1951 p54; NYTBR N 12, 1950 p6.

Miers, Earl Schenck
JUV *We Were There When Grant Met Lee at Appomat-
    tox.*
Grosset & Dunlap 1960.

Miller, Helen Topping
JUV *Christmas with Robert E. Lee.*
Longmans, Green 1958.
BL v55 1958 p214; BRD 1959 p709; KR v26 1958
    p526; LJ v83 1958 p2442.

Monsell, Helen Albee
JUV *Robert E. Lee, Boy of Old Virginia.*
Bobbs-Merrill 1960.
First published in 1937 under title: *Boy of Old Virginia,
    Robert E. Lee.*

Savage, Douglas
The Court Martial of Robert E. Lee.
Combined Books 1993.

Shaara, Michael
The Killer Angels.
McKay 1974.
Won 1975 Pulitzer prize.
BRD 1974 p1098; KR v42 1974 p702; LJ v99 1974
    p2091; NYTBR O 20, 1974 p38.

Turtledove, Harry
The Guns of the South: A Novel of the Civil War.
Ballantine 1992.
KR v60 1992 p947; PW v239 Ag 24, 1992 p63.

Vance, Marguerite
YA *The Lees of Arlington, the Story of Mary and Robert E. Lee.*
Dutton 1949.
BL v46 1949 p105; BRD 1949 p935; KR v17 1949 p554; LJ v74 1949 p1550; NYTBR O 16, 1949 p26.

Vaughan, Matthew
Major Stepton's War.
Doubleday 1978.
KR v46 1978 p572; LJ v103 1978 p1662.

Vinton, Iris
JUV *The Story of Robert E. Lee.*
Grosset & Dunlap 1952.
BRD 1953 p972; LJ v77 1952 p2078.

Willis, Connie
Lincoln's Dreams.
Grafton 1988.
BW v18 Jl 31, 1988 p12; CSM v80 Jl 13, 1988 p18; LARBR F 7, 1988 p11; VOYA v10 O 1987 p182; WCRB v13 no. 1 1987 p26.

850. Lemoyne, Jean-Baptiste
1751-1796
French composer & conductor

Costain, Thomas B.
High Towers.
Doubleday 1949.
BL v45 1948 p129; BRD 1945 p193; FC 9th p115; LJ v74 1949 p155.

851. Lenclos, Ninon de
1620-1705
French courtesan; noted for her beauty & wit

Beamish, Annie O'Meara
The Adorable Ninon de Lenclos.
Hale 1968.

Estey, Norbert
All My Sins: A Novel of the Life and Loves of Ninon de Lenclos.
A.A. Wyn 1954.
BRD 1954 p287; KR v22 1954 p241; LJ v79 1954 p1058; NYTBR My 9, 1954 p27.

852. Lenin, Vladimir Ilyich
1870-1924
Russian statesman & Communist leader

Baker, Nina
YA *Lenin.*
Vanguard Press 1945.
BRD 1945 p32; KR v13 1945 p400; NYTBR D 16, 1945 p13; SatR F 16, 1946 p59.

Brien, Alan
Lenin: The Novel.
Morrow 1988.
BL v84 1988 p1640; KR v56 1988 p636; LJ v113 Je 15, 1988 p67; NYTBR O 16, 1988 p53.

Casey, Jane B.
I, Krupskaya: My Life with Lenin.
Houghton Mifflin 1974.
KR v42 1974 p319; LJ v99 1974 p1846; NYTBR S 29, 1974 p6.

Dangulov, Savva
Lenin Talks to America.
Progress Publishers 1978.

Herlin, Hans
Grishin.
Doubleday 1987.
Also published as *Assassin.*
BL v83 1987 p1563; KR v60 1987 p579; LJ v112 Je 1, 1987 p128.

Hyman, Vernon Tom
Seven Days to Petrograd.
Viking 1988.
BL v84 1988 p973; KR v55 1987 p1641; LJ v113 Ja 1988 p99; NYTBR Jl 10, 1988 p18; PW v232 D 18, 1987 p56.

Kazakevich, Emmanuil
The Blue Notebook.
Foreign Languages Pub. House 1962 (Rpr. 1969).

Linklater, Eric
The Cornerstones: A Conversation in Elysium.
Macmillan 1942.
BRD 1942 p473.

O'Brien, Gregory
Lenin Lives!.
Stein & Day 1984.
KR v52 1984 p164; Nat R v36 Jl 13, 1984 p47; PW v225 Mr 2, 1984 p83.

Sela, Owen
The Petrograd Consignment.
Dial 1979.
KR v47 1979 p290; LJ v104 1979 p1080; NYTBR My 20, 1979 p14.

Solzhenitsyn, Aleksandr
Lenin in Zurich: Chapters.
Farrar, Straus & Giroux 1976.
BL v72 1976 p1084; BRD 1976 p1133; KR v44 1976 p302; LJ v101 1976 p1226; NYTBR Ap 25, 1976 p7.

Spengler, Tilman
Lenin's Brain.
Farrar, Straus & Giroux 1993.
NYTBR Ag 29, 1993 p22.

Stover, Leon E.
The Shaving of Karl Marx: An Instant Novel of Ideas, after the Manner of Thomas Love Peacock, in Which Lenin and H.G. Wells Talk about the Political Meaning of the Scientific Romances.
Chiron Press 1982.

853. Leo Africanus

1465-1554

Travelled widely in Africa; wrote *Description of Africa*, long the chief source of information on the Sudan

Maalouf, Amin
Leo Africanus.
Norton 1989.
BRD 1990 p1134; LJ v114 Ja 1989 p102; NYTBR Mr 12, 1989 p13; PW v234 O 21, 1988 p48.

854. Leonardo da Vinci

1452-1519

Italian painter, scupltor, & scientist

Dreifuss, Jerome
Furlough from Heaven.
Crown 1946.
BRD 1946 p227; NYTBR F 24, 1946 p14.

Frank, Michael
A Florentine Commission.
Souvenir 1989.

Konigsburg, E. L.
YA *The Second Mrs. Giaconda.*
Atheneum 1975.
BL v72 1975 p42; BRD 1976 p661; KR v43 1975 p718; NYTBR O 5, 1975 p8; SLJ v22 S 1975 p121; PW v208 D 1, 1975 p66.

La Mure, Pierre
The Private Life of Mona Lisa.
Little, Brown 1976.
BL v73 1976 p235; BRD 1977 p763; KR v44 1976 p753; LJ v101 1976 p1658.

Lagerkvist, Par
The Dwarf.
Hill & Wang 1945.
BRD 1945 p401; KR v13 1945 p498; NYTBR N 25, 1945 p4; SatR D 1, 1945 p74.

Mankowitz, Wolf
Gioconda: The Misadventures of the Mona Lisa from August, 1911, When She Mysteriously Disappeared from the Louvre. . ..
W.H. Allen 1987.
Books Ap 1987 p33; Lis v117 Mr 26, 1987 p29; TLS Mr 27, 1987 p318.

Mayfield, Sara
Mona Lisa, the Woman in the Portrait.
Grosset & Dunlap 1974.
KR v42 1974 p618; LJ v99 1974 p2176.

Merezhkovsky, Dmitry
The Romance of Leonardo da Vinci, the Forerunner.
Putnam 1902 (Heavily reprinted).
Also published as *The Forerunner.*
BRD 1912 p317; NYTBR Mr 1, 1931 p12; NYTBR Jl 16, 1939 p20.

Miller, Eugenia
YA *The Sign of the Salamander.*
Holt, Rinehart & Winston 1967.
BRD 1967 p903; KR v35 1967 p600; LJ v92 1967 p2022.

Perutz, Leo
Leonardo's Judas.
Arcade Pub. 1989.
BL v85 1989 p1610; BRD 1991 p1465; KR v57 1989 p579; LJ v114 Je 15, 1989 p81; NYTBR S 10, 1989 p37; PW v235 Ap 14, 1989 p53.

Woodhouse, Martin; Ross, Robert
The Medici Emerald.
Dutton 1976.
LJ v102 1977 p129.

Woodhouse, Martin; Ross, Robert
The Medici Guns.
Dutton 1975.
KR v43 1975 p264; LJ v100 1975 p504.

Woodhouse, Martin; Ross, Robert
The Medici Hawks.
Dutton 1978.
KR v46 1978 p573; LJ v103 1978 p2009; PW v213 My 29, 1978 p42.

Woodruff, Elvira
JUV *The Disappearing Bike Shop.*
Holiday House 1992.
BL v88 1992 p1380; SLJ v38 My 1992 p117.

855. Leonidas I

d. 480 BC

King of Sparta

Davis, William Stearns
A Victor of Salamis.
Macmillan 1907 (Heavily reprinted).
BRD 1907 p107; FC 7th p101; NYTBR My 18, 1907 p327.

856. Leonowens, Anna Harriette

1834-1915

English governess who worked for Rama IV, King of Siam

Landon, Margaret
Anna and the King of Siam.
J. Day 1944.
BL v40 1944 p376; BRD 1944 p435; KR v12 1944 p241; NYTBR Jl 9, 1944 p3.

857. Leopold, Nathan Freudenthal

1904-1971

American murderer; committed murder with Richard Loeb in attemmpt to commit the "perfect" crime

Levin, Meyer
Compulsion.
Simon & Schuster 1956.

BL v53 1956 p199; BRD 1956 p562; FC 11th p372; KR v24 1956 p600; LJ v81 1956 p2324; NYTBR O 28, 1956 p7.

Yaffe, James
Nothing But the Night.
Little, Brown 1957.
BRD 1957 p1018; LJ v81 1956 p2952; NYTBR Mr 3, 1957 p5; SatR Mr 9, 1957 p16.

858. Lesseps, Ferdinand Marie de
1805-1894
French diplomat & engineer; builder of the Suez Canal

Carter, Ashley
Against All Gods.
W.H. Allen 1982.

859. Lewes, George Henry
1817-1878
English critic & author; wrote *Life and Works of Goethe*

Glover, Halcott
Both Sides of the Blanket.
Constable 1945.

Glover, Halcott
Louise and Mr. Tudor.
Constable 1946.

860. Lewis, C. S. (Clive Staples)
1898-1963
British medievalist & Christian apologist; wrote children's fantasies, as well as science fiction

Kreeft, Peter
Between Heaven and Hell: A Dialog Somewhere beyond Death with John F. Kennedy, C. S. Lewis, and Aldous Huxley.
InterVarsity Press 1982.

861. Lewis, Meriwether
1774-1809
American explorer

Charbonneau, Louis
Trail: The Story of the Lewis and Clark Expedition.
Doubleday 1989.
BL v86 1989 p426; KR v57 1989 p1347; LJ v114 O 15, 1989 p101; PW v236 S 8, 1989 p54.

Churchill, Winston
The Crossing.
Macmillan 1904 (Heavily reprinted).
FC 10th p99; NYTBR My 28, 1904 p354; NYTBR Je 18, 1904 p405.

Fisher, Vardis
Tale of Valor: A Novel of the Louis and Clark Expedition.

Doubleday 1958.
BRD 1958 p374; KR v26 1958 p322; LJ v83 1958 p2179; NYTBR Je 29, 1958 p20.

Munves, James
JUV *We Were There with Lewis and Clark.*
Grosset & Dunlap 1959.

Seton, Anya
My Theodosia.
Houghton Mifflin 1941.
BRD 1941 p806; FC 7th p311; LJ v66 1941 p220; NYTBR Mr 16, 1941 p7.

Thom, James Alexander
From Sea to Shining Sea.
Ballantine 1984.
BL v80 1984 p1524; KR v52 1984 p502; NYTBR O 7, 1984 p22.

862. Lewis, Sinclair
1885-1951
American novelist & dramatist; won 1930 Nobel Prize; wrote *Babbitt*

Hemingway, Ernest
Across the River and into the Trees.
Scribner 1950 (Heavily reprinted).
BRD 1950 p422; KR v18 1950 p390; LJ v75 1950 p1407; NYTBR S 10, 1950 p1; SatR O 28, 1950 p26; Time v56 S 11, 1950 p110.

863. Liddell, Eric
1902-1945
English track star; subject of the film *Chariots of Fire*

Weatherby, William J.
Chariots of Fire.
Granada 1982.
Based on a screenplay by Colin Welland.

864. Liebknecht, Karl
1871-1919
German Communist leader; founder of the Spartacus League

Doblin, Alfred
Karl and Rosa.
Fromm International 1983.
Sequel to *A People Betrayed.*
FC 11th p1012; KR v51 1983 p1012; PW v224 S 30, 1983 p106.

Doblin, Alfred
A People Betrayed.
Fromm International 1983.
FC 11th p160; KR v51 1983 p17; LJ v108 1983 p516; NYTBR Ap 17, 1983 p11.

865. Liliuokalani, Lydia Kamekeha
1838-1917
Last Hawaiian ruler

Abe, Keith S.
Hawaii Aloha.
TopGallant Pub. Co. 1987.

Paananen, Eloise (Eloise Engle, pseud.)
YA *Princess of Paradise.*
John Day Co. 1962.
LJ v88 1963 p1372.

866. Lin, Piao (Yu-Yung)
1908-1971
Chinese Defense minister, 1959-1972

Jones, Margaret
The Confucius Enigma.
St. Martin's 1982.
BS v42 O 1982 p258; LJ v107 1982 p1348; PW v221
Je 4, 1982 p59.

867. Lincoln, Abraham
1809-1865
16th US President; led Union during the Civil
War; assassinated by John Wilkes Booth

Adicks, Richard
A Court for Owls.
Pineapple Press 1989.
BL v85 1989 p1778; KR v57 1989 p640; LJ v114 Jl
1989 p105.

Anderson, Lavere
JUV *Abe Lincoln and the River Robbers.*
Garrard Co. 1971.

Andrews, Mary Raymond Shipman
The Perfect Tribute.
Scribner 1906 (Heavily reprinted).
BRD 1907 p11; FC 9th p14; SHSLC 10th p477.

Bailey, Bernadine
YA *Abe Lincoln's Other Mother: The Story of Sarah
Bush Lincoln.*
Messner 1941.
BRD 1942 p31; LJ v66 1941 p887; NYTBR Mr 1,
1942 p10; WLB v38 Ap 1942 p69.

Beim, Jerrold
JUV *The Boy on Lincoln's Lap.*
Morrow 1955.
CC 12th p375; LJ v80 1955 p1962.

Carnahan, Walter H.
Hoffman's Row.
Bobbs-Merrill 1963.
LJ v88 1963 p4392.

Cavanah, Frances
JUV *Abe Lincoln Gets His Chance.*
Scholastic Book Services 1959.
BL v55 1959 p575; BRD 1959 p187; KR v27 1959 p9;
LJ v84 1959 p1011.

Churchill, Winston
The Crisis.

Macmillan 1901 (Heavily reprinted).
NYTBR Je 1, 1901 p389; NYTBR S 4, 1904 p595.

Coblentz, Catherine Cate
JUV *Martin and Abraham Lincoln: Based on a True In-
cident.*
Children's Press 1947.
BRD 1947 p172; LJ v72 1947 p1473; NYTBR O 26,
1947 p43.

Colver, Anne
JUV *Bad Jack and the Lincoln Boys.*
Raintree 1976.
SLJ v23 D 1976 p65.

Colver, Anne
Mr. Lincoln's Wife.
Farrar & Rinehart 1943.
BL v39 Jl 1, 1943 p446; BRD 1943 p168; FC 7th p85;
LJ v68 1943 p363; NYTBR My 23, 1943 p6; WLB
v39 Jl 1943 p109.

Cormack, Maribelle
YA *A Recruit for Abe Lincoln.*
Appleton-Century 1942.
BRD 1942 p167; NYTBR F 21, 1943 p12.

Davis, Burke
JUV *Mr. Lincoln's Whiskers.*
Coward, McCann & Geoghegan 1978.
BL v75 1979 p1362; PW v215 Ap 16, 1979 p75; SLJ
v26 S 1979 p134.

Eggleston, Edward
The Graysons: A Story of Illinois.
Century 1887 (Heavily reprinted).

Eifert, Virginia L.
YA *The Buffalo Trace.*
Dodd, Mead 1955.
BL v51 1955 p372; BRD 1955 p275; LJ v80 1955
p1009; NYTBR Mr 13, 1955 p26.

Eifert, Virginia L.
YA *New Birth of Freedom: Abraham Lincoln in the
White House.*
Dodd, Mead 1959.
BL v55 1959 p425; BRD 1959 p322; KR v26 1958
p873; LJ v84 1959 p648; NYTBR F 8, 1959 p30.

Eifert, Virginia L.
YA *Out of the Wilderness; Young Abe Lincoln Grows
Up.*
Dodd, Mead 1956.
BRD 1956 p285; LJ v81 1956 p2731; NYTBR O 7,
1956 p38; SatR N 17, 1956 p72.

Eifert, Virginia L.
YA *Three Rivers South: The Story of Young Abe Lin-
coln.*
Dodd, Mead 1953.

Eifert, Virginia L.
YA *With a Task before Me: Abraham Lincoln Leaves
Springfield.*
Dodd, Mead 1958.

BL v54 1958 p569; BRD 1958 p331; KR v26 1958
p231; LJ v83 1958 p1608; NYTBR Jl 13, 1958 p24.

Everson, David
False Profits.
St. Martin's 1992.
BL v89 1992 p35; KR v60 1992 p695.

Fisher, Aileen
JUV *My Cousin Abe.*
Nelson 1962.

Fraser, George MacDonald
Flash for Freedom!.
Knopf 1972.
Choice v9 Jl/Ag 1972 p644; FC 11th p214; LJ v97
1972 p1825.

Hubbard, Freeman H.
YA *Vinnie Ream and Mr. Lincoln.*
Whittlesey House 1949.
BL v46 1949 p128; BRD 1949 p438; KR v17 1949
p558; LJ v74 1949 p1550; NYTBR Ja 22, 1950 p18.

Kennelly, Ardyth
The Spur.
Messner 1951.
BL v47 1951 p266; BRD 1951 p473; KR v19 1951
p78; LJ v76 1951 p514; NYTBR Ap 15, 1951 p17.

King, Benjamin
A Bullet for Lincoln: A Novel.
Pelican 1993.

Lancaster, Bruce
For Us the Living.
Frederick A. Stokes 1940 (Rpr. 1983).
BL v37 1940 p155; BRD 1940 p529; LJ v65 1940
p923; NYTBR N 3, 1940 p5.

Lawson, John
YA *The Spring Rider.*
Crowell 1968.
BL v65 1968 p254; BRD 1968 p784; KR v36 1968
p699; LJ v93 1968 p4698; NYTBR Ag 18, 1968 p34.

Le Sueur, Meridel
JUV *The River Road: A Story of Abraham Lincoln.*
Knopf 1954 (Rpr. 1991).
BL v50 1954 p403; BRD 1954 p536; LJ v79 1954
p861; NYTBR S 5, 1954 p12.

Lewis, Oscar
The Lost Years: A Biographical Fantasy.
Knopf 1951.
BL v48 1952 p159; BRD 1951 p522; KR v19 1951
p455; LJ v76 1951 p1561; NYTBR O 21, 1951 p20.

McNicol, Jacqueline
JUV *Elizabeth for Lincoln.*
Longmans, Green 1960.
BRD 1961 p914; KR v28 1960 p146; LJ v85 1960
p2479.

Miers, Earl Schenck
JUV *We Were There with Lincoln in the White House.*
Grosset & Dunlap 1963.

Miller, Helen Topping
JUV *Christmas for Tad.*
Longmans, Green 1956.
BL v53 1956 p175; BRD 1956 p644; KR v24 1956
p590.

Monjo, F. N.
JUV *Gettysburg: Tad Lincoln's Story.*
Windmill Books 1976.
BL v72 1976 p1269; KR v44 1976 p324; NYTBR Ap
18, 1976 p24; SLJ v22 My 1976 p61.

Monjo, F. N.
JUV *Me and Willie and Pa: The Story of Abraham Lin-
coln and His Son Tad.*
Simon & Schuster 1973.
BL v70 1974 p544; KR v41 1973 p1269; LJ v99 1974
p575.

Morrow, Honore
Great Captain: Three "Lincoln" Novels.
Morrow 1930 (Rpr. 1958).
Contains: *Forever Free, With Malice toward None,* and
The Last Full Measure.

Neyhart, Louise A.
JUV *Henry's Lincoln.*
Holiday House 1945 (Rpr. 1958).
BRD 1945 p523; HB v21 Jl 1945 p274; KR v13 1945
p271; LJ v70 1945 p688; NYTBR Jl 29, 1945 p21.

O'Toole, G. J. A.
*The Cosgrove Report: Being the Private Inquiry of
a Pinkerton Detective into the Death of President
Lincoln. . . .*
Rawson, Wade 1979.
BL v76 1980 p700; KR v47 1979 p1159; LJ v104 1979
p2484; PW v216 O 1, 1979 p75.

Ryan, Edward J.
Comes an Echo on the Breeze.
Exposition Press 1949.
BRD 1949 p797.

Safire, William
Freedom.
Doubleday 1987.
BL v83 1987 p1539; BRD 1987 p1636; KR v55 1987
p887; LJ v112 Ag 1987 p144; NYTBR Ag 23, 1987
p6.

Stevenson, Augusta
JUV *Abe Lincoln, Frontier Boy.*
Bobbs-Merrill 1959 (Rpr. 1986).
SE v50 Ap 1986 p265.

Steward, Barbara; Steward, Dwight
The Lincoln Diddle.
Morrow 1979.
KR v47 1979 p825; LJ v104 1979 p1591; PW v215 Je
18, 1979 p80.

Stone, Irving
*Love Is Eternal: A Novel about Mary Todd Lin-
coln and Abraham Lincoln.*
Doubleday 1954.

BL v51 1954 p42; BRD 1954 p851; FC 11th p587; KR
v22 1954 p401; LJ v79 1954 p1400; NYTBR Ag 22,
1954 p4.

Teilhet, Darwin Le Ora
Steamboat on the River.
William Sloane 1952.
BL v49 1952 p49; BRD 1952 p876; FC 7th p342; KR
v20 1952 p426; LJ v77 1952 p1506; NYTBR S 21,
1952 p30.

Tucker, Wilson
The Lincoln Hunters.
Rinehart 1958.
FC 7th p354.

Vidal, Gore
Lincoln: A Novel.
Random House 1984.
BL v80 1984 p1130; BRD 1984 p1589; KR v52 1984
p323; LJ v109 1984 p1146; NYTBR Je 3, 1984 p1.

Wahl, Jan
JUV *Abe Lincoln's Beard*.
Delacorte 1971.
KR v39 1971 p117; LJ v97 1972 p1604; NYTBR N 7,
1971 p46.

Williams, Ben Ames
House Divided.
Houghton Mifflin 1947.
KR v15 1947 p368; LJ v72 1947 p1110; NYTBR S 7,
1947 p3.

Wilson, Dorothy Clarke
Lincoln's Mothers.
Doubleday 1981.
BL v77 1981 p1014; LJ v106 1981 p371; PW v218 D
26, 1980 p51.

Wilson, William E.
Abe Lincoln of Pigeon Creek.
Whittlesey House 1949.
BRD 1949 p1001; FC 7th p385; KR v17 1949 p482; LJ
v74 1949 p1557; NYTBR O 16, 1949 p36.

868. Lincoln, Mary Todd
1818-1882
Wife of Abraham Lincoln; suffered from mental
illness after her husband's death

Carnahan, Walter H.
Hoffman's Row.
Bobbs-Merrill 1963.
LJ v88 1963 p4392.

Colver, Anne
Mr. Lincoln's Wife.
Farrar & Rinehart 1943.
BL v39 Jl 1, 1943 p446; BRD 1943 p168; FC 7th p85;
LJ v68 1943 p363; NYTBR My 23, 1943 p6; WLB
v39 Jl 1943 p109.

Miller, Helen Topping
JUV *Christmas for Tad*.
Longmans, Green 1956.

BL v53 1956 p175; BRD 1956 p644; KR v24 1956
p590.

Rhodes, James A.; Jauchius, Dean
The Trial of Mary Todd Lincoln.
Bobbs-Merrill 1959.
BL v55 1959 p453; BRD 1959 p834; FC 7th p287; LJ
v84 1959 p517.

Stone, Irving
*Love Is Eternal: A Novel about Mary Todd Lin-
coln and Abraham Lincoln*.
Doubleday 1954.
BL v51 1954 p42; BRD 1954 p851; FC 11th p587; KR
v22 1954 p401; LJ v79 1954 p1400; NYTBR Ag 22,
1954 p4.

Wilkie, Katherine
JUV *Mary Todd Lincoln, Girl of the Bluegrass*.
Bobbs-Merrill 1954 (Rpr. 1992).

869. Lind, Jenny (Johanna Maria)
1820-1887
Swedish-born soprano; nicknamed the "Swedish
Nightingale"

Cavanah, Frances
JUV *Jenny Lind and Her Listening Cat*.
Vanguard Press 1961.
LJ v86 1961 p4362; SatR Ja 20, 1962 p27.

Cavanah, Frances
YA *Two Loves for Jenny Lind*.
Macrae Smith 1956.
BL v53 1957 p360; BRD 1957 p162; KR v24 1956
p637; LJ v82 1957 p884; NYTBR Ja 20, 1957 p32.

Kyle, Elisabeth
YA *The Swedish Nightingale: Jenny Lind*.
Holt, Rinehart & Winston 1966.
BRD 1965 p718; LJ v90 1965 p5527; SatR N 13, 1965
p62.

Thorp, Roderick
Jenny and Barnum: A Novel of Love.
Doubleday 1981.
KR v49 1981 p834; LJ v106 1981 p1755; PW v220 Jl
17, 1981 p80.

Unnerstad, Edith
YA *Journey to England*.
Macmillan 1961.
BRD 1962 p1226; LJ v87 1962 p336.

870. Lindbergh, Charles A.
1902-1974
American aviator; made first solo nonstop trans-
Atlantic flight

Collins, Max Allan
*Stolen Away: A Novel of the Lindbergh Kidnap-
ping*.
Bantam 1991.
BL v97 1991 p1435; KR v59 1991 p343.

871. Liszt, Franz (Ferencz)

1811-1886

Hungarian composer & pianist

Bagby, Albert Morris
Liszt's Weimar.
T. Yoseloff 1961.

Rousselot, Jean
Hungarian Rhapsody: The Life of Franz Liszt.
Putnam 1961.
BRD 1961 p1221; KR v28 1960 p1055; LJ v86 1961 p792.

Winwar, Frances
The Last Love of Camille.
Harper 1954.
BL v50 1954 p269; BRD 1954 p965; KR v22 1954 p71; NYTBR Ap 18, 1954 p20.

872. Livingstone, David

1813-1873

Scottish missionary & explorer

Albus, Harry J.
"Dr. Livingstone, I Presume": Henry M. Stanley's Search for David Livingstone in the Jungles of Africa.
W.B. Eerdmans 1957.

Jackson, Dave; Jackson, Neta
YA *Escape from the Slave Traders.*
Bethany House Publishers 1992.

Mitchell, Mary
Black Crusade.
Methuen 1949.

873. Lloyd George of Dwyfor, David

1863-1945

British politician & prime minister

Benedictus, David
Lloyd George.
Weidenfeld & Nicolson 1981.
CR v239 Jl 1981 p45; Lis v105 Ja 22, 1981 p109; TLS Ja 23, 1981 p77.

874. Loeb, Richard A.

1907-1936

American murderer; committed murder with Nathan Leopold in attempt to commit the "perfect" crime

Levin, Meyer
Compulsion.
Simon & Schuster 1956.
BL v53 1956 p199; BRD 1956 p562; FC 11th p372; KR v24 1956 p600; LJ v81 1956 p2324; NYTBR O 28, 1956 p7.

Yaffe, James
Nothing But the Night.

Little, Brown 1957.
BRD 1957 p1018; LJ v81 1956 p2952; NYTBR Mr 3, 1957 p5; SatR Mr 9, 1957 p16.

875. London, Jack (John Griffith)

1876-1916

American novelist & short story writer; wrote *The Call of the Wild*

Fenady, Andrew
The Summer of Jack London.
Walker 1985.
KR v52 1984 p1058; PW v226 N 9, 1984 p57.

Lane, Frederick A.
JUV *The Greatest Adventure: A Story of Jack London.*
Aladdin Books 1954.
BRD 1954 p520; KR v22 1954 p438; LJ v79 1954 p2500; NYTBR N 14, 1954 p26.

876. Long, Huey Pierce

1893-1935

American governor & senator; assassinated

Basso, Hamilton
Sun in Capricorn.
Scribner 1942.
BRD 1942 p45; LJ v67 1942 p682; NYTBR S 13, 1942 p6; SatR S 19, 1942 p17.

Dos Passos, John
Number One.
Houghton Mifflin 1943.
BRD 1943 p219; NYTBR Mr 7, 1943 p1; SatR Mr 6, 1943 p7.

Langley, Adria Locke
A Lion Is in the Streets.
Whittlesey House 1945.
BRD 1945 p405; KR v13 1945 p90; LJ v70 1945 p414; NYTBR My 13, 1945 p3; SatR My 12, 1945 p8.

Warren, Robert Penn
All the King's Men.
Harcourt, Brace 1946 (Heavily reprinted).
Won Pulitzer prize in 1947.
BL v43 1946 p18; BRD 1946 p858; KR v14 1946 p301; LJ v71 1946 p1051; NYTBR Ag 18, 1946 p3.

877. Longfellow, Henry Wadsworth

1807-1882

American poet & educator

Melin, Grace Hathaway
JUV *Henry Wadsworth Longfellow: A Gifted Young Poet.*
Bobbs-Merrill 1968.

Wilkinson, Jack
Sunset over Craigie House: A Novel about Henry Wadsworth Longfellow.
Brunswick Pub. Co. 1985.

878. Longstreet, James
1821-1904
Confederate general

Shaara, Michael
The Killer Angels.
McKay 1974.
Won 1975 Pulitzer prize.
BRD 1974 p1098; KR v42 1974 p702; LJ v99 1974
p2091; NYTBR O 20, 1974 p38.

Wells, Lawrence
Let the Band Play Dixie.
Doubleday 1987.
KR v55 1987 p888; LJ v112 Ag 1987 p145.

Williams, Ben Ames
House Divided.
Houghton Mifflin 1947.
KR v15 1947 p368; LJ v72 1947 p1110; NYTBR S 7,
1947 p3.

Williams, Ben Ames
The Unconquered.
Houghton Mifflin 1953.
BL v50 1953 p36; BRD 1953 p1008; FC 11th p663;
KR v21 1953 p227; LJ v78 1953 p1328.

879. Lope de Vega
1562-1635
Spanish dramatist & poet

Flores, Angel
Lope de Vega, Monster of Nature.
Brentano's 1930 (Rpr. 1969).
BRD 1930 p362; NYTBR My 11, 1930 p10; SatR Jl
19, 1930 p1211.

880. Lorca, Federico Garcia
see Garcia Lorca, Federico

881. Lorre, Peter
1904-1964
American actor

Kaminsky, Stuart M.
Think Fast, Mr. Peters.
St. Martin's 1987.
BL v84 1988 p830; KR v56 1988 p90; LJ v113 F 1,
1988 p78; PW v232 D 11, 1987 p51.

882. Lot
Old Testament figure; his wife turned into a pillar of salt

Ilton, Paul
The Last Days of Sodom and Gomorrah.
New American Library 1957.

Ley-Piscator, Maria
Lot's Wife.
Bobbs-Merrill 1954.

BRD 1954 p543; NYTBR O 17, 1954 p42; SatR D 11,
1954 p17.

Rees, Jean A.
Road to Sodom: A Novel.
Random House 1961.

883. Louis XIV
1638-1715
King of France, 1643-1715

Acland, Alice
The Secret Wife.
St. Martin's 1975.
KR v44 1976 p17; LJ v101 1976 p359.

Auchincloss, Louis
The Cat and the King.
Houghton Mifflin 1981.
BL v77 1981 p598; BRD 1981 p66; KR v49 1981 p86;
LJ v106 1981 p468; NYTBR Mr 15, 1981 p14.

Butler, Mildred Allen
Ward of the Sun King.
Funk & Wagnalls 1970.
KR v38 1970 p7; LJ v95 1970 p3634.

Chandernagor, Francoise
The King's Way: Recollections of Francoise d'Aubigne, Marquise de Maintenon, Wife to the King of France.
Harcourt, Brace, Jovanovich 1984.
KR v51 1983 p1262; LJ v109 1984 p191; NYTBR Mr
11, 1984 p22; PW v224 D 16, 1983 p66.

Coryn, Marjorie
Sorrow by Day.
Appleton-Century-Crofts 1950.
BRD 1950 p204; KR v18 1950 p243; LJ v75 1950
p774; NYTBR My 14, 1950 p21.

Deschamps, Fanny
The King's Garden.
Harmony 1985.
CSM v77 Mr 19, 1985 p26; KR v53 1985 p7; PW
v227 Ja 18, 1985 p63.

Dumas, Alexandre
The Man in the Iron Mask.
Original French edition published in 1850. Several
editions exists.
FC 11th p172.

Farely, Alison
The Cardinal's Nieces.
Hale 1976.

Fuller, Iola
All the Golden Gifts.
Putnam 1966.
BL v63 1967 p616; KR v34 1966 p927; LJ v91 1966
p6000.

Golon, Sergeanne
Angelique and the King.
Lippincott 1960 (Rpr. 1974).

BRD 1960 p542; KR v28 1960 p337; LJ v85 1960 p1936.

Hill, Pamela
The Crown and the Shadow: The Story of Francoise d'Aubigne, Marquise de Maintenon.
Putnam 1955.
Also published as *Shadow of Palaces.*
BL v51 1955 p389; BRD 1955 p419; FC 7th p182; KR v23 1955 p144; LJ v80 1955 p647; NYTBR My 15, 1955 p26.

Law, Janice
All the King's Ladies.
St. Martin's 1986.
KR v54 1956 p1236; PW v230 Ag 29, 1986 p386.

Lewis, Janet
The Ghost of Monsieur Scarron.
Doubleday 1959.
BRD 1959 p615; KR v26 1958 p883; LJ v84 1959 p534.

Long, Freda M.
Louis the Divine.
Hale 1982.

Pell, Sylvia
The Shadow of the Sun.
Coward, McCann & Geoghegan 1978.
KR v46 1978 p512; LJ v103 1978 p2008; PW v213 My 22, 1978 p228.

Sanders, Joan
The Marquis, a Novel.
Houghton Mifflin 1963.
NYTBR Ag 11, 1963 p4.

884. Louis XV
1710-1774
King of France, 1715-1774

Bloom, Ursula (Lozania Prole, pseud.)
The Enchanting Courtesan.
Hale 1955 (Rpr. 1975).

Hibbert, Eleanor (Jean Plaidy, pseud.)
Louis, the Well-Beloved.
Hale 1959 (Rpr. 1972).

Kenyon, Frank Wilson
Royal Merry-Go-Round.
Crowell 1954.
BL v50 1954 p193; BRD 1954 p489; KR v22 1954 p39; LJ v79 1954 p550; NYTBR Mr 14, 1954 p23.

Laker, Rosalind
To Dance with Kings.
Doubleday 1988.
KR v56 1988 p1556; LJ v113 D 1988 p133; NYTBR Mr 12, 1989 p22; PW v234 N 18, 1988 p68.

885. Louis XVI
1754-1793
King of France, 1774-1793; husband of Marie Antoinette; guillontined

Chapman, Hester W.
Fear No More.
Reynal 1968.
KR v36 1968 p1072; LJ v94 1969 p215; PW v194 S 23, 1968 p91; Punch v255 S 25, 1968 p452.

Feuchtwanger, Lion
Proud Destiny.
Viking 1947.
BRD 1947 p299; LJ v72 1947 p1193; NYTBR S 14, 1947 p3; SatR S 13, 1947 p9.

Hibbert, Eleanor (Jean Plaidy, pseud.)
Flaunting, Extravagant Queen.
Hale 1957.

Kenyon, Frank Wilson
Marie Antoinette: A Novel.
Crowell 1956.
BL v52 1956 p275; BRD 1956 p510; FC 8th p238; KR v23 1955 p871; LJ v81 1956 p192; NYTBR F 19, 1956 p27.

Laker, Rosalind
To Dance with Kings.
Doubleday 1988.
KR v56 1988 p1556; LJ v113 D 1988 p133; NYTBR Mr 12, 1989 p22; PW v234 N 18, 1988 p68.

886. Louis, Joe
1914-1981
American boxer; world heavyweight champion, 1937-1949

Kaminsky, Stuart M.
Down for the Count.
St. Martin's 1985
BL v81 1985 p1030; KR v53 1985 p206.

887. Lovecraft, H. P. (Howard Phillips)
1890-1937
American author

Lupoff, Nobuko
Lovecraft's Book.
Arkham House 1985.
PW v227 Je 7, 1985 p78.

888. Low, Juliette Gordon
1860-1927
American reformer; founder of the Girl Scouts

Higgins, Helen Boyd
JUV *Juliette Low, Girl Scout.*
Bobbs-Merrill 1959.
LJ v76 1951 p1713.

889. Lowry, Malcolm
1909-1957
English author & poet; wrote *Under the Volcano*

Aiken, Conrad
A Heart for the Gods of Mexico.
Secker 1939 (Rpr. 1964, 1973).

890. Luciano, "Lucky" (Charles)
1897-1962
American criminal

Higgins, Jack
Luciano's Luck.
Stein & Day 1981.
BL v77 1981 p1417; KR v49 1981 p955; LJ v106 1981
p1646; PW v220 Jl 17, 1981 p82.

891. Ludwig II
1845-1886
Bavarian ruler; committed suicide

Freeman, Gillian
The Alabaster Egg.
Viking 1971.
BL v67 Je 1, 1971 p818; BRD 1971 p451; KR v39
1971 p189; NYTBR Ap 18, 1971 p34.

Stacton, David
Remember Me.
Faber & Faber 1957.

892. Lugosi, Bela
1882-1956
American actor; starred in horror films; noted
for his role in *Dracula*

Kaminsky, Stuart M.
Never Cross a Vampire.
St. Martin's 1980.
BL v77 1980 p31; KR v48 1980 p1029; LJ v105 1980
p1754; NYTBR D 7, 1980 p45.

893. Luke, Saint
One of Christ's 12 apostles; believed to be
author of third gospel; physician

Brown, Slater
YA *Luke, Missionary Doctor.*
Association Press 1956.
LJ v81 1956 p2725.

Caldwell, Taylor
Dear and Glorious Physician.
Doubleday 1959 (Rpr. 1981).
BL v55 1959 p228; BRD 1959 p164; LJ v84 1959
p1343; NYTBR Mr 15, 1959 p34.

Perkins, Jacob R.
The Emperor's Physician.
Bobbs-Merrill 1944.
BL v40 1944 p390; BRD 1944 p593; KR v12 1944
p236; NYTBR Jl 16, 1944 p14.

Pickett, Anita
JUV *How Luke Discovered Christmas.*
Beacon Press 1951.

Slaughter, Frank G.
*The Road to Bithynia: A Novel of Luke, the Be-
loved Physician.*
Doubleday 1951.
BL v48 1951 p50; BRD 1951 p819; FC 9th p471; KR
v19 1951 p301; LJ v76 1951 p1223; NYTBR Ag 26,
1951 p14.

Snedeker, Caroline
YA *Luke's Quest.*
Doubleday 1947.
BRD 1947 p836; KR v15 1947 p430; LJ v72 1947
p1695; NYTBR Ja 18, 1948 p27.

Yale, Alfred H.
My Friend Paul: A Novel.
Herald Pub. House 1986.

894. Luther, Martin
1483-1546
Leader of the German Reformation; founder of
the Lutheran Church

Barr, Gladys Hutchison
Monk in Armour.
Abingdon-Cokesbury Press 1950.
BL v47 N 15, 1950 p115; BRD 1951 p52; FC 7th p30;
SatR F 3, 1951 p42.

Charles, Elizabeth Rundle
Luther.
Moody Press 1983.

Jackson, Dave; Jackson, Neta
YA *Spy for the Night Riders.*
Bethany House Publishers 1992.

Ludwig, Charles
Queen of the Reformation.
Bethany House Publishers 1986.
PW v230 O 17, 1986 p31.

Mall, E. Jane
Kitty, My Rib.
Concordia Publishing House 1959.

Vernon, Louise A.
JUV *Thunderstorm in Church.*
Herald Press 1974.
LJ v99 1974 p3270.

895. Luxemburg, Rosa
1870-1919
German socialist leader

Doblin, Alfred
Karl and Rosa.
Fromm International 1983.
Sequel to *A People Betrayed.*
FC 11th p1012; KR v51 1983 p1012; PW v224 S 30,
1983 p106.

Doblin, Alfred
A People Betrayed.
Fromm International 1983.

FC 11th p160; KR v51 1983 p17; LJ v108 1983 p516;
NYTBR Ap 17, 1983 p11.

896. MacArthur, Douglas
1880-1964
American general; accepted Japanese surrender
in WW II

Gibbons, Floyd Phillips
The Red Napoleon.
J. Cape & H. Smith 1929 (Rpr. 1976).
BRD 1929 p351; NYTBR Ag 25, 1929 p9; SatR O 12,
1929 p274.

Kaminsky, Stuart M.
Buried Caesars.
Mysterious Press 1989.
KR v57 1989 p420.

Weaver, John D.
Another Such Victory.
Viking 1948.
BRD 1948 p894; KR v16 1948 p65; NYTBR Ap 18,
1948 p17; SatR Ap 3, 1948 p19.

897. Macbeth
d. 1057
King of Scotland, 1040-1057

Clarke, Brenda (Brenda Honeyman, pseud.)
Macbeth, King of Scots.
Hale 1977.

Copeland, Bonnie
Lady of Moray.
Atheneum 1979.
LJ v104 1979 p2587.

Dunnett, Dorothy
King Hereafter.
Knopf 1982 (Rpr. 1992).
BL v78 1982 p1041; BW v12 Ag 8, 1982 p3; FC 11th
p175; KR v50 1982 p433; LJ v107 1982 p1111.

Dymoke, Juliet
Shadows on a Throne.
Wingate 1976.

Leigh, Michael
He Couldn't Say Amen.
W. Laurie 1951.

Tranter, Nigel G.
Macbeth the King.
Hodder & Stoughton 1978.
TES N 24, 1978 p42.

898. Macdonough, Thomas
1783-1825
American naval officer

Muller, Charles G.
JUV *Hero of Champlain.*

John Day Co. 1961.
LJ v86 1961 p3674.

899. Machiavelli, Niccolo
1469-1527
Italian politician & author; wrote *The Prince*

Maugham, W. Somerset
Then and Now: A Novel.
Heinemann 1946 (Rpr. 1956, 1967, 1977).
Also published as *Fools and Their Folly.*
BL v42 1946 p329; BRD 1946 p557; KR v14 1946
p129; NYTBR My 26, 1946 p4.

Samuel, Maurice
Web of Lucifer: A Novel of the Borgia Fury.
Knopf 1947.
BL v42 1947 p242; BRD 1947 p784; FC 7th p301; LJ
v72 1947 p320; NYTBR F 23, 1947 p5.

900. Mackenzie, Alexander, Sir
1755-1820
Scottish fur trader & explorer

Clarkson, Betty
JUV *Hide-and-Seek.*
Borealis Press 1979.

Lambert, Richard S.
Trailmaker: The Story of Alexander Mackenzie.
McClelland & Stewart 1957.

Shore, Maxine
YA *Knight of the Wilderness: The Story of Alexander
Mackenzie.*
McClelland & Stewart 1943.
BRD 1943 p740; LJ v68 1943 p366; NYTBR Je 13,
1943 p9; SatR My 15, 1943 p30.

901. Mackenzie, William Lyon
1795-1861
Canadian political leader & journalist

Bellasis, Margaret
"Rise, Canadians!".
Hollis & Carter 1955.

Reaney, James
JUV *The Boy with an R in His Hand: A Tale of the
Type-Riot at William Lyon Mackenzie's Print
Office in 1826.*
Porcupine's Quill 1980.
Can Child Lit #23 1981 p96; Quill & Q Je 1980 p36.

902. MacLaine, Shirley
1934-
American actress & author

Vidal, Gore
Live from Golgotha.
Random House 1992.
NYTBR O 4, 1992 p13; NW v120 Ag 31, 1992 p69;
Time v140 S 28, 1992 p64.

903. Maclean, Donald Duart
1913-1983
British diplomat & Soviet spy

Garland, Rodney
The Troubled Midnight.
Coward McCann 1955.
KR v23 1955 p185; LJ v80 1955 p878; NYTBR My 8, 1955 p14.

Harling, Robert
The Enormous Shadow.
Harper 1955.
BRD 1956 p410; KR v24 1956 p602; NYTBR N 25, 1956 p67; SatR D 15, 1956 p40.

Llewellyn, Richard
Mr. Hamish Gleave.
Doubleday 1956.
BRD 1956 p577; LJ v81 1956 p442; NYTBR F 5, 1956 p23; SatR F 11, 1956 p43.

Pape, Richard
Arm Me Audacity.
A. Wingate 1955.

904. Madison, Dolly Payne Todd
1768-1849
Wife of James Madison

Morgan, Helen L.
JUV *Mistress of the White House: The Story of Dolly Madison.*
Westminster Press 1946.
BRD 1946 p588; LJ v71 1946 p829; NYTBR My 12, 1946 p27.

Wilson, Dorothy Clarke
Queen Dolley: The Life and Times of Dolley Madison.
Doubleday 1987.
LJ v112 Ja 1987 p111; NYTBR Ja 4, 1987 p18.

905. Madison, James
1751-1836
Fourth US President; drafted Bill of Rights

Gerson, Noel Bertram
The River Devils.
Doubleday 1968.
KR v36 1968 p529; LJ v93 1968 p2523.

Wilson, Dorothy Clarke
Queen Dolley: The Life and Times of Dolley Madison.
Doubleday 1987.
LJ v112 Ja 1987 p111; NYTBR Ja 4, 1987 p18.

906. Magellan, Ferdinand
1480-1521
Portuguese navigator & explorer

Cameron, Ian
The Wind at Morning.
Morrow 1973.
BL v70 1973 p422; KR v41 1973 p771; LJ v98 1973 p2335; NYTBR S 9, 1973 p42.

Israel, Charles E.
JUV *Five Ships West.*
Macmillan 1966.
BRD 1968 p669; LJ v91 1966 p6192.

Kent, Louise Andrews
JUV *He Went with Magellan.*
Houghton Mifflin 1943.
BL v40 1943 p151; BRD 1943 p447; LJ v68 1943 p831; SatR N 13, 1943 p34.

Lomask, Milton
JUV *Ship's Boy with Magellan.*
Doubleday 1960.
LJ v86 1961 p376.

Mitchell, Mairin
The Odyssey of Acurio: Who Sailed with Magellan.
Heinemann 1956.

Paananen, Eloise (Eloise Engle, pseud.)
YA *Sea Challenge: The Epic Voyage of Magellan.*
C.S. Hammond 1962.
LJ v87 1962 p2031.

Syme, Ronald
JUV *Magellan: First around the World.*
Morrow 1953.
BL v50 1953 p20; BRD 1953 p918; KR v21 1953 p358; LJ v78 1953 p1700; NYTBR N 15, 1953 p30.

907. Maimonides, Moses
1135-1204
Jewish philosopher

Le Porrier, Herbert
The Doctor from Cordova: A Biographical Novel about the Great Philosopher Maimonides.
Doubleday 1979.
BL v75 1979 p1607; KR v47 1979 p594; LJ v104 1979 p2119; PW v215 My 7, 1979 p69.

Morrison, Lester M.; Hubler, Richard G.
Trial & Triumph: A Novel about Maimonides.
Crown 1965.
BL v62 1965 p262; BS v25 Jl 1, 1965 p158; PW v189 My 9, 1966 p80.

908. Maintenon, Francoise d'Aubigne, Marquise de
1635-1719
Second wife of Louis XIV

Acland, Alice
The Secret Wife.
St. Martin's 1975.
KR v44 1976 p17; LJ v101 1976 p359.

Chandernagor, Francoise
*The King's Way: Recollections of Francoise d'Au-
bigne, Marquise de Maintenon, Wife to the King
of France.*
Harcourt, Brace, Jovanovich 1984.
KR v51 1983 p1262; LJ v109 1984 p191; NYTBR Mr
11, 1984 p22; PW v224 D 16, 1983 p66.

Hill, Pamela
*The Crown and the Shadow: The Story of Fran-
coise d'Aubigne, Marquise de Maintenon.*
Putnam 1955.
Also published as *Shadow of Palaces.*
BL v51 1955 p389; BRD 1955 p419; FC 7th p182; KR
v23 1955 p144; LJ v80 1955 p647; NYTBR My 15,
1955 p26.

909. Malibran, Maria Felicita
1808-1836
Spanish opera singer

Myers, Henry
The Signorina.
Crown 1956.
BRD 1956 p675; KR v24 1956 p19; LJ v81 1956 p443;
NYTBR Ap 8, 1956 p36.

910. Mallon, Mary
see Typhoid Mary

911. Mannerheim, Carl Gustav Emil
1867-1951
Finnish field marshall & President of Finland,
1944-1946

Gavin, Catherine Irvine
Give Me the Daggers.
Morrow 1972.
BL v69 1972 p274; KR v40 1972 p874; LJ v97 1972
p2751.

912. Manolete
1917-1947
Spanish bullfighter; died after being gored by
bull

Conrad, Bernaby
Matador.
Capra Press 1988.
LATBR N 27, 1988 p7.

913. Mansfield, Katherine
1888-1923
British short story writer

White, Nelia Gardner
Daughter of Time.
Macmillan 1942.
BL v38 1942 p331; BRD 1942 p828; LJ v67 1942
p225; NYTBR Mr 29, 1942 p7.

914. Manutius, Aldus
1450-1515
Italian printer & scholar

Trease, Geoffrey
YA *Shadow of the Hawk.*
Harcourt, Brace 1949.
BL v46 1949 p17; BRD 1949 p923; KR v17 1949
p362; LJ v74 1949 p1209; NYTBR Ag 21, 1949 p26.

915. Mao Tse-Tung
1893-1976
Chinese Communist leader; first chairman of
the People's Republic of China

Groom, Winston
Forrest Gump.
Doubleday 1986.
BL v82 1986 p706; KR v54 1986 p6; LJ v111 Mr 1,
1986 p108; NYTBR Mr 9, 1986 p31.

Kennedy, Jay Richard
The Chairman.
New American Library 1969.

New, Christopher
Goodbye Chairman Mao.
Coward, McCann & Geoghegan 1979.
KR v46 1978 p1379; LJ v104 1979 p650; NYTBR Ap
8, 1979 p14; PW v215 Ja 1, 1979 p50.

Tuten, Frederic
The Adventures of Mao on the Long March.
Citadel Press 1971.
BRD 1972 p1316; LJ v96 1971 p4031; NYTBR N 7,
1971 p40; VV v16 D 2, 1971 p17.

916. Marco Polo
1254-1324
Italian traveler in China

Buday, Grant
The Venetian.
Oolichan Books 1987.
BIC v17 Je 1988 p35.

Byrne, Donn
Messer Marco Polo.
Century Co. 1921 (Heavily reprinted).
BL v18 1921 p82; BRD 1921 p67; NYTBR O 9, 1921
p18.

Calvino, Italo
Invisible Cities.
Harcourt Brace Jovanovich 1974.
BRD 1975 p198; Choice v12 Ap 1975 p227; FC 9th
p82; LJ v99 1974 p2088; NYTBR N 17, 1974 p35.

Griffiths, Paul
Myself and Marco Polo: A Novel of Changes.
Chatto & Windus 1989.
BL v86 F 15, 1990 p1140; BRD 1991 p750; KR v58 Ja
1, 1990 p8; LJ 115 Mr 1, 1990 p116.

Jennings, Gary
The Journeyer.
Atheneum 1984.
BL v80 1983 p449; BRD 1984 p796; KR v51 1983
p1141; LJ v109 Ja 1984 p111; NYTBR Ja 15, 1984
p18; PW v224 N 11, 1983 p42.

Llewellyn, Richard
Warden of the Smoke and Bells.
Doubleday 1956.
BRD 1956 p577; KR v24 1956 p717; NYTBR N 18,
1956 p5; SatR D 8, 1956 p52.

Marshall, Edison
Caravan to Xanadu: A Novel of Marco Polo.
Farrar, Straus & Young 1953.
BRD 1953 p620; KR v21 1953 p155; LJ v78 1953
p520; NYTBR Mr 29, 1953 p22.

Miles, Keith; Butler, David
Marco Polo.
Dell 1982.
Kliatt v16 Fall 1982 p14.

Walsh, Richard J.
YA *Adventures and Discoveries of Marco Polo.*
E.M. Hale 1953.
NYTBR N 15, 1953 p20.

917. Marconi, Guglielmo
1874-1937
Italian inventor; famous for development of
wireless telegraphy

Frutkin, Mark
The Growing Dawn: Documentary Fiction.
Quadrant 1983.
BIC v13 Ag 1984 p23.

918. Marcus Aurelius Antoninus
121-180
Roman emperor & Stoic; wrote *Meditations*

Gibbs, Willa
A Fig in Winter.
Morrow 1963.
LJ v88 1963 p2725.

Pilpel, Robert H.
Between Eternities.
Harcourt Brace Jovanovich 1985.
KR v53 1985 p902; LJ v110 O 15, 1985 p103; PW
v228 S 27, 1985 p82.

919. Margaret of Anjou
1430-1482
Wife of Henry VI

Hibbert, Eleanor (Jean Plaidy, pseud.)
Red Rose of Anjou.
Putnam 1983.

920. Mariamne the Hasmonaean
d. 29 BC
Wife of King Herod

Lagerkvist, Par
Herod and Mariamne.
Knopf 1968.
Also published as *Mariamne.*
Atl v222 N 1968 p144; BRD 1969 p742; FC 8th p247;
KR v36 1968 p844; LJ v93 1968 p3799.

921. Marie Antoinette
1755-1793
Wife of Louis XVI; guillotined; known for saying, "Let them eat cake"

Bloom, Ursula (Lozania Prole, pseud.)
Sweet Marie Antoinette.
Hale 1969 (Rpr. 1989).

Chapman, Hester W.
Fear No More.
Reynal 1968.
KR v36 1968 p1072; LJ v94 1969 p215; PW v194 S
23, 1968 p91; Punch v255 S 25, 1968 p452.

Dumas, Alexandre
*The Countess de Charny; or, The Fall of the
    French Monarchy.*
T.B. Peterson 1853 (Heavily reprinted).
Translation of *Comtesse de Charny.*

Dumas, Alexandre
Memoirs of a Physician.
T.B. Peterson 1850 (Heavily reprinted).
Translation of *Memoires d'un Medecin.*

Dumas, Alexandre
The Queen's Necklace.
G. Routledge & Sons 1880 (Heavily reprinted).
Translation of *Le Collier de la Reine.*
FC 11th p172.

Feuchtwanger, Lion
Proud Destiny.
Viking 1947.
BRD 1947 p299; LJ v72 1947 p1193; NYTBR S 14,
1947 p3; SatR S 13, 1947 p9.

Gabriel, Gilbert Wolf
I Thee Wed.
Macmillan 1948.
BRD 1948 p295; NYTBR Ap 25, 1948 p12; SatR My
22, 1948 p27.

Hibbert, Eleanor (Jean Plaidy, pseud.)
Flaunting, Extravagant Queen.
Hale 1957.

Holt, Victoria
The Queen's Confession.
Doubleday 1968.
BL v65 1968 p151; KR v36 1968 p417; NYTBR S 8,
1968 p60.

Jordan, Mildred
Asylum for the Queen.
Knopf 1948.
BRD 1948 p434; KR v16 1948 p121; LJ v73 1948
p707; NYTBR My 9, 1948 p6.

Kenyon, Frank Wilson
Marie Antoinette: A Novel.
Crowell 1956.
BL v52 1956 p275; BRD 1956 p510; FC 8th p238; KR
v23 1955 p871; LJ v81 1956 p192; NYTBR F 19,
1956 p27.

Mackin, Jeanne
The Frenchwoman.
St. Martin's 1989.
BL v86 1989 p526; KR v57 1989 p1423; LJ v114 D
1989 p172.

Moody, Laurence
The Austrian Butterfly.
Hale 1975.

Mundt, Klara (L. Muhlbach, pseud.)
Marie Antoinette and Her Son.
Appleton 1867 (Heavily reprinted).

Simpson, Evan John (Evan John, pseud.)
King's Masque.
Dutton 1941.
BRD 1941 p823; LJ v66 1941 p140; NYTBR F 16,
1941 p5; SatR F 15, 1941 p6.

St. Vincent, Isobel
The Fatal Necklace.
Roy 1957.

922. Marie Louise
1791-1847
Second wife of Napoleon I

Gerson, Noel Bertram
The Emperor's Ladies.
Doubleday 1959.
BL v56 1959 p242; BRD 1960 p519; KR v27 1959
p415.

Quigley, Aileen
Empress to the Eagle.
Hale 1975.

923. Marion, Francis
1732-1795
American Revolutionary general; nicknamed
the "Swamp Fox"

Allen, Merritt P.
YA *Battle Lanterns.*
Longmans, Green 1949.
BL v45 Mr 15, 1949 p247; BRD 1949 p8; LJ v74 Ap 1,
1949 p557; NYTBR Mr 20, 1949 p26; SHSLC 8th
p381.

Brown, Marion Marsh
YA *The Swamp Fox.*

Westminster Press 1950.
BL v47 1951 p224; BRD 1951 p124; KR v18 1950
p522; LJ v75 1950 p1673.

Gerson, Noel Bertram
The Swamp Fox, Francis Marion.
Doubleday 1967.
BL v63 1967 p1033; BRD 1967 p490; KR v34 1966
p1303; LJ v92 1967 p230.

Lancaster, Bruce
Phantom Fortress.
Little, Brown 1950.
BRD 1950 p531; LJ v75 1950 p707; NYTBR Mr 12,
1950 p28; SatR Mr 25, 1950 p32.

Leland, John A.
Othneil Jones.
Lippincott 1956.
BRD 1957 p543; LJ v82 1957 p236; NYTBR O 28,
1956 p41.

Lucas, Eric
JUV *Swamp Fox Brigade: Adventures with General
Francis Marion's Guerrillas.*
International Publishers 1945.
BL v42 1945 p113; BRD 1945 p444; KR v13 1945
p400; LJ v70 1945 p1027.

Mayrant, Drayton
The Red Doe.
Appleton-Century-Crofts 1953.

Miller, Helen Topping
Slow Dies the Thunder.
Bobbs-Merrill 1955.
LJ v80 1955 p2303.

Steele, William O.
JUV *Francis Marion, Young Swamp Fox.*
Bobbs-Merrill 1954.
BRD 1954 p838; LJ v79 1954 p1324.

Taylor, David
Sycamore Men.
Lippincott 1958.

924. Mark, Saint
One of Christ's 12 apostles; believed to be
author of second Gospel

Chinn, Laurene
Marcus: A Novel of the Youngest Apostle.
Morrow 1965.
KR v33 1965 p644; LJ v90 1965 p3465.

Mann, Stephen Stafford
The Journal of St. Mark.
Carlton Press 1991.

Williams, Albert N.
YA *John Mark, First Gospel Writer.*
Association Press 1956.
LJ v81 1956 p2725.

925. Marlborough, John Churchill, Duke
1650-1722
English military commander

Bell, Josephine
A Question of Loyalities.
Bles 1974.

Henty, G. A.
JUV *The Cornet of Horse: A Tale of Marlborough's War.*
Sampson Low, Marston, Searle & Rivington 1881 (Heavily reprinted).

Kenyon, Frank Wilson
The Glory and the Dream.
Dodd, Mead 1963.

926. Marlowe, Christopher
1564-1593
English dramatist & poet

De Maria, Robert
To Be a King.
Bobbs-Merrill 1976.
KR v44 1976 p22; LJ v101 1976 p738; PW v209 F 2, 1976 p52.

Dhondy, Farrukh
Black Swan.
Houghton Mifflin 1993.
Sch Lib N 1992 p157.

Garrett, George
Entered from the Sun.
Doubleday 1990.
BL v87 1990 p26; BRD 1991 p669; KR v58 1990 p951; LJ v115 S 1, 1990 p257; NYTBR S 16, 1990 p7; PW v238 Ag 23, 1991 p56.

Lindsay, Philip
One Dagger for Two.
Cassell 1932 (Rpr. 1974).

Lom, Herbert
Enter a Spy.
Merlin 1978.

Wichelns, Lee
The Shadow of the Earth: An Historical Novel Based on the Life of Christopher Marlowe.
Elysian Press 1987.

927. Marquand, John Phillips
1893-1960
American novelist; wrote *The Late George Apley;* won 1937 Pulitzer Prize

Hamburger, Philip P.
J. P. Marquand, Esquire: A Portrait in the Form of a Novel.
Houghton Mifflin 1952.
BRD 1952 p389; LJ v77 1952 p1397; NYTBR O 12, 1952 p10; SatR O 25, 1952 p19.

928. Marshall, John
1755-1835
Chief Justice of the US Supreme Court, 1801-1835

Cunningham, Joe
YA *Remember John Marshall: A Biography of the Great Chief Justice.*
Biographic Press 1956.

Monsell, Helen Albee
JUV *John Marshall, Boy of Young America.*
Bobbs-Merrill 1949.
BRD 1949 p649; LJ v74 1949 p666; NYTBR Jl 17, 1949 p22.

929. Marx Brothers, The
Comedy team made up of Chico Marx, Groucho Marx, Gummo Marx, Harpo Marx, & Zeppo Marx

Kaminsky, Stuart M.
You Bet Your Life.
St. Martin's 1978.
KR v47 1979 p154; LJ v104 1979 p650; NYTBR Ap 22, 1979 p20.

930. Marx, Karl
1818-1883
German journalist & socialist; wrote *Communist Manifesto* and *Das Kapital*

Feuer, Lewis S.
The Case of the Revolutionist's Daughter: Sherlock Holmes Meets Karl Marx.
Prometheus Books 1983.
KR v51 1983 p845; PW v224 Ag 12, 1983 p53.

Roitman, Shlomo
Proze.
Perets 1988.

931. Mary I
1516-1558
Queen of England; daughter of Henry VIII and Katharine of Aragon

Ansle, Dorothy P. (Hebe Elsna, pseud.)
Prelude for Two Queens.
Collins 1972.

Bloom, Ursula (Lozania Prole, pseud.)
The King's Daughter.
Hale 1975 (Rpr. 1984).

Churchill, Rosemary
Daughter of Henry VIII.
Hale 1971.

Hibbert, Eleanor (Jean Plaidy, pseud.)
In the Shadow of the Crown.
Putnam 1988.

Hibbert, Eleanor (Jean Plaidy, pseud.)
The Spanish Bridegroom.
Hale 1954 (Rpr. 1971).
LJ v96 1971 p3158.

Irwin, Margaret
Elizabeth and the Prince of Spain.
Harcourt, Brace 1953.
BL v50 1953 p168; BRD 1953 p467; FC 10th p278;
  KR v21 1953 p552; LJ v78 1953 p1686; NYTBR N
  29, 1953 p46.

Lewis, Hilda
I Am Mary Tudor.
McKay 1972.
BRD 1972 p788; Choice v9 S 1972 p815; FC 11th
  p373; LJ v97 1972 p1740.

Lindsay, Jack
*Fires in Smithfield: A Novel of Mary Tudor's
  Reign.*
Bodley Head 1950 (Rpr. 1972).

Long, Freda M.
The Spanish Tudor: A Novel of Mary Tudor.
Hale 1968 (Rpr. 1973).

McDonald, Eva
The Spanish Wedding.
Hale 1972.

Ormesher, Elizabeth
The Betrayed Tudor.
Hale 1979.

Peters, Maureen
Mary, the Infamous Queen.
Hale 1968 (Rpr. 1971).

Peters, Maureen
Shadow of a Tudor.
Hale 1971.

Player, Robert
Oh! Where Are Bloody Mary's Earrings?.
Harper 1973.
BS v33 My 1, 1973 p55; FC 9th p403; KR v41 1973
  p25; LJ v98 1973 p2152; NYTBR Ap 1, 1973 p33.

Ross Williamson, Hugh
The Cardinal in England.
Joseph 1970.

Ross Williamson, Hugh
The Sisters.
Joseph 1958.
Also published as *Conspirators and the Crown.*
BL v55 1959 p503; BRD 1959 p858; NYTBR Ap 19,
  1959 p6.

Stoker, Mary
Tudor Pavan.
H. Jenkins 1951.

932. Mary Magdalene, Saint

New Testament figure; one of the women who
followed & cared for Jesus in Galilee

Bloom, Ursula (Lozania Prole, pseud.)
A Woman Called Mary.
Severn House 1978.
Originally published in 1966 under the author's
  pseud., Deborah Mann.

Calhoun, Flo
*I Remember Union: The Story of Mary Mag-
  dalena.*
All Worlds Pub. 1992.

Frantz, Mabel
Woman with Alabaster.
Fleming H. Revell 1940.

Gibbs, Willa
According to Mary: A Novel of the Magdalene.
Morrow 1962.
LJ v87 1962 p1629; NYTBR Ap 15, 1962 p38.

Holmes, Marjorie
Three from Galilee.
Harper & Row 1985.
BL v81 1985 p1596; KR v53 1985 p657; LJ v110 S 15,
  1985 p93; PW v227 Je 28, 1985 p62.

Kinstler, Clysta
The Moon under Her Feet.
HarperCollins 1991.

MacClure, Victor
A Certain Woman: The Story of Mary Magdalene.
Pellegrini & Cudahy 1951.
BRD 1951 p549; KR v19 1951 p358; NYTBR S 2,
  1951 p10; SatR S 15, 1951 p28.

Murphy, Edward F.
Road from Olivet.
Bruce Publishing 1946.
BRD 1946 p587; KR v14 1946 p195; LJ v71 1946
  p758; NYTBR Jl 7, 1946 p15.

Murphy, Edward F.
The Scarlet Lily.
Bruce Publishing 1944.
BRD 1944 p547; FC 7th p259.

Saltus, Edgar
Mary Magdalen: A Chronicle.
Belford Co. 1891 (Rpr. 1925, 1970).

Scott, Barbara Montagu
Magdalen.
Hutchinson 1953.

Slaughter, Carolyn
Magdalene: A Novel.
M. Evans 1979.
KR v47 1979 p219.

Slaughter, Frank G.
The Galileans: A Novel of Mary Magdalene.
Doubleday 1953.
BL v49 1953 p190; BRD 1953 p867; FC 9th p470; KR
  v20 1952 p725; NYTBR Ja 11, 1953 p30.

Thompson, Juliet
I, Mary Magdalen.
Delphic Studios 1940.

Williman, Anne C.
Mary of Magdala: A Novel.
Broadman Press 1990.

933. Mary, Queen of Scots
1542-1587
Queen of Scotland, 1542-1567; beheaded

Adamson, Margot Robert
A Rope of Sand.
Sidgwick & Jackson 1965.

Balin, Beverly
King in Hell.
Coward-McCann 1971.
KR v38 1970 p1261; LJ v96 1971 p654.

Benson, Robert Hugh
Come Rack! Come Rope!.
B. Tauchnitz 1913 (Rpr. 1948, 1957).
BL v9 1913 p341; BL v54 1957 p46; BRD 1913 p49;
   BRD 1957 p75; FC 8th p38; KR v25 1957 p106; LJ
   v82 1957 p735; NYTBR F 16, 1913 p76.

Byrd, Elizabeth
*Maid of Honour: A Novel Set in the Court of
   Mary Queen of Scots.*
St. Martin's 1979.
KR v47 1979 p20.

Cartland, Barbara
Hidden Evil.
Hurst & Blackett 1970.

D'Oyley, Elizabeth
The Mired Horse.
M. Joseph 1951.

Dakers, Elaine (Jane Lane, pseud.)
Conies in the Hay.
Hale 1957.

Dakers, Elaine (Jane Lane, pseud.)
JUV *The Escape of the Queen.*
Evans Brothers 1957.

Dakers, Elaine (Jane Lane, pseud.)
Parcel of Rogues.
Rinehart 1948.
BRD 1948 p193; LJ v73 1948 p1090; NYTBR N 14,
   1948 p47; SatR Ag 28, 1948 p31.

Dakers, Elaine (Jane Lane, pseud.)
Queen of the Castle.
Hale 1958 (Rpr. 1971, 1974).

Dunnett, Dorothy
The Game of Kings.
Putnam 1961.
BL v58 1961 p126; BRD 1961 p383; KR v29 1961
   p746; NYTBR O 15, 1961 p4.

Dunnett, Dorothy
Queens' Play.
Putnam 1964.
FC 9th p152; LJ v89 1964 p3183; NYTBR Ag 2, 1964
   p31.

Fallon, Frederic
The White Queen.
Doubleday 1972.
BL v69 1972 p68; KR v40 1972 p423; LJ v97 1972
   p2642.

Fleming, John Arnold
The Four Maries.
W. Maclellan 1951.

George, Margaret
Mary Queen of Scotland and the Isles.
St. Martin's 1992.
BL v88 1992 p1972; KR v60 1992 p800; LJ v117 Ag
   1992 p148; NYTBR N 1, 1992 p20.

Hanley, Clifford
The Red-Haired Bitch.
Houghton Mifflin 1969.
BL v66 1969 p176; BRD 1969 p558; FC 8th p189; KR
   v37 1969 p528; LJ v94 1969 p2639; NYTBR Jl 20,
   1969 p33.

Harwood, Alice
*Seats of the Mighty: A Novel of James Stuart,
   Brother of Mary, Queen of Scots.*
Bobbs-Merrill 1956.
BRD 1957 p402; NYTBR D 9, 1956 p42.

Hendry, Frances Mary
JUV *The Falcon.*
Conongate 1989.
JB v54 F 1990 p41.

Hewlett, Maurice
The Queen's Quair; or, The Six Years' Tragedy.
Macmillan 1904 (Rpr. 1912, 1971).
NYTBR Je 4, 1904 p372; NYTBR Je 18, 1904 p406.

Hibbert, Eleanor (Jean Plaidy, pseud.)
Royal Road to Fotheringay.
Hale 1956 (Rpr. 1968, 1974).
Also published as *Mary, Queen of Scotland, the Trium-
   phant Year.*
LJ v93 1968 p4428.

Hunter, Mollie
YA *You Never Knew Her as I Did!.*
Harper & Row 1981.
BRD 1982 p651; NYTBR Ap 19, 1982 p31; SLJ v28
   O 1981 p142.

Irwin, Margaret
*The Gay Galliard: The Love Story of Mary,
   Queen of Scots.*
Harcourt, Brace 1942.
BL v38 1942 p251; BRD 1942 p391; FC 8th p222; LJ
   v66 1942 p131; NYTBR F 15, 1942 p4.

Jacob, Naomi Ellington
Mary of Delight.
Hutchinson 1949.

Kenyon, Frank Wilson
Mary of Scotland.
Crowell 1957.
BL v53 1957 p527; BRD 1957 p491; FC 8th p238; KR
v24 1956 p913; LJ v82 1957 p1110; NYTBR F 24,
1957 p34.

Kirby, Kate
Footsteps of a Stuart.
Hale 1973.

Lindsay, Philip
Queen Honeypot.
S. Low 1951 (Rpr. 1971).

Long, Freda M.
Three Crowns for Mary.
Hale 1972.

McDonald, Eva
The Reluctant Bridegroom.
Hale 1965.

McDonald, Eva
The White Petticoat.
Hale 1971.

Muir, Marie
The Mermaid Queen.
Constable 1978.

Oliver, Jane
The Lion and the Rose.
Putnam 1958.
BL v55 1959 p382; BRD 1959 p767; KR v27 1959
p111; LJ v84 1959 p863.

Peters, Maureen
Flawed Enchantress.
Hale 1973.

Scott, Walter Sir
The Monastery.
A. Constable 1820 (Heavily reprinted).

Sutherland, May
Uneasy Lies the Head.
Hutchinson 1951.

Uttley, Alison
YA *A Traveler in Time.*
Viking 1964.
BRD 1965 p1278; HB v40 1964 p612; LJ v89 1964
p4653; SHSLC 2nd p363.

Wagenknecht, Edward (Julian Forrest, pseud.)
*Nine before Fotheringhay: A Novel about Mary
Queen of Scots.*
Bles 1966.

Westcott, Jan
The Tower and the Dream.
Putnam 1974.

BL v70 1974 p774; KR v41 1973 p1286; LJ v99 1974
p154; PW v204 D 10, 1973 p30.

934. Mary, the Virgin Mother
Mother of Jesus Christ

Asch, Sholem
Mary.
Putnam 1949 (Rpr. 1985).
BRD 1949 p25; FC 11th p24; KR v17 1949 p436; LJ
v74 1949 p1460; NYTBR O 9, 1949 p5.

Barrett, William E.
The Empty Shrine.
Doubleday 1958.
BL v55 1959 p259; BRD 1959 p59; KR v26 1958
p676; LJ v83 1958 p 3439.

Bauer, Florence A.
Daughter of Nazareth.
Broadman Press 1955.

Bence, Evelyn
Mary's Journal: A Mother's Story.
Zondervan 1992.

Breasted, Mary
Why Should You Doubt Me Now?.
Farrar, Straus & Giroux 1993.
NYTBR N 28, 1993 p17.

Coffey, Thomas M.
JUV *The Donkey's Gift.*
Crown 1984.
KR v52 1984 p811.

Dockman, Elizabeth
The Lady and the Sun
Newman Press 1954.

Eliot, Ethel Cook
Roses for Mexico.
Macmillan 1946.
BRD 1946 p245; KR v14 1946 p183; LJ v71 1946
p917.

Frost, Elizabeth Hollister
Mary and the Spinners.
Coward-McCann 1946.
BRD 1946 p294; LJ v71 1946 p1542.

Gillis, Carroll
A Sword in Her Soul.
Sunburst Press 1986.

Holmes, Marjorie
Two from Galilee: A Love Story.
Revell 1972.
BS v32 S 1, 1972 p247; KR v40 1972 p691; PW v201
Je 19, 1972 p58.

Jeppson, Roxcy
Mary, Behold Thy Son: A Mother's Story.
Covenant Communications 1991.

Kellner, Esther
Mary of Nazareth.

Appleton-Century-Crofts 1958.
BL v55 1958 p126; BRD 1959 p557; KR v26 1958
   p198; NYTBR D 14, 1958 p17.

Lofts, Norah
YA *How Far to Bethlehem?*.
Doubleday 1965.
FC 9th p323; LJ v90 1965 p2871.

Mancini, Anthony
The Miracle of Pelham Park.
Dutton 1982.
BL v78 1982 p586; KR v49 1981 p1424; LJ v107 1982
   p109.

Maugham, W. Somerset
Catalina, a Romance.
Doubleday 1948 (Rpr. 1958, 1967, 1991).
BL v45 1948 p89; BRD 1948 p564; KR v16 1948
   p290; LJ v73 1948 p1091; NYTBR N 7, 1948 p6.

Michael, Arnold
Blessed among Women.
Willing Pub. Co. 1948.

Miller, Calvin
A Symphony in Sand.
Word Pub. 1990.

Milligan, Clarence P.
*Russia and the Woman: A Novel of the Virgin
   Mary, Mother of Jesus*.
Vantage Press 1953.

O'Connell, Charles C.
Light over Fatima.
Mercier Press 1947.

Parish, Helen R.
JUV *Our Lady of Guadalupe*.
Viking 1955.
BRD 1955 p700; HB v31 Ap 1955 p123; LJ v80 1955
   p1259; NYTBR Ap 24, 1955 p32; SatR My 14,
   1955 p57.

Popell, Charles W.
*Bitter Water: An Intriguing Historical Novel of the
   Life and Times*.
Master Book Publishers 1984.

Schroeder, Agustina
Mother of Fair Love.
Bruce Pub. Co. 1957.

Stafford, Ann
Blossoming Rod.
Hodder & Stoughton 1955.

Thomas, Frances
Seeing Things.
Gollancz 1986.
B&B F 1986 p36; Books Je 1987 p32; BritBkN Ap
   1986 p242; NS v111.

Unsworth, Barry
Stone Virgin.
Houghton Mifflin 1986.

BRD 1986 p1638; KR v54 1986 p88; LJ v111 Mr 1,
   1986 p110; NYTBR Ap 6, 1986 p27.

Wallace, Irving
The Miracle: A Novel.
Dutton 1984.
BL v80 1984 p1571; KR v52 1984 p550; LJ v109 1984
   p1688; NYTBR S 16, 1984 p15.

Werfel, Franz
The Song of Bernadette.
Viking 1942.
BL v38 1942 p347; BRD 1942 p818; LJ v67 1942
   p414; NYTBR My 10, 1942 p3.

935. Masaryk, Jan Garrigue
1886-1948
Czech political leader; son of Thomas Masaryk

Lania, Leo
The Foreign Minister.
Houghton Mifflin 1956.
BL v53 1956 p147; BRD 1956 p433; KR v24 1956
   p537; LJ v81 1956 p2593; NYTBR D 23, 1956 p11.

936. Mason, Charles
1730-1787
British surveyor & astronomer; with Jeremiah
Dixon surveyed boundary between Maryland &
Pennsylvania known as the Mason-Dixon Line

Lefever, Barbara S.
The Stargazers: Story of Mason and Dixon.
Printing Express 1986.

937. Masterson, "Bat" (William Barclay)
1853-1921
US marshal; friend of Wyatt Earp

Jones, Kathy
Wild Western Desire.
Kensington Pub. Corp. 1993.
BL v89 1993 p970.

Randisi, Robert
The Ham Reporter: Bat Masterson in New York.
Doubleday 1986.
PW v229 Je 27, 1986 p75.

Swarthout, Glendon
The Old Colts.
Thorndike Press 1985.
BL v81 1985 p1297; KR v53 1985 p347; LJ v110 Je 1,
   1985 p146; PW v227 Mr 29, 1985 p65.

938. Mata Hari
1876-1917
Dutch spy; found guilty of espionage for the Ger-
mans; executed

Huebsch, Edward
The Last Summer of Mata Hari.
Crown 1979.

KR v47 1979 p877; LJ v104 1979 p1719; PW v216 Jl 2, 1979 p96.

Sherman, Dan
The Man Who Loved Mata Hari.
D.I. Fine 1985.
BL v82 1985 p111; KR v53 1985 p749; LJ v110 S 15, 1985 p95.

Wertenbaker, Lael Tucker
The Eye of the Lion: A Novel Based on the Life of Mata Hari.
Little, Brown 1964.
BRD 1964 p1236; LJ v89 1964 p1118; NYTBR F 23, 1964 p31; SatR Ja 4, 1964 p76.

939. Mather, Cotton
1663-1728
American clergyman & author; his writings added to the hysteria of the Salem witchcraft trials

Barker, Shirley
Tomorrow the New Moon.
Bobbs-Merrill 1955.
LJ v80 1955 p460; NYTBR Ja 9, 1955 p5.

Breslin, Howard
The Silver Oar.
Crowell 1954.
BL v51 1954 p83; BRD 1954 p110; KR v22 1954 p454; NYTBR N 14, 1954 p34.

Elliott, Edward E.
The Devil and the Mathers.
Strawberry Hill Press 1989.
KR v57 1989 p1014; PW v236 Jl 28, 1989 p214.

Farber, Norma
YA *Mercy Short: A Winter Journal, North Boston, 1692-93.*
Dutton 1982.
HB v58 D 1982 p655; KR v50 1982 p1195; SLJ v29 O 1982 p160.

Longstreth, Thomas Morris
YA *Time Flight.*
Macmillan 1954.
BRD 1954 p555; KR v22 1954 p117; LJ v79 1954 p866; NYTBR Jl 11, 1954 p20.

940. Mather, Increase
1639-1723
American clergyman; president of Harvard University, 1685-1701; father of Cotton Mather

Elliott, Edward E.
The Devil and the Mathers.
Strawberry Hill Press 1989.
KR v57 1989 p1014; PW v236 Jl 28, 1989 p214.

Newton, J. Edward
The Rogue and the Witch.
Abelard-Schuman 1955.

BL v51 1955 p343; BRD 1955 p674; KR v23 1955 p47; LJ v80 1955 p454.

941. Mathewson, Christy (Christopher)
1880-1925
American baseball player

Greenberg, Eric Rolfe
The Celebrant: A Novel.
Everest House 1983 (Rpr. 1986).
BL v79 1982 p353; KR v50 1982 p949; LJ v108 1983 p516.

942. Matthiesson, Francis Otto
1902-1950
American author

Sarton, May
Faithful Are the Wounds.
Rinehart 1955 (Rpr. 1972, 1985).
BL v51 1955 p317; BRD 1955 p798; KR v23 1955 p18; NYTBR Mr 13, 1955 p6.

943. Maupassant, Guy de
1850-1893
French novelist & short story writer

Coulter, Stephen
Damned Shall Be Desire: The Passionate Life of Guy de Maupassant.
J. Cape 1958.
LJ v84 1959 p3055.

944. Maury, Matthew Fontaine
1806-1873
American oceanographer & naval officer

Latham, Jean Lee
YA *Trail Blazer of the Seas.*
Houghton Mifflin 1956.
BRD 1956 p548; CC 10th p323; HB v32 O 1956 p365; KR v24 1956 p707.

945. Maximilian
1832-1867
Archduke of Austria & emperor of Mexico

Barnes, Nancy
YA *Carlota, American Empress.*
Messner 1943.
BL v40 1943 p150; BRD 1943 p43; NYTBR Ja 30, 1944 p6; SatR N 13, 1943 p46.

Bourne, Peter
Flames of Empire.
Putnam 1949.
BRD 1949 p466; KR v17 1949 p438; LJ v74 1949 p1461; NYTBR S 25, 1949 p30.

Gavin, Catherine Irvine
The Cactus and the Crown.
Doubleday 1962.

BL v58 1962 p477; BRD 1962 p441; FC 11th p231;
KR v29 1961 p1094; LJ v87 1962 p2038; NYTBR F
11, 1962 p34.

Gorman, Herbert
The Breast of the Dove.
Rinehart 1950.
BRD 1950 p368; KR v18 1950 p75; LJ v75 1950 p560;
NYTBR Ap 16, 1950 p43.

Meadows, Rose
Imperial Pawn.
Hurst & Blackett 1972.

Niles, Blair
*Passengers to Mexico; the Last Invasion of the
Americas.*
Farrar & Rinehart 1943.
BRD 1943 p611; LJ v68 1943 p289; NYTBR Ap 4,
1943 p9; SatR Ap 10, 1943 p33.

946. Mayo, Charles Horace
1865-1939
American surgeon; co-founder of Mayo Clinic

Hammontree, Marie
JUV *Will and Charlie Mayo: Doctor's Boys.*
Bobbs-Merrill 1954.
BL v51 1954 p155; BRD 1955 p391; LJ v80 1955 p693.

947. Mayo, William James
1861-1939
American surgeon; co-founder of Mayo Clinic

Hammontree, Marie
JUV *Will and Charlie Mayo: Doctor's Boys.*
Bobbs-Merrill 1954.
BL v51 1954 p155; BRD 1955 p391; LJ v80 1955 p693.

948. Mazarin, Jules, Cardinal
1602-1661
French cardinal, born in Italy; prime minister of
Louis XIV

Farely, Alison
The Cardinal's Nieces.
Hale 1976.

949. McCarthy, Eugene Joseph
1916-
American senator; US presidential candidate,
1968, 1972

Bergstein, Eleanor
Advancing Paul Newman.
Viking 1973.
BRD 1974 p89; KR v41 1973 p900; LJ v98 1973
p3390; NYTBR N 18, 1973 p52.

Tauber, Peter
The Last Best Hope.
Harcourt Brace Jovanovich 1977.

BRD 1977 p1304; KR v45 1977 p689; LJ v102 1977
p1869; NYTBR S 11, 1977 p15.

950. McClellan, George Brinton
1826-1885
Union general in the Civil War

Robertson, Don
By Antietam Creek.
Prentice-Hall 1960.
BRD 1961 p1199; KR v28 1960 p465; LJ v85 1960
p2817; NYTBR O 2, 1960 p40.

951. McCormick, Cyrus Hall
1809-1884
American inventor of the reaper

Nathan, Adele
YA *Wheat Won't Wait.*
Aladdin Books 1952.
BL v49 1952 p92; BRD 1952 p659; KR v20 1952
p557; SatR O 11, 1952 p45.

952. McGovern, George Stanley
1922-
American senator; US presidential candidate,
1972

Max, Nicholas
President McGovern's First Term.
Doubleday 1973.
KR v41 1973 p363; LJ v98 1973 p1826; PW v203 Mr
19, 1973 p69.

953. McLoughlin, John
1784-1857
Canadian fur trader; helped to open Oregon to
permanent settlement

Allen, T. D.
YA *Doctor, Lawyer, Merchant, Chief.*
Westminster Press 1965.
LJ v90 1965 p2026.

Allen, T. D.
Troubled Border.
Harper 1954.
BL v50 1954 p419; KR v22 1954 p244; LJ v79 1954
p982; NYTBR Je 27, 1954 p20.

954. McPherson, Aimee Semple
1890-1944
American evangelist; founded International
Church of Foursquare Gospel

Barber, Elsie Marion
Jenny Angel.
Macmillan 1954.
BRD 1954 p42; KR v22 1954 p405; LJ v79 1954
p1511; NYTBR S 5, 1954 p11; SatR S 11, 1954 p58.

Chevigny, Hector
Woman of the Rock.
A.A. Wyn 1949.
BRD 1949 p161; LJ v74 1949 p311.

Otway, Howard
The Evangelist.
Harper 1954.
BRD 1954 p682; KR v22 1954 p501; LJ v79 1954
    p1826; NYTBR O 10, 1954 p36.

955. Medici, Lorenzo de
1449-1492
Florentine ruler & patron of art

Eliot, George
Romola.
Tauchnitz 1863 (Heavily reprinted).
BRD 1905 p112; BRD 1906 p96; FC 9th p160;
    NYTBR F 4, 1899 p69; NYTBR F 9, 1907 p88.

Ripley, Alexandra
The Time Returns.
Doubleday 1985.
BL v82 1985 p193; BS v45 O 1985 p251; KR v53
    1985 p668; PW v228 Ag 2, 1985 p58.

Shulman, Sandra
The Florentine.
Morrow 1973.
BL v69 1973 p792; KR v40 1972 p1444; LJ v98 1973
    p566.

Woodhouse, Martin; Ross, Robert
The Medici Emerald.
Dutton 1976.
LJ v102 1977 p129.

Woodhouse, Martin; Ross, Robert
The Medici Guns.
Dutton 1975.
KR v43 1975 p264; LJ v100 1975 p504.

Woodhouse, Martin; Ross, Robert
The Medici Hawks.
Dutton 1978.
KR v46 1978 p573; LJ v103 1978 p2009; PW v213
    My 29, 1978 p42.

956. Meir, Golda
1898-1978
First woman prime minister of Israel

Avallone, Michael
A Woman Called Golda.
Leisure 1982.

957. Melbourne, William Lamb, Viscount
1779-1848
British prime minister; favored adviser of Queen
Victoria

Hibbert, Eleanor (Jean Plaidy, pseud.)
The Queen and Lord M.

Hale 1973 (Rpr. 1977).
BL v74 1977 p141; BS v37 S 1977 p169; KR v45 1977
    p553; LJ v102 1977 p2082; PW v211 My 9, 1977
    p88.

Leslie, Doris
This for Caroline.
Heinemann 1964.

958. Melville, Herman
1819-1891
American author; wrote *Moby Dick*

Beaulieu, Victor Levy
Monsieur Melville.
VLB 1978.
Mac v92 Ap 2, 1979 p42.

Metcalf, Paul C.
Genoa: Telling of Wonders.
Nathala Foundation 1965.
NYTBR Je 19, 1966 p32.

Thorn, Michael
Pen Friends.
Macmillan 1988.

959. Mencken, H. L. (Henry Louis)
1880-1956
American editor & satirist

Swaim, Don
*The H. L. Mencken Murder Case: A Literary
    Thriller.*
St. Martin's 1988.
KR v56 1988 p1362; NYTBR D 11, 1988 p34; PW
    v234 S 30, 1988 p52.

960. Mendelssohn, Felix
1809-1847
German composer

La Mure, Pierre
*Beyond Desire: A Novel Based on the Life of Felix
    and Cecile Mendelssohn.*
Random House 1955.
BRD 1955 p523; KR v23 1955 p819; LJ v80 1955
    p2780; NYTBR N 13, 1955 p41.

961. Menendez de Aviles, Pedro
1519-1574
Spanish naval officer & colonizer; founded St.
Augustine, Florida

Cabell, James
*The First Gentlemen of America: A Comedy of
    Conquest.*
Farrar & Rinehart 1942.
BRD 1942 p116; NYTBR F 1, 1942 p6; SatR F 7,
    1942 p7.

962. Mengele, Josef
1911-1979
German Nazi leader

Rosenberger, Joseph
Caribbean Caper.
Manor Books 1974.

Waymire, Ray V.
The Mengele Hoax.
Winston-Derek Publishers 1990.

963. Meredith, George
1828-1909
English novelist & poet

Clarke, Anna
The Lady in Black: A Novel of Suspense.
McKay 1978.
KR v46 1978 p23.

964. Merton, Thomas
1915-1968
Trappist monk; wrote autobiography *Seven Storey Mountain*

Merton, Thomas
My Argument with the Gestapo.
Doubleday 1969.
KR v37 1969 p531; LJ v94 1969 p2641.

965. Mesmer, Franz Anton
1734-1815
German physician & originator of mesmerism

O'Doherty, Brian
The Strange Case of Mademoiselle P..
Pantheon 1992.
BL v88 1992 p1585; KR v60 1992 p562; LJ v117 My 1, 1992 p119; NYTBR Ag 23, 1992 p16.

966. Metternich-Winneburg, Clemens
1773-1859
Austrian political leader

Cartland, Barbara
The Enchanted Waltz.
Hutchinson 1955 (1975).

Hershan, Stella K.
The Naked Angel.
Pinnacle Books 1971.

967. Michelangelo Buonarroti
1475-1564
Italian painter & sculptor

Alexander, Sidney
The Hand of Michelangelo.
Ohio University Press 1977.

Alexander, Sidney
Michelangelo, the Florentine.
Random House 1957 (Rpr. 1965, 1985).
BRD 1957 p12; KR v25 1957 p656; LJ v82 1957 p3207; NYTBR N 17, 1957 p54.

Alexander, Sidney
Nicodemus: The Roman Years of Michelangelo Buonarroti.
Ohio University Press 1984.
BL v81 1985 p756; NYTBR Ja 27, 1985 p22; PW v226 O 12, 1984 p38; TLS Jl 12, 1985 p776.

Stone, Irving
The Agony and the Ecstasy.
Doubleday 1961 (Heavily reprinted).
BL v57 1961 p423; BRD 1961 p1364; KR v29 1961 p67; LJ v86 1961 p1480; NYTBR Mr 19, 1961 p6.

Stone, Irving
JUV *The Great Adventure of Michelangelo.*
Doubleday 1965.
An abridged illustrated edition of *The Agony and the Ecstacy* especially for young readers.
BRD 1965 p1205; LJ v90 1965 p2025; NYTBR Mr 14, 1965 p30; SatR My 15, 1965 p56.

968. Miles, Nelson Appleton
1839-1925
American military leader; commanded forces at Wounded Knee massacre

Burnett, William Riley
Adobe Walls: A Novel of the Last Apache Rising.
Knopf 1953.
BL v50 1953 p34; BRD 1953 p138; KR v21 1953 p314; LJ v78 1953 p1330; NYTBR Ag 16, 1953 p4.

Haines, William Wister
The Winter War.
Little, Brown 1961.
BL v57 1961 p490; BRD 1961 p567; KR v28 1960 p1045; LJ v86 1961 p112; NYTBR Ap 16, 1961 p35.

Van Every, Dale
The Day the Sun Died.
Little, Brown 1971.
FC 9th p526; KR v39 1971 p76; LJ v96 1971 p502; LJ v96 1971 p2146.

969. Millais, John Everett, Sir
1829-1896
English painter

Hale, John
The Love School.
St. Martin's 1975.
BS v36 N 1976 p246.

McDonald, Eva
John Ruskin's Wife.
Hale 1979 (Rpr. 1991).

970. Milton, John
1608-1674
English poet

Figes, Eva
The Tree of Knowledge.
Pantheon 1990.
BL v87 1991 p1452; KR v58 1990 p1356; LJ v116 Mr
   1, 1991 p116; NYTBR Je 16, 1991 p20; PW v238 F
   22, 1991 p209.

Fuller, Edmund
YA *John Milton*.
Harper & Brothers 1944 (Rpr. 1967).
BRD 1944 p266; BRD 1967 p464; LJ v69 1944 p887;
   LJ v92 1967 p2659.

Graves, Robert
Wife to Mr. Milton; the Story of Marie Powell.
Creative Age Press 1944 (Rpr. 1962, 1979).
BRD 1944 p295.

971. Mindszenty, Jozsef, Cardinal
1892-1975
Hungarian cardinal; imprisoned by Communists

Arnothy, Christine
The Captive Cardinal.
Doubleday 1964.
LJ v89 1964 p3034.

972. Mineo, Sal
1939-1976
American actor & singer

Braudy, Susan
Who Killed Sal Mineo?.
Wyndham Books 1982.
KR v50 1982 p216; LJ v107 1982 p1008; NYTBR My
   30, 1982 p9.

973. Mix, Tom
1880-1940
American actor; starred in hundreds of western
films

Irving, Clifford
Tom Mix and Pancho Villa.
St. Martin's 1982.
BL v78 1982 p985; KR v50 1982 p438; LJ v107 1982
   p1010; NYTBR Ag 8, 1982 p13; PW v221 Ap 23,
   1982 p88.

Ponicsan, Darryl
Tom Mix Died for Your Sins.
Delacorte 1975.
KR v43 1975 p871; PW v208 Ag 25, 1975 p285.

974. Moberg, Vilhelm
1898-1973
Swedish author

Moberg, Vilhelm
When I Was a Child.
Knopf 1956.
BRD 1956 p651; KR v24 1956 p93; LJ v81 1956 p716;
   NYTBR Mr 18, 1956 p4.

975. Modigliani, Amedeo
1884-1920
Italian painter

Longstreet, Stephen
The Young Men of Paris.
Delacorte Press 1967.
KR v35 1967 p900; LJ v92 1967 p2943.

Wight, Frederick S.
Verge of Glory.
Harcourt, Brace 1956.
KR v24 1956 p540; LJ v81 1956 p2254.

Wilmot, Anthony
The Last Bohemian: A Novel about Modigliani.
Macdonald & Jane's 1975.
CR v227 O 1975 p216.

Wittlin, Tadeusz
Modigliani: Prince of Montparnasse.
Bobbs-Merrill 1964.
LJ v90 1965 p896.

976. Mohammed
570-632
Prophet; founder of Islam

Hoyt, Edwin Palmer
The Voice of Allah.
J. Day 1970.
KR v38 1970 p274; KR v38 1970 p704; LJ v95 1970
   p1502; PW v197 Mr 16, 1970 p55.

977. Moliere
1622-1673
French dramatist

Arnott, Peter D.
Ballet of Comedians.
Macmillan 1971.
BL v68 1971 p34; KR v39 1971 p602; LJ v96 1971
   p2788.

O'Shaughnessy, Michael
Monsieur Moliere: A Novel.
Crowell 1959.
BRD 1959 p771; LJ v84 1959 p1627; NYTBR Ap 5,
   1959 p38; SatR My 9, 1959 p17.

Thoorens, Leon
The King's Players.
Elek Books 1960.

978. Mona Lisa
see Gioconda, Lisa Gherardini

979. Monet, Claude-Oscar
1840-1926
French impressionist painter

Bjork, Christina
JUV *Linnea in Monet's Garden.*
R. & S. Books 1987.
BL v84 1987 p626; BRD 1988 p155; PW v232 O 30,
1987 p71; SLJ v34 F 1988 p72.

Figes, Eva
Light.
Pantheon 1983.
BRD 1984 p494; KR v51 1983 p830; LJ v108 1983
p2171; NYTBR O 16, 1983 p11.

Howard, Elizabeth
YA *A Scent of Murder.*
Random House 1987.
SLJ v34 O 1987 p139.

980. Mongkut
1804-1868
King of Siam, 1804-1868

Landon, Margaret
Anna and the King of Siam.
J. Day 1944.
BL v40 1944 p376; BRD 1944 p435; KR v12 1944
p241; NYTBR Jl 9, 1944 p3.

981. Monmouth, James Scott, Duke
1649-1685
English political leader & rebel; led unsuccesful
uprising against James II; beheaded

Ansle, Dorothy P. (Hebe Elsna, pseud.)
The King's Bastard.
Collins 1971 (Rpr. 1982).

McDonald, Eva
The Maids of Taunton.
Hale 1963 (Rpr. 1980).

982. Monroe, Marilyn
1926-1962
American actress; died of drug overdose

Korda, Michael
The Immortals: A Novel.
Poseidon Press 1992.
BL v88 1992 p1972; KR v60 1992 p870; LJ v117 Ag
1992 p149; NYTBR S 13, 1992 p9.

Mailer, Norman
Of Women and Their Elegance.
Simon & Schuster 1980.
BRD 1981 p922; LJ v106 1981 p166; NYTBR D 7,
1980 p11.

Rechy, John
Marilyn's Daughter.
Carroll & Graf 1988.

BL v84 1988 p1755; KR v56 1988 p852; NYTBR N 6,
1988 p22.

Staggs, Sam
MM II: The Return of Marilyn Monroe.
D.I. Fine 1991.
BL v87 1991 p1008; KR v58 1990 p1705; LJ v116 F 1,
1991 p107; PW v237 D 7, 1990 p70.

Toperoff, Sam
Queen of Desire.
HarperCollins 1992.
BL v88 1991 p476; KR v59 1991 p1310; LJ v116 D
1991 p201; NYTBR My 3, 1992 p18; PW v238 O
18, 1991 p51.

983. Montagu, Mary Wortley, Lady
1689-1762
English author

Leslie, Doris
A Toast to Lady Mary.
Hutchinson 1954.

Lewis, Hilda
A Toast to Lady Mary.
Heinemann 1968.

984. Montcalm, Louis Joseph de
1712-1759
French general; defeated by Wolfe at Quebec,
1759

Elwood, Muriel
Web of Destiny.
Manor Books 1951.
BRD 1951 p268.

Hays, Wilma Pitchford
JUV *Drummer Boy for Montcalm.*
Viking 1959.
BL v56 1960 p358; BRD 1960 p620; CC 11th p359;
KR v27 1959 p452; LJ v85 1960 p351; NYTBR O
18, 1959 p46.

985. Montez, Lola
1818-1861
Irish dancer & adventuress

Fraser, George MacDonald
Royal Flash.
Knopf 1970.
FC 11th p215; LJ v95 1970 p2715; NYTBR O 18,
1970 p4; Time v96 O 5, 1970 p92.

Marshall, Edison
The Infinite Woman.
Farrar, Straus 1950.
BL v47 1950 p115; BRD 1950 p613; KR v18 1950
p530; LJ v75 1950 p1661; NYTBR D 24, 1950 p11.

Stern, Philip Van Doren
Lola: A Love Story.
Rinehart 1949.

BRD 1949 p876; KR v17 1949 p69; LJ v74 1949 p496;
NYTBR Ap 17, 1949 p18.

986. Montezuma II
1480-1520
Last Aztec emperor of Mexico; conquered by
Cortes

Appel, Benjamin
JUV *We Were There with Cortes and Montezuma.*
Grosset & Dunlap 1959.

Madariaga, Salvado de
The Heart of Jade.
Creative Age Press 1944.
BRD 1944 p493; KR v11 1943 p558; LJ v69 1944
p160; NYTBR Ap 2, 1944 p5.

987. Montfort, Simon de
1208-1265
English soldier & political leader

Bennetts, Pamela
The De Montfort Legacy.
St. Martin's 1973.
B&B v18 Jl 1973 p135; BL v70 1973 p207; KR v41
1973 p265.

Duggan, Alfred Leo
Leopards and Lilies.
Coward-McCann 1954.
BL v51 1954 p108; BRD 1954 p264; KR v22 1954
p502; NYTBR O 10, 1954 p5.

Dymoke, Juliet
The Royal Griffin
Ace Books 1978.

Gibbs, Willa
Simon of Leicester.
Hodder & Stoughton 1960 (Rpr. 1973).

Graham, Alice Walworth
Shield of Honor.
Doubleday 1957.
BRD 1957 p958; FC 7th p158; KR v25 1957 p453; LJ
v82 1957 p2038.

Penman, Sharon Kay
YA *Falls the Shadow.*
Holt 1988.
BL v84 1988 p1202; KR v56 1988 p396; LJ v113 Jl
1988 p96; SLJ v35 S 1988 p211.

Sudworth, Gwynedd
The Bright Sword.
Hale 1974.

Trease, Geoffrey
JUV *The Baron's Hostage.*
T. Nelson 1975.
BL v72 1975 p459; KR v43 1975 p667; LJ v78 1953
p1340; SLJ v22 S 1975 p127.

Trevaskis, Eve
The Lion of England.
Hale 1975 (Rpr. 1979).

988. Montgolfier, Jacques Etienne
1745-1799
French balloonist; invented the first practical
hot air balloon with his brother Joseph Montgol-
fier

Birchman, David F.
JUV *Victorious Paints the Great Balloon.*
Bradbury Press 1991.
BL v88 1991 p695; SLJ v37 O 1991 p119.

989. Moore, Clement Clarke
1779-1863
American poet & author; wrote *A Visit from St.
Nicholas*

Turner, Thyra
JUV *Christmas House.*
Scribner 1943.
BRD 1943 p819; CC 7th p1031; HB v19 N 1943 p401.

990. Moore, Thomas
1779-1852
Irish poet

Brophy, John
Sarah: A Novel.
Collins 1948.

991. More, Thomas, Sir
1478-1535
English chancellor and author; wrote *Utopia*;
canonized in 1935

Beahn, John E.
A Man Born Again: Saint Thomas More.
Bruce Pub. Co. 1954.

Brady, Charles A.
Stage of Fools.
Dutton 1953.
BL v49 1953 p213; BRD 1953 p102; FC 8th p51; KR
v21 1953 p55; LJ v78 1953 p444; NYTBR Ap 5,
1953 p19.

Hibbert, Eleanor (Jean Plaidy, pseud.)
St. Thomas's Eve.
Hale 1954 (Rpr. 1970).
BS v30 D 15, 1970 p407.

Ince, Elizabeth M.
St. Thomas More of London.
Vision Books 1957.

992. Morgan, Daniel
1736-1802
American Revolutionary general

Barry, Jane
The Long March.
Appleton-Century-Crofts 1955.
BL v52 1956 p189; BRD 1956 p54; KR v23 1955
 p671; LJ v80 1955 p2611.

Davis, Burke
The Ragged One.
Rinehart 1951.
BL v47 1951 p301; BRD 1951 p222; KR v19 1951
 p138; NYTBR My 13, 1951 p18.

Dwight, Allan
JUV *Morgan's Long Rifles.*
Putnam 1965.
BRD 1965 p1230; LJ v90 1965 p2424; NYTBR Jl 18,
 1965 p22.

993. Morgan, Henry, Sir
1635-1688
British pirate

Cochran, Hamilton
Windward Passage: A Novel.
Bobbs-Merrill 1942.
BRD 1942 p151.

Dalgheish, James
The Plunderers.
Hale 1975.

Mason, F. van Wyck
Cutlass Empire.
Doubleday 1949.
BL v45 1949 p170; BRD 1949 p615; FC 7th p241; KR
 v17 1949 p8; LJ v74 1949 p377; NYTBR Mr 20,
 1949 p20.

Monjo, F. N.
JUV *Pirates in Panama.*
Simon & Schuster 1970.
KR v38 1970 p1093; LJ v96 1971 p2144.

Nicole, Christopher
The Devil's Own.
St. Martin's 1975.
KR v43 1975 p937; LJ v100 1975 p1570.

Steinbeck, John
Cup of Gold.
R.M. McBride 1929 (Heavily reprinted).
BRD 1929 p911.

Tey, Josephine (Gordon Daviot, pseud.)
The Privateer.
Macmillan 1952.
BRD 1952 p588; FC 7th p99; LJ v77 1952 p1191;
 NYTBR Ag 24, 1952 p17.

994. Morgan, J. P. (John Pierpont)
1837-1913
American financier; formed US Steel Corp.

Doctorow, E. L.
Ragtime.

Random House 1975.
BL v72 1975 p24; BRD 1975 p338; BRD 1976 p313;
 KR v43 1975 p529; LJ v100 1975 p1344; NYTBR Jl
 6, 1975 p1.

Page, Martin
The Man Who Stole the Mona Lisa.
Pantheon 1984.
BL v81 1984 p192; KR v52 1984 p648; LJ v109 1984
 p1773; PW v226 Jl 20, 1984 p69.

995. Morphy, Paul Charles
1837-1884
American chess player; world champion, 1858-
1862

Keyes, Frances Parkinson
The Chess Players.
Farrar, Straus and Cudahy 1960.
BL v57 F 15, 1961 p353; BRD 1961 p757; FC 9th
 p294; KR v28 O 15, 1960 p909; NYTBR Ja 22,
 1961 p33; Time v76 D26, 1960 p58.

996. Morris, Gouverneur
1752-1816
American patriot & diplomat

Bentley, Barbara
Mistress Nancy.
McGraw-Hill 1980.
KR v48 1980 p921; LJ v105 1980 p1750.

Stover, Herbert E.
Song of the Susquehanna.
Dodd, Mead 1949.
BL v45 1949 p338; BRD 1949 p885; NYTBR My 15,
 1949 p21; SatR Je 4, 1949 p2.

997. Morris, Robert
1734-1806
American patriot & financier; signed Declaration of Independence

Benchley, Nathaniel
Portrait of a Scoundrel.
Doubleday 1979.
BL v75 1979 p911; BRD 1979 p95; KR v46 1978
 p1368; LJ v104 1979 p207.

Taylor, David
Mistress of the Forge.
Lippincott 1964.
FC 9th p501; LJ v89 1964 p1117; LJ v89 1964 p2246;
 NYTBR Ap 12, 1964 p37.

998. Morrison, Jim (James Douglas)
1943-1971
American rock star; lead singer for the group,
"The Doors"

Strete, Craig Kee
Burn Down the Night.
Warner 1982.

BL v78 1982 p1226; BS v42 S 1982 p225; KR v50
1982 p444; LJ v107 1982 p1099; PW v221 Ap 30,
1982 p56.

999. Morton, "Jelly Roll" (Joseph Ferdinand)

1885-1941

American jazz musician

Charters, Samuel B.
Jelly Roll Morton's Last Night at the Jungle Inn:
An Imaginary Memoir.
M. Boyars 1984.
Choice v21 1984 p1474; KR v51 1983 p1262; LJ v109
1984 p386.

1000. Morton, William Thomas Green

1819-1868

American dentist; introduced use of ether for anesthesia

Baker, Rachel
YA *Dr. Morton, Pioneer in the Use of Ether.*
Messner 1946.
BRD 1946 p36; KR v14 1946 p73; LJ v71 1946 p669;
NYTBR Ap 14, 1946 p36.

1001. Mosby, John Singleton

1833-1916

Confederate soldier; best known for his raids on
Union outposts with group called "Mosby's
Rangers"

Hogan, Ray
The Ghost Raider.
Pyramid Books 1960.

Hogan, Ray
Mosby's Last Ride.
Curley Publishing 1966 (Rpr. 1989).

Hogan, Ray
The Night Raider.
Avon 1964 (Rpr. 1991).

Icenhower, Joseph B.
YA *The Scarlet Raider.*
Chilton 1961.
BRD 1961 p681; KR v29 1961 p57; LJ v86 1961
p1328; NYTBR My 14, 1961 p6.

Lagard, Garald
Scarlet Cockerel.
Morrow 1948.
BRD 1948 p470; KR v16 1948 p374.

Skimin, Robert
Gray Victory.
St. Martin's 1988.
BL v84 1988 p1096; KR v56 1988 p15; LJ v113 Mr 1,
1988 p79; SLJ v35 D 1988 p132.

1002. Moses

Hebrew prophet & lawgiver; delivered Ten
Commandments to the Israelites

Alloway, Lawrence
Moses the Man.
Vantage Press 1951.

Asch, Sholem
Moses.
Putnam 1951.
BRD 1951 p28; FC 11th p24; LJ v76 1951 p1219;
NYTBR S 23, 1951 p5.

Bell, Sallie Lee
The Bond Slave.
Zondervan 1957.

Bercovici, Konrad
The Exodus.
Beechhurst Press 1947.
BRD 1947 p67; NYTBR My 25, 1947 p3; SatR Ag 23,
1947 p32.

Burnshaw, Stanley
The Refusers: An Epic of the Jews.
Horizon Press 1981.
BRD 1982 p190; KR v49 1981 p1094; LJ v106 1981
p2152; NYTBR Ap 4, 1982 p18.

Fast, Howard
Moses, Prince of Egypt.
Crown 1958.
BRD 1959 p347; FC 8th p142; LJ v83 1958 p606;
NYTBR Mr 23, 1958 p38; SatR Mr 29, 1958 p25.

Gentile, Frank J.
Moses and Nefertiti: The God's Heart Is Pleased.
Vantage Press 1992.

Grant, Joan Marshall
So Moses Was Born.
Methuen 1952 (Rpr. 1980).

Graves, Robert
My Head! My Head!.
M. Secker 1928 (Rpr. 1974).
BRD 1925 p273.

Hardy, W. G.
All the Trumpets Sounded.
Coward-McCann 1942.
BL v39 1942 p102; BRD 1942 p329; LJ v67 1942
p476; NYTBR Jl 26, 1942 p17; WLB v38 D 1942
p187.

Hareven, Shulamith
YA *The Miracle Hater: A Novel.*
North Point Press 1988.
BL v84 1988 p1220; KR v56 1988 p227; LJ v113 Mr
15, 1988 p66; NYTBR Je 12, 1988 p16.

Hayward, Linda
JUV *Baby Moses.*
Random House 1989.
BL v85 1989 p1728; BRD 1990 p791; SLJ v35 D 1989
p95.

Hoffmann, Poul
The Eternal Fire.
Muhlenberg Press 1962.
LJ v87 1962 p2917.

Hurston, Zora N.
Moses, Man of the Mountain.
Lippincott 1939 (Rpr. 1984, 1991).
Also published as *The Man of the Mountain.*
BRD 1939 p490; NYTBR N 19, 1939 p21; SatR N11,
1939 p11.

Ilton, Paul
Moses and the Ten Commandments.
Dell 1956.

Jenks, Kathleen
*The River and the Stone: Mose's Early Years in
Egypt.*
Dutton 1977.
BL v73 1977 p1327; KR v44 1976 p1236.

Keneally, Thomas
Moses the Lawgiver.
Harper & Row 1975.
GW v114 Mr 7, 1976 p22.

Kolb, Leon
Moses, the Near Eastener.
Genuart Co. 1956.

Lawrence, Joan
The Scapegoat: A Life of Moses.
P. Owen 1988.
PW v235 F 17, 1989 p68.

Leibert, Julius A.
The Lawgiver: A Novel about Moses.
Exposition Press 1953.

Levner, I. B.
The Legends of Israel.
J. Clarke 1946.
Volume 2 contains *From the Birth to the Death of Moses.*

Mann, Thomas
The Tables of the Law.
Knopf 1945.
BRD 1945 p465; KR v13 1945 p193.

Sandmel, Samuel
Alone atop the Mountain.
Doubleday 1973.
KR v41 1973 p273; LJ v98 1973 p1511; PW v203 Mr
12, 1973 p63.

Shippen, Katherine B.
JUV *Moses.*
Harper 1949.
BRD 1949 p837; NYTBR F 12, 1940 p18.

Southon, Arthur E.
On Eagle's Wings.
Cassell 1937 (Rpr. 1954).
BRD 1954 p828.

Synge, Ursula
JUV *The People and the Promise.*

S.G. Phillips 1974.
SLJ v21 Mr 1975 p110.

Traylor, Ellen G.
Moses, the Deliverer.
Harvest House 1990.

Wilson, Dorothy Clarke
Prince of Egypt.
Westminster Press 1949.
BRD 1949 p998; FC 8th p443; LJ v74 1949 p1204;
NYTBR N 6, 1949 p28.

1003. Mosley, Oswald Ernald, Sir
1896-1980
English politician

Royce, Kenneth
The Mosley Receipt.
Hodder & Stoughton 1985.
KR v53 1985 p419; NYTBR Je 16, 1985 p25; PW
v227 Ap 19, 1985 p69.

1004. Mott, Lucretia Coffin
1793-1880
American reformer; prominent figure in
women's rights movement in the US

Burnett, Constance Buel
JUV *Lucretia Mott, Girl of Old Nantucket.*
Bobbs-Merrill 1951.
LJ v76 1951 p1573.

Malm, Dorothea
The Woman Question.
Appleton-Century-Crofts 1957.
BL v55 1958 p23; BRD 1958 p712; KR v26 1958 p92;
LJ v83 1958 p2079.

1005. Mountbatten of Burma, Louis Mountbatten, Earl
1900-1979
British naval officer; Viceroy of India

Butler, David
Lord Mountbatten: The Last Viceroy.
Methuen 1985.
BW v16 F 2, 1986 p12.

Cartland, Barbara
Love at the Helm.
Everest House 1981.
BL v77 1981 p1186; KR v49 1981 p370.

Tharoor, Shashi
The Great Indian Novel.
Viking 1989.
BRD 1991 p1837; KR v59 1991 p76; LJ v116 Mr 1,
1991 p118; NYTBR Mr 24, 1991 p16.

1006. Mozart, Wolfgang Amadeus
1756-1791
Austrian composer

Brenneis, Mary A.
JUV *Sky Racket*.
M.W. Cunningham 1989.

Glover, Cedric
The Mysterious Barricades.
Times Press 1964.

Grun, Bernard
The Golden Quill: A Novel Based on the Life of Mozart.
Putnam 1956.
BRD 1956 p391; KR v24 1956 p645; LJ v82 1957 p86; SatR N 3, 1956 p35.

Hersey, John
Antonietta: A Novel.
Knopf 1991.
BL v87 1991 p1435; KR v59 1991 p422; LJ v116 My 15, 1991 p108; NYTBR My 19, 1991 p13; PW v238 Mr 29, 1991 p76.

Kaufmann, Helen
JUV *The Story of Mozart*.
Grosset & Dunlap 1955.
BRD 1955 p483; KR v23 1955 p38; NYTBR Jl 24, 1955 p18.

Mayo, Waldo
YA *Mozart: His Life Told in Anecdotal Form*.
Hyperion Press 1945.
BRD 1945 p482; NYTBR Je 10, 1945 p18; SatR Je 16, 1945 p39.

Monjo, F. N.
JUV *Letters to Horseface: Young Mozart's Travels in Italy*.
Viking 1975 (Rpr. 1991).
PW v238 My 1991 p65.

Morike, Eduard F.
Mozart on the Way to Prague.
Pantheon 1947.
BRD 1948 p599; LJ v72 1947 p1612.

Neider, Charles
Mozart and the Archbooby.
Penguin 1991.
BL v87 1991 p2101; LJ v116 Ag 1991 p146; PW v238 Jl 25, 1991 p46.

Sava, George
Austrian Concerto: A Romantic Life of Mozart.
W. Laurie 1952.

Weiss, David
The Assassination of Mozart.
Morrow 1971.
LJ v95 1970 p2830; NYTBR Ap 4, 1971 p48; PW v225 O 3, 1970 p370.

Weiss, David
Sacred and Profane: A Novel of the Life and Times of Mozart.
Morrow 1968.

BL v65 1969 p483; BRD 1969 p1385; KR v36 1968 p781; LJ v93 1968 p2693; NYTBR D 8, 1968 p76; PW v194 Jl 22, 1968 p55.

1007. Mudgett, Herman W.
d. 1896
American murderer; believed to have killed more than 200 people

Bloch, Robert
American Gothic.
Simon & Schuster 1974.
BL v70 1974 p1080; KR v42 1974 p269; NYTBR Je 30, 1974 p32; PW v205 Ja 21, 1974 p81.

Eckert, Allan W.
The Scarlet Mansion.
Little, Brown 1985.
KR v53 1985 p435; LJ v110 Je 1, 1985 p142; PW v227 My 3, 1985 p67.

1008. Mussolini, Benito
1883-1945
Italian Fascist leader; premier & dictator; executed

Botsford, Keith
Benvenuto.
Hutchinson 1961.

Gallo, Max
With the Victors.
Doubleday 1974.
LJ v99 1974 p2982; NYTBR O 6, 1974 p40.

Garnet, Eldon
I Shot Mussolini.
Impulse Editions 1989.
BIC Mr 1990 p48.

Gelb, Alan
Mussolini.
Pocket Books 1985.
Based on the screenplay by Stirling Silliphant.

Lee, John
Lago.
Doubleday 1980.
BL v76 1980 p1492; KR v48 1980 p465.

Moravia, Alberto
The Fancy Dress Party.
Farrar, Straus & Young 1952.
BRD 1952 p713; KR v20 1952 p327; LJ v77 1952 p1012; NYTBR Jl 27, 1952 p5.

1009. Napoleon I
1769-1821
Emperor of France; overthrown at the Battle of Waterloo

Anthony, Evelyn
Far Flies the Eagle.
Crowell 1955.

BL v51 1955 p468; BRD 1955 p862; KR v23 1955
  p335; LJ v80 1955 p1381; NYTBR Jl 17, 1955 p18.

Bankoff, George A. (George Sava, pseud.)
The Beloved Nemesis.
Hale 1971.

Bell, Neil
A Romance in Lavender: A Novel.
Hale 1946 (Rpr. 1975).

Burgess, Anthony
Napoleon Symphony.
Knopf 1974.
BRD 1974 p165; FC 9th p76; LJ v99 1974 p1406;
  NYTBR Je 9, 1974 p5.

Carr, John D.
Captain Cut-Throat.
Harper 1955 (Rpr. 1980, 1988).
BL v51 1955 p290; BRD 1955 p150; KR v23 1955
  p96; NYTBR Ap 3, 1955 p28.

Chambers, Rosamund M.
Little Creole: A Story of Napoleon and Josephine.
Cassell 1952.

Coryn, Marjorie
Alone among Men.
Appleton-Century 1947.
BL v44 1947 p50; BRD 1947 p194; KR v15 1947
  p402; LJ v72 1947 p1193; NYTBR D 28, 1947 p18.

Coryn, Marjorie
Good-bye, My Son.
Appleton-Century 1943.
BL v39 1943 p293; BRD 1943 p178; LJ v68 1943
  p128; NYTBR F 21, 1943 p20.

Coryn, Marjorie
The Marriage of Josephine.
Appleton-Century 1945.
BRD 1945 p153; KR v13 1945 p380; LJ v70 1945
  p1026.

Costain, Thomas B.
The Last Love.
Doubleday 1963.
BRD 1963 p228; FC 11th p133; LJ v88 1963 p4492;
  NYTBR S 15, 1963 p49.

Delmar, Vina
A Time for Titans.
Harcourt Brace Jovanovich 1974.
FC 9th p130; KR v42 1974 p69; LJ v99 1974 p774;
  PW v205 Ja 21, 1975 p79.

Doyle, Arthur Conan
Uncle Bernac: A Memory of the Empire.
Tauchnitz 1897 (Heavily reprinted).

Eaton, Evelyn
In What Torn Ship.
Harper & Brothers 1944.
BRD 1944 p217; KR v12 1944 p179; LJ v69 1944
  p502; NYTBR Jl 9, 1944 p12.

Fecher, Constance
The Night of the Wolf.
Hale 1972.
KR v42 1974 p1074; LJ v100 1975 p310.

Gerson, Noel Bertram
The Emperor's Ladies.
Doubleday 1959.
BL v56 1959 p242; BRD 1960 p519; KR v27 1959
  p415.

Gibbs, Willa
Tell Your Sons: A Novel of the Napoleonic Era.
Farrar, Straus 1946.
BRD 1946 p309; KR v14 1946 p306; NYTBR O 13,
  1946 p20.

Golubov, Sergei
*No Easy Victories: A Novel of General Bagration
  and the Campaign of 1812.*
Hutchinson 1945.
Also published as *Bragration: The Honour and Glory.*

Herbert, Alan Patrick
Why Waterloo?.
Doubleday 1953.
BRD 1953 p422; KR v20 1952 p731; LJ v78 1953 p54;
  NYTBR Ja 11, 1953 p30.

Kane, Harnett T.
*The Amazing Mrs. Bonaparte: A Novel Based on
  the Life of Betsy Patterson.*
Doubleday 1963.
FC 9th p285; LJ v88 Ap 15, 1963 p1686.

Kenyon, Frank Wilson
*The Emperor's Lady: A Novel Based on the Life of
  the Empress Josephine.*
Crowell 1953.
BRD 1953 p506; KR v21 1953 p198; NYTBR My 31,
  1953 p11; SatR Je 13, 1953 p17.

Kenyon, Frank Wilson
*My Brother Napoleon: The Confessions of
  Caroline Bonaparte.*
Dodd, Mead 1971.

Lambert, Derek (Richard Falkirk, pseud.)
Blackstone and the Scourge of Europe.
Stein & Day 1974.
BL v71 1974 p405; KR v42 1974 p965; LJ v99 1974
  p3150; NYTBR Ja 5, 1975 p24.

Landells, Richard
Night of Napoleon.
Hale 1972.

Leys, Simon
The Death of Napoleon.
Farrar, Straus, Giroux 1991.
KR v60 1992 p804; LJ v117 Ag 1992 p150.

Lofts, Norah
*A Rose for Virtue: The Very Private Life of
  Hortense, Stepdaughter of Napoleon I.*
Doubleday 1971.

BL v68 1971 p319; FC 11th p379; KR v39 1971 p829; PW v200 Ag 9, 1971 p40.

Long, Freda M.
The Hundred Days.
Hale 1975.

Mackie, Philip
Napoleon and Love.
Quartet Books 1974.

Malvern, Gladys
YA *Stephanie.*
Macrae Smith 1956.
BL v52 1956 p391; BRD 1956 p608; KR v24 1956 p77; LJ v81 1956 p1553.

Manceron, Claude
So Brief a Spring.
Putnam 1958.
BL v54 1958 p414; BRD 1958 p714; FC 7th p233; KR v25 1957 p912; LJ v83 1958 p765.

McKenney, Ruth
Mirage.
Farrar, Straus & Cudahy 1956.
BRD 1956 p598; KR v24 1956 p718; LJ v81 1956 p2959; NYTBR D 2, 1956 p66.

Moxon, Lloyd
Before the Wind.
Doubleday 1978.

Powers, Anne
The Thousand Fires.
Bobbs-Merrill 1957.
NYTBR Jl 14, 1957 p24.

Quigley, Aileen
Empress to the Eagle.
Hale 1975.

Raymond, John F.
JUV *The Marvelous March of Jean Francois.*
Doubleday 1965.
LJ v90 1965 p4619; NYTBR N 7, 1965 p55.

Robbins, Ruth
JUV *The Emperor and the Drummer Boy.*
Parnassus Press 1962.
BRD 1963 p852; HB v38 D 1962 p596; LJ v88 1963 p346; LJ v88 1963 p4431; NYTBR Oct 21, 1962 p46.

Schonthan, Gaby von
Madame Casanova.
Meredith Press 1969.
LJ v94 1969 p4026.

Selinko, Annemarie
Desiree.
Morrow 1953.
BL v49 1952 p133; BRD 1953 p843; FC 11th p543; KR v20 1952 p513; LJ v78 1953 p55; NYTBR Ja 18, 1953 p25.

Smith, Frederick E.
Waterloo.
Award Books 1970.

Taylor, Margaret Stewart
Napoleon's Captor.
Hale 1971.

Tolstoy, Leo
War and Peace.
Gottesberger 1886 (Heavily reprinted).
Translation of *Voina i Mir.*

Turnbull, Patrick
A Phantom Called Glory.
Hutchinson 1961.

Unwin, Monica
The Tragic Empress.
Hale 1970.
TLS Ag 21, 1970 p934.

Vernon, John
Peter Doyle: A Novel.
Random House 1991.
BL v87 1991 p980; KR v59 1991 p212; LJ v116 Mr 15, 1991 p119; NYTBR Jl 14, 1991 p9.

Wheatley, Dennis
The Wanton Princess.
Hutchinson 1966.

Wheelwright, Jere H.
Draw Near to Battle.
Scribner 1953.
BL v49 1953 p205; BRD 1953 p998; KR v20 1952 p774; LJ v78 1953 p147; NYTBR F 8, 1953 p24.

Wilkins, William V.
Being Met Together.
Macmillan 1944.
BRD 1944 p813; KR v12 1944 p181; LJ v69 1944 p651; NYTBR S 3, 1944 p5.

Winwar, Frances
The Eagle and the Rock.
Harper 1953.
BL v49 1953 p341; BRD 1953 p1019; KR v21 1953 p158; NYTBR My 3, 1953 p21.

1010. Napoleon III

1808-1873
Emperor of France, 1852-1870; deposed

Boas, Maurits I.
Decisions and the Furies: Two Narratives of Napoleonic Times.
F. Fell 1975.

Kenyon, Frank Wilson
Imperial Courtesan.
Dodd, Mead 1967.
BS v27 Ag 1, 1967 p172; PW v191 Je 12, 1967 p56.

Kenyon, Frank Wilson
That Spanish Woman.
Dodd, Mead 1962.

First published with the title *I, Eugenia*.
FC 9th p293.

Lowndes, Marie A.
She Dwelt with Beauty.
Macmillan 1949.

Wagner, Geoffrey
Nicchia, a Novel.
Ward, Lock 1958.
LJ v84 1959 p3154.

1011. Nasser, Gamal Abdel
1918-1970
Egyptian president of the United Arab Republic, 1958-1970

Aldridge, James
The Last Exile.
Doubleday 1961.
BL v58 1961 p190; BRD 1962 p15; FC 8th p6; LJ v86 1961 p3296; NYTBR O 1, 1961 p4.

1012. Nast, Thomas
1840-1902
American caricaturist

Veglahn, Nancy
YA *The Tiger's Tail: A Story of America's Great Political Cartoonist*.
Harper & Row 1964.
BRD 1965 p1285; LJ v90 1964 p3501; NYTBR Ja 17, 1965 p38.

1013. Nebuchadnezzar II
d. 562? BC
King of Babylon

Garfield, Leon
JUV *The King in the Garden*.
Lothrop, Lee & Shepard 1984.

Petty, Thurman C.
Gate of the Gods.
Pacific Press Pub. Association 1991.

1014. Nefertiti
1390-1360 BC
Queen of Egypt

Drury, Allen
A God against the Gods.
Doubleday 1976.
BL v72 1976 p1451; LJ v101 1976 p1554; PW v209 My 17, 1976 p46.

Gentile, Frank J.
Moses and Nefertiti: The God's Heart Is Pleased.
Vantage Press 1992.

Hamilton, Alexandra
Nefertiti the Beautiful One.

F. Muller 1979.
Obs F 11, 1979 p37.

Hamilton, Alexandra
Nefertiti, the Lady of Grace.
F. Muller 1979.

Hawkes, Jacquetta
King of the Two Lands: The Pharaoh Akhenaten.
Random House 1966.
BRD 1967 p579; KR v34 1966 p856; LJ v91 1966 p4696; NYTBR Ja 22, 1967 p40.

Patterson, Emma L.
YA *Sun Queen: A Novel about Nefertiti*.
D. McKay 1967.
BL v64 1968 p933; KR v35 1967 p1323; LJ v93 1968 p309.

Peters, Elizabeth
The Jackal's Head.
Meredith Press 1968 (Rpr. 1986, 1991).
LJ v93 1968 p2694; LJ v93 1968 p3995.

Stacton, David
On a Balcony.
Faber & Faber 1958.
BRD 1960 p1267; SatR S 26, 1959 p20.

Vidal, Nicole
The Goddess Queen: A Novel Based on the Life of Nefertiti.
D. McKay 1965.
Also published as *Nefertiti*.
BL v62 1962 p1965 p44; KR v33 1965 p584.

1015. Nehemiah
Hebrew prophet

Hyman, Frieda Clark
JUV *Builders of Jerusalem in the Time of Nehemiah*.
Farrar, Straus & Cudahy 1960.
LJ v85 1960 p3863.

Parker, Lois M.
JUV *Return to Jerusalem: A Story of Adventure and First Love*.
Review & Herald Pub. Association 1988.

Swift, Mayme A.
JUV *Nehe: The Story of a Great Builder*.
Pageant Press 1956.

1016. Nehru, Jawaharlal
1889-1964
First prime minister of India

Tharoor, Shashi
The Great Indian Novel.
Viking 1989.
BRD 1991 p1837; KR v59 1991 p76; LJ v116 Mr 1, 1991 p118; NYTBR Mr 24, 1991 p16.

1017. Nelson, Horatio Nelson, Viscount
1758-1805
English naval officer; broke Napoleon's sea
power in the battle of Trafalgar

Bloom, Ursula (Lozania Prole, pseud.)
Nelson's Love.
Hale 1966 (Rpr. 1985).

Foxell, Nigel
Loving Emma.
Harvester Press 1986.
BritBKN D 1986 p710; Lon R Bks v9 Ja 8, 1987 p17;
   TLS D 5, 1986 p1380.

Frye, Pearl
A Game for Empires.
Little, Brown 1950.
BRD 1950 p333; KR v18 1950 p337; LJ v75 1950
   p1291; NYTBR Ag 20, 1950 p5.

Frye, Pearl
The Sleeping Sword: A Biographical Novel.
Little, Brown 1952.
BRD 1952 p330; KR v20 1952 p304; LJ v77 1952
   p1304; NYTBR Jl 6, 1952 p11.

Hackforth-Jones, Gilbert
Hurricane Harbour: Pre-View of a Victor.
Hodder & Stoughton 1958.

Kent, Alexander
The Inshore Squadron.
Putnam 1979.
BL v75 1979 p1357; PW v214 D 11, 1978 p55.

Kenyon, Frank Wilson
Emma.
Crowell 1955.
BL v51 1955 p316; BRD 1955 p492; FC 7th p207; KR
   v23 1955 p16; LJ v80 1955 p561; NYTBR Mr 13,
   1955 p24.

Lewis, Paul
The Nelson Touch.
Holt, Rinehart & Winston 1960.
BRD 1961 p838; LJ v85 1960 p3464.

Sontag, Susan
The Volcano Lover: A Romance.
Farrar, Straus, Giroux 1992.
BL v88 1992 p1733; KR v60 1992 p635; LJ v117 Je
   15, 1992 p103; NYTBR Ag 9, 1992 p1; Time v140
   Ag 17, 1992 p66.

Stacton, David
Sir William: or, A Lesson in Love.
Putnam 1963.
BRD 1963 p958; LJ v88 1963 p4398; NYTBR O 20,
   1963 p46; SatR O 5, 1963 p41.

Styles, Showell
The Admiral's Fancy.
Faber & Faber 1958.
BL v55 1958 p157; BRD 1959 p957; KR v26 1958
   p672.

1018. Nero
37-68
Roman emperor

Comfort, Alex
Imperial Patient: The Memoirs of Nero's Doctor.
Duckworth 1987.
Obs Jl 5, 1987 p20; TLS S 18, 1987 p1027.

Hersey, John
The Conspiracy: A Novel.
Knopf 1972.
BL v68 1972 p795; BRD 1972 p592; FC 9th p245; KR
   v39 1971 p1274; LJ v97 1972 p1034; NYTBR Ap
   2, 1972 p6.

Lindsay, Jack
Thunder Underground: A Story of Nero's Rome.
Frederick Muller 1965.

Robb, John
Nero, Beloved.
Hale 1971.

Ronalds, Mary Teresa
Nero.
Doubleday 1969.
Also published as *Myself My Sepulchre.*
KR v37 1969 p886; NYTBR N 2, 1969 p49.

Sheean, Vincent
Beware of Caesar.
Random House 1965.
BRD 1965 p1143; KR v33 1965 p447; LJ v90 1965
   p2873; NYTBR Ag 8, 1965 p24.

Shipway, George
The Imperial Governor.
Doubleday 1968.
FC 8th p363; KR v36 1968 p619; LJ v93 1968 p3579.

Sienkiewicz, Henryk
"Quo Vadis": A Narrative of the Time of Nero.
Little, Brown 1896 (Heavily reprinted).
BRD 1905 p320; LJ v68 1943 p1052; NYTBR O 17,
   1896 p2.

Waltari, Mika
*The Roman: The Memoirs of Minutus Lausus
   Manilianus. . . . .*
Putnam 1966.
BRD 1966 p1258; LJ v91 1966 p3975; NYTBR N 6,
   1966 p57.

1019. Neruda, Pablo
1904-1973
Chilean poet & diplomat; won 1971 Nobel Prize

Donoso, Jose
Curfew: A Novel.
Weidenfeld & Nicolson 1988.
Translation of *La Desesperanza.*
BL v84 1988 p1476; BRD 1988 p457; KR v56 1988
   p302; LJ v113 Ap 1, 1988 p96; NYTBR My 29,
   1988 p9.

Skarmeta, Antonio
YA *Burning Patience.*
Pantheon 1987.
BL v83 1987 p982; BRD 1987 p1735; LJ v112 F 15,
   1987 p163; NYTBR My 3, 1987 p36.

1020. Ness, Eliot
1903-1957
FBI agent who headed investigation of Al
Capone's gangster activity in Chicago

Albert, Marvin
The Untouchables: A Novel.
Ivy Books 1987.
Based on a screenplay written by David Mamet.

Collins, Max Allan
Murder by the Numbers.
St. Martin's 1993.
BL v89 1993 p1038; KR v61 1993 p24.

Cooke, John Peyton
Torsos.
Mysterious Press 1994.
NYTBR Ja 23, 1994 p23.

1021. Newbery, John
1713-1767
English publisher & bookseller

Dalgliesh, Alice
JUV *Book for Jennifer.*
Scribner 1940.
BL v37 1940 p39; BRD 1940 p221; CSM Ag 26, 1940
   p9; LJ v65 1940 p847; NYTBR Ag 18, 1940 p10.

1022. Newman, John Henry, Cardinal
1801-1890
English theologian

Trevor, Meriol
Shadows and Images.
D. McKay 1962.
BL v58 1962 p608; BRD 1962 p1208; LJ v87 1962
   p1811; NYTBR My 27, 1962 p30.

1023. Nicholas I
1796-1855
Czar of Russia, 1825-1855

Hoover, H. M.
YA *The Lion's Cub.*
Four Winds Press 1974.
BL v71 1974 p290; KR v42 1974 p1201; LJ v99 1974
   p3267.

Leskov, N. S.
JUV *The Steel Flea.*
Harper & Brothers 1943 (Rpr. 1964).
BL v40 1944 p167; BRD 1943 p486; LJ v69 1944 p73;
   NYTBR F 13, 1944 p14.

Trease, Geoffrey
The Iron Tsar.
Macmillan 1975.
GP v14 N 1975 p2743; TLS D 5, 1975 p1450.

1024. Nicholas II
1868-1918
Last czar of Russia; executed

Gavin, Catherine Irvine
The Snow Mountain.
Hodder & Stoughton 1973.
BL v70 1974 p1080.

Haskin, Gretchen
An Imperial Affair.
Dial 1980.
KR v48 1980 p24; LJ v107 1980 p527; PW v217 Ja 11,
   1980 p78.

Hoe, Susanna
God Save the Tsar.
St. Martin's 1978.
KR v46 1978 p1029; LJ v103 1978 p2261; PW v214 O
   16, 1978 p107.

Pazzi, Roberto
Searching for the Emperor.
Knopf 1988.
Translation of *Cercando L'Imperatore.*
BL v85 1988 p449; KR v56 1988 p1352; LJ v113 N 1,
   1988 p110; NYTBR F 12, 1989 p18.

Plowman, Stephanie
YA *My Kingdom for a Grave.*
Bodley Head 1970.
BRD 1972 p1036; LJ 1971 p3479.

Plowman, Stephanie
YA *Three Lives for the Czar.*
Houghton Mifflin 1970.
Sequel: *My Kingdom for a Grave.*
BL v66 1970 p1402; HB v46 Je 1970 p318; KR v38
   1970 p249; LJ v95 1970 p1955.

Quigley, Aileen
A Devil in Holy Orders.
Hale 1973.

Scott, Justin
A Pride of Royals.
Arbor House 1983.
FC 11th p542.

Trease, Geoffrey
YA *The White Nights of St. Petersburg.*
Macmillan 1967.
KR v35 1967 p1477.

Willis, Ted
The Buckingham Palace Connection.
Macmillan 1978.
BL v75 1978 p29; KR v46 1978 p901; LJ v103 1978
   p1666; PW v214.

1025. Nicholas, Saint

Patron saint of children; "Santa Claus" derived from Dutch form of name "Sinte Klaas"

Burland, Brian
JUV *St. Nicholas and the Tub.*
Holiday House 1964.
BRD 1965 p179; LJ v89 1964 p4116; NYTBR N 1, 1964 p46.

Morgenthaler, Verena
JUV *The Legend of St. Nicholas.*
H.Z. Walck 1970.
BRD 1970 p1005; KR v38 1970 p1031; SatR D 19, 1970 p31.

Pyle, Howard
JUV *How the Good Gifts Were Used.*
Lederer, Street & Zeus 1958.
Reprinted from *The Wonder Clock.*

Reifsnyder, Marylou
JUV *The Golden Cup.*
Knopf 1970.
BL v67 1971 p750; LJ v95 1970 p3647; SatR D 19, 1970 p31.

1026. Nicodemus

New Testament figure

Dobraczynski, Jan
The Letters of Nicodemus.
Heinemann 1958.

Roland, Nicholas
Who Came by Night.
Harvill Press 1971.
BRD 1972 p1103; LJ v97 1972 p1827; LJ v97 1972 p2970.

Walsh, John E.
YA *The Man Who Buried Jesus.*
Collier Books 1989.
BL v85 1989 p1434; KR v57 1989 p250.

1027. Nietzsche, Friedrich Wilhelm

1844-1900
German philosopher

Yalom, Irvin D.
When Nietzsche Wept.
Basic Books 1992.
BL v88 1992 p1997; KR v60 1992 p693; NYTBR Ag 9, 1992 p21; Time v140 Ag 17, 1992 p69.

1028. Nightingale, Florence

1820-1910
English nurse in Crimean War

Dengler, Sandy
Florence Nightingale.
Moody Press 1988.

Gordon, Richard
The Private Life of Florence Nightingale.
Heinemann 1978.
B&B v23 S 1978 p59; BL v75 1979 p1422; GW v118 Ja 22, 1978 p22; KR v46 1978 p1322; LJ v103 1978 p2444.

Ridley, Sheila
Nurses and Ladies.
Hale 1967.
B&B v12 My 1967 p39.

Terrot, Charles
The Passionate Pilgrim.
Bantam 1948.
Also published as *Miss Nightingale's Ladies.*
BRD 1949 p909; LJ v74 1949 p1096; NYTBR O 2, 1949 p42.

1029. Nijinsky, Vaslav

1890-1950
Russian dancer & choreographer

Strathern, Paul
Vaslav: An Impersonation of Nijinsky.
Quartet Books 1975.

1030. Nixon, Patricia

1912-1993
Wife of Richard Nixon

Spencer, Colin
How the Greeks Kidnapped Mrs. Nixon.
Quartet Books 1974.
GW v111 N 2, 1974 p21; Obs O 20, 1974 p33.

1031. Nixon, Richard Milhous

1913-
37th US President; first president to resign

Bishop, Michael
The Secret Ascension: Philip K. Dick is Dead, Alas.
Tor 1987.
BL v84 1987 p365; KR v55 1987 p1424; LJ v112 N 15, 1987 p92; NYTBR F 7, 1988 p22.

Burke, Phyllis
Atomic Candy.
Atlantic Monthly Press 1989.
KR v57 1989 p228; LJ v114 Ap 1, 1989 p110; PW v235 F 24, 1989 p220.

Coover, Robert
The Public Burning.
Viking 1977.
BL v74 1977 p266; BRD 1977 p271; KR v45 1977 p798; LJ v102 1977 p1867; NYTBR Ag 14, 1977 p9.

Ehrlichman, John
The China Card: A Novel.
Simon & Schuster 1986.
BL v82 1986 p1338; KR v54 1986 p653; LJ v111 Jl 1986 p106; NYTBR Je 22, 1986 p13.

Roth, Philip
Our Gang (Starring Tricky and His Friends).
Cape 1971.
BRD 1971 p1175; Atl v229 Ja 1972 p97; LJ v96 1971
    p4031; NYTBR D 5, 1971 p84; SatR N 6, 1971 p54.

1032. Noah
Old Testament figure; noted for building ark before the great flood

Askew, Reginald
The Tree of Noah.
Bles 1971.
B&B v16 Mr 1971 p44.

Barnes, Julian
A History of the World in 10 1/2 Chapters.
Knopf 1989.
BRD 1989 p96; LJ v114 Ag 1989 p161.

Benagh, Christine L.
JUV *Noah's Ark*.
Abingdon Press 1986.

Brelich, Mario
Navigator of the Flood.
Marlboro Press 1991.
LJ v117 My 1, 1992 p114; NYTBR Mr 29, 1992 p16.

Findley, Timothy
Not Wanted on the Voyage.
Viking 1984.

Garnett, David
Two by Two.
Longmans 1963.
LJ v89 1964 p653; NYTBR Ja 26, 1964 p38.

Hewitt, Kathryn
JUV *Two by Two: The Untold Story*.
Harcourt Brace Jovanovich 1984.

Loetscher, Hugo
Noah.
Owen 1970.
Obs F 8, 1970 p34; TLS Je 4, 1970 p602.

Lucas, J. R.
Noah: Voyage to a New Earth.
Wolgemuth & Hyatt 1991.

Minshull, Evelyn
And Then the Rain Came.
T. Nelson 1992.

Olson, Arielle North
JUV *Noah's Cats and the Devil's Fire*.
Orchard Books 1992.
BL v88 1992 p1034; HB v68 My 1992 p347; KR v60
    1992 p118; PW v239 F 10, 1992 p81; SLJ v38 My
    1992 p107.

Zehnpfennig, Gladys
Search for Eden.
T.S. Denison 1955.

1033. Nostradamus
1503-1566
French astrologer & physician

Greene, Liz
The Dreamer of the Vine.
Norton 1980.
BS v41 My 1981 p46; KR v49 1981 p92; LJ v106 1981
    p1098; PW v219 Ja 23, 1981 p118.

McCann, Lee
Nostradamus: The Man Who Saw through Time.
Creative Age Press 1941 (Rpr. 1992).
BRD 1941 p573.

Symons, Allene
Vagabond Prophet.
Avon 1983 (Rpr. 1987).
LATBR Ag 21, 1983 p7; LJ v108 1983 p2173; PW
    v224 Jl 29, 1983 p68.

1034. Noyes, John Humphrey
1811-1886
American founder of communist community at
Oneida, NY

Hedden, Worth Tuttle
Wives of High Pasture.
Doubleday, Doran 1944.
BRD 1944 p336.

1035. O'Higgins, Bernardo
1778-1842
South American revolutionary leader; Chilean
dictator

Beals, Carleton
Taste of Glory.
Crown 1956.
BRD 1956 p59.

Nelson, Edna
O'Higgins and Don Bernardo.
Dutton 1954.
BRD 1954 p652; LJ v79 1954 p2099; NYTBR N 28,
    1954 p10.

1036. O'Keeffe, Georgia
1887-1986
American artist

Cheuse, Alan
The Light Possessed.
Peregrine Smith Books 1990.
BRD 1992 p350; NYTBR O 7, 1990 p33.

1037. O'Neill, Eugene Gladstone
1888-1953
American dramatist

Wylie, Max
Trouble in the Flesh.

Doubleday 1959.
BL v55 1959 p628; KR v27 1959 p156; NYTBR My
24, 1959 p41.

1038. O'Shea, Katherine Page
1845-1921
Mistress and later wife of Charles Stewart
Parnell

Eden, Dorothy
Never Call It Loving.
Coward-McCann 1966.
KR v34 1966 p268; LJ v91 1966 p3236.

Leonard, Hugh
Parnell and the Englishwoman.
Atheneum 1991.
BRD 1992 p1168; KR v59 1991 p274; LJ v116 Ap 15,
1991 p127; NYTBR Je 23, 1991 p22; SLJ v370
1991 p160.

1039. Oakley, Annie
1860-1926
American frontierswoman; performed in Buffalo
Bill's Wild West Show

Collier, Edmund
YA *The Story of Annie Oakley.*
Grosset & Dunlap 1956.
BRD 1956 p205; KR v24 1956 p125; LJ v81 1956
p1043; NYTBR Ap 1, 1956 p205.

Heidish, Marcy
The Secret Annie Oakley.
New American Library 1983.
BL v79 1983 p1014; KR v51 1983 p137; LJ v108 1983
p516; PW v223 F 11, 1983 p57.

Shaw, Stanley
Sherlock Holmes Meets Annie Oakley.
Magna 1990.

Wilson, Ellen Janet
JUV *Annie Oakley, Little Sure Shot.*
Bobbs-Merrill 1958 (Rpr. 1962).
LJ v84 1959 p248.

1040. Oates, Titus
1649-1705
English conspirator

Dakers, Elaine (Jane Lane, pseud.)
Thunder on St. Paul's Day.
Hale 1954.

Neill, Robert
Traitor's Moon.
Doubleday 1952.
BL v49 1952 p90; KR v20 1952 p516; NYTBR O 5,
1952 p36.

1041. Oglethorpe, James Edward
1696-1785
English general & colonizer; founder of Georgia

Ethridge, Willie
Summer Thunder.
Coward-McCann 1958.
BL v55 1959 p313; BRD 1959 p340; KR v26 1958
p679; LJ v84 1959 p118; NYTBR Ja 4, 1959 p29.

Mason, F. van Wyck
Rascals' Heaven.
Doubleday 1964.
NYTBR Jl 12, 1964 p28.

Miller, Helen Topping
Dark Sails: A Tale of Old St. Simons.
Bobbs-Merrill 1945.
BL v42 1945 p129; BRD 1945 p492; KR v13 1945
p322; NYTBR N 18, 1945 p16.

Parks, Aileen Wells
JUV *James Oglethorpe, Young Defender.*
Bobbs-Merrill 1960.
LJ v83 1958 p966.

1042. Omar Khayyam
1050-1123
Persian poet

Komroff, Manuel
*The Life, the Loves, the Adventures of Omar
Khayyam.*
New American Library 1957.

Lamb, Harold
Persian Mosaic.
Hale 1943.

Maalouf, Amin
Samarkand.
Quartet Books 1992.
TLS Jl 31, 1992 p19.

1043. Oppenheimer, Julius Robert
1904-1967
American nuclear physicist; director of Los
Alamos laboratory during testing of first atomic
bombs

Silman, Roberta
Beginning the World Again.
Viking 1990.
BL v87 1990 p258; KR v58 1990 p1038; LJ v115 O 1,
1990 p118; NYTBR N 4, 1990 p29.

Smith, Martin Cruz
Stallion Gate.
Random House 1986.
BL v82 1986 p1043; LJ v111 My 1, 1986 p132;
NYTBR My 4, 1986 p14; PW v229 Mr 14, 1986
p102.

Thackara, James
America's Children.
Chatto & Windus 1984.
PW v226 S 14, 1984 p129; SB v20 Mr 1985 p198;
TLS My 18, 1984 p546.

1044. Origen Adamantius
185-254
Early Christian theologian

Vrettos, Theodore
Origen: A Historical Novel.
Caratzas Bros. 1978.
BL v75 1978 p159; KR v46 1978 p716; PW v213 Je
19, 1978 p94.

1045. Orwell, George, pseud.
1903-1950
English author & critic; wrote *Animal Farm* &
1984

Clarke, Thurston
*Thirteen O'Clock: A Novel about George Orwell
and 1984.*
Doubleday 1984.
KR v52 1984 p417; LJ v109 1984 p1251; NYTBR S
16, 1984 p30; PW v225 My 11, 1984 p260.

1046. Osceola Nickanochee
1804-1838
Seminole Indian chief

Clark, Electa
Osceola, Young Seminole Indian.
Bobbs-Merrill 1965.

Hall, Rubylea
Flamingo Prince.
Duell, Sloan & Pearce 1954.
LJ v79 1954 p1953.

McNeer, May Yonge
JUV *War Chief of the Seminoles.*
Random House 1954.
BL v51 1955 p252; BRD 1955 p598; KR v22 1954
p447; LJ v79 1954 p2497; NYTBR N 7, 1954 p50.

Pratt, Theodore
Seminole.
Duell, Sloan & Pearce 1954 (Rpr. 1963).
Novel based on the author's drama: *Seminole.*
LJ v88 1963 p1904; NYTBR Mr 7, 1954 p25.

Robson, Lucia St Clair
Light a Distant Fire.
Ballantine 1988.
KR v56 1988 p1008.

Slaughter, Frank G.
The Warrior.
Doubleday 1956.
Also published as *The Flaming Frontier.*
BL v53 1957 p246; BRD 1957 p851; NYTBR N 18,
1956 p58.

Wilder, Robert
Bright Feather: A Novel.
Putnam 1948.
BL v44 1948 p337; BRD 1948 p922; FC 8th p441; KR
v16 1948 p219; LJ v73 1948 p814; NYTBR My 16,
1948 p5.

1047. Oswald, Lee Harvey
1939-1963
American assassin; shot & killed John F. Kennedy; killed by Jack Ruby

DeLillo, Don
Libra.
Viking 1988.
BL v84 1988 p1625; KR v56 1988 p843; NYTBR Jl
24, 1988 p1; Time v132 Ag 1, 1988 p65.

Ions, Edmund S. (Edmund Aubrey, pseud.)
Sherlock Holmes in Dallas.
Dodd, Mead 1980.
Also published as *The Case of the Murdered President.*
KR v48 1980 p942; LJ v105 1980 p2103.

Thomas, D. M.
Flying in to Love.
Scribner 1992.
BL v89 1992 p5; KR v60 1992 p946; NYTBR O 11,
1992 p13.

1048. Otis, James
1725-1783
American political leader & patriot

Wibberley, Leonard
YA *John Treegate's Musket.*
Ariel Books 1959.
BL v56 1959 p192; BRD 1960 p1432; KR v27 1959
p495; LJ v84 1959.

1049. Ovid
43 BC-AD 17
Roman poet

Horia, Vintila
God Was Born in Exile.
St. Martin's 1961.
BL v58 1961 p226; BRD 1961 p654; FC 8th p213; KR
v29 1961 p628; LJ v86 1961 p3301; NYTBR S 10,
1961 p5.
43 BC-17 AD

Malouf, David
An Imaginery Life.
Braziller 1978.
BRD 1979 p829; LJ v103 1978 p587; NYTBR Ap 23,
1978 p10; Obs S 10, 1978 p34; PW v213 Ja 30,
1978 p125.

Ransmayr, Christoph
*The Last World: A Novel with an Ovidian Reper-
tory.*
Grove Weidenfeld 1990.

BL v86 1990 p1140; BRD 1990 p1493; KR v58 1990
p215; LJ v115 Mr 1, 1990 p117; NYTBR My 27,
1990 p12.

1050. Paganini, Niccolo
1782-1840
Italian violinist & composer

Komroff, Manuel
The Magic Bow: A Romance of Paganini.
Harper & Brothers 1940.
BRD 1940 p522; LJ v65 1940 p874; NYTBR O 20,
1940 p7.

1051. Pahlevi, Mohammed Riza
1919-1980
Iranian ruler, 1941-1979

Parvin, Manoucher
Cry for My Revolution, Iran.
Mazda Pubs. 1987.
SPBR v3 Mr 1988 p24; WCRB v13 #5 1988 p43.

1052. Paine, Thomas
1737-1809
American Revolutionary patriot, author, & political thinker

Fast, Howard
Citizen Tom Paine.
Duell, Sloan and Pearce 1943 (Rpr. 1964, 1983,
1986).
BL v39 1943 p368; BRD 1943 p252; LJ v68 1943
p327; NYTBR Ap 25, 1943 p1.

Hawthorne, Hildegarde
YA *His Country Was the World: A Life of Thomas
Paine.*
Longmans, Green 1949.
BRD 1949 p403; KR v17 1949 p4; LJ v74 1949 p668;
NYTBR Ap 10, 1949 p26.

Levin, Benjamin
To Spit against the Wind.
Citadel Press 1970.
BL v67 1970 p214; LJ v95 1970 p3305; NYTBR O 11,
1970 p44; PW v198 Jl 13, 1970 p149.

Mercer, Charles E.
Enough Good Men.
Putnam 1960.
BL v56 1960 p417; BRD 1960 p920; KR v27 1959
p822; LJ v84 1959 p3791; NYTBR Ja 17, 1960 p31.

1053. Paisley, Ian Richard Kyle
1926-
Irish clergyman & political leader

Gill, Bartholomew
McGarr and the Method of Descartes.
Viking 1984.
KR v52 1984 p878.

1054. Palmer, Arnold
1929-
American golfer

Polakoff, P. Byron
JUV *Arnold Palmer and the Golfin' Dolphin.*
Turnbull & Willoughby 1984.

1055. Palmer, Nathaniel Brown
1799-1877
American polar explorer

Sperry, Armstrong
YA *South of Cape Horn: A Saga of Nat Palmer and
Early Antarctic Exploration.*
J.C. Winston 1958.
BL v54 1958 p570; BRD 1958 p1001; KR v26 1958
p85; LJ v83 1958 p1950; NYTBR Je 8, 1958 p43.

1056. Palmer, William
1824-1856
English murderer

Graves, Robert
They Hanged My Saintly Billy.
Cassell 1957 (Rpr. 1980).
BRD 1957 p368; FC 7th p160; KR v25 1957 p234; LJ
v82 1957 p1065.

1057. Paracelsus, Philippus Aureolus
1493-1541
Swiss alchemist & physician

Connell, Evan S.
The Alchymist's Journal.
North Point Press 1991.
KR v59 1991 p195; LJ v116 Ap 15, 1991 p124; NY
v67 Jl 1, 1991 p88; NYTBR My 12, 1991 p16.

1058. Park, Mungo
1771-1806
Scottish explorer

Boyle, T. Coraghessan
Water Music: A Novel.
Little, Brown 1981.
BRD 1983 p171; LJ v106 1981 p2251; NYTBR D 27,
1981 p9; PW v223 Je 10, 1983 p60.

1059. Parker, Charlie
1920-1955
American jazz musician

Mierau, Maurice
Charlie Parker's Birdland: A Novella.
Boke Books 1984.

1060. Parker, Dorothy
1893-1967
American writer known for her satiric humor

Baxt, George
The Dorothy Parker Murder Case.
St. Martin's 1984.
BL v81 1984 p189; KR v52 1984 p932.

1061. Parker, Quanah
see Quanah

1062. Parker, Robert Leroy
see Cassidy, Butch

1063. Parker, Theodore
1810-1860
American preacher & reformer

Nelson, Truman
The Sin of the Prophet.
Little, Brown 1952.
BL v48 1952 p229; BRD 1952 p661; FC 7th p262; KR v19 1951 p684; LJ v77 1952 p361; NYTBR F 17, 1952 p32.

1064. Parks, Lillian Rogers
1897-
American author; wrote My *Thiry Years Backstairs at the White House*

Bagni, Gwen; Dubov, Paul
Backstairs at the White House.
Prentice Hall 1978.
BL v75 1979 p911; KR v46 1978 p1318; LJ v104 1979 p419.

1065. Parnell, Charles Stewart
1846-1891
Irish political leader

Eden, Dorothy
Never Call It Loving.
Coward-McCann 1966.
KR v34 1966 p268; LJ v91 1966 p3236.

Leonard, Hugh
Parnell and the Englishwoman.
Atheneum 1991.
BRD 1992 p1168; KR v59 1991 p274; LJ v116 Ap 15, 1991 p127; NYTBR Je 23, 1991 p22; SLJ v37 O 1991 p160.

1066. Parr, Catherine
1512-1548
Sixth wife of Henry VIII

Bloom, Ursula (Lozania Prole, pseud.)
Henry's Last Love.
Hale 1958 (Rpr. 1978).

Eady, Carol Maxwell
Her Royal Destiny.
Harmony Books 1985.
BL v81 1985 p1029; KR v53 1985 p381; PW v227 Ap 26, 1985 p79.

Evans, Jean
Katherine, Queen Dowager.
Hale 1973.

Evans, Jean
Royal Widow.
Hale 1971.
Also published as *Katherine Parr.*

Hibbert, Eleanor (Jean Plaidy, pseud.)
The Sixth Wife.
Ulverscroft 1953 (Rpr. 1969).

Luke, Mary M.
The Ivy Crown.
Doubleday 1984.
BL v80 1984 p944; KR v52 1984 p58; LJ v109 1984 p509; PW v225 Ja 20, 1984 p76.

Smith, Jessica
Mistress Parr's Four Husbands.
Hale 1967.

Westcott, Jan
The Queen's Grace.
Crown 1959.
BL v56 1960 p328; BRD 1960 p1424; KR v27 1959 p710.

1067. Pasternak, Boris Leonidovich
1890-1960
Russian author; wrote *Doctor Zhivago*

Krotkov, Yuri
The Nobel Prize.
Simon & Schuster 1980.
BRD 1980 p689; LJ v105 1980 p1187; NYTBR Jl 13, 1980 p1.

1068. Pasteur, Louis
1822-1895
French chemist; developed process of food sterilization known as pasteurization

Malkus, Alidi Sims
JUV *The Story of Louis Pasteur.*
Grosset & Dunlap 1952.
BRD 1953 p609; LJ v77 1952 p2077.

1069. Patrick, Saint
385-461
Patron saint of Ireland

Beahn, John E.
A Man Cleansed by God: A Novel Based on St. Patrick's Confession.
Newman Press 1959.

Hamilton, Joan Lesley
The Lion and the Cross.
Doubleday 1979.
KR v47 1979 p25; LJ v104 1979 p1276.

Polland, Madeleine A.
YA *Flame over Tara.*
Doubleday 1964.
BRD 1964 p939; LJ v89 1964 p2233.

Schofield, William G.
The Deer Cry: A Novel.
Longmans, Green 1948.
BRD 1948 p743; KR v16 1948 p510; LJ v73 1948
p1385; NYTBR N 14, 1948 p48.

1070. Patton, George
1885-1945
American general in WW II

Leopold, Christopher
Blood and Guts Is Going Nuts.
Doubleday 1977.
BL v74 1977 p528; KR v45 1977 p873; LJ v102 1977
p2277; NYTBR O 30, 1977 p24; PW v212 S 5,
1977 p65.

Rohmer, Richard H.
Rommel & Patton.
Irwin 1986.
BIC v16 Ap 1987 p24; Mac v99 O 20, 1986 p66.

Sire, Glen
The Deathmakers.
Simon & Schuster 1960.
BRD 1961 p1309; KR v28 1960 p165; LJ v85 1960
p1939; NYTBR Ap 10, 1960 p43.

Weaver, John D.
Another Such Victory.
Viking 1948.
BRD 1948 p894; KR v16 1948 p65; NYTBR Ap 18,
1948 p17; SatR Ap 3, 1948 p19.

1071. Paul, Saint
d. 64
One of the founders of the Christian religion

Asch, Sholem
The Apostle.
Putnam 1943 (Rpr. 1985).
BL v40 O 1, 1943 p47; BRD 1943 p25; FC 11th p24;
LJ v68 1943 p724; NYTBR Sp 19, 1943 p3;
SHSLC 8th p384.

Ball, Elsie
JUV *Perilous Voyage.*
Abingdon-Cokesbury Press 1951.
BRD 1951 p45; NYTBR N 11, 1951 p6.

Benson, Ginny
JUV *According to Amos.*
A & P Books 1981.
PW v221 Ja 1, 1982 p51; WCRB v8 F 1982 p61.

Berstl, Julius
*The Cross and the Eagle: A Novel Based on the
Life of St. Paul.*
Muhlenberg Press 1955.

Berstl, Julius
The Tentmaker.
Rinehart 1951.
BRD 1952 p72; FC 7th p39; KR v20 1952 p45; LJ v77
1952 p432; NYTBR Ap 13, 1952 p16.

Blandford, Brian
*Breakin' into Life: An Imaginative Reconstruction
of an Episode When the Church Was Young.*
Regal Books 1986.

Blythe, LeGette
Man on Fire: A Novel of the Life of St. Paul.
Funk & Wagnalls 1964.
LJ v89 1964 p2823.

Bremkamp, Gloria Howe
Phoebe: God's Messenger to the Church at Rome.
Here's Life Publishers 1992.

Buckmaster, Henrietta
*And Walk in Love: A Novel Based on the Life of
the Apostle Paul.*
Random House 1956.
BL v53 1956 p21; BRD 1956 p428; FC 7th p58; KR
v24 1956 p363; NYTBR Jl 29, 1956 p18.

Caldwell, Taylor
Great Lion of God.
Doubleday 1970.
BL v66 1970 p1259; KR v38 1970 p123; LJ v95 1970
p1500; NYTBR My 17, 1970 p38.

Call, Max
Phoebe.
Chosen Books 1984.
Also published as *Deadline in Rome.*
SEP v253 Ap 1981 p88

Cash, Johnny
YA *Man in White: A Novel.*
Harper & Row 1986.
BL v82 1986 p1561; KR v54 1986 p1039; SLJ v33 D
1986 p125.

Chinn, Laurene
The Soothsayer: A Novel.
Morrow 1972.
KR v40 1972 p1112; LJ v97 1972 p3614.

De Wohl, Louis
The Glorious Folly.
Lippincott 1957.
BL v54 1957 p136; BRD 1957 p248; FC 7th p106; KR
v25 1957 p651; LJ v82 1957 p2036.

Dobraczynski, Jan
The Sacred Sword.
Heinemann 1959.

Farrell, Gene
Treasure beyond Taurus.
Van Kampen Press 1954.

Goldthorpe, John
The Hidden Splendour.
Cassell 1962.

Kersh, Gerald
The Implacable Hunter.
Heinemann 1961.

McElrath, William N.
JUV *I Sailed with Saul of Tarsus.*
Broadman Press 1980.

Miller, Donald G.
Conqueror in Chains: A Story of the Apostle Paul.
Westminster Press 1951.
BL v48 1951 p128; BRD 1951 p613; KR v19 1951
p612; LJ v77 1952 p70.

Miller, Rex
I, Paul.
Duell, Sloan & Pearce 1940.
BRD 1940 p642.

Neilson, Winthrop; Neilson, Frances
The Woman Who Loved Paul.
Doubleday 1978.
BS v38 N 1978 p239; LJ v103 1978 p1436; PW v213
My 15, 1978 p92.

Petitclerc, Grace
The Magnificent Three.
Crown 1956.
BRD 1956 p731; LJ v81 1956 p2693; NYTBR D 16,
1956 p18.

Poirier, Leon
Saint Paul: A Historical Romance of His Life.
B. Herder Book Co. 1961.

Shrader, Wesley
*Forty Days Till Dawn: Memoirs of the Apostle
Paul.*
Word Books 1972.

Slaughter, Frank G.
God's Warrior.
Doubleday 1967.
FC 9th p471; KR v34 1966 p1240; LJ v92 1967 p137.

Steen, John W.
Barnabas and Paul: Brothers in Conflict.
Broadman Press 1973.

Taylor, Tom
The Sin Bearer: A Novel.
Word Books 1986.

Wolf, Lester A.
*I, Paul: An Autobiography of the Prince among
Missionaries.*
Concordia Pub. House 1948.

Yale, Alfred H.
My Friend Paul: A Novel.
Herald Pub. House 1986.

1072. Payne, John Howard
1791-1852
American actor & playwright

Barragan, Maude
John Howard Payne, Skywalker.
Dietz Press 1953.
BRD 1954 p46; LJ v79 1954 p1592.

1073. Peale, Charles Willson
1741-1827
American portrait painter

Epstein, Sam
JUV *Mister Peale's Mammoth.*
Coward, McCann & Geoghegan 1977.
BRD 1978 p395; KR v45 1977 p488; SLJ v24 S 1977
p126.

Morrow, Barbara
JUV *Help for Mr. Peale.*
Macmillan 1990.
BL v87 1990 p527; BRD 1991 p1328; SLJ v37 Ja 1991
p78.

1074. Peary, Robert Edwin
1856-1920
American arctic explorer; first man to reach
North Pole

Clark, Electa
JUV *Robert Peary, Boy of the North Pole.*
Bobbs-Merrill 1953 (Rpr. 1962).
LJ v78 1953 p2106.

1075. Penn, William
1644-1718
English Quaker; founder of Pennsylvania

Mason, Miriam E.
JUV *William Penn, Friendly Boy.*
Bobbs-Merrill 1944.

Meigs, Cornelia
JUV *The Dutch Colt.*
Macmillan 1952.
BRD 1952 p618; KR v20 1952 p553; LJ v77 1952
p2077; NYTBR N 9, 1952 p52.

1076. Pepys, Samuel
1633-1703
English naval officer & diarist

Abernethy, Cecil
Mr. Pepys of Seething Lane.
McGraw-Hill 1957 (Rpr. 1974).
BRD 1957 p2; LJ v82 1957 p2816; NYTBR N 10,
1957 p16.

Delaforce, Patrick
Pepys in Love: Elizabeth's Story.
Bishopsgate 1986.

McKemy, Kay
YA *Samuel Pepys of the Navy: A Biographical Novel.*
F. Warne 1970.

BRD 1970 p908; LJ v95 1970 p4366; PW v197 Mr 30, 1970 p65.

Trease, Geoffrey
Popinjay Stairs.
Vanguard Press 1977.
TLS S 28, 1973 p1117.

Varble, Rachel McBrayer
YA *Three against London.*
Doubleday 1962.
LJ v87 1962 p4291.

1077. Pericles
495?-429? BC
Athenian political leader

Caldwell, Taylor
Glory and the Lightning.
Doubleday 1974.
FC 10th p81; KR v42 1974 p958; LJ v99 1974 p2870; PW v206 S 2, 1974 p61.

Dimont, Madelon
Darling Pericles.
Atheneum 1972.
KR v40 1972 p274; Obs Ag 13, 1972 p27; PW v201 F 28, 1972 p70.

Plowman, Stephanie
YA *The Road to Sardis.*
Houghton Mifflin 1965.
BRD 1966 p961; LJ v91 1966 p2712; NYTBR My 8, 1966 p30.

Tarnoi, Laszlo
Wingless Victory: A Novel of Pericles.
Delphik Book/Classics 1982.

Twose, Anna
The Lion of Athens.
Chatto & Windus 1976.
Lis v95 Je 24, 1976 p822; Obs Je 27, 1976 p23.

Warner, Rex
Pericles the Athenian.
Little, Brown 1963.
BRD 1963 p1046; LJ v88 1963 p238; NYTBR Ap 7, 1963 p52; SatR My 11, 1963 p74.

1078. Peron, Juan
1895-1974
President of Argentina, 1946-1955, 1973-1974

Martinez, Tomas Eloy
The Peron Novel.
Pantheon 1988.
BL v84 1988 p1220; BRD 1989 p1073; LJ v113 Ap 15, 1988 p94; NYTBR My 22, 1988 p16; PW v233 F 26, 1988 p180.

1079. Perry, Matthew Calbraith, Commodore
1794-1858
American naval officer; noted for opening Japan to US trade

Scharbach, Alexander
JUV *Boy Sailor, Matthew Calbraith Perry.*
Bobbs-Merrill 1955.

1080. Perry, Oliver Hazard, Admiral
1785-1819
American naval officer; defeated British in Battle of Lake Erie

Crosby, Ralph M.
We Have Met the Enemy.
Bobbs-Merrill Co. 1940.
LJ v65 1940 p878.

Lane, Carl D.
The Fleet in the Forest.
Coward-McCann 1943.
BL v40 1943 p146; BRD 1943 p470; LJ v68 1943 p769; NYTBR N 21, 1943 p38.

Rhodes, James A.
The Court-Martial of Commodore Perry.
Bobbs-Merrill 1961.
BRD 1962 p1008; KR v29 1961 p136; LJ v86 1961 p1585.

Schumann, Mary
My Blood and My Treasure.
Dial Press 1941.
BRD 1941 p800; NYTBR My 4, 1941 p23.

1081. Pershing, John J.
1860-1948
American general; commander in chief of American Expeditionary Force in World War I

Blackburn, Thomas Wakefield
A Good Day to Die.
D. McKay 1967.
BL v63 1967 p1032; BRD 1967 p132; KR v35 1967 p17; LJ v92 1967 p1029; NYTBR Mr 19, 1967 p49.

Meggs, Brown
The War Train: A Novel of 1916.
Atheneum 1981.
BL v77 1981 p1434; KR v49 1981 p651; LJ v106 1981 p1443.

1082. Peter the Great
1672-1725
Czar of Russia, 1682-1725

Markish, David
Jesters.
Holt 1988.
KR v56 1988 p925; LJ v113 S 1, 1988 p184.

Price, Jeramie
Katrina.
Farrar, Straus & Cudahy 1955.
BRD 1955 p735; LJ v80 1955 p1382; NYTBR Jl 24,
1955 p16.

Tolstoi, Aleksei
Peter the Great.
Covici, Friede 1932 (Heavily reprinted).
Translated from the Russian by H.C. Matheson.
BL v28 1932 p475; BRD 1932 p955; NYTBR Je 5,
1932 p6.

1083. Peter, Saint

Leading figure amongst Christ's twelve apostles;
first pope

Battle, Gerald N.
JUV *Simon Peter: The Boy Who Became a Fisherman*.
Word Books 1970.

Cosgrove, John
Upon This Rock: A Tale of Peter.
Our Sunday Visitor 1978.

Douglas, Lloyd C.
The Big Fisherman.
Houghton Mifflin 1948 (Rpr. 1952).
BL v45 1948 p103; BRD 1948 p225; LJ v73 1948
p1594; NYTBR N 21, 1948 p6; Time v52 N 22,
1948 p110.

Friedberger, Kurt
Fisher of Men: A Novel of Simon Peter.
Appleton-Century-Crofts 1954.
BRD 1955 p320; KR v22 1954 p687; NYTBR D 5,
1954 p52.

Godwin, Stephani; Godwin, Edward
YA *Roman Eagle*.
Oxford University Press 1951.
BL v48 1951 p105; BRD 1951 p342; KR v19 1951
p488; LJ v76 1951 p2016; NYTBR N 11, 1951 p6.

Joers, Lawrence E. C.
Thou Art Peter.
Vantage Press 1952.

Morrill, Belle Chapman
Simon Called Peter.
Judson Press 1948.

Murphy, Walter F.
Upon This Rock: The Life of St. Peter.
Macmillan 1987.
BRD 1988 p1231; LJ v112 N 15, 1987 p90; NYTBR D
6, 1987 p26.

Ranger, Mary
JUV *Simon the Small: A Young Galilean Wonders Why
Peter Becomes a Fisher of Men*.
Concordia Pub. House 1977.

Slaughter, Frank G.
Upon This Rock: A Novel of Simon Peter.

Coward-McCann 1963.
BRD 1964 p1090; LJ v88 1963 p4101.

Van Greenaway, Peter
The Judas Gospel.
Atheneum 1972.
BRD 1972 p1327; FC 9th p526; KR v40 1972 p752; LJ
v97 1972 p3186; NYTBR S 17, 1972 p45.

Williams, Albert N.
YA *Simon Peter, Fisher of Men: A Fictionalized Auto-
biography of the Apostle Peter*.
Association Press 1954.
BRD 1955 p981; KR v22 1954 p636; LJ v79 1954
p2502; NYTBR Ja 16, 1955 p28.

1084. Petipa, Marius

1822-1910
French dancer & choreographer; developed clas-
sical ballet in Russia

Graham, Harriet
JUV *The Ring of Zoraya*.
Atheneum 1982.
BL v78 1982 p1444; BRD 1983 p593.

1085. Petronius, Gaius

Roman satirist

Sienkiewicz, Henryk
"Quo Vadis": A Narrative of the Time of Nero.
Little, Brown 1896 (Heavily reprinted).
BRD 1905 p320; LJ v68 1943 p1052; NYTBR O 17,
1896 p2.

1086. Philby, Kim (Harold Adrian Russell)

1912-1988
English traitor; defected to Soviet Union

Bennett, Dorothea
The Jigsaw Man.
Coward, McCann & Geoghegan 1976.
LJ v101 1976 p1315; NYTBR Ag 1, 1976 p15;
NYTBR Je 26, 1977 p41; SatR S 1976 p142.

Jute, Andre
Reverse Negative: A Novel of Suspense.
Norton 1979.
NYTBR O 14, 1979 p24.

Williams, Alan
Gentleman Traitor.
Harcourt, Brace, Jovanovich 1975.
BL v72 1976 p837; KR v43 1975 p1147; LJ v101 1976
p363; NYTBR D 21, 1975 p18.

1087. Philip II

382-336 BC
King of Macedonia; father of Alexander the
Great

Eiker, Karl V.
Star of Macedon.

Putnam 1957.
BRD 1957 p283; KR v25 1957 p228; LJ v82 1957
  p1239; NYTBR My 19, 1957 p32.

Renault, Mary
Fire from Heaven.
Pantheon 1969.
BL v66 1970 p543; BRD 1970 p1174; KR v37 1969
  p1086; LJ v94 1969 p4541; NYTBR Je 7, 1970 p2.

1088. Philip II
1165-1223
King of France, 1179-1223

Phillips, Jill M.
The Rain Maiden.
Citadel Press 1987.
PW v231 My 15, 1987 p266.

1089. Philip II
1527-1598
King of Spain, 1556-1598

Benitez-Rojo, Antonio
Sea of Lentils.
University of Massachusetts Press 1990.
BRD 1991 p149; KR v58 1990 p1105; LJ v115 Ag
  1990 p138; NYTBR D 16, 1990 p28.

De Wohl, Louis
The Last Crusader.
Lippincott 1956.
BL v53 1957 p224; BRD 1957 p249; KR v24 1956
  p647; NYTBR N 4, 1956 p37.

Hibbert, Eleanor (Jean Plaidy, pseud.)
The Spanish Bridegroom.
Hale 1954 (Rpr. 1971).
LJ v96 1971 p3158.

Kesten, Hermann
I, the King.
Longmans, Green 1940.
BRD 1940 p507; NYTBR S 15, 1940 p14; SatR S 21,
  1940 p22.

O'Brien, Kate
For One Sweet Grape.
Doubleday 1946 (Rpr. 1985).
Also published as *That Lady.*
BL v42 1946 p348; BRD 1946 p620; KR v14 1946
  p155; LJ v71 1946 p758; NYTBR Je 2, 1946 p12.

Ross Williamson, Hugh
The Princess a Nun!: A Novel without Fiction.
Joseph 1978.

Zara, Louis
In the House of the King.
Crown 1952.
BRD 1952 p990; NYTBR D 28, 1952 p14; SatR O 11,
  1952 p37.

1090. Philip VI
1293-1350
King of France, 1328-1350

Druon, Maurice
The Lily and the Lion.
Scribner 1961.
Final volume of *The Accursed Kings* series.
BL v58 1962 p476; BRD 1962 p324; LJ v87 1962
  p1629; NYTBR F 18, 1962 p40.

1091. Phillips, Wendell
1811-1884
American orator, author, & abolitionist

Nelson, Truman
The Sin of the Prophet.
Little, Brown 1952.
BL v48 1952 p229; BRD 1952 p661; FC 7th p262; KR
  v19 1951 p684; LJ v77 1952 p361; NYTBR F 17,
  1952 p32.

1092. Phips, William, Sir
1651-1695
American colonial governor

Alderman, Clifford L.
The Silver Keys.
Putnam 1960.
BL v56 1960 p326; BRD 1960 p11; KR v27 1959
  p890; LJ v84 1959 p3869.

Cochran, Hamilton
Silver Shoals.
Bobbs-Merrill 1945.
BL v42 1945 p128; BRD 1945 p140; KR v13 1945
  p280; NYTBR N 4, 1945 p37.

Heenan, Barry
The Treasure Seekers: The Story of William Phips.
T.S. Denison 1969.

Mason, F. van Wyck
Log Cabin Noble.
Doubleday 1973.
Also published as *Stand before Kings.*
LJ v98 1973 p2464.

1093. Picasso, Pablo
1881-1973
Spanish-born painter; dominating figure of early
20th-century French art

Kay, Helen
JUV *Henri's Hands for Pablo Picasso.*
Abelard-Schuman 1966.
BRD 1966 p631; LJ v90 1965 p5517; NYTBR N 7,
  1965 p55.

1094. Pike, Zebulon Montgomery
1779-1813
American general & explorer; Pike's Peak named for him

Stevenson, Augusta
JUV *Zeb Pike, Boy Traveler*.
Bobbs-Merrill 1953 (Rpr. 1963).
LJ v78 1953 p2106.

Woodley, Richard
Zebulon Pike: Pioneer Destiny.
Banbury Books 1982.

1095. Pilate, Pontius
Roman procurator of Judaea & Samaria; presided over trial of Jesus

Bekessy, Emery
Barabbas: A Novel of the Time of Jesus.
Prentice-Hall 1946.
BL v43 1947 p132; BRD 1946 p51; FC 10th p42; KR v14 1946 p436; LJ v71 1946 p1542; NYTBR N 24, 1946 p26.

Blythe, LeGette
Hear Me, Pilate!.
Holt 1961.
LJ v86 1961 p2489.

Bono, Elena
The Widow of Pilate.
Hutchinson 1958.

Caillois, Roger
Pontius Pilate.
Macmillan 1963.

Dunscomb, Charles
The Bond and the Free.
Houghton Mifflin 1955.
BL v52 1955 p13; BRD 1955 p261; FC 7th p120; KR v23 1955 p370;.

Franzero, Charles
The Memoirs of Pontius Pilate.
George Allen & Unwin 1947.

Kellner, Esther
The Bride of Pilate.
Appleton-Century-Crofts 1959.
FC 7th p206; NYTBR Jl 12, 1959 p22.

Koch, Werner
Pontius Pilate Reflects.
Putnam 1961.
BRD 1962 p665; LJ v87 1962 p784; NYTBR Ap 8, 1962 p33.

Lang, Theo
The Word and the Sword.
Joseph 1974.
KR v42 1974 p598; LJ v99 1974 p1984; PW v205 Je 3, 1974 p152.

Le Fort, Gertrud
The Wife of Pilate.
Bruce Pub. Co. 1957.

Maier, Paul L.
Pontius Pilate.
Doubleday 1968.
BRD 1968 p876; LJ v93 1968 p3995; LJ v93 1968 p4308.

Mayrant, Drayton
First the Blade.
Peoples Book Club 1950.
BRD 1951 p815; KR v18 1950 p646; NYTBR D 10, 1950 p24; SatR Ja 20, 1951 p13.

Mills, James R.
The Gospel According to Pontius Pilate.
San Francisco Club 1977.
KR v45 1977 p1038; PW v212 Ag 22, 1977 p61.

Slaughter, Frank G.
The Thorn of Arimathea.
Doubleday 1959.
BRD 1959 p918; FC 9th p471; KR v26 1958 p855; LJ v84 1959 p120.

Sullivan, Alan
"And from That Day".
Ryerson Press 1944.

1096. Pinkerton, Allan
1819-1884
American detective; head of US secret service; founder of first detective agency in the United States

Borland, Kathryn Kilby; Speicher, Helen Ross
JUV *Allan Pinkerton, Young Detective*.
Bobbs-Merrill 1962.

1097. Pio da Pietrelcina, Father
1887-1968
Italian monk believed to have been marked by stigmata

Seiden, Othniel
The Capuchin.
Gregory Publications 1981.

1098. Piozzi, Hester Lynch
1741-1821
English diarist & poet; friend of Samuel Johnson

Carter, Winifred
Dr. Johnson's Dear Mistress.
Selwyn & Blount 1949.
BRD 1950 p152; LJ v75 1950 p1397; NYTBR Ja 21, 1951 p20; SatR N 18, 1950 p29.

1099. Pissarro, Camille Jacob
1831-1903
French impressionist painter

Stone, Irving
Depths of Glory: A Biographical Novel of Camille Pissarro.
Doubleday 1985.
BL v82 1985 p91; BRD 1986 p1549; KR v53 1985 p821; LJ v110 O 15, 1985 p103; NYTBR O 20, 1985 p16; PW v228 Ag 9, 1985 p64; Time v126 N 11, 1985 p92.

1100. Pitcher, Molly
1750-1832
Earned her nickname by carrying water for soldiers in the Battle of Monmouth, 1778

Hall, Marjory
JUV *A Hatful of Gold.*
Westminster Press 1964.
LJ v89 1964 p3491.

Stevenson, Augusta
JUV *Molly Pitcher, Girl Patriot.*
Bobbs-Merrill 1952.
Also published as *Molly Pitcher, Young Patriot.*
BRD 1952 p847; LJ b77 1952 p1667.

1101. Pitt, William
1708-1778
English politician

Wyckoff, Nicholas
The Braintree Mission: A Fictional Narrative of London and Boston, 1770-1771.
Macmillan 1957.
BRD 1957 p1015; FC 9th p569; KR v25 1957 p155; LJ v82 1957 p1069; NYTBR Ap 21, 1957 p6.

1102. Pitt, William
1759-1806
English prime minister, 1783-1801, 1804-1806

Maughan, A. M.
The King's Malady.
Hodder & Stoughton 1978.

Maughan, A. M.
Young Pitt: A Novel.
Hodder & Stoughton 1974.
KR v42 1974 p897; LJ v99 1974 p2620; PW v206 S 23, 1974 p148.

1103. Pius IX, Pope
1792-1878
Pope, 1846-1878; convened first Vatican Council

Carpentier, Alejo
The Harp and the Shadow.
Mercury House 1990.
BL v86 1990 p1683; BRD 1991 p303; LJ v115 Ap 15, 1990 p121; NYTBR Je 3, 1990 p18; PW v237 My 4, 1990 p56.

1104. Pizzarro, Francisco
1470-1541
Spanish conqueror of Peru

Muir, Marie
Captive of the Sun.
Hale 1972.

1105. Plato
427-347 BC
Greek philosopher; student of Socrates

Renault, Mary
The Mask of Apollo.
Pantheon 1966.
Atl v218 N 1966 p153; BRD 1966 p1001; FC 11th p514; LJ v91 1966 p3973; NYTBR F 10, 1966 p4.

1106. Pocahontas
1595-1617
American Indian princess; daughter of Powhatan; saved the life of Captain John Smith

Barth, John
The Sot-Weed Factor.
Doubleday 1960.
BRD 1961 p81; KR v28 1960 p462; LJ v85 1960 p3099; NYTBR Ag 21, 1960 p4.

Bowman, John Clarke
Powhatan's Daughter.
Viking 1973.
Also published as *Pocahontas.*
FC 9th p58; KR v41 N 1, 1973 p1219; LJ v98 1973 p3390.

Bulla, Clyde Robert
JUV *Pocahontas and the Strangers.*
Crowell 1971.
BL v68 D 15, 1971 p365; Comw v95 N 19, 1971 p187; KR v39 1971 p1016; LJ v96 1971 p3898.

Carpenter, Frances
JUV *Pocahontas and Her World.*
Knopf 1957.
BRD 1957 p153; KR v25 1957 p219; LJ v82 1957 p1797.

Criss, Mildred
JUV *Pocahontas, Young American Princess.*
Dodd, Mead & Co. 1943.
BRD 1943 p186; LJ v68 1943 p577; SatR Je 19, 1943 p31.

Dixon, Margaret
Pocahontas: The Princess of the Old Dominion.
Garrett & Massie 1958.
Also published as *The Princess of the Old Dominion.*

Donnell, Susan
YA *Pocahontas.*
Berkley Books 1991.
BL v87 1991 p1113; SLJ v37 Ag 1991 p209.

Gerson, Noel Bertram
Daughter of Eve.
Doubleday 1958 (Rpr. 1979).
BL v54 1958 p638; BRD 1958 p423; KR v26 1958
    p343.

Lawson, Marie A.
YA *Pocahontas and Captain John Smith; the Story of
    the Virginia Colony.*
Random House 1950.
BRD 1950 p541; LJ v76 1951 p54; NYTBR N 12,
    1950 p6.

O'Dell, Scott
YA *The Serpent Never Sleeps: A Novel of Jamestown
    and Pocahontas.*
Houghton Mifflin 1987.
BL v84 N 1, 1987 p483; KR v55 1987 p998; PW v232
    Ag 14, 1987 p105; SLJ v34 S 1987 p198.

Wahl, Jan
Pocahontas in London.
Crowell 1971.

1107. Poe, Edgar Allan
1809-1849
American author, poet, & journalist

Avi
YA *The Man Who Was Poe: A Novel.*
Orchard Books 1989.
BL v86 1989 p345; BRD 1990 p82; KR v57 1989
    p1470; SLJ v35 S 1989 p270.

Benet, Laura
YA *Young Edgar Allan Poe.*
Dodd 1941.
BL v38 1942 p161; BRD 1941 p71; LJ v66 1941 p1096.

Davis, Harriet
Elmira; the Girl Who Loved Edgar Allan Poe.
Houghton Mifflin 1966.
KR v34 1966 p989; LJ v91 1966 p5248; NYTBR F 12,
    1967 p20.

Edwards, Anne
Child of Night.
Random House 1975.
BS v35 O 1975 p193; KR v43 1975 p621; LJ v100
    1975 p1573.

Hurwood, Bernhardt J.
*My Savage Muse: The Story of My Life: Edgar Al-
    lan Poe, an Imaginative Work.*
Everest House 1980.
BL v76 1980 p1021; KR v47 1979 p1343; LJ v105
    1980 p225; NYTBR F 3, 1980 p15.

Madsen, David
*Black Plume: The Suppressed Memoirs of Edgar Al-
    lan Poe.*
Simon & Schuster 1980 (Rpr. 1991).
BL v77 1980 p99; KR v48 1980 p862; LJ v105 1980
    p1753; NYTBR O 12, 1980 p15; SLJ v27 My 1981
    p90.

Metcalf, Paul C.
Both.
Jargon Society 1982.
LJ v108 1983 p2300.

Meyers, Manny
The Last Mystery of Edgar Allan Poe.
Lippincott 1978.
KR v46 1978 p904.

Moore, Barbara
The Fever Called Living.
Doubleday 1976.
BL v73 1976 p588; KR v44 1976 p921; LJ v101 1976
    p2394; PW v210 Jl 26, 1976 p69.

O'Neal, Cothburn
The Very Young Mrs. Poe.
Crown 1956.
BL v52 1956 p276; BRD 1956 p706; FC 7th p269; KR
    v23 1955 p901; LJ v81 1956 p771.

Perowne, Barry
A Singular Conspiracy.
Bobbs-Merrill 1974.
KR v42 1974 p266; LJ v99 1974 p776; NYTBR My
    19, 1974 p41; PW v205 Ap 15, 1974 p47.

Rucker, Rudy
*The Hollow Earth: The Narrative of Mason Algiers
    Reynolds of Virginia.*
Morrow 1990.
BL v87 1990 p32; KR v58 1990 p972; LJ v115 Ag
    1990 p147; NYTBR S 2, 1990 p18; PW v237 Je 29,
    1990 p89.

Sinclair, Andrew
The Facts in the Case of E. A. Poe.
Holt, Rinehart & Winston 1980.
KR v48 1980 p1020; LJ v105 1980 p2234; NYTBR O
    12, 1980 p15; PW v218 Ag 15, 1980 p44.

Steward, Barbara
Evermore.
Morrow 1978.
BL v74 1978 p1327; KR v46 1978 p65; LJ v103 1978
    p900; PW v213 Ja 23, 1978 p364.

Steward, Barbara; Steward, Dwight
The Lincoln Diddle.
Morrow 1979.
KR v47 1979 p825; LJ v104 1979 p1591; PW v215 Je
    18, 1979 p80.

Williams, Chancellor
The Raven.
Dorrance 1943 (Rpr. 1975).
BRD 1944 p815; NYTBR Ja 9, 1944 p26.

Zaroulis, N. L.
The Poe Papers: A Tale of Passion.
Putnam 1977.
BL v73 1977 p1709; KR v45 1977 p310; LJ v102 1977
    p1309; NYTBR Je 5, 1977 p53; PW v211 Mr 21,
    1977 p80.

1108. Poinsett, Joel Roberts
1779-1851
American Secretary of War, 1837-1840

Kummer, Frederic A.
YA *Courage over the Andes.*
Winston 1940.
BL v37 1941 p221; BRD 1940 p526; CC 7th p1008.

1109. Polk, James Knox
1795-1849
11th US President

Gerson, Noel Bertram
The Slender Reed: A Biographical Novel of James Knox Polk.
Doubleday 1965.
FC 9th p198; LJ v90 1965 p894.

1110. Polk, Sarah Childress
1803-1891
Wife of James Polk

Crabb, Alfred L.
Lodging at the Saint Cloud, a Tale of Occupied Nashville.
Bobbs-Merrill 1946.
BL v42 1946 p317; BRD 1946 p178; KR v14 1946 p49; NYTBR Ap 21, 1946 p26.

1111. Polo, Marco
see Marco Polo

1112. Pompey the Great
106-48 BC
Roman general & political leader

Duggan, Alfred Leo
Winter Quarters.
Coward-McCann 1956.
BRD 1956 p273; FC 7th p117; KR v24 1956 p590; LJ v81 1956 p1993; NYTBR S 23, 1956 p4.

1113. Ponce de Leon, Juan
1460-1521
Spanish discoverer of Florida

Bailey, Bernadine
YA *Juan Ponce de Leon: First in the Land.*
Houghton Mifflin 1958.
LJ v84 1959 p641.

Baker, Nina
YA *Juan Ponce de Leon.*
Knopf 1957.
BL v53 1957 p535; BRD 1957 p40; KR v25 1957 p180; LJ v82 1957 p1686.

Kaufelt, David A.
American Tropic.
Poseidon Press 1986.

BL v83 1987 p751; KR v54 1986 p1605; LJ v112 F 1, 1987 p92; NYTBR F 1, 1987 p20.

1114. Pontiac
1720-1769
Chief of the Ottawa Indians

Gay, Margaret Cooper
Hatchet in the Sky.
Simon & Schuster 1954.
BL v51 1954 p84; BRD 1954 p346; KR v22 1954 p412; LJ v79 1954 p1832; NYTBR D 5, 1954 p53.

Zara, Louis
This Land Is Ours.
Houghton Mifflin 1940.
BL v36 1940 p346; BRD 1940 p1024; NYTBR Ap 21, 1940 p2; SatR Ap 27, 1940 p7.

1115. Pope, Alexander
1688-1744
English poet; wrote *The Rape of the Lock*

Holdsworth, Jean
The Stooping Falcon: A Novel of the Life of Alexander Pope.
Constable 1977.
Obs Ag 14, 1977 p23.

1116. Porter, William Sydney
see Henry, O., pseud.

1117. Powell, Adam Clayton
1908-1972
American politician

Meriwether, Louise
Daddy Was a Number Runner.
Prentice-Hall 1970 (Rpr. 1972, 1977, 1986).
BL v67 1971 p654; BRD 1970 p968; KR v38 1970 p22; LJ v95 1970 p685; NYTBR Je 28, 1970 p31.

1118. Powhatan
1550-1618
American Indian chief

Bowman, John Clarke
Powhatan's Daughter.
Viking 1973.
Also published as *Pocahontas.*
FC 9th p58; KR v41 N 1, 1973 p1219; LJ v98 1973 p3390.

1119. Presley, Elvis
1935-1977
American rock n' roll idol

Charters, Samuel B.
Elvis Presley Calls His Mother after the Ed Sullivan Show.

Coffee House Press 1992.
PW v239 Mr 2, 1992 p60.

Childress, Mark
Tender: A Novel.
Harmony Books 1990.
BL v87 1990 p139; KR v58 1990 p946; LJ v115 S 1,
1990 p256; NYTBR S 23, 1990 p12; PW v237 Jl
20, 1990 p48; Time v136 S 24, 1990 p90.

Farren, Mick
The Neural Atrocity.
Mayflower 1977.

Kalpakian, Laura
Graced Land.
Grove Weidenfeld 1992.
Also published as *Graceland.*
Obs Ag 9, 1992 p51; PW v239 F 10, 1992 p70.

Levy, Elizabeth
YA *All Shook Up.*
Scholastic 1986.
KR v54 1986 p52; SLJ v33 N 1986 p104.

Marino, Jan
YA *The Day That Elvis Came to Town.*
Little, Brown 1991.
BL v87 1990 p817; KR v59 1991 p48; SLJ v37 Ja 1991
p114.

Townsend, Tom
Trader Wooly and the Ghost in the Colonel's Jeep.
Eakin Press 1991.

1120. Priestly, Joseph
1733-1804
English clergyman & chemist; one of the discov-
erers of oxygen

Gilliam, John Graham
The Crucible: The Story of Joseph Priestly.
Hale 1954.

1121. Princip, Gavrilo
1895-1918
Serbian assassin; assassinated Archduke Ferdinand

Koning, Hans
Death of a Schoolboy.
Harcourt Brace Jovanovich 1974.
BL v70 1974 p977; BRD 1974 p673; KR v41 1973
p1324; LJ v99 1974 p504; NYTBR Ap 7, 1974 p30;
PW v204 D 3, 1973 p35.

1122. Puccini, Giacomo
1858-1924
Italian opera composer

Paul, Barbara
A Cadenza for Caruso.
St. Martin's 1984.

BL v80 1984 p1380; KR v52 1984 p430; NY v60 S 3,
1984 p98; PW v225 My 11, 1984 p262.

1123. Puento, Tito
1923-
American bandleader

Hijuelos, Oscar
The Mambo Kings Play Songs of Love.
Farrar, Straus, Giroux 1989.
Won 1990 Pulitzer Prize.
BL v85 1989 p1943; BRD 1990 p817; KR v57 1989
p860; NYTBR Ag 27, 1989 p1.

1124. Pugachev, Yemelyan I
1741-1775
Russian adventurer & impostor

Carnegie, Sacha
The Banners of Revolt.
Davies 1977.

Kay, Mara
JUV *In Place of Katia.*
Scribner 1963.
LJ v88 1963 p1766.

1125. Pulaski, Kazimierz
1747-1779
Polish patriot & American Revolutionary general

Bell, Kensil
YA *Secret Mission for Valley Forge.*
Dodd, Mead 1956.
BL v51 1955 p346; BRD 1955 p59; LJ v80 1955 p1007.

Flood, Charles B.
Monmouth.
Houghton Mifflin 1961.
BRD 1962 p395; LJ v86 1961 p3300; NYTBR O 8,
1961 p5; SatR N 4, 1961 p41.

1126. Pullman, George Mortimer
1831-1897
American inventor; developed railway sleeping
car

Jakes, John
Homeland.
Doubleday 1993.

Mark, Grace
The Dream Seekers.
Morrow 1992.

1127. Pushkin, Aleksandr Sergeyevich
1799-1837
Russian poet

Grossman, Leonid Petrovich
Death of a Poet: A Novel of the Last Years of Alexander Pushkin.
Hutchinson International Authors 1940.

Killens, John O.
Great Black Russian: A Novel on the Life and Times of Alexander Pushkin.
Wayne State University Press 1989.
NYTBR F 18, 1990 p20; PW v236 S 15, 1989 p108.

Lambert, Lydia
Pushkin, Poet and Lover.
Doubleday 1946.
BRD 1946 p468; LJ v71 1946 p822; NYTBR S 1, 1946 p8.

Petrie, Glen
The Fourth King.
Atheneum 1986.
BL v83 1986 p102; KR v54 1986 p1150; LJ v111 O 15, 1986 p111.

1128. Putnam, Israel
1718-1790
American Revolutionary general

Dean, Leon W.
YA *Old Wolf: The Story of Israel Putnam.*
Farrar & Rinehart 1942.
BL v39 1942 p107; BRD 1942 p196; LJ v67 1942 p741.

Monjo, F. N.
JUV *The Jezebel Wolf.*
Simon & Schuster 1971.
BRD 1972 p916; KR v39 1971 p740; LJ v97 1972 p276.

Stevenson, Augusta
JUV *Israel Putnam, Fearless Boy.*
Bobbs-Merrill 1959.
LJ v84 1959 p3932.

1129. Pyle, Ernie
1900-1945
American journalist; won 1944 Pulitzer Prize

Wilson, Ellen Janet
JUV *Ernie Pyle, Boy From Back Home.*
Bobbs-Merrill 1955.

1130. Pytheas
Greek navigator

Frye, John
North to Thule: An Imagined Narrative of the Famous "Lost" Sea Voyage of Pytheas of Massalia in the Fourth Century B.C..
Algonquin 1985.
PW v227 Mr 22, 1985 p46.

1131. Quanah
1845-1911
Comanche Indian chief

Dugan, Bill
Quanah Parker.
Harper 1993.

Foreman, Paul
Quanah, the Serpent Eagle.
Northland Press 1983.
CAY v5 Summer 1984 p6; SWR v68 Autumn 1983 p410.

Kemper, Troxey
Comanche Warbonnet: A Story of Quanah Parker.
Navajo Community College Press 1991.

Kissinger, Rosemary K.
JUV *Quanah Parker: Commanche Chief.*
Pelican Pub. Co. 1991.
BL v87 1991 p1792.

1132. Quantrill, William Clarke
1837-1865
American Confederate guerrilla leader; killed by Federal troops

Appell, George C.
The Man Who Shot Quantrill.
Doubleday 1957.
BRD 1957 p23; KR v25 1957 p548; LJ v82 1957 p2034; SatR N 23, 1957 p42.

Goede, William
Quantrill.
Quadrant Editions 1982.
BIC v11 Ag 1982 p23; Mac v95 Ap 12, 1982 p57; Quill & Q v48 O 1982 p33.

Gruber, Frank
The Bushwhackers.
Rinehart 1959.
NYTBR Mr 1, 1959 p22.

Gruber, Frank
Quantrell's Raiders.
Ace Books 1953.

Ringler, Laurel O.
Dark Grows the Night.
Pageant Press 1961.

1133. Rachel
Old Testament figure

Cabries, Jean
Jacob.
Dutton 1958.
BL v55 1958 p97; BRD 1958 p177; KR v26 1958 p477; LJ v83 1958 p3152; NYTBR S 14, 1958 p30.

Fineman, Irving
Jacob; an Autobiographical Novel.
Random House 1941.

BRD 1941 p297; NYTBR O 5, 1941 p6; SatR O 11, 1941 p14.

1134. Rachel, Elisa Felix
1820-1858
French actress

Cost, March
Rachel: An Interpretation.
Collins 1947 (Rpr. 1957).
Reprint published as *I, Rachel.*
BRD 1957 p656; KR v25 1957 p700; NYTBR N 17, 1957 p53; SatR D 28, 1957 p26.

Powers, Anne
Rachel.
Pinnacle 1973 (Rpr. 1979).
PW v203 My 28, 1973 p41.

1135. Radisson, Pierre Espirit
1636-1710
French explorer

Edwards, C. A. M.
YA *Son of the Mohawks.*
Ryerson Press 1954.
LJ v80 1955 p1511.

Hough, Edith A.
YA *The Blue-Eyed Iroquois.*
F.E. Faulkner Print Co. 1968.

Ridle, Julia Brown
YA *Mohawk Gamble.*
Harper & Row 1963.
LJ v88 1963 p2154.

1136. Raffles, Thomas Stamford, Sir
1781-1826
English colonial administrator; founded Singapore

George, S. C.
Bright Moon in the Forest.
Jarrolds 1946.

1137. Raleigh, Walter, Sir
1552-1618
English courtier, navigator, & author; beheaded for treason

Anthony, Michael
Bright Road to El Dorado.
Nelson Caribbean 1982.

Garrett, George
Death of the Fox.
Doubleday 1971 (Rpr. 1991).
BL v68 1971 p182; BRD 1971 p477; FC 11th p229; KR v39 1971 p1036; LJ v96 1971 p2540; NYTBR S 26, 1971 p52.

Graham, Winston
The Grove of Eagles.
Doubleday 1963.
BRD 1964 p486; FC 9th p213; LJ v89 1964 p654; NYTBR Ja 12, 1964 p22.

Greenwood, L. B.
Sherlock Holmes and the Case of the Raleigh Legacy.
Atheneum 1986.
BL v83 1986 p474; KR v54 1986 p1474; PW v232 O 2, 1987 p94.

Heaven, Constance
Queen's Delight.
Hale 1966.

Lobdell, Helen
YA *The King's Snare.*
Houghton Mifflin 1955.
BL v51 1955 p324; BRD 1955 p565; KR v23 1955 p83; LJ v80 1955 p1011.

Lofts, Norah
Here Was a Man: A Romantic History of Sir Walter Raleigh, His Voyages, His Discoveries, and His Queen.
Knopf 1936 (Rpr. 1975).

Nye, Robert
The Voyage of the Destiny.
Putnam 1982.
BRD 1983 p1085; LJ v107 1982 p1896.

O'Conor, Joseph
A Lion Trap.
Hutchinson 1969.

Pelham, Randolph
Raleigh's Rival.
Hale 1972.

Rose, Mark
Golding's Tale.
Walker 1972.
BL v68 1972 p888; KR v40 1972 p95; LJ v97 1972 p2435.

Schoonover, Lawrence
To Love a Queen.
Little, Brown 1973.
BL v69 1973 p791; KR v40 1972 p1444; LJ v98 1973 p86.

Sutcliff, Rosemary
Lady in Waiting.
Hodder & Stoughton 1957 (Rpr. 1989).
BRD 1957 p896; FC 9th p497; KR v25 1957 p195; NYTBR Ap 7, 1957 p26; SatR Je 1, 1957 p14.

Trease, Geoffrey
YA *Sir Walter Raleigh, Captain and Adventurer.*
Vanguard Press 1950.
BRD 1950 p910; LJ v75 1950 p1675; NYTBR N 12, 1950 p18; SatR N 11, 1950 p63.

Turner, Judy
Ralegh's Fair Bess.
Hale 1972 (Rpr. 1974).
LJ v99 1974 p1060; PW v205 F 25, 1974 p104.

1138. Rama IV
see Mongkut

1139. Rameses II
King of Egypt; known for building magnificent
monuments & temples

Grant, Joan Marshall
So Moses Was Born.
Methuen 1952 (Rpr. 1980).

Rice, Anne
The Mummy; or, Ramses the Damned.
Ballantine 1989.
BL v85 1989 p1051; KR v57 1989 p328; NYTBR Je
11, 1989 p9; PW v235 My 5, 1989 p70.

1140. Rasputin, Grigori Efimovich
1871-1916
Russian monk & mystic; adviser to Czarina Alexandra; assassinated

Quigley, Aileen
A Devil in Holy Orders.
Hale 1973.

Trease, Geoffrey
YA *The White Nights of St. Petersburg.*
Macmillan 1967.
KR v35 1967 p1477.

Wilson, Colin
The Magician from Siberia.
Hale 1988.

1141. Rathbone, Basil
1892-1967
English actor; known for his Sherlock Holmes
series of films

Kaminsky, Stuart M.
The Howard Hughes Affair.
St. Martin's 1979.
BL v76 1979 p332; BW v9 O 21, 1979 p6; KR v47
1979 p895; LJ v104 1979 p1723; NYTBR O 7,
1979 p35.

1142. Rawlins, John A.
1831-1869
American army officer; General Grant's advisor

Devon, Louis
Aide to Glory.
Crowell 1952.
BL v49 1952 p125; BRD 1952 p248; LJ v77 1952
p1758.

1143. Reagan, Ronald Wilson
1911-
American actor & 40th US President

Ballard, J. G.
The Atrocity Exhibition.
Cape 1970.
KR v38 1970 p529; LJ v95 1970 p2512.

Blumberg, Nathan
*The Afternoon of March 30: A Contemporary His-
torical Novel.*
Wood Fire Ashes Press 1984.

Garnet, Eldon
I Shot Mussolini.
Impulse Editions 1989.
BIC Mr 1990 p48.

Thomsen, Paul
Operation Rawhide.
Wolgemuth & Hyatt 1990.

1144. Red Cloud, Chief
1822-1909
Chief of the Oglala Sioux Indians

Ulyatt, Kenneth
North against the Sioux.
Prentice-Hall 1967.
BL v64 1967 p319; BRD 1967 p1332; KR v35 1967
p329; LJ v92 1967 p1952.

Wheeler, Richard S.
Dodging Red Cloud.
Evans & Co. 1987.
BL v84 1987 p539; LJ v112 N 1, 1987 p123; PW v232
1987 p69.

1145. Reed, John Silas
1887-1920
American journalist & author; wrote *Ten Days
That Shook the World*

Cheuse, Alan
*The Bohemians, John Reed & His Friends Who
Shook the World.*
Apple-Wood Books 1982.
Choice v20 N 1982 p424; KR v50 1982 p20; LJ v107
1982 p1009; NYTBR Mr 28, 1982 p14.

1146. Reed, Walter
1851-1902
American surgeon; proved that transmission of
the yellow fever virus was by mosquitoes

Higgins, Helen Boyd
JUV *Walter Reed, Boy Who Wanted to Know.*
Bobbs-Merrill 1961.

1147. Reinhardt, Django
1910-1953
Belgian jazz musician

Kotzwinkle, William
The Hot Jazz Trio.
Houghton Mifflin 1989.
Contains a novella entitled *Django Reinhardt Played the Blues.*
KR v57 1989 p1354; LJ v114 O 15, 1989 p102; PW v236 S 15, 1989 p109.

1148. Rembrandt (Harmenszoon van Rijn)
1607-1669
Dutch painter

Alcorn, Johnny
JUV *Rembrandt's Beret; or, The Painter's Crown.*
Tambourine Books 1991.
BL v87 1991 p2047; KR v59 1991 p727; SLJ v37 Je 1991 p100.

Heller, Joseph
Picture This.
Putnam 1988.
BL v84 1988 p1754; BRD 1989 p726; KR v56 1988 p923; LJ v113 S 1, 1988 p182; NYTBR S 11, 1988 p9.

Lawrence, Isabelle
YA *The Night Watch.*
Rand McNally 1952.
BL v48 1952 p384; BRD 1952 p541; HB v28 Ag 1952 p240.

Passes, Alan
YA *The Private Diary of Rembrandt Harmenszoon van Rijn, Painter, 1661.*
Pavilion Books 1985.
BFYC v21 Autumn 1986 p16.

Schmitt, Gladys
Rembrandt: A Novel.
Random House 1961.
BL v57 1961 p664; BRD 1961 p1255; FC 9th p447; KR v29 1961 p379; LJ v86 1961 p2494; NYTBR Je 25, 1961 p3.

Strand, Mark
JUV *Rembrandt Takes a Walk.*
C.N. Potter 1986.
BRD 1987 p1808; KR v54 1986 p1859; NYTBR N 9, 1986 p54; SLJ v33 Ja 1987 p68.

Weiss, David
I, Rembrandt.
St. Martin's 1979.
KR v47 1979 p412; LJ v104 1979 p1281; PW v215 Ap 9, 1979 p96.

1149. Remington, Frederic
1861-1909
American painter, sculptor, & illustrator of Western scenes

Blackburn, Thomas Wakefield
A Good Day to Die.
D. McKay 1967.
BL v63 1967 p1032; BRD 1967 p132; KR v35 1967 p17; LJ v92 1967 p1029; NYTBR Mr 19, 1967 p49.

Lynch, Daniel
Yellow: A Novel.
Walker 1992.
KR v60 1992 p1276; LJ v117 N 15, 1992 p102.

Van Every, Dale
The Day the Sun Died.
Little, Brown 1971.
FC 9th p526; KR v39 1971 p76; LJ v96 1971 p502; LJ v96 1971 p2146.

1150. Revere, Paul
1735-1818
American patriot & silversmith

Fisher, Dorthea
YA *Paul Revere and the Minute Men.*
Random House 1950.
BRD 1950 p310; LJ v76 1951 p53; NYTBR N 12, 1950 p6.

Forbes, Esther
JUV *Johnny Tremain.*
Houghton Mifflin 1943 (Heavily reprinted).
Won 1944 Newbery award.
BRD 1943 p273; LJ v68 1943 p832; LJ v68 1943 p965; NYTBR N 14, 1943 p5; SatR N 13, 1943 p44.

Kornblatt, Marc
JUV *Paul Revere and the Boston Tea Party.*
Bantam 1987.
SLJ v34 Ja 1988 p96.

Lawson, Robert
JUV *Mr. Revere and I.*
Little Brown 1953 (Rpr. 1976).
BRD 1953 p549; BL v50 O 15, 1953 p84; LJ v78 1953 p1858; NYTBR N 15, 1953 p26.

Phelan, Mary Kay
JUV *Midnight Alarm: The Story of Paul Revere's Ride.*
Crowell 1968.
BRD 1969 p1038; KR v36 1968 p1055; LJ v93 1968 p3973; NYTBR D 29, 1968 p20; PW v194 O 28, 1968 p60.

Rogers, Frances
YA *Paul Revere, Patriot on Horseback.*
Frederick A. Stokes 1943.
BL v40 1943 p83; BRD 1943 p700; LJ v68 1943 p730; SatR N13, 1943 p45.

Stevenson, Augusta
JUV *Paul Revere, Boy of Old Boston.*
Bobbs-Merrill 1946 (Rpr. 1962).
BRD 1946 p787; KR v14 1946 p198; LJ v71 1946 p983.

Webb, Robert N.
JUV *We Were There at the Boston Tea Party.*

Grosset & Dunlap 1956.
BRD 1956 p974; KR v24 1956 p45; LJ v81 1956
p1045; NYTBR Mr 18, 1956 p40.

1151. Rhodes, Cecil John
1853-1902
British Colonial Administrator in South Africa;
founder of Rhodes Scholarships

Fish, Robert L.
Rough Diamond.
Doubleday 1981.
PW v220 Ag 7, 1981 p64; TLS Ag 6, 1982 p853.

Samkange, Stanlake
On Trial for My Country.
Heinemann 1966.

Young, Francis Brett
The City of Gold.
Heinemann 1939 (Rpr. 1966, 1971).
BL v36 1939 p69; BRD 1939 p1076; NYTBR O 8,
1939 p6; SatR O 14, 1939 p12.

1152. Ricci, Matteo
1552-1610
Italian missionary; founder of the Jesuit missions
in China

Polland, Madeleine A.
YA *Mission to Cathay.*
Doubleday 1965.
BRD 1967 p1047; LJ v90 1965 p3808.

1153. Richard I
1157-1199
King of England, 1189-1199

Adams, Doris Sutcliffe
No Man's Son.
Walker 1969.

Barnes, Margaret Campbell
The Passionate Brood.
Macrae Smith 1945 (Rpr. 1972).
Also published as *Like Us They Live.*
BRD 1945 p37; FC 10th p34; KR v13 F 15, 1945 p72;
WLB v40 O 1945 p101.

Bennetts, Pamela
Richard and the Knights of God.
St. Martin's 1973.
KR v41 1973 p825; LJ v98 1973 p3281; PW v204 S 3,
1973 p50.

Brand, Max
The Golden Knight.
Greystone 1940.

Charques, Dorothy
Men Like Shadows.
Murray 1952.
BL v49 1953 p303; BRD 1953 p171; KR v21 1953
p195; NYTBR Ap 5, 1953 p18.

Haggard, H. Rider
The Brethren.
Cassell 1904 (Rpr. 1907, 1952).
NYTBR D 31, 1904 p940.

Haycraft, Molly
My Lord Brother the Lion Heart.
Lippincott 1968.
BRD 1968 p583; FC 10th p245; LJ v93 1968 p1161;
LJ v93 1968 p2132.

Hibbert, Eleanor (Jean Plaidy, pseud.)
The Heart of the Lion.
Putnam 1980.
KR v48 1980 p1017.

Kaufman, Pamela
Banners of Gold.
Crown 1986.
BL v83 1986 p3; BS v46 D 1986 p328; KR v54 1986
p1314; PW v230 S 12, 1986 p79.

Kaufman, Pamela
Shield of Three Lions.
Crown 1983.
BL v79 1983 p1421; KR v51 1983 p781; LJ v108 1983
p1721; PW v224 Jl 29, 1983 p61.

Leslie, Doris
*The Warrior King: The Reign of Richard the Lion
Heart.*
Heinemann 1977.

Lodge, Thomas
The Life and Death of William Longbeard.
University of Copenhagen Press 1983.

Lofts, Norah
The Lute Player.
Doubleday 1951.
BL v48 1951 p102; BRD 1951 p536; FC 11th p379;
KR v19 1951 p495; NYTBR N 11, 1951 p26.

Peters, Maureen
The Willow Maid.
Hale 1974.

Rofheart, Martha
Lionheart: A Novel of Richard I, King of England.
Simon & Schuster 1981.
KR v49 1981 p1031; LJ v106 1981 p2050.

Scott, Walter Sir
YA *Ivanhoe: A Romance.*
A. Constable 1820 (Heavily reprinted).
FC 11th p543.

Scott, Walter Sir
YA *The Talisman.*
Constable 1825 (Heavily reprinted).

Shelby, Graham
The Devil Is Loose.
Doubleday 1974.
KR v42 1974 p833; LJ v99 1974 p2503; PW v206 Ag
12, 1974 p52.

Shelby, Graham
The Kings of Vain Intent.
Weybright & Talley 1970.
KR v39 1971 p137; LJ v96 1971 p2104.

Tarr, Judith
The Isle of Glass.
Bluejay Books 1985.
BL v81 1985 p824; KR v52 1984 p1172; LJ v110 F 15,
    1985 p182; PW v227 Ja 18, 1985 p64.

Vidal, Gore
A Search for the King: A 12th Century Legend.
Dutton 1950 (Rpr. 1978).
BL v46 1950 p150; BRD 1950 p933; FC 7th p362; KR
    v17 1949 p628; LJ v74 1949 p1819; NYTBR Ja 15,
    1950 p4.

Webb, Robert N.
JUV *We Were There with Richard the Lionhearted in the
    Crusades.*
Grosset & Dunlap 1957.

Welch, Ronald (R. O. Felton, pseud.)
YA *Knight Crusader.*
Oxford University Press 1954 (Rpr. 1979).
BL v51 1955 p370; BRD 1955 p960; KR v23 1955
    p130; LJ v80 1955 p1515; NYTBR Ag 21, 1955 p24.

Williams, Jay
Tomorrow's Fire.
Atheneum 1964.
LJ v89 1964 p3975; NYTBR O 4, 1964 p40.

1154. Richard II
1367-1400
King of England, 1377-1399; son of Edward the
Black Prince

Barnes, Margaret Campbell
Within the Hollow Crown.
Macrae 1947 (Rpr. 1972).
BRD 1948 p46; FC 7th p30; KR v15 1947 p553;
    NYTBR D 28, 1947 p17.

Bennetts, Pamela
The Lords of Lancaster.
St. Martin's 1973.

Clarke, Brenda (Brenda Honeyman, pseud.)
At the King's Court.
Hale 1977.

Dakers, Elaine (Jane Lane, pseud.)
A Summer Storm.
P. Davies 1976.

Doherty, P. C.
The Whyte Harte.
St. Martin's 1988.
BL v85 1988 p617; KR v56 1988 p1566; LJ v114 Ja
    1989 p105; PW v234 O 28, 1988 p64.

Hibbert, Eleanor (Jean Plaidy, pseud.)
Passage to Pontefract.
Hale 1981.

BL v79 1982 p2; KR v50 1982 p897; PW v222 O 8,
    1982 p127.

Leslie, Doris
*Crown of Thorns: The Life and Reign of Richard
    II.*
Heinemann 1979.

Lewis, Hilda
YA *The Gentle Falcon.*
Criterion Books 1957.
BL v54 1957 p82; BRD 1957 p550; KR v25 1957
    p385; LJ v82 1957 p2658; NYTBR S 1, 1957 p14.

Tucker, Terry
The Unravished Bride.
Hale 1970 (Rpr. 1973).

Young, Dorothy V.
King's Tragedy: The Life and Times of Richard II.
Hale 1971.

1155. Richard III
1452-1485
King of England, 1483-1485

Abbey, Margaret
Blood of the Boar.
Hale 1979.

Abbey, Margaret
The Crowned Boar.
Hale 1971.

Abbey, Margaret
The Heart Is a Traitor.
Hale 1978.

Anand, Valerie
Crown of Roses.
St. Martin's 1989.
KR v57 1989 p1344.

Barnes, Margaret Campbell
The King's Bed.
Macrae Smith 1961.
FC 10th p34; LJ v87 1962 p1334.

Belle, Pamela
The Lodestar.
St. Martin's 1987.
KR v57 1989 p642; LJ v114 Je 15, 1989 p76; PW v235
    My 19, 1989 p68.

Bennetts, Pamela
The Third Richard.
Hale 1972.

Davidson, Margaret
My Lord Richard.
Cassell 1979.

Doherty, P. C.
The Fate of Princes.
St. Martin's 1991.
KR v59 1991 p214; NYTBR Ap 7, 1991 p33; PW
    v238 Ja 25, 1991 p48.

Eckerson, Olive
The Golden Yoke: A Novel of the War of the Roses.
Coward-McCann 1961.
LJ v86 1961 p3685.

Edwards, Rhoda
The Broken Sword.
Doubleday 1976.
Also published as *Some Touch of Pity.*
BS v36 N 1976 p245; KR v44 1976 p649; PW v209 My 31, 1976 p191.

Edwards, Rhoda
Fortune's Wheel.
Doubleday 1979.
KR v46 1978 p1263; LJ v104 1979 p647; PW v214 N 20, 1978 p52.

Evans, Jean
The White Rose of York.
Hale 1972.

Fairburn, Eleanor
Winter's Rose.
Hale 1976.

Farrington, Robert
The Killing of Richard the Third.
Scribner 1971.
BRD 1972 p401; KR v39 1971 p891; LJ v96 1971 p3345.

Few, Mary Dodgen
Under the White Boar.
Droke House 1971.

Ford, John M.
YA *The Dragon Waiting.*
Timescape Books 1983.
BL v80 1983 p468; KR v51 1983 p970; LJ v108 1983 p976; PW v224 O 14, 1983 p47; SLJ v30 Mr 1984 p178.

Jarman, Rosemary Hawley
We Speak No Treason.
Little, Brown 1971.
BRD 1971 p688; FC 9th p277; LJ v96 1971 p3159.

Kilbourne, Janet
Garland of the Realm.
Hale 1972.

Leary, Francis W.
Fire and Morning.
Putnam 1957.
BRD 1957 p536; FC 7th p217; KR v25 1957 p189; LJ v82 1957 p1066; NYTBR My 5, 1957 p34.

Lenanton, Carola M. (Carola Oman, pseud.)
Crouchback.
H. Holt 1929 (Rpr. 1953).
BRD 1929 p554; NYTBR N 3, 1929 p14; SRL v6 1930 p1089; TLS My 9, 1929 p385.

Long, Freda M.
Requiem for Richard.
Hale 1975.

McDonald, Eva
Cry Treason Thrice.
Hale 1977.

Nickell, Lesley J.
The White Queen.
St. Martin's 1978.
KR v47 1979 p956; LJ v104 1979 p2238.

Palmer, Marian
The White Boar.
Doubleday 1968.
FC 9th p394; KR v36 1968 p206; LJ v93 1968 p1502.

Penman, Sharon Kay
The Sunne in Splendour.
Holt, Rinehart & Winston 1982.
BL v78 1982 p1483; BRD 1983 p1140; KR v50 1982 p958; LJ v107 1982 p1677; NYTBR D 12, 1982 p34; PW v222 S 3, 1982 p52.

Peters, Elizabeth
The Murders of Richard III.
Dodd, Mead 1974 (Rpr. 1986, 1989).
BRD 1974 p952; LJ v99 1974 p1568; NYTBR Ag 25, 1974 p30; PW v205 Ap 22, 1974 p73.

Potter, Jeremy
A Trail of Blood.
Constable 1970.
BL v67 1971 p896; FC 9th p407; KR v39 1971 p28; LJ v96 1971 p863; NYTBR Mr 28, 1971 p22; Spec v225 N 21, 1970 p648.

Rabinowitz, Ann
YA *Knight on Horseback.*
Macmillan 1987.
BL v84 1987 p572; BRD 1988 p1420; SLJ v34 O 1987 p142.

Stevenson, Robert Louis
YA *The Black Arrow.*
Cassell & Co. 1888 (Heavily reprinted).
JHSLC 5th p418.

Tey, Josephine (Gordon Daviot, pseud.)
The Daughter of Time.
Macmillan 1951 (Heavily reprinted).
BRD 1952 p588; FC 9th p502; LJ v77 1952 p144; NYTBR F 24, 1952 p31; SatR Mr 22, 1952 p45.

Tyler-Whittle, Michael S.
Richard III: The Last Plantagenet.
Chilton Book Co. 1970.
Also published as *The Last Plantagenet.*
BL v67 1970 p265.

Vance, Marguerite
YA *Song for a Lute.*
Dutton 1958.
BL v55 1958 p107; BRD 1959 p1012; KR v26 1958 p418; LJ v83 1958 p3017; NYTBR S 28, 1958 p48.

Viney, Jayne
King Richard's Friend.
Hale 1975.

Viney, Jayne
The White Rose Dying.
Hale 1973.

1156. Richard the Lionhearted
see Richard I

1157. Richelieu, Armand Jean du Plessis, Cardinal
1585-1642
French political advisor; chief minister to Louis XIII; cardinal

Anthony, Evelyn
The Cardinal and the Queen.
Coward-McCann 1968.
FC 11th p20; KR v36 1968 p613; PW v193 Je 3, 1968 p125.

Dumas, Alexandre
The Three Musketeers.
Several editions exists, including some for juvenile and young adult readers.
FC 10th p151.

Dumas, Alexandre
Twenty Years After.
Original French edition published in 1845; several English language editions exists. Sequel to *The Three Musketeers.*
FC 11th p172; SHSLC 7th p383.

James, G. P. R.
Richelieu: A Tale of France.
Henry Colburn 1829 (Heavily reprinted).

Mallet-Joris, Francoise
The Favourite.
Farrar, Straus & Cudahy 1962.
BL v58 1962 p682; BRD 1962 p772; FC 9th p340; KR v30 1962 p250; LJ v87 1962 p1485; NYTBR My 6, 1962 p30.

Vigny, Alfred de
Cinq-Mars; or, A Conspiracy under Louis XIII.
Little, Brown 1826 (Heavily reprinted).

1158. Richthofen, Manfred von, Baron
1892-1918
German aviator; ace pilot in World War I; known as "The Red Baron"

Coursen, H. R.
After the War.
Heidelberg Graphics 1981.
Kliatt v16 Winter 1982 p6.

Mueller, Richard
YA *World War I Flying Ace.*
Bantam 1988.
VOYA v11 O 1988 p189.

1159. Rickover, Hyman George
1900-1986
American naval officer

Stephens, Edward C.
Blow Negative!.
Doubleday 1962.
BRD 1962 p1151; KR v30 1962 p24; LJ v87 1962 p1153; NYTBR Mr 25, 1962 p32.

1160. Riel, Louis David
1844-1885
Canadian insurgent; headed the Red River rebellion, 1870

Constantin-Weyer, Maurice
The Half-Breed.
Macaulay Co. 1930 (Rpr. 1954).
BRD 1930 p224; NYTBR My 11, 1930 p8; SatR Je 21, 1930 p1140.

Lutz, Giles A.
The Magnificent Failure.
Doubleday 1967.
KR v35 1967 p901; LJ v92 1967 p2943.

Palud-Pelletier, Noelie
JUV *Louis, Son of the Prairies.*
Pemmican Publications 1990.
Can Mat v19 My 1991 p160.

Rosenstock, Janet
Riel.
PaperJacks 1979.
BIC v8 Ap 1979 p28.

Truss, Jan
JUV *A Very Small Rebellion.*
J.M. LeBel Enterprises 1976.
SLJ v27 S 1980 p43.

Wiebe, Rudy
The Scorched-Wood People.
McClelland & Stewart 1977.
CF v57 N 1978 p34.

1161. Rimbaud, (Jean Nicolas) Arthur
1854-1891
French poet

Bercovici, Konrad
Savage Prodigal.
Beechhurst Press 1948.
BL v44 1948 p382; BRD 1948 p64; NYTBR Je 20, 1948 p16; SatR Jl 17, 1948 p14.

Strathern, Paul
A Season in Abyssinia: An Impersonation.
Macmillan 1972.
NS v83 My 19, 1972 p680; Obs My 28, 1972 p33; Spec v228 My 20, 1972 p772.

Ullman, James R.
The Day on Fire, Suggested by the Life of Arthur Rimbaud.

World Pub. Co. 1958.
BL v55 1958 p75; BRD 1958 p1070; BRD 1959
  p1004; KR v26 1958 p523; LJ v83 1958 p2324;
  NYTBR S 21, 1958 p5.

1162. Ringling Brothers
American circus owners

Burt, Olive Woolley
JUV *The Ringling Brothers: Circus Boys.*
Bobbs-Merrill 1945 (Rpr. 1962).
LJ v84 1959 p248.

1163. Ringo, Johnny
1844-1882
American outlaw

Aggeler, Geoffrey
Confessions of Johnny Ringo: A Novel.
Dutton 1987.
KR v55 1987 p738.

Garwood, W. R.
Ringo's Tombstone.
Bath Street Press 1981.

Scott, Leslie
Tombstone Showdown.
Arcadia House 1957.

1164. Rivera, Diego
1886-1957
Mexican painter

Brenner, Leah
YA *An Artist Grows Up in Mexico.*
Beechhurst Press 1953 (Rpr. 1987).
BRD 1953 p106; LJ v78 1953 p2216; NYTBR S 13,
  1953 p42; NYTBR Ap 12, 1987 p46.

Poniatowska, Elena
YA *Dear Diego.*
Pantheon 1986.
BL v82 1986 p1358; LJ v111 Jl 1986 p110; NYTBR Jl
  20, 1986 p12; PW v229 Ap 18, 1986 p49.

1165. Robert I
1274-1329
King of Scotland, 1306-1329; known as "Robert
the Bruce"

Hammand, Norman B.
De Monterey and the Losing Side.
Hale 1977.

Henty, G. A.
JUV *In Freedom's Cause: A Story of Wallace and
  Bruce.*
Blackie 1884 (Heavily reprinted).

Hill, Pamela
Marjorie of Scotland.
Putnam 1956.

BL v52 1956 p385; BRD 1956 p440; FC 7th p182; KR
  v24 1956 p139; SatR My 26, 1956 p27.

Mackenzie, Anges Mure
Apprentice Majesty.
Serif Books 1950.

Oliver, Jane
The Lion Is Come.
Collins 1951.
BL v53 1957 p404; BRD 1957 p697; KR v25 1957
  p152; NYTBR Mr 17, 1957 p38.

Oliver, Jane
JUV *Young Man with a Sword: A Novel for Boys and
  Girls.*
Macmillan 1955.
BRD 1955 p690; LJ v80 1955 p1971.

Porter, Jane
YA *The Scottish Chiefs.*
Longman 1810 (Heavily reprinted).

Stephens, Peter J.
JUV *Outlaw King: The Story of Robert the Bruce.*
Atheneum 1964.
BRD 1965 p1196; LJ v89 1964 p3500; NYTBR S 27,
  1964 p34.

Tranter, Nigel G.
Robert the Bruce: The Path of the Hero King.
Hodder & Stoughton 1970.
The second title of a trilogy of novels.
KR v40 1972 p351; KR v41 1973 p81; Obs My 17,
  1970 p31.

Tranter, Nigel G.
Robert the Bruce: The Price of the King's Peace.
Hodder & Stoughton 1971.
The third of a trilogy of novels.

Tranter, Nigel G.
Robert the Bruce: The Steps to the Empty Throne.
Hodder & Stoughton 1969.
The first of a trilogy of novels.
BW v7 Je 10, 1973 p13; TLS O 23, 1969 p1225.

1166. Robert the Bruce
see Robert I

1167. Roberts, Oral
1918-
American evangelist; founder of Oral Roberts
University

Vidal, Gore
Live from Golgotha.
Random House 1992.
NYTBR O 4, 1992 p13; NW v120 Ag 31, 1992 p69;
  Time v140 S 28, 1992 p64.

1168. Robeson, Paul Leroy
1898-1976
American singer & actor

Kaminsky, Stuart M.
Smart Moves.
St. Martin's 1986.
BL v83 1987 p983; KR v55 1987 p177; PW v231 Ja
23, 1987 p64.

Miers, Earl Schenck
Big Ben: A Novel.
Westminster Press 1942.
BL v38 1942 p275; BRD 1942 p533; SatR F 21, 1942
p13.

1169. Robespierre, Maximilien Francois de
1758-1794
French revolutionist; guillotined

Bois, Helma de
*The Incorruptible: A Tale of Revolution and Roy-
alty.*
Crown 1965.

Coryn, Marjorie
The Incorruptible.
Appleton-Century 1943.
Also published as *Ridiculous Dictator.*
BRD 1943 p179; NYTBR S 12, 1943 p4.

Mantel, Hilary
A Place of Greater Safety.
Atheneum 1993.
LJ v118 F 15, 1993 p193; NYTBR My 9, 1993 p21.

Williamson, Joanne S.
YA *Jacobin's Daughter.*
Knopf 1956.
BRD 1956 p1006; LJ v81 1956 p1051; NYTBR Je 24,
1956 p20.

1170. Robin Hood
Legendary hero & outlaw of Sherwood Forest

Bettinson, Ralph
Rogues of Sherwood Forest.
Ward, Lock & Co. 1950.

Blackwood, Gary L.
The Lion & the Unicorn.
Eagle Books 1982.

Carpenter, Richard
JUV *Robin of Sherwood.*
Puffin Books 1984.
GP My 1984 p4247.

Chase, Nicholas
Locksley.
St. Martin's 1983.
KR v51 1983 p894; LJ v108 1983 p1887.

Eager, Edward
JUV *Knight's Castle.*
Harcourt, Brace & World 1956 (Rpr. 1984).
BL v52 1956 p281; BRD 1956 p280; KR v23 1955
p859; LJ v81 1956 p766; NYTBR F 26, 1956 p30.

Fraser, Antonia
JUV *Robin Hood.*
Knopf 1971.
KR v40 1972 p480; LJ v97 1972 p2949.

Godwin, Parke
Sherwood.
Morrow 1991.
BL v87 1991 p1842; KR v59 1991 p748; LJ v116 Jl
1991 p134.

Gray, Nigel
JUV *The One and Only Robin Hood.*
Joy Street Books 1987.
SLJ v34 N 1987 p90.

Green, Simon
*Kevin Costner Is Robin Hood, Prince of Thieves: A
Novel.*
Berkley Books 1991.
Based on the story and screenplay by Pen Densham.

Ingle, Annie
JUV *Robin Hood.*
Random House 1991.

McKinley, Robin
YA *The Outlaws of Sherwood.*
Greenwillow Books 1988.
BL v85 1988 p703; BRD 1989 p1107; KR v56 1988
p1530; PW v234 N 11, 1988 p58; SLJ v35 Ja 1989
p94; SLJ v36 S 1990 p171.

Pyle, Howard
JUV *The Merry Adventures of Robin of Great Renown
in Nottinghamshire.*
Scribner 1883 (Heavily reprinted).
BRD 1946 p669; LJ v72 1947 p84; LJ v91 1966 p6212.

Roberson, Jennifer
Lady of the Forest.
Kensington Pub. Corp. 1992.
BL v88 1992 p1899; KR v60 1992 p876; LJ v117 Ag
1992 p152.

Ryan, David Stuart
The Lost Journal of Robyn Hood, Outlaw.
Kozmik Press 1989.

Singer, Marilyn
JUV *Lizzie Silver of Sherwood Forest.*
Harper & Row 1986.
BL v82 1986 p1544; BRD 1987 p1734; SLJ v33 O
1986 p183.

Stevenson, Jocelyn
JUV *Robin Hood, a High-Spirited Tale of Adventure,
Starring Jim Henson's Muppets.*
Random House 1980.
SLJ v27 D 1980 p56.

Sutcliff, Rosemary
JUV *The Chronicles of Robin Hood.*
Oxford University Press 1950 (Rpr. 1977).

Trease, Geoffrey
JUV *Bows against the Barons.*

International 1934 (Rpr. 1966).
LJ v92 1967 p3192.

Walt Disney Productions
JUV *Robin Hood to the Rescue.*
Golden Press 1973.

Whitby, Sharon
The Last of the Greenwood.
Hale 1975.

Williams, Jay
The Good Yeomen.
Appleton-Century-Crofts 1948.
BL v44 1948 p368; BRD 1948 p926; KR v16 1948
p127; LJ v73 1948 p709; NYTBR My 30, 1948 p4.

1171. Robinson, Jackie
1919-1972
American baseball player; first Black player in
the major leagues

Cohen, Barbara
JUV *Thank You, Jackie Robinson.*
Lothrop, Lee & Shepard Books 1974 (Rpr. 1989,
1990).
BL v70 1974 p1251; KR v42 1974 p423; LJ v99 1974
p2263.

Honig, Donald
The Plot to Kill Jackie Robinson.
Dutton 1992.
BL v88 1992 p1586; KR v60 1992 p356; PW v239 Mr
2, 1992 p50.

1172. Rockefeller, John D.
1839-1937
American capitalist & philanthropist; founded
Standard Oil of Ohio & Rockefeller Foundation

Ferrell, Elizabeth
Full of Thy Riches.
M.S. Mill Co. 1944.
BL v40 1944 p355; BRD 1944 p236; KR v12 1944
p104; LJ v69 1944 p354; NYTBR My 7, 1944 p19.

1173. Rockne, Knute Kenneth
1888-1931
American football coach; head coach for Notre
Dame, 1918-1931

Van Riper, Guernsey
JUV *Knute Rockne, Young Athlete.*
Bobbs-Merrill 1952 (Rpr. 1986).
BL v49 1953 p178; BRD 1953 p965; LJ v77 1952
p2185.

1174. Rockwell, Norman
1894-1978
American illustrator

Hodges, Hollis
Norman Rockwell's Greatest Painting.

Eriksson 1988.
BL v84 1988 p1889; KR v56 1988 p782; LJ v113 S 1,
1988 p182; PW v233 Je 17, 1988 p57.

Moline, Mary
JUV *Anne: The Story of Norman Rockwell's "No Swim-
ming".*
Rumbleseat Press 1985.

Moline, Mary
JUV *Mimi: The Story of Norman Rockwell's "Doctor
and Doll".*
Rumbleseat Press 1980.

1175. Rodia, Simon
1879-1965
American architect

Madian, Jon
JUV *Beautiful Junk.*
Little, Brown 1968.
BL v65 1968 p190; CC 13th p549; HB v44 O 1968
p557; LJ v93 N 15, 1968 p4406.

1176. Rodin, Auguste (Francois Auguste Rene)
1840-1917
French sculptor

Weiss, David
Naked Came I: A Novel of Rodin.
Morrow 1963.
BRD 1964 p1232; FC 9th p542; LJ v88 1963 p4790;
NYTBR N 24, 1963 p60.

1177. Roebling, John Augustus
1806-1869
American designer & engineer; father of Washington Roebling

Browin, Frances W.
YA *Big Bridge to Brooklyn: The Roebling Story.*
Aladdin Books 1956.
BL v53 1956 p50; BRD 1956 p123; KR v24 1956
p404; LJ v81 1956 p2036.

Veglahn, Nancy
YA *The Spider of Brooklyn Heights.*
Scribner 1967.
BL v63 1967 p1103; KR v35 1967 p138; LJ v92 1967
p3857.

1178. Roebling, Washington Augustus
1837-1926
American engineer; succeeded his father, John
Roebling, as chief engineer on the Brooklyn
Bridge

Browin, Frances W.
YA *Big Bridge to Brooklyn: The Roebling Story.*
Aladdin Books 1956.

BL v53 1956 p50; BRD 1956 p123; KR v24 1956
p404; LJ v81 1956 p2036.

Veglahn, Nancy
YA *The Spider of Brooklyn Heights*.
Scribner 1967.
BL v63 1967 p1103; KR v35 1967 p138; LJ v92 1967
p3857.

1179. Rogers, Roy
1912-
American actor & singer

Fannin, Cole
JUV *Roy Rogers, King of the Cowboys*.
Whitman 1956.

Miller, Snowden
JUV *Roy Rogers and the Outlaws of Sundown Valley*.
Whitman 1950.

Rivers, Jim
JUV *Roy Rogers and the Enchanted Canyon*.
Whitmore Pub. Co. 1954.

1180. Rogers, Will
1879-1935
American actor & humorist

Day, Donald
JUV *Will Rogers: The Boy Roper*.
Houghton Mifflin 1950.
BL v47 1951 p224; BRD 1951 p225; LJ v75 1950
p2083.

Van Riper, Guernsey
JUV *Will Rogers, Young Cowboy*.
Bobbs-Merrill 1951.
BRD 1951 p908; LJ v76 1951 p782; NYTBR My 13,
1951 p26; SatR Je 9, 1951 p48.

1181. Romanov, Anastasia
1901-1918?
Daughter of Czar Nicholas II of Russia

St. Rick, William
The Touching Fear.
International University Press 1991.

1182. Romberg, Sigmund
1887-1951
American composer

Arnold, Elliott
*Deep in My Heart: A Story Based on the Life of
Sigmund Romberg*.
Duell, Sloan & Pearce 1949.
BL v46 1949 p81; BRD 1949 p23; KR v17 1949 p319;
LJ v74 1949 p1604; NYTBR D 11, 1949 p26.

1183. Rommel, Erwin
1891-1944
German field marshall in World War II

Rohmer, Richard H.
Rommel & Patton.
Irwin 1986.
BIC v16 Ap 1987 p24; Mac v99 O 20, 1986 p66.

Wells, Lawrence
Rommel and the Rebel.
Doubleday 1986.
BL v82 1986 p946; NYTBR Mr 16, 1986 p16; WCRB
v12 S 1986 p30.

1184. Romulus
Roman legendary figure; founder of Rome

Duggan, Alfred Leo
Children of the Wolf.
Coward-McCann 1959.
Also published as *Founding Fathers*.
BL v56 1959 p183; BRD 1960 p384; LJ v84 1959
p3644; NYTBR S 20, 1959 p4.

1185. Ronsard, Pierre de
1524-1585
French poet

Ingman, Heather
*The Dance of the Muses: A Novel on the Life of
Pierre Ronsard*.
P. Owen 1987.
NS v113 My 15, 1987 p29; PW v233 F 12, 1988 p70.

1186. Roosevelt, Alice Lee
1861-1884
First wife of Theodore Roosevelt

Wilson, Dorothy Clarke
*Alice and Edith: The Two Wives of Theodore
Roosevelt*.
Doubleday 1989.
BL v86 1989 p725; KR v57 1989 p1360; LJ v114 O
15, 1989 p105.

1187. Roosevelt, Edith Kermit Carow
1861-1948
Second wife of Theodore Roosevelt

Wilson, Dorothy Clarke
*Alice and Edith: The Two Wives of Theodore
Roosevelt*.
Doubleday 1989.
BL v86 1989 p725; KR v57 1989 p1360; LJ v114 O
15, 1989 p105.

1188. Roosevelt, Eleanor
1884-1962
Wife of Franklin Delano Roosevelt; social reformer; US delegate to United Nations

Charyn, Jerome
The Franklin Scare.
Arbor House 1977.
BL v74 1977 p461; KR v45 1977 p797; LJ v102 1977 p2080.

Kaminsky, Stuart M.
The Fala Factor.
St. Martin's 1984.
BL v80 1984 p1522; NYTBR Ag 19, 1984 p20.

Lerman, Rhoda
Eleanor: A Novel.
Holt, Rinehart & Winston 1979.
BL v75 1079 p1202; BRD 1979 p749; KR v47 1979 p145; LJ v104 1979 p849; NYTBR My 20, 1979 p14.

Roosevelt, Elliott
A First Class Murder.
St. Martin's 1991.
BL v87 1991 p1099; KR v59 1991 p363.

Roosevelt, Elliott
The Hyde Park Murder.
St. Martin's 1985.
BL v81 1985 p1274; PW v227 My 31, 1985 p47; TLS Mr 7, 1986 p256.

Roosevelt, Elliott
Murder and the First Lady.
St. Martin's 1984.
BL v80 1984 p1361; KR v52 1984 p506; LJ v109 1984 p1147; NYTBR Ag 5, 1984 p21.

Roosevelt, Elliott
Murder at Hobcaw Barony.
St. Martin's 1986.
BL v82 1986 p1184; KR v54 1986 p827; LJ v111 My 1, 1986 p134; PW v229 My 16, 1986 p71.

Roosevelt, Elliott
Murder at the Palace.
St. Martin's 1987.
BL v84 1988 p973; KR v56 1988 p94; PW v232 D 25, 1987 p64.

Roosevelt, Elliott
Murder in the Blue Room.
St. Martin's 1990.
BL v86 1990 p1784; KR v58 1990 p537.

Roosevelt, Elliott
Murder in the Oval Office.
St. Martin's 1989.
BL v85 1988 p666; NYTBR Ap 16, 1989 p31; NYTBR S 9, 1990 p42; PW v237 Ap 27, 1990 p58.

Roosevelt, Elliott
Murder in the Red Room.
St. Martin's 1992.
BL v88 1992 p1643; KR v60 1992 p574.

Roosevelt, Elliott
Murder in the Rose Garden.
St. Martin's 1989.
BL v86 1989 p148; KR v57 1989 p1366.

Roosevelt, Elliott
The White House Pantry Murder.
St. Martin's 1987.
BL v83 1986 p602; KR v55 1987 p266; LJ v112 Ap 1, 1987 p168; PW v231 F 20, 1987 p74.

Weil, Ann
JUV *Eleanor Roosevelt, Courageous Girl.*
Bobbs-Merrill 1965.

1189. Roosevelt, Franklin Delano
1882-1945
32nd US President; served longest term, 1933-1945

Chakovsky, Alexander
Unfinished Portrait.
Progress Publishers 1988.

Charyn, Jerome
The Franklin Scare.
Arbor House 1977.
BL v74 1977 p461; KR v45 1977 p797; LJ v102 1977 p2080.

Kanfer, Stefan
Fear Itself.
Putnam 1981.
KR v49 1981 p1024; LJ v106 1981 p2154; NYTBR N 1, 1981 p15.

Lerman, Rhoda
Eleanor: A Novel.
Holt, Rinehart & Winston 1979.
BL v75 1079 p1202; BRD 1979 p749; KR v47 1979 p145; LJ v104 1979 p849; NYTBR My 20, 1979 p14.

Roosevelt, Elliott
The President's Man.
St. Martin's 1991.
KR v59 1991 p1049.

Roosevelt, James
A Family Matter.
Simon & Schuster 1980.
BL v76 1980 p1492; KR v48 1980 p672; LJ v105 1980 p1542; NYTBR Jl 20, 1980 p12.

Spike, Paul
The Night Letter.
Putnam 1979.
BL v75 1979 p1132; KR v46 1978 p1327; PW v214 D 11, 1978 p56.

Weil, Ann
JUV *Franklin Roosevelt, Boy of the Four Freedoms.*
Bobbs-Merrill 1947.
BRD 1947 p951; LJ v72 1947 p644.

1190. Roosevelt, Theodore
1858-1919
26th US President

Alexander, Lawrence
The Big Stick.
Doubleday 1986.
BL v82 1986 p850; KR v53 1985 p1332; NYTBR Mr
16, 1986 p20.

Alexander, Lawrence
Speak Softly.
Doubleday 1987.
KR v55 1987 p753.

Alexander, Lawrence
*The Strenuous Life: A Theodore Roosevelt Mys-
tery.*
Knightsbridge Pub. Co. 1991.
BL v87 1991 p1009; KR v58 1990 p1709; PW v237 N
16, 1990 p47.

Bowen, Peter
Imperial Kelly.
Crown 1992.
KR v60 1992 p732; PW v239 Je 29, 1992 p55.

DeAndrea, William L.
YA *The Lunatic Fringe: A Novel Wherein Theodore
Roosevelt Meets the Pink Angel.*
M. Evans 1980.
KR v48 1980 p942; SLJ v27 N 1980 p92.

Flack, Ambrose
Room for Mr. Roosevelt.
Crowell 1951.
BRD 1951 p294; NYTBR Jl 29, 1951 p10.

Foster, Genevieve Stump
JUV *Theodore Roosevelt: An Initial Biography.*
Scribner 1954.
BL v50 1954 p424; BRD 1954 p323; KR v22 1954
p312; LJ v79 1954 p1237; NYTBR Jl 11, 1954 p20.

Garfield, Brian
Manifest Destiny.
Penzler Books 1989.
KR v57 1989 p856; PW v235 Je 16, 1989 p59.

Gerson, Noel Bertram
TR.
Doubleday 1970.
LJ v95 1970 p82.

Henry, Marguerite
JUV *Brighty of the Grand Canyon.*
Macmillan 1953.
BL v50 1953 p151; BRD 1953 p422; KR v21 1953
p710; LJ v79 1954 p73; NYTBR N 15, 1953 p34.

Henry, Will
San Juan Hill.
Random House 1962.
LJ v87 1962 p1484; NYTBR Je 3, 1962 p26.

Jakes, John
Homeland.
Doubleday 1993.

Jeffers, Harry Paul
The Adventure of the Stalwart Companions.

Harper & Row 1978.
KR v46 1978 p717.

Miller, Helen Topping
JUV *Christmas at Sagamore Hill with Theodore
Roosevelt.*
Longmans, Green 1960.
BRD 1961 p988; KR v28 1960 p874; LJ v85 1960
p4473.

Monjo, F. N.
JUV *The One Bad Thing about Father.*
Harper & Row 1970.
BRD 1970 p998; LJ v95 1970 p1959; NYTBR My 24,
1970 p43; SatR Mr 21, 1970 p39; SLJ v25 D 1978
p33; SLJ v28 F 1982 p37.

Neilson, Winthrop
YA *The Story of Theodore Roosevelt.*
Grosset & Dunlap 1953.
LJ v78 1953 p742.

Resnick, Michael D.
Bully!.
Axolotl Press 1990.
Analog v110 D 15, 1990 p178; BW v20 D 30, 1990
p11; Locus v25 D 1990 p31; SFChr v12 Mr 1991
p34.

Schorr, Mark
Bully!.
St. Martin's 1985.
BL v82 1985 p110; KR v53 1985 p1052; PW v228 Ag
16, 1985 p64.

Singer, A. L.
YA *Safari Sleuth.*
Random House 1992.

Wilson, Dorothy Clarke
*Alice and Edith: The Two Wives of Theodore
Roosevelt.*
Doubleday 1989.
BL v86 1989 p725; KR v57 1989 p1360; LJ v114 O
15, 1989 p105.

1191. Rosenberg, Ethel Greenglass
1915-1953
American communist convicted of passing on
atomic secrets to the USSR; executed

Coover, Robert
The Public Burning.
Viking 1977.
BL v74 1977 p266; BRD 1977 p271; KR v45 1977
p798; LJ v102 1977 p1867; NYTBR Ag 14, 1977 p9.

Nason, Tema
Ethel.
Delacorte 1990.
KR v58 1990 p1196; LJ v115 S 1, 1990 p258; LJ v116
1991 p152.

1192. Rosenberg, Julius

1918-1953

With wife Ethel convicted of espionage; executed

Coover, Robert
The Public Burning.
Viking 1977.
BL v74 1977 p266; BRD 1977 p271; KR v45 1977 p798; LJ v102 1977 p1867; NYTBR Ag 14, 1977 p9.

1193. Ross, Betsy (Elizabeth Griscom)

1752-1836

Reputed maker of the first American flag

Mandrell, Louise
JUV *A Mission for Jenny.*
Summit Group 1993.

Mayer, Jane
JUV *Betsy Ross and the Flag.*
Random House 1952.
LJ v77 1952 p1666.

Walkington, Ethlyn
JUV *Betsy Ross, the Little Rebel.*
Friends United Press 1990.

Weil, Ann
JUV *Betsy Ross, Girl of Old Philadelphia.*
Bobbs-Merrill 1954.
LJ v79 1954 p1324.

1194. Ross, John

1790-1866

American Indian chief

Forrest, Williams
Trail of Tears.
Crown 1959.
BL v55 1959 p394; LJ v84 1959 p777; NYTBR Mr 1, 1959 p33.

Jordan, Jan
Give Me the Wind.
Prentice-Hall 1973.
FC 9th p283; KR v41 1973 p140; PW v203 F 5, 1973 p83.

Swonger, W. A.
The Trail of Tears.
Moody Press 1976.

1195. Rossetti, Dante Gabriel

1828-1882

English poet & painter

Batchelor, Paula
Angel with Bright Hair.
Methuen 1957.

Hale, John
The Love School.
St. Martin's 1975.
BS v36 N 1976 p246.

Kitchen, Paddy
The Golden Veil: A Novel Based on the Life of Elizabeth Siddall.
H. Hamilton 1981.
KR v50 1982 p25; TLS My 29, 1981 p596.

Savage, Elizabeth
Willowwood.
Little, Brown 1978.
BL v75 1978 p157; KR v46 1978 p658; LJ v103 1978 p1533; PW v214 Jl 3, 1978 p60.

Shute, Nerina
Victorian Love Story: A Study of the Victorian Romantics Based on the Life of Dante Gabriel Rossetti.
Jarrolds 1954.

1196. Rossetti, Elizabeth

see Siddal, Elizabeth Eleanor

1197. Rossini, Gioacchino Antonio

1792-1868

Italian composer

Malvern, Gladys
YA *Blithe Genius: The Story of Rossini.*
Longmans, Green 1959.
BRD 1960 p880; KR v27 1959 p374; LJ v84 1959 p3328; NYTBR N 1, 1959 p10.

1198. Rostropovich, Mstislav Leopoldovich

1927-

Russian cellist; director of Washington's National Symphony

Isele, Elizabeth
JUV *Pooks.*
Lippincott 1983.
KR v51 1983 p61; SLJ v30 O 1983 p150.

1199. Rousseau, Jean Jacques

1712-1778

French philosopher, social theorist, & author

Endore, Guy
Voltaire! Voltaire! A Novel.
Simon & Schuster 1961.
Also published as *The Heart and the Mind.*
BL v58 1961 p63; BRD 1962 p355; KR v29 1961 p344; LJ v86 1961 p2490; NYTBR Je 18, 1961 p4.

Feuchtwanger, Lion
'Tis Folly to Be Wise.
Messner 1953.
BL v49 1953 p303; BRD 1953 p313; FC 7th p132; KR v21 1953 p159.

1200. Roxana
d. 311? BC
Wife of Alexander the Great

Moray, Helga
Roxana and Alexander.
Hale 1971.

1201. Rubens, Peter Paul, Sir
1577-1640
Flemish painter

Braider, Donald
An Epic Joy: A Novel Based on the Life of Rubens.
Putnam 1971.
BL v67 1971 p640; FC 9th p61; KR v38 1970 p1261; LJ v96 1971 p655.

Harsanyi, Zsolt
Lover of Life.
Putnam 1942.
BL v38 1942 p330; BRD 1942 p334; FC 7th p169; NYTBR Mr 29, 1942 p6; SatR Mr 28, 1942 p5.

Wallach, Ira Jan
The Horn and the Roses: A Novel Based on the Life of Peter Paul Rubens.
Boni & Gaer 1947.
LJ v72 1947 p961; NYTBR Je 29, 1947 p18; SatR S 13, 1947 p29.

1202. Rudolf II
1552-1612
Holy Roman emperor, 1576-1612; son of Maximilian II

Perutz, Leo
By Night under the Stone Bridge.
Arcade Pub. 1990.
BL v86 1990 p1140; BRD 1991 p1465; KR v58 1990 p460; LJ v115 Mr 1, 1990 p117; NYTBR My 27, 1990 p16.

1203. Rudolf of Hapsburg
1858-1889
Austrian prince; only son of Emperor Franz Joseph

Anet, Jean
Mayerling: The Love and Tragedy of a Crown Prince.
Hutchinson 1930 (Rp. 1968, 1975).

Arnold, Michael P.
The Archduke.
Doubleday 1967.
BL v63 1967 p717; KR v1966 p1154; NYTBR Ja 15, 1967 p45.

1204. Ruskin, John
1819-1900
English art critic, author, & social theorist

Hoyle, Peter
Brantwood: The Story of an Obsession.
Carcanet 1986.
Atl v258 O 1986 p103; B&B O 1986 p35; BritBkN O 1986 p600; Lis v116 Ag 28, 1986 p22; PW v230 Ag 15, 1986 p69; TLS O 3, 1986 p1115.

McDonald, Eva
John Ruskin's Wife.
Hale 1979 (Rpr. 1991).

Morazzoni, Marta
The Invention of Truth.
Knopf 1993.

Shute, Nerina
Victorian Love Story: A Study of the Victorian Romantics Based on the Life of Dante Gabriel Rossetti.
Jarrolds 1954.

Williams, Lawrence
I, James McNeill Whistler: An Autobiography.
Simon & Schuster 1972.
BL v68 1972 p889; BS v32 Je 1, 1972 p109; FC 9th p560; LJ v97 1972 p1036.

1205. Russell, Bertrand
1872-1970
English philosopher & mathematician

Collins, Randall
The Case of the Philosopher's Ring.
Crown 1978.
KR v46 1978 p1216.

1206. Russell, Lillian
1861-1922
American singer & actress

Brough, James
Miss Lillian Russell: A Novel Memoir.
McGraw-Hill 1978.
BL v75 1978 p153; KR v46 1978 p958; LJ v103 1978 p2443.

1207. Ruth
Old Testament figure; central figure in the Book of Ruth

Fineman, Irving
Ruth.
Harper 1949.
BL v46 1949 p3; BRD 1949 p296; FC 7th p133; KR v17 1949 p403; LJ v74 1949 p1321; NYTBR S 25, 1949 p6.

Henderson, Lois
YA *Ruth: A Novel.*
Harper & Row 1981.
VOYA v4 F 1982 p32.

Kern, Louisa
The Wife of Mahlon.
Pageant Press 1954.

Malvern, Gladys
YA *The Foreigner: The Story of a Girl Named Ruth.*
Longmans, Green 1954.
BL v51 1954 p90; BRD 1954 p586; KR v22 1954
p341; LJ v79 1954 p1673; NYTBR O 17, 1954 p44.

Mayberry, Thomas G.
Ruth: An Unusual Novel.
Savoy Book Publishers 1940.

Murphy, Edward F.
The Song of the Cave: A Tale of Ruth and Noemi.
Bruce Publishing 1950.
BL v47 1950 p97; BRD 1950 p663.

Slaughter, Frank G.
The Song of Ruth: A Love Story from the Old Tes-
tament.
Doubleday 1954.
BL v50 1954 p401; BRD 1954 p815; FC 9th p471; KR
v22 1954 p129; NYTBR Ap 11, 1954 p24.

Traylor, Ellen G.
Ruth: A Love Story.
Tyndale 1986.

1208. Rutherford, Ann
1917-
Canadian actress

Heisenfelt, Kathryn
Ann Rutherford and the Key to Nightmare Hall.
Whitman Publishing 1942.

1209. Sacagawea
1787-1812
American Indian; served as guide on Lewis and
Clark Expedition

Emmons, Della
Sacajawea of the Shoshones.
Binfords & Mort 1943.
BL v40 1943 p59; BRD 1943 p242.

Farnsworth, Frances
JUV *Winged Moccasins: The Story of Sacajawea.*
Messner 1954.
BL v50 1954 p363; BRD 1954 p297; KR v22 1954
p122; LJ v79 1954 p993; NYTBR My 16, 1954 p28.

Nevin, Evelyn C.
JUV *The Lost Children of the Shoshones.*
Westminster Press 1946.
BRD 1946 p607; LJ v71 1946 p983; NYTBR Je 23,
1946 p17.

O'Dell, Scott
YA *Streams to the River, River to the Sea: A Novel of*
Sacagawea.
Houghton Mifflin 1986.

BL v82 1986 p1086; BRD 1987 p1394; KR v54 1986
p719; SLJ v32 My 1986 p107.

Peattie, Donald
Forward the Nation.
Putnam 1942.
BL v38 1942 p442; BRD 1942 p596; LJ v67 1942
p475; NYTBR My 24, 1942 p1.

Waldo, Anna Lee
Sacajawea.
Avon Books 1978 (Rprt. 1980, 1984).
KR v47 1979 p352; LJ v104 1979 p1079.

1210. Sacco, Nicola
1891-1927
Italian political activist in US; together with B.
Vanzetti, executed for murder despite international protest that they were victims of political
bias

Asch, Nathan
Pay Day.
Brewer & Warren 1930 (Rpr. 1990).
BRD 1930 p34.

Fast, Howard
The Passion of Sacco and Vanzetti: A New Eng-
land Legend.
Blue Heron Press 1953.

McKenney, Ruth
Jake Home.
Harcourt, Brace & Co. 1943.
BRD 1943 p528; NYTBR F 28, 1943 p6; SatR Mr 13,
1943 p14.

Rose, Howard
The Pooles of Pismo Bay.
Raymond Saroff 1990.
LJ v115 Je 1, 1990 p184.

Sinclair, Upton
Boston: A Novel.
Boni 1928 (Rpr. 1970, 1978).
BRD 1928 p708; NYTBR N 18, 1928 p6; SatR D 1,
1928 p425.

Vonnegut, Kurt
YA *Jailbird.*
Delacorte 1979.
BRD 1979 p1320; BRD 1980 p1260; LJ v104 1979
p2240; SLJ v26 D 1979 p104; NYTBR N25, 1979
p54.

1211. Sacher-Masoch, Leopold von
1836-1895
Austrian author; the word "masochism" has
been coined to describe the form of eroticism de-
tailed in some of his works

Perutz, Kathrin
Reigning Passions.
Lippincott 1978.

BL v74 1978 p1166; KR v46 1978 p63; LJ v103 1978
p483; PW v213 Ja 30, 1978 p124.

1212. Sade, Marquis (Donatien Alphonse Francoise) de
1740-1814
French author; term "sadism" derived from his name

Endore, Guy
Satan's Saint: A Novel about the Marquis de Sade.
Crown 1965.
KR v33 1965 p197.

Reed, Jeremy
When the Whip Comes Down: A Novel about de Sade.
P. Owen 1992.

1213. Saint Ambrose
see Ambrose, Saint

1214. Saint Anthony of Padua
see Anthony of Padua, Saint

1215. Saint Augustine
see Augustine, Saint

1216. Saint Bartholomew
see Bartholomew, Saint

1217. Saint Benedict
see Benedict, Saint

1218. Saint Brendan of Clonfert
see Brendan of Clonfert, Saint

1219. Saint Clair, Arthur
1736-1818
American military leader

Fast, Howard
The Proud and the Free.
Little, Brown 1950.
BRD 1950 p297; LJ v75 1950 p1825; NYTBR D 3, 1950 p56.

Van Trees, Robert V.
Banks of the Wabash.
R.V. Van Trees 1986.

1220. Saint Columba
see Columba, Saint

1221. Saint Elizabeth of Hungary
see Elizabeth of Hungary, Saint

1222. Saint Francis of Assisi
see Francis of Assisi

1223. Saint Francis Xavier
see Francis Xavier, Saint

1224. Saint George
see George, Saint

1225. Saint Hildegard of Bingen
see Hildegard of Bingen, Saint

1226. Saint James the Greater
see James the Greater, Saint

1227. Saint Joan of Arc
see Joan of Arc, Saint

1228. Saint John Chrysostom
see Chrysostom, John, Saint

1229. Saint John of the Cross
see John of the Cross, Saint

1230. Saint Joseph
see Joseph, Saint

1231. Saint Kateri Tekakwitha
see Tekakwitha, Kateri, Saint

1232. Saint Luke
see Luke, Saint

1233. Saint Mark
see Mark, Saint

1234. Saint Mary Magdalene
see Mary Magdalene, Saint

1235. Saint Mary, the Virgin Mother
see Mary, the Virgin Mother

1236. Saint Nicholas
see Nicholas, Saint

1237. Saint Patrick
see Patrick, Saint

1238. Saint Paul
see Paul, Saint

1239. Saint Peter
see Peter, Saint

1240. Saint Therese of Lisieux
see Therese of Lisieux, Saint

1241. Saint Thomas
see Thomas, Saint

1242. Saint Thomas A' Becket
see Becket, Thomas, Saint

1243. Saint Thomas Aquinas
see Aquinas, Thomas, Saint

1244. Saint Veronica Giuliani
see Veronica Giuliani, Saint

1245. Saint Vincent de Paul
see Vincent de Paul, Saint

1246. Salazar, Antonio de Oliveira
1889-1970
Portuguese politician; premier, & dictator of
Portugal

Slavitt, David R.
Salazar Blinks.
Atheneum 1988.
BL v85 1988 p365; KR v56 1988 p1273; LJ v113 N 1,
1988 p111; NYTBR F 26, 1989 p34.

1247. Salinger, J. D. (Jerome David)
1919-
American author; wrote *Catcher in the Rye*

Kinsella, W. P.
Shoeless Joe.
Houghton Mifflin 1982.
BL v78 1982 p941; BRD 1982 p732; KR v50 1982
p159; LJ v107 1982 p745; NYTBR Jl 25, 1982 p10;
SLJ v28 Ag 1982 p131.

1248. Salome
14-62
Danced before King Herod, and as a reward
asked for, and received, the head of John the
Baptist

Bloom, Ursula (Lozania Prole, pseud.)
The Song of Salome.
Severn House 1978.
First published in 1969 under the author's pseud., De-
borah Mann.

Denker, Henry
Salome, Princess of Galilee.
Crowell 1952.
BRD 1952 p243; KR v20 1952 p93; LJ v77 1952 p590;
NYTBR Ap 20, 1952 p25.

Dieterle, William (William Sidney, pseud.)
The Good Tidings.
Farrar, Straus 1950.
BRD 1950 p249; KR v18 1950 p283; LJ v75 1950
p1045; NYTBR Je 18, 1950 p22.

Jakes, John
Veils of Salome.
Pinnacle Books 1976.

Kadison, Ellis
The Eight Veil.
Nelson Doubleday 1981.

1249. Salomon, Haym
1740-1785
American patriot; helped finance the American
Revolution

Fast, Howard
Haym Salomon, Son of Liberty.
Messner 1941.
BL v37 1941 p444; BRD 1941 p290; LJ v66 1941
p359; NYTBR Ap 27, 1941 p10.

1250. Sampson, Deborah
1760-1827
American woman soldier; served in the Continental Army disguised as a man

Cheney, Cora
YA *The Incredible Deborah: A Story Based on the Life
of Deborah Sampson.*
Scribner 1967.
BRD 1968 p229; LJ v93 1968 p879; NYTBR N 5,
1967 p28; SatR N 11, 1967 p48.

Clapp, Patricia
YA *I'm Deborah Sampson: A Soldier in the War of the
Revolution.*
Lothrop, Lee & Shepard 1977.
BL v73 1977 p1651; KR v45 1977 p284; SLJ v24 N
1977 p68.

1251. Samson
Old Testament figure; known for his physical
strength

Jabotinsky, Vladimir
Prelude to Delilah.
B. Ackerman 1945.

Linklater, Eric
Husband of Delilah: A Novel.
Macmillan 1962.
BRD 1963 p621; LJ v88 1963 p1548.

1252. Samuel
Old Testament prophet

Johnson, Buford M.
Priest of Dagon.
White Wing Pub. House 1952.

Watkins, Shirley
The Prophet and the King.
Doubleday 1956.
BRD 1956 p970; LJ v81 1956 p1513; NYTBR Ag 5,
1956 p16.

1253. Sanchez, Ilitch Ramirez
see Carlos

1254. Sand, George, pseud.
1804-1876
French novelist

Byrne, Marie
Softly, Softly.
Blond 1958.

Kenyon, Frank Wilson
The Questing Heart: A Romantic Novel about George Sand.
Dodd, Mead 1964.
Also published as *The Shadow and the Substance.*
B&B v10 Je 1965 p38.

Leslie, Doris
Polonaise.
Hutchinson 1944.

1255. Sanger, Margaret
1883-1966
American nurse & birth control advocate

Gerson, Noel Bertram
The Crusader: A Novel on the Life of Margaret Sanger.
Little, Brown 1970.
BL v66 1970 p1194; KR v38 1970 p343; LJ v95 1970 p1760; PW v197 Mr 9, 1970 p80; WSJ v175 Je 29, 1970 p12.

1256. Santa Anna, Antonio Lopez de
1794-1876
Mexican president & general

Bryan, Jack Y.
Come to the Bower.
Viking 1963.
LJ v88 1963 p1683; LJ v88 1963 p3374.

Foreman, L. L.
The Road to San Jacinto.
Dutton 1943.
BL v39 1943 p426; BRD 1943 p275; LJ v68 1943 p366; NYTBR Ap 11, 1943 p16.

Gorman, Herbert
The Wine of San Lorenzo.
Farrar & Rinehart 1945.
BRD 1945 p275; LJ v70 1945 p488.

Michener, James A.
The Eagle and the Raven.
State House Press 1990.
BL v86 1990 p1932; KR v58 1990 p827; NYTBR S 30, 1990 p28; PW v237 Jl 20, 1990 p49.

1257. Santos-Dumont, Alberto
1873-1932
Brazilian balloonist; first to combine a gasoline motor with propeller on a balloon

Llewellyn, Richard
A Night of Bright Stars.
Doubleday 1979.
KR v47 1979 p816; Obs Je 24, 1979 p36; PW v216 Jl 9, 1979 p99.

1258. Sappho
b. 612? BC
Greek lyric poet

Frye, Ellen
The Other Sappho: A Novel.
Firebrand Books 1989.
BL D 1, 1989 p723; PW v236 N 10, 1989 p56.

Green, Peter
The Laughter of Aphrodite.
J. Murray 1965.
BL v62 1966 p696; BRD 1966 p469; KR v33 1965 p1168; NYTBR Ja 30, 1966 p4.

Krislov, Alexander
No Man Sings.
Longmans, Green 1956.

Rofheart, Martha
My Name Is Sappho.
Putnam 1974.
KR v42 1974 p1022; LJ v99 1974 p2873; NYTBR Ja 12, 1975 p18.

1259. Sarah
Old Testament figure; wife of Abraham, mother of Isaac

Kellner, Esther
The Promise.
Westminster Press 1956.
BRD 1956 p506; LJ v81 1956 p828.

Reid Banks, Lynne
JUV *Sarah and After: Five Women Who Founded a Nation.*
Doubleday 1975.
BRD 1977 p68; SLJ v23 F 1977 p60.

1260. Sassoon, Siegfried
1886-1967
English poet & novelist

Barker, Pat
Regeneration.
Dutton 1992.
BRD 1992 p118; LJ v117 Mr 1, 1992 p116; NYTBR Mr 29, 1992 p1; TLS My 24, 1991 p20.

1261. Savonarola, Girolamo
1452-1498
Italian religious & political reformer

Eliot, George
Romola.
Tauchnitz 1863 (Heavily reprinted).

BRD 1905 p112; BRD 1906 p96; FC 9th p160;
NYTBR F 4, 1899 p69; NYTBR F 9, 1907 p88.

Merezhkovsky, Dmitry
The Romance of Leonardo da Vinci, the Forerunner.
Putnam 1902 (Heavily reprinted).
Also published as *The Forerunner.*
BRD 1912 p317; NYTBR Mr 1, 1931 p12; NYTBR Jl
16, 1939 p20.

Stowe, Harriet Beecher
Agnes of Sorrento.
Ticknor & Fields 1862 (Heavily reprinted).

1262. Saxe, Maurice
1696-1750
French military leader

Dunlap, Katharine
The Glory and the Dream.
Morrow 1951.
BL v47 1951 p329; BRD 1951 p253; KR v19 1951
p136; NYTBR My 13, 1951 p19.

1263. Sayers, Dorothy Leigh
1893-1957
English detective fiction writer

Larsen, Gaylord
Dorothy and Agatha.
Dutton 1990.
BL v87 1990 p804; KR v58 1990 p1571; SLJ v37 My
1991 p126.

1264. Schliemann, Heinrich
1822-1890
German archaeologist

Stone, Irving
*The Greek Treasure: A Biographical Novel of
Henry and Sophia Schliemann.*
Doubleday 1975.
BL v72 1975 p115; BRD 1976 p1157; KR v43 1975
p801; LJ v100 1975 p1847; NYTBR O 12, 1975
p48.

1265. Schoolcraft, Henry Rowe
1793-1864
American ethnologist & explorer

Derleth, August W.
Land of Sky-Blue Waters.
Aladdin Books 1955.
LJ v80 1955 p1506.

1266. Schubert, Franz Peter
1797-1828
Austrian composer

Goss, Madeleine
YA *Unfinished Symphony: The Story of Franz
Schubert.*
Holt 1941.
BL v38 1941 p135; BRD 1941 p359.

1267. Schultz, Dutch
1900-1935
American criminal

Doctorow, E. L.
Billy Bathgate.
Random House 1989.
BL v85 1989 p818; BRD 1989 p420; BRD 1990 p477;
LJ v114 F 15, 1989 p175; NYTBR F 26, 1989 p1.

1268. Schumann, Clara Josephine Wieck
1819-1896
German pianist; wife of Robert Schumann

Curling, Audrey
Cry of the Heart.
Hurst & Blackett 1971.

Kyle, Elisabeth
YA *Duet: The Story of Clara and Robert Schumann.*
Holt, Rinehart & Winston 1968.
BRD 1969 p740; HB v44 O 1968 p570; KR v36 1968
p1059; LJ v93 1968 p4405.

Painter, Eleanor
Spring Symphony.
Harper & Brothers 1941.
BL v37 1941 p270; BRD 1941 p689; LJ v66 1941 p80;
NYTBR Ja 5, 1941 p7.

White, Hilda
YA *Song without End: The Love Story of Clara and
Robert Schumann.*
Dutton 1959.
BL v56 1960 p423; BRD 1960 p1428; KR v27 1959
p553; LJ v84 1959 p3643; NYTBR N 1, 1959 p10.

1269. Schumann, Robert Alexander
1810-1856
German composer

Curling, Audrey
Cry of the Heart.
Hurst & Blackett 1971.

Kyle, Elisabeth
YA *Duet: The Story of Clara and Robert Schumann.*
Holt, Rinehart & Winston 1968.
BRD 1969 p740; HB v44 O 1968 p570; KR v36 1968
p1059; LJ v93 1968 p4405.

Painter, Eleanor
Spring Symphony.
Harper & Brothers 1941.
BL v37 1941 p270; BRD 1941 p689; LJ v66 1941 p80;
NYTBR Ja 5, 1941 p7.

White, Hilda
YA *Song without End: The Love Story of Clara and Robert Schumann.*
Dutton 1959.
BL v56 1960 p423; BRD 1960 p1428; KR v27 1959 p553; LJ v84 1959 p3643; NYTBR N 1, 1959 p10.

1270. Schweitzer, Albert
1875-1965
Medical missionary, theologian, musician, & philosopher; won 1952 Nobel Peace Prize

Franck, Frederick
JUV *My Friend in Africa.*
P. Davies 1960.
LJ v85 1960 p4566.

Fritz, Jean
JUV *The Animals of Doctor Schweitzer.*
Coward-McCann 1958.
BRD 1959 p384; KR v26 1958 p502; LJ v83 1958 p2498; NYTBR N 2, 1958 p44.

1271. Scott, Robert Falcon
1868-1912
English antarctic explorer

Davis, Paxton
YA *A Flag at the Pole: Three Soliloquies.*
Atheneum 1976.
KR v44 1976 p800; SLJ v23 N 1976 p67.

Holt, Kare
The Race: A Novel of Polar Exploration.
Delacorte 1976.
Translation of *Kapplopet.*
BRD 1977 p625; KR v44 1976 p808; LJ v101 1976 p2086; NYTBR O 31, 1976 p42.

1272. Scott, Walter, Sir
1771-1832
Scottish novelist & poet; wrote *Ivanhoe*

Oliver, Jane
The Blue Heaven Bends over All.
Putman 1971 (Rpr. 1992).
BRD 1972 p983; KR v39 1971 p1093; LJ v97 1972 p791; PW v200 O 11, 1971 p58.

1273. Scott, Winfield
1786-1866
American military leader; led US forces in Mexican War

Gerson, Noel Bertram
The Golden Eagle.
Doubleday 1953.
BL v49 1953 p321; BRD 1953 p357; KR v21 1953 p230; NYTBR Je 14, 1953 p15.

1274. Secord, Laura
1775-1868
Canadian heroine; warned British of surprise American attack during War of 1812

Crook, Connie Brummel
Laura's Choice: The Story of Laura Secord.
Windflower Communications 1993.

1275. Selkirk, Alexander
1676-1721
Scottish sailor, whose story is supposed to have suggested the Robinson Crusoe of Daniel Defoe

Ballard, Martin
JUV *The Monarch of Juan Fernandez.*
Scribner 1968.
BS v28 N 1, 1968 p323; KR v36 1968 p652; PW v194 O 14, 1968 p66.

Carse, Robert
The Fabulous Buccaneer.
Dell 1957.

1276. Seneca, Lucius Annaeus
4-65
Roman Stoic, poltical leader, & statesman

Sheean, Vincent
Beware of Caesar.
Random House 1965.
BRD 1965 p1143; KR v33 1965 p447; LJ v90 1965 p2873; NYTBR Ag 8, 1965 p24.

1277. Sennacherib
705-681 BC
King of Assyria

Ronalds, Mary Teresa
Gateway to the Gods.
Macdonald & Co. 1973.
B&B v18 Jl 1973 p135.

1278. Sennett, Mack
1884-1960
American director & producer; directed Charlie Chaplin and Harold Lloyd; creator of the "Keystone Kops"

Lovesey, Peter
Keystone.
Pantheon 1983.
FC 11th p382; Obs Ag 28, 1983 p25; PW v224 s 2, 1983 p71.

1279. Sequoya
1770-1843
American Indian scholar, who invented a Cherokee syllabary; sequoia tree named for him

Browin, Frances W.

YA *Captured Words: The Story of a Great Indian.*
Aladdin Books 1954.
BRD 1954 p119; LJ v80 1955 p189; NYTBR N 14,
1954 p26.

Jones, Weyman B.

JUV *Edge of Two Worlds.*
Dial 1968.
BL v64 1968 p1286; BRD 1968 p694; CC 16th p512;
KR v36 1968 p466; LJ v93 1968 p1812; NYTBR
My 5, 1968 p32.

Roop, Peter

JUV *Ahyoka and the Talking Leaves.*
Lee & Shepard Books 1992.

Snow, Dorothea J.

JUV *Sequoyah, Young Cherokee Guide.*
Bobbs-Merrill 1960.

1280. Serra, Junipero

1713-1784
Franciscan missionary in California

Blackburn, Edith H.

JUV *The Bells of Carmel: Mission Days of California.*
Aladdin Books 1954.
BRD 1955 p82; KR v22 1954 p437; LJ v79 1954
p2494; NYTBR N 14, 1954 p26.

Cather, Willa

Father Junipero's Holy Family.
Anvil Press 1956.

Lauritzen, Jonreed

The Cross and the Sword.
Doubleday 1965.
BL v61 1965 p1055; FC 8th p251; KR v33 1965 p398;
LJ v90 1965 p2583.

Politi, Leo

JUV *The Mission Bell.*
Scribner 1953.
BRD 1953 p747; KR v21 1953 p694; LJ v78 1953
p2227; NYTBR N 15, 1953 p36.

Scott, Bernice

Junipero Serra, Pioneer of the Cross.
Valley Publishers 1976 (Rpr. 1985).

Teilhet, Darwin Le Ora

The Road to Glory.
Funk & Wagnalls 1956.
BRD 1956 p918; FC 7th p342; KR v24 1956 p101;
NYTBR Jl 1, 1956 p14; SatR My 5, 1956 p46.

Waterhouse, E. B.

Serra, California Conquistador: A Narrative History.
Parker 1968.
BL v65 1968 p152.

Wells, Evelyn

A City for St. Francis.

Doubleday 1967.
KR v35 1967 p580; LJ v92 1967 p2608.

Ziegler, Isabelle Gibson

The Nine Days of Father Serra.
Longmans, Green 1951.
BRD 1951 p983; KR v19 1951 p132; NYTBR Ap 22,
1951 p20; SatR Je 30, 1951 p28.

1281. Seton, Elizabeth Ann Bayley, Saint

1774-1821
Roman Catholic educator; first native-born
American saint

Eaton, Evelyn

Heart in Pilgrimage.
Harper 1948 (Rpr. 1960).
BRD 1948 p234; KR v16 1948 p2; LJ v73 1948 p473;
NYTBR My 9, 1948.

Heidish, Marcy

*Miracles: A Novel about Mother Seton, the First
American Saint.*
New American Library 1984.
BL v80 1984 p1294; KR v52 1984 p267; LJ v109 1984
p995; NYTBR Je 17, 1984 p20; PW v225 Ap 6,
1984 p67.

1282. Sevier, John

1745-1815
First governor of Tennessee

Chapman, Maristan

Rogue's March.
Lippincott 1949.
BL v46 1949 p25; BRD 1949 p154; LJ v74 1949
p1921; NYTBR N 13, 1949 p46.

Henri, Florette

Kings Mountain.
Avon 1950.
BL v47 1950 p136; BRD 1950 p424; KR v18 1950
p432; NYTBR S 24, 1950 p51.

Hubbard, Margaret A.

YA *The Hickory Limb.*
Macmillan 1942.
BRD 1942 p377; LJ v67 1942 p848; NYTBR S 27,
1942 p11.

Miller, Helen Topping

The Sound of Chariots.
Bobbs-Merrill 1947.
BL v44 1947 p69; BRD 1947 p634; LJ v72 1947 p1108.

Steele, William O.

JUV *John Sevier, Pioneer Boy.*
Bobbs-Merrill 1953.

1283. Seymour, Jane

1509-1537
Third wife of Henry VIII

Bloom, Ursula (Lozania Prole, pseud.)
The King's Wife.
Lythway Press 1973.
Originally published by Hutchinson, 1950.

Clark, Frances B.
Jane Seymour.
Ulverscroft 1973.
First published in 1967 under title: *Mistress Jane Seymour.*

Dobson, Phillippa
The Flower of Old England.
Hale 1976.

Evans, Jean
Jane, Beloved Queen.
Hale 1971.

Watson, Julia
The Tudor Rose.
Corgi 1972.

1284. Shackleton, Ernest Henry, Sir
1874-1922
British antarctic explorer

Davis, Paxton
YA *A Flag at the Pole: Three Soliloquies.*
Atheneum 1976.
KR v44 1976 p800; SLJ v23 N 1976 p67.

1285. Shakespeare, William
1564-1616
English dramatist & poet

Alexander, Louis C.
The Autobiography of Shakespeare.
Kennikat Press 1970.

Ashton, Winifred (Clemence Dane, pseud.)
The Godson: A Fantasy.
Norton 1964.

Bennett, John
YA *Master Skylark: A Story of Shakespeare's Time.*
Century Co. 1897 (Heavily reprinted).

Bloom, Ursula (Lozania Prole, pseud.)
How Dark, My Lady! A Novel Concerning the Private Life of William Shakespeare.
Hutchinson 1951.

Bowers, Gwendolyn
JUV *At the Sign of the Globe.*
H.Z. Walck 1966.
BRD 1967 p155; KR v34 1966 p909; LJ v92 1967 p332.

Brahms, Caryl
No Bed for Bacon.
M. Joseph 1941 (Rpr. 1950, 1986).
BRD 1950 p3; LJ v75 1950 p405; NYTBR F 12, 1950 p26; SatR Ap 1, 1950 p16.

Brophy, John
Gentleman of Stratford.
Harper 1940.
BRD 1940 p117; NYTBR Ap 14, 1940 p5.

Buckmaster, Henrietta
All the Living: One Year in the Life of William Shakespeare.
Random House 1962.
BRD 1963 p143; CSM N 8, 1962 p7; FC 8th p60; LJ v87 1962 p4209; NYTBR N 11, 1962 p50.

Bullett, Gerald
The Alderman's Son.
M. Joseph 1954.

Burgess, Anthony
Nothing Like the Sun, a Story of Shakespeare's Love-Life.
Norton 1964.
BRD 1964 p176; Choice v1 Ja 1965 p477; NYTBR S 13, 1964 p5; SatR Jl 15, 1967, p28.

Burton, Philip
You, My Brother: A Novel Based on the Lives of Edmund & William Shakespeare.
Random House 1973.
KR v41 1973 p901; LJ v98 1973 p3390.

Chute, Marchette
YA *The Wonderful Winter.*
Dutton 1954.
BL v51 1954 p114; BRD 1954 p175; KR v22 1954 p534; NYTBR N 14, 1954 p34.

Dhondy, Farrukh
Black Swan.
Houghton Mifflin 1993.
Sch Lib N 1992 p157.

Disher, Maurice
Whitely Wanton: A Story of Mistress and Lover.
Hutchinson 1951.

Fisher, Edward
The Best House in Stratford.
Abelard-Schuman 1965.
Sequel to *Love's Labour Won.*
FC 8th p148; KR v33 1965 p856.

Fisher, Edward
Love's Labour's Won; a Novel About Shakespeare's Lost Years.
Abelard-Schuman 1963.
BRD 1964 p403; FC 8th p148; LJ v89 1964 p1113; NYTBR D 8, 1963 p48.

Fisher, Edward
Shakespeare & Son.
Abelard-Schuman 1962.
BL v58 1962 p786; BRD 1962 p387; FC 8th p148; KR v30 1962 p335; LJ v87 1962 p2398.

Freeman, Don
JUV *Will's Quill.*
Viking 1975.

HB v51 O 1975 p453; KR v43 1975 p708; SLJ v22 O 1975 p89.

Hill, Frank E.
YA *King's Company.*
Dodd, Mead 1950.
BL v47 1951 p224; BRD 1951 p403; LJ v76 1951 p340; SHSLC 6th p1047.

Holland, Edith
One Crown with a Sun.
J. Cape 1952.

Jong, Erica
Serenissima: A Novel of Venice.
Houghton Mifflin 1987.
BL v83 1987 p947; LJ v112 Ap 15, 1987 p99; NYTBR Ap 19, 1987 p12; PW v231 Mr 13, 1987 p70.

Jowett, Margaret
A Cry of Players.
Roy Publishers 1963.
LJ v88 1963 p4854; NYTBR N 17, 1963 p40.

Kellerman, Faye
The Quality of Mercy.
Morrow 1989.
KR v57 Ap 15, 1989 p571; LJ v114 My 15, 1989 p90; PW v235 Ap 28, 1989 p64.

Lenanton, Carola M. (Carola Oman, pseud.)
The Best of His Family.
Hodder & Stoughton 1951.

Lepscky, Ibi
JUV *William Shakespeare.*
Barrons 1989.

Lunn, Hugh Kingsmill
The Return of William Shakespeare.
Bobbs-Merrill 1929 (Rpr. 1978).
BRD 1929 p517; NYTBR Ja 19, 1930 p7.

MacInnes, Colin
Three Years to Play.
Farrar, Straus & Giroux 1970.
FC 9th p334; KR v38 1970 p1122; LJ v95 1970 p4280; NYTBR N 15, 1970 p5.

Malpass, Eric
The Cleopatra Boy.
St. Martin's 1975.
LJ v100 1975 p1014.

Malpass, Eric
A House of Women: A Novel.
St. Martin's 1975.
KR v43 1975 p936; PW v208 Ag 25, 1975 p284.

Mortimer, John
Will Shakespeare: The Untold Story.
Delacorte Press 1977.
BL v74 1978 p1593; LJ v103 1978 p1436.

Nye, Robert
Mrs. Shakespeare: The Complete Works.
Sinclair-Stevenson 1993.
Obs Ja 24, 1993 p53; TLS Ja 29, 1993 p21.

Payne, Robert
The Royal Players.
Hale 1956.

Rooke, Leon
Shakespeare's Dog.
Knopf 1983.
BL v79 1983 p1263; BRD 1983 p1238; KR v51 1983 p267; LJ v108 1983 p921; NYTBR My 29, 1983 p11; PW v223 Mr 11, 1983 p79.

Sisson, Rosemary Anne
JUV *The Stratford Story.*
W.H. Allen 1975 (Rpr. 1986).
Also published as *Will in Love.*

Stuart, Frank
Remember Me.
S. Paul 1951.

Trease, Geoffrey
YA *Cue for Treason.*
Vanguard Press 1941.
BRD 1942 p780; LJ v67 1942 p890; SHSLC 7th p431.

Van Greenaway, Peter
The Destiny Man.
Gollancz 1977.
GP v18 S 1979 p3589; Obs Ag 7, 1977 p29.

Vining, Elizabeth Gray
JUV *I Will Adventure.*
Viking 1962.
BRD 1963 p404; LJ v88 1963 p1361.

Watson, Robert
Whilom.
Atlantic Monthly 1990.
Locus v25 N 1990 p61; WCRB v15 n6 1990 p31.

1286. Shaw, George Bernard
1856-1950
Irish dramatist, essayist, & critic; won Nobel Prize, 1925

Hanley, Tullah Innes
The Strange Triangle of G.B.S..
Bruce Humphries 1956.

1287. Shays, Daniel
1747-1825
American soldier; leader in Shay's Rebellion

Degenhard, William
The Regulators.
Dial 1943.
BL v39 1943 p446; BRD 1943 p203; NYTBR My 2, 1943 p8; SatR My 22, 1943 p44.

Muir, Robert
The Spring of Hemlock: A Novel about Shay's Rebellion.
Longmans, Green 1957.

1288. Sheba, Queen of
Old Testament figure

Ormonde, Czenzi
Solomon and the Queen of Sheba.
Farrar, Straus & Young 1954.
BL v51 1954 p110; BRD 1954 p679; KR v22 1954
p593; LJ v79 1954 p1589; NYTBR Ja 16, 1955 p27.

Williams, Jay
Solomon and Sheba.
Random House 1959.
BL v55 1959 p507; BRD 1960 p1438; KR v27 1959
p18; NYTBR Mr 8, 1959 p42.

1289. Shelley, Mary Wollstonecraft
1797-1851
English author; wrote *Frankenstein*

Aldiss, Brian W.
Frankenstein Unbound.
Random House 1974.
BRD 1975 p15; FC 9th p5; LJ v99 1974 p1988; Time
v104 Ag 5, 1974 p84.

Bolton, Guy
The Olympians.
World Pub. Co. 1961.
BRD 1961 p141; LJ v86 1961 p1475.

Carrere, Emmanuel
Gothic Romance.
Scribner 1990.
KR v58 1990 p599; LJ v115 Je 15, 1990 p132.

Chernaik, Judith
Love's Children: A Novel.
Knopf 1992.
Also published as *Mab's Daughters.*
KR v60 1992 p199.

Edwards, Anne
Haunted Summer.
Coward, McCann & Geoghegan 1972.
KR v40 1972 p1043; LJ v97 1972 p3727; LJ v98 1973
p273; PW v202 S 18, 1972 p72.

West, Paul
Lord Byron's Doctor.
Doubleday 1989.
BL v86 1989 p147; BRD 1991 p1968; KR v57 1989
p1034; LJ v114 S 1, 1989 p298; NYTBR F 3, 1991
p32; PW v236 Jl 21, 1989 p50.

1290. Shelley, Percy Bysshe
1792-1822
English poet

Bolton, Guy
The Olympians.
World Pub. Co. 1961.
BRD 1961 p141; LJ v86 1961 p1475.

Chernaik, Judith
Love's Children: A Novel.
Knopf 1992.
Also published as *Mab's Daughters.*
KR v60 1992 p199.

Edwards, Anne
Haunted Summer.
Coward, McCann & Geoghegan 1972.
KR v40 1972 p1043; LJ v97 1972 p3727; LJ v98 1973
p273; PW v202 S 18, 1972 p72.

Kenyon, Frank Wilson
*The Golden Years: A Novel Based on the Life and
Loves of Percy Bysshe Shelley.*
Crowell 1959 (Rpr. 1974).
BL v56 1959 p154; BRD 1960 p735; FC 7th p207; KR
v27 1959 p384; LJ v84 1959 p2212.

Maurois, Andre
Ariel: The Life of Shelley.
Appleton 1924 (Heavily reprinted).
NYTBR D 2, 1923 p8; BRD 1924 p391.

McDonald, Eva
Shelley's Springtime Bride.
Hale 1971.

Morley, Margaret
Wild Spirit: The Story of Percy.
Hodder & Stoughton 1992.
LJ v117 N 1, 1992 p118.

Shute, Nerina
*Poet Pursued: A Biographical Novel Based on the
Life of Percy Bysshe Shelley.*
Jarrolds 1951.

West, Paul
Lord Byron's Doctor.
Doubleday 1989.
BL v86 1989 p147; BRD 1991 p1968; KR v57 1989
p1034; LJ v114 S 1, 1989 p298; NYTBR F 3, 1991
p32; PW v236 Jl 21, 1989 p50.

1291. Sheppard, Jack (John)
1702-1724
English thief; subject of many plays and ballads

Ainsworth, William Harrison
Jack Sheppard: A Romance.
Richard Bentley 1839 (Heavily reprinted).

1292. Sheridan, Philip Henry
1831-1888
Union Civil War general

Allen, Merritt P.
YA *Blow, Bugles, Blow.*
D. McKay 1956.
BL v53 1956 p98; BRD 1956 p11; LJ v81 1956 p2467;
NYTBR Sp 16, 1956 p38; SHSLC 8th p381.

Catton, Bruce
YA *Banners at Shenandoah: A Story of Sheridan's
Fighting Cavalry.*
Doubleday 1955 (Rpr. 1965).

BL v51 1955 p300; BRD 1955 p158; KR v22 1954
p776; LJ v80 1955 p1008; NYTBR F 13, 1955 p28.

Lampman, Evelyn
Witch Doctor's Son.
Doubleday 1954.
BL v51 1954 p156; BRD 1954 p518; KR v22 1954
p486; SatR N 13, 1954 p92.

Lancaster, Bruce
Roll, Shenandoah.
Little, Brown 1956.
BL v53 1956 p45; BRD 1956 p543; FC 9th p306; KR
v24 1956 p450; LJ v81 1956 p1791; NYTBR S 2,
1956 p14.

1293. Sheridan, Richard Brinsley
1751-1816
British dramatist

Walker, Joan
*Marriage of Harlequin: A Biographical Novel of the
Important Years in the Life of Richard Brinsley
Sheridan.*
McClelland & Stewart 1962.

1294. Sherman, William Tecumseh
1820-1891
Union Civil War general; famous for his march
through Atlanta to the sea

Brick, John
Jubilee.
Doubleday 1956.
BRD 1956 p115; FC 10th p66; KR v24 Ja 1, 1956 p13;
NYTBR Mr 4, 1956 p4.

Odom, John D.
Hell in Georgia.
Corlies Macy 1960.

1295. Shippen, Margaret
1760-1804
Revolutionary spy; second wife of Benedict Arnold

Callahan, North
Peggy.
Cornwall Books 1983.
LATBR Jl 15, 1984 p6.

Duncan, Lois
YA *Peggy.*
Little, Brown 1970.

Pleasants, Henry
Mars' Butterfly.
Christopher Publishing House 1941.
BRD 1942 p607.

1296. Sibeluis, Jean
1865-1957
Finnish composer

Trotter, William R.
Winter Fire.
Dutton 1993.
NYTBR My 16, 1993 p32.

1297. Sickles, Daniel Edgar
1825-1914
American general & politician

Wells, Lawrence
Let the Band Play Dixie.
Doubleday 1987.
KR v55 1987 p888; LJ v112 Ag 1987 p145.

1298. Siddal, Elizabeth Eleanor
1834-1862
English model & artist; wife of Dante Rossetti

Batchelor, Paula
Angel with Bright Hair.
Methuen 1957.

Kitchen, Paddy
*The Golden Veil: A Novel Based on the Life of
Elizabeth Siddall.*
H. Hamilton 1981.
KR v50 1982 p25; TLS My 29, 1981 p596.

Savage, Elizabeth
Willowwood.
Little, Brown 1978.
BL v75 1978 p157; KR v46 1978 p658; LJ v103 1978
p1533; PW v214 Jl 3, 1978 p60.

1299. Siddons, Sarah Kemble
1755-1831
English actress

Brahms, Caryl
*Enter a Dragon—Stage Centre: An Embroidered
Life of Mrs. Siddons.*
Hodder & Stoughton 1979.
BritBkN Ap 1980 p248; NS v98 N 2, 1979 p687.

Durman, Hilda
Artist in Love.
Roy 1954 (Rpr. 1973, 1980, 1989).

1300. Sidney, Philip, Sir
1554-1586
English poet, politician, & soldier

Foote, Dorothy Norris
The Constant Star.
Scribner 1959.
BL v56 1959 p27; BRD 1959 p368; KR v27 1959
p330; LJ v84 1959 p2079; NYTBR Jl 19, 1959 p4.

Willard, Barbara
*He Fought for His Queen: The Story of Sir Philip
Sidney.*

Heinemann 1954.
LJ v81 1956 p245.

Willard, Barbara
Portrait of Philip.
Macmillan 1950.

1301. Simpson, James Young, Sir
1811-1870
Scottish obstetrician; one of the founders of
modern gynecology

Murrell, Shirley
Young Doctor Simpson.
Hale 1971.

1302. Simpson, Wallis (Bessie Wallis War-field)
1896-1986
American-born wife of Edward VIII of England

Edwards, Anne
Wallis: The Novel.
Morrow 1991.
BL v87 1991 p1282; KR v59 1991 p345; NYTBR Je 9,
1991 p40.

Fisher, Graham
The Plot to Kill Wallis Simpson.
St. Martin's 1989.
KR v57 N 1, 1989 p1549; PW v236 O 27, 1989 p55.

Kilian, Michael
Dance on a Sinking Ship.
St. Martin's 1988.
KR v55 1987 p1692; LJ v113 Mr 1, 1988 p77; PW
v232 Ja 8, 1988 p72.

Smith, A. C. H.
Edward and Mrs. Simpson.
Weidenfeld & Nicolson 1978.

1303. Sinclair, Upton Beall
1878-1968
American author; wrote *The Jungle*

Campbell, R. Wright
Fat Tuesday.
Ticknor & Fields 1983.
KR v50 1982 p1345; LJ v108 1983 p145; NYTBR Mr
6, 1983 p10.

1304. Sitting Bull
1831-1890
Sioux Indian chief; defeated Custer at the Battle
of the Little Big Horn

Haines, William Wister
The Winter War.
Little, Brown 1961.
BL v57 1961 p490; BRD 1961 p567; KR v28 1960
p1045; LJ v86 1961 p112; NYTBR Ap 16, 1961
p35.

Jones, Douglas C.
Arrest Sitting Bull.
Scribner 1977.
BL v74 1977 p268; BRD 1978 p688; KR v45 1977
p682; LJ v102 1977 p1678; NYTBR D 11, 1977 p20.

Leeder, Terry
JUV *White Forehead of the Cypress Hills.*
Dundurn Press 1979.

McMurtry, Larry
Buffalo Girls: A Novel.
Simon & Schuster 1990.
BL v87 1990 p5; BRD 1991 p1266; KR v58 1990
p1033; LJ v115 O 1, 1990 p118; NYTBR O 7, 1990
p3; Time v136 O 29, 1990 p103.

Stevenson, Augusta
JUV *Sitting Bull, Dakota Boy.*
Bobbs-Merrill 1960.
LJ v82 1957 p226.

Ulyatt, Kenneth
YA *Custer's Gold: A Story of the American West at
the Time of the Battle of the Little Big Horn.*
Collins 1971.
TLS O 22, 1971 p1319.

Van Every, Dale
The Day the Sun Died.
Little, Brown 1971.
FC 9th p526; KR v39 1971 p76; LJ v96 1971 p502; LJ
v96 1971 p2146.

1305. Smith, Alfred Emanuel
1873-1944
American political leader; governor of New
York; Democratic presidential nominee, 1928

Gibbons, Floyd Phillips
The Red Napoleon.
J. Cape & H. Smith 1929 (Rpr. 1976).
BRD 1929 p351; NYTBR Ag 25, 1929 p9; SatR O 12,
1929 p274.

1306. Smith, Jedediah Strong
1799-1831
American explorer & fur trader

Allen, Merritt P.
YA *Sun Trail.*
Longmans 1943.
BRD 1943 p14; CC 7th p980; HB v19 N 1943 p411;
LJ v68 1943 p729.

Burt, Olive Woolley
JUV *Jed Smith, Young Western Explorer.*
Bobbs-Merrill 1963.

1307. Smith, John
1580-1631
Adventurer & colonist in America; leader of
Jamestown colony

Barren, Charles
Jamestown.
Hale 1961.

Barth, John
The Sot-Weed Factor.
Doubleday 1960.
BRD 1961 p81; KR v28 1960 p462; LJ v85 1960
   p3099; NYTBR Ag 21, 1960 p4.

Barton, Thomas Frank
JUV *John Smith, Jamestown Boy.*
Bobbs-Merrill 1966.
CE v44 Ap 1968 p504.

Bowman, John Clarke
Powhatan's Daughter.
Viking 1973.
Also published as *Pocahontas.*
FC 9th p58; KR v41 N 1, 1973 p1219; LJ v98 1973
   p3390.

Dixon, Margaret
Pocahontas: The Princess of the Old Dominion.
Garrett & Massie 1958.
Also published as *The Princess of the Old Dominion.*

Gerson, Noel Bertram
Daughter of Eve.
Doubleday 1958 (Rpr. 1979).
BL v54 1958 p638; BRD 1958 p423; KR v26 1958
   p343.

Holberg, Ruth Langland
YA *Captain John Smith, the Lad From Lincolnshire.*
Crowell 1946.
BL v43 1947 p138; BRD 1946 p388; KR v14 1946
   p347; LJ v71 1946 p1468.

Latham, Jean Lee
YA *This Dear-Bought Land.*
Harper 1957.
BRD 1957 p530; KR v25 1957 p80; LJ v82 1957
   p1362; NYTBR Mr 31, 1957 p34.

Lawson, Marie A.
YA *Pocahontas and Captain John Smith; the Story of
   the Virginia Colony.*
Random House 1950.
BRD 1950 p541; LJ v76 1951 p54; NYTBR N 12,
   1950 p6.

Marshall, Edison
Great Smith.
Farrar & Rinehart 1943.
BRD 1943 p551; LJ v68 1943 p289; NYTBR Ap 11,
   1943 p7.

Mason, Miriam E.
JUV *John Smith: Man of Adventure.*
Houghton Mifflin 1958.
LJ v84 1959 p644.

Wellman, Manly Wade
JUV *Jamestown Adventure.*
Washburn 1967.
KR v35 1967 p881; LJ v93 1968 p297.

Wohl, Burton
Soldier in Paradise.
Putnam 1977.
KR v45 1977 p751; LJ v102 1977 p2083; NYTBR D
   11, 1977 p24; PW v212 Jl 18, 1977 p128.

1308. Smith, Joseph
1805-1844
American founder of the Mormon sect

Fisher, Vardis
Children of God: An American Epic.
Harper 1939 (Rpr. 1975).
BL v36 S 1939 p8; BRD 1939 p327; NYTBR Ag 27,
   1939 p1.

Furnas, J. C.
The Devil's Rainbow.
Harper 1962.
BRD 1962 p423; LJ v87 1962 p1149; NYTBR Ap 1,
   1962 p40.

Lauritzen, Jonreed
The Everlasting Fire.
Doubleday 1962.
BL v59 N 1, 1962 p206; BRD 1962 p693; LJ v87 1962
   p2775; NYTBR Ag 5, 1962 p20.

Lund, Gerald N.
The Work and the Glory: A Historical Novel.
Bookcraft 1991.

Pryor, Elinor
And Never Yield.
Macmillan 1942.
BL v38 1942 p442; BRD 1942 p618; NYTBR My 3,
   1942 p7; SatR Je 20, 1942 p12.

Stienon, Elaine
The Light of Morning.
Ensign 1988.

1309. Smith, Madeleine Hamilton
1835-1928
Scottish murderer

Kauffmann, Lane
The Villian of the Piece.
Dial 1973.
KR v41 1973 p530; LJ v98 1973 p1192.

Petrie, Glen
Mariamne.
Coward, McCann & Geoghegan 1977.
BL v73 1977 p1327; KR v45 1977 p182; LJ v102 1977
   p949; PW v211 F 28, 1977 p118.

West, Pamela
Madeleine.
St. Martin's 1983.
BL v80 1983 p330; KR v51 1983 p974; LJ v108 1983
   p1890.

1310. Socrates
Greek philosopher

Kraus, Rene
The Private and Public Life of Socrates.
Doubleday, Doran 1940.
BRD 1940 p523; NYTBR Mr 17, 1940 p8; SatR Ap
27, 1940 p20.

Mason, Cora
YA *Socrates: The Man Who Dared to Ask.*
Beacon Press 1953.
BRD 1954 p600; LJ v79 1954 p151; SatR F 5, 1955
p37.

Moessinger, Pierre
JUV *Socrates.*
Creative Education 1993.

Pick, Robert
The Escape of Socrates.
Knopf 1954.
BRD 1954 p706; KR v22 1954 p498; LJ v79 1954
p1590; NYTBR S 12, 1954 p31.

Plowman, Stephanie
YA *The Road to Sardis.*
Houghton Mifflin 1965.
BRD 1966 p961; LJ v91 1966 p2712; NYTBR My 8,
1966 p30.

Renault, Mary
The Last of the Wine.
Pantheon 1956.
BL v53 N 15, 1956 p149; BRD 1956 p773; FC 10th
p440; KR v24 1956 p714; TLS Je 29, 1956 p389.

1311. Solomon, King of Israel

Old Testament figure; known for his wisdom &
wealth

Cassill, R. V.
After Goliath.
Ticknor & Fields 1985.
BL v81 1985 p756; KR v53 1985 p96; LJ v110 Mr 15,
1985 p70; NYTBR Je 16, 1985 p27.

Fisher, Vardis
*The Valley of Vision: A Novel of King Solomon
and His Time.*
Abelard Press 1951.
LJ v76 1951 p773; NYTBR Je 3, 1951 p16; Time v58
Jl 2, 1951 p100.

Heym, Stefan
The King David Report, a Novel.
Putnam 1973.
BL v70 1973 p320; BRD 1974 p546; KR v41 1973
p829; LJ v98 1973 p3283.

Hubler, Richard G.
Love and Wisdom: A Novel about Solomon.
Crown 1968.
BL v65 1968 p43; KR v36 1968 p356; LJ v93 1968
p1915.

Ormonde, Czenzi
Solomon and the Queen of Sheba.
Farrar, Straus & Young 1954.

BL v51 1954 p110; BRD 1954 p679; KR v22 1954
p593; LJ v79 1954 p1589; NYTBR Ja 16, 1955 p27.

Tarr, Herbert
A Time for Loving.
Random House 1973.
BL v69 1973 p620; KR v40 1972 p1268; LJ v97 1972
p4004; NYTBR Ja 21, 1973 p24.

Williams, Jay
Solomon and Sheba.
Random House 1959.
BL v55 1959 p507; BRD 1960 p1438; KR v27 1959
p18; NYTBR Mr 8, 1959 p42.

1312. Solzhenitsyn, Alexandr

1918-
Russian author; won Nobel Prize, 1970; wrote
Gulag Archipelago

Salisbury, Harrison E.
The Gates of Hell.
Random House 1975.
KR v43 1975 p938; LJ v100 1975 p1846.

1313. Son of Sam

see Berkowitz, David

1314. Spartacus

d. 71 BC
Roman gladiator; leader of a rebellion of slaves
against Rome

Fast, Howard
Spartacus.
Crown 1951 (Heavily reprinted).
BRD 1952 p296; LJ v77 1952 p437; NYTBR F 3, 1952
p22; SatR Mr 8, 1952 p17.

Ghnassia, Maurice
Arena: A Novel.
Viking 1969.
BL v66 1969 p438; KR v37 1969 p579; LJ v94 1969
p2807; PW v195 My 26, 1969 p49.

Houghton, Eric
JUV *They Marched with Spartacus.*
McGraw-Hill 1963.
BRD 1964 p587; LJ v88 1963 p4476; NYTBR D 8,
1963 p30.

Koestler, Arthur
The Gladiators.
Macmillan 1939 (Rpr. 1967).
BRD 1939 p553; NYTBR Jl 16, 1939 p6; SatR Jl 15,
1939 p7.

Levy, Elizabeth
YA *Running Out of Time.*
Knopf 1980.
BL v76 1980 p1678; SLJ v27 D 1980 p75; SLJ v27 My
1981 p27.

Mitchell, James Leslie
Spartacus.
Hutchinson 1970.

Perdue, Jacques
Slave and Master: The Story of Spartacus.
Macaulay 1960.

1315. Speke, John Hanning
1827-1864
English explorer

Harrison, William
Burton and Speke.
St. Martin's 1982.
BL v79 1982 p92; KR v50 1982 p951; LJ v107 1982
   p1895; PW v222 Ag 13, 1982 p67.

1316. Springsteen, Bruce
1949-
American rock singer & songwriter

Major, Kevin
YA *Dear Bruce Springsteen: A Novel.*
Delacorte 1987.
BL v84 1988 p1001; BRD 1988 p1091; KR v56 1988
   p57; SLJ v34 My 1988 p110.

1317. Squanto
1585-1622
American Indian; taught Pilgrims survival skills

Anderson, Anita M.
JUV *Squanto and the Pilgrims.*
Wheeler Pub. Co. 1949.

Bulla, Clyde Robert
JUV *John Billington, Friend of Squanto.*
Crowell 1956.
BRD 1956 p138; KR v24 N 1, 1956 p803; LJ v82 1957
   p224; NYTBR N 18, 1956 p48.

Gaggin, Eva
YA *Down Ryton Water.*
Viking 1941.
BL v38 1941 p83; BRD 1941 p329; LJ v66 1941 p886;
   NYTBR Ja 18, 1942 p10.

Malvern, Gladys
YA *Meg's Fortune.*
Messner 1950.
BRD 1950 p606; KR v18 1950 p63; LJ v75 1950
   p1056; NYTBR Mr 26, 1950 p24.

Stevenson, Augusta
JUV *Squanto, Young Indian Hunter.*
Bobbs-Merrill 1962.

Webb, Robert N.
JUV *We Were There with the Mayflower Pilgrims.*
Grosset & Dunlap 1956.

1318. Stalin, Joseph
1879-1953
Premier & dictator of the Soviet Union

Barwick, James
The Kremlin Contract.
Putnam 1987.
BL v83 1987 p1179.

Gibbons, Floyd Phillips
The Red Napoleon.
J. Cape & H. Smith 1929 (Rpr. 1976).
BRD 1929 p351; NYTBR Ag 25, 1929 p9; SatR O 12,
   1929 p274.

Jones, Mervyn
Joseph.
Atheneum 1970.
BRD 1970 p740; LJ v95 1970 p4280; NYTBR Ag 16,
   1970 p5; TLS Ap 30, 1970 p471.

Krotkov, Yuri
The Red Monarch: Scenes from the Life of Stalin.
Norton 1979.
BL v75 1979 p1347; BRD 1979 p714; KR v47 1979
   p144; LJ v104 1979 p976; PW v215 F 12, 1979
   p115.

Melius, Emeric
Enemy of the People.
New Century Pub. 1967.

Noel, Sterling
I Killed Stalin.
Farrar, Strauss & Young 1951.
BRD 1951 p658; KR v19 1951 p357; LJ v76 1951
   p1222; NYTBR Ag 19, 1951 p19.

Nysse, Allen
America Within.
First Amendment Press 1990.

Rybakov, Anatoli
Children of the Arbat.
Little, Brown 1988.
Translation of *Deti Arbata.*
BL v84 1988 p1290; BRD 1988 p1511; KR v56 1988
   p399; LJ v113 Ag 1988 p175; NYTBR My 22, 1988
   p7.

Rybakov, Anatoli
Fear.
Little, Brown 1992.
BW v22 S 6, 1992 p7; KR v60 1992 p877; NYTBR S
   20, 1992 p3; PW v239 Ag 3, 1992 p62.

Ulam, Adam
The Kirov Affair.
Harcourt Brace Jovanovich 1988.
BL v84 1988 p1575; BRD 1989 p1689; KR v56 1988
   p323; LJ v113 Je 1, 1988 p144; NYTBR Je 12, 1988
   p13.

1319. Standish, Miles
1584-1656
Military leader at Plymouth Colony

Gaggin, Eva
YA *Down Ryton Water.*
Viking 1941.
BL v38 1941 p83; BRD 1941 p329; LJ v66 1941 p886;
NYTBR Ja 18, 1942 p10.

Gebler, Ernest
*The Plymouth Adventure: A Chronicle Novel of
the Voyage of the Mayflower.*
Doubleday 1950.
BRD 1950 p349; NYTBR Ap 30, 1950 p32; SatR Ap
29, 1950 p13.

Payne, Robert
O Western Wind.
Putnam 1957.
BRD 1957 p248; LJ v82 1957 p1065.

Stevenson, Augusta
JUV *Myles Standish: Adventurous Boy.*
Bobbs-Merrill 1949.
BRD 1950 p867; LJ v75 1950 p328.

Webb, Robert N.
JUV *We Were There with the Mayflower Pilgrims.*
Grosset & Dunlap 1956.

1320. Stanford, Leland (Amasa Leland)
1824-1893
American railroad builder, politician, & founder
of Stanford University

Jakes, John
California Gold: A Novel.
Random House 1989.
BL v85 1989 p1922; NYTBR O 8, 1989 p24.

McMurtry, Larry
Streets of Laredo.
Simon & Schuster 1993.

1321. Stanley, Henry Morton, Sir
1841-1904
British explorer & journalist; known for finding
David Livingstone in the jungles of Africa

Albus, Harry J.
*"Dr. Livingstone, I Presume": Henry M. Stanley's
Search for David Livingstone in the Jungles of Af-
rica.*
W.B. Eerdmans 1957.

Forbath, Peter
The Last Hero: A Novel.
Simon & Schuster 1988.
BL v84 1988 p1865; KR v56 1988 p998; LJ v113 O
15, 1988 p100; NYTBR S 25, 1988 p38.

Hagerfors, Lennart
The Whales in Lake Tanganyika.
Grove Press 1989.
BRD 1990 p746; LJ v114 Ap 1, 1989 p111; NYTBR Jl
30, 1989 p16.

Mitchell, Mary
Black Crusade.
Methuen 1949.

Smith, B. Webster
JUV *Sir Henry M. Stanley.*
Blackie 1960.

1322. Stanton, Elizabeth Cady
1815-1902
American woman's rights advocate

Jacobs, William J.
JUV *Mother, Aunt Susan and Me: The First Fight for
Women's Rights.*
Coward, McCann & Geoghegan 1979.
BL v76 1979 p120; CBRS v8 1979 p9; KR v47 1979
p1070.

Monfredo, Miriam G.
Seneca Falls Inheritance.
St. Martin's 1992.
KR v60 1992 p144; PW v239 F 10, 1992 p74.

1323. Stark, John
1728-1822
American Revolutionary general

Jennings, John E.
The Shadow and the Glory.
Reynal & Hitchcock 1943.
BL v40 1944 p183; BRD 1943 p425; NYTBR D 19,
1943 p10; SatR D 4, 1943 p55.

1324. Starr, Belle
1848-1889
American pioneer & outlaw

Camp, Deborah
Belle Starr: A Novel of the Old West.
Harmony Books 1987.
LJ v112 My 15, 1987 p95; PW v231 My 15, 1987
p267.

Leaton, Anne
Pearl.
Knopf 1985.
BL v81 1985 p927; BRD 1986 p950; KR v52 1984
p1159; LJ v110 F 15, 1985 p180; NYTBR Mr 31,
1985 p22; PW v227 Ja 25, 1985 p85.

Morgan, Speer
Belle Starr: A Novel.
Little, Brown 1979.
BL v75 1979 p737; KR v46 1978 p1268; LJ v104 1979
p212.

Taylor, Robert
Loving Belle Starr.
Algonquin Books 1984.
KR v52 1984 p169; LATBR Jl 29, 1984 p8; LJ v109
1984 p997; PW v225 F 24, 1984 p125.

1325. Stauffenberg, Claus (Schenk Graf) Von
1907-1944
German army officer; attempted to assassinate Hitler

West, Paul
The Very Rich Hours of Count von Stauffenberg.
Harper & Row 1980 (Rpr. 1989).
BL v76 1980 p1660; LJ v105 1980 p1664; NYTBR N 9, 1980 p14.

1326. Stein, Gertrude
1874-1946
American author

Burnett, Avis
Gertrude Stein.
Atheneum 1972.
BL v69 1972 p189; BRD 1973 p173; KR v40 1972 p1204; LJ v97 1972 p4076; NYTBR D 17, 1972 p8.

Steward, Samuel M.
The Caravaggio Shawl.
Alyson Publications 1989.
BL v86 1989 p264; LJ v114 O 1, 1989 p121; NYTBR D 10, 1989 p41.

Steward, Samuel M.
Murder Is Murder Is Murder.
Alyson Publications 1985.
PW v227 Ap 12, 1985 p98.

Steward, Samuel M.
Parisian Lives: A Novel.
St. Martin's 1984.
BL v80 1984 p847; KR v52 1984 p15; PW v224 D 23, 1984 p53.

1327. Stendhal
1783-1842
French author & critic

Vinogradov, Anatoli Kornelievich
Three Colours of Time: A Novel of the Life of Stendhal.
Hutchinson 1946.

1328. Stephens, John Lloyd
1805-1852
American traveler & archaeologist

Highwater, Jamake
Journey to the Sky: A Novel about the True Adventures of Two Men in Search of the Lost Maya Kingdom.
Crowell 1978.
KR v46 1978 p963; PW v214 S 25, 1978 p127.

1329. Sterne, Laurence
1713-1768
English novelist; wrote *Sentimental Journey* & *Tristram Shandy*; wrote under pseud., "Mister Yorick"

Bill, Alfred H.
Alas, Poor Yorick!.
Little, Brown 1927 (Rpr. 1970).
BRD 1927 p78; NYTBR D 25, 1927 p10; SatR O 29, 1927 p255.

1330. Steuben, Friedrich Wilhelm Augustus
1730-1794
American Revolutionary War general

Brick, John
The Strong Men.
Doubleday 1959.
BL v56 1960 p266; BRD 1960 p159; KR v27 1959 p614; LJ v84 1959 p3150; NYTBR N 8, 1959 p63.

Richter, William Benson
The Life and Loves of Von Steuben.
Christopher Pub. House 1952.

Taylor, David
Farewell to Valley Forge.
Lippincott 1955.
BL v52 1955 p126; BRD 1955 p889; KR v23 1955 p559; LJ v80 1955 p2522; NYTBR N 27, 1955 p47.

1331. Stevens, Thaddeus
1792-1868
American politician

Singmaster, Elsie
I Speak for Thaddeus Stevens.
Houghton Mifflin 1947.
BRD 1947 p826; KR v15 1947 p208; LJ v72 1947 p807; NYTBR Je 8, 1947 p19.

1332. Stevenson, Robert Louis Balfour
1850-1894
Scottish poet & novelist; wrote *Dr. Jekyll and Mr. Hyde* and *Treasure Island*

Howard, Joan
The Story of Robert Louis Stevenson.
Grosset & Dunlap 1958.

Knight, Alanna
The Passionate Kindness: The Love Story of Robert Louis Stevenson and Fanny Osbourne.
Milton House Books 1974.
LR v24 Winter 1975 p376.

Nakajima, Atsushi
Light, Wind, and Dreams: An Interpretation of the Life and Mind of Robert Louis Stevenson.
Hokuseido Press 1962.

Reinstedt, Randall A.
JUV *The Strange Case of the Ghosts of the Robert Louis Stevenson House.*
Ghost Town Publications 1988.

Stern, Gladys B.
No Son of Mine.
Macmillan 1948.
BRD 1948 p802; LJ v73 1948 p814; NYTBR Je 6, 1948 p10.

1333. Stiegel, Henry William
1729-1785
German-born American iron & glass manufacturer

Jordan, Mildred A.
One Red Rose Forever.
Knopf 1941.
BRD 1941 p485; FC 8th p231; LJ v66 1941 p731; NYTBR S 14, 1941 p6; SatR O 4, 1941 p13.

Rogers, Frances; Beard, Alice
YA *Jeremy Pepper.*
Lippincott 1946.
BL v43 Ja 15, 1947 p158; BRD 1947 p765; HB v23 Mr 1947 p115; LJ v72 1947 p168.

1334. Stieglitz, Alfred
1864-1946
American pioneer photographer

Cheuse, Alan
The Light Possessed.
Peregrine Smith Books 1990.
BRD 1992 p350; NYTBR O 7, 1990 p33.

1335. Stoker, Bram
1847-1912
English author; wrote *Dracula*

Douglas, Carole Douglas
YA *Good Night, Mr. Holmes.*
Tor Books 1990.
BL v87 1990 p419; KR v58 1990 p1354; NYTBR D 16, 1990 p33; SLJ v37 Mr 1991 p226.

1336. Stone, Lucy
1818-1893
American feminist & editor

Malm, Dorothea
The Woman Question.
Appleton-Century-Crofts 1957.
BL v55 1958 p23; BRD 1958 p712; KR v26 1958 p92; LJ v83 1958 p2079.

1337. Stowe, Harriet Beecher
1811-1896
American novelist & reformer

Ludwig, Charles
Champion of Freedom.
Bethany House Publishers 1987.

1338. Strachey, (Giles) Lytton
1880-1932
English biographer & historian

Collins, Randall
The Case of the Philosopher's Ring.
Crown 1978.
KR v46 1978 p1216.

1339. Stradivari, Antonio
1644-1737
Italian violin maker

Deverell, Catherine
JUV *Stradivari's Singing Violin.*
Carolrhoda Books 1992.
BL v89 1993 p1059.

Hersey, John
Antonietta: A Novel.
Knopf 1991.
BL v87 1991 p1435; KR v59 1991 p422; LJ v116 My 15, 1991 p108; NYTBR My 19, 1991 p13; PW v238 Mr 29, 1991 p76.

1340. Strauss, Johann
1804-1849
Austrian composer

Ewen, David
YA *Tales from the Vienna Woods: The Story of Johann Strauss.*
Holt 1944.
BRD 1944 p228; KR v12 1944 p482; LJ v69 1944 p1106.

1341. Strindberg, August
1849-1912
Swedish playwright & novelist

Strindberg, August
A Madman's Defence.
Cape 1968.
LJ v92 1967 p597; SatR Ap 29, 1967 p33.

1342. Stuart, "Jeb" (James Ewell Brown)
1833-1864
American Confederate general

Evans, Edna Hoffman
YA *Sunstar and Pepper: Scouting with Jeb Stuart.*
University of North Carolina Press 1947.
BRD 1947 p283; LJ v72 1947 p819; NYTBR Je 15, 1947 p27; SatR S 6, 1947 p35.

Love, Edmund G.
An End to Bugling.
Harper & Row 1963.

LJ v88 1963 p575; LJ v88 1963 p2156; SatR My 4, 1963 p35.

Seifert, Shirley
Farewell, My General.
Lippincott 1954.
BL v50 1954 p452; BRD 1954 p796; FC 7th p310; KR v22 1954 p272.

Skimin, Robert
Gray Victory.
St. Martin's 1988.
BL v84 1988 p1096; KR v56 1988 p15; LJ v113 Mr 1, 1988 p79; SLJ v35 D 1988 p132.

Wellman, Manly Wade
Appomattox Road: Final Adventures of the Iron Scouts.
Washburn 1960.
LJ v85 1960 p2054; SatR Je 18, 1960 p34.

Wellman, Manly Wade
The Ghost Batallion: A Story of the Iron Scouts.
Washburn 1958.
BRD 1958 p1103; KR v26 1958 p231; LJ v83 1958 p2077; NYTBR Je 18, 1958 p44.

Wellman, Manly Wade
Gray Riders, Jeb Stuart and His Men.
Aladdin Books 1954.
LJ v79 1954 p2255; NYTBR N 14, 1954 p26.

Wellman, Manly Wade
Ride, Rebels! Adventures of the Iron Scouts.
Washburn 1959.
LJ v84 1959 p2225.

1343. Stuart, Charles Edward Louis Philip
1720-1788
Known variously as "Bonnie Prince Charlie," and "The Young Pretender"; unsuccessfully tried to seize Hanoverian throne

Anthony, Evelyn
Clandara.
Doubleday 1963.
LJ v88 1963 p1682.

Beatty, John; Beatty, Patricia
YA *The Royal Dirk.*
Morrow 1966.
BL v62 1966 p829; BRD 1966 p78; KR v34 1966 p375; NYTBR Mr 6, 1966 p34.

Binner, Ina
Prince of Adversity.
Hale 1974.

Broster, D. K.
The Dark Mile.
Coward-McCann 1934 (Rpr. 1961, 1974).
Continues *The Flight of the Heron.*
BL v31 1934 p98; BRD 1934 p117; LJ v60 1935 p305; NYTBR N 4, 1934 p10.

Broster, D. K.
The Flight of the Heron.
Coward-McCann 1930 (Rpr. 1975).
BL v26 1930 p401; BRD 1930 p132; NYTBR Mr 16, 1930 p18.

Broster, D. K.
The Gleam in the North.
Heinemann 1927 (Rpr. 1949, 1974).
LJ v56 1931 p1057.

Campbell, Grace Maclennan
Torbeg.
Duell, Sloan & Pearce 1953.
BL v49 1953 p284; LJ v78 1953 p594; NYTBR Ap 5, 1953 p18.

Cormack, Maribelle
YA *Last Clash of Claymores, a Story of Scotland in the Time of Prince Charles.*
Appleton-Century 1940.
BRD 1940 p200; LJ v65 1940 p857; NYTBR N 10, 1940 p44.

Dakers, Elaine (Jane Lane, pseud.)
Farewell to the White Cockade.
Muller 1961 (Rpr. 1975).

De La Torre, Lillian
YA *The White Rose of Stuart.*
T. Nelson 1954.
BRD 1954 p238; LJ v79 1954 p2258.

Duke, Winifred
The Ship of Fools.
Hale 1956.

Fisher, Richard
Masquerader Brett.
Selwyn & Blount 1946.

Gartner, Chloe
The Woman from the Glen.
Morrow 1973.
BL v69 1973 p1007; KR v41 1973 p206; LJ v98 1973 p885.

Gluyas, Constance
Born to Be King.
Prentice-Hall 1974.
BL v70 1974 p1180; KR v42 1974 p262; LJ v99 1974 p774; PW v205 Mr 18, 1974 p48.

Hardwick, Mollie
Charlie Is My Darling.
Coward, McCann & Geoghegan 1977.
BL v74 1978 p1609; KR v45 1977 p1112; LJ v103 1978 p384.

Johnston, Velda
I Came to the Highlands: A Novel of Suspense.
Dodd, Mead 1974.
BL v70 1974 p1180; FC 9th p281; LJ v99 1974 p1848.

Kersey, Clare
The White Cockade.
Hale 1979.

Linklater, Eric
The Prince in the Heather.
Hodder & Stoughton 1965.
BRD 1966 p721; LJ v91 1966 p3931.

Oliver, Jane
Candleshine No More.
Putnam 1967.
BL v64 1968 p626; LJ v92 1967 p4274; LJ v93 1968
   p572.

Rees, Joan
The Queen of Hearts.
Hale 1974.
TLS Ja 17, 1975 p48.

Rossiter, Clare
The White Rose.
St. Martin's 1978.
KR v46 1978 p453; LJ v103 1978 p1085.

Scott, Walter Sir
YA *Redgauntlet: A Tale of the Eighteenth Century.*
A. Constable 1824 (Heavily reprinted).
BRD 1912 p402.

Scott, Walter Sir
Waverley: or, 'Tis Sixty Years Since. . . .
A. Constable 1814 (Heavily reprinted).

Shepard, Odell
*Jenkin's Ear; a Narrative Attributed to Horace
   Walpole, Esq..*
Macmillan 1951.
BRD 1951 p808; FC 7th p315; LJ v75 1950 p1662;
   NYTBR Ap 1, 1951 p5; SatR Ap 14, 1951 p53.

Thomas, Donald S.
Prince Charlie's Bluff.
Viking 1974.
BS v34 Jl 15, 1974 p200; KR v42 Ap 15, 1974 p447;
   LJ v99 1974 p1988; Time v104 Ag 19, 1974 p84.

Watson, Sally
Highland Rebel.
Holt, Rinehart & Winston 1954.
BRD 1954 p929; KR v22 1954 p385; LJ v79 1954
   p2502; NYTBR N 14, 1954 p34.

Wilkins, William V.
Crown without Sceptre.
Macmillan 1952.
BL v48 1952 p281; BRD 1952 p954; KR v20 1952
   p163; NYTBR My 11, 1952 p20.

1344. Stuart, Gilbert Charles
1755-1828
American painter

Bischoff, Ilse
JUV *Painter's Coach.*
Longmans, Green 1943.
BRD 1943 p76; LJ v69 1944 p120; NYTBR Ja 9, 1944
   p8.

Bischoff, Ilse
*Proud Heritage, a Novel Based on the Life of Gil-
   bert Stuart.*
Coward-McCann 1949.
BRD 1949 p76; NYTBR O 23, 1949 p36.

1345. Stuyvesant, Peter (Petrus)
1610-1672
Dutch colonial administrator in America

Holland, Rupert S.
YA *Peter Stuyvesant.*
Messner 1953.
LJ v78 1953 p2226.

Linderholm, Helmer
Land of the Beautiful River.
St. Martin's 1963.
LJ v88 1963 p3102.

Lobel, Arnold
JUV *On the Day Peter Stuyvesant Sailed into Town.*
Harper & Row 1971.
BL v68 1971 p293; HB v47 D 1971 p601; KR v39
   1971 p936; LJ v96 1971 p3893; NYTBR Ja 2, 1972
   p8.

MacKellar, William
JUV *Alfie and Me and the Ghost of Peter Stuyvesant.*
Dodd, Mead 1974.
KR v42 Ag 15, 1974 p977; LJ v99 D 15, 1974 p3268.

Miller, Shane
JUV *Peter Stuyvesant's Drummer.*
Coward-McCann 1959.
BRD 1959 p710; KR v27 1959 p137; LJ v84 1959
   p1014; NYTBR Mr 15, 1959 p36.

Widdemer, Mabel
JUV *Peter Stuyvesant, Boy with Wooden Shoes.*
Bobbs-Merrill 1950.
LJ v75 1950 p881.

1346. Suleiman I
1496-1566
Turkish ruler

Crawley, Aileen
The Bride of Suleiman.
Hutchinson 1981.
KR v49 1981 p1357.

Faulkner, Nancy
YA *Knights Besieged.*
Doubleday 1964.
LJ v89 1964 p5016.

Waltari, Mika
The Wanderer.
Putnam 1951.
BRD 1951 p921; FC 7th p368; KR v19 1951 p491;
   NYTBR O 21, 1951 p4; Time v58 N 5, 1951 p128.

1347. Sulla, Lucius Cornelius
138-78 BC
Roman general & dictator

Green, Peter
*The Sword of Pleasure: Being the Memoirs of the
    Most Illustrious Lucius Cornelius Sulla.*
World Pub. Co. 1957.
BL v55 1958 p98; BRD 1958 p457; KR v26 1958
    p429; NYTBR S 7, 1958 p38.

McCullough, Colleen
The Grass Crown.
Morrow 1991.
BL v87 1991 p2078; KR v59 1991 p959; NYTBR O 6,
    1991 p13.

1348. Sullivan, Anne
1866-1936
American teacher of Helen Keller

Brown, Marion Marsh
YA *The Silent Storm.*
Abingdon Press 1963.
BRD 1964 p161; LJ v88 1963 p3346; NYTBR Ja 26,
    1964 p26.

1349. Sullivan, Arthur Seymour, Sir
1842-1900
English composer, best known for his partner-
ship with Sir William Schwenck Gilbert in the
"Gilbert and Sullivan" light operas

Power-Waters, Alma
YA *The Melody Maker.*
Dutton 1959.
BRD 1960 p1085; LJ v84 1959 p3939.

Ronalds, Mary Teresa
*A Victorian Masque: The Love Story of Arthur Sul-
    livan.*
Macdonald & Jane's 1975.
Spec v234 Je 7, 1975 p692.

1350. Sullivan, John L.
1858-1918
American boxer

Grant, James E.
The Great John L..
World Publishing Co. 1945.

1351. Surratt, Mary Eugenia
1820-1865
American co-conspirator in Abraham Lincoln's
assassination; executed

Russell, Pamela Redford
The Woman Who Loved John Wilkes Booth.
Putnam 1978.
KR v46 1978 p330; LJ v103 1978 p1199; PW v213 Ap
    10, 1978 p66.

1352. Sutter, John Augustus
1803-1880
German-born American pioneer; discovery of
gold on his land started the California gold rush

Candrars, Blaise
*Gold: Being the Marvelous History of General John
    Augustus Sutter.*
M. Kesend 1984.
Choice v22 S 1984 p106; LJ v109 1984 p191; NYTBR
    Mr 18, 1984 p18; PW v225 F 17, 1984 p70.

Lauritzen, Jonreed
Captain Sutter's Gold.
Doubleday 1964.
LJ v89 1964 p1115; NYTBR F 16, 1964 p36.

1353. Swedenborg, Emanuel
1688-1772
Swedish scientist, philosopher, & mystic

Cost, March
Two Guests for Swedenborg.
Cassell 1971.
BS v31 N 15, 1971 p380; KR v39 1971 p962; PW
    v200 S 6, 1971 p42; Spec v226 My 29, 1971 p709.

1354. Swift, Jonathan
1667-1745
English satirist; wrote *Gulliver's Travels*

Clewes, Winston
The Violent Friends.
Appleton-Century 1945 (Rpr. 1972).
BRD 1945 p136; KR v12 1944 p551; NYTBR Mr 18,
    1945 p6.

Myers, Elizabeth
The Basilisk of St. Jame's.
Chapman & Hall 1945.

Sitwell, Edith
I Live under a Black Sun.
Lehmann 1948.

1355. Szold, Henrietta
1860-1945
American Zionist leader

Cone, Molly
JUV *Hurry, Henrietta.*
Houghton Mifflin 1966.
BL v63 1967 p624; KR v34 1966 p1139; LJ v92 1967
    p333.

1356. Tabor, Horace Austin Warner
1830-1899
American government official; gained wealth
from silver mining; known as "Silver Dollar" Tabor

Roberts, Martha Gaby
Honeymaid: The Story of Silver Dollar Tabor.
Golden Bell Press 1977.

1357. Taglioni, Maria
1804-1884
Italian dancer

Racster, Olga
Sylphide: Study of a Great Ballerina.
Hutchinson 1945.

1358. Talleyrand-Perigord, Charles Maurice de
1754-1838
French government official & diplomat

Carr, John D.
Captain Cut-Throat.
Harper 1955 (Rpr. 1980, 1988).
BL v51 1955 p290; BRD 1955 p150; KR v23 1955
p96; NYTBR Ap 3, 1955 p28.

Waldeck, R. G.
Lustre in the Sky.
Doubleday 1946.
BRD 1946 p329; KR v14 1946 p110; NYTBR Ap 28,
1946 p18; SatR Je 1, 1946 p8.

1359. Tamerlane
1336-1405
Mongolian conqueror

O'Neal, Cothburn
Master of the World.
Crown 1952.
BRD 1952 p683; KR v20 1952 p521; LJ v77 1952
p1656; NYTBR N 23, 1952 p52.

1360. Tarbell, Ida Minerva
1857-1944
American muckraking author & editor

Campbell, R. Wright
Fat Tuesday.
Ticknor & Fields 1983.
KR v50 1982 p1345; LJ v108 1983 p145; NYTBR Mr
6, 1983 p10.

1361. Tarleton, Banastre, Sir
1754-1833
English military leader in American Revolutionary War

Bristow, Gwen
Celia Garth.
Crowell 1959.
BL v55 1959 p467; BRD 1959 p139; KR v27 1959
p235; LJ v84 1959 p1917; NYTBR My 31, 1959
p18.

Mason, F. van Wyck
Wild Horizon.
Little, Brown 1966.
BL v63 1966 p442; KR v34 1966 p786; LJ v91 1966
p3973; NYTBR D 11, 1966 p68.

1362. Tartini, Giuseppe
1692-1770
Italian composer & violinist

Spalding, Albert
*A Fiddle, a Sword, and a Lady: The Romance of
Giuseppe Tartini.*
Holt 1953.
BL v49 1953 p197; BRD 1953 p882; KR v21 1953
p78; LJ v78 1953 p445; NYTBR Mr 29, 1953 p5.

1363. Taylor, Ann
1782-1866
English author & poet

Ashton, Agnes
*Two Twinkling Stars: The Story of Ann and Jane
Taylor.*
Merlin Books 1983.
BritBkN F 1984 p113.

1364. Taylor, Elizabeth Rosemond
1932-
English actress

Ballard, J. G.
The Atrocity Exhibition.
Cape 1970.
KR v38 1970 p529; LJ v95 1970 p2512.

1365. Taylor, Jane
1783-1824
English poet; wrote *Twinkle, Twinkle, Little Star*

Ashton, Agnes
*Two Twinkling Stars: The Story of Ann and Jane
Taylor.*
Merlin Books 1983.
BritBkN F 1984 p113.

1366. Taylor, William Desmond
1877-1922
American film director

Peeples, Samuel A.
*The Man Who Died Twice: A Novel about Holly-
wood's Most Baffling Murder.*
Putnam 1976 (Rpr. 1984).
BL v72 1976 p1574; KR v44 1976 p557; LJ v101 1976
p1663; PW v209 My 31, 1976 p142.

1367. Tchaikovsky, Peter Ilyich
1840-1893
Russian composer

Gronowicz, Antoni
YA *Tchaikovsky.*
T. Nelson & Sons 1946.
BRD 1947 p368; KR v14 1946 p527; LJ v71 1946
p1630.

Mann, Klaus
Pathetic Symphony, a Novel about Tchaikovsky.
Allen, Towne & Heath 1948.
BRD 1948 p550; LJ v73 1948 p815; NYTBR Jl 4, 1948
p5; SatR Ap 17, 1948 p38.

Mayo, Waldo
YA *Tchaikovsky: His Life in Told in Anecdotal Form.*
Hyperion Press 1945.
BRD 1945 p482; KR v13 1945 p252; LJ v70 1945
p639; NYTBR Je 10, 1945 p18.

Purdy, Claire Lee
YA *Stormy Victory.*
Messner 1942.
BL v39 1943 p322; BRD 1943 p666; LJ v68 1943 p173.

1368. Teach, Edward
see Blackbeard

1369. Tecumseh
1768-1813
Shawnee Indian chief

Anness, Milford E.
Song of Metamoris: A Story That Remains of a People Who Passed This Way.
Caxton Printers 1964.
LJ v89 1964 p2114.

Card, Orson Scott
YA *Red Prophet.*
TOR 1988.
BL v84 1987 p657; KR v56 1988 p22; LJ v113 F 15,
1988 p180; PW v232 D 25, 1987 p65.

Cooper, Jamie Lee
The Horn and the Forest.
Bobbs-Merrill 1963.
LJ v88 1963 p4394.

Eckert, Allan W.
JUV *Johnny Logan: Shawnee Spy.*
Little, Brown 1983.
KR v51 1983 p828; LJ v108 1983 p1972.

Fuller, Iola
The Loon Feather.
Harcourt, Brace 1940.
BL v36 1940 p283; BRD 1940 p331; NYTBR F 25,
1940 p2; SatR F 24, 1940 p5.

Huston, James A.
Counter Point.
Cosmic House 1985.

Salaz, Ruben Dario
I Am Tecumseh.
Fine Line Publications 1980.

Shepard, Odell
Holdfast Gaines.
Macmillan 1946.
BL v43 1946 p103; BRD 1946 p746; KR v14 1946
p428; LJ v71 1946 p1543; NYTBR N 24, 1946 p28.

Thom, James Alexander
Panther in the Sky.
Ballantine 1989.
BL v85 1989 p1433; KR v57 1989 p85; LJ v114 Mr 1,
1989 p90; PW v235 F 10, 1989 p53.

1370. Tegakovita, Catherine
see Tekakwitha, Kateri, Saint

1371. Teilhard de Chardin, Pierre
1881-1955
French priest & philosopher

Marks, Peter
Skullduggery.
Carroll & Graf 1987.
BL v83 1987 p1718; KR v55 1987 p882; LJ v112 Jl
1987 p96; NYTBR Ag 23, 1987 p11.

1372. Tekakwitha, Kateri, Saint
1656-1680
First American Indian to be made a saint;
known as "Lily of the Mohawks"

Brown, Evelyn M.
YA *Kateri Tekakwitha, Mohawk Maid.*
Vision Books 1958.
BRD 1959 p144; KR v26 1958 p760; LJ v83 1958
p2495.

Casey, Jack
Lily of the Mohawks.
Bantam 1984.
BS v44 O 1984 p245; PW v226 Jl 27, 1984 p141.

1373. Tell, William (Wilhelm)
Swiss legendary figure; known for shooting an
apple from his son's head with an arrow

Brandenberg, Aliki (Aliki, pseud.)
JUV *The Story of William Tell.*
Barnes 1961.

Buff, Mary; Buff, Conrad
JUV *The Apple and the Arrow.*
Houghton Mifflin 1951.
BRD 1951 p131; CC 11th p330; LJ v76 1951 p1342;
NYTBR Sep 2, 1951 p12.

Early, Margaret
JUV *William Tell.*
Harry N. Abrams 1991.
BL v88 1991 p621; BRD 1992 p558; SLJ v38 Ja 1992
p102.

Hurlimann, Bettina
JUV *William Tell and His Son.*

Harcourt, Brace & World 1965.
BRD 1967 p646; LJ v92 1967 p1734; NYTBR My 7, 1967 p50.

1374. Teller, Edward
1908-
Hungarian-born American physicist; "father of the hydrogen bomb"

Smith, Martin Cruz
Stallion Gate.
Random House 1986.
BL v82 1986 p1043; LJ v111 My 1, 1986 p132; NYTBR My 4, 1986 p14; PW v229 Mr 14, 1986 p102.

1375. Tennyson, Alfred, Lord
1809-1892
English poet; wrote *Charge of the Light Brigade*

Byatt, A. S.
Angels and Insects: Two Novellas.
Random House 1993.
Second novella *The Conjugial Angel* deals with Lord Tennyson.
NYTBR Je 27, 1993 p14.

1376. Teresa, Mother
1910-
Catholic nun known for her humanitarian work with the poor; won 1979 Nobel Peace Prize

Bang, Kirsten
JUV *Yougga Finds Mother Teresa: The Adventures of a Beggar Boy in India*.
Seabury Press 1983.
SLJ v30 Ja 1984 p70.

1377. Terry, Ellen
1848-1928
English actress

Ansle, Dorothy P. (Hebe Elsna, pseud.)
The Sweet Lost Years.
Hale 1955 (Rpr. 1974).

1378. Tesla, Nikola
1856-1943
Serbian-born American electrical engineer & inventor

McMahon, Thomas A.
Loving Little Egypt.
Viking 1987.
BW v17 F 22, 1987 p9; KR v54 1986 p1751; LJ v112 F 1, 1987 p93; NYTBR F 8, 1987 p16; PW v230 D 12, 1986 p42.

Zohler, Maxim
Between Thunder and Lightning: A Novel Based on the Life of Nikola Tesla.
J.E. Lebrun 1961.

1379. Thackeray, William Makepeace
1811-1863
English novelist; wrote *Vanity Fair*

Forster, Margaret
Memoirs of a Victorian Gentleman, William Makepeace Thackeray.
Morrow 1979.
BL v75 1979 p1564; BRD 1979 p422; LJ v104 1979 p1257; NYTBR My 6, 1979 p7; PW v215 Mr 12, 1979 p67.

Gould, Jean
JUV *Young Thack (William Makepeace Thackeray)*.
Houghton Mifflin 1949.
BRD 1949 p360; LJ v75 1950 p329.

1380. Thatcher, Margaret
1925-
British political leader

Higgins, Jack
Eye of the Storm.
Putnam 1992.

1381. Thaw, Harry Kendall
1871-1947
American murderer; killed architect Stanford White

Doctorow, E. L.
Ragtime.
Random House 1975.
BL v72 1975 p24; BRD 1975 p338; BRD 1976 p313; KR v43 1975 p529; LJ v100 1975 p1344; NYTBR Jl 6, 1975 p1.

1382. Thayer, Sylvanus
1785-1872
American military leader & educator; superintendent of West Point, 1817-1833

Agnew, James B.
Eggnog Riot: The Christmas Mutiny at West Point.
Presidio Press 1979.
BS v39 S 1979 p214; PW v215 Ap 30, 1979 p110.

1383. Themistocles
524?-460? BC
Athenian general & political leader

Paton Walsh, Jill
Farewell Great King.
Macmillan 1972.
KR v40 1972 p553; LJ v97 1972 p2649.

Paton Walsh, Jill
JUV *The Walls of Athens.*
Heinemann 1977.
GP v16 Mr 1978 p3265; JB v42 Ap 1978 p94; NS v95
My 19, 1978 p680.

1384. Theodora
508-548
Byzantine empress as wife of Justinian I

Bradshaw, Gillian
The Bearkeeper's Daughter.
Houghton Mifflin 1987.
BL v84 1987 p604; KR v55 1987 p1411; LJ v112 N
15, 1987 p89; PW v232 O 30, 1987 p51.

Dixon, Pierson
*The Glittering Horn: Secret Memoirs of the Court
of Justinian.*
J. Cape 1958.

Gerson, Noel Bertram
Theodora: A Novel.
Prentice-Hall 1969.
BL v65 1969 p638; LJ v94 1969 p778.

Lamb, Harold
*Theodora and the Emperor: The Drama of Justin-
ian.*
Doubleday 1952.
BRD 1952 p528; FC 8th p240; KR v20 1952 p312; LJ
v77 1952 p1188; NYTBR Ag 3, 1952 p7.

Masefield, John
Basilissa: A Tale of the Empress Theodora.
Macmillan 1940.
BL v37 1940 p36; BRD 1940 p614; LJ v65 1940 p709;
NYTBR S 22, 1940 p6.

Masefield, John
*Conquer: A Tale of the Nika Rebellion in Byzan-
tium.*
Macmillan 1941.
BL v38 1941 p113; BRD 1941 p606; NYTBR N 9,
1941 p7; SatR N 1, 1941 p8.

Oleck, Jack
Theodora.
M. Joseph 1971.

Wellman, Paul I.
The Female: A Novel of Another Time.
Doubleday 1953.
BL v50 1953 p80; BRD 1953 p994; KR v21 1953
p546; NYTBR S 27, 1953 p35.

1385. Therese of Lisieux, Saint
1873-1897
French religious figure

Clarkson, Tom
*Love Is My Vocation: An Imaginative Study of St.
Therese of Lisieux.*
Allan Wingate 1952.

BRD 1953 p186; KR v21 1953 p443; LJ v78 1953
p1428.

1386. Thomas, Dylan Marlais
1914-1953
Welsh poet & author

Summers, John
Dylan.
New English Library 1970.
B&B v15 Ag 1970 p26; B&B v16 Jl 1971 p58.

1387. Thomas, George Henry
1816-1870
American Union general

Altsheler, Joseph A.
The Rock of Chickamauga.
Appleton-Century 1915 (Rpr. 1943).

1388. Thomas, Saint
One of the 12 Apostles of Christ; known as
"Doubting Thomas"

Malvern, Gladys
According to Thomas.
R.M. McBride & Co. 1947.
BRD 1947 p601; NYTBR Mr 23, 1947 p16.

McNarie, Alan D.
Yeshua: The Gospel of St. Thomas.
Pushcart 1993.
NYTBR My 30, 1993 p14.

1389. Thompson, David
1770-1857
Canadian explorer, fur trader, & mapmaker

Clutton-Brock, Elizabeth
Woman of the Paddle Song.
Copp Clark 1972.

Wood, Kerry
The Map-Maker: The Story of David Thompson.
Macmillan 1955.

1390. Thompson, Francis Joseph
1859-1907
English poet & essayist

Broderick, Robert C.
Wreath of Song.
Bruce Pub. Co. 1948.

1391. Thomson, Tom
1877-1917
Canadian painter

MacGregor, Roy
Shorelines: A Novel.
McClelland & Stewart 1980.

BIC v9 Je 1980 p29; Quill & Q v46 Je 1980 p34; SN
v95 Jl 1980 p58.

1392. Thoreau, Henry David
1817-1862

American essayist; wrote *Civil Disobedience* and
Walden

Colver, Anne
JUV *The Wayfarer's Tree*.
Dutton 1973.
BL v70 1973 p49; HB v49 Je 1973 p270; KR v41 1973
p253; LJ v98 1973 p2191.

Graff, Polly
JUV *The Wayfarer's Tree*.
Dutton 1973.

Longstreth, Thomas Morris
Two Rivers Meet in Concord.
Westminster Press 1946.
BL v42 1946 p317; BRD 1946 p508; LJ v71 1946 p587.

Roach, Marilynne K.
JUV *The Mouse and the Song*.
Parents' Magazine Press 1974.
SLJ v21 Ja 1975 p41; NYTBR N 3, 1974 p55; PW
v206 D 16, 1974 p52.

1393. Thorpe, Jim (James Francis)
1888-1953

American sportsman; won gold medals in 1912
Olympics; played professional baseball & football

Van Riper, Guernsey
JUV *Jim Thorpe, Indian Athlete*.
Bobbs-Merrill 1956.
LJ v81 1956 p2044.

1394. Tiberius
42 BC-AD 37

Roman emperor, 14-37

Douglas, Lloyd C.
The Robe.
Houghton Mifflin 1942.
BL v39 1942 p71; BRD 1942 p217; FC 11th p166;
NYTBR O 25, 1942 p7; SatR O 31, 1942 p16.
42 BC-37 AD

Graves, Robert
*I, Claudius: From the Autobiography of Tiberius
Claudius, Born B.C. 10, Murdered and Deified
A.D. 54*.
Modern Library 1934 (Heavily reprinted).

1395. Titian
1477-1576

Italian painter

Cecchi, Dario
Titian.
Farrar, Straus & Cudahy 1958.
BRD 1958 p203.

Weiss, David
The Venetian.
Morrow 1976.
BS v37 Ap 1977 p7; KR v44 1976 p1153; LJ v102
1977 p220; PW v210 O 18, 1976 p50.

1396. Toklas, Alice B.
1877-1967

American author; close companion of Gertrude
Stein

Steward, Samuel M.
The Caravaggio Shawl.
Alyson Publications 1989.
BL v86 1989 p264; LJ v114 O 1, 1989 p121; NYTBR
D 10, 1989 p41.

Steward, Samuel M.
Murder Is Murder Is Murder.
Alyson Publications 1985.
PW v227 Ap 12, 1985 p98.

1397. Tolstoy, Leo Nikolayevich
1828-1910

Russian author; wrote *Anna Karenina* & *War
and Peace*

Okudzhava, Bulat
*The Extraordinary Adventures of Secret Agent
Shipov in Pursuit of Count Leo Tolstoy, in the
Year 1862*.
Abelard-Schuman 1973.
GW v108 Je 30, 1973 p26; TLS Je 29, 1973 p737.

Parini, Jay
The Last Station: A Novel of Tolstoy's Last Year.
Holt 1990.
BL v86 1990 p2072; BRD 1991 p1432; KR v58 1990
p681; LJ v115 Je 15, 1990 p136; NYTBR Jl 22,
1990 p1.

1398. Torquemada, Tomas de
1420-1498

Spanish grand inquisitor

Andrzejewski, Jerzy
The Inquisitors.
Knopf 1960.
BRD 1960 p28; LJ v85 1960 p2616; NYTBR D 11,
1960 p36; SatR N 5, 1960 p32.

Fast, Howard
Torquemada: A Novel.
Doubleday 1966.
KR v33 1965 p1133; LJ v91 1966 p127; NYTBR F 6,
1966 p42; Time v87 Ja 28, 1966 p91.

1399. Toulouse-Lautrec Monfa, Henri Marie Raymond de
1864-1901
French painter & lithographer

La Mure, Pierre
Moulin Rouge; a Novel Based on the Life of Henri de Toulouse-Lautrec.
Random House 1950.
BRD 1950 p530; FC 7th p214; KR v18 1950 p533; LJ v75 1950 p1824; NYTBR N 5, 1950 p6.

1400. Toussaint L'Ouverture, Pierre Dominique
1743-1803
Haitian revolutionary & political leader

Bedford-Jones, Henry
Drums of Dambala.
Covici-Friede 1932 (Rpr. 1953).
BL v28 1932 p389; BRD 1932 p65.

Bourne, Peter
Drums of Destiny.
Putnam 1947.
Also published as *Black Saga.*
BL v44 1947 p32; BRD 1947 p464; FC 9th p57; KR v15 1947 p369; LJ v72 1947 p1269.

Carpentier, Alejo
The Kingdom of This World.
Knopf 1957.
Atl v200 Ag 1957 p84; FC 11th p99; NYTBR My 19, 1957 p4.

Delmar, Vina
A Time for Titans.
Harcourt Brace Jovanovich 1974.
FC 9th p130; KR v42 1974 p69; LJ v99 1974 p774; PW v205 Ja 21, 1975 p79.

Heckert, Eleanor
The Little Saint of St. Domingue.
Doubleday 1973.
KR v41 1973 p769; LJ v98 1973 p2333.

Turner, Adam
Voodoo Queen.
New English Library 1972.

1401. Trotsky, Leon
1879-1940
Organized 1917 Russian revolution

Burgess, Anthony
The End of the World News.
McGraw-Hill 1983.
BL v79 1983 p641; BRD 1983 p217; FC 11th p87; KR v51 1983 p14; LJ v108 1983 p411; NYTBR Mr 6, 1983 p3; Time v121 Mr 21, 1983 p76.

Elliott, John
Blood on the Snow.
St. Martin's 1977.

Roth, Joseph
The Silent Prophet.
Overlook Press 1980.
LJ v105 1980 p1753.

Wolfe, Bernard
The Great Prince Died.
Scribner 1959.
Also published as *Trotsky Dead.*
BL v55 1959 p453; BRD 1959 p1078; KR v27 1959 p60; LJ v84 1959 p1154; NYTBR Mr 29, 1959 p5.

1402. Trujillo (Molina), Rafael Leonidas
1891-1961
Dictator of the Dominican Republic, 1931-1961

Vazquez Montalban, Manuel
Galindez.
Atheneum 1992.
KR v60 1992 p429; LJ v117 1992 p119; NYTBR Ag 23, 1992 p19.

1403. Truman, Harry S.
1884-1972
33rd US President

Robertson, Don
A Flag Full of Stars.
Putnam 1964.
BRD 1964 p995; LJ v89 1964 p3036.

1404. Tubman, Harriet Ross
1826-1913
American abolitionist

Erens, Pamela
Fight for Freedom: A Slave Girl's Escape.
Shameless Hussy Press 1978.

Heidish, Marcy
A Woman Called Moses: A Novel Based on the Life of Harriet Tubman.
Houghton Mifflin 1976.
BRD 1976 p523; LJ v101 1976 p635; NYTBR Je 20, 1976 p32; SLJ v22 My 1976 p82.

Parrish, Anne
YA *A Clouded Star.*
Harper & Brothers 1948.
BL v45 O 15, 1948 p67; BRD 1948 p646; FC 9th p395; NYTBR N 14, 1948 p50.

Petry, Ann
Harriet Tubman, Conductor on the Underground Railroad.
Crowell 1955 (Heavily reprinted).
BRD 1955 p715; KR v23 1955 p366; LJ v80 1955 p1971.

Ringold, Faith
JUV *Aunt Harriet's Underground Railroad.*
Crown 1993.
KR v60 1992 p1507; SLJ v38 D 1992 p22.

Rogers, Frances
YA *Mr. Brady's Camera Boy.*
Lippincott 1951.
BRD 1951 p753; LJ v76 1951 p1717; NYTBR S 16,
1951 p28.

Swift, Hildegarde Hoyt
YA *The Railroad to Freedom: A Story of the Civil
War.*
Harcourt, Brace 1932 (Rpr. 1960).
BL v29 1932 p121; BRD 1932 p926; NYTBR Ja 22,
1933 p15; SatR N 19, 1932 p257.

1405. Turner, Joseph Mallord William
1775-1851
English painter

Noonan, Michael
The Sun Is God.
Delacorte Press 1973.
KR v42 1974 p73; LJ v99 1974 p1328; PW v205 Ja 28,
1974 p296.

1406. Turner, Nat
1800-1831
Led only effective slave rebellion in US history

Panger, Daniel
Ol' Prophet Nat.
J.F. Blair 1967.
Choice v5 1969 p1583; LJ v93 1968 p1654.

Styron, William
The Confessions of Nat Turner.
Random House 1967 (Rpr. 1970, 1976, 1979).
BRD 1967 p1274; LJ v92 1967 p3448; LJ v92 1967
p4581; NYTBR O 8, 1967 p1; Time v90 O 13,
1967 p110.

1407. Turpin, Dick (Richard)
1706-1739
English criminal

Ainsworth, William Harrison
Rookwood: A Romance.
Richard Bentley 1834 (Heavily reprinted).

Ellacott, S. E.
Until You Are Dead.
Abelard-Schuman 1972.
B&B v18 Ja 1973 p120.

Lanzol, Cesare
The Turpin Affair.
Hale 1971.

Lanzol, Cesare
The Turpin Tryst.
Hale 1971.

1408. Tussaud, (Marie Gresholtz), Madame
1760-1850
Swiss wax modeler; creator of Madame Tussard's
wax museum

Martin, Sylvia Pass
I, Madame Tussaud.
Harper 1957.
BRD 1957 p611; FC 8th p282; KR v25 1957 p47; LJ
v82 1957 p752.

Willumsen, Dorrit
*Marie: A Novel about the Life of Madame Tus-
saud.*
Bodley Head 1986.
CR v249 Jl 1986 p48; TLS Jl 18, 1986 p793.

1409. Tutankhamen
1358-1340 BC
Egyptian pharaoh

Bell, Clare
YA *Tomorrow's Sphinx.*
McElderry Books 1986.
BL v83 1986 p344; JHSLC 1987 p59; KR v54 1986
p1372.

Bruckner, Karl
YA *The Golden Pharaoh.*
Pantheon 1959.
BRD 1959 p148; KR v27 1959 p761; LJ v85 1960
p851; NYTBR N 15, 1959 p58.

Drury, Allen
Return to Thebes.
Doubleday 1977.
Sequel to *A God against the Gods.*
BL v73 1977 p792; BRD 1977 p357; KR v45 1977
p111; LJ v102 1977 p512; NYTBR Mr 20, 1977 p29.

Holland, Cecelia
Valley of the Kings: A Novel of Tutankhamun.
V. Gollancz 1978.
Obs Je 18, 1978 p28; TLS Ag 4, 1978 p897.

Reig, June
JUV *Diary of the Boy King: Tut-Ankh-Amen.*
Scribner 1978.
CBSR v7 Ap 1979 p90; SLJ v25 Ap 1979 p61.

1410. Twain, Mark, pseud.
1835-1910
American author, journalist, & humorist; wrote
Huckleberry Finn & *Tom Sawyer*

Brock, Darryl
If I Never Get Back.
Crown 1990.
KR v57 1989 p1692; NYTBR Mr 11, 1990 p18.

Carkeet, David
I Been There Before.
Harper & Row 1985.

BL v82 1985 p309; KR v53 1985 p801; NYTBR Ja 26, 1986 p28; PW v228 Ag 23, 1985 p61; SLJ v33 S 1986 p152.

Davids, Hollace
The Fires of Pele: Mark Twain's Legendary Lost Journal.
Pictorial Legends 1986.

Davis, Sam P.
The Typographical Howitzer.
Meteroite Press 1944.

Lane, Blaise
Mark Twain: Adventure in Old Nevada.
Aladdin Books 1956.
LJ v81 1956 p2464.

Malzberg, Barry
The Remaking of Sigmund Freud.
Ballantine 1985.
LJ v110 Ag 1985 p121; NYTBR Ag 4, 1985 p20.

Miers, Earl Schenck
YA *Mark Twain on the Mississippi.*
Cleveland Pub. Co. 1957.
BL v53 1957 p435; BRD 1957 p634; KR v25 1957 p78; LJ v82 1957 p1695; NYTBR Mr 31, 1957 p34.

Miller, Albert G.
JUV *Mark Twain in Love.*
Harcourt Brace Jovanovich 1973.
KR v41 1973 p819; LJ v98 1973 p3455; PW v204 AG 13, 1973 p55.

Mitchell, Kirk
Never the Twain.
Ace Books 1987.
SFChr v9 F 1988 p43.

Wright, Cynthia
Brighter Than Gold.
Ballantine 1990.
PW v237 Mr 9, 1990 p59.

Yep, Laurence
YA *The Mark Twain Murders.*
Four Winds Press 1982.
BL v79 1982 p50; KR v50 1982 p497; SLJ v28 My 1982 p85.

1411. Tweed, "Boss" (William Marcy)
1823-1878
Tammany Hall boss; his corruption exposed by Nast cartoons

Renek, Morris
Bread and Circus.
Weidenfeld & Nicolson 1987.
BL v83 1987 p1562; KR v60 1987 p588; LJ v112 Je 15, 1987 p86; NYTBR Je 14, 1987 p28; PW v231 My 8, 1987 p60; Time v130 Jl 27, 1987 p66.

Stewart, Ramona
Casey.
Little, Brown 1968.

BL v64 1968 p901; BRD 1968 p1281; KR v36 1968 p73; LJ v93 1968 p1504.

Train, Arthur C.
Tassels on Her Boots.
C. Scribner's Sons 1940.
BRD 1940 p924; SatR Ag 17, 1940 p11.

1412. Tyler, Wat
d. 1381
English revolutionary; led Peasant's Revolt, 1381

Bolton, Ivy
YA *Son of the Land.*
J. Messner 1946.
BRD 1947 p91; KR v14 1946 p389; LJ v72 1947 p168; NYTBR Ja 19, 1947 p31.

Israel, Charles E.
Who Was Then the Gentleman?.
Simon & Schuster 1963.
LJ v88 1963 p1902.

Lindsay, Philip
The Golden Cage.
Hale 1961.

Morris, William
A Dream of John Ball and a King's Lesson.
Reeves & Turner 1888 (Heavily reprinted).

Woods, William H.
Riot at Gravesend: A Novel of Wat Tyler's Rebellion.
Duell, Sloan & Pearce 1952.
BL v49 1952 p49; BRD 1952 p979; KR v20 1952 p470; NYTBR O 12, 1952 p25.

1413. Tyndale, William
1484-1536
English Protestant reformer; Bible translator

Chaikin, L. L.
Recovery of the Lost Sword.
Broadman Press 1990.

Jackson, Dave; Jackson, Neta
YA *The Queen's Smuggler.*
Bethany House Publishers 1991.

O'Dell, Scott
YA *The Hawk That Dare Not Hunt by Day.*
Houghton Mifflin 1975.
BL v72 O 15, 1975 p305; KR v43 O 1, 1975 p1139; NYTBR F 22, 1976 p18; SLJ v22 D 1975 p60.

Oliver, Jane
Flame of Fire.
Putnam 1961.
BL v58 1961 p127; BRD 1962 p900; KR v29 1961 p506; LJ v86 1961 p3303; NYTBR Ag 6, 1961 p22.

Oliver, Jane
JUV *Watch for the Morning.*
St. Martin's Press 1964.
BRD 1965 p962; LJ v89 1964 p4651.

Vernon, Louise A.
JUV *The Bible Smuggler.*
Herald Press 1967.

1414. Typhoid Mary
1870-1938
Infamous typhoid fever carrier

Federspiel, J. F.
YA *The Ballad of Typhoid Mary.*
Dutton 1983.
BRD 1985 p503; LJ v109 1984 p110; NYTBR F 12,
1984 p11; PW v234 N 4, 1983 p57.

1415. Tz'u Hsi
1835-1908
Empress dowager of China, 1861-1908

Buck, Pearl S.
Imperial Woman.
John Day 1956 (Rpr. 1991).
BRD 1956 p135; FC 10th p74; KR v24 1956 p89; LJ
v81 1956 p633; NYTBR Ap 1, 1956 p5.

Hunter, Bluebell M.
The Manchu Empress.
Dial 1945.
BRD 1945 p345; KR v13 1945 p229; SatR Je 23, 1945
p32.

Jernigan, Muriel Molland
Forbidden City.
Crown 1954.
BL v51 1955 p203; BRD 1955 p467; KR v22 1954
p685; LJ v79 1954 p2319; NYTBR Ja 2, 1955 p20.

1416. Utrillo, Maurice
1883-1955
French artist

Baylis, Sarah
Utrillo's Mother.
Pandora 1987.
KR v57 1989 p138; NYTBR Ag 19, 1990 p28; PW
v235 Mr 3, 1989 p88; TLS Ag 21, 1987 p896.

Longstreet, Stephen
*Man of Montmartre: A Novel Based on the Life of
Maurice Utrillo.*
Funk & Wagnells 1958.
BL v54 1958 p503; BRD 1958 p683; KR v26 1958
p89; LJ v83 1958 p1230; NYTBR Mr 23, 1958 p38.

1417. Valadon, Suzanne
1869-1938
French artist; mother of Maurice Utrillo

Baylis, Sarah
Utrillo's Mother.
Pandora 1987.
KR v57 1989 p138; NYTBR Ag 19, 1990 p28; PW
v235 Mr 3, 1989 p88; TLS Ag 21, 1987 p896.

Longstreet, Stephen
*Man of Montmartre: A Novel Based on the Life of
Maurice Utrillo.*
Funk & Wagnells 1958.
BL v54 1958 p503; BRD 1958 p683; KR v26 1958
p89; LJ v83 1958 p1230; NYTBR Mr 23, 1958 p38.

1418. Valentino, Rudolph
1895-1926
Italian-born American actor

Sapia, Yvonne
Valentino's Hair.
Fiction Collective Two 1991.
Winner of the 1991 Charles H. and N. Mildred Nilon
Excellence in Minority Fiction Award, Sponsored
by the University of Colorado and Fiction Collec-
tive Two.
BL v88 1991 p495; KR v59 1991 p1178; LJ v116 1991
p133.

1419. Van Buren, Martin
1782-1862
Eighth US President

Gerson, Noel Bertram
*The Slender Reed: A Biographical Novel of James
Knox Polk.*
Doubleday 1965.
FC 9th p198; LJ v90 1965 p894.

1420. Van Eyck, Jan
1371-1440
Flemish painter

Mullins, Edwin B.
The Master Painter.
Doubleday 1989.
Also published as *Lands of the Sea.*

1421. Van Gogh, Vincent
see Gogh, Vincent Willem van

1422. Van Lew, Elizabeth
1818-1900
American spy during Civil War

Stevenson, Janet
Weep No More.
Viking 1957.
BL v54 1957 p45; BRD 1957 p881; KR v25 1957
p425; LJ v82 1957 p1909.

1423. Vancouver, George
1757-1798
English navigator & explorer

Bowering, George
Burning Water.
Beaufort Books 1980.
KR v48 1980 p1173; PW v218 O 3, 1980 p57.

1424. Vanderbilt, Cornelius

1794-1877
American financier; Vanderbilt University
named after him

Porter, Donald
Jubilee Jim and the Wizard of Wall Street.
Dutton 1990.
BL v86 1990 p1071; KR v58 1990 p133; LJ v115 Ap
1, 1990 p138.

1425. Vanderbilt, Gloria

1924-
American fashion designer

Van Rensselar, Philip
That Vanderbilt Woman.
Playboy Press 1978.

1426. Vanzetti, Bartolomeo

1888-1927
Italian political activist in US; together with Ni-
cola Sacco, executed for murder despite international protest that they were victims of political
bias

Asch, Nathan
Pay Day.
Brewer & Warren 1930 (Rpr. 1990).
BRD 1930 p34.

Fast, Howard
*The Passion of Sacco and Vanzetti: A New Eng-
land Legend.*
Blue Heron Press 1953.

McKenney, Ruth
Jake Home.
Harcourt, Brace & Co. 1943.
BRD 1943 p528; NYTBR F 28, 1943 p6; SatR Mr 13,
1943 p14.

Rose, Howard
The Pooles of Pismo Bay.
Raymond Saroff 1990.
LJ v115 Je 1, 1990 p184.

Sinclair, Upton
Boston: A Novel.
Boni 1928 (Rpr. 1970, 1978).
BRD 1928 p708; NYTBR N 18, 1928 p6; SatR D 1,
1928 p425.

Vonnegut, Kurt
YA *Jailbird.*
Delacorte 1979.
BRD 1979 p1320; BRD 1980 p1260; LJ v104 1979
p2240; SLJ v26 D 1979 p104; NYTBR N25, 1979
p54.

1427. Vaughan, Henry

1622-1695
Welsh poet

Ashton, Helen
The Swan of Usk: A Historical Novel.
Macmillan 1940.
BRD 1940 p489; NYTBR Mr 31, 1940 p16; SatR Ap
6, 1940 p22.

1428. Vega Carpio, Lope Felix de

see Lope de Vega

1429. Velazquez, Diego Rodriquez de Silva

1599-1660
Spanish painter

Trevino, Elizabeth Borton
YA *I, Juan de Pareja.*
Farrar, Straus & Giroux 1965 (Rpr. 1988).
Won the 1966 Newbery award.
BRD 1965 p1261; LJ v90 1965 p3136; NYTBR Ag 22,
1965 p18; SatR Ag 21, 1965 p32.

1430. Verdi, Giuseppe

1813-1901
Italian composer

Werfel, Franz
Verdi: A Novel of the Opera.
Simon & Schuster 1925 (Rpr. 1947).
BL v22 1926 p332; BRD 1926 p738.

1431. Verlaine, Paul Marie

1844-1896
French poet

Aerde, Rogier van
*The Tormented: A Biographical Novel of Paul Ver-
laine.*
Doubleday 1960.
Also published as *The Poor Wedding Guest.*
BRD 1961 p1191; KR v27 1959 p928; LJ v85 1960
p682.

1432. Veronica Giuliani, Saint

Legendary woman who wiped Jesus' face as he
bore the cross

Slaughter, Frank G.
The Thorn of Arimathea.
Doubleday 1959.
BRD 1959 p918; FC 9th p471; KR v26 1958 p855; LJ
v84 1959 p120.

1433. Vespasian

8-79
Roman emperor; began erection of the Co-
losseum, 69-79

Davis, Lindsey
YA *The Iron Hand of Mars.*
Crown 1992.

BL v90 S 15, 1993 p130; KR v61 1993 p892; LJ v118
Ag 1993 p159; PW v240 Jl 12, 1993 p72; TLS Ag
14, 1992 p19.

Davis, Lindsey
YA *Shadows in Bronze.*
Crown 1990 (Rpr. 1992).
BL v87 1991 p1320; KR v59 1991 p142; LJ v116 Mr
15, 1991 p114; PW v238 F 1, 1991 p68; SLJ v37 Jl
1991 p96.

Davis, Lindsey
YA *Silver Pigs.*
Crown 1989 (Rpr. 1991).
BL v85 1989 p1948; KR v57 1989 p854; LJ v114 S 1,
1989 p215; TLS N 17, 1989 p1271.

1434. Vespucci, Amerigo
1451-1512
Italian navigator & explorer; America named after him

Baker, Nina
YA *Amerigo Vespucci.*
Knopf 1957.
BL v52 1956 p345; BRD 1956 p40; KR v24 1956
p126; LJ v81 1956 p1041; NYTBR Jl 29, 1956 p20.

1435. Victoria
1819-1901
Queen of England, 1837-1901

Ansle, Dorothy P. (Hebe Elsna, pseud.)
Mrs. Melbourne.
Collins 1958 (Rpr. 1972).

Anthony, Evelyn
Victoria and Albert: A Novel.
Crowell 1958.
BL v54 1958 p503; BRD 1958 p1012; FC 10th p17;
KR v26 1958 p90; NYTBR Mr 30, 1958 p35.

Bloom, Ursula (Lozania Prole, pseud.)
The Little Victoria.
Hale 1957 (Rpr. 1982).

Bonnet, Theodore
The Mudlark.
Doubleday 1949 (Rpr. 1978).
BRD 1949 p87; FC 11th p64; LJ v74 1949 p1092;
NYTBR Ag 14, 1949 p5.

Byrd, Elizabeth
*The Long Enchantment: A Novel of Queen Victo-
ria and John Brown.*
Macmillan 1973.
B&B v18 S 1983 p134; GW v109 Ag 25, 1973 p20.

Fleming, H. K.
The Day They Kidnapped Queen Victoria.
Frewin 1969 (Rpr. 1978).
BL v74 1978 p1718; KR v46 1978 p563; LJ v103 1978
p1438.

Hibbert, Eleanor (Jean Plaidy, pseud.)
The Queen and Lord M.
Hale 1973 (Rpr. 1977).
BL v74 1977 p141; BS v37 S 1977 p169; KR v45 1977
p553; LJ v102 1977 p2082; PW v211 My 9, 1977
p88.

Hibbert, Eleanor (Jean Plaidy, pseud.)
The Queen's Husband.
Hale 1973 (Rpr. 1978, 1982).
BL v74 1978 p1674; KR v46 1978 p131; LJ v103 1978
p899.

Hibbert, Eleanor (Jean Plaidy, pseud.)
Victoria in the Wings.
Hale 1972 (Rpr. 1990).

Hibbert, Eleanor (Jean Plaidy, pseud.)
The Widow of Windsor.
Hale 1974 (Rpr. 1978).
BL v75 1979 p1040; KR v46 1978 p1089.

Lambert, Derek (Richard Falkirk, pseud.)
Blackstone and the Scourge of Europe.
Stein & Day 1973.
B&B v18 D 1972 p121; FC 9th p165; KR v41 1973
p77; LJ v98 1973 p769.

Long, Freda M.
For the Love of Albert.
Hale 1977.

Ludwig, Charles
Defender of the Faith.
Bethany House Publishers 1988.

Mayerson, Evelyn Wilde
Princess in Amber.
Doubleday 1985.
BL v81 1985 p1238; KR v53 1985 p57; PW v227 Ja
25, 1985 p84.

McDonald, Eva
Lament for Lady Flora.
Hale 1974.

Player, Robert
Oh! Where Are Bloody Mary's Earrings?.
Harper 1973.
BS v33 My 1, 1973 p55; FC 9th p403; KR v41 1973
p25; LJ v98 1973 p2152; NYTBR Ap 1, 1973 p33.

Routh, Jonathan
The Secret Life of Queen Victoria.
Doubleday 1980.
B&B v25 D 1979 p53; LJ v105 1980 p1734; PW v218
Jl 4, 1980 p79.

Tyler-Whittle, Michael S.
Albert's Victoria.
St. Martin's Press 1972.
Sequel to *Young Victoria.*
BL v69 1973 p472; KR v40 1972 p883; LJ v97 1972
p2650.

Tyler-Whittle, Michael S.
The Young Victoria.
St. Martin's 1971.

BL v69 1972 p30; KR v40 1972 p159; LJ v97 1972 p1349.

Wilkins, Vaughan
Consort for Victoria.
Doubleday 1959.
Also published as *Husband for Victoria.*
BL v55 1959 p228; BRD 1959 p1062; KR v26 1958 p885; LJ v84 1959 p536.

1436. Viereck, George Sylvester
1884-1962
American author & editor

Lupoff, Nobuko
Lovecraft's Book.
Arkham House 1985.
PW v227 Je 7, 1985 p78.

1437. Vigee-Lebrun, Marie Louise Elisabeth
1755-1842
French painter

Dunlop, Agnes M. (Elizabeth Kyle, pseud.)
JUV *Portrait of Lisette.*
Nelson 1963.
BRD 1963 p585; LJ v88 1963 p2781; NYTBR My 12, 1963 p34.

1438. Villa, "Pancho" (Francisco)
1878-1923
Mexican revolutionary leader; assassinated

Bonds, Parris Afton
Blue Moon.
Fawcett Columbine 1985.
KR v53 1985 p592; PW v228 Jl 12, 1985 p49.

Brandewyne, Rebecca
Desperado.
Warner Books 1992.

Burroway, Janet
Cutting Stone.
Houghton Mifflin 1992.
BRD 1992 p293; LJ v117 Ap 1, 1992 p145; NYTBR Je 7, 1992 p11.

Day, Douglas
The Prison Notebooks of Ricardo Flores Magon.
Harcourt Brace Javanovich 1991.
BL v88 1991 p676; KR v59 1991 p1106; LJ v116 O 15, 1991 p119.

Gonzales, Laurence
El Vago.
Atheneum 1983.
KR v51 1983 p324; LJ v108 1983 p918; NYTBR O 30, 1983 p33.

Irving, Clifford
Tom Mix and Pancho Villa.
St. Martin's 1982.

BL v78 1982 p985; KR v50 1982 p438; LJ v107 1982 p1010; NYTBR Ag 8, 1982 p13; PW v221 Ap 23, 1982 p88.

Meador, Nancy
JUV *Paco and the Lion of the North: General Pancho Villa Teaches a Boy about Life and Death during the Mexican Revolution.*
Eakin Press 1987.
SLJ v34 O 1987 p127.

Morrell, David
Last Reveille: A Novel.
Fawcett Crest Books 1977.
KR v45 1977 p15; LJ v102 1977 p730.

Patten, Lewis B.
Villa's Rifles.
Doubleday 1977.
BL v74 1978 p1084; FC 10th p411.

Reachi, Santiago
Pancho Villa and the Revolutionist.
Exposition Press 1976.

Shorris, Earl
Under the Fifth Sun.
Delacorte 1980.
KR v48 1980 p937; LJ v105 1980 p2109; NYTBR O 5, 1980 p14; PW v218 Ag 1, 1980 p46.

1439. Villon, Francois
1431-1463
French poet

Deutsch, Babette
Rogue's Legacy: A Novel about Francois Villon.
Coward-McCann 1942.
BRD 1942 p208; NYTBR F 22, 1942 p5; SatR F 21, 1942 p7.

Leslie, Doris
I Return: The Story of Francois Villon.
Doubleday 1969.
Uniform title: *Vagabond's Way.*

Stevenson, Robert Louis
A Lodging for the Night.
First published in 1882 as part of the author's *New Arabian Nights.* Heavily reprinted.

1440. Vincent de Paul, Saint
1581-1660
French priest & philanthropist

Williamson, Denise
JUV *The King's Reward: A Story of Vincent de Paul.*
Wolgemuth & Hyatt 1991.

1441. Virgil
70-19 BC
Roman poet

Broch, Hermann
The Death of Virgil.
Pantheon 1945.
BRD 1945 p83; KR v13 1945 p269; NYTBR Jl 8, 1945
    p1; SatR Je 30, 1945 p11.

Davidson, Avram
The Phoenix and the Mirror.
Doubleday 1969 (Rpr. 1978, 1984).
FC 8th p106; LJ v94 1969 p1159.

1442. Voltaire, Francois Marie Arouet de
1694-1778
French author & philosopher

Brophy, Brigid
*The Adventures of God in His Search for the Black
    Girl.*
Macmillan 1973.
A novella in a collection of short stories.
BRD 1974 p150; Choice v11 O 1974 p1132; FC 9th
    p68; NYTBR Ag 25, 1974 p4; TLS N 23, 1973
    p1417.

Endore, Guy
Voltaire! Voltaire! A Novel.
Simon & Schuster 1961.
Also published as *The Heart and the Mind.*
BL v58 1961 p63; BRD 1962 p355; KR v29 1961
    p344; LJ v86 1961 p2490; NYTBR Je 18, 1961 p4.

Feuchtwanger, Lion
Proud Destiny.
Viking 1947.
BRD 1947 p299; LJ v72 1947 p1193; NYTBR S 14,
    1947 p3; SatR S 13, 1947 p9.

1443. Wagner, Richard
1813-1883
German composer

Gurr, David
The Ring Master.
McClelland & Stewart 1987.
KR v55 1987 p1014; LJ v112 O 1, 1987 p108; NYTBR
    N 1, 1987 p24.

Harding, Bertita
Magic Fire: Scenes around Richard Wagner.
Bobbs-Merrill 1953.
BL v50 1953 p99; BRD 1953 p401; NYTBR D 20,
    1953 p10.

Tims, Hilton
Prelude: A Novel about Richard Wagner.
Macdonald's & Janes 1975.
CR v228 Ja 1976 p48.

1444. Walker, William
1824-1860
American adventurer & South American revolutionary

Bellah, James Warner
The Journal of Colonel De Lancey.
Chilton Books 1967.
KR v35 1967 p217.

Gerson, Noel Bertram
YA *Sad Swashbuckler: The Life of William Walker.*
T. Nelson 1976.
BL v73 1976 p540; BRD 1976 p432; KR v44 1976
    p544; NYTBR My 2, 1976 p34; SLJ v22 My 1976
    p69.

Houston, Robert
The Nation Thief.
Pantheon 1984.
KR v51 1983 p1175; LJ v109 F 1, 1984 p192; NYTBR
    Ja 22, 1984 p22.

Maxwell, Patricia
The Notorious Angel.
Fawcett 1977.
PW v211 My 23, 1977 p244.

Neumann, Alfred
Look upon This Man: A Novel.
Hutchison 1950.

Teilhet, Darwin Le Ora
The Lion's Skin.
Sloane Associates 1955.
BL v51 1955 p452; BRD 1955 p893; KR v23 1955
    p258; LJ v80 1955 p1217; NYTBR Je 19, 1955 p17.

1445. Wallace, George Corley
1919-
American politician; governor of Alabama

Baker, Russell
Our Next President.
Atheneum 1968.
BRD 1968 p59; LJ v93 1968 p2227; NYTBR Mr 17,
    1968 p10; SatR My 18, 1968 p61.

1446. Walpole, Horace
1717-1797
English author; wrote *The Castle of Otranto*

Shepard, Odell
*Jenkin's Ear; a Narrative Attributed to Horace
    Walpole, Esq..*
Macmillan 1951.
BRD 1951 p808; FC 7th p315; LJ v75 1950 p1662;
    NYTBR Ap 1, 1951 p5; SatR Ap 14, 1951 p53.

1447. Walsingham, Francis, Sir
1530-1590
English secretary of state to Elizabeth I

Meadows, Denis
Tudor Underground.
Devin-Adair 1950.
KR v18 1950 p338; NYTBR Ag 20, 1950 p5.

1448. Wanamaker, John
1838-1922
American merchant; started Wanamakers department stores

Burt, Olive Woolley
JUV *John Wanamaker, Boy Merchant.*
Bobbs-Merrill 1952.
LJ v77 1952 p1664.

1449. Washington, Booker T.
1856-1915
American educator; founded Tuskegee Institute

Stevenson, Augusta
JUV *Booker T. Washington, Ambitious Boy.*
Bobbs-Merrill 1950 (Rpr. 1960).
BRD 1951 p843; LJ v76 1951 p121.

1450. Washington, George
1732-1799
First US President & Revolutionary general

Alter, Robert E.
JUV *Listen, the Drum!: A Novel of Washington's First Command.*
Putnam 1963.

Blair, Anne Denton
JUV *Hurrah for Arthur!: A Mount Vernon Birthday Party.*
Seven Locks Press 1982.
BW v12 D 12, 1982 p12; PW v223 Ja 28, 1983 p86; SLJ v30 S 1983 p102.

Bourne, Miriam Anne
JUV *The Children of Mount Vernon: A Guide to George Washington's Home.*
Doubleday 1981.
BW v11 Mr 8, 1981 p12.

Bourne, Miriam Anne
JUV *Nelly Custis' Diary.*
Coward, McCann & Geoghegan 1974.
KR v42 1974 p680; LJ v99 1974 p2261; PW v206 Jl 29, 1974 p57.

Boyce, Burke
Man from Mt. Vernon.
Harper 1961.
BL v57 1961 p488; BRD 1961 p152; FC 9th p58; KR v28 1960 p644; LJ v85 1960 p4005; NYTBR Ja 22, 1961 p32.

Boyce, Burke
Morning of a Hero.
Harper & Row 1963.
LJ v89 1964 p132; LJ v89 1964 p413.

Brandenberg, Aliki (Aliki, pseud.)
JUV *George and the Cherry Tree.*
Dial Press 1964.
BRD 1964 p11; LJ v89 1964 p1439; NYTBR F 16, 1964 p28; SatR F 22, 1964 p61.

Clark, Mary Higgins
YA *Aspire to the Heavens: A Portrait of George Washington.*
Meredith Press 1969.
BS v28 Mr 1, 1969 p490; LJ v94 1969 p1792.

Davis, Burke
Yorktown.
Rinehart 1952.
BL v49 1952 p125; BRD 1952 p228; FC 7th p99; KR v20 1952 p520; LJ v77 1952 p1654; NYTBR N 2, 1952 p22.

Fast, Howard
The Unvanquished.
Duell, Sloan & Pearce 1942.
BRD 1942 p244; LJ v67 1942 p533.

Flood, Charles B.
Monmouth.
Houghton Mifflin 1961.
BRD 1962 p395; LJ v86 1961 p3300; NYTBR O 8, 1961 p5; SatR N 4, 1961 p41.

Ford, Paul Leicester
Janice Meredith; a Story of the American Revolution.
Dodd, Mead & Co. 1899 (Heavily reprinted).
FC 9th p179; NYTBR Ap 14, 1900 p247; NYTBR O 21, 1899 p710.

Frankel, Ellen
JUV *George Washington and the Constitution.*
Bantam 1987.

Frey, Ruby Frazier
Red Morning.
Putnam 1946.
BL v43 1946 p16; BRD 1946 p292; KR v14 1946 p278; LJ v71 1946 p978; NYTBR Jl 28, 1946 p14.

Fritz, Jean
JUV *The Cabin Faced West.*
Coward-McCann 1958.
BL v54 1958 p450; BRD 1958 p401; KR v26 1958 p33; LJ v83 1958 p1284; NYTBR Jl 20, 1958 p24.

Fritz, Jean
JUV *George Washington's Breakfast.*
Coward-McCann 1969.
BL v65 1969 p1174; KR v37 1969 p54; LJ v94 1969 p1326; PW v195 My 10, 1969 p73.

Heron, Virginia
JUV *Pedro's Gift.*
Denison 1970.

Hill, John H.
Princess Malah.
Associated Publishers 1933 (Rpr. 1972).

Holland, Janice
JUV *They Built a City: The Story of Washington, D.C..*
Scribner 1953.
BRD 1953 p441; KR v21 1953 p70; LJ v78 1953 p454; NYTBR F 15, 1953 p26.

Kantor, MacKinlay
Valley Forge: A Novel.
M. Evans 1975.
BL v72 1975 p432; KR v43 1975 p867; LJ v100 1975
p1949; NYTBR O 19, 1975 p45.

Longstreet, Stephen
A Few Painted Feathers.
Doubleday 1963.
BRD 1964 p746; LJ v89 1964 p135; SatR D 7, 1963
p64.

Longstreet, Stephen
War in the Golden Weather.
Doubleday 1965.
KR v33 1965 p268; LJ v90 1965 p2158.

Maciel, Judith
JUV *Martin's Important Day.*
Harvey House 1972.
LJ v97 1972 p2939.

Mandrell, Louise
JUV *A Mission for Jenny.*
Summit Group 1993.

Mason, F. van Wyck
Valley Forge, 24 December 1777.
Doubleday 1950.
KR v18 1950 p536.

Meadowcroft, Enid La Monte
JUV *Silver for General Washington: A Story of Valley
Forge.*
Crowell 1944 (Rpr. 1957).
BL v40 1944 p393; BRD 1944 p515; KR v12 1944
p118; LJ v69 1944 p464; NYTBR Ag 20, 1944 p25.

Meadowcroft, Enid La Monte
JUV *The Story of George Washington.*
Grosset & Dunlap 1952.
LJ v77 1952 p2077.

Miers, Earl Schenck
JUV *We Were There When Washington Won at York-
town.*
Grosset & Dunlap 1958.

Miller, Helen Topping
JUV *Christmas at Mount Vernon with George and
Martha Washington.*
Longmans, Green 1957.
BL v54 1957 p201; BRD 1957 p637; SatR D 7, 1957
p22.

Myers, Maan
The Kingsbridge Plot.
Doubleday 1993.

Pier, Arthur S.
The Young Man from Mount Vernon.
F.A. Stokes 1940.
BRD 1940 p724; LJ v65 1940 p118.

Roop, Peter
JUV *Buttons for General Washington.*

Carolrhoda Books 1986.
BL v83 1986 p583; SLJ v33 1986 p124.

Stevenson, Augusta
JUV *George Washington, Boy Leader.*
Bobbs-Merrill 1942 (Rpr. 1959, 1986).
BRD 1942 p739; LJ v67 1942 p911.

Vance, Marguerite
JUV *The Beloved Friend.*
Colonial Williamsburg 1963.
BRD 1964 p1191; LJ v88 1963 p4097; NYTBR Ja 5,
1964 p18.

Wilson, Dorothy Clarke
Lady Washington.
Doubleday 1984.
BL v80 1984 p1440; KR v52 1984 p324; LJ v109 1984
p997; PW v225 Ap 20, 1984 p79.

Wise, William
JUV *The Spy and General Washington.*
Dutton 1965.
KR v33 1965 p313; LJ v90 1965 p2889.

Woodruff, Elvira
JUV *George Washington's Socks.*
Scholastic 1991.
PW v238 O 4, 1991 p88; SLJ v37 N 1991 p125.

1451. Washington, Martha Dandridge Curtis
1732-1802
Wife of George Washington

Boyce, Burke
Man from Mt. Vernon.
Harper 1961.
BL v57 1961 p488; BRD 1961 p152; FC 9th p58; KR
v28 1960 p644; LJ v85 1960 p4005; NYTBR Ja 22,
1961 p32.

Hill, John H.
Princess Malah.
Associated Publishers 1933 (Rpr. 1972).

Miller, Helen Topping
JUV *Christmas at Mount Vernon with George and
Martha Washington.*
Longmans, Green 1957.
BL v54 1957 p201; BRD 1957 p637; SatR D 7, 1957
p22.

Wilson, Dorothy Clarke
Lady Washington.
Doubleday 1984.
BL v80 1984 p1440; KR v52 1984 p324; LJ v109 1984
p997; PW v225 Ap 20, 1984 p79.

1452. Watts, George Frederick
1817-1904
English painter

Ansle, Dorothy P. (Hebe Elsna, pseud.)
The Sweet Lost Years.
Hale 1955 (Rpr. 1974).

1453. Wayne, Anthony
1745-1796
American Revolutionary general; known as
"Mad Anthony"

Bell, Kensil
YA *Secret Mission for Valley Forge.*
Dodd, Mead 1956.
BL v51 1955 p346; BRD 1955 p59; LJ v80 1955 p1007.

Brick, John
The Strong Men.
Doubleday 1959.
BL v56 1960 p266; BRD 1960 p159; KR v27 1959
 p614; LJ v84 1959 p3150; NYTBR N 8, 1959 p63.

Fast, Howard
The Proud and the Free.
Little, Brown 1950.
BRD 1950 p297; LJ v75 1950 p1825; NYTBR D 3,
 1950 p56.

Gerson, Noel Bertram
*I'll Storm Hell: A Biographical Novel of "Mad An-
 thony" Wayne.*
Doubleday 1967.
LJ v92 1967 p4027; LJ v92 1967 p4273.

Miers, Earl Schenck
YA *The Magnificent Mutineers.*
Putnam 1968.
KR v36 1968 p51; LJ v93 1968 p1326.

Seifert, Shirley
Let My Name Stand Fair.
Lippincott 1956.
BL v53 1956 p23; BRD 1956 p836; FC 7th p311; KR
 v24 1956 p322; SatR Jl 28, 1956 p29.

Stevenson, Augusta
JUV *Anthony Wayne, Daring Boy.*
Bobbs-Merrill 1962.

Wiener, Willard
Morning in America.
Farrar & Rinehart 1942.
BRD 1942 p832; LJ v67 1942 p952; NYTBR N 1,
 1942 p22.

Zara, Louis
This Land Is Ours.
Houghton Mifflin 1940.
BL v36 1940 p346; BRD 1940 p1024; NYTBR Ap 21,
 1940 p2; SatR Ap 27, 1940 p7.

1454. Webster, Daniel
1782-1852
American political leader, diplomat, & orator

Benet, Stephen Vincent
The Devil and Daniel Webster.

Farrar & Rinehart 1937 (Heavily reprinted).
BRD 1937 p80; FC 11th p52; SHSLC 13th p579.

Breslin, Howard
The Tamarack Tree.
Whittlesey House 1947.
BRD 1947 p102; FC 7th p51; LJ v72 1947 p1374;
 NYTBR N 23, 1947 p7.

Gerson, Noel Bertram
*The Slender Reed: A Biographical Novel of James
 Knox Polk.*
Doubleday 1965.
FC 9th p198; LJ v90 1965 p894.

1455. Weizmann, Chaim
1874-1952
First elected president of Israel; first president of
the World Zionist Organization

Davidson, Lionel
The Sun Chemist.
Knopf 1976.
BL v73 1976 p452; BRD 1977 p309; KR v44 1976
 p749; LJ v101 1976 p1796; NYTBR O 17, 1976
 p38.

1456. Welk, Lawrence
1903-
American bandleader

Welk, Lawrence; McGeehan, Bernice
JUV *Lawrence Welk's Bunny Rabbit Concert.*
Saturday Evening Post 1977.
WCRB v4 Mr 1978 p42.

1457. Wellington, Arthur Wellesley, Duke
1769-1852
English military leader & political leader

Baldwin, Michael
The Gamecock.
Faber & Faber 1980.
B&B v25 My 1980 p47; BritBkN S 1980 p564; GW
 v122 Mr 16, 1980 p22; TLS My 9, 1980 p537.

Henty, G. A.
JUV *Under Wellington's Command.*
Blackie 1899 (Rpr. 1954).

Heyer, Georgette
An Infamous Army.
Doubleday, Doran 1938 (Rpr. 1965).
FC 8th p207.

Nelson, Cholmondeley
YA *With Wellington at Waterloo.*
Reilly & Lee 1962.
LJ v88 1963 p876.

Smith, Frederick E.
Waterloo.
Award Books 1970.

1458. Wells, H. G. (Herbert George)
1866-1946
English author; wrote *The Invisible Man, The Time Machine, & The War of the Worlds*

Alexander, Karl
Time after Time.
Delacorte 1979.
BS v39 My 1979 p43; KR v47 1979 p74; LJ v104 1979 p850; PW v215 Ja 29, 1979 p106.

Hughes, David
The Man Who Invented Tomorrow.
Constable 1968.
GW v98 Mr 7, 1968 p11; Lis v79 F 29, 1968 p279; NS v75 Mr 1, 1968 p275; Obs F 25, 1968 p29; TLS F 29, 1968 p213.

Stover, Leon E.
The Shaving of Karl Marx: An Instant Novel of Ideas, after the Manner of Thomas Love Peacock, in Which Lenin and H.G. Wells Talk about the Political Meaning of the Scientific Romances.
Chiron Press 1982.

1459. Wesley, John
1703-1791
British founder of Methodism

Andrew, Prudence
A New Creature.
Putnam 1968.
B&B v14 Ag 1969 p42; BS v28 Ja 1, 1969 p402; LJ v94 1969 p214.

Drakeford, John W.
Take Her, Mr. Wesley.
Word Books 1973.

Williamson, Glen
Sons of Susanna.
Tyndale House Publishers 1991.

1460. West, Benjamin
1738-1820
American painter

Henry, Marguerite
JUV *Benjamin West and His Cat Grimalkin.*
Bobbs-Merrill 1947 (Rpr. 1987).
BL v43 1947 p349; BRD 1947 p410; HB v23 Jl 1947 p26; KR v15 1947 p67; LJ v72 1947 p962; NYTBR Je 22, 1947 p27.

1461. West, Mae
1892-1980
American actress

Kaminsky, Stuart M.
He Done Her Wrong.
St. Martin's 1983.
BL v79 1983 p763; KR v50 1982 p1361.

1462. Wharton, Edith
1862-1937
American author; wrote *The Age of Innocence*; won 1921 Pulitzer Prize

Hill, Carol DeChellis
Henry James' Midnight Song.
Poseidon Press 1993.
NYTBR S 5, 1993 p10.

1463. Wheatley, Phillis
1753-1784
American poet

Du Bois, Shirley Graham
YA *The Story of Phillis Wheatley.*
Messner 1949.
BL v46 1949 p69; BRD 1949 p364; KR v17 1949 p432; LJ v74 1949 p1549; NYTBR N 13, 1949 p30.

1464. Wheeler, Joseph
1836-1906
American Confederate general

Steele, William O.
JUV *The Perilous Road.*
Harcourt, Brace 1958 (Rpr. 1990).
Won 1958 Newbery award.
BRD 1958 p1007; LJ v83 1958 p1605; NYTBR Ap 27, 1958 p36; SLJ v41 My 10, 1958 p47.

1465. Whistler, James Abbott McNeill
1834-1903
American artist

Berkman, Ted
To Seize the Passing Dream.
Doubleday 1972.
BL v68 1972 p751; KR v39 1971 p1327; LJ v97 1972 p1033; NYTBR Mr 19, 1972 p40; PW v201 Ja 17, 1972 p56.

Williams, Lawrence
I, James McNeill Whistler: An Autobiography.
Simon & Schuster 1972.
BL v68 1972 p889; BS v32 Je 1, 1972 p109; FC 9th p560; LJ v97 1972 p1036.

1466. White, Stanford
1853-1906
American architect

Doctorow, E. L.
Ragtime.
Random House 1975.
BL v72 1975 p24; BRD 1975 p338; BRD 1976 p313; KR v43 1975 p529; LJ v100 1975 p1344; NYTBR Jl 6, 1975 p1.

1467. Whitman, Marcus
1802-1847
American physician & missionary

Allen, T. D.
YA *Doctor in Buckskin.*
Harper 1951.
BL v47 1951 p11; BRD 1951 p13; LJ v76 1951 p1218;
SHSLC 10th p477.

Cranston, Paul
To Heaven on Horseback.
Messner 1952.
BL v48 1952 p339; BRD 1952 p212; FC 7th p94; LJ
v77 1952 p1758; WLB v48 Jl 1952 p172.

Lampman, Evelyn
YA *Cayuse Courage.*
Harcourt, Brace & World 1970.
BL v66 1970 p1280; KR v38 1970 p58; LJ v95 1970
p1640; NYTBR Ap 12, 1970 p26.

1468. Whitman, Walt
1819-1892
American poet

Aronin, Ben
Walt Whitman's Secret.
Argus Books 1955.

Vernon, John
Peter Doyle: A Novel.
Random House 1991.
BL v87 1991 p980; KR v59 1991 p212; LJ v116 Mr
15, 1991 p119; NYTBR Jl 14, 1991 p9.

1469. Whitney, Eli
1765-1825
American inventor & manufacturer; invented
cotton gin in 1793

Burlingame, Roger
Whittling Boy: The Story of Eli Whitney.
Harcourt, Brace & Co. 1941.
BRD 1941 p128; LJ v66 1941 p887.

Snow, Dorothea J.
JUV *Eli Whitney, Boy Mechanic.*
Bobbs-Merrill 1948.
LJ v73 1948 p1601.

1470. Whittington, Dick (Richard)
1358-1423
Lord Mayor of London, England

Burlingame, Cora
JUV *Lord of London.*
Appleton-Century 1944.
BRD 1944 p109; KR v12 1944 p434; LJ v69 1944
p1051; NYTBR N 12, 1944 p20.

Gibson, Katherine
JUV *Bow Bells.*

Longmans 1943.
BRD 1943 p302; HB v19 N 1943 p412; LJ v68 1943
p826.

Harnett, Cynthia
JUV *The Sign of the Green Falcon.*
Lerner Publications 1984.
Also published as *Ring Out, Bow Bells.*
Cur R v24 N 1984 p96.

Sitwell, Osbert
*The True Story of Dick Whittington: A Christmas
Story for Cat-Lovers.*
Home & Van Thal Ltd. 1945.

Sudworth, Gwynedd
Richard Whittington, London's Mayor.
Ulverscroft 1977.

1471. Whymper, Edward
1840-1911
English wood-engraver; explorer, & mountaineer

Ullman, James R.
YA *Banner in the Sky.*
Lippincott 1954.
BRD 1954 p903; KR v22 1954 p392; LJ v79 1954
p2258; NYTBR S 12, 1954 p32.

1472. Wiggin, Kate Douglas
1856-1923
American author; wrote *Rebecca of Sunnybrook
Farm*

Mason, Miriam E.
JUV *Kate Douglas Wiggin, the Little Schoolteacher.*
Bobbs-Merrill 1958.
LJ v83 1958 p966.

1473. Wilde, Oscar
1856-1900
Irish poet & playwright

Ackroyd, Peter
The Last Testament of Oscar Wilde.
Harper & Row 1983.
BL v80 1983 p28; KR v51 1983 p821; LJ v108 1983
p1500; PW v224 Ag 19, 1983 p70.

Brown, Russell
*Sherlock Holmes and the Mysterious Friend of Os-
car Wilde.*
St. Martin's 1988.
KR v56 1988 p1639; LJ v114 Ja 1989 p105; PW v234
O 21, 1988 p50.

Buruma, Ian
Playing the Game.
Farrar, Straus & Giroux 1991.
BL v87 1991 p2090; KR v59 1991 p620; LJ v116 Jl
1991 p131; NYTBR Ag 4, 1991 p11.

Cameron, William
The Day Is Coming.

Macmillan 1944.
BRD 1944 p120; KR v12 1944 p47; LJ v69 1944 p203;
   NYTBR Je 18, 1944 p6.

Douglas, Carole Douglas
YA *Good Night, Mr. Holmes.*
Tor Books 1990.
BL v87 1990 p419; KR v58 1990 p1354; NYTBR D
   16, 1990 p33; SLJ v37 Mr 1991 p226.

Farren, Mick
The Neural Atrocity.
Mayflower 1977.

Hall, Desmond
I Give You Oscar Wilde: A Biographical Novel.
New American Library 1965.
LJ v90 1965 p1742.

Hichens, Robert Smythe
The Green Carnation.
Appleton 1894 (Rpr. 1970, 1984).
Choice v8 Mr 1971 p66.

Marks, Peter
Skullduggery.
Carroll & Graf 1987.
BL v83 1987 p1718; KR v55 1987 p882; LJ v112 Jl
   1987 p96; NYTBR Ag 23, 1987 p11.

Reilly, Robert
The God of Mirrors.
Atlantic Monthly Press 1986.
KR v53 1985 p1354; LJ v111 F 1, 1986 p95; NYTBR
   Mr 2, 1986 p17; PW v228 N 29, 1985 p38.

Satterthwait, Walter
Wilde West.
St. Martin's 1991.
KR v59 1991 p828; LJ v116 Ag 1991 p147.

Stokes, Sewell
Beyond His Means.
Davies 1955.

Wood, Clement
*The Sensualist: A Novel of the Life and Times of
   Oscar Wilde.*
J. Swift 1942.

1474. Willard, Frances Elizabeth
1839-1898
American temperance leader

Mason, Miriam E.
JUV *Frances Willard, Girl Crusader.*
Bobbs-Merrill 1961.

1475. William III
1650-1702
King of England, 1689-1702

Gerson, Noel Bertram
The Queen's Husband.
McGraw-Hill 1960.

BL v56 1960 p540; BRD 1960 p519; KR v28 1960
   p103; LJ v85 1960 p985.

Hibbert, Eleanor (Jean Plaidy, pseud.)
The Three Crowns: The Stuart Saga.
Putnam 1965.

Kenyon, Frank Wilson
The Glory and the Dream.
Dodd, Mead 1963.

1476. William the Conqueror
1027-1087
King of England, 1066-1087

Anand, Valerie
The Norman Pretender.
Scribner 1979.
KR v47 1979 p1272; LJ v105 1980 p118; PW v216 D
   10, 1979 p59.

Bennetts, Pamela
A Crown for Normandy.
Hale 1971.

Bryher, Winifred
This January Tale.
Harcourt, Brace & World 1966.
BL v63 1966 p300; KR v34 1966 p926; LJ v91 1966
   p6109; NYTBR N 27, 1966 p69.

Bulwer-Lytton, Edward
Harold, the Last of the Saxon Kings.
B. Tauchnitz 1848 (Heavily reprinted).

Gerson, Noel Bertram
The Conqueror's Wife.
Doubleday 1957.
BL v53 1957 p558; BRD 1957 p347; KR v25 1957
   p233; SatR Jl 6, 1957 p31.

Heyer, Georgette
The Conqueror.
Dutton 1931 (Rpr. 1933, 1956, 1966).
FC 8th p206.

Hibbert, Eleanor (Jean Plaidy, pseud.)
The Bastard King.
Hale 1974 (Rpr. 1979).
KR v47 1979 p30; LJ v104 1979 p753; PW v215 Ja 22,
   1979 p364.

Holland, Cecelia
The Firedrake.
Atheneum 1966.
BL v62 1966 p566; BRD 1966 p561; KR v33 1965
   p1134; LJ v91 1966 p714; NYTBR Ja 30, 1966 p5.

Lewis, Hilda
YA *Harold Was My King.*
D. McKay 1970.
BL v67 1971 p602; LJ v96 1971 p1528.

Lewis, Hilda
Wife to the Bastard.
Hutchinson 1966.

BL v64 1967 p169; LJ v92 1967 p2809; LJ v92 1967 p4274.

Muntz, Hope
The Golden Warrior: The Story of Harold and William.
Scribner 1949.
BL v45 1949 p225; BRD 1949 p665; FC 9th p372; KR v16 1948 p581; LJ v74 1949 p312; NYTBR Mr 6, 1949 p26.

Oliver, Jane
JUV *Faraway Princess.*
St. Martin's 1962.
LJ v87 1962 p3204; NYTBR O 14, 1962 p34.

Prescott, Hilda
Son of Dust.
Macmillan 1956.
BRD 1956 p750; KR v24 1956 p795; LJ v81 1956 p2959; NYTBR N 25, 1956 p4.

Quigley, Aileen
King Bastard: The Story of William the Conqueror.
Hale 1973.

Todd, Catherine
Bond of Honour.
St. Martin's 1981.
BL v78 1982 p849; KR v49 1981 p1487; LJ v107 1982 p475; SLJ v28 1982 p94.

Wingate, John
William the Conqueror.
F. Watts 1983.
TLS Ag 3, 1984 p875.

1477. Williams, "Hank" (Hiram King)
1923-1953
American singer & songwriter

Deal, Babs H.
High Lonesome World.
Doubleday 1969.
FC 9th p125; KR v37 1969 p795; LJ v94 1969 p3466; PW v196 Jl 28, 1969 p55.

1478. Williams, Roger
1603-1683
English clergyman in America & founder of Rhode Island

Cannon, Le Grand
Come Home at Even.
Holt 1951.
BL v47 1951 p165; BRD 1951 p148; KR v19 1951 p35; LJ v76 1951 p406; NYTBR Mr 11, 1951 p406.

Eaton, Jeanette
YA *Lone Journey: The Life of Roger Williams.*
Harcourt, Brace & World 1944.
BRD 1944 p217; KR v12 1944 p406; LJ v69 1944 p867; SatR O 21, 1944 p29.

Rees, Gilbert
I Seek a City.
Dutton 1950.
BRD 1950 p755; KR v18 1950 p368; LJ v75 1950 p1293; NYTBR D 10, 1950 p25.

Schofield, William G.
Ashes in the Wilderness.
Macrae-Smith 1942.
BRD 1942 p686; LJ v67 1942 p739; NYTBR O 18, 1942 p24.

1479. Willkie, Wendell Lewis
1892-1944
American politician

Stacton, David
Tom Fool.
Faber & Faber 1962.

1480. Wilson, Woodrow
1856-1924
28th US President

Monsell, Helen Albee
JUV *Woodrow Wilson, Boy President.*
Bobbs-Merrill 1950.
BRD 1950 p648; LJ v75 1950 p1835.

Vidal, Gore
Hollywood: A Novel of America in the 1920s.
Random House 1990.
BRD 1990 p1879; NYTBR Ja 21, 1990 p1.

1481. Winchell, Walter
1897-1972
American journalist

Herr, Michael
Walter Winchell: A Novel.
Knopf 1990.
BRD 1990 p807; NYTBR My 20, 1990 p12; PW v237 F 23, 1990 p206; TLS S 14, 1990 p970.

1482. Windsor, Wallis Warfield, Duchess of
see Simpson, Wallis (Bessie Wallis Warfield)

1483. Wingate, Orde Charles
1903-1944
English army officer; expert on mobile tactics

Taylor, Thomas
Born of War.
McGraw-Hill 1988.
KR v56 198 p85; LJ v113 F 1, 1988 p76.

1484. Winthrop, John
1588-1649
English colonial administrator in America

Auchincloss, Louis
The Winthrop Covenant.
Houghton Mifflin 1976.
BRD 1976 p57; LJ v101 1976 p546; NYTBR Mr 28,
1976 p10.

Heidish, Marcy
Witnesses: A Novel.
Houghton Mifflin 1980.
BL v77 1980 p31; KR v48 1980 p666; LJ v105 1980
p1540; NYTBR S 14, 1980 p12; SLJ v27 N 1980
p92.

Rushing, Jane Gilmore
Covenant of Grace.
Doubleday 1982.
BL v78 1982 p1301; KR v50 1982 p367; LJ v107 My
1, 1982 p906; PW v221 Mr 26, 1982 p66.

1485. Wittgenstein, Ludwig
1889-1951
British philosopher

Collins, Randall
The Case of the Philosopher's Ring.
Crown 1978.
KR v46 1978 p1216.

Duffy, Bruce
The World as I Found It.
Ticknor & Fields 1987.
BRD 1989 p439; LJ v112 Ag 1987 p140; NYTBR O
11, 1987 p18; PW v231 Je 19, 1987 p115.

Eagleton, Terry
Saints and Scholars.
Verso 1987.
BRD 1988 p484; LJ v113 F 15, 1988 p178; NYTBR O
18, 1987 p30; PW v232 S 25, 1987 p95.

Markson, David
Wittgenstein's Mistress.
Dalkey Archive Press 1988.
BL v84 1988 p1572; NYTBR My 22, 1988 p12.

1486. Wittgenstein, Paul
1887-1961
American pianist; brother of Ludwig Wittgenstein

Barchilon, John
The Crown Prince: A Novel.
Norton 1984.
BL v80 1984 p1292; KR v52 1984 p361.

Bernhard, Thomas
Wittgenstein's Nephew: A Friendship.
Quartet Books 1986.
BL v85 1988 p616; KR v56 1988 p1621; LJ v114 Ap
1, 1989 p109; PW v234 N 11, 1988 p41.

1487. Woffington, Margaret
1714-1760
Irish actress

Mahon, Brid
A Time to Love.
Poolbeg 1992.

Reade, Charles
Peg Woffington: A Novel.
R. Bentley 1853 (Heavily reprinted).

1488. Wolfe, James
1727-1759
British general; captured Quebec from the
French on the Plains of Abraham

Elwood, Muriel
Web of Destiny.
Manor Books 1951.
BRD 1951 p268.

Henty, G. A.
JUV *With Wolfe in Canada.*
Blackie 1887 (Rpr. 1961).
LJ v87 1962 p848.

O'Brien, Vincent
The White Cockade: An Historical Novel.
Abelard-Schuman 1963.
LJ v88 1963 p4397.

Spicer, Bart
The Tall Captains.
Dodd, Mead 1957.
SatR F 23, 1957 p34.

Styles, Showell
Wolfe Commands You.
Faber & Faber 1959 (Rpr. 1975).

White, Leslie Turner
His Majesty's Highlanders.
Crown 1964.

1489. Wollstonecraft, Mary
1759-1797
English feminist; wrote paper *The Vindication of
the Rights of Women*; mother of Mary Shelley

Sherwood, Frances
Vindication.
Farrar, Straus, Giroux 1993.
KR v61 1993 p180; NYTBR Jl 11, 1993 p21.

1490. Wolsey, Thomas, Cardinal
1475-1530
English Cardinal & government official in the
courts of Henry VII and Henry VIII

Barnes, Margaret Campbell
Brief Gaudy Hour: A Novel of Anne Boleyn.
Macrae Smith 1949.
BRD 1949 p42; FC 11th p41; KR v17 1949 p371; LJ
v74 1949 p1320; NYTBR O 2, 1949 p42.

Clynes, Michael
The White Rose Murders.

St. Martin's 1993.
LJ v118 F 15, 1993 p190.

1491. Woodhull, Victoria Claflin
1838-1927
American publisher & social reformer

Becker, Beril
Whirlwind in Petticoats.
Doubleday 1947.
BRD 1947 p55.

McCall, Dan
Beecher: A Novel.
Dutton 1979.
BL v76 1979 p432; KR v47 1979 p880; LJ v104 1979
    p1720; NYTBR Ja 20, 1980 p15; PW v216 Ag 6,
    1979 p86.

1492. Woolf, Virginia
1882-1941
English author & critic

Collins, Randall
The Case of the Philosopher's Ring.
Crown 1978.
KR v46 1978 p1216.

Hawkes, Ellen; Manso, Peter
*The Shadow of the Moth: A Novel of Espionage
    with Virginia Woolf.*
St. Martin's 1983.
BRD 1983 p658; KR v50 1982 p1350; LJ v108 1983
    p224; NYTBR My 22, 1983 p49; PW v222 D 17,
    1982 p63.

1493. Woolman, John
1720-1772
American Quaker preacher & social reformer

Fager, Charles
JUV *John Woolman and the Slave Girl.*
Kimo Press 1977.

1494. Woolworth, Frank Winfield
1852-1919
American merchant; founder of F.W. Woolworth Co.

Myers, Elisabeth P.
JUV *F. W. Woolworth, Five and Ten Boy.*
Bobbs-Merrill 1962.

1495. Wovoka
1856-1932
American Indian mystic & religious leader

Murray, Earl
Song of Wovoka.
TOR 1992.
KR v60 1992 p562.

1496. Wren, Christopher, Sir
1632-1723
English architect; helped rebuild London after
1666 fire

Laker, Rosalind
Circle of Pearls.
Doubleday 1990.
BL v86 1990 p1957; KR v58 1990 p601; SLJ v36 O
    1990 p150.

Weiss, David
Myself, Christopher Wren.
Hodder & Stoughton 1973.
BL v70 1973 p417; KR v41 1973 p1286; LJ v98 1973
    p3579.

1497. Wright, Frank Lloyd
1869-1959
American architect

Levin, Meyer
The Architect.
Simon & Schuster 1981.
BL v78 1981 p266; KR v49 1981 p1362; LJ v106 1981
    p2332; NYTBR Ja 3, 1982 p9.

1498. Wright, Orville
1871-1948
American aviation pioneer

Harris, John
JUV *A Tale of a Tail.*
Hutchinson 1975.
GP v14 N 1975 p2743.

Stevenson, Augusta
JUV *Wilbur and Orville Wright, Boys with Wings.*
Bobbs-Merrill 1959.
BL v48 1951 p110; BRD 1952 p847; LJ v76 1951
    p1715.

Sutton, Felix
JUV *We Were There at the First Airplane Flight.*
Grosset & Dunlap 1960.

1499. Wright, Wilbur
1867-1912
American aviation pioneer

Harris, John
JUV *A Tale of a Tail.*
Hutchinson 1975.
GP v14 N 1975 p2743.

Stevenson, Augusta
JUV *Wilbur and Orville Wright, Boys with Wings.*
Bobbs-Merrill 1959.
BL v48 1951 p110; BRD 1952 p847; LJ v76 1951
    p1715.

Sutton, Felix
JUV *We Were There at the First Airplane Flight.*
Grosset & Dunlap 1960.

1500. Wyatt, Thomas, Sir
1503-1542
English poet

Wiat, Philippa
The Heir of Allington.
Hale 1973.

Wiat, Philippa
The Knight of Allington.
Hale 1974.

Wiat, Philippa
The Rebel of Allington.
Hale 1974.

1501. Wycliffe, John
1320-1384
English religious reformer

Floyd, John Fletcher
The Moring Star: A Historical Novel with Ecclesiastical Overtones.
Star Bible Publications 1990.

Vernon, Louise A.
JUV *The Beggar's Bible.*
Herald Press 1971.

1502. Xerxes I
519-465 BC
King of Persia, 486-465 BC

Andrews, Gini
Esther: The Star and the Sceptre.
Zondervan 1980.

Davis, William Stearns
A Victor of Salamis.
Macmillan 1907 (Heavily reprinted).
BRD 1907 p107; FC 7th p101; NYTBR My 18, 1907 p327.

De Camp, Lyon Sprague
The Dragon of the Ishtar Gate.
Doubleday 1961 (Rpr. 1982).
LJ v86 1961 p4307; NYTBR D 10, 1961 p48.

Hutchinson, Polly A.
Oh, King, Live Forever.
Beta Books 1977.

Weinreb, Nathaniel Norsen
Esther.
Doubleday 1955.
BL v52 1956 p191; BRD 1956 p976; LJ v81 1956 p1053.

1503. Yezierska, Anzia
1885-1970
American author

Rosen, Norma
John and Anzia: An American Romance.
Dutton 1989.
BRD 1991 p1594; KR v57 1989 p1426; NYTBR Ja 28, 1990 p23.

1504. Young, Brigham
1801-1877
American Mormon leader

Fisher, Vardis
Children of God: An American Epic.
Harper 1939 (Rpr. 1975).
BL v36 S 1939 p8; BRD 1939 p327; NYTBR Ag 27, 1939 p1.

Gordon, Leo V.
Powderkeg.
Presido Press 1991.
KR v59 1991 p1109; LJ v116 O 15, 1991 p120; PW v238 S 27, 1991 p43.

Jordan, Polly Carver
JUV *Brigham Young: Covered Wagon Boy.*
Bobbs-Merrill 1962.

Lauritzen, Jonreed
The Everlasting Fire.
Doubleday 1962.
BL v59 N 1, 1962 p206; BRD 1962 p693; LJ v87 1962 p2775; NYTBR Ag 5, 1962 p20.

Williams, Barbara
JUV *Brigham Young and Me, Clarissa.*
Doubleday 1978.
BL v75 1978 p388; KR v46 1978 p1018; SLJ v25 N 1978 p71.

1505. Younger, Cole (Thomas Cole)
1844-1916
American outlaw

Harte, Bryce
Betrayed.
Berkley Books 1992.

Leaton, Anne
Pearl.
Knopf 1985.
BL v81 1985 p927; BRD 1986 p950; KR v52 1984 p1159; LJ v110 F 15, 1985 p180; NYTBR Mr 31, 1985 p22; PW v227 Ja 25, 1985 p85.

1506. Zaharias, "Babe" Didrikson
1914-1956
American golfer

De Grummond, Lena
JUV *Babe Didrikson, Girl Athlete.*
Bobbs-Merrill 1963.

1507. Zapata, Emiliano
1879-1919
Mexican revolutionary

Gonzales, Laurence
El Vago.
Atheneum 1983.
KR v51 1983 p324; LJ v108 1983 p918; NYTBR O 30, 1983 p33.

1508. Zenger, John Peter
1697-1746
German-born colonial printer & journalist

Cooper, Kent
Anna Zenger: Mother of Freedom.
Farrar, Straus 1946.

BL v43 1947 p132; BRD 1946 p170; FC 7th p89; KR v14 1946 p413; LJ v71 1946 p1542; NYTBR N 17, 1946 p5.

Galt, Thomas
YA *Peter Zenger, Fighter for Freedom.*
Crowell 1951.
BL v48 1951 p52; BRD 1951 p323; KR v19 1951 p298; LJ v76 1951 p1236; NYTBR S 9, 1951 p30.

Long, Laura
JUV *John Peter Zenger, Young Defender of a Free Press.*
Bobbs-Merrill 1966.

Stone, Eugenia
YA *Free Men Shall Stand.*
T. Nelson & Sons 1944.
BL v41 1944 p128; BRD 1944 p724; KR v12 1944 p482; LJ v70 1945 p72; NYTBR N 12, 1944 p14.

Author Index

Occupation Index

Political Leader, Venezuelan
Bolivar, Simon, 161

Prince
Charles, Prince of Wales, 299
Edward the Black Prince, 470
Frederick Louis, 543
Henry the Navigator, 674
Rudolf of Hapsburg, 1203
Stuart, Charles Edward Louis
  Philip, 1343

Princess
Diana, Princess of Wales, 415
Jezebel, 756

Printer
Caxton, William, 277
Franklin, Benjamin, 537
Gutenberg, Johannes, 626
Manutius, Aldus, 914
Zenger, John Peter, 1508

Producer
DeMille, Cecil B., 407
Disney, Walt, 426
Hughes, Howard Robard, 717
Sennett, Mack, 1278

Prophet
Abraham, 3
Amos, 42
Daniel, 385
Deborah, 398
Elijah, 478
Hosea, 706
Isaiah, 735
Jeremiah, 754
John the Baptist, 762
Mohammed, 976
Moses, 1002
Nehemiah, 1015
Samuel, 1252

Psychiatrist
Jung, Carl Gustav, 786

Psychoanalyst
Freud, Sigmund, 547

Publisher
Brannan, Samuel, 194
Gollancz, Victor, Sir, 597
Hearst, William Randolph, 656
Newbery, John, 1021
Woodhull, Victoria Claflin, 1491
Zenger, John Peter, 1508

R

Radio Performer
Coughlin, Father (Charles Edward), 360

Railroad Executive
Hill, James Jerome, 689
Stanford, Leland (Amasa Leland), 1320

Rancher
Goodnight, Charles, 599

Reformer
Addams, Jane (Laura Jane), 12
Anthony, Susan B., 54
Barton, Clara Harlowe, 106
Beecher, Henry Ward, 124
Blackwell, Antoinette Louisa
  Brown, 148
Booth, Catherine Mumford, 171
Dix, Dorothea Lynde, 428
Donnelly, Ignatius, 434
Forten, James, 523
Howe, Julia Ward, 712
Howe, Samuel Gridley, 713
Low, Juliette Gordon, 888
Mott, Lucretia Coffin, 1004
Nightingale, Florence, 1028
Parker, Theodore, 1063
Roosevelt, Eleanor, 1188
Sanger, Margaret, 1255
Stanton, Elizabeth Cady, 1322
Stowe, Harriet Beecher, 1337
Szold, Henrietta, 1355
Willard, Frances Elizabeth, 1474
Woodhull, Victoria Claflin, 1491
Woolman, John, 1493

Religious Figure
see also Biblical Character, New
  Testament; Biblical Character, Old Testament

Religious Figure, American Indian
Wovoka, 1495

Religious Figure, Anglican
Cranmer, Thomas, 363

Religious Figure, Baha'i
Baha'u'llah, 90

Religious Figure, Bohemian
Hus, Jan, 723

Religious Figure, Buddhist
Buddha, 217

Religious Figure, Catholic
Alexander VI, Pope, 26
Bernadette of Lourdes, 138
Catherine of Siena, 270
Coughlin, Father (Charles Edward), 360
Damien, Father, 383
Heloise, 662
John Paul II, Pope, 761
Mazarin, Jules, Cardinal, 948
Merton, Thomas, 964
Mindszenty, Jozsef, Cardinal, 971
Pio da Pietrelcina, Father, 1097
Pius IX, Pope, 1103
Ricci, Matteo, 1152
Savonarola, Girolamo, 1261
Serra, Junipero, 1280
Teresa, Mother, 1376
Torquemada, Tomas de, 1398

Religious Figure, Christian
Jesus Christ, 755
Mary, the Virgin Mother, 934

Religious Figure, Christian Scientist
Eddy, Mary Baker Morse, 461

Religious Figure, Evangelical
Booth, William, 173
Graham, Billy (William Franklin), 608
McPherson, Aimee Semple, 954
Roberts, Oral, 1167

Religious Figure, Hindu
Gandhi, Mahatma, 559

Religious Figure, Islamic
Mohammed, 976

Religious Figure, Jewish
Ba'al Shem Tov, Israel, 83
Gamaliel the Elder, 557
Maimonides, Moses, 907

Religious Figure, Lutheran
Knox, John, 816
Luther, Martin, 894

Religious Figure, Methodist
Heck, Barbara Ruckle, 657
Wesley, John, 1459

Religious Figure, Mormon
Smith, Joseph, 1308
Young, Brigham, 1504

Religious Figure, Puritan
Cotton, John, 359
Hutchinson, Anne, 726
Williams, Roger, 1478

Religious Figure, Quaker
Fox, George, 527
Woolman, John, 1493

Religious Figure, Saint
Ambrose, Saint, 39
Anthony of Padua, Saint, 53
Aquinas, Thomas, Saint, 59
Augustine, Saint, 78
Becket, Thomas, Saint, 120
Benedict, Saint, 131
Brendan of Clonfert, Saint, 197
Chrysostom, John, Saint, 313
Columba, Saint, 340
Columban, Saint, 341
Elizabeth of Hungary, Saint, 482
Francis of Assisi, Saint, 531
Francis Xavier, Saint, 532
George, Saint, 576
Gregory the Great, Saint, 614
Hildegard of Bingen, Saint, 688
Ignatius of Loyola, Saint, 729
Joan of Arc, Saint, 757
John of the Cross, Saint, 760
More, Thomas, Sir, 991
Patrick, Saint, 1069

Title Index